Contemporary Issues in Family Studies

D0788016

Contemporary Issues in Family Studies

Global Perspectives on Partnerships, Parenting and Support in a Changing World

Edited by

Angela Abela and Janet Walker

WILEY Blackwell

This edition first published 2014
© 2014 John Wiley & Sons, Ltd

Registered Office
John Wiley & Sons, Ltd, The Atrium, Southern Gate, Chichester, West Sussex, PO19 8SQ, UK

Editorial Offices
350 Main Street, Malden, MA 02148-5020, USA
9600 Garsington Road, Oxford, OX4 2DQ, UK
The Atrium, Southern Gate, Chichester, West Sussex, PO19 8SQ, UK

For details of our global editorial offices, for customer services, and for information about how to apply for permission to reuse the copyright material in this book please see our website at www.wiley.com/wiley-blackwell.

The right of Angela Abela and Janet Walker to be identified as the authors of the editorial material in this work has been asserted in accordance with the UK Copyright, Designs and Patents Act 1988.

All rights reserved. No part of this publication may be reproduced, stored in a retrieval system, or transmitted, in any form or by any means, electronic, mechanical, photocopying, recording or otherwise, except as permitted by the UK Copyright, Designs and Patents Act 1988, without the prior permission of the publisher.

Wiley also publishes its books in a variety of electronic formats. Some content that appears in print may not be available in electronic books.

Designations used by companies to distinguish their products are often claimed as trademarks. All brand names and product names used in this book are trade names, service marks, trademarks or registered trademarks of their respective owners. The publisher is not associated with any product or vendor mentioned in this book.

Limit of Liability/Disclaimer of Warranty: While the publisher and author(s) have used their best efforts in preparing this book, they make no representations or warranties with respect to the accuracy or completeness of the contents of this book and specifically disclaim any implied warranties of merchantability or fitness for a particular purpose. It is sold on the understanding that the publisher is not engaged in rendering professional services and neither the publisher nor the author shall be liable for damages arising herefrom. If professional advice or other expert assistance is required, the services of a competent professional should be sought.

Library of Congress Cataloging-in-Publication Data

Contemporary issues in family studies : global perspectives on partnerships, parenting and support in a changing world / edited by Angela Abela and Janet Walker.
    pages cm
  Includes bibliographical references and index.
  ISBN 978-1-119-97103-0 (cloth)
1. Families. 2. Marriage. 3. Parenting. I. Abela, Angela. II. Walker, Janet (Janet A.)
  HQ503.C657 2013
  306.85–dc23

                    2013020786

A catalogue record for this book is available from the British Library.

Cover image: Images from Shutterstock (© Kudryashka / © Nowik Sylwia / © vectorgirl / © Imagewell / © red rose)
Cover design by Richard Boxall Design Associates

Set in 10/12pt Galliard by SPi Publisher Services, Pondicherry, India
Printed in Malaysia by Ho Printing (M) Sdn Bhd

1   2014

To all our families

Contents

Part IV   Looking to the Future: The Role of States in Supporting Families

List of Figures

List of Tables

Preface

The inspiration for this book came from a colloquium held on the Mediterranean island of Malta in 2009. The Cana Movement, a leading NGO which has been providing services to Maltese families for over fifty years, invited one of us, Angela Abela, to assist in the organisation of a colloquium on supporting families in a changing world. Dr Anna Maria Vella, the then President of the Cana Movement, invited a group of leading scholars from around the world to meet at the magnificent Presidential Palace in Valletta for two days in October 2009 to debate global changes in marriage and family life and consider the kinds of supports that are necessary to buttress strong, stable couple relationships and strengthen parenting practices.

The colloquium was held under the patronage of His Excellency the President of the Republic of Malta, Dr George Abela, and under the auspices of the Standing Committee on Social Affairs of the Maltese Parliament. It was made possible by the financial support of the Doha International Institute for Family Studies and Development (DIIFSD). The DIIFSD was established in 2006 to promote and strengthen the family, and it provides a platform for networking opportunities between international scholars, practitioners and organisations working on issues related to the protection of families.

During the colloquium, the participants agreed with Angela Abela's suggestion that the papers presented should be collated in a book which would discuss contemporary issues and global changes impacting on family life across the world. Dr Vella and Dr Richard Wilkins, the then Executive Director of DIIFSD, both of whom had attended and contributed to the colloquium, readily endorsed the idea. Angela Abela took responsibility for developing the proposal and invited one of the key speakers, Janet Walker, to join her as co-editor.

The Contributors

Over the following months, in consultation with the colloquium participants, we invited a range of other scholars from different cultures and a variety of disciplines to contribute to a book which would take a truly global perspective. We were delighted with the overwhelmingly positive response from the colleagues we invited to contribute to the book and with the glowing endorsement by other leading scholars of the book as a whole. We were extremely pleased when Wiley Blackwell accepted the proposed book for publication.

The contributors to this book live and work in various countries around the world, and in different cultural contexts. As a consequence, they have access to research studies that are not available in the English language and can offer perspectives on major issues which reflect specific cultural traditions and values: this, we hope, is one of the key strengths of the book. The messages emerging from this book are, in fact, remarkably consistent regarding the importance of strong, stable families for the development and maintenance of strong, stable societies. The contributors also highlight the challenges and opportunities associated with increasing choice in family structures and the need to understand the impacts of diversity and globalisation on partnerships and parenting.

About the Book

The book captures the most significant changes in partnerships, parenting and family life in the second decade of the twenty-first century, drawing on the most recent research findings about the impact of global demographic, economic, social and cultural changes. Within the chapters are examples and vignettes of how families are responding to change, and descriptions of good practice and constructive approaches to family policy in many different parts of Europe, North America, North Africa, the Middle East, the Far East, Australia and New Zealand. We believe that these contribute to the richness of the content and significantly extend our understanding of similarities and differences within and between nations. The authors include recommendations for ways in which policymakers and practitioners can support children, adults, and all kinds of families, to build and maintain strong, stable personal and intimate relationships across the life course.

The book contains twenty-seven chapters, grouped into four separate sections. After our introductory chapter, Part I explores changing couple and family relationships; Part II focuses on parenthood, parenting and family life; Part III examines global impacts on family life; and Part IV looks to the future and considers the role of governments in supporting families. An introduction at the beginning of each of these parts highlights the key issues addressed in the chapters that follow.

We believe that this book presents a unique perspective on contemporary issues that are relevant to families in all parts of the globe, and that it will make a significant contribution to our understanding of and thinking about the importance of couple relationships and family life in the modern world. Froma Walsh has remarked that '[t]he changing landscape of family life in a turbulent world has become "the new normal"'.[1] It is timely, therefore, to reflect on the extent and level of changes in different societies and on what they mean for current and future generations.

---

[1] Walsh, F. (ed.) (2012) *Normal Family Process: Growing Diversity and Complexity*, 4th edn (New York: Guilford).

Acknowledgements

We wish to offer our heartfelt thanks to Dr Vella and the Cana Movement for providing the impetus for the writing of this book. We would also like to thank His Excellency the President of the Republic of Malta and the Social Affairs Committee in Parliament for their interest, support and encouragement in helping us to achieve this.

We are extremely grateful to DIIFSD for its generous financial contribution towards our preparation of the book for publication. Our special thanks go to: Dato Fatima Saad, who was until December 2012 Director of Implementation and Social Research at DIIFSD, and who gave us her total support throughout the time it has taken us to complete the book; Dr Marya Reed, Director of Operations, who offered her support in the later stages of the book; and H. E. Noor Al-Malki Al-Jehani, Executive Director of DIIFSD. But above all, we pay tribute to the late Dr Richard Wilkins. As Executive Director of DIIFSD until early 2012, he was an unswerving and constant supporter of our venture, and it was with great sadness that we learned of his sudden and unexpected death in November 2012. Dr Wilkins had dedicated his life to championing and protecting families around the world. As a law professor, he had established the World Family Policy Centre at Brigham Young University and was a staunch advocate of traditional family values. Although he was opposed to many of the changes taking place in marriage and family life in recent decades, Dr Wilkins nevertheless acknowledged the importance of debate and of ensuring that research could inform our understanding of these changes. We trust that this book will be a fitting tribute to his life's work.

A special thank you goes to the Malta Community Chest Fund, a distinguished charitable institution chaired by His Excellency the President of Malta, for its generous financial support in the latter stages of the preparation of this publication. Its support highlights the importance the Maltese accord to families, and the President of Malta's determination to put family life at the centre of his presidency. We are very grateful for this support.

This book would not exist without the contributions of all the authors. They have been a pleasure to work with, and we trust that those who were fortunate enough to participate in the 2009 colloquium in Malta will consider this to be an exciting output. We very much hope that the contributors to the book will enjoy reading all the chapters. We offer our thanks to all of them.

During the preparation of the book we were fortunate to be able to call on the expertise of several colleagues. We have been helped enormously by the unstinting support of Jane Tilbrook, Janet Walker's personal assistant at Newcastle University, who made sure that all the elements of the book's preparation were managed and implemented efficiently and effectively, liaised with authors and staff at Wiley Blackwell and, in the latter stages, prepared the whole manuscript for publication. Claire Casha, Angela Abela's research officer at the University of Malta, provided support in Malta, and Michael Ayton, our excellent copy editor, worked tirelessly to ensure that our book is acceptable and intelligible to a wide range of readers. In particular, Michael's careful attention to detail was indispensable to authors whose first language is not English. Our final task was to undertake the indexing, and we were fortunate to secure the professional services of Ingrid Lock. To all four we offer our very sincere thanks for making sure the book has become a reality.

Finally, we would like to offer our very sincere thanks to the team at Wiley Blackwell, Darren Reed, Karen Shield and Olivia Evans, who have been enthusiastic and committed to this project, extremely patient when timelines have slipped, and consistently supportive of our endeavours. We very much hope that this will be a worthy addition to their portfolio.

Angela Abela
Department of Family Studies
University of Malta

Janet Walker
Institute of Health and Society
Newcastle University, UK

Contributors' Biographies

Professor Angela Abela is Head of the Family Studies Department at the University of Malta. She is a clinical psychologist and a UKCP-registered family therapist and supervisor. Angela is a consultant in the area of children and families for the Maltese government. Her research interests are in the area of children in out-of-home care, the relationship between adolescents and their parents, families living in poverty, and marital and couple relationships. She also has a long-standing research interest in how culture shapes relationship behaviour within the family. On an international level, she is frequently engaged as an expert of the Council of Europe. She has published widely in the area of children and families and supervision practice and is an associate editor of *Clinical Child Psychology and Psychiatry* and an international advisory editor of *Contemporary Family Therapy*.

Paul R. Amato is Arnold and Bette Hoffman Professor of Family Sociology and Demography at Pennsylvania State University, USA. His research interests include the causes and consequences of divorce, marriage and marital quality, and psychological wellbeing over the life course. He has received the Distinguished Career Award from the Family Section of the American Sociological Association, the Stanley Cohen Distinguished Research Award from the American Association of Family and Conciliation Courts, the Ernest Burgess Distinguished Career Award from the National Council on Family Relations, and the Distinction in the Social Sciences Award from Pennsylvania State University.

Layachi Anser is Professor of Sociology at Qatar University, Doha. He has taught and conducted research for over twenty years, covering various topics relating to North African and Middle Eastern societies, including economic development and political participation, civil society and social movements, family, marriage and gender. He has published a number of books and numerous journal articles in his area of interest.

Sabah Ayachi is a sociologist specialising in family studies and Head of the Laboratory of Family, Development, Prevention Delinquency and Criminality, University of Algiers, Algeria. In 2011, she founded a new academic BA entitled 'Sociology of family and childhood'. She has published many papers relating to youth, family and social change. She is co-author of a book on sociology (1998). She is a member of the European Early Childhood Education Research Association and of the Algerian National Family and Woman's Condition's Council.

Dr Eva Bernhardt is Professor Emerita of Demography, Stockholm University, Sweden. She specialises in the analysis of changing family dynamics in contemporary Sweden. Her main research area is family demography, with an emphasis on the intersection between work and family life, in particular from a gender perspective.

Karen Bogenschneider is Rothermel Bascom Professor of Human Ecology at the University of Wisconsin-Madison and a Family Policy Specialist at the University of Wisconsin-Extension, USA. She directs the Wisconsin Family Impact Seminars and the Policy Institute for Family Impact Seminars. Her book *Family Policy Matters: How Policymaking Affects Families and What Professionals Can Do* is in its third edition. She co-authored, with Thomas Corbett, *Evidence-Based Policymaking: Insights from Policy-minded Researchers and Research-minded Policymakers*. She was invited to write the family policy decade review in 2000 and 2010 for the *Journal of Marriage and Family*. She has received the Extension Specialist Lifetime Achievement Award and was named a fellow of the National Council on Family Relations. She has received several awards for faculty excellence, land grant scholarship, and quality outreach.

Professor John Bond is Strategic Research Advisor at the Institute of Health and Society at Newcastle University, UK. He trained as a sociologist and has worked since 1970 as a social gerontologist and applied health researcher. He was co-editor of three editions of the textbook *Ageing in Society* in 1990, 1993 and 2007. He is also author of *Quality of Life and Older People* (2004), with Lynne Corner, and *The Social World of Older People* (2009), with Christina Victor and Sasha Scambler. He has also written widely on psychosocial aspects of dementia and social support.

Lisa M. Boyd is a graduate student in Sociology and Demography at Pennsylvania State University, USA. Her research interests include romantic and sexual behaviour across the life course, biosocial and developmental determinants of relationship outcomes, interpersonal processes in families, marriage, and fertility decision-making. Her Masters thesis, 'Romantic and Sexual Experiences in Adolescence and Later Relationship Instability: How Do Family of Origin Factors Inform the Relationship Life Course?', looks at family structure and parent-child closeness as predictors of sexual and romantic outcomes in adolescence and early adulthood.

Simon B. Burnett is the Programme Manager of Working Families, the UK's leading work–life balance organisation. He is responsible for the Happy Homes, Productive Workplaces project, investigating the links between work engagement and relationship quality. Prior to this he focused on the effects of flexible working practices on the physiological and psychological health of working fathers. He is the author of a research monograph detailing the political and organisation use of happiness, and also lead- and co-author of numerous peer-reviewed articles on health and wellbeing at work, flexibility and work–life balance.

Dr John Coleman is a clinical and developmental psychologist and founder of the Trust for the Study of Adolescence in the UK. He has been a Policy Advisor at the Department of Health in England and is currently a Senior Research Fellow at the Department of Education at the University of Oxford. He has an international reputation for his work on adolescence. His best-known book is *The Nature of Adolescence* (Routledge, 2011), now in its fourth edition. He has a particular interest in parenting and has written widely on this topic. In 2001, he was awarded an OBE for his services to young people.

Cary Cooper is Distinguished Professor of Organisational Psychology and Health at Lancaster University, UK. He is the author/editor of over 120 books (on occupational stress, women at work and industrial and organisational psychology), has written over 400 scholarly articles for academic journals, and is a frequent contributor to national newspapers, TV and radio. He is currently Founding Editor of the *Journal of Organisational Behaviour* and Editor-in-Chief of the medical journal *Stress & Health*. He is a Fellow of the British Psychological Society, the Royal Society of Arts, the Royal Society of Medicine, the Royal Society of Public Health and the British Academy of Management, and Chair of the Academy of Social Sciences.

Dr Fabrizio D'Esposito is a Research Fellow at the Parenting Research Centre, Melbourne, Australia with an honorary position at the Murdoch Children's Research Institute. He has a PhD in Pharmacy and five years of experience in medical and clinical research. In recent years he has completed retraining in public health. His research interests include the study of the social determinants of physical and socio-emotional wellbeing in children and families from disadvantaged backgrounds, and the utilisation of evidence-based information and practice in parenting and family support programmes.

Dr Ruth Farrugia is an advocate and Senior Lecturer at the University of Malta. She lectures and researches in family law, child law and human rights. In Malta, she has served as consultant on family law and child law to the deputy Prime Minister and Minister for Social Policy, the Minister for Family and Social Solidarity, the Social Affairs Committee in Parliament, and the Commissioner for Children. She is an expert to the PRMIII Experts Group of the European Commission and the Child Access to Justice and Violence against Children programmes of the Council of Europe, country expert with the Comparative European Family Law Commission, the Common Core in Family Law Group and the Euro-Med Human Rights Group, and a Vice-President of the International Academy of Jurisprudence of the Family. She has published widely in the field of family law, child law and human rights.

Frank D. Fincham obtained a doctoral degree in social psychology while a Rhodes Scholar at Oxford University. He currently holds the Eminent Scholar Chair in Human Sciences, and is Director of the Family Institute at Florida State University, USA. He is the author of over 250 publications and his research has been widely recognised by numerous awards, including the Berscheid-Hatfield Award for 'sustained, substantial, and distinguished contributions to the field of personal relationships' from the International Network on Personal Relationships, and the President's Award for 'distinguished contributions to psychological knowledge' from the British Psychological Society. A Fellow of five different professional societies, he has been listed among the top 25 psychologists in the world in terms of impact (defined by number of citations per paper).

Dr W. Kim Halford is Professor of Clinical Psychology at the University of Queensland, Australia, and earned his doctorate at La Trobe University. Prior to that he was Professor of Clinical Psychology at Griffith University, and before that he held a joint appointment as Chief Psychologist of the Royal Brisbane Hospital and as a faculty member of the Department of Psychiatry of the University of Queensland. He has published five books and over 150 articles, primarily focused on couple therapy and couple relationship education. He works with couples adjusting to major life challenges, including developing committed relationships, coping with chronic health problems in a partner, becoming a parent, forming a stepfamily, negotiating co-parenting after separation, and living in intercultural couple relationships.

Lydia N. Hayes is a graduate student in the Sociology Programme at Pennsylvania State University, USA. Her research interests include romantic relationships, gender, and union formation. Her Masters thesis was entitled 'The Role of Facebook in the Formation of Romantic Relationships among College Students'.

Danika N. Hiew is a PhD candidate at the School of Psychology at the University of Queensland, Australia, where she graduated with the degree of Bachelor of Psychological Science with First Class Honours and as Valedictorian. She is a registered psychologist who has worked with couples and individuals coping with a variety of psychological and physical health conditions and family and couple relationship difficulties. As part of her PhD research, she has interviewed and conducted relationship assessments with over 100 Chinese, European and intercultural Chinese-European couples.

Dr Shuang Liu is Senior Lecturer in Communication at the School of Journalism and Communication at the University of Queensland, Australia. She obtained her PhD in communication from Hong Kong Baptist University, and has been researching in the areas of cross-cultural psychology, intercultural communication and intergroup relations. Her books, book chapters and refereed papers on culture and communication have been published in North America, Europe, Australia and Asia.

Nina Lucas (MPH) is a Research Officer at the Parenting Research Centre, Melbourne, Australia, with honorary/visiting positions at the Murdoch Children's Research Institute and the National Centre for Epidemiology and Population Health at the Australian National University. Her work primarily involves analysis of the Longitudinal Study of Australian Children, and she has a particular interest in the wellbeing of parents and children in separated families.

Ubaldo Martínez Veiga is Professor of Anthropology at the Universidad Nacional de Educación a Distancia, Spain. He obtained doctorates at the universities of Rome and

Madrid before teaching at the Universidad Autónoma de Madrid. He was a Fulbright Scholar at Columbia University (USA) and has been Visiting Professor at Johns Hopkins and Monash Universities, the London School of Economics, and, most recently, La Trobe University, Australia. He has authored more than 15 books on economic and ecological anthropology, labour problems, racism and immigration. His most recent research has focused on African migrants to Spain.

Melinda Mills is Professor of Sociology at the University of Groningen in the Netherlands, and is Editor-in-Chief of the *European Sociological Review*. Her research focuses on family formation, fertility and partnerships, the life course, flexible work arrangements, globalisation and event history methods. She currently leads a large-scale sociogenetics project linking sociological and genetic research on the family.

Dr Gabriela Misca is a developmental psychologist and Senior Lecturer in Psychology at the Institute of Health and Society at the University of Worcester, UK where she is also director of the MSc in Applied Psychology and of the BSc in Developmental Psychology pathway. After gaining degrees in psychology and social work at Babes-Bolyai University in Romania, she undertook her doctoral research at Newcastle University, UK in child and adolescent development. Her research interest is within the applied developmental psychology field. She has researched and taught in the interdisciplinary fields of child and adolescent development and their interface with social policy and practice. Her current research is in the specialist areas of resilience in child abuse and neglect, attachment and non-parental childcare, inter-country adoption and same-gender parenting.

Professor Jan M. Nicholson is the Research Director of the Parenting Research Centre, Melbourne, Australia, with Adjunct/Honorary positions at the Murdoch Children's Research Institute and Queensland University of Technology. A psychologist by background, with post-doctoral public health training, she has expertise in parenting and family influences on child development, with a particular interest in the influences of social inequalities and families' work and community environments. She is the Design Team Leader for parenting and family functioning in the Longitudinal Study of Australian Children, a national study tracking the health and development of two cohorts of 5000 children.

Dr Turid Noack is Senior Researcher at the research department at Statistics Norway. Her main focus of research has been on fertility, family formation and dissolution, and the relationship between family behaviour and family policies. Her current work involves research on grandparenthood, including on grandparents in both biological and step-grandparent relationships.

Charlotte J. Patterson is Professor of Psychology and Director of the interdisciplinary programme on Women, Gender and Sexuality at the University of Virginia, USA. Her interests focus on sexual orientation, human development and family lives. Best-known for her work on children of lesbian and gay parents, she recently coedited, with Anthony R. D'Augelli, the *Handbook of Psychology and Sexual Orientation* (Oxford University Press, 2013).

Dr Jan Pryor retired recently as Director of the McKenzie Centre for the Study of Families at Victoria University, Wellington, New Zealand. She is currently an Honorary Research Fellow in the School of Psychology at Auckland University and an Adjunct Professor at Victoria University. Her research includes the impact of separation and divorce on children and adults, and the dynamics of stepfamilies and stepfamily formation. She co-authored the book *Children in Changing Families: Life After Parental Separation* with Bryan Rodgers, and edited the *International Handbook of Stepfamilies*. She is currently writing a textbook on stepfamilies for family studies students in the USA.

James M. Raymo is a Professor in the Department of Sociology and the Center for Demography and Ecology at the University of Wisconsin-Madison, USA. He received his doctoral degree from the University of Michigan. Much of his research has focused on recent changes in patterns of family formation and socioeconomic differences in family behaviour, especially in Japan. In other work, he has examined life course influences on work, health and family outcomes at older ages in Japan and the USA. This work has appeared in journals such as *Demography*, *American Sociological Review*, *Journal of Marriage and Family*, and the Journal of *Gerontology: Social Psychology and Social Sciences*.

Marie-Cécile Renoux is the delegate of ATD Quart Monde to the European Union. A permanent volunteer with ATD Quart Monde since 1977, she has been involved in several actions supporting families in situations of extreme poverty in France. From 1999 to 2004, she was the delegate on family-related questions in ATD Quart Monde. As part of this role, she was a member of the committee of experts in the European Council. She is the author of *Réussir la Protection de l'Enfance avec les Familles en Precarité*.

Rachel G. Riskind, MA, is a doctoral candidate in psychology at the University of Virginia, USA. Her research deals with sexual orientation and human development, focusing on adolescence and young adulthood. She has studied adolescent girls' sexual and reproductive health, predictors of parenthood, and social climates surrounding members of sexual minority groups.

Jo Smith has been a Research Assistant in the Institute of Health and Society at the University of Worcester, UK. She is contributing to a research project on same-gender couples choosing parenthood through adoption and fostering. Her research interests are in child development, including clinical applications such as mental health. She is currently conducting a study of dementia and carer stress.

Jonathan Swan is Policy and Research Officer for Working Families in the UK. He has researched and written on a wide range of work–life integration issues, including fathers and work, flexible working in senior roles, productivity and performance, organisational culture and active ageing. He is responsible for the annual work–life balance benchmark for organisations and the *Time, Health and the Family* series of reports.

Maria Letizia Tanturri is Assistant Professor in Demography at the University of Padua, Italy. She has undertaken research in the area of reproductive behaviour, focusing on the link between gender roles, time-use and fertility, and on childlessness. Her research interests cover a variety of fields in demography, ranging from the characteristics of the foreign presence in Italy to the economic condition of the elderly in Europe. She has published on these topics in various international journals, including *Population and Development Review, European Journal of Population, Demographic Research, Population* and *Feminist Economics.* She is involved in a number of national and international research projects on reproductive behaviour and family change.

Samantha L. Tornello, MA, is a doctoral student in psychology at the University of Virginia, USA. Her research interests include parenting, couple functioning, and child development in the context of family systems, with an emphasis on families headed by members of sexual minorities. She has also conducted research on adolescent girls' sexual and reproductive health.

Justine van Lawick is a clinical psychologist and family therapist, and Director of Training at the Lorentzhuis Centre for Systemic Therapy, Training and Consultation in Haarlem, the Netherlands. She is a senior trainer in the Netherlands and abroad. Her areas of interest focus on addressing violent behaviour and demonisation in couples, couple groups and families, with compassion for all involved family members and without blaming. Children are central to her work, while another area of interest is working with marginalised families. She has published numerous articles and is co-author with Martine Groen of *Intimate Warfare: Regarding the Fragility of Family Relations* (Karnac Books, 2009).

Janet Walker is Emeritus Professor of Family Policy in the Institute of Health and Society at Newcastle University, UK. She studied social sciences and has worked as a probation officer, family therapist and family mediator. She was the Director of four research centres, retiring as Director of Newcastle Centre for Family Studies in 2006. She has led over 50 studies in the fields of marriage, divorce, parenting, youth justice, family law and family communication, and has published widely. She has been expert advisor to the Council of Europe and has served on several UK government committees. She has received the Stanley Cohen Distinguished Research Award, USA, is an Academician of the Academy of Learned Society of Social Sciences, and was awarded an OBE in 2010 for her work on the UK government's Social Security Advisory Committee.

Dr Elizabeth M. Westrupp is a Research Fellow and a registered Clinical Psychologist at the Parenting Research Centre, Melbourne, Australia and an Honorary Fellow at the Murdoch Children's Research Institute. She has experience with clinical and population-level longitudinal research, and with randomised control trials of parenting interventions across both the hospital and community settings. Her primary research interest is in exploring models of differential susceptibility, by investigating the effects of biological, and modifiable social and environmental, determinants on long-term developmental outcomes of children and families.

Monica T. Whitty is Professor of Contemporary Media in the Department of Media and Communication at the University of Leicester, UK. She is the first author of *Cyberspace Romance: The Psychology of Online Relationships* with Adrian Carr, and of

Truth, Lies and Trust on the Internet with Adam Joinson. She has published widely on the following topics: the online dating romance scam, cyber-relationships, internet infidelity, online identity, online deception, cyber-stalking, cyber-ethics, internet surveillance in the workplace, and taboos in video games.

Dr Kenneth Aarskaug Wiik, is a Senior Researcher in the research department at Statistics Norway. His main research area is in family demography, including socio-economic inequalities in union formation and relationship behaviour, with particular emphasis on differences between marriage and cohabitation.

Part I

Changing Couple and Family Relationships

The chapters in the first part of this book explore the changes taking place in couple and family relationships. The first four chapters focus on marriage. For centuries, marriage has signified a committed couple relationship via a legal contract which binds partners together, ostensibly for life. Marriage is influenced by a range of factors, however, including the norms and laws of each society, and by religious beliefs. The institution of marriage, like all social institutions in a given society, is continually adapting to internal and external changes. Over the last fifty years, however, these changes have been extensive; the more traditional pathways to getting married are being eroded and are giving way to a range of options for making, breaking and remaking couple relationships. It is these options which are explored in the chapters which follow.

One option is cohabitation. In the first chapter of this section, Chapter 2, Turid Noack, Eva Bernhardt and Kenneth Aarskaug Wiik explore the development of cohabiting relationships since 1800 and examine the current rise, and variation, in cohabitation patterns across the Western world. They consider different types of cohabitation in different countries and point out that while cohabitation as a partnership type of choice has become commonplace in the Nordic countries and France, the number of those cohabiting in eastern and southern Europe is low. Nevertheless, living together in an intimate couple relationship without being married is becoming increasingly acceptable in many countries, although statutory regulation of cohabitation is not well-developed, except in countries with high cohabitation rates. The extent to which cohabitation is replacing marriage is debatable, however, particularly since the symbolic importance of marriage remains high. The authors conclude that

Contemporary Issues in Family Studies: Global Perspectives on Partnerships, Parenting and Support in a Changing World, First Edition. Edited by Angela Abela and Janet Walker.
© 2014 John Wiley & Sons, Ltd. Published 2014 by John Wiley & Sons, Ltd.

it is still reasonable to consider marriage and cohabitation as distinct aspects of partnership formation.

Emerging forms of marriage and couple relationships are explored further in Chapter 3. Paul Amato and Lydia Hayes describe a form of marriage in the USA that they term 'alone together' marriages, and 'living apart together' (LAT) relationships, which are more common in Europe. Drawing on cross-sectional data sets, the authors show how marriage in the USA has changed, and use measures of happiness and interaction to create a typology of marriages. They present vignettes to illustrate this typology.

Amato and Hayes point to a shift in the USA from companionate to individualistic marriages, which are successful only insofar as they continue to meet each partner's innermost psychological needs and deepest wishes. They argue that the rise in alone together marriages can be seen as indicating a natural adaptation to and extension of the growing individualism of American society. By contrast, in LAT relationships, unmarried partners in an intimate relationship maintain dual households. Data about LATs are relatively sparse, but evidence suggests that while most LAT relationships are transitory, others are long-lasting, and a deliberate alternative to marital and non-marital cohabitation. Amato and Hayes suggest that long-term LATs face different challenges and may be particularly fragile when problems occur in the relationship.

The discussion of fragility in couple relationships is developed by Jan Pryor in her review of marriage and divorce in the Western world (Chapter 4). In order to understand the rapid increase in divorce in the last half of the twentieth century, she considers the role of religion, individualism, connectedness, and the changing characteristics of marriage. She argues that connectedness and commitment have not weakened in the Western world. She highlights the distress which accompanies divorce, and argues for a more holistic view of intimate relationships in the twenty-first century and more inclusive approaches for promoting wellbeing and stability in couple relationships. Within this context, she examines different levels of commitment in relationship wellbeing and makes a case for strengthening relational commitment.

Although high rates of divorce have been associated with the USA and countries in Northern Europe, divorce is having an increasing impact across the globe. Layachi Anser (Chapter 6) focuses on the challenge posed by divorce in Gulf societies, enabling us to understand changes in marriage and divorce in the Arab world. Muslim societies have always upheld the sanctity of marriage and divorce is regarded as a last resort in a troubled relationship. Nevertheless, the rapid economic and global transformations which have made the Gulf region the richest in the world have had far-reaching impacts on family life, despite the existence of very strong kinship ties. Anser suggests that a complex interaction between internal and external factors has resulted in increasing opportunities being open to women while, at the same time, mate selection and marriage are still strongly influenced by kinship and tribal frameworks. The chapter provides a powerful illustration of the tensions and contradictions which emerge as global changes compete with long-revered traditional values and processes.

The next three chapters in Part I examine three different aspects of family life which have global relevance. The first (Chapter 6) looks at couple and family dynamics in respect of family violence; the second (Chapter 7) examines the growing significance of intercultural couple relationships; and the third (Chapter 8) considers the challenges and opportunities in family life as people grow older.

Family violence has received increasing attention over the last fifty years. In her chapter, Justine van Lawick discusses different perspectives on family violence, considers the evidence relating to both male and female violence, and describes innovative approaches to treatment. She asserts that it is possible to link escalations in violence to the frustrations in human relationships and stress factors in day-to-day family life, and argues that unless these complex dynamics are fully understood treatment programmes will be ineffective. Since family violence is a universal phenomenon, in van Lawick's view contextualisation is necessary to avoid simplistic perspectives on and approaches to a very serious issue in couple relationships.

Danika Hiew, Kim Halford and Shuang Liu examine the complexities of intercultural couple relationships, looking specifically at relationships between spouses of European and Chinese ancestry. Although intercultural partnerships were rare in the past, opportunities today to form relationships across cultural divides are growing. Using vignettes, the authors examine communication between a partner brought up in an individualistic culture and a partner brought up in a collectivist culture. This insightful overview emphasises the powerful role of culture in shaping expectations of relationships, and introduces the innovative Yin and Yang relationship measure. Importantly, this chapter reminds us of the tendency to view one's own culture's way of doing things as necessarily right and of the need to transcend any one single cultural tradition when developing policies and programmes to support couple relationships in a changing world.

In the final chapter in this section, John Bond also reminds us of the dangers of adopting cultural stereotypes stemming from a Westernised view of family life. He reviews the impact of global changes as perceived by older people. Life expectancy is increasing worldwide, although there are clear regional variations. Societal attitudes to ageing shape both the lived experience of growing older and the predominant discourse, which sees ageing as either an opportunity or a problem. Bond highlights ways in which the changes in couple relationships and family life discussed in earlier chapters will impact on the availability of family support in later life, but he questions whether intergenerational ties are any weaker than previously, and argues that reciprocity in families is as strong as it has ever been. This optimistic perspective nevertheless signals the important role of the state in preparing people for later life and ensuring that older people can live independently within community and family networks.

In all these chapters, cultural context emerges as a key factor influencing the ways in which people are responding to changes in relationships and living arrangements. References to the Second Demographic Transition are made in several chapters throughout the book as a means of contextualising the ideological shifts towards individualism in modern societies.

1

Global Changes in Marriage, Parenting and Family Life
An Overview

ANGELA ABELA AND JANET WALKER

Introduction

We live in a time of unprecedented diversity in household living arrangements, and of extensive social, cultural and economic change, both of which have far-reaching implications for marriage, parenting and family life in the twenty-first century. While families across the globe have always taken a variety of forms, certain functions, such as the nurture of children and care of family members, are universal. The concept of family denotes stability, and most societies have placed a high value on the institution of marriage as providing the best environment in which to bring up children.

Contemporary global variations in partnership formation and decreasing marriage rates have generated concerns that family stability is under threat and family values are in decline. Expressions of a looming crisis in family relationships, however, can be traced through hundreds of years of social history. Such concerns primarily revolve around the weakening of the nuclear family, comprising a married couple and their children, widely regarded as the traditional family structure in Western societies. But this kind of family is by no means a universal phenomenon, nor is it essential for carrying out family functions. As diversity increases, it is vitally important to examine the nature and extent of the changes in marriage, parenting practices and family life taking place across the globe; to understand the impacts of these changes on adults' and children's wellbeing, on communities, and on societies as a whole; and to assess the steps that might need to be taken by governments and others to develop family-friendly policies and support services that can enable families to foster strong, stable, loving environments in which family members can flourish and reach their potential in the modern world.

Contemporary Issues in Family Studies: Global Perspectives on Partnerships, Parenting and Support in a Changing World, First Edition. Edited by Angela Abela and Janet Walker.
© 2014 John Wiley & Sons, Ltd. Published 2014 by John Wiley & Sons, Ltd.

This book has drawn on the expertise of scholars around the world to consider the challenges and opportunities currently facing families in different societies and to review the evidence about changes in partnership and parenting. In this first chapter, we provide a brief overview of the key changes and set the global context for the more in-depth discussions in subsequent chapters about how these changes are affecting people in different societies at a time when long-established cultural traditions and belief systems are having to accommodate modern conceptions and expectations of intimate couple relationships and varying approaches to child rearing.

In developing this book, we were influenced by evidence that points to the importance of family bonds and strong, stable family relationships for the development and maintenance of strong stable societies. It is clear to us that the quality of the relationships between parents as partners and between parents and their children are critical determinants in enabling us to assess the risk and protective factors in children's lives. An understanding of the interrelationships between these factors and how resilience may be fostered is, we would argue, critical to the development of policies which can support families at times of stress and increased vulnerability to global conditions which might increase risk. Reviewing the wide variety of couple relationships and modern approaches to marriage was the obvious starting point for the book. Love and marriage are symbolic constructions that derive their meaning from the social, cultural and historical contexts in which they are embedded (Albas and Albas, 1989). As McKie and Callan (2012) have pointed out, it is a Western assumption that couple relationships now result exclusively from emotional response and the process of 'falling in love'. Nevertheless, Balfour *et al.* (2012, p. xxix) have argued that, irrespective of family structure, couple relationships shape our world:

> … the qualities of our relationships have profound implications from our earliest years, for the emotional, cognitive, and physical development of our children, to our latest years—in old age, affecting the likelihood of hospitalisation, the rate of progression of disease in dementia, and even mortality rates.

Changes in Marriage and Couple Relationships

While married couples still constitute the main type of adult couple partnerships in most countries, many people enter marriage having experienced earlier sexual relationships and, increasingly, both men and women exercise choice about the kind of partnership they enter into. Although many social commentators believe that marriage provides the most secure foundation for raising children and healthy family life, marriage is a multi-faceted concept. Until well into the seventeenth century in England, for example, love and companionship were secondary considerations in the marriage relationship, which was primarily an economic union, with the choice of marital partner less a matter of mate selection and more a matter of suitable living arrangements having been made. In the twentieth century, increasing emphasis on achieving personal emotional satisfaction and self-fulfilment in marriage began to change people's expectations about the marriage relationship.

In some cultures, couple formation has been orchestrated by families and arranged marriages are still in evidence. Parental control over mate selection is decreasing, however, and there is now a shift towards a more romantic approach to marriage in countries such as Turkey, Japan (Roopnarine and Gielen, 2005), China (Xiaohe and Whyte, 1998) and India (Leeder, 2004). Increased choice in mate selection is being reflected in increased choice about whether and when to marry. Marriage still carries a distinctive symbolic importance (Cherlin, 2009) and remains an aspiration for many people, including those forming same-sex partnerships. Vigorous campaigning for legal recognition for same-sex marriage has been successful in several countries.

Increasingly, getting married is no longer an expected prerequisite for living together as a couple. In the past, living together as an unmarried couple was socially and culturally prohibited, and it tended to be the last resort for people who were unable to marry for one reason or another. Today, living together in a cohabiting relationship is increasingly common both as a precursor to getting married and as the partnership of choice. As a consequence, increasing numbers of children are born into cohabiting relationships in the USA, the UK and countries in northern Europe, although the stability of these relationships has been questioned. Initial indications are that cohabiting partnerships are less stable and more prone to breakdown, but recent evidence from countries in which cohabitation has become the norm challenges these concerns and raises questions about the extent to which cohabitation increases the risk of relationships breaking down (Reinhold, 2010). Nevertheless, there is a strong pro-marriage movement in some countries, such as the USA, which illustrates a continuing tension between welcoming choice in mate selection and greater diversity in living arrangements on the one hand, and valuing the continuity provided by the institutional structures associated with marriage on the other. The advantages of marriage over cohabitation are now being questioned by research which demonstrates that both marriage and cohabitation increase wellbeing, putting the focus firmly on the quality of relationships rather than on their legal status (Musick and Bumpass, 2012).

Marriage has undergone a process of de-institutionalisation in recent decades, particularly in Western societies. Nevertheless, marriage represents a rite of passage which gives public recognition to statements of commitment between the partners, whereas no such transformative process is associated with cohabitation. Recent research which seeks to understand the nature of commitment suggests that commitment-forming behaviour in relationships is triggered differentially in men and women, resulting in a lack of congruence (Stanley, 2010). This suggests that partners' commitments to each other are not necessarily linked to the status of their relationship, and further research is needed to understand the influences on commitment in all kinds of couple relationships.

Greater choice in personal relationships is reflected in patterns of partnership formation around the world and in the growing number of individuals who choose to remain single, both in the Western world (Wilkes Karraker and Grochowski, 2012) and in Asian and Arab countries. Moreover, polygyny, although not widely practised, is decreasing as societal pressures against men having many wives have increased and the exclusivity of a monogamous relationship has become ever more highly valued.

What, then, are the changes in marriage and couple relationships that we need to understand better in order to promote and foster personal and structural commitment and stable relationships? The changes that are deemed critical to policy formation and the development of supportive interventions are shown in the box below. These are discussed in more detail in Part I of the book.

> ## Key changes in marriage and couple relationships
>
> We need to understand more about:
>
> 1. The impact increasing choice has in:
>   (a) the forming of intimate relationships
>   (b) decisions about whether to marry, when to marry, and choice of marital partner
>   (c) couples' living arrangements (e.g. living apart together)
> 2. Shifting expectations of couple relationships in respect of:
>   (a) individualism versus connectedness and commitment
>   (b) the intricacies of same-sex partnerships
>   (c) marriage as optional

Changes in Parenting

Bringing up children has been regarded as one of the most important tasks that adults perform. Marriage has traditionally been the prerequisite for legitimate procreation and child rearing across the globe. Indeed, being married and having children have traditionally brought with them the status of being a family, but shifts in partnership formation have inevitably impacted on the transition to parenthood. One of the key contradictions in family life today relates to the increased freedom of choice in respect of partnership formation on the one hand, and the expectations and constraints associated with being a parent on the other. A very high value is placed on the importance of good parenting and on fathers and mothers being involved in parental activities that support child development, yet parenthood requires no particular form of intimate relationship or family structure.

The increase in cohabitation and the deferment of marriage means that parenting takes place in the context of a multiplicity of family forms, including single-parent families, reconstituted families and same-sex partnerships. There has been a marked increase in same-sex couples forming families and bringing up children—a shift which engenders deep prejudices about the importance of children having both a mother and a father and generates passionate debates about the conditions that foster a positive environment for child rearing. Assertions that the demise of the 'traditional' family has resulted in increases in antisocial behaviour and juvenile offending, drug and alcohol misuse, behavioural disorders in children, rates of teenage pregnancy and education failure are challenged in a report by Goodman and Greaves (2010) that indicates that children's cognitive, social and emotional development does not appear to be affected by the marital status of their parents. This assertion is consistent with research indicating that healthy, well-functioning parental relationships facilitate the wellbeing of and positive outcomes for children. Moreover, parental sexual orientation does not appear to be associated with child adjustment. Until relatively recently, however, it would have been inconceivable that, in an increasing number of countries, same-sex couples could both legitimise their relationship and raise children.

These changes have reopened the debate about child attachment. The psychological literature has moved away from a belief in the exclusiveness of the mother–child relationship in child development towards the realisation that children form multiple attachments and that fathers as well as mothers play a critical role in child development. The prevailing view has been that children brought up in single-parent families will do less well on a range of outcomes than those living in two-parent households. An informed review of the evidence, however, points to a number of characteristics and factors that negatively impact on the parenting and wellbeing of single parents. Single mothers who are not in a relationship are exposed to a wide variety of risk factors which compromise their parenting ability: they tend to be young, and to have poor education and limited financial resources, and they may live in poor and hostile neighbourhoods, factors which place them at risk of poor mental health and their children at risk of poor outcomes. Moreover, the majority of single-parent families are formed following parental separation and divorce, and this transition in family life exposes children and parents to additional risk factors.

The impact of separation and divorce

Up until the twentieth century, divorce was not a feature of daily life. When relationships broke down, economic, social and emotional constraints kept many women locked into unhappy and, often, violent relationships. Divorce was the privilege of the rich, of the clergy, and of men. Those women who did separate and form new partnerships were not able either to divorce or to remarry. Only during the twentieth century did divorce become a real option in most countries. In Catholic countries, the sacramental nature of marriage rendered it indissoluble, though the Roman Catholic Church has always permitted annulments. Nevertheless, only in the twenty-first century has divorce been legalised in Catholic countries such as Chile and Malta.

During the twentieth century, the possibility of legally terminating a marriage brought relief to many intensely unhappy people, particularly those who had been subject to domestic abuse and had been unable to leave the relationship, and the chance to find happiness with another partner and remarry. Nevertheless, the rapid increase in the number of families experiencing separation and divorce, described by some social historians as a 'gigantic moral, religious and legal revolution' (Stone, 1977, p. 422), has caused great concern in the last fifty years.

Although more marriages survive than end in divorce, large numbers of children across the globe will experience parental separation, the remarriage or repartnering of their parents, and multiple transitions in family living arrangements. Repeated disruptions increase children's vulnerability and these children are the most likely to be adversely affected by the break-up of their parents' relationship. Evidence accumulated from around the world points to the potential negative outcomes for children and their parents. Although no direct causal relationship has been found between parental separation and detrimental outcomes for children, a number of factors contribute towards enhanced risks. These include: economic hardship; continuing parental conflict; multiple transitions and changes in household structures and living arrangements; the loss of parental relationships (most often with fathers); one or both partners being unable to make a satisfactory adaptation to the dissolution of the couple relationship; and failure to keep children informed about what is happening and to hear their voice.

Many of the concerns being expressed about the demise of marriage and family life have focused on the perceived ease with which a divorce can be obtained and the decreasing element of social stigma associated with a failed relationship. Yet research shows that the decision to end a relationship is rarely taken lightly and that the vast majority of parents think very seriously about the impacts before taking action. Parents face many dilemmas as they weigh up the consequences of separation, and those who stay in unhappy relationships for the sake of their children are acutely aware of the damaging effects of ongoing parental conflict and disharmony (Walker *et al.*, 2004).

Increasingly, the view being taken is that people do not divorce simply as an overt expression of individualistic behaviour or because marriage is not important to them, but because expectations of marriage and intimate couple relationships have become so high that staying in a less than satisfactory relationship is not to be tolerated. It is not surprising, therefore, that people continue to seek a fulfilling partnership and remarry or form a new relationship, often quite quickly. The breakdown rate of second and subsequent marriages remains high, however, and the unresolved emotions carried forward from one relationship to another can seriously undermine attempts to create a more stable relationship second or third time round. This is particularly challenging for parents who have to accommodate child contact arrangements with a former partner while trying to build a new family environment. While some people manage to rebuild shattered lives and to create more stable, healthier family units, others continue to live on the cusp of breakdown, with a range of stressors characterising their daily lives. Parents and children are rarely well-prepared for the enormity of the changes they face when families split up, and one of the most challenging tasks for parents is working out how they will live separately and continue to parent. This is hugely demanding and frequently leads to disputes between parents, and may result in one parent (usually the father) losing contact with their children.

Making sense of changes in parenting

In seeking to understand contemporary changes in parenting and family life and the implications for policy and practice, it is important to determine what is genuinely different between the situation today and in times past. In the mid-nineteenth century in the UK, for example, just as many marriages ended through death within 15 years as now end in divorce in the same time period. As a result, large numbers of children lost a parent through death by the age of 15, and step-parents were a normal feature of Victorian family life. Then as now, many children were born out of wedlock. Death is final, however, whereas divorce is not. Furthermore, the coexistence in the twenty-first century of so many choices, and of alternative legally acceptable ways of partnering and organising family life, in any one society renders relationships today qualitatively different (Coontz, 2004). The contributors to this book have sought to explore this diversity and address a number of key issues in Part II of the book. These issues are indicated in the box below.

Changes in parenting: key issues

1. Raising children in single-parent families.
2. Sexual orientation and parenting.
3. Child development theories and processes.
4. The roles of mothers and fathers.
5. The impact of increasing parental separation and divorce.

Global Changes in Family Life

Family structures and parenting practices are heavily influenced by social, cultural and economic factors, but the global changes explored primarily in Part III of this book are being felt across cultures and boundaries. Increased globalisation and significant demographic and social shifts are also shaping the way we live our lives. An understanding of these is central to the quest for more supportive family environments irrespective of family structures. We have focused our attention on six global issues, indicated in the box below, and we refer briefly here to each in turn.

Global impacts on partnerships and parenting

1. Changing roles of men and women—combining work and family life.
2. Demographic changes.
3. Wealth inequality and poverty.
4. Migration.
5. Technological advances in communication.
6. Religion and belief systems.

Changing roles of men and women: combining work and family life

Traditional conceptions of family life have regarded men as breadwinners and women as homemakers and carers. These ascribed roles paint a picture of complementarity within a patriarchal model of family stability. It is doubtful whether this idealised image ever reflected the kind of family life experienced by most people, but it is nevertheless clear that gender roles are being transformed across the globe as women postpone the formation of committed couple relationships to pursue advanced education and meaningful careers. The twentieth century witnessed a feminist movement which campaigned for gender equality at home, in the workplace and in society in general. The achievement of gender equality is a fairly slow process, however, and a disproportionate amount of unpaid work and caring responsibilities continue to be undertaken by women, even when they are in employment outside the home.

In many societies, the pressure on women to contribute to the household income is rising and the number of dual-earner families is increasing. This has significant impacts on childbearing as women delay the transition to parenthood, rendered increasingly possible by effective methods of birth control. The result tends to be smaller families and a tension between undertaking caring responsibilities and engaging in the world of paid work. In the Western world, women's participation in paid work is greater than at any previous period other than during the two World Wars of the twentieth century. The policy in many European countries, for example, of encouraging families to be economically self-sufficient and independent of welfare benefits has shifted social expectations firmly away from gender divisions in employment towards family life characterised by both parents working outside the home. Increasingly, women's earnings have become a necessary part of family income. There is, nevertheless, a distinct gender pay gap in most countries, which reinforces gender discrimination.

The challenge for many women is how to balance work commitments with caring responsibilities towards children and older family members. This can create tensions in the home and have a detrimental impact on couple relationships, particularly when incomes are low and couples are worried about their finances. Single parents are the hardest hit as they have to balance caring responsibilities with being the sole breadwinner. Moreover, many single mothers are likely to be in low-paid jobs, which are frequently precarious. This kind of employment can have a devastating effect on parents' mental and physical health and on their capacity to parent effectively. Many have to make difficult choices about how to prioritise the expectations placed on them and yet fulfil their caring obligations.

While there is global recognition that families are responsible for raising children and offering care and support to older generations, the burden of care still falls on women in most societies, irrespective of family structures. This reality increasingly impacts on the choices women make and on gender equality. Even when a couple has forged an equal partnership and created well-balanced gender roles in the home, the transition to parenthood can easily destabilise the status quo, with serious consequences for relationship stability, particularly during the postnatal period (Borg Xuereb *et al.*, 2012). The gendered allocation of household and caring tasks can be stressful and tiring, leaving little time for couple-focused activities.

Demographic changes

Global demographic changes are among the most significant in twenty-first-century family life. A decline in fertility rates and an increase in life expectancy are changing the shape of populations in all corners of the globe. As countries move from pre-industrial to industrialised economies there tends to be a transition in birth and death rates from high to low. As choices about family formation increase and women improve their access to education and work opportunities, fertility rates tend to decline. Moreover, there are still parts of the world, such as sub-Saharan Africa, where both infant and maternal mortality rates remain high, reflecting huge global differences in life chances and choices (McKie and Callan, 2012).

The increasing numbers of people who are living longer is one of the greatest demographic challenges for the twenty-first century. There are concerns in Europe about fertility rates being lower than the minimum rate required for generation replacement, and global concerns about how to support an increasingly elderly population. Not all older people are well-off and Eurostat 2012 figures show that 20 per cent of older people in Europe are at risk of poverty and social exclusion (Eurostat, 2012). There are considerable regional disparities: for example, people over sixty-five in Eastern European countries are at a higher risk of poverty than those living in northern Europe. Furthermore, increasing numbers of older people are living alone and are dependent on family support. One of the consequences of family breakdown is that older people may find themselves severed from family support. The more traditional approach to providing intergenerational care is increasingly threatened.

Wealth inequality and poverty

The changes explored in this book are taking place during a period of severe global recession and fiscal austerity. Recovery from recession is expected to be slow and income inequalities may continue to increase in OECD countries (OECD, 2008).

Cherlin (2010) has argued that the income gap is causing a marriage gap, whereby poorer people are least likely to get married and most likely to get divorced.

Since the 1980s, average family incomes have increased across OECD countries but in many countries child poverty rates have also increased, although there are considerable variations between countries. Poverty in childhood is known to have a damaging effect on children's development and wellbeing, and to contribute to a range of problems for children and for their mothers, particularly in respect of health. Unemployment is the single biggest risk factor for poverty and, across the OECD, being unemployed as a single parent can almost triple the risk of poverty. Poverty falls disproportionately on women, resulting from a combination of unpaid and paid work, limited access to well-paid jobs, the gender pay gap, and limited choices because of caring responsibilities.

There are still parts of the world where poverty is extreme, presenting a continuing global challenge. The World Bank (2012) has estimated that 1.29 billion people were living in absolute poverty in 2008. The highest incidence of absolute poverty is in sub-Saharan Africa, India and China. Although both India and China are increasing their rate of economic growth, poverty and its impacts on families will continue to be a significant concern.

Migration

Migration has long been an important response to the impact of poverty: families have migrated to other countries in the hope of finding employment and a better quality of life. This has resulted in huge cultural diversity within the populations of many Western countries and in growing numbers of cross-cultural households. Immigration flows have a range of impacts on family life and on partnership formation and parenting. Hochschild (2003) noted that at the millennium, about half of the world's 120 million legal and illegal (irregular)[1] immigrants were female, indicating a new trend in migration patterns and increasing numbers of children being left behind in the care of extended family members. Migration is set to continue, and the number of cross-cultural marriages is expected to increase. The demographic characteristics of migrants are increasingly varied: whereas in the past many migrants were poor, greater numbers of migrants now are well-educated, highly qualified and taking advantage of the opportunities open to them in both developed and developing countries. Nevertheless, the world economic recession has highlighted tensions in migration policies.

Technological advances in communication

The most significant global change impinging on partnerships, parenting and family life today is, arguably, the rapid development of electronic communications, and in particular the Internet. Children in many countries are growing up with a remarkable capacity to use digital technology in all aspects of their lives, and this will undoubtedly change work patterns and the ways in which people communicate. It is possible, for

[1] Diverse terminology is used in respect of migrants with irregular or unauthorised status. The term 'illegal' immigration is typically used in the US context. See http://www.migrationpolicy.org/pubs/tcmirregular-migration.pdf [Accessed 31.1.2013.]

example, for partners to live far apart and communicate daily, offering increased autonomy within an intimate relationship.

Social networking is a central part of many young people's daily lives, and is already changing concepts of identity and the ways relationships are forged. Social networking sites, email, texting, Facebook and Twitter increase the opportunities for people to develop large global networks well beyond family and local community boundaries. Daily life will increasingly be affected by the technological advances of the last twenty years, and advances continue at an extraordinary rate. The implications of these opportunities and their impacts are only just now being explored, and it will be essential, in the years to come, for policymakers and practitioners to understand them fully.

Religion and belief systems

Religion and belief systems have long provided the context for marriage, parenting and family life. Religious beliefs have strongly influenced debates about cohabitation, divorce, civil partnerships and same-sex relationships, and assisted reproduction. The global changes in family life continue to be influenced by a range of belief systems. The challenge facing governments is how to embrace new conditions which enhance economic development, increase mobility and open new opportunities without colliding with beliefs and cultural norms which favour more traditional approaches to family life. Partnerships and parenting are shaped by a wide range of factors and, in the twenty-first century, the boundaries of what is socially acceptable are being challenged as never before. As expectations change, the values of commitment and connectedness within families are being confronted. Adaptations are inevitable as new norms emerge and social institutions take account of world economic, social, technological and political systems. Yet, there is strong evidence that reciprocity, support and companionship continue to be hallmarks of family life, even in countries in which personal relationships are increasingly individualistic (Smart, 2007).

Looking Ahead

Partnerships and parenting practices in the twenty-first century are influenced by social, cultural and economic changes on a global scale. There is no doubt that stable, supportive families are important to growth and development, rendering it essential to understand the pressures, opportunities and challenges families face. Collaboration and cooperation among policymakers and practitioners at a local, national and international level should inform the kind of investment that needs to be made to support families and embrace diversity. The role of the state in supporting families is explored in Part IV.

In the chapters which follow, leading scholars examine the key changes of relevance to families and governments today in order to ensure a greater understanding of the ways in which family-friendly policies and interventions can be promoted and a constructive balance between continuity and change can be maintained. We hope that the policy and practice recommendations at the end of each chapter will, as well as being informative, inspire debate and innovative thinking.

References

Albas, D. and Albas, C. M. (1989) Love and marriage, in K. Ishwaran (ed.), *Family and Marriage: Cross-cultural perspectives* (Toronto, Ont.: Wall & Thompson), 125–144.

Balfour, A., Morgan, M. and Vincent, C. (2012) *How Couple Relationships Shape Our World: Clinical practice, research and policy perspectives* (London: Karnac).

Borg Xuereb, R., Abela, A. and Spiteri, G. (2012) Early parenting—portraits from the lives of first-time parents, *Journal of Reproductive and Infant Psychology*, 30(5): 468–482.

Cherlin, A. J. (2009) *The Marriage-go-round: The state of marriage and the American family today* (New York: Knopf).

Cherlin, A. J. (2010) Demographic trends in the United States: a review of research in the 2000s, *Journal of Marriage and Family*, 72(3): 403–419.

Coontz, S. (2004) The world historical transformation of marriage, *Journal of Marriage and Family*, 66(4): 974–979.

Eurostat (2012) *At Risk of Poverty or Social Inclusion in the EU27* (news release 21/2012). http://epp.eurostat.ec.europa.eu/cache/ITY_PUBLIC/3-08022012-AP/EN/3-08022012-AP-EN.PDF [Accessed 14.1.2013.]

Goodman, A. and Greaves, E. (2010) *Cohabitation, Marriage and Child Outcomes* (London: Institute for Fiscal Studies).

Hochschild, A. (2003) *The Commercialisation of Intimate Life: Notes from home and work* (Berkeley, CA: University of California Press).

Leeder, E. (2004) *The Family in Global Perspective* (Thousand Oaks, CA: Sage).

McKie, L. and Callan, S. (2012) *Understanding Families: A global introduction* (London: Sage).

Musick, K. and Bumpass, L. (2012) Re-examining the case for marriage: union formation and changes in well-being, *Journal of Marriage and Family*, 74(1): 1–18.

OECD (2008) *Growing Unequal? Income distribution and poverty in OECD countries* (Paris: OECD).

http://dx.doi.org/10.1787/9789264044197-en DOI:%2010.1787/9789264044197-en [Accessed 15.1.2013.]

Reinhold (2010) Reassessing the link between premarital cohabitation and marital instability, *Demography*, 47(3): 719–734.

Roopnarine, J. L. and Gielen, U. P. (2005) Families in global perspective: an introduction, in J. L. Roopnarine and U. P. Gielen (eds), *Families in Global Perspective* (Boston, MA: Pearson): 3–13.

Smart, C. (2007) *Personal Life: New directions in sociological thinking* (Cambridge: Polity Press).

Stanley, S. M. (2010) *What Is It with Men and Commitment Anyway?* Working paper. http://www.catholicmarriagenz.org.nz/LinkClick.aspx?fileticket=heMvkVXifVE%3D&tabid=8358&mid=16310&language=en-US [Accessed 25.1.2013.]

Stone, L. (1977) *The Family, Sex and Marriage in England, 1500–1800* (London: Weidenfeld & Nicolson).

Walker, J., McCarthy, P., Stark, C. and Laing, K. (2004) *Picking Up the Pieces: Marriage and divorce two years after information provision* (London: Department for Constitutional Affairs).

Wilkes Karraker, M. and Grochowski, J. R. (2012) *Families with Futures: Family studies into the 21st century* (New York and London: Routledge).

World Bank (2012) *Poverty Reduction and Equity*. http://web.worldbank.org/WBSITE/EXTERNAL/TOPICS/EXTPOVERTY/EXTPA/0,,contentMDK:20040961~menuPK:435040~pagePK:148956~piPK:216618 ~ theSitePK:430367 ~ isCURL:Y,00.html [Accessed 15.1.2013.]

Xiaohe, X. and Whyte, W. T. (1998) Love matches and arranged marriages: a Chinese replication, in S. Ferguson (ed.), *Shifting the Center: Understanding contemporary families* (Mountain View, CA: Mayfield): 115–133.

2

Cohabitation or Marriage? Contemporary Living Arrangements in the West

TURID NOACK, EVA BERNHARDT AND
KENNETH AARSKAUG WIIK

Introduction

Forming a co-residential union, usually with a person of the opposite sex, is one of the most important transitions in the life course of an individual. This event has social significance in most societies. Traditionally, this has usually meant getting married. In Western countries today, however, many decisions which in the past were made in order to conform with socially prescribed behaviour have now become free choices. New stages in the life course have emerged, resulting in a de-standardisation of family formation patterns. Cohabitation, and living independently without a partner before moving into a couple relationship, both constitute such new stages. Cohabitation has thus been viewed as just one component of many in the formation of a co-residential union, a process during which individual behaviour is less determined by tradition and institutional arrangements, and is more open to individual choice (Giddens, 1992). In Scandinavian countries, where unmarried cohabitation has emerged as a well-established phenomenon over many decades, it would now seem to be quite normative, at least for young people, to cohabit before (possibly) getting married. Indeed, to marry directly without previous cohabitation is seen as deviant behaviour (Bernhardt, 2001).

Cohabitation can be defined as non-marital co-residential union—of, that is, partners who maintain an intimate relationship and live together in the same dwelling but without being married to each other (Prinz, 1995). This kind of union can be constituted by opposite-sex as well as by same-sex couples. Our knowledge about same-sex cohabitation is rather sparse, however, especially when it comes to international comparisons. More recently, in some countries same-sex partners have also been able to formalise their union by entering marriage or marriage-like unions.

Contemporary Issues in Family Studies: Global Perspectives on Partnerships, Parenting and Support in a Changing World, First Edition. Edited by Angela Abela and Janet Walker.
© 2014 John Wiley & Sons, Ltd. Published 2014 by John Wiley & Sons, Ltd.

In most countries we find that somewhat similar terms are used to describe cohabitation. The terminology tends to be more uniform with the increasing number of cohabitations. Unlike marriage, cohabitation has normally not been regulated by law, nor has its occurrence been officially registered. Therefore, cohabitation is often referred to as an informal union. Over recent years, however, there has been increasing regulation of cohabitation in some countries.

Cohabitation is increasing in prevalence all over the Western world—in Europe, North America, Australia and New Zealand (Kiernan, 2004). This trend is regarded as an inherent part of the transformation of family patterns that has been called the Second Demographic Transition (Lesthaeghe, 1995). Although cohabitation has been the focus of increasing research interest since the 1990s (see e.g. Brown, 2004; Kiernan, 2001; Le Bourdais and Lapierre-Adamcyk, 2004; Moors and Bernhardt, 2009; Wiik *et al.*, 2009, 2010), it is probably still the case that less is known about cohabitation than about most other demographic phenomena. Detailed information about cohabitation comes mainly from surveys, such as the Gender and Generation Survey (GGS) and the European Social Survey (ESS).

The Nordic countries have the highest levels of cohabitation in Europe, followed by France. According to the 2008 European Social Survey in Sweden, Norway and Finland, between 30 and 40 per cent of those in the 18–55 age group who were living with a co-residential partner were not married to that partner, as against 10 per cent in most Eastern and Southern European countries.

Cohabitation is often now regarded as being a union of choice primarily among young people, that is, among those in their twenties and early thirties. But there is a noticeable trend in many countries for older men and women to choose cohabitation over marriage following the dissolution of a marital union. This is referred to as post-marital cohabitation (Kiernan, 2001; Lesthaeghe and Moors, 2000; Loomis and Landale, 1994; Wu and Balakrishnan, 1994). Noack (2010), for example, reports that in Norway about half of cohabitees in the 50–59 age group have previously been married.

Historical Background

Historically, there have been numerous examples of couples cohabitating in many societies. Nevertheless, it is difficult to see an evident connection between unmarried cohabitation in earlier times and the development of cohabitation since the late 1960s. In some countries unmarried cohabitation was prohibited by law. This was the case in Norway, where the so-called 'concubinage paragraph', a part of the Norwegian Penal Code, was abolished only in 1972. Although this paragraph existed for seventy years, no cases of judicial punishment were reported and most people were unaware of the paragraph (Noack, 2010).

Cohabitation occurring between the 1800s and the late 1960s can be divided into two categories. These are described in the box overleaf.

The first category was by far the most common. An important function of wedding parties in that period was to symbolise the fact that the partners were accepted as worthy members of the neighborhood and the family, forming a couple that could return favours on other occasions. Unmarried cohabitation was quite common among the poor rural Norwegian population around the 1850s and among the working class

Two categories of cohabitation: 1800–late 1960s

1. Cohabitation as a result of partners having been unable to afford to marry, particularly because of the expenses associated with the wedding itself.
2. Cohabitation chosen by radical groups of intellectuals and artists who opposed marriage and argued for an alternative union which was easier to start and to end.

in Stockholm some decades later (Noack, 2010). Unmarried cohabitation among the underprivileged urban population has also been reported in other countries, including Great Britain, France and Germany (Gillis, 1985; Kiernan, 2001; Murphy, 2000).

The second category—unmarried cohabitation as an ideological alternative to marriage—was far more debated than practised. Some of the supporters of alternatives to marriage were intellectuals such as the British philosopher Bertrand Russell (Russell, 1929). Another supporter was the American judge Ben Lindsey, who became well-known for his highly debated book about companionate marriage (Lindsey and Evans, 1927). In contrast to the modern form of cohabitation that has evolved since the late 1960s, these historical examples of cohabitation were limited to sub-groups in society, and were not widespread in the population at large.

In some countries, it has been possible to identify pioneers in the process towards the modern form of cohabitation. In Sweden, people in the Stockholm area, and especially young middle-class women, are defined as forerunners (Bernhardt and Hoem, 1985). In France, however, cohabitation was more common among the working class (Villeneuve-Gokalp, 1991). In other countries, like Great Britain, the shift in union formation happened so quickly that it is difficult to point out typical forerunners (Kiernan, 1989), although cohabitation had been the only practical way of forming a partnership for those who were unable to terminate a marriage that had broken down and were forced to live in what was often erroneously termed a 'common law marriage'. In the USA cohabitation was and still is most common among those with lower levels of education (Cherlin, 2009).

One of the main functions of the traditional institution of marriage was to regulate the transfer of property and inheritance in ways that benefited society. Another important function was to guarantee safety for the economically weaker parties in a union, usually children and women (Coontz, 2005). The development of the modern form of cohabitation coincided with a major shift in the role of women, rendering the functions of the traditional marriage less important. For instance, new contraceptive methods and a more liberal abortion practice in many countries made it easier for women to decide when and with whom they wanted to have their children. Moreover, women born in the late 1950s and after were more educated, and more likely to be gainfully employed, than those who were born in the 1930s and the 1940s, who formed part of the typical housewife generation.

The Scandinavian welfare system has also replaced some of the functions of the traditional marriage. By giving single mothers economic support and other kinds of benefits, the system has acted as what has been described as a safety net in case of union dissolution. This may have made it less important to marry in the 'defamiliarised'

Scandinavian welfare state (Esping-Andersen, 1990) than in other countries where the welfare system is more family-based, although lone parents in many countries have received welfare benefits.

Current Empirical Patterns

How common is cohabitation?

Levels of cohabitation vary a great deal between European countries, as can be seen from Table 2.1. Presenting data from the 2008 European Social Survey (ESS), this table shows the distribution by civil status (currently married, formerly married, never married) for the 18–55 age group in 28 countries (columns 1–3), together with four different measures of the frequency of unmarried cohabitation in this age group. Here, we first relate the number of cohabitees to those not currently married (thus either formerly married or never married) (column 4), then to those living with a partner (whether married or not to that partner) (column 5), and finally to the total population aged 18–55 (column 6).

Looking first at the distributions by marital status in Table 2.1 (columns 1–3), we see that the percentage of currently married respondents in the 28 countries ranges between 39 and 67. It is clear that marriage is the dominating civil status category in countries like Bulgaria, Cyprus, Greece, Romania, Turkey and Ukraine, with more than 60 per cent of people currently married. This is combined with very low percentages of unmarried people who live with a partner (the exception being Bulgaria, with as many as 16% of those not married cohabiting). These countries represent the traditional pattern of living arrangements in the twenty-first century, whereby cohabitation is still a relatively marginal phenomenon.

The other extreme is the Nordic countries, primarily Sweden and Norway, where approximately 40 per cent of people are currently married (column 1), and over 40 per cent of those not currently married are living with a partner (column 4). Also, in Finland and Denmark a substantial proportion of couples are unmarried, and well over one-third of those not married are cohabiting. The only country outside Scandinavia with low levels of currently married people and a substantial proportion (about one-third) of unmarried cohabiting people is France.

Measuring cohabitation in terms of the proportion of those living with a partner who are unmarried (Table 2.1, column 5) provides the same general pattern. The percentage ranges between 1 and 42, and again it is the Nordic countries plus France which have the highest levels—more than 25 per cent. In the UK, more than one in five of those living with a partner are cohabiting. If we define 10 per cent as the lowest threshold in order to claim that cohabitation has made its breakthrough in a particular country, 15 out of the 28 countries included can be defined as 'breakthrough' countries.

Further, Table 2.1 (column 6) shows that from below 1 per cent to more than 28 per cent of the total populations in the 28 countries are cohabiting. More precisely, in six countries (Croatia, Greece, Romania, Slovenia, Turkey and Ukraine) less than 3 per cent of the total population aged 18–55 is cohabiting, as against around 20 per cent in the Nordic countries and France. Germany, Hungary, Latvia, the Netherlands, Switzerland and the UK, on the other hand, constitute a middle group where 10 to

Table 2.1 Marital status and cohabitation frequencies by age and country: men and women aged 18–55 ($N = 33995$)

		Marital status[1]			Cohabitation[2]			
	n	% currently married	% divorced, separated or widowed	% never married	% cohabiting of all unmarried respondents	% cohabiting of all respondents living with a partner	% of sample currently cohabiting	% of sample who have ever cohabited
Belgium	967	54.4	11.4	34.2	16.8	12.3	7.7	23.2
Bulgaria	1159	66.6	7.5	25.9	15.9	7.4	5.3	9.6
Croatia	918	58.4	5.7	35.9	6.9	4.7	2.9	19.0
Cyprus	792	61.4	7.7	30.9	8.2	4.9	3.1	28.1
Czech Republic	1209	55.5	10.7	33.8	14.0	10.1	6.2	23.8
Denmark	884	53.4	10.5	36.1	38.4	25.1	17.9	56.9
Finland	1271	45.7	11.7	42.6	37.8	31.0	20.5	47.4
France	1195	48.5	10.5	41.0	38.6	29.0	19.9	41.0
Germany	1599	52.6	11.6	35.8	25.0	18.4	11.8	30.3
Greece	1451	64.2	5.8	30.0	6.4	3.5	2.3	12.8
Hungary	944	51.9	12.2	35.9	21.5	16.6	10.3	22.2
Ireland	1098	55.1	6.5	38.4	21.1	14.7	9.5	23.7
Israel	1566	58.6	13.1	28.3	10.4	6.8	4.3	16.4
Latvia	1206	52.9	18.0	29.1	21.6	16.1	10.2	38.0
Norway	959	42.9	12.6	44.5	40.3	35.0	23.4	44.6
Poland	1062	58.2	6.9	34.9	10.7	7.2	4.5	13.3
Portugal	1144	59.9	8.3	31.8	16.0	9.7	6.4	8.9
Romania	1386	65.8	7.6	26.6	7.4	3.7	2.5	6.8
Russia	1536	57.1	16.5	26.4	8.7	6.1	3.7	16.4
Slovakia	1050	54.0	13.0	33.0	12.9	9.9	5.9	12.0
Slovenia	662	56.9	7.0	36.1	2.8	2.1	1.2	12.5
Spain	1539	53.4	8.3	38.3	15.6	11.8	7.2	14.1
Sweden	1067	39.5	9.2	51.3	46.8	41.8	28.3	46.2
Switzerland	1090	54.2	13.6	32.2	21.9	15.6	10.0	39.4
The Netherlands	997	57.2	10.0	32.8	28.8	17.8	12.4	32.9
Turkey	1848	67.0	3.0	30.0	1.7	0.8	0.6	1.6
UK	1323	51.5	13.2	35.3	29.7	21.9	14.4	34.9
Ukraine	1070	62.2	14.4	23.4	4.9	2.9	1.9	20.5

Note. Table is weighted using ESS design weights. [1]Respondents in a civil partnership ($n = 758$) are omitted from the table. [2]The columns for cohabitation are not mutually exclusive and do not add up to 100%.

Source. European Social Survey (2008). Authors' own computation.

14 per cent of the total population aged 18–55 are cohabiting. We can discern three distinct groups of countries in respect of cohabitation: those that follow a traditional pattern of marriage, those combining couples who marry and those who cohabit, and those in which cohabitation is common.

Three groups of cohabitation countries

Traditional pattern—Greece, Romania, Turkey, Ukraine, Croatia, Cyprus, Slovenia, Bulgaria, Israel, Poland, Russia

- around 60% married
- 16% or less of those unmarried living with a partner
- 5% or less of the total population cohabiting

Middle group—Germany, Hungary, Latvia, the Netherlands, Switzerland, the UK, Belgium, Czech Republic, Ireland, Portugal, Slovakia, Spain

- around 50% married
- 30% or less of those unmarried living with a partner
- 6 to 14% of the total population cohabiting

High prevalence countries—Sweden, Norway, Denmark, Finland, France

- around 40% married
- 38% or more of those unmarried living with a partner
- 18% or more of the total population cohabiting

Clearly, in the early twenty-first century unmarried cohabitation has spread far beyond its forerunners in the Scandinavian countries, which is not to argue that all countries will eventually have levels of cohabitation similar to those in Scandinavia.

Non-marital childbearing

In the past several decades, there has been a dramatic rise in non-marital childbearing in nearly every European country. Most of the increase has taken place within cohabiting unions, not to single mothers (Perelli-Harris *et al.*, 2009). Looking at how the relationship between first birth and union status has changed over time from the 1970s to the early 2000s across 11 European countries, we see that Norway has the highest proportion of first births within cohabitation in the period 1995–2004: 54 per cent, as against 20 per cent in the 1970s (Perelli-Harris *et al.*, 2012). In France too, around half of the first births took place within cohabitation in the last period. A much smaller increase is observed in the Netherlands and the UK, from 3–4 per cent to 26–29 per cent, and in Italy fewer than one in ten first births took place within cohabitation.

Although cohabitation has increased in every country, the patterns do not develop along the same trajectories in all countries and can hardly be interpreted as sequential stages. Further research is needed to investigate why countries develop different trajectories. The reasons seem to be embedded in differences in cultural norms, attitudes and values, but the behaviour may also be affected by social welfare arrangements and how more marriage-like cohabitation is treated in the laws in different countries (Perelli-Harris and Gassen, 2012).

By and large, cohabitation in Europe is still not regarded as an alternative to marriage (Heuveline and Timberlake, 2004) with respect to childbearing and early child rearing. While there is considerable variation in the frequency of births outside marriage, there is, however, no doubt that, overall, marriage is no longer an absolute prerequisite for child rearing in Europe.

Marriage intentions

Using data from the GGS for eight countries (Bulgaria, Germany, Hungary, the Netherlands, Norway, France, Romania and Russia) we can shed some light on whether cohabitation should be regarded mostly as an alternative or as a prelude to marriage. In this survey, cohabitees were asked whether they intended to get married within the next three years or not. Figure 2.1 shows that among these eight countries Norway and France stand out as having the highest frequency of cohabitation (roughly half of all partnered respondents aged 18–35). Moreover, most of the cohabitees did not plan to marry in the short term. This is especially noticeable for Norway, where four out of five cohabitees aged 18–35 did not intend to marry, at least not within the next three years.

In the intermediate group we find Germany, Hungary and the Netherlands, where between 30 and 40 per cent of those living with a partner in the 18–35 age group were cohabiting rather than married. In Germany, as in Norway and France, most of the cohabitees had no immediate plans to marry, while the majority in Hungary and the Netherlands did have such plans.

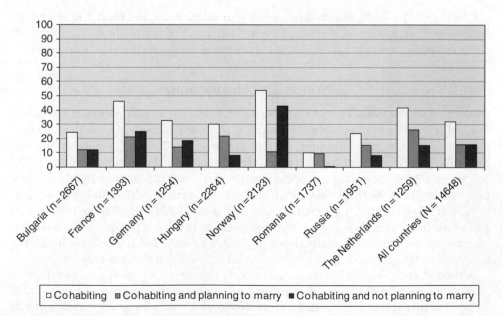

Figure 2.1   Percentages of all cohabiting respondents aged 18–35 with and without plans to marry (GGS round 1, 2003–2007) (N = 14648)

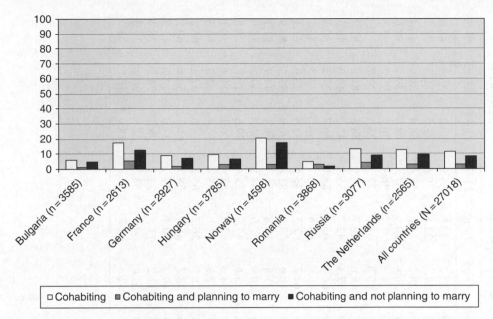

Figure 2.2 Percentages of all cohabiting respondents aged 36–55 with and without plans to marry (GGS round 1, 2003–2007) (N = 27018)

Looking at Bulgaria, Romania and Russia, all of which are characterised as having a low frequency of cohabitation, we see that the majority of cohabitees seem intent on marrying (in Bulgaria it is about 50–50). So there seems to be a clear relationship between frequencies of cohabitation in the ages below 35 and marriage intentions— the less people cohabit, the more they plan to marry. Figure 2.2 shows that the proportion of those cohabiting with a partner in the older age group (35–55) is on average one-third of the level of the younger age group in each country. With one exception, Romania, the majority of cohabitees in this age group had no plans to marry.

To conclude, it appears that among the young cohabitees (those aged 18–35) cohabitation is mostly a preface to marriage in the low-frequency countries in Eastern Europe (Bulgaria, Romania and Russia), as well as in Hungary and the Netherlands. On the other hand, in high-frequency countries, such as Norway and France, a majority of those cohabiting have not formed any marriage plans, at least not yet. Whether this means that they view cohabitation as a perfectly acceptable alternative to marriage on a long-term basis cannot be ascertained on the basis of these cross-sectional figures. However, we can shed more light on this issue after analysing ESS information on attitudes to cohabitation in different countries.

Attitudes to cohabitation

The 2006 wave of the ESS contained a question about approval of cohabitation (i.e. 'How much do you approve or disapprove if a man/woman lives with a partner without being married to her/him?'). The response options went from 1 ('Disapprove completely') to 5 ('Approve completely'). In Table 2.2 we have grouped the two

Table 2.2 Percentages of sample who disapprove or approve of unmarried partners living together, by age and country ($N = 27204$)

Country	n	Disapproving 15–24	Disapproving 25–34	Disapproving 35–55	Disapproving 15–55	Neither disapproving nor approving 15–24	Neither disapproving nor approving 25–34	Neither disapproving nor approving 35–55	Neither disapproving nor approving 15–55	Approving 15–24	Approving 25–34	Approving 35–55	Approving 15–55
Austria	1753	5.6	6.5	9.2	7.7	30.5	37.3	52.2	43.5	64.0	56.2	38.5	48.8
Belgium	1195	7.7	6.3	5.3	6.1	21.7	20.2	24.1	22.8	70.6	73.5	70.5	71.1
Bulgaria	779	19.0	21.2	31.9	27.3	22.4	24.3	28.2	26.3	58.6	54.4	39.9	46.4
Cyprus	650	12.8	9.6	24.8	19.0	19.5	20.4	35.8	29.0	67.8	69.9	39.4	52.0
Denmark	891	2.9	2.8	3.4	3.2	0.7	0.5	1.4	1.1	96.4	96.7	95.2	95.7
Estonia	962	16.6	8.9	21.5	17.6	56.1	67.5	65.8	63.6	27.3	23.6	12.7	1.8
Finland	1122	7.5	2.5	3.4	4.1	14.5	12.7	15.6	14.7	78.0	84.8	81.0	81.2
France	1252	8.9	6.7	9.6	8.8	35.3	50.0	42.4	42.7	55.8	43.3	48.0	48.5
Germany	1831	5.8	6.4	6.6	6.4	59.2	56.9	66.1	63.1	35.0	36.7	27.2	30.5
Hungary	828	7.1	5.9	9.8	8.3	49.7	43.5	46.9	46.6	43.2	50.6	43.3	45.1
Ireland	1129	5.3	11.1	14.4	11.5	49.1	55.5	61.7	57.3	45.6	33.4	23.9	31.1
Norway	1206	5.7	3.3	4.0	4.2	12.5	5.8	10.4	9.8	81.8	90.9	85.5	85.9
Poland	1215	18.1	19.6	33.8	26.2	25.5	22.2	21.4	22.8	56.4	58.1	44.9	51.1
Portugal	1226	4.1	4.5	9.4	7.1	32.1	32.3	40.9	37.0	63.8	63.2	49.7	55.9
Russia	1583	26.1	23.0	34.6	29.7	44.6	37.4	45.6	43.5	29.4	39.6	19.8	26.8
Slovakia	1253	24.9	2.8	31.1	26.9	39.7	43.1	44.6	43.0	35.4	36.1	24.4	30.1
Slovenia	950	10.1	6.5	15.2	12.0	24.5	17.1	22.5	21.8	65.4	76.4	62.3	66.3
Spain	1291	5.4	6.2	8.7	7.4	29.3	19.8	28.7	26.3	65.3	74.0	62.6	66.3
Sweden	1211	3.9	2.4	2.7	2.9	38.0	31.5	38.7	36.8	58.1	66.1	58.6	60.2
Switzerland	1098	7.9	6.1	9.5	8.5	42.9	56.9	50.3	50.1	49.2	37.0	40.2	41.3
The Netherlands	1179	8.3	10.7	10.3	10.1	12.8	11.3	11.2	11.5	78.9	78.1	78.5	78.4
UK	1416	12.6	8.1	9.8	10.1	54.1	59.0	64.0	60.7	33.3	32.9	26.2	29.3
Ukraine	1194	46.6	35.8	48.4	45.3	28.7	36.2	32.8	32.7	24.7	28.0	18.7	21.9

Note. Table is weighted using ESS design weights.
Source. European Social Survey (2006). Authors' own computation.

lowest and the two highest values respectively, creating the three categories 'Disapproving', 'Neither disapproving nor approving' and 'Approving'.

With some exceptions, most notably Estonia, Slovakia, Ukraine, Russia, Germany, the UK and Ireland, the levels of approval of unmarried cohabitation in the 15–55 age range were surprisingly high. Germany, Ireland and the UK all have close to two-thirds in the 'Neither' category and low percentages disapproving, so living together while not being married to one's partner is neither frowned upon nor seen as generally socially acceptable.

In most countries, however, over half of those in the 15–55 age range have no objection to people living together without being married. The highest levels of approval are, not surprisingly, found in the Scandinavian countries, particularly in Denmark, where 96 per cent agree that unmarried cohabitation is completely acceptable.

Denmark and Ukraine are clearly the two extremes among the countries included in this survey. In Denmark there is almost universal acceptance of unmarried cohabitation, while acceptance is a minority view in Ukraine. These positions are combined with very high and very low levels of actual cohabitation, respectively, in these two countries.

Less consistent are France and Sweden, which both have high frequencies of actual cohabitation, combined with moderate levels of approval. In both countries, around 40 per cent of people are in the 'Neither' category, indicating perhaps that, although few people disapprove of unmarried cohabitation, neither is there a great deal of enthusiasm about this kind of living arrangement. Interestingly enough, in Sweden there seems to have been a marriage revival since the late 1990s (Ohlsson-Wijk, 2011), while in France there are no signs of an upturn in marriage trends (Prioux *et al.*, 2010). The recent upturn in Sweden does not seem to be due to compositional changes in the population (e.g. more men and women being of 'marriageable' ages) but suggests the increasing popularity of marriage, for hitherto unknown reasons.

Same-Sex Cohabitation and Marriage

The legalisation of same-sex partnerships and marriages, which in recent decades has taken place in several countries, has contributed to more reliable data being available on the prevalence of these unions. The trend of granting people in same-sex relationships more or less equal legal rights and duties as people in heterosexual marriages started in Denmark in 1989, when so-called registered partnerships were legalised, and the other Nordic countries followed suit (Andersson *et al.*, 2006). Registered partnerships were also recognised in the Netherlands in 1998. With few exceptions, people in these registered partnerships have the same legal rights and duties as those in marriages.

Same-sex marriage was first legalised in the Netherlands in 2001. Since then, same-sex marriage has been introduced in six other European countries (Belgium in 2003, Spain in 2005, Norway and Sweden in 2009 and Iceland and Portugal in 2010) and in Canada in 2005 (Chamie and Mirkin, 2011). Same-sex marriage has also been legalised in many states in the USA, where marriage is a particularly important cultural ideal (Cherlin, 2009). The Coalition Government in England has also announced its approval of a proposal for same-sex couples to be allowed to marry.

Analyses of data from the Scandinavian countries have so far proved that, in the first year after the legalisation, more men than women entered same-sex marriages. This has, however, become reversed in recent years. The same-sex partners are older than the opposite-sex ones and there is a much higher divorce risk among the female couples than among the male couples and heterosexual couples (Andersson *et al.*, 2006; Andersson and Noack, 2011). Recently, more female couples have started to have children, a change that could reduce their comparatively high risk of divorce.

The debate about granting same-sex couples the right to marry has been strong and has been pursued with varying intensity in different countries. Some opponents (e.g. Kurtz, 2004) have claimed that a legalisation of same-sex marriage will more or less destroy the institution of marriage. Marriage trends in the Scandinavian countries do not support such an interpretation. Others have maintained that when same-sex marriages became legal, cohabitation had already undermined traditional marriage, a fact that may have made it easier to go a step further and accept same-sex marriage (Moxnes, 1993).

Legal Status of Cohabitation and Its Policy Implications

Although there is a development towards increased regulation and rights for cohabitation in many countries, there are significant differences between countries. Generally, statutory regulation of unmarried cohabitation is most developed in countries with high cohabitation rates. In Sweden and Norway, for instance, 'marriage-like' cohabiting relationships (i.e. ones where there are children and where the relationship has lasted two years or more) mostly carry the same rights and obligations as those relating to couples who are married when it comes to social security, pensions and taxation. There are, however, still differences in private law (Noack, 2010). Cohabiting couples are still free to make private arrangements, and in some areas, such as inheritance, they have to make individual contracts if they want to secure themselves fully without marrying. In other countries it is left to cohabitees themselves to register a contract (France) or formally register their partnership (the Netherlands), or else the legal protection of the family is mainly restricted to marriage (Germany) (Kiernan, 2004).

In no country have cohabiting couples themselves acted as a pressure group to be treated more like married people. One reason may be that in most countries those who cohabit are a heterogeneous group with mixed interests. More importantly, however, many cohabiting couples seem to regard their cohabitational status as temporary and believe that they will get the rights they need when they marry. In addition, being treated as single may be advantageous in many situations.

Analysing the amendments in the regulation of cohabitation in Norway, Noack (2010) concluded that such regulations were brought about by the increasing number of cohabitations. Formal civil status, not whether someone was living in a union or not, was for a long time a criterion for being entitled to social security and pensions, and determined how much tax the person had to pay. Compared to married couples, cohabiting couples benefited strongly economically because they were treated as living alone. So, after a couple of decades, the more marriage-like cohabitating unions were given largely the same rights and duties as married couples. The need for changing the rules was discussed and recognised early on, but it proved difficult to work out rules to identify cohabiting couples without infringing on the right to privacy. There was no wish to give privileges to married couples, as there is in some other countries. In practice, the Norwegian system is now based upon self-reporting, with withdrawal of some economic subsidies if people do not report.

Possible Future Developments

International comparisons of cohabitation were few in the beginning and were often used only as indirect measures for calculating decreasing marriage rates and increasing rates of extramarital births. Lack of data, problems in combining different data sources, less suitable time-series information and uncertainty about the validity of extrapolating from one study to another have been and continue to be common problems in comparative studies of cohabitation (e.g. Prinz, 1995). In recent years, the data situation has improved, as is illustrated by the two internationally comparative surveys referred to in this chapter (i.e. ESS and GGS). These data confirm that although there are considerable differences between countries, unmarried cohabitation is a phenomenon that has spread far beyond the 'forerunners' in Scandinavia.

So why do people cohabit? Should cohabitation be viewed as an alternative to marriage, or is it just a prelude to moving into a seriously committed relationship? Rindfuss and VandenHeuvel (1990) argued that, at least in the USA until some decades ago, cohabitation was mostly an alternative to being single, and thus a (short-term) prelude rather than a long-term alternative to marriage. Drawing on in-depth interviews with cohabitees from the working and lower middle classes in the USA, Smock *et al.* (2005) found that financial issues were important factors in the decision to marry. Their results showed that these people did not want to marry before they had obtained an economic package including home ownership and financial stability. Wiik and colleagues (2009) found that in Sweden and Norway the relationships of cohabitees who reported that they planned to marry their current partner differed much less from those of married respondents than from those of cohabitees without marriage plans. The latter were less satisfied with their current relationship and were more likely to have plans to split up. Clearly, cohabiting couples form a rather heterogeneous group and the meaning and practical functions of this kind of living arrangement differ across national contexts.

Whether cohabitation currently is viewed as a perfectly acceptable alternative to marriage on a long-term basis cannot be ascertained on the basis of the cross-sectional figures presented here. However, judging from the figures on the marriage intentions of those who cohabit presented in this chapter, it seems that among young people (aged 18–35) cohabitation is viewed mostly as a prelude to marriage in the low-frequency countries in Eastern Europe, as well as in Hungary and the Netherlands. In high-frequency countries, such as Norway and France, as well as among older cohabitees (aged 36–55), a majority of those cohabiting had no concrete marriage plans. Also, the fact that very few ESS respondents in high-frequency countries disapprove of cohabitation does imply that cohabitation is more often considered to be an acceptable alternative to marriage.

Cherlin (2000) underlined the need for social scientists to develop theories of family formation that include cohabitation, not just marriage. Moreover, they should explain not just why people cohabit, but also why cohabiting couples marry. What are the benefits (and possible costs) of transforming a co-residential relationship into a marriage? When people live together without being married, they have already completed the searching and matching process that precedes the start of a union, and thus have already obtained (or have a chance to obtain) the benefits of a living-together arrangement, such as pooling their incomes and sharing their costs. To the extent that people continue to get married in societies where there is no longer any social stigma attached to living with a partner without being married, marriage is clearly still viewed by many people as a positive option and as *the* preferred form for a long-term partnership under the same roof, especially if there are children in the household (Perelli-Harris *et al.*, 2009). One reason could be that in many countries those who cohabit still lack some of the normative and legal benefits that married individuals have. Although the practical importance of marriage has decreased, its symbolic importance has remained high and may even have increased, at least in the USA (Cherlin, 2004). Moreover, marriage and the wedding party may be important status symbols in themselves. To marry could also mark a new stage in a relationship or it could be an indicator of achievement or a way to symbolise difference from cohabitation. The marriage revival in Sweden is a very interesting development. More qualitative research is needed to help us understand the motivations behind the choice of living arrangements in the different countries.

Family researchers disagree on whether country differences related to the prevalence of cohabitation are likely to disappear over time, or whether they represent persistent fundamental structural and cultural differences between societies (Kalmijn, 2007). In this regard, diffusion theory can be used to describe the spread of any given practice within a society. In a first phase, unmarried cohabitation constitutes a distinct deviation from the prevailing norms, one practised only by small groups who oppose the institution of marriage or, more commonly, have insufficient means to get married. In a second phase, cohabitation constitutes a short-lived (and childless) introduction to marriage. Finally, once social acceptance of cohabitation has become established, cohabiting relationships of long duration will become common, as well as childbearing within these unions.

According to the typology proposed by Heuveline and Timberlake (2004), the role of cohabitation in family formation evolves from a marginal position associated with a clearly negative public attitude to one where cohabitation is largely identical to marriage. The next-to-last category is called an 'alternative to marriage'. Here long-term arrangements are common, and a low proportion of cohabiting couples choose to marry. In the last category, according to the authors, there is no social distinction between cohabitation and marriage, though cohabiting couples with children are fairly likely to get married. Heuveline and Timberlake base their conclusions on the Family and Fertility Surveys from the early 1990s, thus largely reflecting the situation in the 1980s.

In this chapter we have presented more recent data from the late 2000s, which has given us a more up-to-date picture of a rapidly changing phenomenon. Sobotka and Toulemon (2008) have commented:

> Family and living arrangements are currently heterogeneous across Europe, but all countries seem to be making the same shifts: towards fewer people living together as a couple, especially in marriage; an increased number of unmarried couples; more children born outside marriage, and fewer children living with their two parents. (p. 85)

That fewer people live together as a couple nowadays is usually due to more frequent relationship break-ups than to fewer people entering a co-residential union.

Nevertheless, most people still spend the bulk of their lives living in a co-residential union. If cohabitation continues to spread and becomes a normative experience across the Western world, and extends to countries where it currently remains rare, cohabitation and marriage could become more alike and fewer cohabiting couples could choose to marry. At present, however, it is still reasonable to consider both marriage and cohabitation as two distinct aspects of the pairing process in most Western countries.

References

Andersson, G. and Noack, T. (2011) Legal advances and demographic developments of same-sex unions in Scandinavia, *Zeitschrift für Familienforshung* [Journal of Family Research], Sonderheft 2010: 87–101.

Andersson, G., Noack, T., Seierstad, A. and Weedon-Fekjær, H. (2006) The demographics of same-sex marriages in Norway and Sweden, *Demography*, 43: 79–98.

Bernhardt, E. (2001) Att gifta sig—eller bara bo ihop? [To marry—or just live together?], *Välfärdsbulletinen*, 4/2001: 4–5.

Bernhardt, E. and Hoem, B. (1985) Cohabitation and social background: trends observed for Swedish women born between 1936 and 1960, *European Journal of Population*, 1: 375–395.

Brown, S. L. (2004) Moving from cohabitation to marriage: effects on relationship quality, *Social Science Research*, 33: 1–49.

Chamie, J. and Mirkin, B. (2011) Same-sex marriage: a new social phenomenon, *Population and Development Review*, 37: 529–551.

Cherlin, A. J. (2000) Toward a new home socio-economics of union formation, in L. Waite (ed.), *Ties That Bind: Perspectives on marriage and cohabitation* (New York: de Gruyter).

Cherlin, A. J. (2004) The deinstitutionalisation of American marriage, *Journal of Marriage and Family*, 66(4): 848–861.

Cherlin, A. J. (2009) *The Marriage go-round: The state of marriage and the family in America today* (New York: Knopf).

Coontz, S. (2005) *Marriage, A History: How love conquered marriage* (New York: Penguin).

Esping-Andersen G. (1990) *The Three Worlds of Welfare Capitalism* (Cambridge: Polity Press).

European Social Survey (2006) *ESS Round 3: European Social Survey Round 3 Data (2006). Data file edition 3.3* (Bergen: Norwegian Social Science Data Services).

European Social Survey (2008) *ESS Round 4: European Social Survey Round 4 Data (2008). Data file edition 4.0* (Bergen: Norwegian Social Science Data Services).

Giddens, A. (1992) *The Transformation of Intimacy: Sexuality, love and eroticism in modern societies* (Cambridge: Polity Press/Blackwell).

Gillis, J. R. (1985) *For Better, for Worse: British marriages, 1600 to the present* (Oxford: Oxford University Press).

Heuveline, P. and Timberlake, J. M. (2004) The role of cohabitation in family formation: the United States in a comparative perspective, *Journal of Marriage and Family*, 66: 1214–1230.

Kalmijn, M. (2007) Explaining cross-national differences in marriage, cohabitation and divorce in Europe, 1990–2000, *Population Studies*, 61: 243–263.

Kiernan, K. (1989) The family: fission or fusion?, in H. Joshi (ed.), *The Changing Population of Britain* (Oxford: Blackwell).

Kiernan, K. (2001) The rise of cohabitation and childbearing outside marriage in Western Europe, *International Journal of Law, Policy and the Family*, 15: 1–21.

Kiernan, K. (2004) Redrawing the boundaries of marriage, *Journal of Marriage and Family*, 66(4): 980–987.

Kurz, S. (2004) The end of marriage in Scandinavia: the 'conservative case' for same-sex marriages collapses, *The Weekly Standard*, 9(20): 26–33.

Le Bourdais, C. and Lapierre-Adamcyk, E. (2004) Changes in conjugal life in Canada: is cohabitation progressively replacing marriage?, *Journal of Marriage and Family*, 66: 929–942.

Lesthaeghe, R. (1995) The second demographic transition in Western countries: an interpretation, in K. O. Mason and A.-M. Jensen (eds), *Gender and Family Change in Industrialised Countries* (Oxford: Clarendon Press), 17–62.

Lesthaeghe, R. and Moors, G. (2000) Recent trends in fertility and household formation in the industrialized world, *Review of Population and Social Policy*, 9: 121–170.

Lindsey, B. B. and Evans, W. (1927) *The Companionate Marriage* (New York: Boni & Liveright).

Loomis, L. S. and Landale, N. S. (1994) Nonmarital cohabitation and childbearing among black and white American women, *Journal of Marriage and Family*, 56: 949–962.

Moors, G. and Bernhardt, E. (2009) Splitting up or getting married? Competing risk analysis of transitions among cohabiting couples in Sweden, *Acta Sociologica*, 52: 227–247.

Moxnes, K. (1993) Partnerskapsloven—et uttrykk for parforholdets endrede karakter, *Løvetann*, 3: 30–31.

Murphy, M. (2000) The evolution of cohabitation in Britain, 1960–95, *Population Studies*, 54: 43–56.

Noack, T. (2010) *En stille revolusjon: Det moderne samboerskapet I Norge* (Oslo: Universitetet i Oslo).

Ohlsson-Wijk, S. (2011) Sweden's marriage revival: an analysis of the new-millennium switch from long-term decline to increasing popularity, *Population Studies*, 65: 183–200.

Perelli-Harris, B. *et al.* (2009) Examining nonmarital childbearing in Europe: how does union context differ across countries? MPIDR Working Paper 2009-021.

Perelli-Harris, B. *et al.* (2012) Changes in union status during the transition to parenthood in eleven European countries, 1970s to early 2000s, *Population Studies*, 66(2): 167–182.

Perelli-Harris, B. and Gassen, N. S. (2012) How similar are cohabitation and marriage? Legal approaches to cohabitation across Western Europe, *Population and Development Review* 38(3): 435–467.

Prinz, C. (1995) *Cohabiting, Married or Single? Portraying, analyzing, and modeling new living arrangements in the changing societies of Europe* (Aldershot: Avebury).

Prioux, F., Mazuy, M. and Barbieri, M. (2010) Recent demographic developments in France: fewer adults live with a partner, *Population-E*, 65(3): 363–414.

Rindfuss, R. and VandenHeuvel, A. (1990) Cohabitation: a precursor to marriage or an alternative to being single? *Population and Development Review*, 16: 703–726.

Russell, B. (1929) *Marriage and Morals* (London: Allen & Unwin).

Smock, P. J., Manning, W. D. and Porter, M. (2005) 'Everything's there except money': how money shapes decisions to marry among cohabitors, *Journal of Marriage and Family*, 67: 680–696.

Sobotka, T. and Toulemon, L. (2008) Changing family and partnership behaviour: common trends and persistent diversity across Europe, *Demographic Research*, 19: 85–138.

Villeneuve-Gokalp, C. (1991) From marriage to informal union: recent changes in the behaviour of French couples, *Population: An English selection*, 3: 81–111.

Wiik, K. A., Bernhardt, E. and Noack, T. (2009) A study of commitment and relationship quality in Sweden and Norway, *Journal of Marriage and Family*, 71: 465–477.

Wiik, K. A., Bernhardt, E. and Noack, T. (2010) Love or money? Marriage intentions among young cohabitors in Norway and Sweden, *Acta Sociologica*, 53: 269–287.

Wu, Z. and Balakrishnan, T. R. (1994) Cohabitation after marital disruption in Canada, *Journal of Marriage and Family*, 56: 723–734.

3
'Alone Together' Marriages and 'Living Apart Together' Relationships

Paul R. Amato and Lydia N. Hayes

Introduction

Marriages in the USA have changed more during the last 50 years than during any comparable period in US history. During this period, with respect to demographic trends, age at first marriage increased, cohabitation became common as a prelude to marriage, marital fertility declined, the divorce rate rose, and the percentage of marriages in which one or both spouses had been married previously increased. Changes also occurred in spousal relationships: wives increasingly entered the labour force and became co-providers, husbands took on a larger share of household chores and child-rearing responsibilities, and decision-making equality between spouses became more common. Corresponding to changes in behaviour were shifts in attitudes, with people becoming more accepting of alternatives to the traditional two-parent family. These trends were not limited to the USA. Indeed, similar trends have occurred in many Western societies.

In this chapter we describe an emerging form of marriage in the USA that we refer to as *alone together marriage*. Amato *et al.* (2007) first drew attention to this phenomenon when they compared married individuals in 1980 and 2000. During this two-decade period, substantial declines occurred in people's reports of activities shared with their spouses, despite the fact that overall levels of marital happiness remained constant. Similarly, people reported having fewer friends in common with their spouses and were less likely to belong to the same clubs and organisations. The authors argued that American marriages were becoming more individualistic, with an increasing number of spouses pursuing independent interests and lifestyles at the expense of shared goals.

Contemporary Issues in Family Studies: Global Perspectives on Partnerships, Parenting and Support in a Changing World, First Edition. Edited by Angela Abela and Janet Walker.
© 2014 John Wiley & Sons, Ltd. Published 2014 by John Wiley & Sons, Ltd.

Owing to a lack of data, we do not know if similar trends are occurring in other Western countries. Observers in several places around the world, however, have referred to a related phenomenon: *living apart together* (LAT) relationships. Partners in these unions maintain long-term, sexually exclusive ties yet choose to live in separate households rather than cohabit or marry. We suspect that LAT relationships, like alone together marriages, are reflections of the growing individualism of Western culture—a topic to which we return later in this chapter.

'Alone Together' Marriage

To show how marriage in the USA has changed in recent decades, we draw on two cross-sectional data sets. The first was the original wave of data from the Marital Instability over the Life Course study (collected in 1980). The second was the cross-sectional Survey of Marriage and Family Life (collected in 2000). Both surveys involved telephone interviews with randomly selected, married individuals living in the USA (sample sizes were 2033 in 1980 and 2100 in 2000). Because both surveys included identically worded questions, it was possible to compare response distributions across time.

Two measures of marital quality were included in both surveys. Marital happiness was measured with 10 items, including: 'How happy are you with the amount of understanding received from your spouse? … the amount of love and affection received from your spouse? … the extent to which you and your spouse agree about things? … your sexual relationship with your spouse? … your spouse as someone to do things with?' (1 = *not too happy*, 2 = *pretty happy*, 3 = *very happy*). When added up, these items yielded an alpha reliability coefficient of 0.88. Marital interaction was measured with five items: 'How often do you and your spouse engage in the following activities together? Eating the main meal of the day together? Shopping? Visiting friends? Working on projects around the house? Going out for recreation, such as playing cards, movies, or bowling?' (1 = *never*, 2 = *occasionally*, 3 = *usually*, 4 = *almost always*). When added, these items yielded an alpha reliability coefficient of 0.65.

We used cluster analysis to create a typology of marriages based on happiness and interaction. Because different clustering algorithms yielded nearly identical results, we present the results from K-Means clustering—one of the most commonly used methods of cluster analysis (Bailey, 1994). The analysis produced four groups (clusters) of marriages. Figure 3.1 shows the means of these groups on Z-score (standardised) versions of marital happiness and interaction.

The first group consisted of marriages with very low levels of marital happiness and interaction. We refer to these as *troubled marriages*. The second group was characterised by a low level of marital happiness and an above-average level of interaction. These spouses appeared to be acting like married couples (e.g. going shopping together,

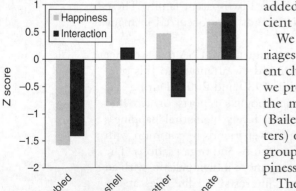

Figure 3.1 Mean levels of marital happiness and interaction in four marriage types

visiting friends together) but experienced little satisfaction from their relationships. Consequently, we refer to these as *empty shell marriages*. The third group involved marriages with a high level of happiness and a low level of interaction. These are *alone together marriages*—the group of special interest in this chapter. The final group was characterised by high levels of happiness and interaction. We refer to these as *companionate marriages*.

Marital happiness and interaction

Four key groups:

1. Troubled marriages—low levels of happiness and interaction.
2. Empty shell marriages—a low level of happiness and an above-average level of interaction.
3. Alone together marriages—a high level of happiness and a low level of interaction.
4. Companionate marriages—high levels of happiness and interaction.

Figure 3.2 shows the percentage of marriage types in 1980 and 2000, weighted to be nationally representative of all US marriages in each year. The percentage of companionate marriages declined from 44 per cent in 1980 to 35 per cent in 2000. Correspondingly, the percentage of alone together marriages increased from 22 per cent to 30 per cent during the same period. Taken together, there were about as many happy marriages in 2000 as there had been two decades earlier. That is, the decline in companionate marriages was essentially offset by the increase in alone together marriages. Also during this period, troubled marriages increased (from 12% to 17%) and empty shell marriages declined (from 23% to 18%). The overall shift in distributions between decades was statistically significant ($\chi^2 = 83.80$, $df = 3$, $p < .001$).

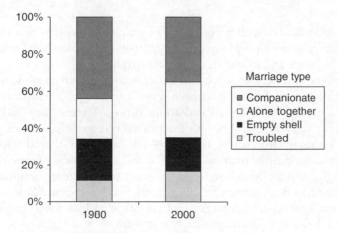

Figure 3.2   Percentages for four types of marriage in 1980 and 2000

To illustrate these types of marriages, we present vignettes drawn from the interviews in 2000. The first describes David and Barbara, a couple with a troubled marriage. (We have changed the names of all spouses to protect their anonymity.) Their relationship was typical of most troubled marriages, with little shared interaction, modest levels of happiness and love, many serious problems, and a high risk of divorce.

A troubled marriage: David and Barbara

When we interviewed David in 2000, he was 42 and Barbara was 41. They had been married for 14 years and had three children. Both spouses were white and were high school graduates. Despite their lack of college degrees, they both worked full-time, and their combined earnings came to over $110000 per year. Although Barbara made a substantial contribution to household income, they had a traditional division of labour, with Barbara doing most of the childcare and housework and David making most of the important decisions. Although they 'occasionally' attended church together, neither was particularly religious. David and Barbara usually ate their main meal of the day together, but 'never' worked on projects around the house together or went out for recreation together. David said that he was 'somewhat' rather than very happy with most aspects of the marriage, and he described his feelings of love for Barbara as 'somewhat' rather than 'very' strong. David also saw many serious issues in the marriage, including problems with one or both spouses getting angry easily, being jealous, being critical, refusing to talk, not being home enough, and spending money foolishly. At one point during the interview David acknowledged that his marriage 'was in trouble'. David sometimes felt that he would like to live apart from Barbara, and he had thought seriously about divorce on several occasions during the previous three years.

The second vignette describes Frank and Christine, a couple with a companionate marriage. Their relationship was typical of many successful marriages, with high levels of happiness and love and frequent, close interaction.

The third vignette describes Jacob and Susan, a couple with an alone together marriage. A notable aspect of this relationship was a low level of interaction and the lack of any shared friends or organisational affiliations—a feature they had in common with David and Barbara. Yet, although the marital relationship was not perfect, they appeared to be reasonably happy together—a feature they shared with Frank and Christine. Typically, happily married couples spend a good deal of time together and, correspondingly, unhappily married couples tend to minimise the amount of time they spend together. But contrary to this general trend, Jacob and Susan were happily married despite their separate interests and activities: and, as noted earlier, marriages like Jacob and Susan's are becoming more common.

Companionate marriage: Frank and Christine

At the time of the interview in 2000, Frank and Christine were both 41 years old. They had been married for sixteen years and had no children. Both were African-American. They were high-school graduates, but neither had attended college. Frank was a semi-skilled factory worker, and Christine held a lower-level professional position. Both spouses earned similar salaries, and their combined earnings came to $90000 a year. They were buying a small home together, but had few other financial assets. Their marriage was egalitarian, and they shared housework as well as making all important decisions equally. Religion was very important to Christine and Frank, and they attended church together every week. Although neither belonged to any clubs or organisations, they held all their good friends in common. Frank was 'very happy' with all aspects of the marriage, and described his feelings of love for Christine as 'extremely strong'. The couple almost always ate their main meal of the day together, and they frequently went shopping, visited friends, worked on projects around the house, and went out for fun together. Although they occasionally disagreed on issues, they rarely quarrelled, and Frank saw no serious problems in the relationship. Moreover, he said that the thought of divorce had 'never' crossed his mind.

Alone together marriage: Jacob and Susan

When we interviewed Jacob in 2000, he was 41 years old and had been married to Susan (age 37) for eight years. Both spouses were white and had Bachelor's degrees. They had one pre-school-age child. Although Jacob worked around fifty hours a week, and Susan was employed for 35 hours a week, their combined income was a modest $48000 per year. Jacob did about half of the housework and childcare, and they shared important decisions equally. Although Susan was very religious Jacob was not, and they never attended religious services together. Although they 'almost always' ate their main meal of the day together, they only occasionally or rarely went out for recreation together, went shopping together, or worked on projects around the house together. Although they had several good friends, they did not hold any of these friends in common. Not surprisingly, they rarely visited friends together. They also did not belong to any of the same organisations or clubs. Despite their infrequent interaction, Jacob was 'very happy' with the amount of understanding, love and affection he received from his wife. He also reported that his feelings of love for his wife were 'very strong'. Jacob did admit, however, that he was only 'pretty happy' with their sexual relationship. He saw few problems in the marriage, with two exceptions: both he and his wife sometimes became angry and were critical of one another. Jacob also admitted that there had been a time in the past when he had thought the marriage was in trouble, but he did not feel that way currently.

We examined the data to see if we could locate clues about why alone together marriages might have increased between 1980 and 2000. Compared with spouses in companionate marriages, spouses in alone together marriages were somewhat older (a little over one year, on average) and had been married for longer durations (nearly two years, on average). These findings suggest that some companionate marriages turn into alone together marriages with the passage of time. Consistent with this notion, alone together marriages made up 25 per cent of marriages of seven years' duration or less, as against 33 per cent of marriages of eight years' duration or longer. But even if some alone together marriages were formerly companionate marriages, the average duration of marriage did not change between 1980 and 2000. Consequently, changes in marital duration across the decades cannot account for the growth of alone together marriages.

With respect to children, couples in alone together marriages had more children, on average, than did those in companionate marriages. This finding is consistent with the notion that children tend to decrease the amount of time that spouses spend together. Nevertheless, the mean number of children per marriage has declined (not increased) since 1980, so changes in childbearing cannot account for the increase in alone together marriages.

As regards employment, husbands in alone together marriages worked more hours than did husbands in companionate marriages—a finding that might help to explain why spouses in the former group spent less time together. Husbands' work hours, however, did not change between 1980 and 2000, so this variable cannot account for the growth in alone together marriages. In contrast to the figures for husbands, the percentage of wives in the labour force, and the weekly hours of employed wives, increased substantially after 1980. These changes in wives' employment, however, were nearly identical across all four marriage types.

We also looked at education, family income and church attendance, but we were unable to locate any demographic variables that could account for the rise in alone together marriages. These findings suggest that the increase in this marriage form is related primarily to cultural shifts—especially shifts in individualism—rather than to changes in the demographic characteristics of American marriages.

Individualism in American Culture

Ernest Burgess, a sociologist who wrote on marriage and family life in the middle of the twentieth century, argued that marriage was shifting from an institution to a form of companionship (Burgess and Wallin, 1953; Burgess et al., 1963). By an institution, Burgess meant a formal union strictly regulated by law, social norms, and religion—the dominant form of marriage during most of the country's agrarian, rural past. But in the late nineteenth century and the first half of the twentieth century, the USA became increasingly industrialised and urbanised. As people became more mobile, better educated and less religious, the social regulation of marriage weakened and, correspondingly, the notion emerged that marriage should be based primarily on the emotional bonds between spouses. 'Modern' marriages, according to this view, are formed when couples fall in love, and these couples stay together because they engage in cooperative teamwork to achieve mutually valued goals (such as achieving economic security, owning a home and raising children). By the middle of the twentieth century, this companionate ideal of marriage was firmly entrenched in American society (Mintz and Kellogg, 1988).

American culture has always had a strong current of individualism. This is not surprising, given that the first European colonists were escaping from societies that they viewed as overly restrictive and oppressive. In an insightful volume, Bellah *et al.* (1985) distinguished between two forms of individualism. Utilitarian individualism is the belief that people should work hard, be as self-sufficient as possible, and find success through their own efforts. This form of individualism has been pervasive throughout American history. Indeed, the search for opportunity and a better way of life is what motivated people of European descent to migrate and populate the central and western parts of the USA during the nineteenth century.

Utilitarian individualism is still pervasive and influential. But in the second half of the twentieth century, a second form of individualism emerged: expressive individualism (Bellah *et al.*, 1985). Expressive individualism is based on the assumption that people have an intrinsic need to express their innermost feelings, and that close relationships exist primarily to enhance individual happiness and maximise psychological growth. These ideas were popularised in the Human Potential Movement, as reflected in the writings of psychologists such as Carl Rogers (1961) and Abraham Maslow (1962).

As this new form of individualism spread throughout the country, it had a major impact on people's views about marriage. A number of observers (e.g. Amato, 2004; Cherlin, 2004, 2009) have argued that marriages in the USA have become more individualistic in recent decades, with self-development and personal fulfilment replacing the earlier emphasis on companionship and successful teamwork. According to this new understanding, love is absolutely necessary to form a union. But these unions are successful only to the extent that they continue to meet each partner's innermost psychological needs. In this sense, marriage came to have a new 'therapeutic' function in which personal growth became the *raison d'être* for forming and maintaining unions. The earlier notion of a spouse as a supportive partner with whom the partner cooperates to achieve practical goals was replaced with the notion of a spouse as a 'soul mate' who fulfils the partner's deepest wishes.

Although the potential for satisfaction is high in these marriages, individualistic unions also tend to be unstable. As Nock (1995) argued, passionate love and personal fulfilment, although important, also can be problematic, given that emotional closeness is likely to ebb and flow during the course of marriage. Consequently, if one or both spouses fall out of love, or if the union fails to meet one or both spouses' innermost needs, they will view divorce as a necessary—and even a positive—outcome.

Corresponding to the rise of individualistic marriage was a tendency for married couples to value privacy and to disengage from other social groups and networks. Putnam (2000) documented trends during the last several decades for people to be less involved in community organisations, including civic associations, political parties, recreational groups (e.g. bowling teams) and church social groups. Apparently, as we noted earlier, this trend has also extended into marriages, with spouses having fewer friends in common and sharing activities (like eating together) less often than in the past.

The changing focus of marriage

A socially regulated and institutionalised union → A private form of companionship → A therapeutic relationship that enhances personal growth

One might say that the focus of these three forms has been the society, the couple and the individual, respectively. Of course, we do not want to oversimplify the complexity of marriage. In the early years of American history, many married couples enjoyed companionate relationships. Correspondingly, many couples today have institutional marriages based firmly on religious beliefs and practices. It would not be unreasonable to say that all marriages contain some mix of institutional, companionate and individualistic elements. Nevertheless, the rise in alone together marriages in recent decades can be seen as a natural adaptation to, and extension of, the growing expressive individualism of American society.

'Living Apart Together' Relationships

Just as alone together marriages challenge traditional marriage ideals, living apart together (LAT) relationships stand at odds with conventional definitions of romantic relationships. These relationships (romantic, committed, dual-residence) do not appear to be common in the USA, but they are prevalent throughout Europe, especially in the UK and the Scandinavian countries. For example, one study estimated that the number of LAT relationships in Britain is roughly equal to the number of non-marital cohabitations (Haskey, 2005). Despite the prevalence of these relationships, social researchers have only recently begun to recognise that for many adults LATs are becoming an accepted alternative to single-residence relationships. Unfortunately, most national surveys do not allow for measuring these relationships, and individuals in LATs often are classified as single. Given the lack of data, our understanding of which couples choose LATs and why they do so is limited. Nevertheless, a research literature on this topic is growing, and it is possible to discern the emerging outline of a new field of study.

Although it is necessary to define a phenomenon before it can be studied, existing definitions of LAT relationships are ambiguous. Most observers appear to agree on three relevant conditions. First, as with marriage and non-marital cohabitation, LATs are romantic relationships that generally include a sexual component. Second, as Levin (2004) suggested, 'the couple has to agree that they are a couple; [and] others have to see them as such' (p. 226). Duncan and Phillips (2010) added that 'being a couple' means maintaining an exclusive relationship marked by fidelity. Third, LATs are dual-residence relationships, with partners voluntarily residing in separate homes.

Beyond these three criteria, however, there is little consensus about how these relationships should be measured. As Duncan and Phillips (2010) stated:

> A particular problem in researching LATs is that there is no easily defined 'cut-off' point in the same way that is apparently provided by formal marriage (a legal status) or cohabitation (physically living together) ... What is the difference between a boyfriend or girlfriend, especially one who is 'special' or long term, and living apart together? (p. 117)

As these authors pointed out, it is not clear when a conventional dating relationship transitions into an LAT relationship. Some researchers have sought to solve this problem by prescribing a minimal amount of time that a couple has been together (Castro-Martín *et al.*, 2008; Haskey, 2005) or by relying on partners' self-definitions of commitment (Levin, 2004; Levin and Trost, 1999). But because there is no broad agreement on these criteria, a great deal of heterogeneity exists in the types of relationships that researchers label as LATs.

Because of this ambiguity, counting the number of people who participate in and maintain these relationships is challenging, and estimates of the number of LATs vary greatly. Using the British Office of National Statistics' Omnibus survey, Haskey (2005) estimated that 4 million Britons aged 16–59 (around 6%) had a regular partner not living with them. Eliminating full-time students and young people living with their parents reduced the estimate to around 2 million. Despite the huge implications of this decision, many researchers include students as LATs (e.g. Billari *et al.*, 2008; Castro-Martín *et al.*, 2008). Similarly, using the British Social Attitudes Survey, Duncan and Phillips (2010) determined that 40 per cent of respondents in self-defined LATs were actually 'dating casually' and not in committed partner relationships. These findings demonstrate that determining the frequency of LATs will hinge on the general acceptance of an explicit definition of what it means to be living apart together.

Although it is difficult to estimate the actual number of LATs, the number of people living apart from their partners appears to be increasing. Roseneil (2006) reported that 19 per cent of people in the UK did *not* live with a partner in 1979, as against nearly 30 per cent in 2004. Although these data do not directly address the frequency of LATs, it is clear that an increasing number of people are neither married nor cohabiting, and it is likely that a significant number of these people are in LATs. Levin (2004) found a large increase in the number of self-defined LAT relationships in Sweden during the 1990s. In 1993, 6 per cent of Swedes not living with a partner were in LATs, as against 14 per cent in 2001. Although LATs appear to be more common in Sweden than in most other Western countries (Levin, 2004), corresponding increases appear to have occurred throughout much of Europe. The LATs appear to be most common in the UK, Scandinavia, the Netherlands and Germany, and less common in southern European countries such as Spain and Italy.

Types of LAT relationship

The term 'living apart together' appears to describe at least two distinct types of relationship. *Transitory LATs* (a name suggested by Reimondos *et al.*, 2009) are relatively short-term partnerships with a modest level of commitment. These relationships, however, eventually may lead to highly committed long-term relationships, such as marriage. The second type of LAT represents the final goal of a relationship progression rather than an intermediate step. *Stable LATs* are long-lasting, committed relationships that function as deliberate alternatives to marital or non-marital cohabitation.

Transitory LATs provide opportunities to try out relationships with partners before entering into more lasting (and confining) commitments. Duncan and Phillips (2010) asked 320 British respondents in LAT relationships about their reasons for living apart, and more than a third (37%) said that they were not ready to live together or that it was too early to move in together. Similarly, in a study of German LATs (aged 30–50), Reuschke (2010) found that 26 per cent of the 188 respondents were not living with their partners because they did not know each other well enough. Although people in transitory LATs are not ready for co-residential relationships with their partners, many expect that they will live together in the future. For example, Milan and Peters (2003) found that about one-third of the approximately 2100 Canadian LATs in the 2001 General Social Survey expected to live with their current partners in the future. This was especially true of younger LATs: nearly 60 per cent of respondents aged 20–29 (as against around 45 per cent of those age 30–49 and around 25 per cent of those older than 50) expected to live with their partners eventually. Similarly, Reimondos *et al.* (2009), in a study of Australian LATs, found that 64 per cent of all respondents and 79 per cent of young adult respondents (age 25–35) expected to live with their partners within the next three years. These findings indicate that many people in LATs are not deliberately avoiding co-residential relationships and, instead, see living together as a desirable future outcome.

Many relationships classified as LATs are of relatively short duration. Reimondos *et al.* (2009) found that around 40 per cent of the Australian LAT relationships in their study had begun less than 12 months before the survey, and the median duration of LAT relationships was 1.5 years. In a study of 22 British LATs, Roseneil (2006) found that 15 respondents (67%) had been with their partner for less than three years, three (14%) for 4–6 years, and the remaining four (18%) for more than seven years. Using the longitudinal German Socio-Economic Panel 1991–2005, Ermisch and Siedler (2009) found that the average LAT lasted around four years. They also found that around 45 per cent dissolved, 35 per cent became non-marital cohabitations, and 10 per cent became marriages. (Presumably the remaining 10% of LATs continued past 10 years.) These data illustrate the transitory nature of most LATs.

Rather than being a new phenomenon, transitory LATs do not appear to be essentially different from conventional dating relationships, with the potential to develop into more deeply committed unions. What is new is the fact that these types of relationship have become more common during the last few decades. Stable LATs, in contrast, appear to be a relatively new phenomenon. These long-duration relationships are strikingly unconventional because partners, although committed to one another and presumably in love, have no desire or plans to live together—ever. Theoretically speaking, it makes little sense to combine the two types of LATs, because the causes and consequences of these two types of relationships are likely to differ considerably.

In some countries, LATs are, almost exclusively, transitory relationships involving young adults. In Spain, 2 per cent of women aged 35–49 have LAT partners, as against one quarter of women aged 25–29 and nearly one-third of women aged 20–24 (Castro-Martín *et al.*, 2008). To put these figures in context, around 93 per cent of women between the ages of 20 and 30 still live with their parents

(Castro-Martín *et al.*, 2008). In their study of Spanish LATs, Castro-Martín and colleagues suggested that the high occurrence of LATs is not a product of non-traditional values, but of social constraints. They point to the difference in the proportion of LATs (23%) to cohabitees (7%) among young women aged 25–29 as evidence for 'the difficulties faced by young adults in reaching economic and residential independence rather than compliance with traditional family values' (p. 462). In Italy too, LAT relationships function almost exclusively among young adults and serve as a step in the progression towards cohabitation or marriage, as well as a means of extending time in young adulthood before family formation (Billari *et al.*, 2008).

LATs over the life course

Understanding how the frequency of LATs varies over the life course is challenging, since some of the most comprehensive studies of this topic either did not include adults over 60 or did not distinguish between middle-aged and older adults (Ermisch and Siedler, 2009; Haskey, 2005; Milan and Peters, 2003; Reimondos *et al.*, 2010). The exclusion of older couples with LAT relationships is unfortunate, because these couples appear to differ from their younger counterparts in many respects. For example, older adults in LAT relationships are especially unlikely to share financial costs or obligations.

Nevertheless, available studies lead to two conclusions. First, the majority of LATs occur among people under 30 (Haskey, 2005; Milan and Peters, 2003). Second, younger adults almost exclusively form transitory LATs, whereas adults over 35 tend towards stable LATs. One study, for example, found that around 60 per cent of people under 35 in LATs anticipated shifting into single-residence relationships (either non-marital cohabitation or marriage), as against around 40 per cent of people over 35 (Ermisch and Siedler, 2009). This same study also found that adults over 35 tend to stay in LAT partnerships longer than their younger counterparts. According to Ermisch and Siedler (2009), age 35 is an important marker in the life course, with the incidence of LATs (especially transitory ones) declining substantially after this.

The relationship expectations of older adults differ from those of younger adults, for three reasons, as given in the box overleaf.

LATs and the Second Demographic Transition

Earlier, we argued that the increase in alone together marriages is a reflection of growing individualism—especially expressive individualism—in the USA. Correspondingly, the rise in LAT relationships in Europe can be understood within the context of the Second Demographic Transition (Lesthaeghe, 1983, 2010). Features of the Second Demographic Transition include an increase in the acceptance and occurrence of pre-marital sex, divorce and non-marital cohabitation; a decline in the importance of marriage and fertility; and (with the exception of non-marital births) a general delay in family formation. Strohm *et al.* (2009) suggested that these factors represent 'the behavioural manifestation of a long-term normative shift toward individualism and egalitarianism' (p. 179). The LAT relationships are a logical product of this recent ideological shift, since they seemingly offer opportunities for independence, self-fulfilment and egalitarianism within the context of a committed partnership.

Relationship expectations of older adults

1. LAT relationships among those over the age of 35 are especially likely to follow marital dissolution, and many of these individuals are apprehensive about repeating this experience (Levin, 2004; Trost, 2010).
2. Older adults have invested considerably more time in their careers, homes and hobbies than younger adults. It is not surprising, therefore, that some older adults are reluctant to adapt their single lifestyles to accommodate live-in partners. Indeed, one-third of respondents in a study of French LATs stated that they maintained dual-residence relationships primarily to retain their independence (Villeneuve-Gokalp, 1997).
3. Older adults often have responsibilities to others, especially children or age-ing parents, and these responsibilities may decrease their willingness to take on new commitments. For example, Ermisch and Siedler (2009) found that 50 per cent of LAT mothers did not expect to marry or cohabit with their current partners, as against 62 per cent of women who were not mothers.

Theoretical work on the Second Demographic Transition suggests why both types of LATs have increased. With regard to transitory LATs, the declining importance of early marriage means that young adults are spending more time as single persons. Strohm *et al.* (2009) pointed out that although the number of marriages is declining, the rise in non-marital cohabitations signals that 'individuals are not rejecting partnerships *per se* … They still seek intimate relationships, but not necessarily marriage' (p. 179). Transitory LATs, even more than non-marital cohabitations, allow young people to explore roman-tic, sexual relationships during the expanded time before marriage and parenthood. Many young adults are postponing relationship commitments because they feel that a degree of self-development should occur prior to (rather than follow) union formation. In particular, the early adult years are now seen as a time to focus on education and employment. Consequently, it is not surprising that many LATs are students and young professionals, many of whom still live with their parents (Haskey, 2005).

The same values of expressive individualism and self-fulfilment also help to explain the rise of stable LATs among older adults. Increasing numbers of older adults are taking advantage of the range of alternative relationship styles now available in Western countries. Stable LATs, which were viewed as 'incomplete' in the past, can now serve as an acceptable relationship option for adults apprehensive about the personal costs of living together. This option may be especially appealing to people following divorce or separation from a long-term partner. For younger as well as older adults, LATs allow for a substantial degree of freedom and personal growth within the context of emotionally close, mutually supportive, romantic relationships.

Implications for the Future

The cultural changes that underlie the rise in expressive individualism and the Second Demographic Transition have altered family formation processes, and alone together marriages and living apart together relationships are reflections of this shift. Although we have addressed alone together marriages in the USA, it is likely that this marriage type has increased in other Western countries as well. Similarly, although we have discussed LAT relationships in Europe, it is probable that the number of these relationships has increased in the USA as well, although few American studies on this topic have taken place. Further attention from family and relationship scholars will be needed if we are to ascertain the frequency of these relationship forms, as well as their distributions across various countries around the world.

With respect to LATs, we argue that the umbrella term 'living apart together' has been used to describe two distinct phenomena: transitory LATs and stable LATs. Among (primarily) young adults, transitory LATs reflect the delay in family formation in favour of self-development. Among (primarily) older adults, stable LATs represent the acceptance of alternative long-term relationships that maximise the possibilities of personal autonomy within the context of a committed relationship. A clearer under-standing of the difference between the two types of LATs, and an understanding of how these relationships differ from marital and non-marital cohabitation, is an impor-tant task for future research.

Conducting new studies of transitory and stable LATs will not be possible, how-ever, without clearer definitions of these phenomena. Moreover, few existing data sets include information on participants' perceptions of LAT relationships and their moti-vations to enter and remain in these types of unions. Qualitative measures may prove to be especially useful for these purposes. A better understanding of LATs will almost certainly require the collection of new data as well as greater theoretical development.

Observers should recognise that these emerging relationship forms include risks along with potential benefits. Although alone together marriages can provide spouses with a considerable degree of valued autonomy, they are likely to be fragile when relationship problems emerge. Because these spouses are independent of one another in many ways, they can divorce without greatly disrupting their individual lifestyles. In contrast, spouses in companionate marriages (who share multiple activities, inter-ests, friends, and organisational affiliations) are more resilient in the face of the inevi-table ups and downs of relationships. These spouses must, of necessity, give up a great deal if they divorce. Consequently, spouses in companionate marriages are highly motivated to resolve relationship problems through negotiation and compromise. Because the costs of divorce are high for interdependent spouses in companionate marriages, a considerable degree of security is gained at the expense of a modest level of autonomy.

The LAT relationships face different challenges. First, couples who choose to live apart forgo the economies of scale gained through living together. Because maintain-ing two households is costly, this relationship form is beyond the financial means of many couples. Second, LAT relationships involve benefits for adults who value auton-omy, but it is unlikely that children from these relationships will receive comparable benefits. The vast majority of studies have shown that children have the best chance of developing into well-adjusted, competent adults when they grow up with two resi-dential parents with a healthy relationship (Amato, 2005). For this reason, LATs may be appealing to young adults not yet ready to make deeper commitments, or to older adults who have already raised children (or who prefer to remain childless). But they have little utility for most people in middle adulthood raising children. The one exception might involve stepfamilies. It is possible that some single parents, following separation or divorce, would prefer a long-term non-resident relationship with a partner to a live-in relationship. Arrangements like this might reduce the level of conflict between step-parents and stepchildren—a common problem in traditional residential stepfamilies (Hetherington and Jodl, 1994). The topic of LAT stepfamilies, like many others in this chapter, would make a fine starting point for future research. Moreover, these family types need to be carefully considered as family policies are developed, and support services will have to take account of and be able to respond to very different kinds of relationships.

References

Amato, P. R. (2004) Tension between institutional and individual views of marriage, *Journal of Marriage and Family*, 66: 959–965.

Amato, P. R. (2005) The impact of family formation change on the cognitive, social, and emotional well-being of the next generation, *The Future of Children*, 15(2): 75–96.

Amato, P. R., Booth, A., Johnson, D. and Rogers, S. J. (2007) *Alone Together: How marriage in America is changing* (Cambridge, MA: Harvard University Press).

Bailey, K. D. (1994) *Typologies and Taxonomies: An introduction to classification techniques* (Beverly Hills, CA: Sage).

Bellah, R. N., Madsen, R., Sullivan, W. M., Swidler, A. and Tipton, S. M. (1985) *Habits of the Heart: Individualism and commitment in American life* (New York: Harper & Row).

Billari, F. C., Rosina, A., Ranaldi, R. and Romano, M. C. (2008) Young adults living apart and together (LAT) with parents: a three-level analysis of the Italian case, *Regional Studies*, 42(5): 625–639.

Burgess, E. W., Locke, H. J. and Thomes, M. M. (1963) *The Family: From institution to companionship* (New York: American Book Company).

Burgess, E. W. and Wallin, P. (1953) *Engagement and Marriage* (Chicago, IL: Lippincott).

Castro-Martín, T., Domínguez-Folgueras, M. and Martín-García, T. (2008) Not truly partnerless: non-residential partnerships and retreat from marriage in Spain, *Demographic Research*, 18: 443–468.

Cherlin, A. J. (2004) The deinstitutionalisation of American marriage, *Journal of Marriage and Family*, 66(4): 848–861.

Cherlin, A. J. (2009) *The Marriage-go-round: The state of marriage and the family in America today* (New York: Knopf).

Duncan, S. and Phillips, M. (2010) People who live apart together (LATs)—how different are they?, *The Sociological Review*, 58(1): 112–134.

Ermisch, J. and Siedler, T. (2009) Living apart together, in M. Brynin and J. Ermisch (eds), *Changing Relationships* (London: Routledge): 29–43.

Haskey, J. (2005) Living arrangements in contemporary Britain: having a partner who usually lives elsewhere and living apart together (LAT), *Population Trends*, 122: 35–45.

Hetherington, E. M. and Jodl, K. M. (1994) Stepfamilies as settings for child development, in A. Booth and J. Dunn (eds), *Stepfamilies: Who benefits? Who does not?* (Hillsdale, NJ: Lawrence Erlbaum), 55–79.

Lesthaeghe, R. (1983) A century of demographic and cultural change in Western Europe: an exploration of underlying dimensions, *Population and Development Review*, 9(3): 411–435.

Lesthaeghe, R. (2010) The unfolding story of the Second Demographic Transition, *Population and Development Review*, 36(2): 211–251.

Levin, I. (2004) Living apart together: a new family form, *Current Sociology*, 52(2): 223–240.

Levin, I. and Trost J. (1999) Living apart together, *Community Sociology*, 2(3): 279–294.

Maslow, A. (1962) *Toward a Psychology of Being* (Princeton, NJ: Van Nostrand).

Milan, A. and Peters, A. (2003) Couples living apart, *Canadian Social Trends*, Summer: 2–6.

Mintz, S. and Kellogg, S. (1988) *Domestic Revolutions: A social history of American family life* (New York: Free Press).

Nock, S. L. (1995) Commitment and dependency in marriage, *Journal of Marriage and Family*, 57: 503–514.

Putnam, R. D. (2000) *Bowling Alone: The collapse and revival of American community* (New York: Simon & Schuster).

Reimondos, A., Evans, A. and Gray, E. (2009) *Living-Apart-Together (LAT) Relationships in Australia: An overview*, presented at the annual meeting of the Australian Sociological Association, December, Canberra, Australia. http://melbourneinstitute.com/downloads/hilda/conf-papers/Reimondos_LAT_TASA09.pdf. [Accessed 20.6.2011.]

Reuschke, D. (2010) Living apart together over long distances—time–space patterns and consequences of a late modern-living arrangement, *Erdkunde*, 64(3): 215–226.

Rogers, C. (1961) *On Becoming a Person* (Boston, MA: Houghton Mifflin).

Roseneil, S. (2006) On not living with a partner: unpicking coupledom and cohabitation, *Sociological Research Online*, 11(3). http://www.socresonline.org.uk/11/3/Roseneil.html. [Accessed 20.6.2011.]

Strohm, C. Q., Seltzer J. A., Cochran, S. D. and Mays, V. M. (2009) Living apart together relationships in the United States, *Demographic Research*, 21: 177–214.

Trost, J. (2010) The social institution of marriage, *Journal of Comparative Family Studies*, Summer: 507–514.

Villeneuve-Gokalp, C. (1997) *Vivre en couple chacun chez soi*, *Population*, 5: 1050–1082.

4

Marriage and Divorce in the Western World

Jan Pryor

Introduction

In all countries that constitute the Western world, there has been a remarkable and, in many ways, unforeseen change in the nature of marriage and divorce. The 'Western world', however, is far from homogeneous. This chapter considers the state of marriage and divorce in the twenty-first century, and examines several themes that are important in considering the changes that are evident.

Differences between the USA and Europe

In a discussion of marriage and other family dynamics such as divorce, we need to distinguish the USA, which has produced the bulk of the literature on marriage and divorce, from European countries. Table 4.1 gives an overview of the differences for several Western countries. It is apparent that in the USA people marry more, marry younger, divorce more readily, and cohabit less than in other Western countries.

The history of marriage and divorce in the USA is broadly similar to that of marriage and divorce in north-west European countries (Thornton, 2009). There are several commonalities, including the shift in economic activity from the household to the workplace during the industrial revolution, and the movement of women into the workplace in the twentieth century. These and other factors have changed the nature of marriage and family life.

Contemporary Issues in Family Studies: Global Perspectives on Partnerships, Parenting and Support in a Changing World, First Edition. Edited by Angela Abela and Janet Walker.
© 2014 John Wiley & Sons, Ltd. Published 2014 by John Wiley & Sons, Ltd.

Table 4.1   Marriage and divorce: an international comparison[1]

Country	Marriage rate	Age at first marriage (m/f)	Divorce rate	Cohabitation rate
Australia	5.4	29.6/27.7	1.9	8.9
Canada	4.2	29.5/28	1.7	8.9
Denmark	6.0	33.5/31.5	2.8	11.5
France	4.0	32/30	1.5	14.4
UK	4.1	32/28.5	2.2	8.7
USA	6.8	28/26	3.5	5.5

[1]The crude marriage rates are the number of marriages per 1000 population in 2009; the crude divorce rates are the number of divorces per 1000 population in 2008; the cohabitation rate represents the percentage of population in both sexes.

Based on data from OECD Family Database, www.oecd.org/els/social/family/database. [Accessed on 13.3.2013.].

The role of religion

Cherlin (2009) points to some specific aspects of US culture that contribute to the fact that Americans marry, divorce and remarry more readily than people in other countries. He suggests that Puritanism, accompanying the early migration of north-western Europeans to the USA, has had the dual and contradictory roles of encouraging formal commitment to partnership, at the same time as emphasising an individual's direct relationship with God, meaning that personal development is also imperative. So important was marriage that some colonies in the seventeenth century forbade people to live alone, and church attendance was high—70 to 80 per cent of households belonged to a church (Cherlin, 2009).

By the twentieth century the trajectories of church membership in the USA and much of Europe were going in different directions; there was a burgeoning diversity of religions in the USA and an attendant rise in religiosity, while in England in particular there has been a steady process of secularisation as citizens have moved away from churches. Table 4.2 compares religious belief and behaviour in the UK and USA. In the UK and elsewhere in Europe, the church in the twenty-first century clearly does not play such a pivotal role in people's lives as it does in the USA. The prominent place of religion in the USA continues, and so too does the tension between, on the one hand, the desirability of marriage and, on the other, the acceptance by churches of divorce.

Individualism versus connectedness

A major debate about the possible causes of lower rates of marriage and the higher dissolution rates centres on the rise of individualism in Western societies. Wages have become individualised rather than family-based, and indeed, many aspects of society focus on the individual rather than the couple or family as a group. European writers such as Elisabeth Beck-Gernsheim (2002) and Anthony Giddens (1992) emphasise the dramatic impact of self-actualisation on the fragility of marriages.

Table 4.2   Comparison between USA and UK on religious factors[1]

Country	No religion	Christian	Never go to church	Don't believe in God
UK	43%	50%	62%	18%
USA	15%	76%	22%	3%

[1]Statistics compiled, with the authors' permission, from data presented in Voas and Ling (2010), Ch. 4.

Pure relationship

Anthony Giddens describes 'pure relationship' as 'a social relation [which] is entered for its own sake, for what can be derived by each person from a sustained association with another and which is continued only in so far as it is thought by both parties to deliver enough satisfactions for each individual to stay within it'. (Giddens, 1992, p. 58)

Giddens suggests that intimate relationships are becoming more and more like 'confluent love', and that 'the "separating and divorcing" society of today here appears as an effect of the emergence of confluent love rather than its cause' (Giddens, 1992, p. 61). Beck-Gernsheim's theory of individualisation has two parts: the loss of external imperatives as to how to live, resulting in individuals having to 'decide for themselves how to shape their lives' (Gernsheim, 2002, p. ix); and the focus of institutions on the individual rather than on families, 'enjoining the individual to lead a life of his or her own beyond any ties to the family or other groups' (p. ix).

In contrast, in the UK writers such as Smart (2007) and Lewis (2001) suggest that connectedness and commitment have not declined in recent decades. Smart proposes a connectedness thesis as a framework for studying relationship, reciprocity and other aspects of being connected that she finds evident in families she studies. Lewis focuses on commitment and finds that commitment is widespread in relationships regardless of their legal status. In the USA, too, Bengston and his colleagues (Bengston *et al.*, 2002) have documented the similarities, across four generations, in levels of collectivism and family commitment, suggesting that 'our findings challenge the myth that … families are declining in functioning and influence' (p. 157). The differences in the implications of these perspectives are discussed later in the chapter.

Marriage

Historians have identified three kinds of marriage characteristic of the last 110 years: institutional marriage, companionate marriage, and individualised marriage. *Institutional* marriage was a feature of the first half of the twentieth century. Roles and behaviour in marriage were dictated by church and state; the marital relationship was patriarchal, as much practical as it was affectionate, and neither partner expected self-fulfilment in the marriage (Amato, 2009).

By the mid-twentieth century, marital bonds were increasingly affectionate and based on sentiment. Roles were still gendered; women were homemakers and men were providers. Despite women being often as well-educated as their husbands, men were the 'senior partners' in the family (Amato, 2009). It was still unacceptable to have children outside marriage, and sex before marriage, although no doubt practised, was not condoned. This *companionate* marriage represented the nuclear family. Most recently, we have seen the rise of the *individualised* marriage, characterised by self-development, flexibility, and open communication (Cherlin, 2004).

Gillis (2004) suggests that the period from 1870 to 1970 was a time when marriage was almost mandatory, and that today's acceptance of informal partnerships, such as cohabitation, signals a return to the situation that was the norm preceding the mid-nineteenth century. Marriage, it seems, is becoming an ideal to which people aspire, but which many do not achieve. As Cherlin suggests, marriage is 'a marker of prestige, not conformity' (2004, p. 855). The nature of marriage is thus changing from a formally recognised and, in the past, socially necessary institution to one that is chosen.

Government agencies and others in the USA are endeavouring to change the culture of individualistic marriage back towards companionate or institutional styles of partnership, and highly educated middle-class people show indications of a move towards these, while less educated people endorse aspects of individualistic marriage (Amato, 2009). The Pew Survey suggests, however, that a shift towards liberal views of marriage is continuing (Taylor, 2010). For example, 39 per cent of those polled agreed that marriage is becoming obsolete, and liberal attitudes to family change are particularly high in young adults. Yet in the same survey, over half said that they were closer to their partner than their parents were in their relationships. Similarly, only 43 per cent of participants objected to cohabitation and to unmarried and same-sex couples raising children. Notably, however, in Europe only 14–20 per cent of people disapprove of childbirth outside marriage, and 10–14 per cent disapprove of cohabitation (Harrison and Fitzgerald, 2010). The difference in attitudes between the USA and Europe is evident, although both are becoming more liberal.

In 2010, the Pew Research Center carried out a survey of 2691 adults in the USA in order to describe changes in behaviours and attitudes to marriage and families. It was accompanied by an analysis of demographic data drawn in the main from the US census. The survey oversampled divorced or separated people, single people and adults who were parenting a child under the age of 18, and data were weighted in order to achieve a sample representative of the general population of adults in the USA.

The Pew Survey found that, in the USA, education, race and socio-economic status are linked to marriage rates, with college-educated and white adults most likely to be married (Taylor, 2010). In 1960, those who never attended college and college graduates were almost equally likely to marry; in 2008, 64 per cent of graduates were married, as against 48 per cent of adults with a high school diploma or less (Taylor, 2010). The drop is particularly dramatic for African-American women. In 1950, 96 per cent of African-American women with a less than high-school level of education were ever married; by 2006, only 61.7 per cent were ever married (Peters and Kamp Dush, 2009).

Non-marital cohabitation

One of the most momentous changes in the nature of marriage is the unforeseen increase in pre-marital cohabitation; the majority of couples now cohabit before marrying (Manning *et al.*, 2009). Changes in marriage patterns must be understood in the context of the increasing rates of cohabitation; although people form partnerships at similar rates, the increase in the popularity of cohabitation as a prelude to, or a replacement for, formal marriage means that as marriage rates have fallen so too have divorce rates, since dissolution of cohabitation is not legally recorded. In turn, many higher-order partnerships are cohabitations. It is comparatively recently that partnership research has addressed cohabitation as well as marriage, and in many instances people who cohabit are still not included in studies of intimate relationships.

Pre-marital cohabitation has been linked in several studies with a higher risk of marriage breakdown (Kamp Dush *et al.*, 2003). Studies using more recent cohorts suggest, however, that in the USA cohabitation before marriage no longer increases the risk of divorce (Reinhold, 2010). This is also the case in Denmark (Svarer, 2004) and Australia (Hewitt and DeVaus, 2009). Soons and Kalmijn (2009) examined the 'cohabitation gap' across European countries and demonstrated that differences in wellbeing between married and cohabiting couples not only were predicted by selection factors (religiosity and material resources) but were also related closely to the institutionalisation of cohabitation. Those countries where cohabitation was firmly embedded had either no gap or, in a few cases, a negative gap—people in cohabiting relationships were happier than those who were married.

The advantages of marriage over cohabitation have also been questioned by Musick and Bumpass (2012), who found, using data from the National Survey of Families and Households, that both marriage and cohabitation increase wellbeing, and that differences between marriage and cohabitation were insignificant on a wide range of outcomes, including health, happiness, self-esteem and depression. They also found that, when union dissolutions were excluded from analyses, levels of health were higher for married individuals but that levels of self-esteem and happiness were higher for those who were cohabiting.

The impact of same-sex marriage

Another factor contributing to changes is the rise of civil unions, brought about in the main by the desire of gay and lesbian couples to achieve formal partnership status. This arises from the lack of rights same-sex couples have in terms of medical choices and other rights granted by formal marriage, and from their desire to have a legally and socially recognised relationship. Their success in achieving this varies internationally, with same-sex marriage now legal in many countries. Civil unions, which confer very similar rights to marriage, have burgeoned in some parts of the USA, in European countries and in New Zealand. In the UK, for example, the Civil Partnership Act 2004 gives lesbian and gay couples access to the same inheritance tax, social security exemptions and pension benefits as married couples.

In most jurisdictions only same-sex couples are able to enter civil unions. However, in those where heterosexual couples do have access to civil unions a remarkable number choose this option.

In France, there are two civil unions for every marriage and it is predicted that the numbers of marriages and civil unions will become equal in the near future. Furthermore, 95 per cent of civil unions in France are undertaken by heterosexual couples. In New Zealand in 2010, almost one-third of civil unions were entered by heterosexual couples.

A few states in the USA allow civil unions, the most recent being Illinois. Rarely, however, are heterosexual couples able to enter a civil union in the USA. The effect of this is that couples have reduced choices relative to those of couples in France and New Zealand; they can cohabit or they can marry.

Why has marriage declined in popularity?

There are four possible explanations for the decline in popularity of marriage. First, cohabitation may be chosen not by those who are marriage-averse, but by those who are divorce-averse. The dissolution of a marriage involves legal proceedings and the social approbation of becoming divorced. Cohabitation, at least in a legal sense, is not so difficult to end. Second, Giddens and others would argue that marriage in its traditional form does not allow for the development of the individual and for the self-realisation that is encouraged in Western societies.

Third, the elevation of marriage to a state which represents the ideal relationship, to be achieved only if and when one's partner and relationship are perfect, means that for many couples cohabitation is the best they feel they can achieve. Gillis, for example, sees cohabitation as a way of managing the overly high expectation of marriage that it meet both partners' needs for self-fulfilment.

A fourth explanation, and one linked with the first three, is that legally marriage and cohabitation increasingly resemble each other. In some countries (e.g. New Zealand, Australia and Sweden), cohabitation and marriage are virtually indistinguishable, and this is becoming increasingly the case in many states in the USA (Kiernan, 2004). Legal similarities are accompanied by the fact that the traditional functions of marriage—legitimising sexual activity, having babies, providing economic support for women—have been largely removed from its exclusive ambit. Marriage, then, becomes primarily a site of intimacy and personal fulfilment.

Marriage today

Given that marriage has become optional for sexual intimacy and child rearing, and that it has few legal advantages over cohabitation and civil union, why do people still marry? While it is true that marriage rates are declining and that people marry later, it remains the case that 90 per cent of Americans eventually marry. Cherlin (2004, 2009) suggests the role of 'enforceable trust' in marriage—a public commitment to fidelity and a lifelong relationship that is witnessed by family and friends, and brings with it constraints (financial, legal and social) on leaving the relationship.

More than this, Cherlin argues that the symbolic importance of marriage has increased. Rather than being an integral aspect of being an adult and of gaining respectability, it is now an individualised achievement, something that is gained and earned by first establishing compatibility, financial stability and, sometimes, parenting ability. So, possibly because the alternative of civil union is not available but also because marriage carries considerable status in the USA, Americans continue to marry at high rates in comparison with European couples. When asked why they married, the main reason respondents in the Pew Survey gave was love, followed by making a lifelong commitment, and companionship. Having children came fourth in the ranking of reasons (Taylor, 2010). Similar reasons were given by a group of married parents interviewed in New Zealand (Pryor and Roberts, 2005). Finally, the role of religious beliefs is significant for a considerable number of couples who are not comfortable living outside a partnership sanctioned by their church.

Marital quality

Family scholars have long believed that marital happiness forms a U-shaped curve over time, with high levels in the early years of marriage and a dip during child rearing, and a return towards high levels once children have left home. So strong was the belief in the U-shaped curve that Glenn (1999) suggested that 'a curvilinear relationship between family stage and some aspects of marital quality is about as close to being certain as anything ever is in the social sciences' (p. 33). Most studies, however, have used cross-sectional analyses to examine marital happiness. Recent longitudinal studies show that there is a pervasive decline throughout the duration of marriages in the quality of the relationship (see also Musick and Bumpass, 2012).

Overall, formal marriage is a declining phenomenon in Western countries. Its status has changed, from that of near-universal means to attaining adult roles and responsibilities to an optional relationship that is increasingly seen as unattainable or unnecessary. As other forms of partnership flourish alongside marriage its place in the future is uncertain. Nevertheless, there is little doubt that most people will continue to want a conjugal relationship; what the future balance and characteristics of diverse partnerships will be is far from clear.

> Degrees of formal and informal commitment are available to couples, ranging from living apart together, cohabitation and in some cases civil union, to formal marriage, and covenant marriage (available in some states in the USA) that encompasses legal enticements and barriers to ending the marriage.

Divorce

Rates of divorce in the Western world have climbed in the last 75 years. In the USA, rates reached their peak in 1980, when the crude rate was 5.2 per 1000 people. In 2008 they had dropped to 3.5, related in considerable measure to the increase in the proportion of people cohabiting, since rates of dissolution of cohabiting relationships are not recorded. Nevertheless, the rate of divorce in the USA remains high in comparison with that of other Western countries (Table 4.1).

Why are divorce rates so high in the USA? Amato points to the deep ambivalence in US society about divorce: on the one hand people will endorse statements that personal happiness is more important than staying in a marriage, and on the other they will endorse the statement that children are frequently harmed when their parents divorce (Amato and Irving, 2006). Cherlin notes (2009) that whereas in England divorce was not allowed until 1857, in the USA divorce was allowed under certain circumstances from the country's inception. The USA, then, began as a country on a very different footing with respect to attitudes and laws about marriage and divorce.

Predictors of divorce

Considerable effort has been made to explain why relationships end. Most research has focused on the breakdown of marriages, although a body of literature is developing, especially in Europe, that addresses the dissolution of cohabiting unions (Lyngstad and Jalovaara, 2010). Demographic correlates include time factors such as age at marriage and duration of the marriage. Low educational levels, low socioeconomic status and unemployment are factors which are positively associated with the dissolution of marriage (Amato, 2010; Lyngstad and Jalovaara, 2010). Education, however, shows a complex relationship with divorce. Generally, husbands' high education levels are negatively associated; wives' education levels appear to be negatively related in the USA and Scandinavia, but not in Italy (Lyngstad and Jalovaara, 2010) or the Netherlands (Poortman and Kalmijn, 2002), where divorce is more likely for women with university degrees. Recent research from Italy, however, suggests that the relationship may be reversing (Salvini and Vignoli, 2011). Educational heterogamy (differences in educational levels between spouses) appears also to be a risk factor for divorce in Scandinavian countries (Svarer and Verner, 2006) and the USA (Tzeng, 1992).

Linked with educational levels are employment and income, and here the picture is also complicated. The effect of the income of wives is referred to as the 'independence effect', where the higher a wife's income, the more likely divorce becomes. Evidence for this is found in several European countries (Jalovaara, 2001). In the USA the effect is dependent on a wife's relative contribution to the household income (Rogers, 2004). Schoen and colleagues concluded that increased hours of employment of wives increased marital conflict, but that the increased income contribution to the family improved other aspects of the relationship, resulting in a zero net effect of wives' employment (Schoen *et al.*, 2006). A more recent study by Teachman also shows a complicated relationship between women's economic resources and the risk of divorce for white women, where both absolute and relative income increases the risk of dissolution, while labour market participation increases the likelihood of stable marriages (Teachman, 2010). It may also be the case that being employed makes it easier for women to leave an unhappy marriage. This is supported by findings that increased employment predicts divorce in unhappy but not in happy marriages (Schoen *et al.*, 2002).

A major predictor of divorce is its intergenerational transmission. For children of divorce, there is a higher risk that their own marriages will break down (Lyngstad and Engelhardt, 2009; Teachman, 2002). Explanations for the relationship between parental and offspring divorce include selection effects, such as inherited mental health issues, and lack of relationship skills. The most convincing explanation so far is the lack of commitment to marriage in the generation that has experienced parental divorce (Wolfinger, 2003). It is likely, however, that all three explanations, and possibly others, are valid.

> Gender roles and agreement about division of household labour appear to be related to the likelihood of divorce or separation, with higher agreement lowering the risk, especially for cohabiting couples (Hohmann-Marriott, 2006).
>
> The social context, however, is important. In Germany a gendered division of labour is encouraged, and unequal earnings and involvement in household labour predicted lower divorce rates, whereas in the USA this is not the case (Cooke, 2006).
>
> Religious belief is consistently related to lower levels of dissolution (Lehrer, 2004). The relationship is both direct and indirect. Religious belief usually encompasses a moral aspect—the feeling that one ought to try to keep a relationship together—and regular church attendance is also likely to be a social deterrent to divorce.

Multiple marriages and divorces

Adults who divorce are more likely than not to repartner, either into a cohabitation or a remarriage. In the USA over half of divorced women remarry within five years, and 75 per cent remarry within ten years of divorce (Bramlett and Mosher, 2001). Second partnerships are less stable than first ones. In the UK, for example, the proportion of divorcing men and women who have had a previous marriage that has ended in divorce doubled between 1980 and 2009 (Office for National Statistics, 2011). If we take into account the rates of cohabitation and non-legal separation that take place, it is apparent that multiple transitions are increasingly common, and that one transition increases the likelihood of further changes in partnerships and households. The impact of multiple family transitions on children is well documented, and includes elevated levels of behaviour problems (Osborne and McLanahan, 2007), lower academic achievement (Hill *et al.*, 2001) and reduced psychological wellbeing Fomby and Cherlin, 2007), and the effect on the adults involved is, also, undoubtedly disruptive.

The Implications of Changes in Marriage and Divorce for Families in the Western World

The most significant aspect of change in marriage and divorce is the *rate* at which change is occurring: and demographic change is accompanied by changes in attitudes and behaviour. Marriage has changed, from being a universal norm in the Western world to becoming a super-relationship to be aspired to rather than taken for granted. Taking the place of conventional marriage is an array of options, ranging from 'living apart together', cohabitation and civil union to marriage and covenant marriage. The situation in France, where couples flock to enter civil unions, suggests that, although for many marriage is not the favoured option, most want some formal recognition of their relationship.

Given the correlation between behaviour and attitudes, we might expect that family and relationship diversity will increase rather than return to the levels evident in the mid-twentieth century. Dissolution of a partnership, however, remains both distressing and potentially damaging to family members; the need to promote stability in families is evident. In the USA, measures tend to focus on encouraging marriage, in the belief that marriage is best for children. Stability, however, is not ensured by marriage—children raised by married parents in the USA are more likely to experience separation than those raised by cohabiting parents in Sweden (Cherlin, 2009). The challenge for policy and practice, therefore, is to understand change and to promote wellbeing in the diverse relationships that exist side by side. More encompassing views of intimate relationships are needed.

The role of commitment

Given the existing diversity of relationships, levels of commitment may be more crucial to relationship wellbeing and durability than are legal considerations. The tripartite model of commitment developed by Johnson *et al.* (1999) distinguishes three components of commitment that offer a nuanced approach to its relevance to relationship stability, as shown in the box below.

> ### Three levels of commitment
>
> 1. Personal commitment—focuses on the satisfaction felt with the partner, and is characterised by *wanting* to stay in a relationship.
> 2. Moral/relational commitment—focuses on the partnership (in contrast to the individual). It carries the moral aspect of feeling one 'ought' to stay in a relationship and implies a will to address problems that might arise.
> 3. Structural, or constraint, commitment—focuses on factors that act as barriers to leaving the relationship, including emotional, social and financial costs. It implies compulsion—people feel they *have* to stay in their relationship.

In parallel with the shift in the character of partnerships, it may be that the focus of commitment is shifting from structural to personal and relational commitment as the constraints of formal marriage diminish. The constraint commitment characteristic of institutional marriages is undoubtedly diminishing as external structures lose their impact. It is evident, too, that personal commitment, focusing on individual satisfaction, is not conducive to the stability of relationships.

There is, then, a case for the promotion of relational commitment. This implies a rebalancing of the focus on the relationship in contrast to the focus on the individual. There is a wealth of information offered about relationships, but a wider and wiser approach is perhaps needed: for example, one that expands the provision of information in high schools as young people form partnerships, and aims to strengthen commitment in partnerships whether or not they are formalised. One way of doing this might be to introduce a form of civil union that is available to heterosexual couples as well as same-sex couples. Civil union represents a step beyond cohabitation by conferring some legal rights (in the case of France, the ability to file joint tax returns, for example). The French example suggests that the availability of a specifically secular option for heterosexual couples that grants legal rights similar to those of marriage might provide a recognised form of partnership that avoids the perceived disadvantages of marriage while encompassing a public commitment to the relationship.

We need more than this, however. Relational commitment applies not just to an intimate relationship between adults, but to other family relationships as well. Parents make commitments to children, siblings to each other, and grandparents to grandchildren. The pessimistic view is that these qualities in families are disappearing, although there is considerable evidence that they are not. A change of policy focus, then, away from individualism and a deficit model of relationships to identifying and valuing connectedness and (secular) commitment to family members, is needed. Starting from the basis of a connectedness thesis rather than an individualist perspective would help researchers and policymakers to reframe their approaches. For policymakers, this implies focusing not on individuals as units, but on policies that reduce stress on families by, for example, encouraging flexible work patterns, parental leave, and adequate income levels.

Practitioners, in turn, might work to encourage overt commitment by couples, as a prelude to their becoming parents. Cherlin (2009) has emphasised the wisdom of moving slowly towards parenthood; taking time to think about the future of a relationship and the children in it is wise advice.

Carol Smart has noted that values associated with being part of a close, supportive kin network were particularly important after the Second World War, because of the trauma and stress associated with enforced separations and war generally. It may be that we are returning to a situation where current external threats can foster similar values of family cohesion and commitment. These values are alive and well in families today, although they manifest themselves in different ways in the mid-twentieth century because of the social changes that have taken place. And although individual wellbeing is undoubtedly a social good, families throughout the Western world are finding ways of nurturing wellbeing at many levels in the new family forms we see now. What they need is recognition and support. Policymakers must no longer assume that there is just one model of well-functioning families. Instead, flexibility in policies and approaches that matches the adaptability we see in families is a more appropriate response.

References

Amato, P. R. (2009) Institutional, companionate, and individualistic marriage: a social psychological perspective on marital change, in E. K. D. Peters (ed.), *Marriage and Family: Perspectives and complexities* (New York: Columbia University Press), 75–92.

Amato, P. R. (2010) Research on divorce: continuing trends and new developments, *Journal of Marriage and Family*, 72 (June): 650–666.

Amato, P. R., Booth, A., Johnson, D. R. and Rogers, S. J. (2007) *Alone Together: How marriage in America is changing* (Cambridge, MA: Harvard University Press).

Amato, P. R. and Irving, S. (2006) Historical trends in divorce in the United States, in M. A. Fine and J. H. Harvey (eds), *Handbook of Divorce and Relationship Dissolution* (Mahwah, NJ: Lawrence Erlbaum), 41–58.

Beck-Gernsheim, E. (2002) *Reinventing the Family: In search of new lifestyles* (Cambridge: Polity Press).

Bengston, V. L., Biblaraz, T. J. and Roberts, R. E. L. (2002) *How Families Still Matter: A longitudinal study of youth in two generations* (Cambridge: Cambridge University Press).

Bramlett, M. D. and Mosher, W. D. (2001) *First Marriage Dissolution, Divorce, and Remarriage* (Washington, DC: National Center for Health Statistics).

Cherlin, A. (2004) The deinstitutionalisation of American marriage, *Journal of Marriage and Family*, 66(4): 848–861.

Cherlin, A. (2009) *The Marriage-go-round: The state of marriage and the family in America today* (New York: Knopf).

Cooke, L. P. (2006). 'Doing' gender in context: household bargaining and the risk of divorce in Germany and the United States, *American Journal of Sociology*, 112(2): 442–472.

Fomby, P. and Cherlin, A. J. (2007) Family instability and child wellbeing, *American Sociological Review*, 72(2): 181–204.

Giddens, A. (1992) *The Transformation of Intimacy: Sexuality, love and eroticism in modern societies* (Cambridge: Polity Press/Blackwell).

Gillis, J. R. (2004) Marriages of the mind, *Journal of Marriage and Family*, 66(4): 988–991.

Glenn, N. D. (1999) Quantitative research in marital quality in the 1980s: a critical review, *Journal of Marriage and Family*, 55: 818–831.

Harrison, E. and Fitzgerald, R. (2010) A chorus of disapproval? European attitudes to non-traditional family patterns, in A. Park, J. Curtice, K. Thomson, M. Phillips, E. Clery and S. Butt (eds), *British Social Attitudes 2009–2010* (London: Sage), 135–158.

Hewitt, B. and DeVaus, D. (2009) Change in the association between premarital cohabitation and separation, Australia 1945–2000, *Journal of Marriage and Family*, 71(2): 353–361.

Hill, M. S., Yeung, W. J. and Duncan, G. J. (2001) Child family structure and young adult behaviors, *Journal of Population Economics*, 14: 271–299.

Hohmann-Marriott, B. E. (2006) Shared beliefs and the union stability of married and cohabiting couples, *Journal of Marriage and Family*, 68(4): 1015–1028.

Jalovaara, M. (2001) Socio-economic status and divorce in first marriages in Finland 1991–93, *Population Studies*, 55(2): 119–133.

Johnson, M., Caughlin, J. P. and Huston, T. L. (1999) The tripartite nature of marital commitment: personal, moral, and structural reasons to stay married, *Journal of Marriage and Family*, 61 (Feb.): 160–177.

Kamp Dush, C. M., Cohan, C. L. and Amato, P. (2003) The relationship between cohabitation and marital quality and stability, *Journal of Marriage and Family*, 65: 539–549.

Kiernan, K. (2004) Redrawing the boundaries of marriage, *Journal of Marriage and Family*, 66(4): 980–988.

Lehrer, E. L. (2004) Religion as a determinant of economic and demographic behavior in the United States, *Population and Development Review*, 30(4): 707–726.

Lewis, J. (2001) *The End of Marriage? Individualism and intimate relations* (Cheltenham: Edward Elgar).

Lyngstad, T. H. and Engelhardt, H. (2009) The influence of offspring's sex and age at parents' divorce on the intergenerational transmission of divorce. Norwegian first marriages *1980–2003, Population Studies*, 63(2): 173–185.

Lyngstad, T. H. and Jalovaara, M. (2010) A review of the antecedents of union dissolution, *Demographic Research*, 23 (July–Dec.): 257–291.

Manning, W. D., Smock, P. J. and Bergstrom-Lynch, C. (2009) Cohabitation and parenthood. Lessons from focus groups and in-depth interviews, in H. E. Peters and C. M. Kamp Dush (eds), *Marriage and Family: Perspectives and complexities* (New York: Columbia University Press), 115–142.

Musick, K. and Bumpass, L. (2012) Reexamining the case for marriage: union formation and changes in well-being, *Journal of Marriage and Family*, 74 (Feb.): 1–18.

Office for National Statistics (2011) *Divorces in England and Wales 2009* (Newport: ONS).

Osborne, C. and McLanahan, S. (2007) Partnership instability and child wellbeing, *Journal of Marriage and Family*, 69: 1065–1083.

Peters, H. E. and Kamp Dush, C. M. (eds) (2009) *Marriage and Family: Perspectives and complexities* (New York: Columbia University Press).

Poortman, A. R. and Kalmijn, M. (2002) Women's labor market position and divorce in the Netherlands: evaluating economic interpretations of the work effect, *European Journal of Population*, 18(2): 175–202.

Pryor, J. and Roberts, J. (2005) What is commitment? How married and cohabiting parents talk about their relationships, *Family Matters*, 71 (Winter): 24–31.

Reinhold, S. (2010) Reassessing the link between premarital cohabitation and marital instability, *Demography*, 47(3): 719–734.

Rogers, S. (2004) Dollars, dependency, and divorce: four perspectives on the role of wives' income, *Journal of Marriage and Family*, 66(1): 59–74.

Salvini, S. and Vignoli, D. (2011) Things change: women's and men's marital disruption dynamics in Italy during a time of social transformations, 1970–2003, *Demographic Research*, 24 (Jan.–June): 145–174.

Schoen, R., Astone, N. M., Rothert, K., Standish, N. J. and Kim, Y. J. (2002) Women's employment, marital happiness, and divorce, *Social Forces*, 81: 643–662.

Schoen, R., Rogers, S. and Amato, P. (2006) Wives' employment and spouses' marital happiness: assessing the direction of influence using longitudinal couple data, *Journal of Family Issues*, 27(4): 506–528.

Smart, C. (2007) *Personal Life: New directions in sociological thinking* (Cambridge: Polity Press).

Soons, J. P. M. and Kalmijn, M. (2009) Is marriage more than cohabitation? Well-being differences in 30 European countries, *Journal of Marriage and Family*, 71(5): 1141–1157.

Svarer, M. (2004) Is your love in vain? Another look at premarital cohabitation and divorce, *Journal of Human Resources*, 39: 523–535.

Svarer, M. and Verner, M. (2006) Do children stabilise Danish marriages?, *Journal of Population Economics*, 21(2): 395–417.

Taylor, P. E. (2010) *The Decline of Marriage and Rise of New Families* (Washington, DC: Pew Research Center Social and Demographic Trends Project).

Teachman, J. (2002) Stability across cohorts in divorce risk factors, *Demography*, 65, 507–524.

Teachman, J. (2010) Wives' economic resources and risk of divorce, *Journal of Family Issues*, 31: 1305–1323.

Thornton, A. (2009) Historical and cross-cultural perspectives on marriage, in H. E. Peters and C. M. Kamp Dush (eds), *Marriage and Family: Perspectives and complexities* (New York: Columbia University Press), 3–32.

Tzeng, M. S. (1992) The effects of socio-economic heterogamy and changes in marital dissolution for first marriages, *Journal of Marriage and Family*, 54(3): 609–619.

Voas, D. and Ling, R. (2010) Religion in Britain and the United States, in A. Park, J. Curice, K. Thomson, M. Phillips, E. Clery and S. Butt (eds), *British Social Attitudes 2009–2010* (London: Sage), 65–86.

Wolfinger, N. H. (2003) Family structure homogamy: the effects of parental divorce on partner selection and marital stability, *Social Science Research*, 32: 80–97.

5

Divorce in the Arab Gulf Countries
A Major Challenge to Family and Society

LAYACHI ANSER

Introduction

In Arab Gulf societies, the right to divorce has always been one that Islam has granted to women, but the actual practice has been widely distorted, since decisions as to whether to divorce have generally been taken by men. Considering how significant conjugal life is for family stability, Muslim societies, like others, have always upheld the sanctity of marriage and family. Therefore, reconciliation between disputing couples has always been encouraged and given priority. Conversely, divorce is always regarded as a last resort. The Prophet Mohammed has been quoted as saying: 'The most despised Halal [permissible act], for God, is divorce.'

Estimating divorce rates in the Gulf Cooperation Council (GCC) countries (which include Bahrain, Kuwait, Oman, Qatar, Saudi Arabia and the UAE) is no easy task given that not all separations are officially declared. For various reasons, many people choose not to declare their divorce. Other difficulties include the lack of reliable data, the poor performance of specialised institutions, and variation in the methods used to calculate divorce rates.

Different studies of divorce use different methods to calculate the divorce rate, making it very difficult to compare rates between countries and time periods. Nonetheless, available data reveal a gradual increase in divorce rates, reaching worrying proportions. The idea that divorce seriously dismantles the family and threatens communal life is widely supported around the world. Nevertheless, as Philippe Bourgeois (1996) has explained, public sentiment that families should stay together at all costs may also serve to keep abusive fathers/husbands in place. Bourgeois argued

Contemporary Issues in Family Studies: Global Perspectives on Partnerships, Parenting and Support in a Changing World, First Edition. Edited by Angela Abela and Janet Walker.
© 2014 John Wiley & Sons, Ltd. Published 2014 by John Wiley & Sons, Ltd.

> ## Methods of calculating divorce rates
>
> 1. Calculate the percentage of divorce cases relative to the number of people married in a given year.
> 2. Calculate the gross divorce rate by determining the number of divorce cases relative to every 1000 married people.
> 3. Calculate the number of divorced women relative to every 1000 married women aged 15 and over.

that within his subject population (poor/urban/black), divorce and separation help preserve some semblance of normality for families who have been experiencing or witnessing abuse in the confines of their own homes.

This chapter is presented in six sections. The first section provides background information about divorce in the GCC countries. This is followed by an outline of some of the structural changes that are transforming the family in these countries. The third section provides a discussion of the effects of globalisation on marriage and the family, followed by a discussion of the competing views regarding current changes in family life. The fifth section presents the available data on marriage and divorce between 1996 and 2005, and the final section looks at the causes of divorce in the GCC countries and reviews the major effects. At the end of the chapter, a number of policy recommendations are made.

The Socio-economic Context in the GCC Countries

Over the last 40 years, especially between the 1970s and the 1990s, the GCC countries have witnessed rapid economic development and social transformation, while the Gulf region has attained the status of being the richest in the world in terms of per capita income. This enormous wealth has been invested in major projects, building basic infrastructure and developing modern services. Although family and tribe are still influential components of society and play an important role in the lives of individuals and communities, such as ensuring their members access to resources, careers and positions in government institutions, alternative ways of mobility, including education and employment, have become progressively available to large numbers of people. Families and society generally have been facing the challenges of modernity and the growing pressures of globalisation for the last few years. New phenomena have been observed, including a change in the status and roles of women, the decline of traditional authority, delays in marriage, increases in spinsterhood and high divorce rates (Ahmed, 2008).

All the GCC countries—except for Saudi Arabia, Oman and Bahrain—face an important demographic imbalance since nationals represent only a minority of the population. At present, however, children aged under 15 constitute over 44 per cent of the national population in these countries. In the circumstances, high fertility is regarded as a priority for all governments. This concern can be seen in the institutional support for marriage, such as represented by the Fund for Marriage in the UAE and

Table 5.1 GCC population trends (thousands), 1950–2050

Country	1950	2007	2050[1]	Total fertility rate
Bahrain	116	753	1173	2.6
Kuwait	152	2851	5240	2.4
Oman	456	2595	4639	3.4
Qatar	25	841	1333	2.8
Saudi Arabia	3201	24735	45030	4.5
UAE	70	4380	8521	2.2

[1]Projected.

Source. Compiled from Roudi-Fahimi and Mederios Kent (2007), p. 5 (Table 1), p. 8 (Table 3).

Table 5.2 GCC population by sex, 2005

Country	Population (1000s)	Males (%)	Females (%)
Bahrain	727	57.63	42.37
Kuwait	2688	62.69	37.31
Oman	2567	52.75	47.25
Qatar	813	72.57	27.43
Saudi Arabia	24574	54.35	45.65
UAE	4496	76.69	23.31

Source. Compiled from Shamsi (2007), p. 141.

the regular campaigns undertaken by Charity organisations in Qatar to finance group marriages among young nationals. However, this endeavour to increase fertility rates faces many obstacles as couples tend to delay their marriage and, when married, have fewer children. High divorce rates among the younger generation of couples in the first years of marriage are also a major problem. On the basis of this trend, the traditional family structure and its values may continue to decline.

Table 5.1 shows the general trend of population growth in GCC countries. It is important to note, first, that the data represent only nationals and, second, that the fertility rates are noticeably high, while there are indications that such rates may drop below existing figures. Consequently, population estimates could change and the population imbalance characterising some GCC countries may become greater. Such prospects will have serious effects on family and marriage as the age structures of local populations change and become dominated by older people, with lower fertility rates.

Table 5.2 reveals yet another problem in the population structure of GCC societies. They suffer not only an acute imbalance between nationals and migrants (Figure 5.2), but also an imbalance in terms of sex ratios. The majority of the population in most GCC countries comprises single male non-nationals. These are guest workers living in camps segregated from the local population. Except for a relatively small expatriate Arab community, these guest workers are not potential marriage partners.

Figure 5.1 shows the median age of populations in the GCC countries. It can be seen that in Oman and Saudi Arabia the median age is under 23 years, whereas in Qatar, Bahrain, Kuwait and the UAE, it is noticeably higher. Both Oman and Saudi Arabia also have the lowest percentage of migrants. The relatively low age of the population and the low percentage of migrants could have positive effects on the

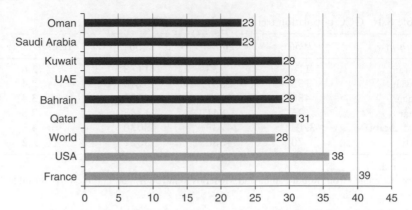

Figure 5.1   Median age of populations in the GCC countries, France, the USA and the world
Source. Compiled from Roudi-Fahimi and Mederios Kent (2007), p. 15 (Figure 7).

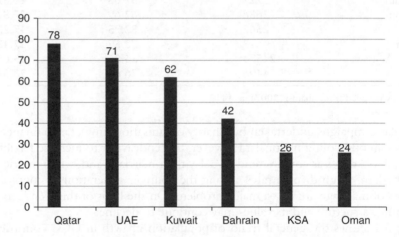

Figure 5.2   Percentage of non-nationals in the GCC countries in 2005
Source. Shamsi (2007), p. 167.

family given the relatively lower median age at marriage. In the case of Qatar, Bahrain, Kuwait and the UAE the situation is more problematic, for two reasons. First, non-nationals are largely single males who contribute little to the marriage market. Second, the local population with a higher median age tends to have low fertility rates because of delayed marriage, spinsterhood and high rates of divorce.

Figure 5.2 points to the population imbalance in the GCC, which brings about a unique situation whereby the large majority of a region's population is made up of single guest workers. This fact has been an enduring characteristic of the region for decades. Although guest workers have helped these countries to realise numerous achievements, their presence is also a source of serious threat in terms of economic dependence, financial haemorrhage, demographic imbalance, social and cultural influences and political volatility. Some have argued that migrant workers may also have negative consequences for the morality and cohesion of society (Ahmed, 1993).

Changes in Family Structure and Values

Studies of the family in the Gulf region have generally tended to stress the transitional nature of family life as it gradually moves from an extended family type to a conjugal nuclear one. Nevertheless, the family in the GCC countries is still very important and kinship ties are very strong (El-Haddad, 2003). Indeed, family size has changed very little over the last two decades. The average family in Qatar consists of eight persons, and in the UAE of seven persons. The move towards a smaller nuclear family is undoubtedly slow, and the extended family and the tribe retain important powers over behaviour, marital alliances, business life and politics. A recent study in Qatar confirms the central position of the family in GCC societies. Data show that the number of families has doubled in two decades, from 48783 in 1986 to 102184 in 2004. This shows that the marriage market is very active as the population increased from 369079 to 744029 over that period. The same study confirms a steady increase in the percentage of conjugal nuclear families, from 74 per cent in 1976 to 82.5 per cent in 2004. Conversely, extended families gradually reduced from 26 to 18 per cent. The average size of the nuclear family in Qatar has remained stable at 5.7 persons, while the overall average family size increased from 8.5 in 1997 to 9.5 in 2008. This indicates that while the prevalence of the extended family is diminishing with the advent of the nuclear family, commitment to having relatively large families is still strong (Permanent Committee for Population, 2009).

The Effect of Globalisation on Families in the GCC Countries

It would be unrealistic to suggest that changes in the structure and function of the family have been brought on solely by globalisation. In fact, changes in GCC societies, including in family and marriage, are a product of the complex interaction between external and internal dynamics. Globalisation may have promoted some processes, modified others or done away with others, including the foundations of the patriarchal family. There are strong observable signs of change in the position and role of spouses and in their relationships, particularly between them and their children. These changes include shifts in the sharing of authority, task negotiation, participation in decision making, and the sharing of responsibility in child raising (Anser, 2008).

As was suggested earlier, these changes have resulted from the interplay between internal and external factors. Women's educational and professional achievements, new legislation, mass media, travel and tourism, migration, trade and commerce have all been intensified, modified or reoriented through a complex interaction with globalisation. The task of socialisation, which is so important for the development of personality and communal life, including family and marriage, has changed. It is no longer the responsibility of parents and close relatives: other social agents and actors have a greater share. They include the mass media (especially television), the Internet, films and videos. Schools and books represent an important category, and it is interesting to note that many foreign schools, colleges and universities, particularly US-owned institutions, have increased exponentially in the GCC countries. Clubs and societies and foreign domestic servants represent yet another significant category.

Domestic labour, both male and female, has become a feature of all GCC societies. There is a mass of literature on the influences of this phenomenon on family, marriage and the socialisation of children (see Al-Swidi *et al.*, 1994; Ismail, 1991).

Globalisation, and its various influences, is making deep headway into the social fabric of the GCC societies, including in the areas of marriage and divorce. Paradoxically, it has gained the explicit blessing of the Fouqaha (religious intellectuals), who provide *fatwas* (religious legal opinions) about marriage and divorce through television, Internet and cell phones (Torr, 2009). Besides, a growing number of marriages take place subsequent to Internet and mobile phone communication. Shopping malls serve as ideal dating and meeting areas. New technologies, readily accessible to people regardless of sex, age, language, religious belief, class or residence, contribute to the breaking of barriers and shift the boundaries between private and public domains. It has become relatively easy to communicate, to meet and converse not only in virtual communities (via cell phones, the Internet and social media), but in person also (Anser, 2010). Furthermore, sex tourism contributes to marriage breakdown as disappointed wives angrily react to husbands taking holidays with other men in search of new and exciting sexual experiences in distant countries, including South East Asia. Travelling and studying abroad also results in mixed marriages, which are more prone to breakdown because of the divergent cultural backgrounds (Baqer, 2004).

Competing Views on Current Changes in Family Life

The literature on family and marriage, in the Middle East generally and the GCC countries in particular, tends to fall into two competing perspectives. The first supports the current changes in family structure and functions in which patriarchal structures are weakened in favour of more flexible and negotiated arrangements, such as diminished parental authority, males sharing in household duties, wives entering the labour force and children gaining more freedom. Zayed (1998) explained how the expansion of education and the ever-increasing numbers of people in employment, and women's accession to the public sphere in particular, have helped the spread of liberal values between the sexes, including the ability to choose a partner.

The second perspective advocates a more cautious view of the effects of modernisation. It acknowledges substantial advances made at different levels without denying the various complex problems arising from that process. Hence, modernisation is not regarded as a linear process enabling smooth transition, but as a dialectic including significant advances, drawbacks and resistance. Consequently, individualism and liberalism among women in the GCC societies are considered cautiously.

Despite much discussion of these opposing viewpoints, most women are still unable to play an active part in choosing their husbands, since there are few opportunities for this to happen. Marriage is still highly influenced by kinship and tribal frameworks. Although women have gained access to education and employment, most have yet to gain the right to self-determination (El-Haddad, 2003). Advocates rightly argue that education and employment do not operate in a vacuum, but within a framework of values, norms and traditions that imposes specific perceptions and actions. The education system, as Bourdieu (1998) has shown, does not necessarily foster values of autonomy and freedom, but reproduces the dominant values of inequality and subordination.

Marriage and Divorce: A Statistical Overview

Despite the prevalence of traditional values important changes in the concept of marriage are apparent, including a gradual move away from arranged marriages, relative delay in the age of marriage, and emergence of marriages across ethnic and class boundaries. A new phenomenon is also on the rise in that GCC societies are facing a real 'spinsterhood crisis' (Sultan, 2002), especially among well-educated middle-class people, as shown in the box below.

The spinsterhood crisis

In Bahrain, Kuwait, Qatar and the UAE:

* the divorce rate ranged between 34% and 46%
* 15%–20% of women failed to marry, mostly for lack of opportunity

In Saudi Arabia:

* the divorce rate stood at 20%
* 1.5 million women failed to marry, mostly for lack of opportunity

It would seem that well-educated women with high aspirations are disillusioned and frustrated by the dominant patriarchal order. Consequently, they decide to concentrate on their career and pursue their dreams of freedom and achievement. This phenomenon is gaining ground everywhere, becoming a major characteristic of all Arab countries today.

In Arab countries, brides also insist on including specific conditions in the marriage contract, such as the right to continue education, the right to work, and the right to have their own separate residence. In other cases, the right of divorce under the law of Khula', whereby divorce is granted in return for a financial payment, has been invoked to prevent situations of polygamy. Breaking engagements and splitting up before the wedding have become commonplace (Baqader, 1985).

In the meantime, general rates of marriage have increased simultaneously with population growth and economic development. In Qatar, for instance, the general marriage rate in the 1990s was 28 cases per 1000 people aged 15 and over. It gradually increased to reach 35 cases in 2006 (Permanent Committee for Population, 2009). Experts have concluded that economic growth positively affects marriage markets, arguing that government support boosts marriage rates and population growth as strategic objectives for GCC countries. The average age at first marriage also increased for both sexes. In Saudi Arabia, 28.6 per cent of females aged 15–19 were married, as against 75.5 per cent for the 20–24 age group and 90.4 per cent for those aged 25–29. Hence, there is a strong positive correlation between marriage rates and age. The average age at marriage in the GCC countries is 20–24 years for females and 25–29 for males (El-Haddad, 2003). A typical case is provided by Qatar, where the average age at first marriage is relatively stable at 23–24 for females and 26–27 for males.

The expansion in education and employment, especially among females, did not seem to delay their marriage or result in lower fertility rates, as had been feared (Permanent Committee for Population, 2009). This provides yet further proof that high fertility rates and population growth can be achieved via adequate state policies providing support for family and marriage (Permanent Committee for Population, 2009).

A statistical overview of marriage and divorce in the GCC societies for the decade 1996–2005 indicates that in Bahrain there was a steady increase in marriage and divorce.[1] The rate of increase in divorce (12.4%) was greater than that in marriage (8.1%), challenging the assumption that Bahrain is the Gulf country least hit by divorce. Kuwait shows a low increase in marriages and a surge in divorces: it had one of the highest divorce rates over the same period, 35.4 per cent in 1996 and 36.6 per cent in 2005.[2]

Between 1996 and 2005, the marriage rate in Qatar increased by 12.6 per cent. On the other hand, divorce dropped by a rate of 3.5 per cent. However, in 2009 the Permanent Committee for Population reported that Qatar had the highest rate of divorce in the GCC countries, and in the rest of the Arab world. In Saudi Arabia, the largest and richest country in the GCC, marriage increased by a rate of 65.8 per cent during the period 1996–2005. However, the divorce rate was even higher, at 73.0 per cent. The UAE, too, has a reputation for high divorce rates. Current data, however, provide a different picture. Over the same period, the number of marriages in the UAE has effectively doubled, reaching the highest rate of 103.8 per cent, while divorce has increased by only 67.2 per cent. In Kuwait, however, both marriage and divorce rates registered the lowest increase (3.0 and 1.1% respectively), although rates for both were among the highest in the GCC countries during the same period.

Marriage duration and divorce

Available statistics show a negative correlation between marriage duration and propensity to divorce. The divorce rate tends to be higher in the first few years of marriage, then appears to decrease in later years. The first three years of marriage seem to be the most risky period. In the period 1986–2007, divorce in the first three years of marriage made up between 57 and 63 per cent of all divorce cases (Permanent Committee for Population, 2009). Data from Qatar show that the rate of divorce decreases over the duration of the marriage. In 1986, the divorce rate dropped from 15 per cent in the first year to 4 per cent in the fourth year, and in 2007 from 10 to 5 per cent (Permanent Committee for Population, 2009). On the other hand, the number of couples splitting up before the wedding increased from 10 in 1986 to 215 in 2007, representing a surge from 4.4 to 13.9 per cent. In the Islamic tradition, marriages are officially declared in the mosque, where the imam (religious leader) reads the Fatiha, the opening verses of the Qur'ān, and announces the marriage of the couples, after having consulted with their families. Many couples come to divorce between then and the wedding night.

[1]   The 1996 data for Bahrain represent nationals and non-nationals, while those for 2001–2005 represent nationals only.
[2]   'Rate' means percentage of divorces among married couples, and the figures refer to successive periods.

Although divorce during the first year of marriage was volatile in Qatar, with most divorce cases occurring in the first three years, the number dropped significantly, from 29 per cent in 1986 to 14 per cent in 2007. In Kuwait, the divorce rate within five years of marriage reached 70 per cent in 2004, with 30 per cent of divorces occurring in the first year. Official reports in the UAE show that divorce rates before the wedding night and in the first two years of marriage have reached 66 per cent. It confirms that young couples face great problems during the first years of marriage. This is a world trend: for example, data from Japan show that 34 per cent of divorces occur in the first five years (Ahmed, 2008). In Dubai, however, a special committee in the Dubai court succeeded in reducing divorce among new couples from 16 to 6 per cent within one year, by adopting various measures including compulsory family training programmes for new couples. The courses are offered either for partners separately before the wedding, or for the couple after the wedding (Darwish, 2009). These types of programmes were first designed by the Malaysian government in the early 1990s: couples have to undergo training sessions and sit exams to obtain a licence to marry. In the UK, couples wishing to marry in the Roman Catholic Church are also required to participate in marriage preparation courses.

Age group and divorce

Data from GCC countries show that divorce rates were highest among relatively younger couples. In Qatar, for example, the highest rate of divorce was among women in their twenties, with half of them divorcing in 2007. This was followed by women in their thirties. Men in their twenties and thirties were also more prone to divorce. Almost half of those who married in these two groups have divorced, without noticeable variation through the years. As for the relationship with age, evidence shows that more men than women were divorcing relatively late in their forties (Permanent Committee for Population, 2009). In Kuwait, men and women in their twenties have very similar divorce rates; almost half of those married in this age group were divorced. Although women in their mid-twenties had the highest rate of divorce, for men the most susceptible age range for divorce was the late twenties. These differences may be linked to the age gap between partners at their first marriage. The tendency for divorce to occur among couples in their twenties seems to be a global trend, as studies from Europe (Mozny and Katrnak, 2005), Japan (Pearson, 2004) and America (Ahmed, 2008) reveal. This global trend shows that age is inversely related to divorce and this can be explained by factors such as maturity, employment and career plans, which tend to stabilise couples and reduce the propensity for divorce.

Education and divorce

As public resources started to be shared more equitably by all GCC countries, the level of education of men and women in these countries increased. This was especially so for women. Lubna Ahmed reports that divorce rates in Kuwait tended to increase among men and women with a higher level of education, whereas the rate is well under 1 per cent for those who are illiterate or have a primary level of education, and reaches 1 per cent for those with an intermediate level of education. This rate goes up to 2.8 per cent among men and 2.3 per cent among women with a diploma level of education, although it drops again, to 1.7 and 1.5 per cent respectively, for people with a university level of education (Ahmed, 2008). The study by the GSPD also reveals that before 1997 the educational level of female divorcees was lower than that of male divorcees, but this trend has completely reversed during the last few years. In 1997, the percentage for divorced women with higher education was 25.5 and that for men 20.9 (Permanent Committee for Population, 2009).

Younger generations are also better educated, but they also have higher divorce rates. Data in GCC countries show that more women are demanding a divorce. One might argue that it is women's higher educational achievement that is contributing to their higher rates of demand for divorce. Their participation in paid employment in an expanding labour market gives them more independence, and renders them more conscious of their rights, more independent-minded, and less prepared to accept inferior positions within the family. In Qatar, the proportion of women requesting divorce increased from 16 per cent in 1997 to 23 per cent in 2004, then sharply dropped to 5.9 per cent in 2010 (Qatar Statistical Authority, 2011). This sharp decline can be explained by a change in the legislation in the mid-1990s, providing women for the first time with the right to initiate divorce under the law of Khula'. This is highly indicative of the changing context in which the family is evolving and attests to the decisive role played by education, the mass media and employment in the liberalisation of Qatari society.

Polygamy and divorce

Polygamy is a frequent practice in most Islamic societies and in the GCC countries in particular. Islamic law (Shariah) tolerates polygamy, but not without restrictions. Empirical evidence has suggested that polygamy was responsible for weakening families and breaking marriages (Salah, 2009). Monogamous marriages increased from 80 to 85 per cent in the years 1986–2004 and continued to do so in 2007, leading polygamous marriages to drop from over 20 per cent to 15 per cent (Permanent Committee for Population, 2009). In 2007, over 90 per cent of men entering into a marriage had no other partner. The proportion of men with one wife at the time of contracting a new marriage was 3.8 per cent, and the number of marriages involving men who already had two or three wives did not exceed 0.3 per cent (Permanent Committee for Population, 2009). Young women marrying for the first time are seeking contractual promises and other insurances that their marriage will remain monogamous.

Children and divorce

Although systematic data confirming a relationship between having children and rates of divorce are scarce, the evidence from Qatar and Kuwait offers contradicting indications. A study by the Justice Ministry of Kuwait shows that 52 per cent of divorced women had no children. It also reveals a tendency for divorce rates to decline as the number of children increases. Probably, many women with children chose to remain in troubled marriages for the sake of their children (Ahmed, 2008). A study of divorced couples in Qatar in 1995, however, found that 66 per cent of them had children, 44 per cent of whom had three children or more. This indicates that, in many cases, having children in the marriage does not prevent divorce (Salah, 2009).

Major Causes of Divorce in the GCC Countries

Many studies have dealt with divorce and its causes in the GCC countries. However, opinions differ between scholars as to the real causes of divorce. Some point to traditionally arranged marriages depriving young couples of free choice (Al-Ansari, 2000). Some emphasise factors such as differences in perceptions, incompatibility and failure of communication (Al-Thaqeb, 1999; El-Haddad, 2003; Shah, 2004), while others argue that governmental provision of higher education and wage employment to larger numbers of people have delayed marriage and seriously changed perceptions about family and marriage among the younger generation (Ahmed, 2008).

Other major causes of divorce in GCC societies include high expectations on the part of one or both partners, especially men, regarding factors such as physical beauty, sexual appeal and sexual performance of partners (most likely influenced by ideals perpetuated by the use of models in the media). In a recent survey, 50 per cent of respondents (mostly men) cited failure or lack of sexual satisfaction with partners as the reason for divorce (Permanent Committee for Population, 2009). Also important is incompatibility between couples in education and socio-economic status (Al-Ghanim, 2003). In addition, the absence of individual choice results from many social barriers related to traditions which do not permit full acquaintance between the future spouses (Al-Ansari, 2000). Furthermore, some people marry under family pressure; some are even forced into marriage without knowledge or consent, leading to incompatible partnerships (Al-Munajjed, 2010). Another cause is age difference between partners, in which middle-aged, and often elderly, men take teenage girls as wives in a second or third marriage (Ahmed, 1993). Equally important, particularly among young people, is the failure to understand that a family requires hard work, commitment and maintenance (Ahmed, 1993). Significantly, there is a lack of commitment on the part of husbands, who are frequently absent and fail to share in household duties and child rearing (Lualuaa and Khalifa, 1996).

Other causes may include polygamous marriages resulting in unfair treatment between wives. This is particularly true of young, well-educated women who are pressured into such marriages (Ahmed, 1993). Women's employment and career aspiration are also a source of disagreement between partners, leading to disputes and ultimately divorce. Conflicting consumption patterns, different lifestyles and spending behaviour, in addition to avaricious husbands, provoke angry reactions from wives, leading to endemic disputes. The high divorce rates in GCC countries are also due to profound changes in social structures that have come about as a result of strong economic development, rapid urbanisation, expansion of education, paid employment, consumerism, the leisure industry and the influence of globalisation (Baqer, 2004; El-Haddad, 2003). This in turn has influenced people's perceptions, values and aspirations regarding marriage and family.

The Major Effects of Divorce

It is necessary here to refer to some of the major effects of divorce on women, men and children. Effects on women include states of severe depression because of pressure from the family and society. In addition to assuming responsibility for children, divorced women, especially middle-aged women with children in their custody, have fewer chances to remarry. On the other hand, younger divorcees provoke major worries and fears around family honour. Divorced women generally suffer from social stigma and a bad reputation, even when they are victims (Saeed, 2007).

Men too suffer from various effects related to divorce, including severe psychological problems. In many cases, men carry bitter and conflicting sentiments, often feeling resentful and guilty at the same time. They may feel responsible for the breakdown of their families and loss of their children, especially in cases where custody is given to women. Also, men feel disoriented: they find themselves isolated after having lived in families surrounded by friends and acquaintances. Although a high proportion of men remarry soon after their divorce, they find it hard to fully reintegrate into social life and establish a new circle of friends (Al-Munajjed, 2010).

While perceptions of divorce remain culturally situated around the world, the evidence suggests that the impacts on children are universally acknowledged (Hughes, 2009; Kelly and Emery, 2003). Children may suffer psychologically, socially and economically as a result of their parents' divorce. As Paul Amato demonstrates very clearly in Chapter 16 (this volume), the impacts are many. Socially, children may feel insecure and disoriented. Evidence from studies of the GCC countries revealed that children may fall victim to various violent behaviours and often suffer as a result of the lack of enforcement of child maintenance payments (Saeed, 2007).

Some Policy Recommendations

The evidence suggests that divorce has far-reaching effects in the Gulf countries, and a number of policy recommendations may be suggested for reducing the number of divorces and strengthening marriage. These are listed in the box below and discussed in turn.

Policy recommendations

1. Promote nationwide programmes for spreading awareness about the importance of marriage and family.
2. Establish counselling services to help young couples before and after marriage.
3. Introduce new legislation to prevent men from pronouncing divorce in the absence of their wives.
4. Provide relevant government institutions with powers and resources pertaining to the rights of divorced women and their children.
5. Promote freedom of choice regarding marriage partners.
6. Use the mass media to convey clear messages about the sanctity of marriage and family life.
7. Provide material support for young couples.
8. Provide material support for divorced women and their children.

In a number of Western countries, programmes have been developed to emphasise the importance of strong, stable family relationships. Relationship education in schools can increase awareness about the importance of marriage, and media campaigns can alert people to the need to foster marriage relationships for the wellbeing of individuals and families and the cohesion and stability of communities. Programmes to spread awareness can promote a culture of mutual respect, tolerance and dialogue among young people.

It is increasingly recognised that most couples face challenges in their relationship and that counselling services can provide advice and support to deal with these. Counselling agencies can also provide programmes which prepare couples for marriage, alerting them to the pressures they might face and providing them with the skills which can protect the relationship through the life course.

In the Gulf countries, it would be useful to introduce new legislation that would prevent husbands from being able to pronounce a divorce in the absence of their wives. Instead, divorce should be valid only if it is registered in a court and in the presence of each party to the marriage. The Saudi authorities have already embarked on law reform in this area (Glass, 2000). In addition, legislation should review the status of divorced women and arrangements for the custody of children in order to safeguard their best interests. It is particularly important for the judiciary to have the power and resources to enforce the law relating to the rights of divorced women and their children. In many Western countries, family courts have been established which specialise in addressing the consequences of separation and divorce.

There is an urgent need to increase freedom of choice in respect of a marriage partner. This is especially the case for women who are illiterate or living in rural areas, who are often kept in the dark about their marriage partner until the marriage is consummated. Regulations should be enforced which require each partner's signature on the marriage contract to be formally witnessed.

Given the knowledge about the potentially detrimental impact of family breakdown, it is important to ensure that consistent messages are given via the mass media about the importance of protecting marriage and family life. All too often, the impacts are unknown until it is too late to save the marriage. Marriage funds could be established to provide material support for young couples when they first marry. Such funds already exist in the UAE and Kuwait. It is equally important to provide material assistance to divorced women, particularly those caring for their children. This support can reduce marginalisation and the poverty that is frequently associated with family breakdown. It can also act as a protective factor, reducing the likelihood that women and children may resort to deviant and immoral activity (Al-Thani, 2006; Al-Thaqeb, 1999). Material assistance can also be used to train women to re-enter the labour market. Since 2004, Bahrain has provided material assistance to divorced women.

Some people have suggested that women should be insured against divorce. The idea is the subject of discussion between a number of Islamic countries, including the GCC countries, and a number of European insurance companies (Salah, 2004). The aim is to provide an insurance policy for women as part of their marriage contract package. In this way, if women became divorced their autonomy and independence would be provided for.

Concluding Comments

This chapter has shown that the GCC countries are experiencing divorce rates which are among the highest in the Middle East. The sudden and profound changes which have been sweeping the region for the last few decades have had an enormous impact on family structures and functions. Family life and marriage were the first to come under pressure: ancestral traditions regulating family and marriage were exposed to new norms and values. Education, employment and the effects of globalisation are important factors driving the sweeping changes. The average age of marriage is now significantly delayed. Divorce rates are highest in the first few years of marriage and among people in their late twenties and early thirties. The causes of divorce include incompatibility between partners in terms of education and socio-economic status, the high and unreasonable expectations of young couples, and a lack of commitment to family life and parental responsibilities. The lack or absence of choice for spouses ensures that arranged marriages are a prevailing feature of modern life, denying the right of prospective partners to meet and get to know each other before marriage. This explains the high rates of divorce in the first years of marriage. The GCC countries are undergoing a period of intense change and are open to the contradictory effects and influences of tradition and modernity at the same time. Effective and efficient social policies are needed to address this critical situation.

References

Ahmed, A. (1993) Family problems and socialization in the UAE, in *Family Problems in the UAE* (Sharjah, UAE: Emirates Sociological Association), 103–132. [In Arabic.]

Ahmed, L. (2008) Divorce: a structural problem not just a personal crisis, *Journal of Comparative Family Studies*, March: 1–18.

Al-Ansari, I. A. (2000) Delay in marriage and high divorce in Gulf societies: the reasons and solutions, *The Journal of the Gulf and Arabian Peninsula Studies*, 26(97): 151–180. [In Arabic.]

Al-Ghanim, K. A. (2003) *Divorce in Qatari Society* (Doha: Centre for Studies and Documents in Humanities, Qatar University). [In Arabic.]

Al-Munajjed, M. (2010) *Divorce in the Gulf Cooperation Countries: Risks and implications* (Dubai: Booz Consulting).

Al-Swidi, E. M. *et al.* (1994) *Domestic Labour in the UAE* (Dubai, UAE: Ministry of Labour and Social Affairs). [In Arabic.]

Al-Thani, S. A. (2006) *Family Breakup: Treatment and Solutions.* http://www.islamweb.net/newlibrary/display_umma.php?lang=A&BabId=4&ChapterId=4&BookId=283&CatId=201&startno=0 [Accessed 15.6.2010.] [In Arabic.]

Al-Thaqeb, F. (1999) *Woman and Divorce in Kuwaiti Society: Psychological, social and economic dimensions* (Kuwait: Council for Scientific Publication, Kuwait University).

Anser, L. (2008) The prospects for change in the Arab family: from patriarchy to partnership, *Alem Al-Fikr*, 36(3): 218–325. [In Arabic.]

Anser, L. (2010) *The Changing Status of Qatari Women* (accepted for publication).

Baqader, A. (1985) Marriage trends in Jiddah City in the light of marriage contracts, *Journal of College of Arts and Human Sciences* (King Abdulaziz University, KSA), 5: 196–218. [In Arabic.]

Baqer, A.-N. (2004) Challenges of globalisation and the future of the family in the Arabian Gulf, *Al-Mustaqbal Al-Arabi*, 380: 129–142. [In Arabic.]

Bourdieu, P. (1998) *La Domination Masculine* (Paris: Seuil).

Bourgeois, P. (1996) *In Search of Respect: Selling crack in El Barrio* (New York and Cambridge: Cambridge University Press), 7th edn.

Darwish, A. (2009) *Roundtable Discussion on Marriage, Netherlands' International Radio*, posted 12.5.2009, 13:34. http://www.rnw.nl/hunaamsterdam/society/talaq [Accessed 15.9.2010.]

El-Haddad, Y. (2003) *Major Trends Affecting Families in the Gulf Countries: A background document* (New York: UN Dept of Economic and Social Affairs).

GCC Secretariat General (2006) GCC Information Centre, Statistical Department. http://library.gcc.sg.org/gccstatvol16/genstat/g7.htm [Accessed 17.9.2010 but nla.]

Glass, A. (2008) *Soaring Saudi Divorce Rate Sparks New Law.* http://arabianbusiness.com [Accessed 25.7.2010.]

Hughes, R. (Jr) (2009) *Parenting.* http://parenting247.org/article.cfm?ContentID=646 [Accessed 21.5.2011.]

Ismail, F. M. (1991) *Domestic Labour: Foreign nannies and their effects on the socialisation of Qatari children* (n.p.) [In Arabic.]

Kelly, J. B. and Emery, R. E. (2003) Children's adjustment following divorce: risk and resilience perspectives, *Family Relations*, 52: 352–362.

Lualuaa, A. and Khalifa, A. (1996) *Gulf Family: Areas of change and future orientations* (Abu Dhabi, UAE: Ettihad Enterprise for Publication and Distribution). [In Arabic.]

Mozny, I. and Katrnak, T. (2005) The Czech family, in B. N. Adams and J. Trost (eds), *The Handbook of World Families* (Thousand Oaks, CA: Sage), 235–252.

Pearson, N. O. (2004) *More Japanese Untie the Knot* (New York: Associate Press, CBS News), Jan.

Permanent Committee for Population (2009) *Marriage and Divorce in Qatar* (Doha: General Secretariat for Development Planning, State of Qatar). [In Arabic.]

Qatar Statistical Authority (2011) The General Population Census: Social Statistics.

Roudi-Fahimi, F. and Mederios Kent, M. (2007) Challenges and opportunities—the population of the Middle East and North Africa, *Population Bulletin*, 62(2): 7.

Saeed, M. N. (2007) *Divorce in Islamic Societies: Causes, effects and solutions.* http://barasy.com/index.pht? [Accessed 24.8.2010.]

Salah, M. (2004) *Divorce a Threat over Arab Households* (Beirut: Dar Al-raya). [In Arabic.]

Salah, M. (2009) *Divorce on the Rise in Qatar: A report on the study of GSDP 2009.* http://alraya.com/qa [Accessed 2.9.2010.] [In Arabic.]

Shah, N. M. (2004) Women's socioeconomic characteristics and marital patterns in a rapidly developing Muslim society; Kuwait, *Journal of Comparative Family Studies*, 35(2): 163–183.

Shamsi, M. (2007) Demographic effects of international migration on Gulf Countries, Proceedings of a Regional Symposium on Foreign Workers in GCC, Doha, 17–19 April (Doha: Permanent Committee for Population), 65–172.

Sultan, I. (2002) *Spinsterhood and Divorce: A threat over Arab societies* (Riyadh, KSA: Selman Social Studies Centre). http://www.Arabiyat.com/Magazine/Publish/Printer_285.Shtml [Accessed 2.9.2010.]

Torr, R. (2009) Religious *fetwas* on Internet, *Gulf Daily News*[n.d.]. http://www.gulf-daily-news.com [Accessed 29.7.2010.]

Zayed, A. (1998) Family, city and social services—the sociological perspective, in Council of Ministries of Labor and Social Affairs of the GCC, *Family, City and Social Transformations: Between development and modernization* (Manama: Executive Bureau of the Council of Ministers of Labor and Social Affairs of the GCC).

6

Couple and Family Dynamics and Escalations in Violence

Justine van Lawick

Introduction

Family violence has received major attention since the 1960s, and the debate around this subject has become increasingly complex. Perpetrators can be victims and victims are often perpetrators. In respect of domestic violence, women can be as violent as men. Scientists, politicians and clinicians need to rethink family violence.

This chapter defines family violence, discusses the different views that contribute to the debate about family violence, taking into account the way violence has been understood over the years, describes innovative types of treatment, and suggests a number of policy proposals.

Defining Family Violence

When does certain behaviour in a family become defined as an act of violence? This has been, and continues to be, debated in varying and different contexts, including those of researchers, practitioners, lay people and politicians. Violence can affect all family relations. Domestic violence mostly refers to partner violence, but it can also be directed against a child, a sibling, a parent, the elderly or any other family member. Defining starts with naming. We can talk about physical, sexual or emotional abuse, maltreatment, domestic violence or family violence. All of these terms refer to behaviour that is not respectful or loving, and which goes against the human worth, autonomy, integrity and safety of the other person.

Contemporary Issues in Family Studies: Global Perspectives on Partnerships, Parenting and Support in a Changing World, First Edition. Edited by Angela Abela and Janet Walker.
© 2014 John Wiley & Sons, Ltd. Published 2014 by John Wiley & Sons, Ltd.

The definition of violence represents a social, cultural and time-bound construction. Thus, corporal punishment of women and children was acceptable until the first half of the last century and was not regarded as violence. Currently, many people do not speak of violence when a woman beats her husband. In research and literature many different definitions are found. Sometimes the definition focuses on the effects: family violence involves injuring someone, physically, emotionally or sexually. Other definitions concentrate on power differences: family violence is used by a person in a position of power to create pain and fear in order to control and oppress, and to have his or her way against the will of the other person.

The American Academy of Family Physicians (2002) defines family violence as 'the intentional intimidation or abuse of children, adults or elders by a family member, intimate partner or caretaker to gain power and control over the victim' (p. 1). The problem here is the word 'intentional'. Is all violent behaviour intentional? When a parent is strongly contrite or upset after losing control and spanking a child, can we say that the beating was intentional? A woman who attacks her male partner out of intense frustration with his behaviour can have the intention of reaching him, not of hurting him. Many argue that violent behaviour can occur without intention when conflicts run out of control (Groen and van Lawick, 2009).

The debate continues into the area of severity, frequency and intensity. All behaviour that brings damage to family relations and the individuals involved constitutes violence. Indeed, psychological violence can be more damaging than physical violence. Many people who have been able to stop physical violence being perpetrated against them have said that they can forget the beating, but cannot forget the humiliating words, or that they continue to have nightmares about the threatening eyes. It may only take one big escalation in rage to damage a family relationship severely.

A further question concerns the use of corporal punishment of children. Is this inherently abusive, or is it acceptable when used in a conscious and controlled way to discipline children? As Straus and Runyan (1997) noted, most cases of physical abuse happen when corporal punishment gets out of control. Corporal punishment that gets out of hand puts children at risk of injury, both psychological and physical. That is why, in most European countries, all forms of corporal punishment are forbidden by law. In the USA there has been considerable resistance among professionals, as well as lay people, to a ban on the corporal punishment of children. One of the problems is that even the most abusive parents frequently believe that their spanking of a child is a normal response to behaviour that requires discipline (Benjet and Kazdin, 2003).

It is true that children's behaviour can be intensely frustrating, and it can be very difficult for parents always to calm down in sufficient time to stay in control and not to be physical with children, but understanding the situation of parents does not make uncontrollable behaviour excusable. The positive aspect of a law that bans all corporal punishment is that parents cannot hide their behaviour behind educational motives. The negative aspect is the criminalisation of common behaviour. We have to set a course between Scylla and Charybdis, making it clear that violence against children causes a lot of suffering and problems—both biological and psychological—while, at the same time, attempting to understand and support parents in the enormous task of raising children in these complex times.

Not only have the debates on the definition of violence not been resolved, there also is no consensus on the causes or motivations that lead to violent behaviour. A broad range of possible causes is mentioned in the literature. One theory is that violence stems from patriarchy: men want to control and possess their women and children (Ylö, 1984). A contrary view is that today, as a result of emancipation, women have become so strong in societal and family life that men suffer an existential crisis and feel unsatisfied and meaningless, and that this can be grounds for family violence (Groen, 2009). Others argue that psychopathology is the main cause of violent behaviour in families (Dutton, 2006). Further theories suggest that social circumstances, such as discrimination, lack of resources and bad housing, lead to major frustration and violent behaviour, or that a culture of honour and shame is the basis of violence (Levinson, 1989).

It therefore seems important to focus not only on the relational effect violence has on the victim but also on contextualising violent behaviour in families. Thus, in order to understand family violence we have to take into account the relevant contexts of culture and socialisation, social circumstances, gender differences, power differences, psychopathology, physical illness and other stress factors.

It is therefore clear that we have to differentiate between various types of domestic violence, according to the different contexts and family dynamics. Two main types of violent behaviour, intimate terrorism and situational violence, have to be distinguished and they will have different consequences for legal action and therapeutic treatment.

Two types of family violence

1. *Intimate terrorism*. There is a type of violence where a person wants to dominate and control others. Johnson (2008) refers to this type of violence as intimate terrorism, where one person terrorises the other(s). It is mostly men who are the perpetrators. The need for control is a major preoccupation in this type of behaviour.
2. *Situational violence*. Violence also occurs in situations where conflicts get out of hand and *loss of control* becomes a central characteristic of the dynamics at play. In this, so-called situational violence (Johnson, 2008), there is no significant difference in the frequency and severity of violent behaviour perpetrated by men and women (Dutton, 2006; Straus, 2009).

Prevalence of Violence in the Family

Connected to the debates about definitions and causes of family violence are the controversies surrounding the statistics generated by research around this topic. It is such a complex, multi-dimensional problem that no single piece of research or single statistic can capture the phenomenon. Nobody knows exactly how much family violence takes place. Moreover, family violence is not a new phenomenon. It has probably existed since the beginning of mankind, and it will probably always be part of human life. The idea that we could extinguish family violence with effective law and treatment is illusory. Societies, however, have started to realise that family violence is a social problem with huge consequences for health, social life and the economy. So we have to do what we can to set limits to family violence, to diminish the problem and its related consequences. In 2002, the World Health Organisation recognised family violence as a global health problem.

People are more likely to be hit, kicked, humiliated, threatened, raped, seriously physically abused, hurt or killed by family members in their own home than anywhere else. This seems to be the case all over the world (Barnett *et al.*, 2005; Hamel and Nicholls, 2007). It is hard to accept the image of the family unit as the most violent institution of society; a preferable image is that of the family as the warm, intimate, safe and relaxing nest, the 'haven in a heartless world' (Lasch, 1977).

Prevalence in the USA

In the USA, social service agencies received approximately 3 million reports of child maltreatment—a rate of 12.2 per 1000 children (Barnett *et al.*, 2005). The most common form of abuse was neglect (62%), followed by physical abuse (19%), sexual abuse (10%) and psychological abuse (8%). Parents were the perpetrators in 84 per cent of the cases, with mothers the most likely perpetrators in physical abuse and neglect cases and fathers the most likely perpetrators in sexual abuse cases (Barnett *et al.*, 2005). We have to keep in mind that these figures refer to reported child maltreatment. The actual figures are likely to be much higher as most child maltreatment is never reported. Findings from national surveys suggest that 75 per cent of parents use some method of physical punishment in child rearing and disciplining practices (Krug *et al.*, 2002).

Prevalence in the Netherlands

In the Netherlands, research demonstrates much higher figures. Every year, 3 in 100 children are physically maltreated—107200 children each year. The research differentiates between sexual abuse (25%) and physical punishment (75%). Only maltreatment that leads to visible physical injuries was taken into account (IJzendoorn, 2007).

More than 9 per cent of the Dutch population had been victims of moderate to severe domestic violence in the five years 2002–2007 (Veen and Bogaerts, 2010). Only around 50 per cent of the Dutch population had never experienced any form of domestic violence in the family circle. Approximately 60 per cent of the victims of domestic violence were women. This demonstrates a considerable shift in the gender proportion of victims from the proportion found by a survey conducted in 1997. This shift appears to be continuing: in the past few years the estimated numbers of male victims have risen faster than the estimated numbers of female victims. Analyses of amalgamated victim and perpetrator data show that 60–65 per cent of domestic violence is related to partner or ex-partner violence. Women reported that they had experienced partner violence, both as victim and perpetrator, more frequently than men.

The group of perpetrators involved in intimate terrorism was found to commit significantly more partner violence (of all kinds) than the group of perpetrators of situational violence. In the former group, the percentage of women was lower than in the latter group. Nearly two-thirds of perpetrators in both groups were also victims, and more than two-thirds of victims were also perpetrators. A significant statistical relationship was observed between the circumstances of being a victim and of being a perpetrator of physical and other forms of violence. This is in line with research that shows that women can be as violent as men (Archer, 2000; Capaldi *et al.*, 2007; Capaldi and Owen, 2001; Fiebert, 2004; Moffitt *et al.*, 2001; Straus, 2005, 2007).

The evidence showing gender symmetry in situational violence has been overwhelming (Archer, 2000; Capaldi *et al.*, 2007; Capaldi and Owen, 2001; Fiebert, 2004; Moffitt *et al.*, 2001; Straus, 2005, 2007). On the basis of the figures it seems reasonable to suppose that with intimate terrorism and sexual assault, around 80 per cent of perpetrators are men. In cases of situational violence there seems to be gender symmetry between perpetrators and victims, with partners often taking both positions.

The History of Family Violence

Children

Attention to the welfare of children in general is a rather young phenomenon. It was not until the mid-to-late 1800s that child neglect and maltreatment was uncovered. A child-saving movement in the Western world began when a group of professionals promoted the protection of children. They argued that children need to be loved and nurtured and that the state should take over this task when parents fail to do so. At the end of the nineteenth century, scholars studied and described the development of children and the connected developmental tasks of parents and other caretakers. Child protection became an important issue all over the Western world.

Child maltreatment increasingly became a criminal act, and children could be removed from their homes when parents did not care well enough or were maltreating their children. A counter-movement, however, raised questions about the wisdom of removing children from the parental home. Are children always better off when removed from their homes? Isn't it a better strategy to support the parents so that they are better able to care for their children? 'You can take a child out of the family, but you cannot take the family out of the child' became a well-known saying and the debate still goes on (Turnell and Essex, 2008).

When a child is found to be seriously maltreated or is killed while professional services are involved child advocates are understandably furious, and many placements of children into care may follow in order to avoid misjudgements and a possible repeat case. But the next incident might be the maltreatment of a child in a foster family, or sexual abuse in a children's home. Then, the advocates of keeping families together are upset and, in many cases, supporting the involved families is the strategy of preference (Turnell and Essex, 2008). The positive consequence of the continuing debate is that it keeps us alert in assessing when it is wise to keep the family together and when it would be better to save the child from a very destructive family. This process will never end, because we will never be able to find the final answer. Life is not totally controllable and neither are people.

Partner violence

In the case of intimate partner violence, attention to the oppression and maltreatment of women was part of the women's rights movement that started in the USA and Europe around the middle of the nineteenth century. In the first liberation wave, the focus was on the right to vote. The second wave of the feminist movement, from the

1960s onwards, drew attention to the subordination and victimisation of women in families. Early marriage law actually gave men the right to hit their women. Because husbands were expected to control their wives the law supported the violence that was involved in controlling behaviour.

Feminists made it clear that domestic violence connected to this kind of patriarchy is not an exception to the rule, but a serious social, medical and psychological problem. The feminists concentrated on the consequences of patriarchy and the victimisation of women. Wife abuse began to receive a great deal of public and political attention and feminism influenced politics around family matters. Safe houses, where women and their children could find shelter and help to survive, were started all over the world. The first shelter for battered women was opened in England in 1971. Many shelters followed in Europe and the USA. Most shelters started as secret hiding places for women and their children; places where their furious and violent men could not find them, where they were safe and protected. This concept of a safe, secret haven, however, raised many problems for the women and children. They had to leave their homes, neighbourhoods, schools, workplaces and social networks. They had to find refuge in a totally unknown and new social environment. The workers in the shelters tried to support women to divorce their violent husbands and find a new, safe life in a new place. To the surprise and shock of the professionals many women chose to go home again, many to the violent husband. It became clear that in violent relationships there can also be love and a strong couple connection (van Lawick, 2009).

Nevertheless, in the Western world, law changed in the area of family violence at a national and international level. Violence against women and against children was no longer considered a private matter and became a criminal act. In the USA the Violence Against Women ACT 1994 (expanded in 1998 and 2002) was designed to provide women with broad protections against violence in their communities and at home.

New perspectives

At the end of the twentieth century, researchers and clinicians added another perspective to family violence by demonstrating that women can also be violent and men can be victims. Domestic violence is not confined to abuse perpetrated by men on women. Male and female adolescent children can maltreat their parents and adult children can be violent with elderly parents. Brothers and sisters can maltreat each other. Among same-sex couples the amount of violence is the same as among heterosexual couples (Colemen, 2007). The picture emerges that family violence is a huge and complex problem for everyone: men and women, adults and children, the elderly and adolescents.

Although there is much evidence supporting gender symmetry in family violence, women advocates deny or fight the evidence. One of the important researchers in this field, Murray Straus (2009), suggests that it is hard to accept gender symmetry because in all other crimes, the majority of perpetrators are men and the fear and injuries of women are more serious, and many women advocates have had to change their belief system about the behaviour of men and women. The realisation that women perpetrate violence just as much as men has been the most difficult of all to achieve, despite the fact that over 200 studies have found that around the same percentage of women and men physically assault partners, and that the risk factors and motivations are mostly the same for women as they are for men (Archer, 2000;

Capaldi *et al.*, 2007; Capaldi and Owen, 2001; Fiebert, 2004; Moffitt *et al.*, 2001; Straus, 2005, 2007). Gender symmetry is not true for sexual assault, however. There is no controversy concerning the fact that almost all heterosexual rapes are perpetrated by men.

It is not only through research that the violence of women becomes clear. It is also evident in clinical practice. It is often rather difficult to decide which partner is the perpetrator and which the victim: often a partner is both. It is for this reason that understanding the family dynamic should be at the centre of treatment. Towards the end of the past century and from the beginning of the present century, interest has grown in couple dynamics (Goldner, 1998; Groen and van Lawick, 2009; van Lawick and Groen, 1998; Vetere and Cooper, 2007).

Policy regarding family violence in Europe has changed. Beginning in Austria and some Scandinavian countries, a new strategy was initiated. In a case of family violence a risk assessment is carried out, mostly by well-trained police. The risk assessment makes it possible to take the perpetrator out of the house for ten days or longer. In this period, support and treatment is organised not only for each partner, but for the couple as a unit, their children, the wider family, and sometimes their social network. The positive advantage of this approach is that the children and one of the caretakers can remain in the house, and the social network around the caretaker and the children is not destroyed. However, another problem has arisen as a result of this new strategy. Most of the time, it is the men who are taken out of the house whereas the women and children remain. Police and professionals have increasingly realised that it is often not easy to decide who is the perpetrator and who is the victim. This led to professionals in Amsterdam changing the terminology from 'perpetrator' and 'victim' to 'leaving partner' and 'staying partner'.

In the Netherlands, there is a new problem. Politicians take the high figures for family violence seriously and want to do something about it. The cities of the Netherlands have set a target for the number of house bans that are expected to occur when domestic violence is discovered or reported. Paradoxically, a competitive element appears to have crept in and cities are considered to be doing a good job according to the number of house bans they implement. Even individual police officers have been given targets. As a consequence, some families are ripped apart when this is not necessary or helpful. There are now also cases where the woman is threatened by other family members after a house ban because she is considered to have shamed her husband and her family. The police need to be extremely careful in their interventions not to inflame violent behaviour. This is only possible if the professionals involved understand the dynamics of family violence.

Understanding the Dynamics

We can link escalations in violence to certain frustrations within human relationships. The grounds for many frustrations are romantic illusions about partner and family life. People who have been neglected and hurt as children may have an expectation that their partner and their children will make up for the suffering by loving them for ever (van Lawick, 2009). In reality, this brings about many frustrations. When people are asked about the kinds of frustration that can provoke violent behaviour the same triggers emerge.

Frustrations that can trigger violent behaviour

Frustrations cluster around:

- Iniquity—injustice; betrayal
- Disrespect—attacks; bullying; humiliation
- Neglect—not getting attention; being misjudged; being ignored (not being seen, heard or understood); being abandoned
- Powerlessness—resistance of the other; opposition; being wrongly accused; bureaucracy; victim behaviour; authoritarian behaviour

All these triggers of violence are intensified by substance abuse, such as alcohol and drugs, and also by stress factors, such as exhaustion, too much work-related pressure, financial problems, bad housing, noise, illness, relational problems and other life issues. Frustrations can lead to escalations. This is represented schematically in Figure 6.1.

Figure 6.1 helps to explain how conflicts within families escalate. It demonstrates visually why calming down and creating distance is necessary in order to stop an escalation. Explanations of the process of escalations lead to the notion of calming down in time. Each escalation starts with a source of frustration, which irritates. When this frustration proceeds or grows, irritation is transformed into anger and later into rage

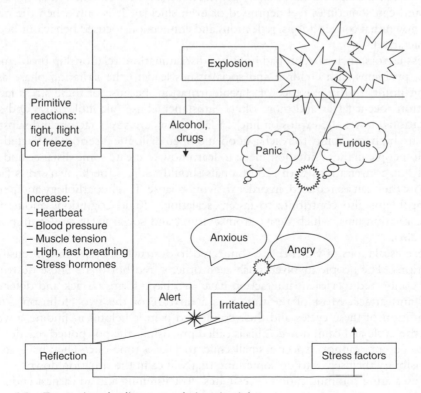

Figure 6.1   Frustrations leading to escalations in violence

until, finally, people cross a line. Several expressions refer to this process: 'going too far', 'going off the rails' or 'stepping out of line'. Every culture and language has similar expressions concerning this condition.

When stress levels keep rising, the body will reach an alarm phase; blood pressure, heartbeat, muscle tension and stress hormone levels increase and respiration is high, fast and shallow. Conscious reflection is hindered and primitive parts of the brain are activated. In the primitive brain three functions dominate: fight, flight or freeze. In this state the other partner becomes an enemy, an enemy one wants to attack or escape from, or one who paralyses by fear. In the fight mode the other person is attacked with words and physical action. Solution-aimed behaviour and reflection is, in this state of mind, not possible. High stress levels make people irrational and cause them to harm the other.

This process often starts because one partner wants to convince the other of being right. He or she does not listen, but tries to persuade the other. Objections are seen as reproach. Everything becomes attack and defence. When no one wins, more and more techniques of persuasion are used: voices are raised, others are involved, threatening behaviour is used. Communication becomes more and more contrasted, 'everything or nothing', 'always or never'. The other person becomes a caricature with no nuances, an enemy. Because neither party listens well, nobody feels heard or acknowledged. Both conclude the other does not *want* to understand. Such conversations lead to increasing frustration and to escalations in violence.

When a person calms down, it is often incomprehensible to them that they could hurt and harm someone else. Family members usually feel ashamed after the explosion, and can sometimes feel depressed or even suicidal. It is only when the person calms down that conversations, reflections and connection-focused behaviour become possible again.

Stress factors, such as debt, bad housing, discrimination, relationship problems, illnesses, problems with children and social issues lead to the irritation phase as the starting point. In the presence of chronic irritation, because of these stress factors, escalations occur faster and more often. Substance abuse (alcohol, drugs and some medications) lower the explosion line. In families where stress factors and substance abuse are high, the ability to reach a good and open dialogue is seriously affected. Not only do people in these situations need to learn how to create some distance and calm down, but conversations with professionals should address the known stress factors and how they can be reduced, in order to avoid relapse. Psychopathology and personality problems also contribute to faster escalations. Rigid cognitions about male–female relationships, which derive from cultural and social ideas, are an important factor also.

These escalations of violence are connected to destructive cycles that intensify the escalations. The people involved push each other's 'red buttons'. These destructive cycles connected to violent interaction have two basic forms: attack and defend, or attack and attack. Most of the time it is a mixture of the two (Johnson, 2004). Recognition of these cycles and their connected pain is helpful in finding a way to break the cycle and calm down. This is called practising 'the postponed reaction'. Of course, parents cannot expect a small child to take a time-out. They have to take responsibility themselves to do something that will calm the situation down.

De-escalating communication necessitates close listening and an earnest endeavour to understand the underlying feelings and intentions of the other person. Such an attitude fosters positive feelings in the other person, who feels that they are being taken seriously, heard and acknowledged. This does not mean that each person has to agree with the other; one person may still think differently. The result could be 'we agree not to agree'. The acceptance of different points of view turns out to be a crucial factor in handling conflicts. It prevents starkly opposed thinking and focuses more on nuances and toning down. It also provides a meeting ground where people may be more willing to compromise. In this way, the other person remains someone it is possible to agree or disagree with, rather than an enemy who wants to dominate or coerce the other in one way or another.

Treatment Issues

Creating safety for all family members is the ultimate objective of all treatment programmes. Treatment began in the twentieth century with a focus on battered women. Shelters and groups worked to emancipate and strengthen battered women so that they were better able to look after their own safety and that of their children.

From 1980 onwards programmes for male batterers started, mostly founded on the idea that men abuse women because they think they are entitled to do so in order to control them. Men have had to be re-educated or resocialised to accept that women are of equal worth and to make appropriate choices to balance power in intimate relationships. For some men these programmes are helpful, but the amount of recidivism appears to be so high that it is not possible to conclude that they are successful in addressing family violence (Babcock *et al.*, 2004). It may be that these programmes are based on a one-dimensional explanation of family violence which is rooted in patriarchy. Couple dynamics, the social and family context and psychopathology are not taken into account. In the Western world, family violence is more connected to the latter than to old patriarchical belief systems.

As has already been argued, it is essential to differentiate between different dynamics in family violence. In the case of those (mostly men) for whom the control of the other family members takes the upper hand, the behaviour can be connected to the patriarchal belief system, as is true for some fundamentalist groups. However, psychopathology, personality problems and antisocial behaviour can also come into play, and this means that female perpetrators can also be involved. Good assessment is therefore essential given that any treatment programme should be tailored to the different groups.

When men (and a few women) are recidivists in criminal acts and violent behaviour antisocial behaviour is often involved. These perpetrators can best be treated by forensic psychiatrists. They have to be trained to control themselves and to treat other human beings as equals. Professionals are still searching for effective treatments for this group. Training programmes, where perpetrators are behaviourally trained to refrain from being violent, can sometimes be effective. The law can also be helpful in reinforcing this training by sentencing perpetrators to imprisonment if violence is repeated. Should perpetrators wish to avoid incarceration they have no option other than to stop being violent.

Other programmes utilise group-based or individual psychotherapy based on attachment theory. Women (and a few men) can be trained to set their limits, be more present in family relations, and take responsibility for their own safety and that of other vulnerable family members. Often substance abuse is a problem and this needs to be addressed too.

The programmes described in this chapter appear to be partially effective, but the results are not convincing. Recidivism is a recurring problem. This is because victims and perpetrators are submitted to the same programme and no clear differentiation is made between the intimate terrorists and those who engage in situational violence. In the case of situational violence, the dynamics that lead to escalations can become clear in couple and family therapy. The escalation spiral can be explained and, together with the family members, a strategy to stop escalations can be discussed. Learning how to calm down oneself and to help the other person calm down before violence escalates is crucial.

Therapists have a role in trying to understand all family members. They ask open questions and let family members tell their stories about the frustrations, goodwill, pain and sorrow. Via the questions of the therapist and close listening to the different voices, family members can listen to each other again. This can be one of the most effective interventions (Yerden, 2008).

These interventions can be performed in individual couple or family therapy, and also in couple and family groups, and can be very effective. Observation by couples of other couples and families fighting can serve to hold a mirror up to their own fights so that they can see themselves. Seeing one's own behaviour as others might see it is an effective therapeutic tool in groupwork (Stith *et al.*, 2004).

Policy Implications

In the light of this new understanding of the dynamics at play when violence erupts in families, the following policy proposals should be considered:

1   Violence in the family is a criminal act, and laws should set limits of acceptable behaviour. A treatment order can be an indispensable part of the sentence. Assessment is needed to decide on the most fitting treatment. In the case of a controlling partner and antisocial behaviour, the approach should involve perpetrator treatment in a forensic setting and supportive attention for the victim and other family members. When partners want to live together again, much attention has to be given to future safety. Children who witness violence between parents or other caretakers may be psychologically damaged (Dalpiaz, 2007), so attention to and support for children is always important.

2   Social/welfare services are often needed to help with financial difficulties, housing and other issues connected with social life. Domestic violence is not simply a criminal matter, however. Well-trained professionals who are not afraid of violence and who are able to assess the dynamics of violence from a systemic perspective can make an indispensable intervention. Together with family members, they can assess what interventions are useful in each individual case. Open dialogue around a possible house ban could be facilitated by such professionals, discussing whether it would be useful, who could best leave the house for a period of time, what help is needed, and how safety could be organised immediately and in the longer term.

To diminish or stop family violence effectively, a connected network of professionals is needed. Network meetings with professionals, and sometimes with the family members, where decisions are taken about possible helpful interventions, are raising the effectiveness of those interventions and often serve to reduce the number of professionals involved. Sometimes more than ten professionals are involved in helping the same family, and this often complicates the problems. Polarising fights between a couple, for example, can provoke a parallel process between professionals, with each taking a particular side. Professionals have, like their clients, to accept that there is no single truth and that they have to work together in order to be effective.

Concluding Comments

Contextualising family violence is necessary to avoid a simplistic perpetrator–victim perspective. The complexity of family violence necessitates high-quality assessment in order to analyse the family and couple dynamics and the context in which violence is occurring. Interventions from the police, social workers and mental health professionals should ensure a joined-up approach to multi-level assessment and intervention.

References

American Academy of Family Physicians (2002) http://www.aafp.org/online/en/home/policy/policies/f/familyandintimatepartner-violenceandabuse.html [Accessed 15.7.2012.]

Archer, J. (2000) Sex differences in aggression between heterosexual partners: a meta-analytic review, *Psychological Bulletin*, 126(5): 651–680.

Babcock, J. C., Green, C. E. and Robie, C. (2004) Does batterers' treatment work? A meta-analytic review of domestic violence treatment, *Clinical Psychology Review*, 23(8): 1023–1053.

Barnett, O., Miller-Perrin, L. C. and Perrin, R. D. (eds) (2005) *Family Violence across the Lifespan: An introduction* (Thousand Oaks, CA: Sage), 2nd edn.

Benjet, C. and Kazdin, A. E. (2003) Spanking children: the controversies, findings, and new directions, *Clinical Psychology Review*, 23: 197–224.

Capaldi, D. M., Kim, H. K. and Shortt, J. W. (2007) Observed initiation and reciprocity of physical aggression in young, at-risk couples, *Journal of Family Violence*, 22(2): 101–111.

Capaldi, D. M. and Owen, L. D. (2001) Physical aggression in a community sample of at-risk young couples: gender comparisons for high frequency, injury, and fear, *Journal of Family Psychology*, 15(3): 425–440.

Colemen, V. E. (2007) Dangerous dances: treatment of domestic violence in same sex couples, in J. Hamel and T. L. Nicholls (eds), *Family Interventions in Domestic Violence. A handbook of gender inclusive theory and treatment* (New York: Springer), 397–417.

Dalpiaz, C. M. (2007) Healing child victims and their parents in the aftermath of family violence, in J. Hamel and T. L. Nicholls (eds), *Family Interventions in Domestic Violence: A handbook of gender inclusive theory and treatment* (New York: Springer), 541–561.

Dutton, D. G. (2006) *Rethinking Domestic Violence* (Vancouver: UBC Press).

Fiebert, M. S. (2004) References examining assaults by women on their spouses or male partners: an annotated bibliography, *Sexuality and Culture*, 8(3–4): 140–177.

Goldner, V. (1998) The treatment of violence and victimisation in intimate relationships, *Family Process*, 37(3): 263–286.

Groen, M. (2009) Apprehensive heroes, in M. Groen and M. J. van Lawick (2009) *Intimate Warfare: Regarding the fragility of family relations* (London: Karnac), 253–273.

Groen, M. and van Lawick M. J. (2009) *Intimate Warfare: Regarding the fragility of family relations* (London: Karnac).

Hamel, J. and Nicholls, T. L. (eds) (2007) *Family Interventions in Domestic Violence: A handbook of gender inclusive theory and treatment* (New York: Springer).

IJzendoorn, M. H. van (ed.) (2007) *Kindermishandeling in Nederland Anno 2005:* De Nationale Prevalentiestudie Mishandeling van Kinderen en Jeugdigen (Den Haag: Ministerie van Justitie).

Johnson, M. P. (2008) *A Typology of Domestic Violence* (Boston, MA: Northeastern University Press).

Johnson, S. (2004) *The Practice of Emotionally Focused Couple Therapy* (New York: Brunner Routledge).

Krug, E. G., Dahlberg, L. L., Mercy, J. A., Zwi, A. and Lozano, R. (eds) (2002) *World Report on Violence and Health* (Geneva: World Health Organisation).

Lasch, C. (1977) *Haven in a Heartless World* (New York: Basic Books).

Levinson, D. (1989) *Family Violence in Cross-cultural Perspective* (Newbury Park, CA: Sage).

Moffitt, T. E., Caspi, A., Rutter, M. and Silva, P. A. (2001) *Sex Differences in Antisocial Behaviour* (Cambridge: Cambridge University Press).

Stith, S. M., Rosen K. H., McCollum, E. E. and Thomsen, C. J. (2004) Treating intimate partner violence within intact couple relationships: outcomes of multi-couple versus individual couple therapy, *Journal of Marital and Family Therapy*, 30: 305–318.

Straus, M. A. (2005) Women's violence toward men is a serious social problem, in D. R. Loseke, R. J. Gelles and M. M. Cavanaugh (eds), *Current Controversies on Family Violence* (Newbury Park, CA: Sage), 2nd edn, 55–77.

Straus, M. A. (2007) Dominance and symmetry in partner violence by male and female university students in 32 nations, *Children and Youth Services Review*, 30: 252–275.

Straus, M. A. (2009) Current controversies and prevalence concerning female offenders of intimate partner violence: why the overwhelming evidence on partner physical violence by women has not been perceived and is often denied, *Journal of Aggression, Maltreatment and Trauma*, 18: 1–19.

Straus, M. A. and Runyan, D. K. (1997) Physical abuse in adolescence, in S. B. Friedman, D. K. Schomberg, M. Fisher and E. M. Alderman (eds), *Comprehensive Adolescent Health Care* (St Louis, MO: Mosby Year-Book), 2nd edn, 723–728.

Turnell, A. and Essex, S. (2008) *Working with 'Denied' Child Abuse: The resolutions approach* (Maidenhead: Open University Press).

Van Lawick, M. J. and Groen, M. (1998) *Intieme Oorlog* (Amsterdam: van Gennep).

Van Lawick, M. J. (20w09) The downward spiral of violence between partners, in M. Groen and M. J. van Lawick, *Intimate Warfare: Regarding the fragility of family relations* (London: Karnac), 25–71.

Veen, H. C. J. van der and Bogaerts, S. (2010) *Huiselijk Geweld in Nederland 2007–2010* (Den Haag: Ministerie van Justitie).

Vetere, A. and Cooper, J. (2007) Couple violence and couple safety: a systemic attachment-oriented approach to working with complexity and uncertainty, in J. Hamel and T. L. Nicholls (eds), *Family Interventions in Domestic Violence* (New York: Springer), 381–397.

Yerden, I. (2008) Families onder druk. Huiselijk geweld in Marokkaanse en Turkse gezinnen (Amsterdam: van Gennep).

Yllö, K. (1984) The status of women, marital equality, and violence against wives, *Journal of Family*, 5: 307–320.

7

Loving Diversity
Living in Intercultural Couple Relationships

Danika N. Hiew, W. Kim Halford
and Shuang Liu

Introduction

Mee Ling [Chinese woman married to a Western man]. [mimicking affectionate tones] I don't like 'Honey, Honey' ... 'Love'. It [physical and verbal affection]'s not important. Affection is when we work together. Let's say we need to prepare food for Chinese New Year—this is where the affection comes in.

Janet [Western woman married to Yang, a Chinese man]. For me, communication is the key. It's vital that both partners are able to express their emotions, and there has to be an understanding response.

Yang. She treats me like a rubbish bin to fill with her negative stuff. It's not right. I keep my negative feelings out of her sight.

The remarks quoted above were among the responses we received when asking adults of European and Chinese ancestry what they thought made for a successful marriage. An important influence on the standards individuals hold regarding what makes a relationship good, and on their behaviour within their relationships, is the culture in which they are raised. This chapter examines the complexities of intercultural relationships when spouses come from distinctly different cultures. How could Janet and Yang reconcile their different beliefs about expressing feelings and foster a strong relationship? We begin the chapter by describing the significance of intercultural relationships, then analyse the effects of culture on couple relationships, particularly communication and relationship standards (what people think a good relationship should be like). Finally, we consider the implications of cultural issues

Contemporary Issues in Family Studies: Global Perspectives on Partnerships, Parenting and Support in a Changing World, First Edition. Edited by Angela Abela and Janet Walker.
© 2014 John Wiley & Sons, Ltd. Published 2014 by John Wiley & Sons, Ltd.

for social policy and the provision of relationship education and therapy, particularly for intercultural couples.

This chapter focuses predominantly on intercultural relationships between spouses of European and Chinese ancestry. This focus was chosen because the majority of research on couple relationships has focused on couples of European ancestry, while people of Chinese ancestry are the most populous cultural group in the world. These two cultural groups differ in important ways in relationship expectations and behaviour, and intercultural pairings between spouses of European and Chinese ancestry are common across the world. While the focus is mainly on Chinese–European couples, the concepts and implications have broad applicability to other intercultural couples.

The Significance of Intercultural Couple Relationships

Historically, intercultural relationships have been rare, and often the subject of disapproval (Lombardo, 1988). For example, laws banning the intermarriage of different racial groups existed in many US states until 1967 and in South Africa until 1985, and they remain in Malaysia today (Daniels, 2005; Lee and Edmonston, 2005). While discrimination against intercultural marriages still exists, this is changing in many parts of the developed world, and social barriers to intercultural couple relationships have decreased. For example, a survey conducted in 2002 revealed that the majority of US Americans had by then accepted interracial couple relationships (Lee and Edmonston, 2005).

The number of couple relationships formed across cultural divides increased dramatically in the later decades of the twentieth century. For example, the number of interracial marriages in the USA increased by more than 1000 per cent between 1960 and 2002 (Zhang and Kline, 2009). Sharp increases in intercultural marriage rates have been reported in the Americas, East and South-East Asia, Europe, Australia and New Zealand (Cook, 2000; Ferreira and Ramos, 2008; Jones and Shen, 2008; Neyrand and M'Sili, 1998; Statistics Canada, 2009). The proportion of marriages identified as intercultural or interracial is around 30 per cent in Australia, Hawaii, Singapore and Taiwan, and over 10 per cent in France, South Korea, and some areas of Japan and the US mainland (Australian Bureau of Statistics, 2007; Jones and Shen, 2008; Lee and Edmonston, 2005; Neyrand and M'Sili, 1998).

Data from Australia, the Netherlands, France and the USA indicate that rates of distress (Bratter and Eschbach, 2006) and divorce are higher for intercultural than for intracultural relationships (Bramlett and Mosher, 2002; Kalmijn *et al.*, 2005; Neyrand and M'Sili, 1998). Furthermore, divorce risk increases as a function of the extent of difference between partners' cultures (Kalmijn *et al.*, 2005). These statistics underscore the importance of understanding the factors contributing to successful intercultural relationships.

Cultural Differences and Couple Relationships

Individualism–collectivism

Individualism–collectivism is a key cultural dimension that influences interpersonal behaviour (Bond, 2009; Trubinsky *et al.*, 1991). Members of individualistic cultures tend to perceive people as independent agents with unique internal attributes that determine their behaviour across situations. Expression of one's unique abilities, ideas, feelings and preferences, the pursuit of individual goals, and the development of independence are valued, and form the basis of self-esteem. In contrast, members of collectivistic cultures tend to view the self as part of an interdependent network of social relationships. Working harmoniously in a network of interdependent relationships is regarded as the way to achieve fulfilment, and the ability to fulfil one's role and obligations forms the basis of self-esteem (Markus and Kitayama, 1991). Cross-national studies identify individualism as predominant in European countries and former European colonies, and collectivism as predominant in Asia, Africa and Latin America (Hofstede, 2001; Triandis *et al.*, 1986).

Individualism–collectivism is a key cultural dimension that influences interpersonal behaviour

Mary, a 28-year-old Australian woman of British ancestry, and Jonathan, a 29-year-old Chinese man, have been married for one year. Neither perceived their difficulties as cultural, believing that Jonathan was 'more Australian than Chinese' owing to his residence in Australia since the age of 5. Mary reported that they spent a lot of time working together at a charitable organisation, but spent little one-on-one time together. In addition, Jonathan stayed up late finishing work for the charity, with the result that they rarely had sex. Mary suggested occasionally missing a week at the charity, but Jonathan insisted that they had made a commitment and must attend. Mary had begun to doubt that Jonathan cared about her, as to her, caring for her meant attending to her needs. In contrast, Jonathon saw honouring their commitments to others, and working together as a couple on such commitments, as evidence of a strong couple relationship.

Individualism–collectivism and communication

Orientation to individualism or collectivism influences communication behaviour. Low-context communication tends to be used in individualistic cultures (Gudykunst and Matsumoto, 1996). Low-context communication involves transmission of meaning through explicit verbal codes. The speaker is responsible for ensuring successful communication by encoding thoughts and feelings in a clear and easily comprehensible message (Ting-Toomey, 1999). High-context communication tends to be used in collectivistic cultures (Gudykunst and Matsumoto, 1996). In high-context communication, meaning is primarily conveyed through non-verbal signals and the context. As the speaker is expected to communicate in ways that maintain relational harmony, the explicit message might be inconsistent with the speaker's true feelings. The listener is responsible for accurately interpreting the implicit intent of the speaker (Ting-Toomey, 1999).

Koreans are more likely to speak indirectly and look for cues signalling implicit messages than US Americans (Holtgraves, 1997), Asian Americans report more use of indirect communication than European Americans (Park and Kim, 2008), and mainland Chinese are more likely than US Americans to signal their desire for help by showing less than they actually feel, and to associate this with appropriateness (Mortensen, 2009). Mainland Chinese express greater confidence in understanding their partners' attitudes and feelings from indirect information than US Americans (Gao and Gudykunst, 1995). This appears to be an important skill in Chinese relationships, as sensitivity to indirect emotional cues is associated with marital adjustment among Taiwanese Chinese (Lewinsohn and Werner, 1997).

Cultural differences in reliance on contextual cues can create difficulty in intercultural relationships. Collectivistic partners can misinterpret individualistic spouses' remarks, assuming they mean more than explicitly stated, while individualistic partners who are not sensitive to indirect cues can miss their collectivistic partners' messages. Furthermore, indirect communication can appear inscrutable and manipulative to individualistic spouses, while explicit statements of 'wants and needs' can appear demanding, rude and selfish to collectivistic partners.

Jonathan complained about Mary's 'selfishness' and 'lack of objectivity'. He explained that he tried to describe things 'objectively' (using the third person), even when he was expressing his own needs, whereas Mary used the first person and described her needs as what she wanted. He interpreted this as 'What she wants, other people should do'. He stated that if, for example, she wanted ice-cream, she would say 'I want ice-cream', whereas if he wanted ice-cream he would say 'I'm a little bit thirsty. How about we get drinks, or maybe coffee, or ice-cream?' He described his approach as giving options so they could be discussed and a decision made together. However, Mary often responded by stating the choice she wanted, and then became upset if Jonathan then stated he wanted something different.

Individualism and collectivism are associated with different conflict style preferences (Ting-Toomey et al., 1991). These differences can be conceptualised using the orthogonal dimensions of emphasis on meeting one's own needs and emphasis on meeting others' needs (Ting-Toomey et al., 2001). Combinations of these dimensions define five conflict styles: integrating, obliging, dominating, avoiding and compromising (Figure 7.1). Members of collectivistic cultures tend to use the avoiding and obliging styles, while members of individualistic cultures tend to use the integrating and dominating styles (see e.g. Boonsathorn, 2007; Oetzel and Ting-Toomey, 2003). Furthermore, perceptions of the appropriateness and effectiveness of the conflict styles differ along these cultural dimensions (Oetzel et al., 2000).

These differences can be understood in relation to the different self-concepts and communication styles that predominate in individualistic and collectivistic cultures. The dominating and integrating styles favoured in individualistic cultures involve expression of one's needs and preferences, which are considered legitimate and important in individualistic cultures. Needs and preferences are stated directly, in the belief that it is each party's responsibility to present his or her views and that the other party will reciprocate. The avoiding and obliging styles are regarded as strategies for maintaining relationship harmony in collectivistic cultures (Ting-Toomey *et al.*, 2000), where people are expected to be aware of others' unstated needs and preferences.

The communication research outlined above suggests that when conflicts arise in relationships comprising an individualistic partner and a collectivistic partner, partners are likely to engage in different conflict strategies based on different cultural expectations. Partners might feel offended and frustrated by each other's behaviour, owing to differences in the perceived appropriateness of conflict styles. Since couple communication is associated with relationship satisfaction across cultures (Christensen *et al.*, 2006; Halford *et al.*, 1990; Rehman and Holtzworth-Munroe, 2007), negotiation of these differences is crucial to intercultural relationship success.

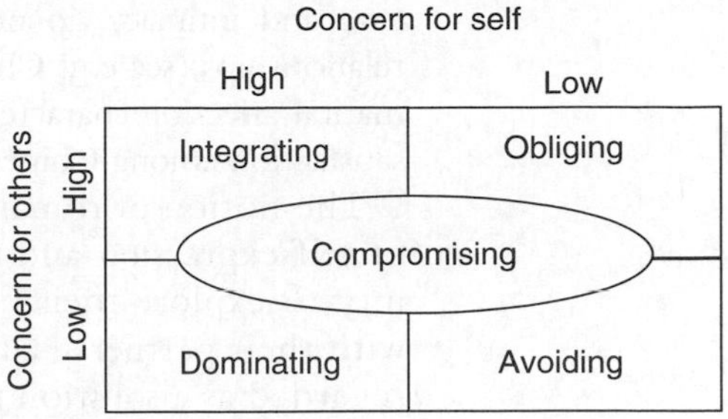

Figure 7.1 The dual-concern model of styles of handling interpersonal conflict
Source. Rahim, M. A. (2002). Toward a theory of managing organizational conflict, *International Journal of Conflict Management*, 13, p. 217. Used with permission from the © Center for Advanced Studies in Management. Further use or reproduction of the instrument without written permission is prohibited.

Individualism–collectivism and relationship standards

Relationship standards are beliefs about what partners and relationships should be like (Baucom *et al.*, 1996). The extent to which partners' standards are realistic, discrepant and fulfilled has been associated with relationship functioning across cultures (Barazandch *et al.*, 2006; Baucom *et al.*, 1996; Epstein *et al.*, 2005). However, the extent to which particular standards are perceived to be realistic or fulfilled varies along the dimension of individualism–collectivism.

The belief that romantic love and psychological intimacy are essential for couple relationships characterises individualistic cultures (see e.g. Dion and Dion, 1993; Sastry, 1999). North Americans are more likely than Chinese, Japanese or Koreans to believe love in marriage is essential (Kline *et al.*, 2008) and to perceive passionate love as necessary for entering marriage (Sprecher and Toro-Morn, 2002). In addition, US Americans report experiencing greater passion in their relationships than Chinese (Gao, 2001), and rate sexual pleasure as more important for maintaining marriage (Sprecher and Toro-Morn, 2002). Asians seem to conceptualise love in a less 'romantic' manner than Westerners. Asian research participants generally use words such as 'respect', 'mutual understanding' and 'support' to describe love, whereas Western research participants generally discuss 'love' and 'going out together' (Kline *et al.*, 2008).

Psychological intimacy between partners also holds less importance in collectivistic than in individualistic cultures. Intimacy has been described as involving reciprocal self-disclosure, sharing of activities and the revealing of strong personal feelings (Chen and Li, 2007; Sastry, 1999). While intimacy correlates strongly with relationship satisfaction in Western couples (Sanderson and Evans, 2001), one of the few surveys of married couples in China showed that interaction between spouses outside the family (couple time) was not strongly related to marital quality (Pimental, 2000). Furthermore, in a sample of 73 Chinese spouses separated owing to occupational, economic or educational reasons the majority reported no decrease in marital satisfaction associated with the separation (Abbott and Meredith, 1994). Chinese psychologists claim that Western concepts such as love and intimacy do not adequately describe the Chinese concept of good marital relationships (see e.g. Chen and Li, 2007). The Chinese concept of *enqing*—a form of marital affection characterised by feelings of gratitude and admiration—predicts marital satisfaction among Chinese couples (Li and Chen, 2002).

The notion of romantic love can be seen as meeting the individualistic needs of self-expression and discovery, in that it provides partners with the opportunity to explore their emotional selves, as they seek to share their 'real selves' with their partners (Dion and Dion, 1993; Sastry, 1999). Romantic love is also regarded as a solution to the relational disconnection of individualistic societies (Ting-Toomey, 1991). It has been argued that there is less need for love and intimacy within couple relationships in collectivistic societies, as these are shared across the broader family network (Lewinsohn and Werner, 1997). Moreover, the mutual absorption and disregard of others' views that characterise romantic love in individualistic societies are regarded as dysfunctional in collectivistic societies, in which group needs are prioritised over personal desires (Dion and Dion, 1993).

Cultural preference for high-context communication also appears to contribute to the lesser role of intimacy in collectivistic couple relationships. Chinese scholars report that Chinese people regard feelings as something to be sensed and discerned, rather than spoken about (Gao and Ting-Toomey, 1998). Love is expressed through helping and caring for one's partner (such as repairing their bicycle), rather than through verbal expression or symbolic gestures (such as sending flowers). Control of emotional expression is considered a sign of maturity, physical demonstration of affection is rare, and expression of personal preferences is similarly restrained (Gao and Ting-Toomey, 1998). This does not mean collectivistic couple relationships have less demanding standards than individualistic relationships, but rather, different standards. Taiwanese couples report significantly less verbal communication than US American couples, but similar levels of marital adjustment (Juang and Tucker, 1991). However, Chinese couples' standards reflect an expectation of greater instrumental investment in the relationship than US American couples' standards (Epstein *et al.*, 2005).

Some aspects of collectivistic, high-context communication appear likely to hinder achievement of the Western ideal of intimacy, and, potentially, to be misinterpreted by an individualistic spouse as indicating secretiveness and lack of care. For example, on average, US Americans receive higher levels of emotional support from their spouses than Chinese, while Chinese receive more informational and problem-solving support from their spouses than US Americans (Burleson and Mortensen, 2003; Xu and Burleson, 2001). Collectivists' lack of provision of emotional support might be misinterpreted by individualists as lack of care. However, provision of comfort in collectivistic cultures is aimed at restoration of social harmony. The focus is recovery of social composure and avoidance of loss of face or excessive emotionality. Chinese regard escaping and dismissing negative feelings, and messages low in person-centredness, as more appropriate support strategies than do US Americans (Barbee and Cunningham, 1995).

Culture also shapes standards regarding family relationships. While individualistic cultures emphasise family members' independence, autonomy and self-sufficiency, collectivistic cultures emphasise interdependence of family members throughout the lifespan (Dion and Dion, 1993; Lee and Mock, 2005). In the USA, spouses report stronger desire to have boundaries around their relationship (less sharing of information and acceptance of advice from others) than mainland Chinese spouses (Epstein *et al.*, 2005), reflecting the US perception of the couple as a separate system. In contrast, in China the marital relationship is considered a continuation of the parents' family, rather than a separate system (Lewinsohn and Werner, 1997). The belief that a potential partner will support one's parents has more influence on Chinese than American marital intentions and relationship commitment (Zhang and Kline, 2009). Parental approval of mainland Chinese marriages is associated with high marital closeness (Pimental, 2000); and relationships with significant others are ranked among the most important dimensions of marriage by Hong Kong Chinese (Chan and Rudowicz, 2002).

In summary, research into cross-cultural relationships indicates substantial cultural variation in relationship standards. In particular, individualistic and collectivistic partners seem likely to hold different beliefs about love, intimacy, support and relationships with the (extended) family. The pan-cultural association between discrepant standards and relationship dissatisfaction (see e.g. Barazandeh *et al.*, 2006; Baucom *et al.*, 1996; Epstein *et al.*, 2005) suggests that management of these discrepancies is likely to be a key contributor to intercultural relationship outcomes.

Practice and Policy Implications

Implicit cultural focus in couple interventions

Psychologists' attempts to assist couples to have better relationships can be broadly classified into two categories of intervention: couple relationship education (CRE) and couple therapy. The CRE intervention works with couples who are currently satisfied in their relationship, and are committed to that relationship (Halford, 2011). It builds upon the high level of positive emotion typical of currently satisfied couples, and has a strong emphasis on building the positive foundations for a good life together. In contrast, couple therapy is for people who are distressed in their relationship. Couple therapy often has to manage high levels of negative affect in the relationship, and address the ambivalence many distressed couples feel about whether they wish the relationship to continue (Halford, 2001). Couple therapy is often extensive in duration, with evidence-based approaches often involving 15, 20 or more sessions of therapy (Halford and Snyder, 2012).

Both CRE and couple therapy have been developed in individualistic cultures, and contain implicit acceptance of an individualistic approach to couple communication and relationship standards. For example, the most widely used curriculum-based CRE programmes, such as Markman *et al.*'s (1988) Prevention and Relationship Enhancement Program (PREP) and Bodenmann and Shantinath's (2004) Couples Coping Enhancement Training (CCET), teach direct communication, assertive conflict management and positive expression of affection. Similarly, there are a number of different evidence-based approaches to couple therapy that seem similarly effective (Halford and Snyder, 2012), and all focus on relationship attributes valued in individualistic cultures. For example, Benson *et al.* (2012) provide what they see as overarching principles of couple therapy common to each evidence-based approach. These include promoting direct, low-context communication between spouses.

In contrast, collectivistic cultural values such as preserving others' face, attention to family responsibilities, and filial piety (respect for parents and other elders) are rarely explicated in Western couple therapy.

Couple interventions with intercultural couples

Intercultural partners bring to the relationship different values, ways of relating, and ways of communicating and resolving conflict (Cools, 2006). Despite the growing number of intercultural marriages, there is no empirical research testing how best to assist intercultural couples to have mutually satisfying, stable relationships. However, research on cultural accommodation seems relevant to intercultural couples. Accommodation refers to people modifying their communication styles to more closely resemble those of the people they interact with, and to the seeking of shared goals or desires (Burgoon and Ebesu Hubbard, 2005). Communication similarity between spouses from the same cultural background is associated with relationship satisfaction (Burleson and Denton, 1992).

We suggest that similarity of communication and relationship standards helps sustain high relationship satisfaction, and that similarity in intercultural couples is enhanced by accommodation. For example, a partner from an individualistic culture can reduce overt expression of concerns and become more subtle, while a partner from a collectivistic culture can increase overt expression of concerns, to make it easier to achieve mutual understanding. Similarly, an individualistic spouse might increase attention to family responsibilities and duties, while a collectivistic spouse might give increased attention to romance and couple time.

When working with intercultural couples, we have often found it helpful to assist spouses to identify how their cultures of origin have shaped their relationship standards and patterns of communication, and to assist the couple to work out how to accommodate the differences between them. We have been developing the Yin and Yang Couple Relationship Standard Measure that assesses standards derived from both individualistic and collectivistic cultures. Examples of items from this measure are presented in Table 7.1. Respondents rate how important each item is for sustaining a good relationship on a six-point scale ranging from 'not important' to 'extremely important'. Exploring relationship standards such as these can help spouses recognise the different assumptions they bring to the relationship, and explore how they can accommodate each other.

In some ways, every couple relationship is 'cross-cultural' because there is a degree of challenge for the partners in understanding each other's world, but this challenge is escalated when intercultural partners unite two worlds, each with its own completely different definition of what might constitute 'normal' and 'good' relationships and completely different framework for communication. People are often unaware of the extent to which their relationship standards and behaviours are culturally determined. Furthermore, there is a tendency to perceive one's own culture's way of doing things as right, and those of other cultures as abnormal (Ting-Toomey, 1999).

The task of intercultural couple relationship education and therapy is to reduce destructive attributions and conflict by helping partners separate culturally normative behaviour from personal idiosyncrasies and relationship dysfunction (Hsu, 2001), and to recognise and respect that there are advantages and disadvantages to each

Table 7.1 Examples of items from the Yin and Yang Couple Relationship Standard Measure

Construct	Behaviour
	Partners:
Demonstration of love	Express their love for each other in words every day (e.g. say 'I love you', write loving letters/emails/text messages). Have regular sex.
Relational harmony	Do not speak about things that may lead to conflict. Avoid saying 'no' to each other (say 'yes' or 'maybe').
Relations with extended family	Visit or call their parents at least once a week, even when it is not convenient or enjoyable. Offer to host any family members who come to their area, without needing to be asked.
Intimacy—self-expression	Tell each other about the things they dislike. Tell each other about their private thoughts and ideas.
Intimacy— responsiveness	Know what each other is thinking without having to be told. Know what each other needs without having to be told.
Face/*Mian zi*	Avoid doing things that might lower other people's opinions of the other partner or the couple. Conceal or exaggerate the truth when this will enhance the other partner's social image.

culture's way of doing things. Facilitating couple discussion of the pros and cons of different cultural norms within that couple's context, and mutual development of a shared set of standards, can be helpful. One way to achieve shared standards is for professionals to help partners identify the similar values that may underlie their culturally different behaviour. For example, a Chinese spouse's long work hours, and a European spouse's reduced work hours, may each reflect a desire to provide the best possible environment for their children.

In many developed countries, such as the USA, Japan, Australia and Norway, government and community agencies promote dissemination of CRE and couple therapy in an attempt to reduce the negative personal, social and economic effects associated with high rates of divorce and relationship distress. However, such services often fail to reach ethnic minorities (Halford and van Acker, 2012).

To be able to assist intercultural couples, the professionals in couple services need to be aware of their own cultural biases, and those of the research and training they draw upon. They also need to understand the values underpinning different cultural standards, in order to be able to help partners explore the bases of their beliefs and behaviour. Governments and community agencies need to promote cultural competence in their professionals, ensuring that their training and professional development help them understand cultural variations in relationship standards and patterns of communication. In addition, services need to present themselves in ways that encourage engagement by couples with diverse cultural backgrounds (e.g. by advertising their services in multiple languages, representing ethnic diversity in their workforce).

Case example of relationship education for an intercultural couple

Wee Hong (38) is a Chinese computer consultant who is married to Suzie (29), an Anglo-Australian teacher. They present for relationship education reporting some difficulties in communication and conflict about where to live. Wee Hong would like to return to Hong Kong, his place of birth and residence until five years ago, while Suzie wishes to continue living in Australia. Suzie reports that their relationship is emotionally distant, they rarely communicate, sex occurs infrequently, and 'Wee Hong is obsessed with work and making money'. Wee Hong states that Suzie is not being a good wife, although he is reluctant to state exactly what he means.

The educator asked each partner to write down some thoughts they had about their respective parents' marriage, and what each saw as the strengths and weaknesses of those relationships. Wee Hong said love was not expressed in words by his parents. Instead they worked together, made many sacrifices to build a good life for each other and their whole family, and demonstrated love by carrying out their duties and being considerate. Wee Hong was proud of providing well for himself and Suzie. He felt a duty to return to Hong Kong to assist his ageing parents, even though that would mean career sacrifices for him and Suzie leaving her friends in Brisbane. Suzie described how her parents had prioritised their relationship with each other, planning regular weekends away together. She often saw them holding hands and heard them saying loving words. Suzie wanted such expressions of affection in her relationship. The educator invited the couple to discuss how they might draw on the strengths of both cultural traditions, valuing the sharing of work and family duties, and also romance and affection, in their relationship.

At one point Wee Hong stated: 'My parents are ageing, it is hard for them.' We noted that he was being indirect, and Suzie suggested that, if expressed directly, what he said meant 'I worry about my parents and I feel it is my duty to do more for them. I also think it is your duty, as my wife, to understand this and help me do the right thing.' (Wee Hong nodded vigorously when she made this interpretation.) We also reflected on a statement by Suzie, 'We need to have secure work … it is not like we have a lot of money saved up', that had elicited some irritation from Wee Hong. We agreed she had been direct in her communication and had meant no more than she had stated. However, in the context of the conversation Wee Hong had interpreted her meaning as: 'You have not provided well enough for us. We cannot afford to go to Hong Kong to do our duty to your parents. We might not be able to have children.' As the couple explored the interplay of their implicit relationship standards (the importance of family and duty versus couple romance and intimacy) and different communication styles (indirect versus direct), they began the process of accommodating to each other.

Conclusion

Intercultural relationships have become increasingly common in many countries. A key cultural dimension influencing couple relationships is individualism–collectivism, which is associated with different relationship standards and styles of communication. Successful intercultural relationships require spouses to accommodate their differences in relationship standards and communication styles. Couple relationship education and therapy have evolved within an individualistic cultural context. Interventions and services for intercultural couples need to transcend any single cultural tradition, and assist partners to understand and value their different cultural traditions and develop mutually satisfying intercultural relationships.

References

Abbott, D. A. and Meredith, W. H. (1994) Unintended marital separation in the People's Republic of China: a pilot study, *Journal of Comparative Family Studies*, 25: 269–277.

Australian Bureau of Statistics (2007) *Marriages, Australia, 2006* [electronic version]. http://www.abs.gov.au/AUSSTATS/abs@.nsf/Lookup/3306.0.55.001Main+Features1006?OpenDocument [Accessed 4.8.2008.]

Barazandeh, H., Aminyazdi, A., Sahebi, A. and Mahram, B. (2006) The relationship between marital adjustment and relationship standards, *Journal of Iranian Psychologists*, 2: 319–330.

Barbee, A. P. and Cunningham, M. R. (1995) An experimental approach to social support communications: interactive coping in close relationships, in B. R. Burleson (ed.), *Communication Yearbook 18* (Thousand Oaks, CA: Sage), 381–413.

Baucom, D. H., Epstein, N., Rankin, L. A. and Burnett, C. K. (1996) Assessing relationship standards: the Inventory of Specific Relationship Standards, *Journal of Family Psychology*, 10: 72–88.

Benson, L. A., McGinn, M. M. and Christensen, A. (2012) Common principles of couple therapy, *Behavior Therapy*, 43: 25–35.

Bodenmann, G. and Shantinath, S. D. (2004) The Couples Coping Enhancement Training (CCET): a new approach to prevention of marital distress based upon stress and coping, *Family Relations*, 53: 477–484.

Bond, M. H. (2009) Believing in beliefs: a scientific but personal quest, in K. Leung and M. H. Bond (eds), *Psychological Aspects of Social Axioms* (New York: Springer), 319–342.

Boonsathorn, W. (2007) Understanding conflict management styles of Thais and Americans in multinational corporations in Thailand, *International Journal of Conflict Management*, 18: 196–221.

Bramlett, M. D. and Mosher, W. D. (2002) Cohabitation, marriage, divorce, and remarriage in the United States, *Vital and Health Statistics*, 23(22) (Hyattsville, MD: National Center for Health Statistics). http://www.cdc.gov/nchs/data/series/sr_23/sr23_022.pdf [Accessed 4.2.2013.]

Bratter, J. L. and Eschbach, K. (2006) 'What about the couple?' Interracial marriage and psychological distress, *Social Science Research*, 35: 1025–1047.

Burgoon, J. K. and Ebesu Hubbard, A. S. (2005) Cross-cultural and intercultural applications of Expectancy Violations Theory and Interaction Adaptation Theory, in W. B. Gudykunst (ed.), *Theorizing about Intercultural Communication* (Thousand Oaks, CA: Sage), 149–171.

Burleson, B. R. and Denton, W. H. (1992) A new look at similarity and attraction in marriage: similarities in social-cognitive and communication skills as predictors of attraction and satisfaction, *Communication Monographs*, 59: 268–287.

Burleson, B. R. and Mortensen, S. T. (2003) Explaining cultural differences in evaluations of emotional support behaviours: exploring the mediating influences of value systems and interaction goals, *Communication Research*, 30: 113–146.

Chan, Y.-W. and Rudowicz, E. (2002) The Chinese version of the Marital Comparison Level Index revisited, *Psychological Reports*, 91: 1143–1147.

Chen, F.-M. and Li, T.-S. (2007) Marital enqing: an examination of its relationship to spousal contributions, sacrifices, and family stress in Chinese marriages, *Journal of Social Psychology*, 147: 393–412.

Christensen, A., Eldridge, K., Catta-Preta, A. B., Lim, V. R. and Santagata, R. (2006) Cross-cultural consistency of the demand/withdraw interaction pattern in couples, *Journal of Marriage and Family*, 68: 1029–1044.

Cook, L. (2000) The big shifts now in train: changes in society, *Looking Past the 20th Century*. http://www2.stats.govt.nz/domino/external/web/nzstories.nsf/092edeb76ed5aa6bcc256afe0081d84e/0b5780700395e6f6cc256b2400769964?OpenDocument. [Accessed 27.6.2009.]

Cools, C. A. (2006) Relational communication in intercultural couples, *Language and Intercultural Communication*, 6: 262–274.

Daniels, T. P. (2005) *Building Cultural Nationalism in Malaysia* (London: Routledge).

Dion, K. K. and Dion, K. L. (1993) Individualistic and collectivistic perspectives on gender and the cultural context of love and intimacy, *Journal of Social Issues*, 49: 53–69.

Epstein, N. B., Chen, F. and Beyder-Kamjou, I. (2005) Relationship standards and marital satisfaction in Chinese and American couples, *Journal of Marital and Family Therapy*, 31: 59–74.

Ferreira, A. C. and Ramos, M. (2008) Patterns of marriage among immigrants in Portugal, *Revista de Estudos Demográficos*, 43. http://www.ine.pt/xportal/xmain?xpid=INE&xpgid=ine_pesquisa&frm_accao=PSQUISAR&frm_show_page_num=1&frm_modo_pesquisa=PESQUISA_SIMPES&frm_modo_texto=MODO_TEXTO_ALL&frm_texto=patterns+of+marriage+mong+immigrants. [Accessed 19.4.2011.]

Gao, G. (2001) Intimacy, passion, and commitment in Chinese and US American romantic relationships, *International Journal of Intercultural Relations*, 25: 329–342.

Gao, G. and Gudykunst, W. B. (1995) Attributional confidence, perceived similarity, and network involvement in Chinese and American romantic relationships, *Communication Quarterly*, 43: 431–445.

Gao, G. and Ting-Toomey, S. (1998) *Communicating Effectively with the Chinese* (Thousand Oaks, CA: Sage).

Gudykunst, W. B. and Matsumoto, Y. (1996) Cross-cultural variability of communication in personal relationships, in W. B. Gudykunst, S. Ting-Toomey and T. Nishida (eds), *Communication in Personal Relationships Across Cultures* (Thousand Oaks, CA: Sage), 19–56.

Halford, W. K. (2001) *Brief Couple Therapy* (New York: Guilford).

Halford, W. K. (2011) *Marriage and Relationship Education: What works and how to provide it* (New York: Guilford).

Halford, W. K., Hahlweg, K. and Dunne, M. (1990) The cross-cultural consistency of marital communication associated with marital distress, *Journal of Marriage and Family*, 52: 487–500.

Halford, W. K. and Snyder, D. K. (2012) Universal processes and common factors in couple therapy and relationship education: introduction to the Special Section, *Behavior Therapy*, 43: 1–12.

Halford and van Acker, E. (2012) Are governments and marriage strange bedfellows? Social policy and couple relationship education, in P. Noller and G. Karantzas (eds), *Positive Pathways for Couples and Families: Meeting the challenges of relationships* (Oxford: Wiley-Blackwell), 453–466.

Hofstede, G. (2001) *Culture's Consequences* (Thousand Oaks, CA: Sage), 2nd edn.

Holtgraves, T. (1997) Styles of language use: individual and cultural variability in conversational indirectness, *Journal of Personality and Social Psychology*, 73: 624–637.

Hsu, J. (2001) Marital therapy for intercultural couples, in W. Tseng and J. Streltzer (eds), *Culture and Psychotherapy* (Washington DC: American Psychiatric), 225–242.

Jones, G. and Shen, H.-H. (2008) International marriage in East and Southeast Asia: trends and research emphasis, *Citizenship Studies*, 12: 9–25.

Juang, S.-H. and Tucker, C. M. (1991) Factors in marital adjustment and their interrelationships: a comparison of Taiwanese couples in America and Caucasian American couples, *Journal of Multicultural Counseling and Development*, 19: 22–31.

Kalmijn, M., de Graaf, Paul M. and Janssen, J. P. G. (2005) Intermarriage and the risk of divorce in the Netherlands: the effects of differences in religion and in nationality, 1974–94, *Population Studies*, 59: 71–85.

Kline, S. L., Horton, B. and Zhang, S. (2008) Communicating love: comparisons between American and East Asian university students, *International Journal of Intercultural Relations*, 32: 200–214.

Lee, E. and Mock, M. R. (2005) Chinese families, in M. McGoldrick, J. Giordano and N. Garcia-Preto (eds), *Ethnicity and Family Therapy* (New York: Guilford Press), 302–318.

Lee, S. M. and Edmonston, B. (2005) New marriages, new families: US racial and Hispanic intermarriage, *Population Bulletin*, 60: 3–36.

Lewinsohn, M. A. and Werner, P. D. (1997) Factors in Chinese marital process: relationship to marital adjustment, *Family Process*, 36: 43–61.

Li, T.-S. and Chen, F.-M. (2002) Affection in marriage: a study of marital enqing and intimacy in Taiwan, *Journal of Psychology in Chinese Societies*, 3: 37–59.

Lombardo, P. (1988) Miscegenation, eugenics, and racism: historical footnotes to *Loving* v. *Virginia*, *University of California Davis Law Review*, 21: 425–432.

Markman, H. J., Floyd, F. J., Stanley, S. M. and Storaasli, R. D. (1988) Prevention of marital distress: a longitudinal investigation, *Journal of Consulting and Clinical Psychology*, 56: 210–217.

Markus, H. R. and Kitayama, S. (1991) Culture and the self: implications for cognition, emotion, and motivation, *Psychological Review*, 98: 224–253.

Mortensen, S. T. (2009) Interpersonal trust and social skill in seeking social support among Chinese and Americans, *Communication Research*, 36: 32–53.

Neyrand, G. and M'Sili, M. (1998) Mixed couples in contemporary France: marriage, acquisition of French nationality and divorce, *Population: An English selection*, 10: 385–416.

Oetzel, J. G. and Ting-Toomey, S. (2003) Face concerns in interpersonal conflict: a cross-cultural empirical test of the face negotiation theory, *Communication Research*, 30: 599–624.

Oetzel, J. G., Ting-Toomey, S., Yokochi, Y., Masumoto, T. and Takai, J. (2000) A typology of facework behaviors in conflicts with best friends and relative strangers, *Communication Quarterly*, 48: 397–419.

Park, Y. S. and Kim, B. S. K. (2008) Asian and European American cultural values and communication styles among Asian American and European American college students, *Cultural Diversity and Ethnic Minority Psychology*, 14: 47–56.

Pimental, E. E. (2000) Just how do I love thee?: marital relations in urban China, *Journal of Marriage and Family*, 62: 32–47.

Rahim, M. A. (2002) Toward a theory of managing organizational conflict, *International Journal of Conflict Management*, 13: 206–235.

Rehman, U. S. and Holtzworth-Munroe, A. (2007) A cross-cultural examination of the relation of marital communication behaviour to marital satisfaction, *Journal of Family Psychology*, 21: 759–763.

Sanderson, C. A. and Evans, S. M. (2001) Seeing one's partner through intimacy-colored glasses: an examination of the processes underlying the intimacy goals–relationship satisfaction link, *Personality and Social Psychology Bulletin*, 27: 463–473.

Sastry, J. (1999) Household structure, satisfaction and distress in India and the United States: a comparative cultural examination, *Journal of Comparative Family Studies*, 30: 135–152.

Sprecher, S. and Toro-Morn, M. (2002) A study of men and women from different sides of Earth to determine if men are from Mars and women are from Venus in their beliefs about love and romantic relationships, *Sex Roles*, 46: 131–147.

Statistics Canada (2009) Ethnic diversity and immigration, *Canada Year Book Overview 2008*. http://www41.statcan.ca/2008/30000/ ceb30000_000_e.htm. [Accessed 27.6.2009.]

Ting-Toomey, S. (1991) Intimacy expressions in three cultures: France, Japan, and the United States, *International Journal of Intercultural Relations*, 15: 29–46.

Ting-Toomey, S. (1999) *Communicating Across Cultures* (New York: Guilford Press).

Ting-Toomey, S., Gao, G., Trubinsky, P., Yang, Z., Kim, H. S., Lin, S.-L. *et al.* (1991) Culture, face maintenance, and styles of handling interpersonal conflict: a study in five cultures, *International Journal of Conflict Management*, 2: 275–296.

Ting-Toomey, S., Oetzel, J. G. and Yee-Jung, K. (2001) Self-construal types and conflict management styles, *Communication Reports*, 14: 87–104.

Ting-Toomey, S., Yee-Jung, K. K., Shapiro, R. B., Garcia, W., Wright, T. J. and Oetzel, J. G. (2000) Ethnic/cultural identity salience and conflict styles in four US ethnic groups, *International Journal of Intercultural Relations*, 24: 47–81.

Triandis, H. C., Bontempo, R., Betancourt, H., Bond, M., Leung, K., Brenes, A. *et al.* (1986) The measurement of etic aspects of individualism and collectivism across cultures, *Australian Journal of Psychology*, 38: 257–267.

Trubinsky, P., Ting-Toomey, S. and Lin, S.-L. (1991) The influence of individualism–collectivism and self-monitoring on conflict styles, *International Journal of Intercultural Relations*, 15: 65–84.

Xu, Y. and Burleson, B. R. (2001) Effects of sex, culture, and support type on perceptions of spousal social support: an assessment of the 'support gap' hypothesis in early marriage, *Human Communication Research*, 27: 535–566.

Zhang, S. and Kline, S. L. (2009) Can I make my own decision? A cross-cultural study of perceived social network influence in mate selection, *Journal of Cross-Cultural Psychology*, 40: 3–23.

8

Growing Older in a Changing World
Opportunities and Challenges for Family Life and Social Support

JOHN BOND

Introduction

Families, family relationships and the practices of families are changing across the world as a consequence of population ageing, economic development, urbanisation and globalisation. The nature and rate of change in family life as experienced by older people, however, is extremely diverse, not only between different regions of the world but also within different countries, cultures and socio-economic groups. This chapter reviews the impact of our changing world on the family lives of older people and examines the opportunities and challenges for the individual and society by highlighting the continued significance through the world of family connection and solidarity in later life.

Family and ageing studies are well established within Europe, North America and Australasia, with a wide range of studies and data for scholars to examine and interpret. There is a paucity of studies from other parts of the world and for many countries even basic demographic data are lacking (National Research Council, 2006). For the Western English-speaking scholar the challenge of providing a balanced view of family life and later life in non-Western cultures is also compounded by the linguistic and cultural barriers to retrieving and interpreting data. This chapter, therefore, provides a primarily Eurocentric perspective on families in later life.

The idea of family is often taken for granted in family studies, perhaps reflecting the common stereotypes of Western politicians and policymakers. To avoid reinforcing such stereotypes this chapter takes both a constructionist and a life-course perspective. Within a critical gerontological tradition, a constructionist perspective on the family

Contemporary Issues in Family Studies: Global Perspectives on Partnerships, Parenting and Support in a Changing World, First Edition. Edited by Angela Abela and Janet Walker.
© 2014 John Wiley & Sons, Ltd. Published 2014 by John Wiley & Sons, Ltd.

moves beyond the conventional structuralist view of family and kinship that focuses on marriage, parenthood and residence, to one that puts the experiences of older people at the centre of our understandings of family life. In the case of many accounts this will reflect conventional views of the family, but other accounts will highlight the diversity and complexity of social relations in later life within different cultural and global contexts. In taking a life-course perspective in the study of ageing and people's family lives, it is useful to reflect on four key life-course constructs.

Key life-course constructs (Giele and Elder, 1998)

- 'Linked lives'—builds on ideas of social integration that highlight the way that different levels of social action (cultural, institutional, social, psychological or socio-biological) interact and influence the lives of people and families, who have shared experiences.
- 'Timing'—reflects the chronological order of events in a person's life or family biography that incorporates personal, group and historical milestones.
- 'Human agency'—is critical for both the development of individual and family or group identity, and one's sense of self as embodied through the active pursuit of personal goals.
- 'Time and place'—highlights the effect that both general and unique aspects of location of place have on family and individual experience; remains critical to understanding ageing and families through a life-course perspective.

Population Ageing

It can be argued that, along with global warming and ongoing geopolitical struggles, population ageing is one of the greatest challenges facing individuals and governments. Economic and technological development over the last century has seen an unprecedented change, that began in Europe and North America and has, at an increasing rate, spread throughout the globe. Population ageing is the consequence of this 'regular stream of continuing progress' (Oeppen and Vaupel, 2002, p. 1029), including increases in absolute income and wealth; improvements in education, nutrition, and sanitation; and developments in preventive and therapeutic medicine. This 'continuing progress' has benefited the regions of the world in different ways and there remain substantial inequalities in the experience of individual citizens within and between countries.

There is no denying population ageing. Life expectancy is increasing worldwide while fertility rates have declined and are unlikely to rise again to the levels experienced in the past (United Nations, 2009). Population ageing occurs when the proportion of people aged 60 or over is accompanied by a reduction in the proportion of children under the age of 15 and a subsequent decline in the proportion of people of working age (defined by the United Nations as 16–59 years). Across the world the proportion of older people has increased from 8 per cent in 1950 to 11 per cent in 2009, and is projected to increase to 22 per cent by 2050. In absolute terms this means a rise in the number of older people living in the world, from 205 million in

1950 to 737 million in 2009 and an anticipated 2 billion in 2050, a tripling of this population over 50 years (United Nations, 2009).

There are marked differences in the proportion of older people in different regions, the more developed regions having a higher proportion than the less developed regions. For example, Japan (29.7%) and Italy (26.4%) have the highest proportion of people aged 60 or over while Sierra Leone (3.5%) and United Arab Emirates (1.9%) have the lowest (United Nations, 2009). However, the pace of population ageing is more marked in less developed regions of the world than in the more developed regions. It is projected that by 2050 nearly one-third of the population in the more developed regions will be aged 60 or over while the comparative proportion for less developed regions is one-fifth. Even in the countries of sub-Saharan Africa, so devastated by the impact of HIV/AIDS (by 2020 it is projected that some 75 million Africans will have died prematurely owing to AIDS/HIV; Velkoff and Kowal, 2006), it is expected that at least one in ten of the population will be aged 60 or over by 2050 (equivalent to many countries in Europe in 1950). Nevertheless, countries with large populations such as Brazil and China will more than double the size of their older populations in the first 25 years of the twenty-first century (United Nations, 2009).

The older population itself is ageing, with increasing numbers of people aged 80 or over and 100 or over, particularly in the more developed regions. In 2009, one in seven older people was aged 80 or over; this is expected to increase to one in five by 2050 (United Nations, 2009). Ageing affects men and women in different ways. Women are living four to five years longer on average than men (United Nations, 2009). Such gender differences in survival affect the numbers of women living alone in all world regions, with an estimated 19 per cent of women and 9 per cent of men living alone (United Nations, 2009). In less developed regions such as sub-Saharan Africa few older people live alone, but households are frequently split across geographical locations in order to diversify risk and maximise incomes (National Research Council, 2006). This reflects the migration of working-age adults from rural to urban areas.

Family structures and population ageing

Although the demographic structure of families varies between regions and cultures, changes in family structures experienced in the more developed regions are likely to be replicated in other regions as population ageing accelerates. In developed regions the combination of increased life expectancy, increased lifespan and decreasing fertility has seen the emergence of what Bengston *et al.* (1990) called the 'beanpole family'. Horizontal ties between siblings and cousins are reduced in number while the number of vertical ties between different generations, for example grandparents and grand-children, increase in frequency but also in complexity.

Ageing across the life course

Ageing is a biological, psychological and social process. For bio-gerontologists, 'ageing is nothing more nor less than the gradual, lifelong accumulation of subtle faults in the cells and organs of the body' (Westendorp and Kirkwood, 2007, p. 20). Biological ageing 'is a continuous process, starting early and developing gradually, instead of being a distinct phase that begins in middle to late life' (Westendorp and

Kirkwood, 2007, p.). Chronological age is therefore not a good proxy for the ageing process. We only have to look at images of the ageing body to see that the process of biological ageing affects individuals in different ways and at different rates. Both genetic and environmental factors play key roles in the process. Nevertheless, different age bands are often linked to phases of the life course that have been constructed for administrative and policy purposes. But personal accounts of the experience of ageing from people of different cultures and generations[1] highlight the diversity of lived experience across the life course.

Attitudes to ageing

Societal attitudes to ageing and the meaning we each give to older age play an important role in the lived experience of ageing. Although the experience of later stages of the life course and particularly the 'third age' (Laslett, 1987) is seen as increasingly positive (Gilleard and Higgs, 2000), many scholars see media reporting of politicians' and policymakers' attitudes to ageing as being essentially negative, reflecting the lived experience of the fourth age and prevalent discourses about the burden of population ageing. One current stereotype of an older person is of someone with frail health, who is unproductive and in need of support. In the past and in other cultures, ageing and family life were often viewed more positively, but such a view often involved rose-tinted spectacles. As the interpretations of historians and the accounts of oral history would suggest (Bond and Corner, 2004), ageing was not always regarded so positively: it has always been seen as a social problem (McIntyre, 1977).

Contemporary scholars of ageing working within the critical gerontological perspective highlight the complexity and diversity of ageing. In their examination of social attitudes to ageing and later life, Westerhof and Tulle (2007) highlight the importance of discursive contexts including biomedicine, the making of social policy, social gerontological knowledge, the mass media, and works of fiction. The biomedicalisation of ageing (Estes and Binney, 1989) remains an important influence on our negative attitudes to ageing with the continuing emphasis on bodily deterioration and debilitation. Social policy discourses have a similar perspective on ageing and physical decline but also highlight increasing dependency and decreasing productivity. For social policy, old age produces social problems to be solved. Within European societies, solutions have changed over time since the end of the nineteenth century with the development of national insurance policies for sickness and retirement. The establishment of the so-called welfare states of the post-World War II era and the associated ideology of collective responsibility provided support in housing, pensions, health and long-term care. During the last 25 years of the twentieth century the impact of globalisation and the ageing of the population led to the emergence of an alarmist discourse referring to an increasing burden of older people within Europe and North America (Katz, 1992; Robertson, 1997). Policy responses have included increasing privatisation of services (particularly long-term care services) and a decline in public-sector provision (Estes *et al.*, 2001), the development of an ideology of personal responsibility, and recognition of the importance of older people as an economic and social resource.

---

[1] The idea of generation used here is not one based on chronological age, but draws on Mannheim's concept of a generational cohort based on shared lived experience (Mannheim, 1952).

Increasing biomedicalisation and the changing nature of policy discourses have intensified public debate about population ageing and attitudes towards older people. Ageing is now a common topic for the mass media, which both reflect and manipulate lay perceptions of older people and older people's attitudes. Although the media are an important vehicle for advertising 'anti-ageing' products, older people are often invisible in television programmes and the visual arts. There are a variety of images of older people, and some of these are positive, but most presentations of older people concern the problems of old age, and where older people are presented they are 'the object of pity or … victims of scandalous practices' (Westerhof and Tulle, 2007).

Social Diversity and the Lived Experience of Later Life

Within and between the different regions of the world, older people live in a variety of different ways and will have experienced a diversity of life courses. Gerontologists have long argued the need for a life-course approach to the study of ageing and later life (Neugarten *et al.*, 1976), but it has been the critical gerontologists who have highlighted the fact that life-course experience is a major determinant of the lived experience in later life (Townsend, 1981; Walker, 1981, 1982, 2005). Social diversity is present in most societies and can be mapped against traditional structural features including gender, ethnicity, cultural background, religion, socio-economic status, social class, educational history and place. There are strong associations between many of these social and environmental characteristics, and a number of empirical and theoretical contributions in gerontology have focused on social inequalities and the cumulative nature of social advantage and disadvantage (Dannefer, 2003; Ferraro and Shippee, 2009; Higgs and Gilleard, 2006; Scharf *et al.*, 2004; Townsend and Davidson, 1982; Walker, 1993). Yet the importance of agency and social identity (Hockey and James, 2003) should not be ignored. Social structures provide the context in which life is lived but the diversity of personal characteristics will mediate experiences of the life course.

Health and wellbeing

Health and wellbeing are important issues for older people (Bowling, 1995, 2005; Victor *et al.*, 2009). In different societies and cultures and within these societies and cultures, both health and wellbeing and ageing may be described and defined from a range of perspectives and seen through a variety of lenses. Life-course experience will influence the way health and wellbeing are perceived in later life. Reflecting both the availability of statistical information and the dominance of the biomedical perspective and Western medicine, health is most often described in terms of the presence of physical and mental medical conditions or diseases such as heart disease, cancer and Alzheimer's disease. Mortality statistics describing the causes of death and morbidity statistics describing the signs and symptoms of illness are widely reported by the United Nations and World Health Organisation (World Health Organisation, 2008). Traditional medical paradigms such as Chinese medicine are poorly reflected within the International Classification of Diseases (World Health Organisation, 1992), although traditional medicine and understandings of health and wellbeing play a continuing role within lay health beliefs throughout the world. International statistics on

Table 8.1 Leading causes of death by income group[1] (% of deaths)

Cause of death	Low-income countries	Middle-income countries	High-income countries	World
Ischemic heart disease	9.4	3.4	16.3	12.2
Cerebrovascular disease	5.6	14.2	9.3	9.7
Lowe respiratory infections	11.2	3.8	3.8	7.1
Chronic obstructive pulmonary disease	3.6	7.4	3.5	5.1
Diarrhoeal diseases	6.9	−[2]	−[2]	3.7
HIV/AIDS	5.7	−[2]	−[2]	3.5
Tuberculosis	3.5	2.2	−[2]	2.5
Trachea, bronchus and lung cancers	−[2]	2.9	5.9	2.3
Road traffic accidents	−[2]	2.8	−[2]	2.2
Prematurity and low birth weight	3.2	−[2]	−[2]	2.0

Notes. [1] Countries grouped by gross national income per capita—low income ($825 or less), high income ($10066 or more).
[2] Less than 1% of deaths.
Source. World Health Organisation (2004) *The Global Burden of Disease: 2004 update.* ISBN 978 92 4 156371 0 (NLM classification: W74). http://www.who.int/healthinfo/ global_burden_disease/ 2004_report_update/ en/index.html [Accessed 4.2.2013.]

mortality and morbidity show different patterns between low-, middle- and high-income countries (Table 8.1). Increasing globalisation of disease, with a decline in mortality due to infectious disease and an increase in mortality due to chronic disease, particularly cancer and heart disease, is predicted over the next 30 years (World Health Organisation, 2008).

With globalisation, Western medicine has probably had an increasing influence on lay health beliefs, but the beliefs of older people about health and illness continue to be particular to the individual and reflect the dominant ideologies and traditional cultures of particular societies and social groups (Calnan, 1987; Charmaz, 2000). Reporting studies of older people from Europe and North America, Bond and Cabrero (2007) highlight that older people's perceptions of health and wellbeing go well beyond biomedical explanations of disease and can only readily be understood within their social and cultural context. For many older people, the perception that ill health and disease are simply part of normal ageing will depend on individual personality and the culture, time and place in which they live (Bond and Comer, 2004). Older people's perceptions of their own state of health are highly influenced by their own sense of self (Charmaz, 1983) and especially their sense of control over mind and body (Stainton Rogers, 1991). Within Europe and North America the values of capitalism and individualism play an important role in defining our conceptions of health and illness (Nettleton, 1995). They are imbued with notions of self-discipline, self-denial, self-control and will-power.

Health and wellbeing remain important for older people because of the consequences of ill health in terms of disability and dependency. Although both these concepts are highly contested (see Bond and Cabrero, 2007), from a public policy perspective they remain useful concepts for summarising the impact of disease and biological ageing on older people and their support needs and preferences.

Income and poverty

An important aspect of the lived experience of people in later life is their access to material resources. Poverty and deprivation have been a recurring theme in geronto-logical research over many years and there exists good evidence for significant levels of poverty and deprivation in older people in low-, medium- and high-income coun-tries.[2] Poverty in later life reflects the experience of people across the life course. It can be measured in absolute and relative terms. An absolute measure of poverty that is often used is the proportion of the population who live on less than \$1.25 per day. Within the European Union (EU) and OECD[3] countries a relative definition of pov-erty is used. Individuals or families are poor when their financial means are such that they are excluded from the way of living that is regarded as the acceptable minimum in the country in which they live. In EU and OECD countries, people in poverty are those who live in households where household incomes are less than 60 per cent of the median household income. A consequence of this approach is that poor people in Scandinavian countries can afford a higher level of consumption than poor people in the Mediterranean countries. In the EU, poverty rates for people aged 65 or over range from 31 per cent in Ireland to less than 1 per cent in the Netherlands (Naegele and Walker, 2007). Income inequalities in later life are also compounded by gender, ethnic, educational and socio-economic status. Other high-income countries experi-ence similar inequalities. Older people living in middle- and lower-income countries, as well as experiencing absolute poverty (around one quarter of the population (United Nations, 2011), are also likely to experience even greater income inequalities. According to the GINI Index[4] income inequalities are highest in African and South American countries (e.g. Botswana 61.0, Brazil 55.0) and lowest in most European countries (e.g. Norway 25.8, UK 36.0) (World Bank, 2009).

In low- and middle-income countries chronic poverty is often associated with the health of older people and their capacity to remain physically active and participate in formal and informal work (Heslop and Gorman, 2002). A decline in working hours as people age reflects their capacity to do hard manual labour. Older people who are unable to support themselves fully as a result of reduced earnings are often reliant on families to maintain their income. Those for whom the only source of support is their own physical labour are progressively more vulnerable to long-term poverty. A consequence of later-life poverty and the need for increasing family support is the perpetuation of chronic intergenerational poverty (Heslop and Gorman, 2002). The absence of even an embryonic social protection system for older people sustains chronic poverty and therefore increases income inequalities in many low- and middle-income countries.

Poverty within both high- and low-income countries is gendered. Evidence from across Europe shows that women are at a persistently higher risk of poverty than

[2] Countries are defined by the World Bank (http://data.worldbank.org/about/country-classifications) according to their Gross National Income (GNI per capita). In 2010, countries were divided into four groups: low-income (\$1005 or less), lower-middle-income (\$1006–\$3976), higher-middle-income (\$3976–\$12275) and high-income (\$12276 or more). Low-income and middle-income countries are sometimes referred to as developing countries.

[3] Organisation of Economic Cooperation and Development.

[4] The GINI Index is a number between 0 and 100 (United Nations, 2011), where 0 corresponds to perfect equality and 100 to perfect inequality.

men owing to a reduced earnings capacity across the life course and lower pension contributions (Naegele and Walker, 2007). Similarly, in countries without well-developed pensions systems older women who are dependent on male family members to support them at times of widowhood or physical or mental incapacity are more at risk of chronic poverty.

Living arrangements

In high-income countries, particularly in Europe and North America, the last sixty years have seen a marked change in the living arrangements of older people. The most common arrangement in high-income countries is for older people to live apart from their children. This contrasts with middle- and low-income countries, in which around three-quarters of older people live with a child or grandchild (United Nations, 2005). Overall, there has been an increase in the numbers of older people living alone or with a partner only and a decrease in those of older people living with other family members and in intergenerational households. Over the whole world, 8 per cent of older men and 19 per cent of older women live alone (United Nations, 2005; Table 8.2). Regional differences persist within Europe. Older men and women in southern Europe are more likely to live with one of their children than those living in other parts of northern and Western Europe, where they tend to live alone or with their partner (Iacovou, 2000). Urban/rural differences have also been observed: older people are more likely to live alone in urban areas and more likely to live in multi-generation households in rural areas (Mollenkopf *et al.*, 2005). As regards other parts of the world, the proportion of older people living alone is lowest in Asia and Africa and higher in countries whose populations are mainly of European origin. Latin America and the Caribbean have slightly higher proportions than Asia or Africa. Older women are more likely to live alone or in skipped-generation households or with other relatives, whereas older men are more likely to live in couple-only households. Skipped-generation households tend to be especially disadvantaged in low-income countries. As within Europe, there is much variation between countries in the developing regions. For example, the median percentage living alone for Africa is 8 per cent but in Ghana 22 per cent live alone (United Nations, 2005).

Differences in living arrangements probably reflect different economic and cultural conditions. High-income countries are more likely to possess the housing

Table 8.2 Estimated percentages of men and women aged 60 years or over living alone in different regions of the world 1995 (%)

Region	Men	Women	Total
Africa	6	11	8
Asia	5	9	7
Europe	13	35	26
Latin America and Caribbean	7	10	9
North America	15	34	26
Oceania	16	34	25
World	8	19	14

Source. Compiled from the United Nations (2005), p. 22 (Table 11.2).

infrastructure to support smaller family units, and in high-income countries where formal pension systems are developed a higher proportion of families and their older generations can afford to live in separate housing units. However, other cultural and institutional contexts will also constrain living arrangements—for example, where grandparents care for children owing to premature mortality of their parents or the childcare needs of working mothers, or in communities where small farms and family-run businesses provide an incentive for co-residence. In countries with poorly developed care services for older people, increasing dependency and infirmity militate against older people living alone. Shared intergenerational households remain a significant characteristic of living arrangements in such countries (Ruggles and Heggeness, 2008).

Family and Social Relations in Later Life

Not only are family structures and the living arrangements of older people changing, but also family relations and family practices are becoming more fluid, with traditional patterns of older people's family relations being replaced by a complex array of relationships and behaviours (Askham *et al.*, 2007). In the more developed regions of the world these may involve patchwork families of partners with children and relatives, new forms of partnership, and a growth in cohabitation, divorce, homosexual relationships and more flexible partnerships in the form of living apart together (de Jong Gierveld and Peeters, 2003). In European culture, family and other personal relationships in later life have been reported to have at least one of the characteristics shown in the box below (Askham *et al.*, 2007). Much of the research on the family lives of older people has generally ignored many of these characteristics, with an emphasis on the gendered nature of caregiving and domestic labour (Carroll and Campbell, 2008).

Characteristics of personal relationships in later life

- Intimate communication takes place, and there is a confidante relationship, or one of 'disclosing intimacy', where people gain 'shared detailed knowledge about each other' (Jamieson, 1998).
- Activities or goods are shared (held in common). This may mean sexual activity, shared home or household goods, and shared possession of children, shared leisure activities or other joint enterprises.
- The relationship is emotionally laden, with love or affection, trust, loyalty, and caring about the other.
- Practical care, personal service to the other, or exchange of resources takes place.

Social support in later life

A dominant discourse in the North American and European gerontological literature has been the view that as societies modernise and families become smaller, there is a decline in the type and level of social support provided by families. This discourse, driven by policy and political rhetoric, has little empirical support, although the potential decline in the availability of family members owing to declining fertility rates and smaller family sizes gives some credibility to policymakers' concerns. Yet this is not the first time in recent history when fertility rates have declined. The impact of the Great War (1914–18) in Europe left a whole generation of childbearing-age women bereft of male partners. Yet fertility rates recovered, particularly in the post-war 1950s. Other factors may also challenge the Doomsday scenario. Although the population is ageing there is evidence that the onset of disability and physical dependency is delayed. There is also increased joint survival of lifelong partners owing to improved survival rates for older men (Agree and Glaser, 2009).

The concerns of policymakers in North America and Europe about the future of social support in later life are also shared by low- and middle-income societies. A decline in fertility rates in a number of countries in Asia, notably China, is a particular policy concern. The absence or low availability of formal services that limits their potential substitution for informal support by family and kinship structures within local communities adds to policy concerns. Families of older people are also increasingly fluid, with more divorce and separation. Rural-to-urban migration of younger cohorts has raised concerns about rural ageing, with an increasing reliance for social support on extended kin and more distant relatives (van der Geest *et al.*, 2004). However, as with European societies, older people living in urban areas are more often isolated than their rural counterparts. Urban living increases the likelihood of poor family and social support (Ezeh *et al.*, 2006). In sub-Saharan Africa, the generation missing owing to AIDS/HIV (Velkoff and Kowal, 2006) has seen the establishment of many skipped-generation households where reciprocal support between grandparents and grandchildren has become the norm.

Dependency and interdependency—intergenerational social support

What evidence is there to support the dominant policy discourse fuelled by the analysis of demographic and epidemiological data provided by the World Bank and other dominant international institutions? Is there evidence for a decline in intergenerational support for older people in Europe, North America and other high-income industrialised societies? Is there an erosion of traditional family support for older people in developing nations through the process of modernisation and industrialisation? As we have seen, the assumptions about worldwide population ageing and changing family structures are generally supportable, but what is the evidence that family practices of intergenerational social support are changing?

In researching family practices in later life, Chambers and colleagues (2009) argue that family and kinship ties in later life are more complex than the traditional common-sense understandings of policymakers and early gerontological theories. Diverse and complex relationships exist between older people, their children and grandchildren in all cultures and societies around the world. Family relationships are actively constructed in later life, being situated within individual and collective biographies that reflect continuities and discontinuities across individual life courses. Although structures may change, families are more resilient and open to change than traditional gerontological theory suggests. Intergenerational ties, in whatever form, continue to provide a major source of reliable emotional and practical support across the generations as well as providing a key role in maintaining personal and social identities. Family and intergenerational reciprocity is arguably as strong as it ever has been (Izuhara, 2010b).

Why should this be? In different regions of the world very similar cultural and religious values underpin the support of older people. All the major world religions revere the older generations. Judaism, Christianity, Islam, Buddhism and Hinduism all articulate the doctrine and values of filial piety: the practice of respecting and caring for older parents based on the moral obligation that children owe their parents (Hashimoto and Ikels, 2005). But the practice of filial piety takes different forms within the context of different family, kinship and gender structures. In most Asian countries filial piety is situated within a strong patriarchal family system that reinforces the formal Confucian hierarchies of age and gender. In practice the eldest son is responsible for his older parents, and his wife (the daughter-in-law) is expected to undertake caregiving duties at times of illness and infirmity. Although the same hierarchy of age and gender exists in societies where Judaism and Christianity dominate, the doctrine of filial piety and social obligations to support older relatives is less explicit in secular laws derived from this tradition.

Although some European societies legislate that children should support their aged parents in times of infirmity the hierarchy of age and gender is not enshrined in law. Children of any birth order or gender are deemed responsible. In practice, in European societies and societies of predominantly European descent, it is the daughters (and in their absence any other female family member) who provide the emotional and practical caregiving role (Qureshi and Walker, 1989; RIS MRC CFAS Study Group, 1999). Evidence for the continuing role of filial piety in the support of older people across the world is based on a number of small case studies: for example, of South East China and Taiwan (Cyrus Chu *et al.*, 2011; Zhan, 2004); Tokyo and Shanghai (Izuhara, 2010a); Ghana (Aboderin, 2003); the USA and the Netherlands (Cooney and Dykstra, 2011); and the UK (Finch, 1989).

Public Policy and Later Life

As Izuhara (2010b) rightly explains, family practice and intergenerational relations are strongly influenced by societal structures and policies. In general, government policies, where they exist, are all based on the premise that population ageing, urbanisation and domestic and international migration will erode contemporary family practice and intergenerational relations further than described to date. Yet, as we have seen, analysts who have taken a life-course perspective and investigated contemporary family practice at the micro level are more optimistic about how different societies will respond to the challenges of population ageing. They have highlighted shifts in the way families have supported older people from practical support to emotional, financial and organisational support, reflecting a transition from material reciprocity to psychological independence. Some have suggested that families and intergenerational relations may hold the key to resolving many of the challenges due to rapid population ageing. The very nature of families—relatedness, interdependence and solidarity, and age integration—can influence and transform societal practice through the continuation of a viable social contract between generations (Bengston and Putney, 2006).

Historically, all societies have managed the support of dependent older people with different degrees of dignity. The support of older people in the community by families and kin dominates in all regions of the world, but is often hidden from view (Patel and

Prince, 2001; Prince *et al.*, 2008). In countries of European descent there has been a long tradition of institutional care where the immediate family have been unable or unwilling to support dependent family members (Thomson, 1983). Thus the boundary between family and community support and state support has long been fluid and this is set to continue, but with increasing pressure to reduce the financial burden on the state (Estes *et al.*, 2001). How, then, should public policy respond to the challenge of the ageing population?

Future public policies will be driven by dominant economic and political discourses. In societies with established welfare states the ethic of collectivism is being undermined by the individualisation of risk and privatisation of social policy (Phillipson, 2006). Although families rather than states will remain at the forefront of supporting older people, continuing state support will be essential if older citizens are to be able to age with dignity. At times when individuals and families are encouraged by the ubiquitous consumerism of the twenty-first century to live for the present, and those without resources are obliged to survive in the present, long-term planning for later life is a minority activity for many world citizens. Those who have resources will adapt and provide for the future, but for the majority, who lack sufficient resources to maintain an adequate standard of living relative to the society in which they live, little preparation for later life will be possible. With continuing globalisation and industrialisation there will always be a continuing role for the state in preparing citizens for later life. Depending on the culture, such planning would include legislative and societal structures to enable people of all ages in good health to maintain a flexible work portfolio, to support families and community networks, and to support individuals to provide financially for later life. Compulsory contributions towards an old age pension and long-term care insurance will continue to be essential to enable older people to live independently within their traditional community and family networks.

References

Aboderin, I. (2003) 'Modernisation' and economic strain: the impact of social change on material family support for older people in Ghana, in V. L. Bengston and A. Lowenstein (eds), *Global Ageing and Families* (New York: de Gruyter), 284–302.

Agree, E. M. and Glaser, K. (2009) Demography of informal caregiving, in P. Uhlenberg (ed.), *International Handbook of Population Ageing* (New York: Springer), 647–668.

Askham, J., Ferring, D. and Lamura, G. (2007) Personal relationships in later life, in J. Bond, S. Peace, F. Dittmann-Kohli and G. Westerhof (eds), *Ageing in Society: European perspectives on gerontology* (London: Sage), 186–208.

Bengston, V. L. and Putney, N. M. (2006) Future conflicts across generations and cohorts, in J. A. Vincent, C. R. Phillipson and M. Downs (eds), *The Futures of Old Age* (London: Sage), 20–29.

Bengston, V. L., Rosenthal, C. and Burton, L. M. (1990) Families and ageing: diversity and heterogeneity, in R. Binstock and L. K. George (eds), *Handbook of Ageing and the Social Sciences* (San Diego, CA: Academic Press), 3rd edn, 263–287.

Bond, J. and Cabrero, G. R. (2007) Health and dependency in later life, in J. Bond, S. Peace, F. Dittmann-Kohli and G. Westerhof (eds), *Ageing in Society: European perspectives on gerontology* (London: Sage), 3rd edn, 113–141.

Bond, J. and Corner, L. (2004) *Quality of Life and Older People* (Maidenhead: Open University Press).

Bowling, A. (1995) What things are important in people's lives? A survey of the public's judgements to inform scales of health related quality of life, *Social Science and Medicine*, 41(10): 1447–1462.

Bowling, A. (2005) *Ageing Well: Quality of life in old age* (Maidenhead: Open University Press).

Calnan, M. (1987) *Health and Illness: The lay perspective* (London, New York: Tavistock).

Carroll, M. and Campbell, L. (2008) Who now reads Parsons and Bales? Casting a critical eye on the 'gendered styles of caregiving' literature, *Journal of Ageing Studies*, 22: 24–31.

Chambers, P., Allan, G., Phillipson, C. and Ray, M. (2009) *Family Practices in Later Life* (Bristol: The Policy Press).

Charmaz, K. (1983) Loss of Self: a fundamental form of suffering in the chronically ill, *Sociology of Health and Illness*, 5(2): 168–195.

Charmaz, K. (2000) Experiencing chronic illness, in G. L. Albrecht, R. Fitzpatrick and S. C. Scrimshaw (eds), *Handbook of Social Studies in Health and Medicine* (London: Sage), 277–292.

Cooney, T. M. and Dykstra, P. A. (2011) Family obligations and support behaviour: a United States–Netherlands comparison, *Ageing and Society*, 31(6): 1026–1050.

Cyrus Chu, C. Y., Xie, Y. and Yu, R. R. (2011) Coresidence with elderly parents: a comparative study of Southeast China and Taiwan, *Journal of Marriage and Family*, 73: 120–135.

Dannefer, D. (2003) Cumulative advantage/disadvantage and the life course: cross-fertilising age and social science theory, *Journal of Gerontology*, 58B(6): SS327–337.

De Jong Gierveld, J. and Peeters, A. (2003) The interweaving of repartnered older adults' lives with their children and siblings, *Ageing and Society*, 23(2): 187–205.

Estes, C. L., Alford, R. R., Binney, E. A., Bradsher, J. E., Close, L., Collins, C. A., Egan, A. H., Harrington, C., Linkins, K. W., Lynch, M., Mahakian, J. L., Pellow, D. N., Wallace, S. P. and Weitz, T. A. (2001) *Social Policy and Ageing: A critical perspective* (Thousand Oaks, CA: Sage).

Estes, C. L. and Binney, E. (1989) The biomedicalisation of ageing: dangers and dilemmas, *Gerontologist*, 29(5): 587–596.

Ezeh, A. C., Chepngeno, G., Kasiira, A. Z. and Woubalem, Z. (2006) The situation of older people in poor urban settings: the case of Nairobi, Kenya, in B. Cohen, J. Menken and Division of Behavioural and Social Sciences and Education Committee on Population (eds), *Aging in Sub-Saharan Africa: Recommendations for furthering research* (Washington DC: National Academies Press), 189–213.

Ferraro, K. F. and Shippee, T. P. (2009) Ageing and cumulative inequality: how does inequality get under the skin, *Gerontologist*, 49(3): 333–343.

Finch, J. (1989) *Family Obligations and Social Change* (Cambridge: Polity Press).

Giele, J. Z. and Elder, G. H. (1998) *Methods of Life Course Research: Qualitative and quantitative approaches* (Thousand Oaks, CA: Sage).

Gilleard, C. and Higgs, P. (2000) *Cultures of Ageing: Self, citizen and the body* (Harlow: Prentice Hall).

Hashimoto, A. and Ikels, C. (2005) Filial piety in changing Asian societies, in M. L. Johnson, V. L. Bengston, P. G. Coleman and T. Kirkwood (eds), *The Cambridge Handbook of Age and Ageing* (Cambridge: Cambridge University Press), 437–442.

Heslop, A. and Gorman, M. (2002) *Chronic Poverty and Older People in the Developing World*, CPRC Working Paper No. 10 (London: HelpAge International).

Higgs, P. and Gilleard, C. (2006) Class, power and inequality in later life, in S. Daatland and S. Biggs (eds), *Ageing and Diversity: Multiple pathways and cultural migrations* (Bristol: The Policy Press), 207–222.

Hockey, J. and James, A. (2003) *Social Identities Across the Life Course* (Basingstoke: Palgrave Macmillan).

Iacovou, M. (2000) *The Living Arrangements of Elderly Europeans* (University of Essex: Institute for Social and Economic Research).

Izuhara, M. (2010a) Housing wealth and family reciprocity in East Asia, in M. Izuhara (ed.), *Ageing and Intergenerational Relations: Family reciprocity from a global perspective* (Bristol: The Policy Press), 77–94.

Izuhara, M. (2010b) New patterns of family reciprocity: policy challenges in ageing societies, in M. Izuhara (ed.), *Ageing and Intergenerational Relations: Family reciprocity from a global perspective* (Bristol: The Policy Press), 149–159.

Katz, S. (1992) Alarmist demography: power, knowledge and elderly population, *Journal of Ageing Studies*, 6(3): 203–225.

Laslett, P. (1987) The emergence of the third age, *Ageing and Society*, 7: 133–160.

McIntyre, S. (1977) Old age as a social problem, in R. Dingwall, C. Health, M. Reid and M. Stacy (eds), *Health Care and Health Knowledge* (London: Croom Helm), 41–63.

Mannheim, K. (1952) The problem of generations, in P. Kecskemeti (ed.), *Essays on the Sociology of Knowledge* (London: Routledge & Kegan Paul), 276–320.

Mollenkopf, H., Marcellini, F., Ruoppila, I., Szeman, Z. and Tacken, M. (2005) *Enhancing Mobility in Later Life—Personal coping, environmental resources and technical support. The out-of-home mobility of older adults in urban and rural regions of five European countries* (Amsterdam: IOS Press).

Naegele, G. and Walker, A. (2007) Social protection: incomes, poverty and the reform of the pension systems, in J. Bond, S. Peace, F. Dittmann-Kohli and G. Westerhof (eds), *Ageing in Society: European perspectives on gerontology* (London: Sage), 3rd edn, 142–166.

National Research Council (2006) Aging in Sub-Saharan Africa: recommendations for furthering research, panel on policy research and data needs to meet the challenges of aging in Africa, in B. Cohen, J. Menken and Division of Behavioural and Social Sciences and Education Committee on Population (eds), *Aging in Sub-Saharan Africa: Recommendations for furthering research* (Washington DC: National Academies Press), 7–45.

Nettleton, S. (1995) *The Sociology of Health and Illness* (Cambridge: Polity Press).

Neugarten, B. L., Hagestad, G. O., Binstock, R. H. and Shanas, E. (1976) Age and the life course, in R. H. Binstock and E. Shanas (eds), *Handbook of Ageing and the Social Sciences* (New York: Van Nostrand Reinhold).

Oeppen, J. and Vaupel, J. W. (2002) Demography. Broken limits to life expectancy, *Science*, 296: 1029–1031.

Patel, V. and Prince, M. (2001) Ageing and mental health in a developing country: who cares? Qualitative studies from Goa, India, *Psychological Medicine*, 31: 29–38.

Phillipson, C. (2006) Ageing and globalisation: issues for critical gerontology and political economy, in J. Baars, D. Dannefer, C. Phillipson and A. Walker (eds), *Ageing, Globalisation and Inequality* (New York: Baywood), 43–58.

Prince, M., Acosta, D., Albanese, E., Arizaga, R., Ferri, C., Guerra, M., Huang, Y., Jacob, K., Jimenez-Velazquez, I. Z., Rodriguez, J. L., Salas, A., Sosa, A. L., Sousa, R., Uwakwe, R., van der Poel, R., Williams, J. and Wortmann, M. (2008) Ageing and dementia in low and middle income countries—using research to engage with public and policymakers, *International Review of Psychiatry*, 20(4): 332–343.

Qureshi, H. and Walker, A. (1989) *The Caring Relationship: Elderly people and their families* (London: Macmillan).

RIS MRC CFAS Resource Implications Study Group of the Medical Research Council Cognitive Function and Ageing Study (1999) Informal caregiving for frail older people at home and in long-term care institutions: who are the key supporters?, *Health and Social Care in the Community*, 7(6): 434–444.

Robertson, A. (1997) Beyond apocalyptic demography: towards a moral economy of interdependence, *Ageing and Society*, 17: 425–446.

Ruggles, S. and Heggeness, M. (2008). Intergenerational coresidence in developing countries, *Population and Development Review*, 34(2): 253–281.

Scharf, T., Phillipson, C., Smith, A. E., Walker, A. and Hagan Hennessy, C. (2004) Poverty and social exclusion: growing older in deprived urban neighbourhoods, in A. Walker (ed.), *Growing Older: Quality of life in old age* (Maidenhead: Open University Press).

Stainton Rogers, W. (1991) *Explaining Health and Illness* (Hemel Hempstead: Harvester Wheatsheaf).

Thomson, D. (1983) Workhouse to nursing home: residential care of elderly people in England since 1840, *Ageing and Society*, 3: 41–69.

Townsend, P. (1981) The structured dependency of the elderly: a creation of social policy in the twentieth century, *Ageing and Society*, 1: 5–28.

Townsend, P. and Davidson, N. (1982) *Inequalities in Health: The Black Report* (Harmondsworth: Penguin).

United Nations (2005) *The Living Arrangements of Older People Around the World* (New York: Department of Economic and Social Affairs/Population Division).

United Nations (2009) *World Population Ageing 2009* (New York: United Nations).

United Nations (2011) *The Millennium Development Goals Report 2011* (New York: United Nations).

Van der Geest, S., Mul. A. and Vermeulen, H. (2004) Linkages between migration and the care of frail older people: observations from Greece, Ghana and the Netherlands, *Ageing and Society*, 24(3): 431–450.

Velkoff, V. A. and Kowal, P. R. (2006) Ageing in Sub Saharan Africa: the changing demography of the region, in B. Cohen, J. Menken and Division of Behavioural and Social Sciences and Education Committee on Population (eds), *Aging in Sub-Saharan Africa: Recommendations for furthering research* (Washington DC: The National Academic Press), 55–91.

Victor, C., Scambler, S. and Bond, J. (2009) *The Social World of Older People: Understanding loneliness and social isolation in later life* (Maidenhead: Open University Press).

Walker, A. (1981) Towards a political economy of old age, *Ageing and Society*, 1: 73–94.

Walker, A. (1982) Dependency and old age, *Social Policy and Administration*, 16: 115–135.

Walker, A. (1983) Poverty and inequality in old age, in J. Bond, P. Coleman and S. Peace (eds), *Ageing in Society: An introduction to social gerontology* (London: Sage), 2nd edn, 280–303.

Walker, A. (2005) Towards an international political economy, *Ageing and Society*, 25(6): 815–838.

Westendorp, R. G. J. and Kirkwood, T. B. L. (2007) The biology of ageing, in J. Bond, S. Peace, F. Dittmann-Kohli and G. J. Westerhof (eds), *Ageing in Society: European perspectives on gerontology* (London: Sage), 3rd edn, 15–37.

World Bank (2009) *World Bank 2009 World Development Indicators* (Washington, DC: World Bank).

World Health Organisation (1992) *ICD-10 International Statistical Classification of Diseases and Related Health Problems* (Geneva: WHO), 10th revision, version for 2007.

World Health Organisation (2004) *The Global Burden of Disease: 2004 update*. ISBN 978 92 4 156371 0 (NLM classification: W74). http://www.who.int/ healthinfo/ global_burden_disease/ 2004_report_ update/en/index.html [Accessed 4.2.2013.]

World Health Organisation (2008) *The Global Burden of Disease: 2008 update* (Geneva: World Health Organisation).

Zhan, H. J. (2004) Willingness and expectations: intergenerational differences in attitudes toward filial responsibility in China, *Marriage and Family Review*, 36: 175–200.

Part II

Parenthood, Parenting and Family Life

The chapters in Part II of the book look specifically at global changes in respect of parenthood and parenting. Some of these changes, such as same-sex parenting, are not universally accepted, and indeed, this section considers issues which cause controversy in debates about modern approaches to parenthood and addresses concerns about the potential detrimental effects on children and young people. This objective review of the evidence is essential if we are to understand parenting within a broad, global context and encourage policymakers and practitioners to provide appropriate support for parents in a range of circumstances.

In the first chapter (Chapter 9), Janet Walker reflects on the potential for parenthood to place additional stressors on couple relationships. Referring to a study of couple relationships in England, she draws attention to societal expectations that having a baby is a rewarding and joyful experience when the reality for many parents, particularly mothers, is often different. A growing number of women across the globe have more choice than ever before about whether, and when, to have children, but they are not always well-prepared for the impact parenthood has on couple relationships and on other aspects of family life. Walker argues for greater understanding about how the transition to parenthood can destabilise couple relationships and calls for more supportive interventions that do not simply focus on the wellbeing of the baby, and which include fathers as well as mothers.

Choice in parenthood has also contributed to low fertility rates, delayed motherhood and an increase in childlessness among younger generations in Europe. Maria Letizia Tanturri (Chapter 10) carefully examines the factors contributing to low fertility and highlights constraints which indicate that couples are not necessarily fulfilling their reproductive desires. A critical analysis of a number of explanatory

Contemporary Issues in Family Studies: Global Perspectives on Partnerships, Parenting and Support in a Changing World, First Edition. Edited by Angela Abela and Janet Walker.
© 2014 John Wiley & Sons, Ltd. Published 2014 by John Wiley & Sons, Ltd.

models leads Tanturri to the conclusion that low fertility is the result of a plurality of factors, all of which must be understood if demographic growth is to be encouraged. The economic recession also contributes to declining fertility rates and, in Tanturri's view, a consistent set of family-friendly policies is essential to counteract the impacts.

The significant changes in couple relationships and the diversity of family structures have reopened interest in theories of child development and placed renewed focus on the important role fathers can play. Gabriela Misca and Jo Smith (Chapter 11) investigate the continuity of attachment relationships across the life course and apply Bronfenbrenner's ecological model of development in order to understand the implications of various family structures on child development. They ask the question 'How important is the traditional two-parent household for children's wellbeing?' They reach the conclusion that the quality of the family environment, including the relationship between the parents/carers, irrespective of family structures, is a key factor in the healthy adjustment, development and wellbeing of children. All kinds of parenting arrangements, including those involving same-sex parents, can provide an environment in which children can thrive.

These themes are discussed further in the following two chapters. In Chapter 12, Jan Nicholson and her colleagues at the Parenting Research Centre in Melbourne, Australia, use three waves of longitudinal data relating to two cohorts of Australian children in order to tease out the factors which impact on the parenting and mental health of single mothers. This robust study assessed parenting across seven domains and showed that exposure to adverse risk factors was very different for single and couple mothers. While these findings are consistent with studies elsewhere, Nicholson and her colleagues have demonstrated just how stark the differences are between family types in contemporary Western society, particularly with respect to socio-economic disadvantage and poverty. This chapter challenges the negative labelling of single mothers as being worse parents than mothers in couple relationships and demands that we should be seeking ways to support parents who face adversity.

This message is reinforced in Chapter 13, in which Charlotte Patterson, Rachel Riskind and Samantha Tornello explore the experiences of same-sex couples as parents. Around the world views are divided about the acceptability of same-sex parenting, and this chapter addresses the concerns expressed by some commentators that children brought up by same-sex parents do less well. The authors refer to contemporary research which has shown that the mental health and adjustment of children and parents are not linked with sexual orientation and that children born to or adopted by lesbian or gay parents are as likely as other children to thrive. Many of the stresses same-sex parents experience are just the same as those reported by parents in all kinds of family structure. Nevertheless, attitudes towards same-sex couples vary considerably and a more liberal legal climate does not necessarily reduce the negative stereotyping of same-sex relationships or the deeply held beliefs about the pre-eminence of heteronormative models.

The final three chapters in Part II focus on specific aspects of parenting that, rightly, are receiving increased attention. John Coleman (Chapter 14) examines the challenges associated with parenting teenagers; Simon Burnett, Jonathan Swan and Cary Cooper (Chapter 15) discuss the effects of balancing work and domestic commitments; and Paul Amato and Lisa Boyd (Chapter 16) take a global perspective in considering the impact of parental divorce on children's wellbeing.

The increased focus in recent years on parenting and children's wellbeing has drawn attention to the complexities facing parents in a world where social and economic changes are having a significant impact on family life. Until recently, relatively little research had been undertaken with a specific focus on adolescence and parental relationships. John Coleman reminds us that the way in which teenagers relate to their families is very variable across the globe, and he distinguishes between different parenting styles within the context of different family structures and different cultural and ethnic contexts. He also points to the key roles played by friends, particularly when young people are experiencing conflict and disruption at home. He takes the view that parenting teenagers in the modern world is an increasingly challenging task.

Chapter 15 returns to a theme which is referred to in many chapters in this book: the pressures and expectations placed on parents today to be economically self-sufficient and combine caring responsibilities with employment outside the home. Taking Britain as a case study, Burnett and colleagues examine the impact of the long-hours work culture found in capitalist economies on relationships within the family, and on increasing stress-related illnesses and stress-induced behaviours. There is increasing recognition of the importance of flexible working patterns, but work–life balance remains a sensitive issue, particularly during a time of global economic turmoil when employment is less secure and quality-of-life issues are often subordinate to business stability and growth. Inevitably, this chapter touches on changing gender roles and changing attitudes towards who should provide care for family members. The authors argue strongly for policies that place a high priority on parental care for children without reinforcing traditional gender roles or restricting mothers' progression in the labour market.

In the final chapter in this part of the book, Amato and Boyd provide a meta-analysis of research conducted across the globe into parental divorce and children's wellbeing. Many concerns have been expressed about the detrimental impact of divorce on children's wellbeing and developmental outcomes and many reviews on this subject have been published in recent years. Whereas most of these reviews have focused on research undertaken in predominantly English-speaking countries, this review takes a far broader approach. The chapter builds on the discussions about divorce in Chapters 4 and 5, and highlights studies undertaken in Mexico, China and Norway. The analysis points to the complexities in understanding the effects of divorce on children and clearly illustrates that the association between family structure and child wellbeing depends on a variety of contextual factors. The authors offer the tentative conclusion that there is a need to protect children from what they have found to be the potentially harmful consequences of high levels of family disruption.

All the chapters in Part II focus on changes in parenting and on the implications for children's overall wellbeing. This dual focus reminds us of the obvious tension between promoting continuity in the best interests of children and facilitating change which embraces choice and new opportunities. All the chapters in Parts I and II assist in identifying more clearly the family processes that foster wellbeing and resilience in adults and in children living in all types of family.

9

The Transition to Parenthood
Choices and Responsibilities

Janet Walker

Introduction

The family unit is widely regarded as the ideal human community in which a child's physical, developmental and emotional needs will be met, even though family structures have been evolving and changing throughout history. Raising children has always been an integral part of family life, and until relatively recently having a baby and the responsibilities associated with parenthood have received little public attention. For centuries, marriage, parenthood and family life have gone hand in hand, in what can be described as 'a package deal' (Struening, 2002), and scant attention has been paid to how couples have managed the transition to parenthood and its impact on the couple relationship. The increased interest shown by policymakers and health and social care practitioners in parenting and parental relationships in recent years has been prompted, primarily, by two factors: first, the unparalleled shifts in the ways in which families are formed and re-formed; and, second, the growing acknowledgement that the quality of family relationships and the quality of parenting have far-reaching implications for the long-term health and wellbeing of children and young people. In short, good parenting matters: being a parent is now recognised as one of the most important tasks adults undertake and research has shown that having children has significant consequences for the quality of couple relationships.

This chapter examines the changing patterns of family life and parenthood, the responsibilities and expectations associated with parenting in the twenty-first century, the choices adults make about whether and when to have children, and the policy and practice implications of these changes and choices. The discussion focuses specifically

Contemporary Issues in Family Studies: Global Perspectives on Partnerships, Parenting and Support in a Changing World, First Edition. Edited by Angela Abela and Janet Walker.
© 2014 John Wiley & Sons, Ltd. Published 2014 by John Wiley & Sons, Ltd.

on the transition to parenthood and explores the growing literature about how this impacts on couple relationships and family stability. It also considers how families, and parents in particular, can be supported to meet their parenting responsibilities and nurture their relationships.

The Drivers of Change

Traditionally, marriage has been viewed as the precursor to becoming a parent: indeed, Christianity regards the procreation of children as a key function of marriage, and many other religions put similar emphasis on the importance of procreation. Moreover, families, usually comprising a married couple and their children, have increasingly been regarded as the bedrock of stable societies. An evidence paper prepared by the UK Government (Cabinet Office/Department for Children, Schools and Families, 2008) emphasised the important role of child rearing:

> Families are the bedrock of our society, providing a wide range of functions. They nurture children, help to build strength, resilience and moral values in young people, and provide the love and encouragement that helps them lead fulfilling lives. Families are vital in ensuring all children have good life chances ... (p. 7)

There can be little doubt about the value placed on parenting. In Western countries, the structural-functional concept of the ideal family has been extremely influential in promoting what is widely referred to as the 'traditional' family. Within the traditional family, paternal and maternal roles are clearly defined and delineated and designed to be complementary. Fathers are expected to be the breadwinner—instrumentally oriented—while mothers are expected to be the homemaker and to look after the children—expressively oriented (Walker, 2013). Gender role complementarity and division of labour are commonly considered to offer stability for adults and children and to meet the needs of wider society. Not surprisingly, therefore, the substantial changes in family life over the last half century have been viewed by some as a severe threat.

This structural-functional conceptualisation has been criticised from a number of perspectives (Dahlström, 1989). Although there have been clear differences between the roles of men and women in the home, they have not been mutually exclusive and there has always been considerable diversity in family forms. Nevertheless, it has long been popular for social commentators to view the decline of the traditional family and the blossoming and acceptance of other family constellations (e.g. stepfamilies, gay and lesbian families, lone-parent families) as signalling the demise of stability within society. Such fears are not new: this tendency to agonise about the decline of traditional family life has been evident for centuries.

A review of the historical evidence, however, questions the idealised image of stability in family life in previous centuries, and highlights the realities of extramarital sex and out-of-wedlock conceptions, stepfamilies, domestic abuse, lone motherhood and poverty, all of which have been in existence for hundreds, if not thousands, of years (Thane, 2010). Nevertheless, the unequal economic status of men and women continued until the last half of the twentieth century, reinforced by traditional conceptions of marriage and parenthood. It was not until the 1970s in Western

Europe that the strong pro-traditional perspective on family life began to give way to a more balanced view of family roles and responsibilities as both marriage and birth rates declined and the employment of women outside the home increased. As a consequence of these changes, men and women today are managing their personal relationships in a variety of ways. Although most young people still expect to marry at some time in their lives, people are delaying marriage and parenthood, and cohabitation is commonplace, either as a precursor to or as an alternative to getting married.

There is strong evidence, however, that family life and parenthood are still highly valued (Anderson *et al.*, 2000; Walker *et al.*, 2010). This suggests that the choices adults make are influenced by both the traditional notions of familism and the more modern shifts towards individualism. Dahlström (1989), in a comparative analysis of 14 European countries, identified four contradictions or tensions in modern family life, all of which can influence how couples experience the transition to parenthood. These are indicated in the box below and considered in turn.

Tensions in modern family life

- Between production—paid employment outside the home—and reproduction.
- Between privacy in family life and increased attempts by governments to regulate and influence how families behave.
- Between increased freedom of choice in conjugal relations and the need for stability in children's lives.
- Between a patriarchal heritage and the quest for gender equality.

Paid employment and childbearing

In many countries there is increased acceptance of a wide variety of family structures, and greater equality and economic independence for women. The dramatic increase in opportunities for women, particularly in respect of access to education and the ability to develop a career outside the home, has undoubtedly had an impact on traditional gender roles and the division of labour within the home, as well as on the gender power balance in couple relationships. In the twenty-first century, the majority of mothers in developed societies are working outside the home, either through economic necessity or as a matter of choice, or both. The idealised picture of a male provider and female carer no long captures the reality of people's everyday lives (Williams, 2004). Within Europe, a central tenet of modern social policy is the encouragement of both men and women to be economically self-sufficient through paid employment. Indeed, the strong work ethic which has underpinned welfare reform in Britain since the 1990s provides the rationale to reduce dependency on state support, alleviate and eradicate child poverty and encourage people to take responsibility for their own lives and wellbeing. These shifts are in stark contrast to the marginalisation and condemnation of families in which mothers took full-time work to support their children in the 1950s and 1960s: mothers who moved to Britain from the Caribbean countries, for example, were accused of neglecting their children when they routinely sought paid employment. Combining childcare and paid work is not easy, however, and it creates tensions, particularly for mothers (see Chapter 15, this volume). While gender roles may be more fluid, they are still influenced by enduring conceptions of gender differences, and the choices women make tend to be embedded in moral considerations and normative ideas about what is best for children (Duncan, 2003). Some UK studies (Duncan and Smith, 2002) have noted the significance of local context on patterns of partnering and parenting and the construction of family lives. The norms embedded in local social networks and institutions, such as around what it means to be a good mother or father, have a strong influence on the choices people make.

The regulation of family life

Concerns about the demise of the traditional family and the potential adverse consequences for children have resulted in increased intervention by governments keen to restore and protect stable family environments. Supporting families in order to support parenting has been evident in UK government policies, for example, since the turn of the century, despite research evidence that non-traditional family forms are not necessarily harmful to children. Williams (2004), in a review of a five-year study of changes in parenting and partnering, noted four shifts in the way policies have reshaped an understanding of marriage and family relations. These are indicated in the box below.

> ### Shifts in policies relating to marriage and family relations
>
> 1. Economic and welfare policy has moved away from the male breadwinner model towards an adult worker model in which both men and women are expected to be in paid employment.
> 2. Couple relations, including partnerships, marriage, separation and divorce, have become a private matter for the adults involved to negotiate; and marriage and parenthood are no longer regarded as necessarily going together.
> 3. Parenthood and parenting, by contrast, have become less private and more an issue of public regulation to ensure that parental responsibilities are fulfilled in the best interests of children's wellbeing and development.
> 4. Recognition of previously excluded partnerships, most significantly same-sex partnerships and legally permitted civil partnerships, has increased and gay marriage/parenting is no longer a taboo issue.

These policy shifts mean that the status of couple relationships has become less important in public policy debates while the quality and continuity of parenting have assumed far greater significance. There are far greater expectations of parents and parenting than in times past, irrespective of whether parents are married, divorced, living alone or in same-sex partnerships. Parenthood is regarded as carrying a range of responsibilities—something parents do (family practices), rather than something they are (Department for Education and Skills, 2007). The concept of family practices focuses attention on everyday interactions and the ways in which relationships are negotiated and shaped. Family practices are fluid and determined less by the traditional obligations and expectations associated with a male-breadwinner model of family life, and more by reference to what is in children's best interests—providing the optimal conditions in which children are healthy, safe, able to achieve educationally and enjoy life, and prepared for making an economic contribution as adults.

Freedom of choice and the need for stability

Greater privacy in respect of couple relationships and acceptance of a variety of family forms have given men and women greater choice about how and when they form a relationship with another adult, the kind of relationship they seek and the expectations they have of an intimate and enduring partnership (Cabinet Office/Department for Children, Schools and Families, 2008), as well as ever-higher expectations of what that partnership can offer in terms of personal emotional benefits beyond the procreation of children (Walker, 2008).

There are, nevertheless, some conundrums. Vastly improved methods of birth control have facilitated a more liberal attitude towards sexual behaviour outside marriage, and most people enter marriage having experienced previous sexual relationships: an increasing trend that has been in evidence for over a hundred years. By contrast, expectations of fidelity in marriage are substantially greater than in the past and adulterous relationships are more likely to threaten the stability and durability of marital relationships than in previous generations. A renewed emphasis on the privacy of family life, an increased expectation of achieving emotional companionship and gender equality in couple relationships, and a positive focus on sexuality beyond its function in procreation have all added to the opportunities and the pressures in modern partnerships.

A number of leading social theorists (Beck, 1992; Giddens, 1992; Beck and Beck-Gersheim, 1995) have long argued that we are living in a period of de-traditionalisation and increased individualism in which adults are increasingly compelled to make their own choices as they are freed from externally imposed constraints, moral codes and traditional customs. People no longer face pre-ordained life trajectories but can search for a family of choice. Moreover, they can decide whether and when to have children, and the transition to parenthood is no longer intrinsically linked to marital status. One consequence of this is the potential conflict between adults' need for intimacy and emotional satisfaction and children's need for stability. Struening (2002) has suggested that the voluntary nature of modern partnerships, freely entered into, has rendered them both fragile and strong: fragile, because feelings are changeable and when intimacy is not satisfied there are few economic and social constraints keeping partners together in an unhappy relationship, even when they have children; and strong because freely chosen relationships carry with them an integrity and dignity which those embedded in economic dependence or coercion do not.

The tension between familism and individualism is at its most fraught when one partner is no longer convinced that their couple relationship is fulfilling the need for intimacy, and intimate relations are often disrupted during and after the transition to parenthood. Faced with disappointment in their couple relationship, parents struggle to 'do the right thing', aware that their own search for fulfilment may have seriously damaging consequences for their children's health and wellbeing. The research evidence indicates that the vast majority of parents do not end relationships and disrupt family life without thinking long and hard about their choices and their responsibilities (Walker, 2006). Nevertheless, the increasing number of children who experience the break-up of their parents' relationship and face severe disruption in their daily living arrangements has caused increasing concern throughout the Western world. While the vast majority of people expect a committed relationship, usually symbolised by marriage, to last for life, the reality is that increasing numbers of relationships are ended by one or both parties. These trends are fully explored in Chapter 4 in this volume. Without doubt, the emphasis on achieving personal fulfilment has changed the ways in which young adults view and form partnerships and approach parenthood.

Children thrive best in families characterised by predictable and consistent care (Coleman and Glenn, 2009) and such care is closely associated with stable and harmonious relationships between the parents. A significant body of research also documents the benefits in psychological and physical health that are evident across the lifespan for adults and children living in stable, supportive relationships (Kiecolt-Glaser and Newton, 2001). Conversely, there is an unequivocal association between couple relationship breakdown and adult ill health and mortality (Murphy, 2007) and negative health outcomes for children (Strohschein, 2005). The quality of adult couple relationships has both direct and indirect effects on the partners and on their children (Davies *et al.*, 2004). Not surprisingly, therefore, governments in many countries have sought to protect children and to support families by putting increasing emphasis on promoting good parenting and preventing family breakdown. Understanding the stresses associated with parenthood has become a critical dimension in the development of appropriate support services.

Patriarchal heritage, gender equality and the transition to parenthood

Modern partnerships demand a high level of personal maturity and good communication and negotiation skills. Although men and women in Western societies are able to contract an equal partnership as they enter a cohabiting or marital relationship with only themselves to consider, when they have children the allocation of parenting tasks tends to be far from equal. The responsibilities for childcare still fall primarily on mothers, even though the majority are in paid work outside the home. The increased freedoms within conjugal relationships often conflict with the constraints and decisions inherent in parenthood, and the majority of fathers continue to see their role as breadwinners as the central aspect of being a good father (Walker, 2006). Hence, the transition to parenthood can severely test the stability of modern couple relationships and everyday family life as the patriarchal heritage threatens newly found gender equality. While the psychological literature has moved away from a belief in the exclusivity of the mother–child relationship, accepting that children form multiple attachments (explored more fully in Chapter 11, this volume), fathers usually spend less time than mothers with their children and are less likely to take responsibility for their everyday care (Clarke and O'Brien, 2004). The resulting role strain for mothers can have a detrimental impact on conjugal relationships. Whereas having a baby inevitably disrupts mothers' working patterns, few men shift their work commitments to accommodate the transition to parenthood, even when paternity leave is available, except, perhaps, in Scandinavia. The enormous changes that having a baby entails and the high societal expectations of them as parents are associated by many couples with a period of very high stress.

Becoming a Parent

The declining birth rate has been one of the two most important demographic changes across Europe in recent decades (see Chapter 10, this volume). The other is the decrease in mortality and longer life expectancies (see Chapter 8, this volume). Historically, fertility has followed a series of oscillations, but the fertility decline across Europe in recent decades denotes a significant change in the reproductive models of the European population as a whole (Saporiti, 1989). In traditional societies, reproductive behaviour was supported by religious values, moral codes, laws and customs, while in modern societies it has increasingly become a matter of individual choice, principally that of women.

In the past, women could exercise little choice about whether and when to have a baby. Pregnancy followed marriage, and repeated pregnancies followed childbirth. High infant mortality rates often meant successive pregnancies. Having children was not always a cause for celebration, and many mothers died during or shortly after childbirth while others experienced a regular cycle of pregnancy, about which they had little choice. Women in Western societies today have far more choice, and couple relationships and family life have changed as a consequence. Moreover, as cohabitation increasingly becomes the couple relationship of choice, more babies are being born outside marriage, either to cohabiting couples or into single-parent households (see e.g. ONS, 2008). Having children is no longer an inevitable outcome of adults deciding to live together as a couple and many people choose to delay parenthood in order to establish their career, have fewer children (see e.g. ONS, 2009) or reject parenthood altogether. Individuals are able to make their own reproductive choices and, as a result, the transition to parenthood has assumed greater significance. While parenting and caring continue to be central elements in modern family life, the transition to parenthood appears to present a number of challenges for those in companionate relationships.

A large body of research (Hirschberger et al., 2009) has shown that the vast majority of couples begin their lives together with a high level of relationship satisfaction, but that this declines over the next 15 years. It is normal to experience disappointment and to evaluate relationships more negatively as time goes on, and the transitions which are commonplace across the lifespan often trigger increased stress and relationship strain. Family transitions have been described as 'long term processes that result in a qualitative reorganisation of both inner life and external behaviour' (Cowan and Cowan, 2012, p. 5). Becoming a parent leads to changes in identity and a restructuring of roles and relationships, but each partner may experience these changes differently and react in markedly different ways. Although both partners may well be experiencing the same life event when they have a baby, they may make the transition to parenthood in different ways and at different speeds.

The growing number of divorces in the early years of marriage, often when couples have young children, has put renewed focus on how couples manage the transition to parenthood. Qualitative research that sought to understand the stressors in couple relationships in order to help policymakers and practitioners find better ways of supporting couple relationships during key transitions highlighted the often unacknowledged difficulties faced by new parents (Walker *et al.*, 2010). The study involved over a thousand people in England who had been or continued to be in a committed couple relationship. The transition to parenthood emerged as the most frequently cited stressor on their relationship. Four aspects were shown to be particularly significant, listed in the box below.

Significant aspects of the transition to parenthood

1. The decision to have children.
2. Problems associated with pregnancy and the postnatal period.
3. Changes in roles and responsibilities.
4. The pressures associated with becoming a parent and their impact on the couple relationship.

These issues were highlighted by men and women of all ages, and by those whose relationship was still intact as well as those whose relationship had broken down. Since they point to the need for better support for couples during the transition to parenthood, the findings from this study are explored here in further detail.

The decision to have children

While most mothers and fathers in the study had been looking forward to starting a family, in retrospect they described becoming a parent as one of the most difficult and stressful moments in their relationship. The comments in the box below (Walker *et al.*, 2010, pp. 28, 27, 33) were typical of many.

We had her [a daughter] after we had been together for a year. It adds a complication. It brings so many challenges—there's more need for discussion. Parenting is the hardest thing. (young mother)

Having a baby is the hardest thing you can do. I look back and think … people are right, having kids is the hardest thing you'll ever do. (young father)

I remember when my child was born, first one, I felt as if my life had been bombed and all the bits blown up into the air and it was absolute chaos, and they all settled down again to different patterns, but it was a huge change. (father)

It became clear during interviews with parents that not everyone had felt ready to become a parent, and some had felt under pressure from the other partner to have a baby. A common theme to emerge was that of not being in control of the transition, and for some this marked the beginning of difficulties in the relationship. Furthermore, discussions about whether and when to have more than one child often involved further tensions between the parents. It was not unusual for mothers to want a gap between pregnancies, while fathers were often keen to increase the size of their family. Both mothers and fathers described how having several children in quick succession had been hard work and had put strains on their relationship, and for some it caused significant financial difficulties. Some mothers had experienced domestic violence: an unplanned pregnancy had sometimes been the start of an abusive relationship from which there was no turning back. It is clear that many couples had not explicitly talked about whether and when to have children and pregnancy could be fraught with anxiety. Other parents faced a range of anxieties associated with IVF treatment in attempts to become pregnant, or the stresses associated with adoption.

Problems associated with pregnancy and postnatal depression

Problems that women faced in becoming pregnant, during pregnancy and in the postnatal period, were also associated with difficulties between partners. Women who struggled repeatedly to become pregnant and those who experienced miscarriages spoke about just how stressful this had been and how their relationship with their partner had deteriorated as a result. It was common for men to have found it difficult to know how to respond during IVF treatment or after a miscarriage, and the loss of a baby tends to provoke different reactions in men and women. Women described the loss of a baby as having left them feeling mentally and physically drained, and some spoke about having had their dreams shattered. Handling their partner's intense emotions had been difficult for many men: they spoke of their partner's grief as something that had led to emotional detachment in the relationship, and this had driven a wedge between them.

Postnatal stress and depression, too, are extremely upsetting and challenging. Women who had suffered from postnatal depression referred to the negative effect this had had on their capacity to sustain an intimate relationship with their partner. It is now some thirty-five years since the potential for mothers to become depressed when trying to cope with a baby was recognised in a seminal study by Brown and Harris (1978). They alluded to the complexities in couple relationships which might enhance the depression, including unhappy marriages and other day-to-day problems. Such complexities were highlighted in the study by Walker *et al.* (2010): while some men had been very supportive and understanding of their partner during and after pregnancy, others had withdrawn, often not really understanding why their partner was so unhappy. The comment by a father shown in the box below was typical of those given in many of the research narratives (Walker *et al.*, 2010, p. 32).

> During that first year, my wife suffered from postnatal depression and we found it really difficult to communicate. I didn't know that my wife was suffering from postnatal depression. I just thought that was sort of normal, having never been in that situation before.

Nearly all the people who had had to face difficulties and problems associated with pregnancy and childbirth had felt isolated at some time, primarily because there seemed to be little understanding within their communities of the stresses and strains and consequently they had received little, if any, support.

Changing roles and responsibilities

Not all couples experience difficulties associated with having a baby and, for many, it is a joyful event. Some parents in the study (Walker *et al.*, 2010) regarded the transition to parenthood as a positive next step once they had made a commitment to be together. Nevertheless, both men and women described a range of challenges and increased stress associated with parenthood. When babies are very young, parents have to manage disruptions to their sleeping patterns and cope with considerable tiredness, particularly when babies do not sleep well. Although some fathers had tried to combine work commitments with caring for a baby, many mothers had felt isolated at home during the day and were exhausted by the time their partner returned from work. This was clearly a point at which some couples first began to grow apart as the roles and responsibilities of the man and the woman diverged. It was easy for resentment and jealousy to build up. Many parents described how hard they had found it to meet the demands of young children, of the workplace and of each other as partners, and also to meet their own need for support and recognition. Lack of time, lack of sleep, lack of energy and lack of money featured prominently in the accounts of new parents.

It is well documented that fathers sometimes feel jealous of a new baby and resentful of the amount of time their partner has to devote to childcare (Mansfield and Collard, 1988). More traditional gender roles often reassert themselves and both men and women often experience confusion about what is expected of them. The research evidence demonstrates that more traditional gender roles come to the fore, with mothers focusing primarily on childcare and fathers seeing their role as being to provide for their family.

A new baby can change the couple dynamic for better or worse. For some couples, the arrival of a baby can make a poor relationship stronger, but more commonly it creates additional strain. Forty-four per cent of mothers in a survey in England reported that they began to argue more with the baby's father after the birth (Centre for Social Justice, 2012). One of the key changes is in respect of the couple's sex life—dealing with a crying baby, feeling tired and exhausted and coping with a myriad of changes can easily spoil any opportunities for intimacy. Moreover, worries about financial pressures can add to the general malaise in the couple relationship. Unemployment or a shift from having two incomes to just one can undermine a relationship rapidly because of the stresses involved in paying bills. As relationships are put under pressure, couples tend to argue more. Finding time and the energy to resolve arguments becomes more difficult and poor relationships can fester and deteriorate. Accounts by parents (Walker *et al.*, 2010, p. 33) refer to the necessity to put intimate relationships on hold while a baby is very young and lack of time alone together makes it difficult to talk about the things that really matter day to day. The comments in the box overleaf attest to this disruption in the couple relationship.

Some men opted out when life at home became difficult—going out drinking with friends or looking for companionship elsewhere. This rarely improved the situation at home and, more commonly, led to the parents' relationship falling apart altogether. The evidence from a range of studies is unequivocal: the transition to parenthood marks a critical moment in most couples' relationships. This transition is particularly challenging for those who have to accommodate children from previous relationships within new stepfamily households. As the number of stepfamily households increases, the challenges become more marked, not only for biological parents but also for

... you need to put your relationship on hold or, like, to the back seat at least, and you just have to focus on getting the baby sorted, and—you know—dressed and fed and cared for. I think that was something that was a big shock for us. (father)

We didn't talk about the really important things—like about having and wanting children. We stopped having time together and talking about our lives ... At the birth of our second child, who was very seriously ill, we didn't and couldn't talk about this. The baby died when only six weeks old ... at this point we grew apart. (mother)

step-parents, who have to take on new caring responsibilities at the same time as they are building a new couple relationship. It is not surprising that many stepfamily relationships break down because of serious strains associated with complex transitions.

The obligations of parenthood are not related to marriage but to the fact of being a parent. These obligations can be overwhelming if the parental relationship is under so much strain that it is in danger of disintegrating. Moreover, coping as a lone parent is extremely challenging: lone mothers experience higher rates of depression and greater psychological distress than other women (Loxton *et al.*, 2006) and often live in more disadvantaged neighbourhoods with a lack of social support. These factors can seriously compromise parents' ability to provide stable and consistent care for their children, thus increasing the risk factors for children's wellbeing and development.

While parenthood requires no particular form of adult relationship or family structure, parenting denotes expectations about behaviours, tasks and commitments which can be extremely challenging. As the meaning of parenthood has increasingly been transformed marital relationships have been reconstructed (Walker, 2013). When parenting does not go hand in hand with a conjugal partnership, mothers and fathers have to negotiate and define their parental roles and these are open to a complex set of influences. A British social attitudes survey at the turn of the century (Barlow *et al.*, 2002) found little support for the view that 'married couples make better parents than unmarried ones', and young people were considerably less likely to believe that 'people who want to have children ought to get married'. Nevertheless, married couples still represent the main type of adult couple partnership in the UK and the majority of babies are born to married or cohabiting parents. Since the evidence indicates that the quality of the adult couple relationship has profound implications for the emotional, cognitive and physical development of children, the rate of progression of disease in old age, and mortality rates (Balfour *et al.*, 2012), it is important to consider how couple relationships can be strengthened and supported, particularly during challenging and potentially disruptive transitions.

Supporting Couple Relationships During the Transition to Parenthood

If the transition to parenthood is a known stressor in couple relationships, it is reasonable to ask whether parents receive enough and the right support as partners, and whether there is too much focus on the baby and on parents acquiring practical parenting skills. The study by Walker *et al.* (2010) described above asked those questions of parents, and found that most had received information during antenatal and/or postnatal support provided by health professionals about childbirth, and practical advice about looking after the baby, but rarely had parents received information about the impact of having a baby on the couple relationship or advice about how to adapt to changing roles, responsibilities and expectations. Parents agreed that more advice is needed about how roles and responsibilities have to adapt to accommodate a new baby and how the adult couple relationship will inevitably change. Men in particular frequently felt marginalised during pregnancy and beyond, commenting that all the attention was focused on the mother and her baby. Most parents had not been encouraged to consider the impact of the transition to parenthood on their own intimate relationship, and there was a clear view that relationship advice and how to nurture that relationship would have been helpful.

The focus on parenting skills

While increased attention has been given to helping parents to improve their parenting skills in order to promote positive child development, little attention has been given to supporting the parents with their own relationship. In the UK and elsewhere during the first decade of this century a plethora of initiatives and programmes were designed in order to improve parenting skills in families experiencing difficulties associated with child behaviour. In 2007, for example, the Labour Government set out a strategy to ensure that parents were able to make confident informed choices for their family, work in partnership with services to optimise children's outcomes, and access additional support when they needed it (Department for Education and Skills, 2007). A range of parenting interventions emerged, informed by evidence that shows that parenting skills are one of the strongest predictors of good outcomes for children: positive, consistent, supportive parenting predicts low levels of child problem behaviour and child abuse, and enhanced cognitive development. By contrast, harsh and inconsistent parenting is predictive of poor youth outcomes, problem behaviour, delinquency, poor educational attainment and poor marital and physical health (Hoeve *et al.*, 2011). While multiple deprivation increases the risks for children, good parenting is said to be protective of children's wellbeing. A number of systematic research reviews have added to our knowledge about effective parenting interventions (Barlow *et al.*, 2012; Furlong *et al.*, 2012). Most are derived from social learning theory aiming to change parent and child behaviour, attachment theory aiming to build on parent–child relationships, and cognitive behaviour theory aiming to address parent stress and anger. The focus tends to be on helping parents to develop positive child interactions, improve parent–child bonding and reduce punitive parenting strategies.

Although parenting patterns are highly variable across cultures, research indicates that parenting interventions developed in the USA and Australia are effective in many other countries in Europe as well as in Hong Kong, Iran and New Zealand (Knerr *et al.*, 2011). This suggests not only that parenting interventions are flexible enough for adaptation to different cultural contexts, but also that many aspects of parenting practices are universal. Not surprisingly, therefore, policymakers and practitioners in many countries around the world have implemented parenting skills programmes (such as Triple P and the Incredible Years) with parents experiencing difficulties with their children.

Focusing on couple relationships

There has been much less interest in developing programmes which can support the couple relationship during the transition to parenthood. With a new focus on the importance of prevention and early intervention to support and strengthen family relationships, efforts are being made to develop programmes that focus on the quality of couple relationships. Theories about the stressors and crises associated with developmental life changes generally reflect on two kinds of transitions—normative and non-normative (Cowan and Cowan, 2012). Almost all adults experience the normative transitions of establishing an intimate relationship with a partner, forming a committed married or cohabiting relationship and becoming a parent. Non-normative transitions might include serious ill health, accidents and natural disasters. Both normative and non-normative transitions create disorder, sometimes only temporary, and displacement in the person's personal life and relationships. Whenever a life transition occurs, individuals and couples have to manage changes in their emotional responses, in their sense of identity (their inner world) and in their roles, responsibilities and relationships with others (their social world). These shifts have the potential to create negative and positive outcomes. The transition to parenthood can result in greater closeness and stability between the parents, or trigger the beginning of a downward spiral within which the couple relationship becomes distant and dysfunctional.

Over the last thirty years, Carolyn and Philip Cowan have pioneered preventive interventions for couples in the USA at the transition to parenthood. These interventions have shown statistically significant differences between intervention and control groups. The Becoming a Family project (Cowan and Cowan, 2000) prevented marital quality and satisfaction from declining for both men and women during the child's first six years of life, whereas the relationships of couples in the control group declined in quality. In two other projects, School Children and Their Families (Cowan et al., 2005) and Supporting Father Involvement (Cowan et al., 2009), the Cowans demonstrated that when parenting skills could be enhanced alongside the provision of support for couple relationships, outcomes were extremely positive. Maintaining the quality of marital relationships resulted in couples developing parenting styles that were more responsive and less harsh. Moreover, their children showed fewer academic, social and emotional behaviour problems over the following ten years than children of parents in the control group.

The conclusion to be drawn from these studies is that while enhanced parenting skills are not necessarily accompanied by improved couple relationships, enhanced couple relationship satisfaction and quality seem to bolster the quality of both parent–child and couple relationships. It is essential for policymakers and practitioners to find ways of sustaining and nurturing couple relationships, thereby complementing strategies which focus on enhancing parenting skills. A review of parenting support across 12 European and non-European non-English speaking countries (Boddy et al., 2009) identified and distinguished levels of accessibility in parenting support. In-depth examination in five countries (Germany, France, Denmark, Italy and the Netherlands) revealed four levels of support, shown in the box overleaf.

In all five countries, individualised parenting support was available through universally accessible services such as family centres. The approaches used were informed by social pedagogic theory, reflecting the prominent role of social pedagogy in policy and practice in all five countries. The emphasis was on interventions that focused on

Four levels of parenting support

1. Support embedded in universal services, delivered by workers in a universal setting.
2. Support activated as part of a universal service (e.g. health or childcare), delivered by workers linked to the universal service, for example through multidisciplinary or cross-agency teams.
3. Universally accessible support, delivered through services which are available to all but which require the parents/families to access them.
4. Targeted specialist support, whereby parents and families have to meet specific criteria to be referred to the service.

parents' strength and competency building. The review points to the potential for a broader conceptualisation of parenting support which includes counselling-based interventions that target couples rather than parents as individuals. Antenatal parenting classes in Italy and Denmark, for example, actively target couples, while in Germany and the Netherlands there is a focus on stepfamily relationships, where the transition to parenting can be especially challenging for everyone concerned and put considerable strain on the step-parent couple relationship. There is considerable potential for the development of services that focus on nurturing strong couple relationships during key transitions in family life.

Furthermore, clinical experience shows that outcomes for children and their parents are significantly better when interventions target the relationship between the parents and not just parenting practices (Hertzmann, 2012). As more and more children around the world experience the breakdown of their parents' relationship, interventions and support that promote couple-focused relationship skills and facilitate more adaptive relationships between parents would appear to be a more effective approach to ensuring positive outcomes for children, parents and families.

Parents in the study by Walker *et al.* (2010) described the emotional distance that occurred between partners when they faced stressful transitions which caused disequilibrium in the couple relationship. Parents who are emotionally withdrawn from each other to the extent that the relationship is devoid of warmth or affection may put children at risk of emotional and behavioural problems. Harold and Leve (2012) have argued that the quality of interparental relationships not only serves as a factor directly related to the psychological wellbeing of children, but serves as an orienting influence on the experiences and expectations children have of other family relationships. Programmes that enhance couple relationship skills may address the negative consequences of family stressors and reduce the numbers of families that experience parental breakdown (Pruett *et al.*, 2005).

Policy Implications

Research indicates the critical importance of supporting couples during the transition to parenthood. A number of interventions, indicated in the box overleaf, would be widely welcomed by parents.

Interventions to support the transition to parenting

1. Information and advice about the impact of parenthood on the couple relationship within universal services such as antenatal classes.
2. Peer group discussions and support provided by other new parents about ways to nurture the couple relationship.
3. Training for health professionals to detect potential stresses and strains for new parents and signpost couples to appropriate support, such as counselling and therapy.
4. Helplines, websites and online services that remove barriers to talking about couple relationships and encourage couples to seek help.

Enhancing our understanding about how couples experience the transition to parenthood, the choices they make and the responsibilities they face can enable policymakers and practitioners to develop services that facilitate smoother transitions and reduce stressors within couple relationships.

References

Anderson, A., Tunaley, J. and Walker, J. (2000) *Relatively Speaking: Communication in families* (London: BT Forum).

Balfour, A., Morgan, M. and Vincent, C. (2012) *How Couple Relationships Shape Our World: Clinical practice, research, and policy perspectives* (London: Karnac).

Barlow, A., Duncan, S., James, G. and Park, A. (2002) Just a piece of paper? Marriage and cohabitation, in A. Park, J. Curtice, K. Thomson, L. Jarvis and C. Bromley (eds), *British Social Attitudes: Public policy, social ties* (London: Sage), 29–57.

Barlow, J., Smailagic, N., Bennett, C., Huband, N., Jones, H. and Coren, E. (2012) *Individual and Group Based Parenting Programmes for Improving Psychological Outcomes for Teenage Parents and Their Children (Review)* (The Cochrane Collaboration, Chichester: Wiley).

Beck, U. (1992) *Risk Society: Towards a new modernity* (London: Sage).

Beck, U. and Beck-Gersheim, E. (1995) *The Normal Chaos of Love* (Cambridge: Polity Press).

Boddy, J., Statham, J., Smith, M., Ghate, D., Wigfall, V. and Hauari, H. (2009) *International Perspectives on Parenting Support: Non-English language sources*, Research Report DCSF-RB114 (London: Thomas Coram Research Unit and Department for Children, Schools and Families).

Brown, G. and Harris, T. O. (1978) *The Social Origins of Depression* (London: Tavistock).

Cabinet Office/Department for Children, Schools and Families (2008) *Families in Britain: An evidence paper* (London: Crown Copyright).

Centre for Social Justice (2012) *Forgotten Families? The vanishing agenda* (London: Centre for Social Justice).

Clarke, L. and O'Brien, M. (2004) Fathers' involvement in Britain: the research and policy evidence, in R. Day and M. Lamb (eds), *Reconceptualising and Measuring Fatherhood* (Hillsdale, NJ: Lawrence Erlbaum), 34–52.

Coleman, J. and Glenn, F. (2009) *When Couples Part: Understanding the consequences for adults and children* (London: OnePlusOne).

Cowan, C. P. and Cowan, P. A. (2000) *When Partners Become Parents: The big life change for couples* (Mahwah, NJ: Lawrence Erlbaum).

Cowan, C. P. and Cowan, P. A. (2012) Prevention: intervening with parents at challenging transition points, in A. Balfour, M. Morgan and C. Vincent (eds), *How Couple Relationships Shape our World: Clinical practice, research, and policy perspectives* (London: Karnac), 1–14.

Cowan, C. P., Cowan, P. A. and Herring, G. (2005) Two validations of a preventive intervention for couples: effects on parents and children during the transition to school, in P. A. Cowan, C. P. Cowan, J. C. Ablow, V. K. Johnson and J. R. Measelle (eds), *The Family Context of Parenting in Children's Adaptation to Elementary School*, Monographs in Parenting Series (Mahwah, NJ: Lawrence Erlbaum), 277–312.

Cowan, P. A., Cowan, C. P., Pruett, M. K., Pruett, K. D. and Wong, J. (2009) Promoting fathers' engagement with children: preventive interventions for low-income families, *Journal of Marriage and Family*, 71, 663–679.

Dahlström, E. (1989) Theories and ideologies of family functions, gender relations and human reproduction, in K. Boh, M. Bak, C. Clason, M. Pankratova, J. Qvortrup, G. B. Sgritta and K. Waerness (eds), *Changing Patterns of European Family Life* (London: Routledge), 31–52.

Davies, P. T., Cummings, E. M. and Winter, M. A. (2004) Pathways between profiles of family functioning, child security in the interparental subsystem, and child psychological problems, *Development and Psychopathology*, 16(3), 525–550.

Department for Education and Skills (2007) *Every Parent Matters* (London: Department for Education and Skills).

Duncan, S. (2003) *Mothers, Care and Employment: Values and theories*, CAVA working paper (Leeds: CAVA).

Duncan, S. and Smith, D. (2002) Geographies of family formation: spatial differences and gender cultures in Britain, *Transactions of the Institute of British Geographers*, 27: 471–493.

Furlong, M., McGilloway, S., Bywater, J., Hutchings, J., Smith, S. M. and Donnelly, M. (2012) *Behavioural and Cognitive-behavioural Group-based Parenting Programmes for Early-onset Conduct Problems in Children Aged 3–12 (Review)* (The Cochrane Collaboration, Chichester: Wiley).

Giddens, A. (1992) *The Transformation of Intimacy: Sexuality, love and eroticism in modern societies* (Cambridge: Polity Press/Blackwell).

Harold, G. T. and Leve, L. D. (2012) Parents as partners: how the parental relationship affects children's psychological development, in A. Balfour, M. Morgan and C. Vincent (eds), *How Couple Relationships Shape our World: Clinical practice, research, and policy perspectives* (London: Karnac), 25–56.

Hertzmann, L. (2012) Commentary on Chapter One, in A. Balfour, M. Morgan and C. Vincent (2012), *How Couple Relationships Shape Our World: Clinical practice, research, and policy perspectives* (London: Karnac), 15–24.

Hirschberger, G., Srivastava, S., Marsh, P., Cowan, C. P. and Cowan, P. A. (2009) Attachment, marital satisfaction and divorce during the first fifteen years of parenthood, *Personal Relationships*, 16(3): 401–420.

Hoeve, M., Dubas, J. S., Gerris, J. R. M., van der Laan, P. H. and Smeenk. W. (2011) Maternal and paternal parenting styles: unique and combined links to adolescent and early adult delinquency, *Journal of Adolescence*, 34(5): 813–827.

Kiecolt-Glaser, J. K. and Newton, T. L. (2001) Marriage and health: his and hers, *Psychological Bulletin*, 27(4): 472–503.

Knerr, W., Gardner, F. and Cluver, L. (2011) *Reducing harsh and abusive parenting and increasing positive parenting in low- and middle-income countries: A systematic review* (Pretoria, SA: Oak Foundation and South African Medical Research Council).

Loxton, D., Mooney, R. and Young, A. F. (2006) The psychological health of sole mothers in Australia, *Medical Journal of Australia*, 184: 265–268.

Mansfield, P. and Collard, J. (1988) *The Beginning of the Rest of Your Life: A portrait of newly-wed marriage* (London: Macmillan).

Murphy, M. (2007) Family living arrangements and health, in ONS, *Focus on Families* (London: The Stationery Office).

ONS (2008) *Social Trends 38: Households and families* (London: Palgrave Macmillan).

ONS (2009) *Social Trends 40. Households and Families* (London: Palgrave Macmillan).

Pruett, M. K., Insabella, G. M. and Gustafson, K. (2005) The Collaborative Divorce Project: a court-based intervention for separating parents with young children, *Family Court Review*, 43: 38–51.

Saporiti, A. (1989) Historical changes in the family's reproductive patterns, in K. Boh, M. Bak, C. Clason, M. Pankratova, J. Qvortrup, G. B. Sgritta and K. Waerness (eds), *Changing Patterns of European Family Life* (London: Routledge), 191–216.

Strohschein, L. (2005) Parental divorce and child mental health trajectories, *Journal of Marriage and Family*, 67: 1286–1300.

Struening, K. (2002) *New Family Values: Liberty, equality and diversity* (Lanham, MD: Rowman & Littlefield).

Thane, P. (2010) *Happy Families? History and policy* (London: British Academy Policy Centre).

Walker, J. (2006) Supporting families in democratic societies: public concerns and private realities, in C. Clulow (ed.), *Families and Democracy: Compatibility, incompatibility, opportunity or challenge* (London: ICCFR), 41–48.

Walker, J. (2008) Family life in the 21st century: the implications for parenting policy in the UK, *Journal of Children's Services*, 3(4): 17–29.

Walker, J. (2013) Partnership and parenting, in M. Davies (ed.), *Blackwell Companion to Social Work* (Oxford: Blackwell), 4th edn, pp. 109–120.

Walker, J., Barrett, H., Wilson, G. and Chang, Y-S. (2010) *Relationships Matter: Understanding the needs of adults (particularly parents) regarding relationship support*, Research Report RR33 (London: Department for Children, Schools and Families).

Williams, F. (2004) *Rethinking Families* (London: Calouste Gulbenkian Foundation).

10

Why Fewer Babies? Understanding and Responding to Low Fertility in Europe

Maria Letizia Tanturri

Introduction

The EU population is characterised by low fertility rates, delayed motherhood and an increase in childlessness among the younger generations. All EU member states now have total fertility rates[1] of below 2.1, which is the level needed for the replacement of generations. Shrinking and ageing populations are two of the most important side-effects of prolonged low fertility. The impact of uninterrupted low fertility on the size of successive generations can be exceptionally rapid: with a fertility level of 1.3 children per woman, the second generation after the present one would be 40 per cent of the present generation's size, and the fourth generation after the present one 15 per cent (McDonald, 2008). Population ageing is an even more important consequence of prolonged low fertility, particularly given the increasing longevity in Western Europe. In most European countries, the over-65 population is around 20 per cent and is projected to increase to 35 per cent when the baby-boomers born in the 1960s will grow old. At the same time, young people account for 15 per cent of the population. As a consequence, problems arise in respect of the sustainability of welfare, the replacement of the workforce in the labour market, and solidarity ties among generations.

Low fertility also deserves attention because surveys show that couples seem not to fulfil their reproductive desires, owing to a number of constraints (Goldstein *et al.*,

---

[1] The total fertility rate is the average number of children who would be born alive to a woman during her lifetime if she were to pass through all childbearing years conforming to the age-specific fertility rate for a given year.

Contemporary Issues in Family Studies: Global Perspectives on Partnerships, Parenting and Support in a Changing World, First Edition. Edited by Angela Abela and Janet Walker.
© 2014 John Wiley & Sons, Ltd. Published 2014 by John Wiley & Sons, Ltd.

2003). Therefore, it is of paramount importance to understand why European families are having fewer children than they would originally have wished for. This chapter focuses on the issues relating to low fertility in modern society. It is structured in three parts. The first presents data on fertility levels in European countries. The second provides a review of both classical and contemporary theories currently still under study, which explain the emergence and maintenance of low fertility. The final section analyses the possible (controversial) role of policies responding to low fertility in the European population. A reflection on possible future scenarios is offered in conclusion.

Low Fertility, Delayed Motherhood and Childlessness

Major trends

If we follow the average trends for all the EU countries excluding Romania and Bulgaria, we find that the total fertility rate (TFR) declined from 2.7 in 1963 to 2.1 (the replacement level) in 1973, then reached a minimum level of 1.4 in 1995 and increased slightly to 1.6 in the most recent year for which figures are available (2010) (Table 10.1). Total fertility rates fell to previously unseen levels in a large number of countries beginning in the early 1990s. Italy and Spain were the forerunners of a new regime of *lowest-low fertility*[2] (Kohler *et al.*, 2006), characterised by a pronounced delay in childbearing, a sharp decline in the number of large families and a rise in the prevalence of childlessness. This phenomenon has spread all over Eastern and Central Europe, and in South-East Asia. Kohler *et al.* (2002) expected that lowest-low fertility would be a persistent pattern for several decades, especially in Eastern Europe. Similarly, Lutz *et al.* (2006) suggested that very low birth rates may persist because of self-reinforcing mechanisms: the negative *population momentum* (i.e. fewer potential mothers in the future will result in fewer births, other things being equal) and the declining ideal family size for the younger cohorts.

Differences across countries

As Table 10.1 shows, fertility trends are far from being homogeneous, and divergence among European countries is a major characteristic of fertility rates (Coleman, 2007). From a demographic perspective Europe is divided into three groups. One demographic group comprises both north-western and Anglophone countries, namely Sweden, the UK, Ireland, Denmark, Finland, Belgium and the Netherlands (where fertility levels remain comparatively close to the replacement level); these face a relatively benign demographic future, primarily owing to positive migration inflows. Southern European and German-speaking countries make up a second group, with much lower birth rates—1.4 or less. These countries will face population decline and more severe population ageing in spite of immigration. The third group of countries

---

[2] Kohler *et al.* (2002, 2006) and Billari and Kohler (2004) coined the label 'lowest low fertility' for a period TFR below 1.3. Other authors (Caldwell and Schindlmayr, 2003; McDonald, 2008) consider a TFR below 1.5 a threshold for lowest-low fertility.

Table 10.1   Total fertility rate in selected developed countries

	1980	1990	2010
Higher fertility EU countries			
Ireland	3.24	2.11	2.07
France	1.95	1.78	2.00
UK	1.89	1.83	1.98
Sweden	1.68	2.13	1.99
Denmark	1.55	1.67	1.88
Finland	1.63	1.78	1.87
Belgium	1.68	1.62	1.84
Netherlands	1.60	1.62	1.75
Lower fertility EU countries			
Greece	2.23	1.39	1.55
Czech Republic	2.10	1.90	1.49
Austria	1.65	1.46	1.44
Italy	1.64	1.33	1.41
Germany	1.56	1.45	1.39
Poland	2.26	2.05	1.38
Spain	2.20	1.36	1.37
Portugal	2.25	1.57	1.32
Romania	2.43	1.84	1.30
Hungary	1.91	1.87	1.26
Other developed countries			
New Zealand	2.02	2.16	2.2[a]
USA	1.85	2.08	2.0
Australia	1.89	1.9	1.9
Canada	1.64	1.68	1.7[a]
Japan	1.76	1.54	1.4[a]

Data source: Eurostat database.
a: data source = UN.

includes countries in Eastern Europe, which is suffering dramatic demographic change characterised by extremely rapid fertility decline, relatively high mortality and net emigration (Coleman, 2007).

Among developed areas outside Europe, all the Anglo-Saxon countries (with the exception of Canada, which has more resemblance to continental Europe) have a TFR around the replacement level (McDonald, 2010). Conversely, Japan (together with South Korea) represents a case of lowest-low fertility very similar to those found in Southern European countries.

Paradoxically, in Europe, fertility is higher in north-western countries, where family institutions seem to be particularly weak, couple instability is common, and women's labour market participation is high (Kohler *et al.*, 2006). Indeed, since 1975 there has been a reversal in cross-country correlations in Europe between the total fertility and the total first marriage rate, the proportion of extramarital births and the labour force participation of women. In addition, since the end of the 1990s, divorce levels are no longer negatively associated with fertility levels (Billari and Kohler, 2004).

Delayed childbirth

Delayed childbirth is considered the most common feature of fertility change in Europe: so much so, that it has been referred to as a distinctive postponement transition towards a late-childbearing regime (Kohler *et al.*, 2006). A sharp decrease in the fertility rates of women under 30 started around the 1960s, but in the first decade of the twenty-first century this was accompanied by an increase in the fertility of women in their 30s (OECD, 2011). On average, half of the births registered in the EU have been to mothers over 30. The proportions are much higher in Ireland, Spain, Italy, the Netherlands, Sweden, Denmark, Germany, Greece and Finland (European Commission, 2010).

Delay in first childbirth is a relevant cause of reduction in completed fertility, for two reasons. First, the compressed reproductive span may affect the possibility of women fulfilling their desired level of fertility owing to possible sub-fecundity or even sterility impediments (Beets, 2006). Second, the period indicator of fertility (TFR) is sensitive to changes in the timing of childbirth. Given the current delay, the TFR will inevitably fall initially, since this would not account for the women who might still wish to have the same number of children at a later stage. Once the general process of postponement of childbirth in a country has stopped, the TFR will rise again (Goldstein *et al.*, 2009; van Nimwegen, 2008).

'Childless' and 'child-free'

Europe's fertility decline has been associated with a decrease in the number of large families, and also with a rise in childlessness (Billari and Kohler, 2004; Rowland, 2007). Recent estimates of permanent childlessness for the cohorts born around 1965 reveal that childless women have become an increasingly large group in Italy (~25%), Germany and Finland (~20%), and Austria, Belgium, England and Wales, Greece, Ireland, the Netherlands, Poland and Sweden (~15%) (Figure 10.1). At present, countries with similar levels of completed fertility can be characterised by different proportions of childless women (e.g. Austria and Spain in Figure 10.1). The patterns suggest that theoretical explanations for childlessness need to be somewhat different from those concerned with low fertility as a whole, although a comprehensive theory of childlessness is not yet well-developed (Tanturri and Mencarini, 2008).

Literature identifies the following macro factors as being associated with changes in rates of childlessness: trends in partnership formation (e.g. median age at first union and the proportions of those entering a union), trends in family formation (e.g. median age at the first birth and average family size), and the different role of voluntary and involuntary factors (Hakim, 2005; Rowland, 2007). In the last decades, the increase in childlessness has been accompanied by changes in attitudes and values, since in many countries not having a child is now acceptable and even seen by some women as the better option (Sobotka and Testa, 2008). A distinction is usually made between women who voluntarily refuse motherhood (described as *child-free*) and those who are unable to have children (described as *childless*). Voluntary childlessness is an interesting new phenomenon that breaks with the norm maintaining that motherhood is instinctive in the human race (Foster, 2000).

It is not easy to identify the individual determinants of this behaviour. On the one hand, data specifically collected to assess voluntary childlessness are rare and fragmentary. On the other hand, predictors depend on context and time, and results

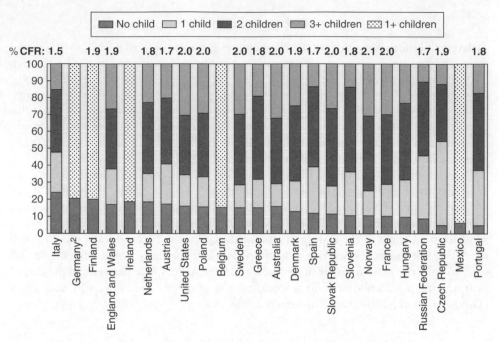

Figure 10.1 Cross-national variation in the number of children women have[1]

[1]Countries are ranked by decreasing proportion of women with no child at the end of their reproductive period. The numbers above the columns reflect the completed fertility rate (CFR) which is the number of children actually born per woman in a cohort of women by the end of their childbearing years (normally, women who are 45 or over are considered to have completed their childbearing years; this end-year is often set at 49). CFRs are not available for Belgium, Germany, Hungary, Ireland and Mexico.

  The figure shows achieved fertility by parity distribution, in per cent, 1965 or latest available birth cohort: 1962–66 for Australia; 1963 for Greece, Portugal and Spain; 1964 for Hungary, England and Wales, Sweden; 1959 for Finland; 1955 for Belgium, Germany and the United States; 1953 for Norway. Unfortunately, cohort data for the same year are not readily available, but the use of data on cohorts of women born within ten years of each other provides an adequate picture of the main cross-country differences.

[2]Estimates for the Western *Länder* of Germany only.

Source. OECD (2011), compiled from Australian Bureau of Statistics; Andersson *et al.* (2009); Frejka (2008); Sardon (2006); Frejka and Sardon (2007); Speder and Kamaras (2008); McDonald (2010).

are not always consistent. Hakim (2005), for instance, finds that in Europe child-free women are a distinctive group in terms of attitudes and values, but far less so in terms of social and economic characteristics. Other studies suggest that education, social class and employment status are important determinants of being child-free, irrespective of partnership status. Usually, this is associated with higher levels of education (Keizer *et al.*, 2008; Kneale and Joshi, 2008), but recent studies provide contrasting results. For instance, in Norway and Denmark women with low levels of education are more likely to opt to be child-free (OECD, 2011). Two comparative studies, by Hoem *et al.* (2006) and Neyer and Hoem (2008), found that other factors may influence the relationship between education and childlessness. In particular, the institutional context in which education is provided and the choices made about which subjects to study may have a decisive impact on a woman's future employment and her attitude to childbearing (e.g. in Sweden, women born in 1995–9 educated for jobs in teaching and health have much lower permanent childlessness at each educational level than any other groups, while those educated in arts and humanities show uncommonly high proportions of permanent childlessness). The type and level of education a woman receives appear to be determinants of her career opportunities, job and income security, her work environment, and, ultimately, her reproductive behaviour. Welfare policies such as those relating to parental leave and the provision of childcare may also influence women's choices about childbearing and, therefore, fertility patterns. Further research is needed to explore these influences in greater depth.

Women opting for voluntary childlessness in Italy: insights from a specific case study

The first quantitative and qualitative study carried out in urban geographical areas in Italy (Tanturri, 2006; Tanturri and Mencarini, 2008) reveals that as many as a third of the women without children interviewed (born around 1960) who live with a partner and do not suffer from any particular physical impediment to childbearing opted to be child-free. Assuming that the proportion of child-free women across Italy is the same as observed in the five cities studied, it is conceivable that around 8 per cent of women born around 1965 would deliberately reject motherhood. This is in stark contrast to the 1.5 per cent of the women born just one or two decades previously.

In line with other studies carried out in other countries (Kiernan, 1989; Murphy and Wang, 2001), voluntarily childless women in Italy tend to have greater gender equity within marriages, to be less traditional, to be non-religious, to be employed in professional occupations, and to have experienced marital disruption. Other significant factors include being an only child, or marrying late. These women have little leisure time, find sources of fulfilment other than motherhood, and in some cases consider a child to be an obstacle to their achievements. Moreover, child-related benefits are perceived to be insufficient compensation for the high costs involved in parenthood, especially when taking into account the time devoted to childcare and the impacts parenthood has on the mother's and the couple's lifestyle. Voluntary childlessness is very rarely related to mere monetary constraints: child-free women are almost impervious to generous family-friendly policies.

The Main Drivers of Low Fertility

Two types of explanations are traditionally offered for the decline in fertility (see box below). Each of these is examined in turn.

Traditional explanations for the decline in fertility

1. The first explanation is based on economic theory and rational choice, re-elaborated by the Chicago School (Becker, 1960, 1981; Hotz *et al.*, 1997; Willis, 1973).
2. The second explanation is based on the Second Demographic Transition (SDT) framework (Lesthaeghe, 1995; van de Kaa, 1987), and focuses on cultural and value changes.

Economic theory—the high costs of children

Economic theory presupposes that the decision to have children is a rational one whereby couples balance the costs and benefits of having children, taking into account their level of income and their personal preferences (Becker, 1960, 1981). According to the economic paradigm, couples have fewer children as soon as they become more expensive. The historical link between economic development and fertility is negative because children's costs increase, both in terms of *direct costs* (expenses, education and housing) and in terms of *opportunity costs* (the cost of forgone labour market opportunities) (Willis, 1973).

In terms of direct costs a child accounts for around 15–30 per cent of the budget of a couple without children (see e.g. De Santis, 2004 for Italy; Hourriez and Olier, 1997 for France; OECD, 2011 for developed countries). The cost of the first child is often found to be greater than that of each subsequent child because of the economies of scale related to shared infrastructure (e.g. bedrooms) or the re-use of items (e.g. clothes and equipment) (De Santis, 2004). The costs associated with children increase with age, reaching a peak in adolescence and during the transition to adulthood, when post-secondary education, transport and leisure costs can be considerable.

Housing is the biggest budget item for families with children in Europe, amounting to up to 25 per cent of budgets for households with children in many EU countries (OECD, 2011). It is a common strategy for families to secure good-quality housing before having children and increasing family size (Mulder and Billari, 2010). Deciding to become a home owner, however, can conflict with having a first or a second child (Mulder, 2006).

The rise in the opportunity cost of children is generally seen as a key driver of fertility decline in European countries. Childbearing compels women to withdraw temporarily from the labour market. This not only determines a short-term drop in resources owing to income loss, but also affects future earnings. Some commentators have referred to this as the 'childbearing penalty' (Joshi, 2002); it is estimated to be between 42 and 89 per cent of lifetime earnings, depending on the degree of work and family compatibility in each country (Sigle-Rushton and Wadfogel, 2007). This loss also varies with education, human capital and career perspectives: for instance, the opportunity cost of having children is greater for women with higher levels of education, who are probably more committed to career progression. It should, however, be noted that, at the macro level, there has been a reversal in the negative relationship between women's employment and fertility levels. In countries where family-friendly policies have been implemented, the more highly educated women do not have fewer children than those who are less well educated, as was the case in the past.

In addition, as income grows, even the negative macro relationship between economic development and fertility levels seems to be questionable: recent studies find a j-shaped relationship (i.e. first negative and after a certain threshold positive) between TFR and GDP per capita (Luci and Thévenon, 2011). In other words, after a certain threshold of income, the connection with the TFR becomes a positive one. The limited success of the conventional economic models of fertility has shifted attention to theories emphasising the effect of cultural change.

Cultural change as an explanation for low fertility

According to the Second Demographic Transition (STD) paradigm (Lesthaeghe, 1995), low fertility is the result of profound cultural changes, in particular, the passage from traditional value systems that maximise the wellbeing of the family to systems that favour self-realisation and individual options. Childbearing is predicted to occupy an increasingly less central role in the life of individuals. Secularisation, the spread of post-materialist values, and an increasingly individualistic life course make reproduction more a matter of choice than an obligation. According to the SDT theory, the weakening of marriage bonds, the replacement of this form of union by other arrangements, high divorce and separation rates, and the growing number of births outside marriage are also associated with low fertility.

However, in countries where the fertility rate is among the lowest, that is in Italy, Spain and Japan, the SDT does not seem to have taken place: family institutions are strong, the divorce rate is relatively low, and reproduction usually occurs within the framework of marriage. The desire for individual affirmation does not seem to affect the traditional family system. On the contrary, a structured and profound familism is in force (Dalla Zuanna and Micheli, 2004; Livi Bacci, 2001). Where family ties are stronger, as in Southern Europe (Reher, 1998), protecting the wellbeing of the family (e.g. in the case of a family business) implies having few children—in most instances only one—on whom to concentrate social expectations and family investment (Dalla Zuanna, 2001; Livi Bacci, 2001). Therefore, aspiration for social mobility can also be an ideational rationale for reducing fertility in a traditional context.

The delay in the transition to adulthood

Increasing returns in human capital and high economic uncertainty in early adulthood have made late childbearing a rational response for individuals and couples (Blossfeld *et al.*, 2005). Childbearing is a no-return choice, which is difficult to make in a poorly defined context. So couples put off having children while they attain other objectives which they consider priorities, as indicated in the box below.

The major causes of delayed parenthood

Among the major causes of delayed parenthood (Nicoletti and Tanturri, 2008; OECD, 2007, 2011) are:

- the higher educational attainment of successive generations of women
- women's growing aspirations to be economically active and financially independent
- high housing costs
- the difficulties of combining parenthood with paid employment
- parents' desire to gain financial security before starting a family

Social interaction reinforces behavioural adjustments and contributes to the extensive and persistent postponement of first birth (Kohler *et al.*, 2002). In Southern European countries, childbearing deferment can be seen as part of a more general 'delay syndrome', as young people delay all the steps in the transition to adulthood and live in their parental home until their mid-thirties (Livi Bacci, 2001).

New Explanations for Low Fertility

More recently, attention has turned from classic theories to other explanations for low fertility (see box below). Some of these theories take into account the role of institutions in shaping individuals' and couples' reproductive choices, while others focus on women's preferences and on their aspirations to lead a happy life. Each theory is considered in turn.

New explanatory models for low fertility

These include:

- Gender-equity theory.
- Preference theory.
- The theory of happiness.

The gender-equity theory

McDonald, in a seminal theoretical article (2000), suggests that very low fertility may be related to a *hiatus* that has enlarged in some developed countries between 'high levels of gender equity in individual-oriented social institutions and sustained gender inequity in family-oriented social institutions' (p. 1). In other words, if recently women have been given the same opportunities as men in education and, to some extent, in the labour market, this has not occurred within the family. In most countries, indeed, the participation of women in the labour market has not triggered a change in the division of domestic labour between men and women. This has resulted in a dual and heavy burden for women. The gender imbalance deteriorates further when couples have children (see Chapter 9, this volume).

In recent years, a growing body of empirical research has emerged which highlights the fact that, where women are not overloaded with domestic duties and men are collaborative, couples are more likely to have (or to wish to have) a further child (see Olah, 2003 on the transition to second child in Hungary and Sweden; Miller Torr and Short, 2004 on the USA; Cooke, 2009 on Italy and Spain; Mencarini and Tanturri, 2004 on urban Italian contexts; Mills *et al.* 2008 on comparing Italy with the Netherlands). The level and extent of welfare support for gender equity as well as for work–family reconciliation have been pinpointed as influencing reproductive choices across Europe.

The preference theory

According to the preference theory (Hakim, 2000, 2002) women are heterogeneous and, in the first period of their life, develop dissimilar preferences with regard to child-bearing and lifestyle which determine their subsequent behaviour. Hakim distinguishes three different types of women: family-oriented women regard family life and children as their main priorities and decide not to work, unless economic needs force them to enter the labour market; career-oriented women value work and frequently remain unmarried and/or childless; and adaptive women (between 40 and 80% of the total) have no prevailing preference orientation—they combine work and family. The weakening of moral and social norms encourages women to follow their innermost wishes, including refusing motherhood without being stigmatised. Hakim's conclusion is that fertility policies should take into account women's heterogeneity and implement specific measures only for women who are more family-oriented. Results from a comparative study conducted in a variety of European countries (Vitali *et al.*, 2009) confirm the links between individual-level preferences and fertility outcomes and intentions.

The theory of happiness

The theory of happiness is a recent theory that explains fertility differences on the basis of a possible connection between happiness and reproductive behaviour. Billari (2009) states that, on the one hand, happiness is a crucial determinant of childbearing and, on the other, having children is one of the ways to reach happiness. According to this theory, societies with very low fertility are characterised by low compatibility between happiness and childbearing. Descriptive analyses from selected countries show a positive, although modest, effect of children on happiness. Interestingly, it appears that parental happiness is highest in France (Billari, 2009).

Childbearing, however, is not associated with greater happiness everywhere and for everyone. Margolis and Myrskylä (2011) point out that the association between happiness and fertility evolves from negative to neutral to positive above the age of 40. Moreover, a negative association between fertility and happiness for younger adults is weakest in countries with high public support for families, while the positive association above age 40 is strongest in countries where old-age support depends mostly on the family.

In another comparative paper, Aassve *et al.* (2012) indicate that fathers' happiness, unlike that of mothers, is not greatly affected by different welfare regimes. Not surprisingly, it is mothers in the Nordic countries who are the happiest. For both fathers and mothers, being in a partnership is an important precondition for enjoying a higher level of happiness derived from having children. Working fathers are always happier, whereas working mothers are not (Aassve *et al.*, 2012).

The Need for Family-Friendly Policies

Removing the obstacles that dissuade European couples from having children is an important consideration for policymaking. In this respect, the European Commission (COM/2006/571) actively promotes demographic renewal through the Lisbon Strategy. Aiming to increase jobs and at the same time promote gender equality, the strategy aims to foster a balance between professional and private life, so that member states could help Europeans have their ideal number of children.

Numerous authors, working within different theoretical frameworks, have focused on the effect of family-friendly policies on fertility within different welfare regimes. In this regard, the empirical evidence is open to question (Gauthier, 2007; OECD, 2011; Thévenon and Gauthier, 2011, Neyer, 2006). It is very difficult to disentangle the effects that a single measure may have on fertility, since often only aggregated information is available or policies have not been in place long enough to be evaluated properly. Moreover, in some cases the effect of specific measures seems to be context-dependent. At the macro level, however, the literature confirms that where there is a higher investment in public policy, fertility levels are also higher (Castles, 2003).

Cross-national studies on the effect of policies suggest that cash transfers (e.g. lump-sum grants, family allowances and tax rebates) seem to have a positive effect on TFR, albeit temporarily given that they only impact on fertility timing (OECD, 2011). The reconciliation policies' effect depends very much on the kind of measure adopted. An increase in the duration of paid leave entitlement, for instance, seems to have a small effect: on the one hand, it supports income around childbirth, but it is simultaneously an incentive to postpone childbirth until parents are well-established in the labour market. Payment conditions during leave are found mainly to affect the timing of fertility. The few studies addressing public contributions to childcare services (and their coverage) suggest a positive effect on family size. While long working hours usually discourage childbearing, part-time employment opportunities are found to have a positive effect on fertility rates among more educated women. Policies on gender equity may contribute towards a more equal share in unpaid work between men and women. Since the 1980s, several European countries have established different types of paternity leave, but the impact on fertility is still under debate (Various authors, 2011). Emerging evidence from a range of countries, however, suggests that the involvement of fathers in caring for the first child increases the probability of the couple having a second child.

Germany provides an interesting case study in respect of fathers' behaviour and paternity leave. German fathers who take parental leave are more often found among

How the changes in parental leave laws in Germany affect fathers' behaviour

1996–2006. The Federal Child-Raising Allowance Act permitted mothers and fathers to share child-raising leave for up to three years after the birth of a child and also receive means-tested benefits if their income was below a certain threshold—result, take-up rates of parental leave by fathers stagnated, to between 2.1 and 3.3 per cent.

2007. The Parental Allowance and Parental Leave Act permitted parents to share 14 months' parental leave between them (but two months are reserved exclusively for fathers) while receiving a parental benefit of 67 per cent of monthly net income (Reich, 2010)—result, take-up rates by fathers increased sharply, to 18 per cent in 2009.

highly educated and urban men who are believed to be the leaders in terms of new values and ideas (Reich 2010). They are more frequently employed in the public sector and in large companies, and are likely to have a permanent contract and be in a leading position. Their partner's characteristics are also significant: a father is more likely to take parental leave if he has a partner who is highly educated or older (Geisler and Kreyenfeld, 2011).

Looking at family-friendly policies in Europe, we find that the Nordic countries enjoy a wide variety of funded childcare services, rather short (but highly subsidised) periods of maternity leave, and compulsory leave for fathers. The Nordic countries' approach to service provision for working parents with very young children is more intensive than that of other European countries (Gstrein *et al.*, 2007; Thévenon, 2011). As a result, these countries benefit from high female employment and relatively high fertility rates.

France provides strong family benefits for larger families, early childcare provision (primary school from age two) and a fast reintegration of females into the labour market. By contrast, Anglo-Saxon countries provide much less public support for working parents with very young children, and financial support is targeted at low-income families and focused on pre-school and early elementary education. Continental and Eastern European countries form a more heterogeneous group (Thévenon, 2011). Countries where there is limited public policy support may still be family-friendly, although childcare is considered to be a private matter, since the preferred choice of part-time working arrangements may still allow for good work–care balances (e.g. in the Netherlands) at low cost to the taxpayer (Gstrein *et al.*, 2007). Conversely, the support received by families in Southern Europe is much less in all dimensions (Thévenon, 2011), and both fertility and women's employment rates are low.

Looking into the Future

The evidence shows that both value shifts and economic transformations have a role in determining low fertility. However, low and late fertility is the result of a plurality of factors with which couples have to struggle. Since 2000 there has been a slight but significant fertility rebound, not only in the lowest-fertility countries, but also in higher-fertility countries such as Sweden, the UK and France. The German-speaking countries, where fertility has remained unchanged, are the only exception to this trend reversal in Europe. The number of countries with TFRs below 1.3 fell from 21 in 2003 to 5 in 2008 (Goldstein *et al.*, 2009). In Southern Europe, TFRs have exceeded 1.4 in Italy, Spain and Greece. It remains to be seen whether this is a temporary phenomenon or a significant and enduring change.

Goldstein *et al.* (2009) conclude that formerly lowest-low fertility countries will continue to see increases in fertility as the transitory effects of shifts to later childbearing become less important. The economic crisis of the twenty-first century, however, seems to have challenged these optimistic conclusions: evidence shows that in most countries the recession has brought a decline in the number of births and fertility rates, often marking a sharp halt to the previous decade of rising fertility rates (Sobotka *et al.*, 2011). Most studies find that fertility tends to be pro-cyclical and often rises and falls with the ups and downs of the business cycle. It has been observed that pro-cyclical effects are relatively small (a few percentage points) and of short duration; in addition they often influence, especially, the timing of childbearing, and in most cases do not leave an imprint on cohort fertility levels (Sobotka *et al.*, 2011).

A further negative effect on the future number of births in the EU will be triggered by the so-called negative 'population momentum': the number of women of childbearing age is shrinking after three decades of low fertility, and this will have an unavoidable impact on the number of births and population ageing (Lutz *et al.*, 2006). Governments should, therefore, continue to fund policies promoting demographic growth. A consistent system of policies (and not just a single measure) could make Europe a more family-friendly place, where couples can fulfil their fertility desires, even under adverse economic conditions.

References

Aassve, A., Goisis, A. and Sironi, M. (2012) Happiness and childbearing across Europe, *Social Indicators Research*, 108(1): 65–86.

Andersson, G., Knudsen, L, Neyer, G., Teschner, K., Ronsen, M., Lappegard, T., Skrede, K. and Vikat, A. (2009) Cohort fertility patterns in the Nordic countries, *Demographic Research*, 20, Article 14: 314–352.

Australian Bureau of Statistics (2008) How many children have women in Australia had?, *Australian Social Trends*, Catalogue No. 4102.0.

Becker, G. (1960) An economic analysis of fertility, in A. J. Coale, H. Gille, G. Z. Johnson and C. V. Kiser (eds), *Demographic and Economic Change in Developed Countries* (Princeton, NJ: Princeton University Press), 209–240.

Becker, G. (1981) *A Treatise on the Family* (Cambridge, MA: Harvard University Press), 1st edn.

Beets, G. (2006) *Research Note: An Assessment of the Size and Cost of Involuntary Infertility That May Be Attributed to Postponement* (Brussels: European Observatory on the Social Situation and Demography, European Commission).

Billari, F. C. (2009) The happiness commonality: fertility decisions in low fertility settings, in UNECE, *How Generations and Gender Shape Demographic Change* (New York and Geneva: United Nations), 7–38.

Billari, F. C. and Kohler, H.-P. (2004) Patterns of low and very low fertility in Europe, *Population Studies*, 58(2): 161–176.

Blossfeld, H.-P., Klijzing, E., Mills, M. and Kurz, K. (eds) (2005) *Globalisation, Uncertainty and Youth in Society* (London/New York: Routledge).

Caldwell, J. and T. Schindlmayr (2003) Explanations of the fertility crisis in modern societies: a search for commonalities, *Population Studies*, 57(3): 241–263.

Castles F. G. (2003) The world turned upside down: below replacement fertility, changing preferences and family-friendly public policy in 21 OECD countries, *Journal of European Social Policy*, 13(3): 209–227.

Coleman, D. (2007) The road to low fertility, *Aging Horizons*, 7: 7–15.

Cooke, L. P. (2009) Gender equity and fertility in Italy and Spain, *Journal of Social Policy*, 38(1): 123–140.

Dalla Zuanna, G. (2001) The banquet of Aeolus: a familistic interpretation of Italy's lowest-low fertility, *Demographic Research*, 4(5): 133–161.

Dalla Zuanna, G. and Micheli, G. A. (eds) (2004) *Strong Family and Low Fertility: A paradox? New perspectives in interpreting contemporary family and reproductive behaviour* (Dordrecht: Kluwer).

De Santis, G. (2004) The monetary cost of children. Theory and empirical estimates for Italy, *Genus*, 60(1): 161–183.

European Commission (2010) *The Demographic Report* (Brussels: European Commission).

Foster, C. (2000) The limits to low fertility: a biosocial approach, *Population and Development Review*, 26(2), 209–234.

Frejka, T. (2008) Parity distribution and completed family size in Europe. Incipient decline of the two-child family model, *Demographic Research*, Special Collection No. 7, *Childbearing Trends and Policies in Europe*, 19, Ch. 2: 47–72.

Frejka, T. and Sardon, J. P. (2007) Cohort birth order, parity progression ratio and parity distribution trends in developed countries, *Demographic Research*, 16(11): 315–374.

Gauthier, A. (2007) The impact of family policies on fertility in industrialised countries: a review of the literature, *Population Research and Policy Review*, 26(3): 323–346.

Geisler, E. and Kreyenfeld, M. (2011) Against all odds: fathers' use of parental leave in Germany, *Journal of European Social Policy*, 21(1): 88–99.

Goldstein, J., Lutz, W. and Testa, M. R. (2003) The emergence of sub-replacement family size ideals in Europe, *European Demographic Research Papers No. 2* (Vienna: Vienna Institute of Demography, Austrian Academy of Sciences).

Goldstein, J. R., Sobotka, T. and Jasilioniene, A. (2009) The end of 'lowest-low' fertility?, *Population and Development Review*, 35: 663–699.

Gstrein, M., Mateeva, L. and Schuh, U. (2007) *Research Note: Deficiencies in the Supply of Family Friendly Services* (Brussels: European Commission, Directorate-General 'Employment, Social Affairs and Equal Opportunities', Unit E1—Social and Demographic Analysis). http://ec.europa.eu/social/BlobServlet?docId=3946&langId=en [Accessed 17.12.2012.]

Hakim, C. (2000) *Work–lifestyle Choices in the 21st Century: Preference theory* (Oxford: Oxford University Press).

Hakim, C. (2002) A new approach to explaining fertility patterns: preference theory, *Population and Development Review*, 29(3): 349–373.

Hakim, C. (2003) Childlessness in Europe: Research Report to the Economic and Social Research Council (ESRC) on the project funded by research grant RES-000-23-0074. London, LSE/ESRC. http://www.esrcsocietytoday.ac.uk/my-esrc/grants/RES-000-23-0074/outputs/Read/66c5d0b8-ca7a-4688-949a-423588329820 [Accessed 17.12.2012.]

Hoem J., Neyer, G. and Andersson, G. (2006) Education and childlessness. The relationship between educational field, educational level, and childlessness among Swedish women born in 1955–59, *Demographic Research*, 14(15): 331–380.

Hotz, V. J., Klerman, J. A. and Willis, R. (1997) The economics of fertility in developed countries, in M. Rosenzweig and O. Stark (eds), *Handbook of Population and Family Economics, Vol. 1A* (Amsterdam: Elsevier), 276–347.

Hourriez, J. M. and Olier, L. (1997) Niveau de vie et taille des ménages: estimation d'une échelle d'équivalence, *Economie et Statistique*, 308–309–310: 65–94.

Joshi, H. (2002) Production, reproduction, and education: women, children, and work in a British perspective, *Population and Development Review*, 28(3): 445.

Keizer, R. P. A., Dykstra, P. and Jansen, M. D. (2008) Pathways into childlessness: evidence of gendered life course dynamics, *Journal of Biosocial Science*, 40(6): 863–878.

Kiernan, K. (1989) Who remains childless?, *Journal of Biosocial Science*, 21: 387–398.

Kneale, D. and Joshi, H. (2008) Postponement and childlessness: evidence from two British cohorts, *Demographic Research*, 19: 1935–1964.

Kohler H.-P., Billari, F. C. and Ortega, J. A. (2002) The emergence of lowest-low fertility in Europe during the 1990s, *Population and Development Review*, 28(4): 641–680.

Kohler H.-P., Billari, F. C. and Ortega, J. A. (2006) Low fertility in Europe: causes, implications and policy options, in F. R. Harris (ed.), *The Baby Bust: Who will do the work? Who will pay the taxes?* (Lanham, MD: Rowman & Littlefield), 48–109.

Lesthaeghe, R. (1995) The Second Demographic Transition in Western countries: an interpretation, in K. Oppenheim Mason and A.-M. Jensen (eds), *Gender and Family Change in Industrialised Countries* (Oxford: Clarendon Press), 17–62.

Livi Bacci, M. (2001) Too few children and too much family, *Daedalus*, 130(3): 139–156.

Luci A. and Thévenon O., (2011) Does economic development explain the fertility rebound in OECD countries?, *Population & Societies*, 481. http://www.ined.fr/fichier/t_publication/1551/publi_pdf2_pesa481.pdf [Accessed 17.12.2012.]

Lutz, W., Skirbekk, V. and Testa, M. R. (2006) The low-fertility trap hypothesis: forces that may lead to further postponement and fewer births in Europe, *Vienna Yearbook of Population Research* 2006: 167–192.

McDonald, P. (2000) Gender equity, social institutions and the future of fertility, *Journal of Population Research*, 17(1): 1–16.

McDonald, P. (2008) Very low fertility. Consequences, causes and policy approaches, *Japanese Journal of Population* 6(1): 19–23.

McDonald, P. (2010) Pourquoi la fécondité est-elle élevée dans les pays anglophones?, *Politiques Sociales et Familiales*, 100: 23–40.

Margolis, R. and Myrskylä, M. (2011) A global perspective on happiness and fertility, *Population and Development Review*, 37(1): 29–56.

Mencarini, L. and Tanturri, M. L. (2004) Time use, family role-set and childbearing among Italian working women, *Genus*, 60(1): 111–137.

Miller Torr, B. M. and Short, S. E. (2004) Second births and the second shift: a research note on gender equity and fertility, *Population and Development Review*, 30: 109–130.

Mills, M., Mencarini, L., Tanturri, M. L. and Begall, K. (2008) Gender equity and fertility intentions in Italy and the Netherlands, *Demographic Research*, 18(1): 1–26.

Mulder, C. (2006) Home-ownership and family formation, *Journal of Housing and the Built Environment*, 21(3): 281–298.

Mulder, C. and Billari, F. C. (2010) Home-ownership regimes and low fertility, *Housing Studies*, 25(4): 527–541.

Murphy, M. and Wang, D. (2001) Family-level continuities in childbearing in low fertility societies, *European Journal of Population*, 17: 75–96.

Neyer, G. (2006) Family policies and fertility in Europe: fertility policies at the intersection of gender policies, employment policies and care policies, MPIDR Working Paper WP2006-010, (Rostock: Max Planck Institute for Demographic Research), Apr.

Neyer, G. and Hoem, J. (2008) Education and permanent childlessness: Austria vs. Sweden: a research note, MPIDR Working Paper WP 2008-007 (Rostock: Max Planck Institute for Demographic Research), Feb.

Nicoletti, C. and Tanturri M. L. (2008) Differences in delaying motherhood across European countries: empirical evidence from the ECHP, *European Journal of Population*, 24(2): 157–183.

OECD (2007) *Babies and Bosses: Reconciling work and family life, a synthesis of findings for OECD countries* (Paris: OECD Publications).

OECD (2011) *Doing Better for Families* (Paris: OECD Publications).

Olah, L. S. (2003) Gendering fertility: second births in Sweden and Hungary, *Population Research and Policy Review*, 22: 171–200.

Reher, D. S. (1998) Family ties in Western Europe: persistent contrasts, *Population and Development Review*, 24(2): 203–234.

Reich, N. (2010) *Who Cares? Determinants of the fathers' use of parental leave in Germany*, Hamburg Institute of International Economics (HWWI), paper 1-31.

Rowland, D. T. (2007) Historical trends in childlessness, *Journal of Family Issues*, 28(10): 1311–1337.

Sardon, J. P. (2006) Recent demographic trends in developed countries, *Population (English Edition)*, 61(3): 225–300.

Sigle-Rushton, W. and Waldfogel, J. (2007) Motherhood and women's earnings in Anglo-American, continental European, and Nordic countries, *Feminist Economics*, 13(2): 55–91.

Sobotka, T., Skirbekk, V. and Philipov, D. (2011) Economic recession and fertility in the developed world, *Population and Development Review*, 37: 267–306.

Sobotka, T. and Testa, M. R. (2008) Attitudes and intentions towards childlessness in Europe, in C. Höhn, D. Avramov and I. Kotowska (eds), *People, Population Change and Policies: Lessons from the Population Policy Acceptance Study, Volume 1* (Berlin: Springer), 177–211.

Speder, Z. and Kamaras, F. (2008) Hungary: secular fertility decline with distinct period fluctuations, *Demographic Research*, 19 (Special Issue, 'Childbearing Trends and Policies in Europe'), 599–664.

Tanturri, M. L. (2006) Le donne senza figli: una tela cubista, in F. Ongaro (ed.), *Scelte riproduttive tra costi, valori e opportunità* (Milan: Franco Angeli), 109–130.

Tanturri, M. L. and Mencarini, L. (2008) Childlessness by choice or by constraints. Paths to voluntary childlessness in Italy, *Population and Development Review*, 34(1): 51–77.

Thévenon, O. (2011) Family policies in OECD countries: a comparative analysis, *Population and Development Review*, 37(1): 57–87.

Thévenon, O. and Gauthier, A. (2011) Family policies in developed countries: a 'fertility-booster' with side-effects, *Community, Work and Family*, 14(2): 197–216.

van de Kaa, D. J. (1987) Europe's Second Demographic Transition, *Population Bulletin*, 42: 1–59.

van Nimwegen, N. (2008) *Demographic Trends, Socio-Economic Impacts and Policy Implications in the European Union—2007*, Executive Summary of Monitoring Report (Brussels: European Observatory on the Social Situation and Demography, European Commission).

Various authors (2011) Rostock debate on demographic change, *Demographic Research*, Special Collection 9, 24,175–250.

Vitali, A., Billari F. C., Prskawetz, A. and Testa, M. R. (2009) Preference theory and low fertility: a comparative perspective, *European Journal of Population*, 25(4): 413–438.

Willis, R. (1973) A new approach to the economic theory of fertility behaviour, *Journal of Political Economy*, 81: SS14–64.

11

Mothers, Fathers, Families and Child Development

Gabriela Misca and Jo Smith

Introduction

Across the globe, family trajectories have become increasingly diverse, thus driving us away from an understanding of child development within the 'traditional' family unit that was once so prevalent, towards an examination of child development within more non-traditional structures (Atter-Schwartz *et al.*, 2009; Kouvo and Silvén, 2010; Magnuson and Berger, 2007). Parallel with this, conceptualising the term 'family' has become increasingly difficult (Dunn, 2002), and this has important implications for our understanding of factors that promote positive child development (Carlson and Corcoran, 2001). Newly emergent family structures resulting from social and demographic changes, including single-parent families, stepfamilies, adoptive and foster care families and same-gender parents, have heightened the need to understand how mothers, fathers and families influence child development (Atter-Schwartz *et al.*, 2009; Carlson and Corcoran, 2001).

In this chapter, we review the main tenets of attachment theory, one of the most popular and traditional approaches to conceptualising the relationship between caregivers and child development. Our review highlights the limitations of attachment theory in achieving a holistic understanding of child development in current societal structures. We propose, as an alternative, an ecological approach to understanding how children adjust within different family structures, and consider the advantages of taking this approach to the development of practice and policy. Key messages for policy and practice will be highlighted.

Contemporary Issues in Family Studies: Global Perspectives on Partnerships, Parenting and Support in a Changing World, First Edition. Edited by Angela Abela and Janet Walker.
© 2014 John Wiley & Sons, Ltd. Published 2014 by John Wiley & Sons, Ltd.

Attachment Theory Revisited

Most professionals working with children and families in Western cultures will be familiar with attachment theory, most probably in its initial formulations by Bowlby (1951, 1969). John Bowlby, a British psychiatrist, developed a highly influential framework which encapsulates the effects of initial attachment formation on a child's subsequent emotional, social and cognitive development whilst offering a theoretical perspective on development across the life course. Bowlby (1969, p. 94) defined attachment as a 'psychological connectedness between two human beings'. Attachment theory suggests that infants elicit proximity-seeking behaviours from their attachment figures to ensure survival and fulfilment of their needs; this in turn assists the development of the internal working model, which promotes lifelong emotional development (Bolen, 2000). Failure to form stable attachments within a 'critical period' (usually thought to be up to the end of the first year of life) may result in behavioural, social, cognitive and emotional difficulties in later life (Atwool, 2006). Several aspects of attachment theory as they were initially put forward have been challenged by a vast body of research. These are shown in the box below and will be summarised in turn.

Challenges to attachment theory

1. The role of mothers *vis-à-vis* fathers as primary caregivers.
2. The critical period of early attachment.
3. The continuity of attachment across the lifespan.

The role of mothers *vis-à-vis* fathers as primary caregivers

Bowlby (1969) initially proposed that the primary caregiving role is assumed by the mother, consequently neglecting the importance of the father in child development. Until some decades afterwards the importance of fathers as caregivers was not explored (Lamb, 1987, 2010), and recent reviews (Mercer, 2011) offer insightful evidence that challenge and revolutionise the basic tenets and core assumptions of attachment theory. Whilst attachment remains conceptualised as an intimate emotional bond between infant and caregiver, Mercer establishes that bonds can be formed with any person who provides long-lasting connectedness with the child, and that these are not necessarily restricted to a mother–child relationship.

The critical period of early attachment

The importance of the critical period of attachment during the first year of life has been challenged. Rutter (2002) argued that, given the right circumstances, new attachments can be formed when children are placed in a positive stable environment, enabling children to benefit from interventions such as adoption. Such conclusions are well supported by adoption research, including research on the adoption of children who have experienced severe neglect and abuse or institutionalisation (Chisholm, 1998;

Garvin *et al.*, 2012; Rutter *et al.*, 2007a, 2010; Smyke *et al.*, 2010). The importance of the environment is accentuated when examining the influences on child development, supporting arguments that children can develop and thrive in non-biological families and shedding new light on debates about the role of same-gender carers and children conceived as a result of assisted reproduction technologies.

The continuity of attachment across the lifespan

The assumption that internal working models are fixed throughout the life course (Bowlby, 1969) has had important implications for child development research, particularly as family structures have changed and continue to transition to include non-traditional arrangements. Recent research (reviewed by Mercer, 2011) challenges this notion, asserting that the child's internal working models are flexible and have the ability to adapt to new environments. These conclusions have been reinforced by studies of Romanian institutionalised children, who, despite their previous lack of early stable attachment relationships, were able to form attachments after placement within adoptive families, even though some of these attachments displayed features of 'indiscriminate friendliness' (Chisholm, 1998; Chisholm *et al.*, 1995). Research studies that followed up these children into their teens (Rutter *et al.*, 2007a) show that features of disinhibited attachment (such as indiscriminate friendliness) were reduced in frequency at age 11 (Rutter *et al.*, 2007b), and a quarter of the children who displayed 'quasi-autistic' features lost these as they were growing into their teenage years (Rutter *et al.*, 2007c). Overall longitudinal research attests to the remarkable resilience in these children's development. Recent reports on children at age 15 indicate that although some features of the effects of institutional deprivation persist, positive, major changes took place, such as the fading of the autistic features and problematic social disinhibition (Rutter *et al.*, 2010), reinforcing the fact that the effects of institutional deprivation are by no means fixed and irreversible. The evidence, then, suggests that poor early attachment experiences may not irreversibly hamper social and emotional adjustment as was once believed.

Public policy and practice in the UK and worldwide have embraced the original principles of attachment theory, and these have influenced child welfare systems and childcare policies, including custody decisions and adoption and fostering policies, for over 50 years. However, the challenges presented by increasingly diverse family structures (Walker, 2008), coupled with advances in current attachment theory, prompt a rethink of how decisions 'in the best interest of the child' are made. The current drive for evidence-based practice and a more highly skilled child workforce will hopefully provide the framework for a more positive integration of theory and practice.

Towards an Ecological Perspective in Understanding Child Development

This chapter proposes an alternative perspective for exploring the impact of family structure on child development. The bio-ecological model, also known as ecological systems theory, provides an evolving theoretical approach for human development, advocating that the objective and subjective elements of an individual and their environment dynamically drive their development (Bronfenbrenner, 2005). Comprehensive in its nature, the bio-ecological model consists of several hierarchical systems, the micro-, meso-, exo-, macro- and chronosystems that interrelate to influence human development (Bronfenbrenner, 2005), as indicated in the box below.

Bronfenbrenner's ecological model of development

The ecological model of development was put forward by Urie Bronfenbrenner, a distinguished American developmental psychologist, also well-known as a co-founder of the Head Start programme in the USA for disadvantaged pre-school children. His ecological systems model identifies five levels of environment that interact with an individual's development:

1. *Microsystem.* Comprises factors that impact directly on the child's development (e.g. family, school, peers, etc.).
2. *Mesosystem.* Refers to relations between microsystems (e.g. the relationship between parents and school).
3. *Exosystem.* Involves factors from the larger social system that impact on the child's development by interacting with a structure in the microsystem (e.g. community resources).
4. *Macrosystem.* Refers to the cultural contexts in which individuals live, including cultural values, customs, and laws (e.g. socioeconomic status, poverty, ethnicity, etc.).
5. *Chronosystem.* Encompasses the time dimension and transitions over the life course, as well as socio-historical circumstances.

An individual's own biology may be considered to be part of the microsystem, thus creating the 'bio-ecological model'. The bio-ecological model of development (Bronfenbrenner, 1979) has been applied to investigations of an array of developmental processes and to examinations of the ways in which multi-dimensional environments and a variety of family patterns shape child development, adjustment and wellbeing (Evans and Wachs, 2011). For example, Pedrosa *et al.* (2011) explored the ecology of adolescent adjustment and development, concluding that developmental processes are primarily associated with familial influences and relational variables. Similarly, friendship duration has been examined through the application of the ecological model to provide a framework for development.

Troutman and Fletcher (2010) advocated that individual development is influenced by direct interactions with family (process), the characteristics of the individual (person), the context in which development occurs (context), and changes over time (time), supporting the notion that peer relationships are dynamic and influenced by time and context. This understanding has important implications for developmental research: since peer relationships are context-specific and shaped by change over time, this may also hold true for child development within different types of families.

The reconceptualised tenets of Bowlby's attachment theory suggest that internal working models are flexible and susceptible to change in various environments (Mercer, 2011). Evans and Wachs (2011) reinforced this notion and emphasised the importance of the environment, suggesting that chaos and dysfunctional relationships can occur within any given environment. Therefore it may be conceivable that the emphasis on 'family' may be overstated, while the role of the 'environment' might be more salient.

In order to understand fully the ecology of child development and the implications of various family patterns on developmental processes, it is important to unravel the micro- and mesosystems in more detail, and we examine these in turn below. The remaining hierarchical environments in the ecological model of development— although not considered here in detail—filter down through to the individual and are influential regarding the processes involved in the first two hierarchical stages. The exosystem considers the social context in which children develop, for instance the social settings children engage with. The macrosystem envisages the cultural context (socio-economic status, poverty, ethnicity, public policy) that shapes the development of the child.

The Microsystem

At the micro level, the immediate environmental processes that influence child development include the relationship between the child and his or her parents as a unified structure. However, the microsystem further explores the role of the mother–child relationship independent of the father, and vice versa, to clarify the unique contribution each parent makes (Bronfenbrenner, 2005). Moreover, the role of siblings, extended family and day care/schooling arrangements may be considered in light of the effects on child development. Quality of relationship with the immediate family profoundly impacts on how children continue to develop during periods of stability or change (Bronfenbrenner, 2005).

The traditional family unit

There has been a long-held belief that the traditional family, consisting of two parents and their biological children, is the best environment for raising children (Lansford *et al.*, 2001). It is important, therefore, to consider further the microsystem of the traditional family unit and its impact on child development, and to ask the question 'How important is the traditional two-parent household on children's wellbeing?' It is well-established that children growing up in a traditional two-parent household exhibit more enhanced development, particularly within the social, cognitive and emotional aspects of child development, than children living in diverse family structures (Amato, 2005). Likewise, the quality of attachment towards two parents enhances children's wellbeing across the life course (Liu, 2006) and further assists the stabilisation of romantic relationships and peer friendships in adolescence (Dykas *et al.*, 2006). Alternatively, evidence from meta-analysis posits that both parents may influence the development of mental health disturbances, in the presence of maternal and/or paternal psychopathology, which suggests that the mother and father are equally influential on child development (Connell and Goodman, 2002).

Exposure to a positive, stable environment offers the child a greater opportunity to develop security and a secure attachment to both parents, which consequently enhances academic competence (Diener *et al.*, 2007) and emotional wellbeing (Baxter *et al.*, 2011). Similarly, Magnuson and Berger (2007) advocate that a stable two-parent household is likely to earn significantly more income, achieve a better socio-economic status and live in a higher-quality environment, all of which are assets to child development. Moreover, a unified mother–father relationship facilitates child development by offering two role models, enhanced supervision and stability (Hetherington and Stanley-Hagan, 1999), which act as protective factors against substance misuse, violence and risky behaviour (Barratt and Turner, 2006). Involvement with two parents optimises development and psychological wellbeing, especially in quality relationships (Bulando and Majumdar, 2008). Similarly, stable long-term autonomous parenting enhances adjustment to social situations and also influences gender behaviour (Kouvo and Silvén, 2010). These themes are illustrated in the box below.

The potential advantages of living in a two-parent family

Three themes emerge from the research on children living in a two-parent family:

1. Children living in a two-parent household have better outcomes than their peers who do not (Lansford *et al.*, 2001).
2. Children have the opportunity to benefit from two role models (Barratt and Turner, 2006).
3. Living in a stable two-parent family environment enhances the development of secure attachments, which the mesosystem reinforces (Bronfenbrenner, 2005).

Analysis at the micro level offers only a partial view of the role of the mothers and fathers in child development, however. As much research on divorce has shown (see e.g. Chapter 16, this volume), the relationship between parents is crucial in determining the influence that parents have on their children. This will be explored further at the mesosystem level.

The Mesosystem

Beyond the microsystem, a study at the mesosystem level shows how different family structures may impact on children's development and adjustment in the light of newly emerging family structures (Palacios, 2009). Dramatic shifts in family arrangements have increased single parenthood and reduced the number of multi-generational households in industrialised societies (Ginsburg, 2007). By considering the mesosystem it is possible to examine child development relating to children living in a range of family structures. Thus, we can consider children whose parents are cohabiting, divorced, remarried or gay or lesbian, as well as children who are adopted. The microsystem and the mesosystem are salient for the understanding of child adjustment in diverse family structures because they take account of the immediate environment and the interrelation of contexts in relation to the child (Bronfenbrenner, 2005; Palacios, 2009).

Cohabiting and conflictual couples

There are no significant differences between the contributions to child development made by cohabiting and married parents (Liu, 2006). The development of children growing up with cohabiting parents has been shown to be considerably better than that of children who have minimal contact with one parent and, perhaps more importantly, children of cohabiting parents do not fare worse than children of married parents (Heiland and Liu, 2006).

Exposure to high conflict in any kind of family increases the psychological distress experienced by children, which in turn impacts on the child's sense of security (Harold *et al.*, 2004). Exposure to observed and covert conflict impacts on the parental relationship and, consequently, hinders child adjustment (Finger *et al.*, 2009). This has important implications for child adjustment. Irrespective of marital status, the evidence suggests that parental conflict is far more damaging to the child's wellbeing in increasing the risk of behavioural disturbances, psycho-social problems and poor adjustment (Pedro-Carroll, 2001). Consequently, a stable environment enhances positive child development and adjustment (Amato, 2005).

Single parenthood: mothers and fathers

Research exploring the impact on children of living in single-parent households is less consistent (see Chapter 12, this volume). Single parenthood, whether through choice, death, or separation and divorce, is shown to have adverse consequences on child development and adjustment (Belsky and Pasco-Fearon, 2011). However, while there is greater risk of ambivalent behaviour and conflict than in two-parent households, research shows that children simultaneously experience greater intimacy with their parent (Walker and Hennig, 1997). Growing up in a single-parent household further emphasises the independent roles played by mothers and fathers.

Parental separation is a significant contributing factor to single parenthood (Carlson and Corcoran, 2001; Ginsburg, 2007). Amato (2005) ascertained that children in single-parent families experience weaker relationships with their primary parent, and exhibit less secure attachments than their peers whose families remain intact (Hamilton, 2000). These impacts are closely associated with conflict. Risk factors associated with divorce heighten the prevalence of behavioural problems among children and adolescents (Pasco Fearon and Belsky, 2011). When the parental relationship is hostile post-separation, this environment has negative consequences for the child's emotional wellbeing (Baxter *et al.*, 2011). The risks of children of divorced parents engaging in delinquent behaviour and leaving education early are three times those of children of non-divorced parents doing so (Hetherington and Stanley-Hagan, 1999), indicating that there are significant disadvantages relating to lone parenting, parental conflict and economic hardship (Carlson and Corcoran, 2001). Moreover, children with divorced parents are at risk of unresolved attachment representations in adolescence and adulthood, subsequently affecting their own romantic relationships and peer friendships (Aikins *et al.*, 2009).

Sharing close relationships with siblings and other kin, by contrast, aids adjustment to parental separation and negative life events (Ainsworth, 1989). Child development is significantly associated with the time and attention that the child receives from its parents or caregiver. Magnuson and Berger (2007) argue that single parents are significantly disadvantaged with regard to parenting in terms of the time they can give to their children. As a result of parental separation, time for lone parents to engage in play with their child is reduced, which has a major impact on the child's social, emotional and cognitive development (Ginsburg, 2007).

Single mothers

The assumption that the mother assumes the role of the primary caregiver (Ainsworth, 1989; Bowlby, 1969) has heavily influenced public policy and custodial arrangements when parents separate, with the result that the majority of children live with their mothers and spend less time with their fathers (Stevenson and Black, 1988). A positive maternal attitude has been shown to alleviate the negative effects of parental divorce (Ricciuti, 2004), indicating that the stability of the new environment is influential on child adjustment and wellbeing. The role of the mother has been shown to be highly important in peer relationships, particularly influencing friendship quality in childhood and assisting social and emotional development across the life course (McElwain and Volling, 2004; Steele, 2002).

Nevertheless, transitioning to a single-mother household increases the risk of a child having behavioural problems during childhood, which can escalate to affect emotional adjustment (Magnuson and Berger, 2007). Furthermore, single mothers are susceptible to poverty, which increases the risk of alcohol misuse, and both of these factors have major implications for children's adjustment and development (O'Connor et al., 2002). In turn, poverty and scarcity of economic resources significantly affect the child's cognitive and emotional wellbeing and adjustment (Ram and Hou, 2003).

The role of the father in child development

After decades of an exclusive focus on mother–child relationships, researchers have come to recognise the important roles that fathers play in socialising their children (see Lamb, 2010, for a review). Most fathers and father figures have a significant impact on children's development, both directly and indirectly. Fathers in heterosexual couples, and increasingly those in gay relationships, are taking a more active role in child rearing.

Evidence from research that has explored the importance of the father–child relationship has increased significantly in recent decades. While there is evidence that the absence of a father does not necessarily hinder child development (MacCallum and Golombok, 2004), critics argue that lack of a father figure hinders emotional wellbeing and promotes exposure to hostile environments (Magnuson and Berger, 2007). The risk of aggressive behaviour is more prevalent among sons whose father is absent than among sons who have stable or frequent contact with their father (Lewis and Lamb, 2003). This supports more recent findings that children who receive greater paternal support exhibit fewer aggressive tendencies (Harper et al., 2006). Although some research has minimised the importance of the father–child relationship, Allgood et al. (2012) have highlighted the profound positive effect fathers have on their child's self-esteem, independence and psychological wellbeing. Lone fathers bringing up children can claim to promote significant benefits for children's romantic relationships and their social and emotional development (Hall, 2009). Single fathers offer protection for their children and enable positive adjustment, particularly among sons who are able to relate to their father (Hetherington and Stanley-Hagan, 1999). Moreover, the father's role is crucial for learning about the outer social world and developing peer relationships in adolescence (Steele, 2002), and for assisting the child's development (Lewis and Lamb, 2003) and wellbeing (Wilson and Prior, 2010). Fathers have a critical role to play in providing care for their child. As fathers frequently report feeling emotionally detached from their child in the presence of the mother (Miall and March, 2005), providing the child with a secure paternal relationship benefits the child's socio-emotional development and adjustment (Lewis and Lamb, 2003).

Conversely, the lack of a maternal influence significantly hampers child development, particularly for young girls. For example, adolescent girls have reported difficulties in approaching their lone father about personal issues which they would typically discuss with their mother (Kalman, 2003). The research indicates that both parents are equally important contributors to child development and that the absence of either parent can have detrimental effects on a child's wellbeing.

Various single-parent arrangements reinforce the importance of the environment and the significance of stability on child development (Baxter *et al.*, 2011). More important than the family structure *per se* is the quality of the environment that parents provide, whether stable or hostile, which predicts child development and adjustment (Evans and Wachs, 2011; Gunnar *et al.*, 2000; Lansford *et al.*, 2001; Rutter, 2002).

The evidence suggests that mothers and fathers are equally important in shaping child development. However, in the absence of one parent, adverse effects can be overcome if the transitioning environment is stable and positive (Baxter *et al.*, 2011). When children move into a harmonious environment having experienced a conflictual parental divorce, they are likely to exhibit fewer behavioural problems (Hetherington and Stanley-Hagan, 1999). Such transitions may include moving into a stepfamily owing to the remarriage or repartnering of one or both birth parents or more harmonious shared care arrangements between the parents. How these transitions are managed is critically important for child development.

In respect of parenting post-divorce or post-separation, finding the solution which is 'in the best interests of the child' presents many challenges. While parent–child contact after parental separation receives paramount consideration in judicial decisions, recent research evidence from Australia indicates that shared childcare (defined as childcare taking place five nights or more per fortnight) post-divorce or post-separation is developmentally challenging for infants and pre-school children (McIntosh *et al.*, 2010). This new evidence is important, as it identifies the developmental stage of the child as an important factor in children's outcomes in shared post-separation arrangements:

> ... regardless of socio-economic background, parenting or inter-parental cooperation, shared overnight care of children under four years of age had an independent and deleterious impact on several emotional and behavioral regulation outcomes ... By kindergarten or school entry at around age 4–5 years of age, these effects were no longer evident. (McIntosh *et al.*, 2010, p. 9)

These findings have important implications for policy and practice, unequivocally placing the developmental needs of the child at the centre of decisions on childcare arrangements post-divorce or separation.

Stepfamilies

The effect of stepfamily life on children's development is unclear, as research has so far failed to draw a clear conclusion. Family transitions become problematic for child wellbeing and adjustment when there is heightened stress, a change in family roles and ongoing familial conflict (Magnuson and Berger, 2007). The complexities of stepfamily arrangements are more apparent when the step-parent also has children from a previous relationship. This complexity is more likely to be associated with adjustment problems and poor psychological wellbeing for children living in complex stepfamilies than for those living in non-complex stepfamilies (Dunn, 2002).

Wagmiller et al. (2010) have challenged previous negative findings relating to stepfamilies, suggesting that mothers from advantaged single-parent households who remarry facilitate their child's academic achievement since their children re-enter a unified household that provides a more stable environment. Conversely, adjustment problems as a result of acquiring a stepfamily tend to change the parent–child relationship and maintain residual conflict (Dunn, 2002). Consequently, Saint-Jacques and colleagues (2006) have reported that stepfamilies increase children's vulnerability to behavioural problems, although these are usually short-lived, and in the long term are reduced.

The negative effects of family transitions can be overcome when step-parents offer support to their stepchildren (Kinniburgh-White et al., 2010), but if step-parents portray dominance this can increase adjustment difficulties, conflict and the risk of emotional and behavioural problems (Cartwright et al., 2009). Moreover, an increasingly negative relationship with stepfamilies reduces attachment security (Planitz et al., 2009). Research suggests that the effects of transitioning to a new family structure affects children differently, and some may develop resilience to the impact of changes which accompany family reorganisation, thereby negating adverse childhood experiences (Magnuson and Berger, 2007).

Adoption and child development

A fundamental question in applied child development research is whether children can develop normally in terms of their psychological, emotional and social wellbeing after experiencing abuse and neglect and, consequently, having been removed from their birth families and placed in state care or with foster parents, or having been adopted. Researchers are essentially interested in how adopted children engage with their microsystem (school and family life) and how their past experience impacts on their later development, including how their internal working models coexist with the internal working models of their adoptive parents (Palacios, 2009).

The evidence indicates that a positive caregiving environment has the ability to reverse the effects of neglect and deprivation and assist normal child development (Smyke et al., 2010). This suggests that past experiences need not hamper a child's future development and adjustment. Moreover, parenting quality can mediate the potentially detrimental effects of early institutionalisation (Garvin et al., 2012), especially if the child is adopted before reaching the age of 2, as they are still able to form a secure attachment within this early critical period (Smyke et al., 2010).

On the basis of Bowlby's original (1969) assumptions, adoption policy and practice maintain that failure to initiate a bond with or separation from the primary caregiver within the first two years of life has detrimental consequences for the child's social and emotional development (Chisholm, 1995). However, as the tenets of attachment theory have evolved, new light has been shed on the understanding of adoption and attachment. While research into the effects of institutionalisation among Romanian children has highlighted the importance of attachment formation (Audet and Mare, 2010), evidence pertaining to the assumption of attachment continuity is not uniform.

Child institutionalisation reportedly hinders the ability to form an attachment (Stein, 2006), so that later exposure to a positive environment cannot always negate impaired development because the increased risk of developmental disorders prevails (Audet and Mare, 2010). Likewise, long-term absence of a primary caregiver increases antisocial behaviour and the risk of irreversible developmental consequences (Muris and Maas, 2004). It is well established that attachment insecurity remains higher among adopted than among non-adopted children (Feeney et al., 2007). Yet, despite many children continuing to exhibit socio-emotional difficulties, problem behaviour and cognitive delays, these effects can be eradicated by post-adoption care when the child is exposed to a positive and stable environment (Gunnar et al., 2000). Palacios et al. (2011) proposed that adoption offers a remarkable opportunity to facilitate positive child development and overcome past negative experiences.

Gay and lesbian parenthood

The impact of same-gender parenthood is the focus of Chapter 13 in this volume. Here we summarise the main messages from a child development perspective. Many of the negative stereotypes about gay or lesbian parenting have been challenged by research conducted over the past three decades (Anderssen et al., 2002; Tasker, 2005). A strong body of empirical evidence, emerging in particular from studies of lesbian-headed families, indicates that children with same-gender parents are indistinguishable from children with heterosexual parents with respect to their psychological adjustment, quality of peer relationships and psychosexual development. Moreover, children raised by lesbian women do not develop more poorly than children in general and, indeed, they experience family lives which are very similar to those experienced by children in heterosexual families (Tasker, 2005). As is the case in heterosexual families, the quality of the couple relationship is a strong predictor of the quality of children's adjustment (see e.g. Bos, 2004; Brewaeys et al., 1997; Chan et al., 1998; Patterson et al. 2004). Research on outcomes for children raised in same-gender families has progressed our understanding of children's social development by highlighting the importance of factors such as family harmony, and by raising questions about the presumed importance of same-sex and heterosexual role models in shaping gender development and the development of sexual preferences (Golombok and Tasker, 1996). Research on the impact of same-gender families in respect of child development does not detract from the importance of mothers or fathers in child development, but highlights ways in which different gender roles are provided through extended family, kin and social networks.

Implications for Policy and Practice

For many years, attachment theory influenced social policy and the child welfare system (Walker, 2008) and new assumptions, research findings and reformulations have not always filtered into practice. In the light of new evidence, we can see that the quality of the home environment and the quality of the relationship with the caregiver both facilitate positive child development more than the type of family structure in which children live (Baxter *et al.*, 2011): a positive and stable environment has the ability to negate the harmful effects of family transitions and divorce, and any damaging experiences before adoption (Diener *et al.*, 2007; Liu, 2006). Despite the need to reconceptualise attachment theory's basic assumptions and understand that attachment styles are not inflexible across the life course, so that the sooner a deprived child is moved into a harmonious environment the sooner they can readjust, in reality the primacy of birth parents is frequently maintained to the detriment of children's wellbeing. Research recognises the important role that both mothers and fathers play in child development (Amato, 2005), but, as the traditional family structure is changing, it is important to adequately support alternative family structures, including those involving single parents, stepfamilies and same-gender parents.

The evidence reviewed in this chapter has important implications for child welfare policy and practice. An ecological perspective that is child-centred contributes to a holistic understanding of how families, in all their variety of forms, influence child development. Such a perspective will support child-centred practice and policy. With an adequate environment and appropriate and stable care, children will thrive. The quality of the family environment, including the relationship between the parents, whether living in the same household or sharing parenting after separation, is a key factor for the healthy adjustment, development and wellbeing of children. However, it is equally imperative that judicial decisions, and in particular post-separation parenting arrangements, take into account the ages and developmental stages of children.

The existing evidence supports the idea that both mothers and fathers are equally important in child development and that this should be acknowledged. This has implications for decisions about the provision of childcare and family support, or about family support, which all too often tend to be mother-centred in practice. Equally, the evidence should not be interpreted too narrowly in practice—as evidence from research on same-gender families shows, same-sex parents can provide an environment in which children may thrive. At a time when many governments are seeking to support parents and families so that they can ensure healthy outcomes for children, four key messages from the research need to be taken into account:

1. An ecological perspective that is child-centred contributes to a holistic understanding of how families, in all their variety of forms, influence child development.
2. Such a perspective will support child-centred policy and practice.
3. The quality of the family environment, including the relationship between the parents, whether living in the same household or sharing parenting after separation, is a key factor for the healthy adjustment, development and wellbeing of children.
4. Taking into consideration the developmental age/stage of the child is paramount when making decisions in the best interests of the child.

References

Aikins, J. W., Howes, C. and Hamilton, C. (2009) Attachment stability and the emergence of unresolved representations during adolescence, *Attachment & Human Development*, 11(5): 491–512.

Ainsworth, M. D. S. (1989) Attachments beyond infancy, *American Psychologist*, 44(4): 709–716.

Allgood, S. M., Beckert, T. E. and Peterson, C. (2012) The role of father involvement in the perceived psychological well-being of young adult daughters: a retrospective study, *North American Journal of Psychology*, 14(1): 95–110.

Amato, P. R. (2005) The impact of family formation change on the cognitive, social, and emotional well-being of the next generation, *The Future of Children*, 15(2): 75–96.

Anderssen, N., Amlie, C. and Ytteroy, E. A. (2002) Outcomes for children with lesbian or gay parents: a review of studies from 1978 to 2000, *Scandinavian Journal of Psychology*, 43: 335–351.

Attar-Schwartz, S., Tan, J. P., Buchanan, A., Flouri, E. and Griggs, J. (2009) Grandparenting and adolescent adjustment in two-parent biological, lone-parent, and step-families, *Journal of Family Psychology*, 23(1): 67 75.

Atwool, N. (2006) Attachment and resilience: implications for children in care, *Child Care in Practice*, 12(4): 315–330.

Audet, K. and Mare, L. L. (2010) Mitigating effects of the adoptive caregiving environment on inattention/overactivity in children adopted from Romanian orphanages, *International Journal of Behavioural Development*, 35(2): 107–115.

Barratt, A. E. and Turner, J. (2006) Family structure and substance use problems in adolescence and early adulthood: examining explanations for the relationship, *Addiction*, 101: 109–120.

Baxter, J., Weston, R., and Qu, L. (2011) Family structure, co-parental relationship quality, post-separation paternal involvement and children's emotional well-being, *Journal of Family Studies*, 17(2): 86–109.

Bolen, R. M. (2000) Validity of attachment theory, *Trauma, Violence, and Abuse*, 1(2): 128–153.

Bos, H. (2004) *Parenting in Planned Lesbian Families* (Amsterdam: Vossiuspers UvA).

Bowlby, J. (1951) *Maternal Care and Mental Health* (Geneva: World Health Organisation).

Bowlby, J. (1969) *Attachment and Loss: Attachment* (London: Hogarth Press/Institute of Psycho-analysis).

Brewaeys, A., Ponjaert, I., van Hall, E. and Golombok, S. (1997) Donor insemination: child development and family functioning in lesbian mother families, *Human Reproduction*, 12(6): 1349–1359.

Bronfenbrenner, U. (1979) *Ecology of Human Development* (Cambridge, MA: Harvard University Press).

Bronfenbrenner, U. (2005) *Making Human Beings Human: Bioecological perspectives on human development* (Thousand Oaks, CA: Sage).

Bulands, R. E. and Majumbar, D. (2008) Perceived parent–child relations and adolescent self-esteem, *Journal of Child Family Studies*, 18: 203–212.

Carlson, M. J. and Corcoran, M. E. (2001) Family structure and children's behavioural and cognitive outcomes, *Journal of Marriage and Family*, 63: 779–792.

Cartwright, C., Farnsworth, V. and Mobley, V. (2009) Relationships with step-parents in the life stories of young adults of divorce, *Family Matters*, 82: 30–37.

Chan, R. W., Brooks, R. C., Raboy, B. and Patterson, C. J. (1998) Division of labor among lesbian and heterosexual parents: associations with children's adjustment, *Journal of Family Psychology*, 12(3): 402–419.

Chisholm, K. (1998) A three year follow-up of attachment and indiscriminate friendliness in children adopted from Romanian orphanages, *Child Development*, 69(4): 1092–1106.

Chisholm, K., Carter, M. C., Ames, E. W. and Morison, S. J. (1995) Attachment security and indiscriminately friendly behaviour in children adopted from Romanian orphanages, *Development and Psychopathology*, 7: 283–294.

Diener, M. L., Isabelle, R. A. and Behunin, M. G. (2007) Attachment to mothers and fathers during middle childhood: associations with child gender, grade, and competence, *Social Development*, 17(1): 84–101.

Dunn, J. (2002) The adjustment of children in stepfamilies: lessons from community studies, *Child and Adolescent Mental Health*, 7(4): 154–161.

Dykas, M. J., Woodhouse, S. S., Cassidy, J. and Waters, H. S. (2006) Narrative assessment of attachment representations: links between secure base scripts and adolescent attachment, *Attachment & Human Development*, 8(3): 221–240.

Evans, G. W. and Wachs, T. D. (2011) Chaos and its influence on children's development: an ecological perspective, *East Asian Archives of Psychiatry*, 21(2): 85–86.

Feeney, J. A., Passmore, N. L. and Peterson, C. C. (2007) Adoption, attachment, and relationship concerns: a study of adult adoptees, *Personal Relationships*, 14: 129–147.

Finger, B., Hans, S. L., Bernstein, V. J. and Cox, S. M. (2009) Parent relationship quality and infant–mother attachment, *Attachment & Human Development*, 11(3): 285–306.

Garvin, M. C., Tarullo, A. R., Ryzin, M. V. and Gunnar, M. R. (2012) Postadoption parenting and socioemotional development in postinstitutionalised children, *Development and Psychopathology*, 24: 35–48.

Ginsburg, K. R. (2007) The importance of play in promoting health child development and maintaining strong parent–child bonds, *American Academy of Pediatrics*, 119(1): 182–191.

Golombok, S. and Tasker, F. (1996) Do parents influence the sexual orientation of their children? Findings from a longitudinal study of lesbian families, *Developmental Psychology*, 32(1): 3–11.

Gunnar, M. R., Bruce, J. and Grotevant, H. D. (2000) International adoption of institutionally reared children: research and policy, *Development and Psychopathology*, 12: 677–693.

Hall, S. S. (2009) Paternal influences on daughters' heterosexual relationship socialisation: attachment style and disposition toward marriage, *Family Science Review*, 14(2): 1–17.

Hamilton, C. E. (2000) Continuity and discontinuity of attachment from infancy through adolescence, *Child Development*, 71(3): 690–694.

Harold, G. T., Sheltin, K. H., Goeke-Morey, M. C. and Cummings, M. (2004) Marital conflict, child emotional security about family relationships and child adjustment, *Social Development*, 13(3): 350–376.

Harper, F. W. K., Brown, A. M., Arias, I. and Brody, G. (2006) Corporal punishment and kids: how do parent support and gender influence child adjustment?, *Journal of Family Violence*, 21(3): 197–207.

Heiland, F. and Liu, S. H. (2006) Family structure and wellbeing of out-of-wedlock children: the significance of the biological parents' relationship, *Demographic Research*, 15(4), 61–104.

Hetherington, E. M. and Stanley-Hagan, M. (1999) The adjustment of children with divorced parents: a risk and resiliency perspective, *Journal of Child Psychology*, 40(1): 129–140.

Kalman, M. B. (2003) Adolescent girls, single-parent fathers, and menarche, *Holistic Nursing Practice*, 17(1): 36–40.

Kinniburgh-White, R., Cartwright, C. and Seymour, F. (2010) Young adults' narratives of relational development with stepfathers, *Journal of Social and Personal Relationships*, 27(7): 890–907.

Kouvo, A. M. and Silvén, M. (2010) Finnish mother's and father's attachment representations during child's first year predict psychosocial adjustment in pre-adolescence, *Attachment & Human Development*, 12(6): 529–549.

Lamb, M. E. (ed.) (1987) *The Father's Role: Cross cultural perspectives* (Hillsdale, NJ: Lawrence Erlbaum).

Lamb, M. E. (ed.) (2010) *The Role of the Father in Child Development* (Hoboken, NJ and Chichester, UK: Wiley), 5th edn.

Lansford, J. E., Ceballo, R., Abbey, A. and Stewart, A. J. (2001) Does family structure matter? A comparison of adoptive, two-parent biological, single-mother, stepfather, and stepmother households, *Journal of Marriage and Family*, 63: 840–851.

Lewis, C. and Lamb, M. E. (2003) Fathers' influences on children's development: the evidence from two-parent families, *European Journal of Psychology of Education*, 18(2): 211–228.

Liu, Y. L. (2006) Paternal/maternal attachment, peer support, social expectations of peer interaction, and depressive symptoms, *Adolescence*, 41(164): 705–721.

MacCallum, F. and Golombok, S. (2004) Children raised in fatherless families from infancy: a follow-up of children of lesbian and single heterosexual mothers at early adolescence, *Journal of Child Psychology and Psychiatry*, 45(8): 1407–1419.

McElwain, N. L. and Volling, B. L. (2004) Attachment security and parental sensitivity during infancy: associations with friendship quality and false-belief understanding at age 4, *Journal of Social and Personal Relationships*, 21(5): 639–667.

McIntosh, J., Smyth B., Kelaher, M., Wells, Y. and Long, C. (2010) *Post-separation Parenting Arrangements: Patterns and developmental outcomes for infants and children*, Collected reports (three reports prepared for the Australian Government Attorney-General's Department, Canberra), http://www.ag.gov.au/Families/Familylawpublications/Pages/Researchonsharedcareparentingandfamilyviolence.aspx [Accessed 17.10.2012.]

Magnuson, K and Berger, L. M. (2007) *Associations of Family Structure States and Transitions During Middle Childhood* (University of Michigan: National Poverty Center).

Mercer, J. (2011) Attachment theory and its vicissitudes: toward an updated theory, *Theory & Psychology*, 21(1): 25–45.

Miall, C. E. and March, K. (2005) Community attitudes toward birth fathers' motives for adoption placement and single parenting, *Family Relations*, 54(4): 535–546.

Muris, P. and Maas, A. (2004) Strengths and difficulties as correlates of attachment style in institutionalised and non-institutionalised children with below-average intellectual abilities, *Child Psychiatry and Human Development*, 34(4): 317–328.

O'Connor, M. J., Kogan, N. and Findlay, R. (2002) Prenatal alcohol exposure and attachment behaviour in children, *Alcoholism, Clinical and Experimental Research*, 26(10): 1592–1602.

Palacios, J. (2009) The ecology of adoption, in G. M. Wrobel and E. Neil (eds), *International Advances in Adoption Research for Practice* (Chichester: Wiley), 71–94.

Palacios, J., Román, M. and Camacho, C. (2011) Growth and development in internationally adopted children: extent and timing of recovery after early adversity, *Child: Care, Health and Development*, 37(2): 282–288.

Patterson, C. J., Sutfin, E. L. and Fulcher, M. (2004) Division of labor among lesbian and heterosexual parenting couples: correlates of specialized versus shared patterns, *Journal of Adult Development*, 11(3): 179–189.

Pedro-Carroll, J. (2001) The promotion of wellness in children and families: challenges and opportunities, *American Psychologist*, 56(11): 993–1004.

Pedrosa, A. A., Pires, R., Carvalho, P., Canavarro, M. C. and Dattilio, F. (2011) Ecological contexts in adolescent pregnancy: the role of individual, sociodemographic, familial and relational variables in understanding risk of occurrence and adjustment patterns, *Contemporary Family Therapy*, 33: 107–127.

Planitz, J. M., Feeney, J. A. and Peterson, C. C. (2009) Attachment patterns of young adults in stepfamilies and biological families, *Journal of Family Studies*, 15(1): 67–81.

Ram, B. and Hou, F. (2003) Changes in family structure and child outcomes: roles of economic and familial resources, *The Policy Studies Journal*, 31(3): 309–330.

Ricciuti, H. N. (2004) Single parenthood, achievement, and problem behavior in white, black, and Hispanic children, *The Journal of Educational Research*, 97(4): 196–207.

Rutter, M. (2002) Nature, nurture, and development: from evangelism through science toward policy and practice, *Child Development*, 73: 1–21.

Rutter, M., Beckett, C., Castle, J., Colvert, E., Kreppner, J., Mehta, M., Stevens, S. and Sonuga-Barke, E. (2007a) Effects of profound early institutional deprivation: an overview of findings from a UK longitudinal study of Romanian adoptees, *European Journal of Developmental Psychology*, 4(3): 332–350.

Rutter, M., Colvert, E., Kreppner, J., Beckett, C., Castle, J. and Groothues, C. (2007b) Early adolescent outcomes for institutionally deprived and non-deprived adoptees. I. Disinhibited attachment, *Journal of Child Psychology and Psychiatry*, 48: 17–30.

Rutter, M., Kreppner, J., Croft, C., Murin, M., Colvert, E., Beckett, C., Castle, J. and Sonuga-Barke, E. J. S. (2007c) Early adolescent outcomes of institutionally deprived and non-deprived adoptees. III. quasi-autism, *Journal of Child Psychology and Psychiatry*, 48(12): 1200–1207.

Rutter, M., Sonuga-Barke, E. J., Beckett, C., Castle, J., Kreppner, J., Kumsta, R., Schlotz, W., Stevens, S. and Bell, C. (2010) Deprivation-specific psychological patterns: effects of institutional deprivation, *Monographs of the Society for Research in Child Development*, 75: 1–20.

Saint-Jacques, M. C., Cloutier, R., Pauze, R., Simard, M., Gagne, M. H. and Poulin, A. (2006) The impact of serial transitions on behavioural and psychological problems among children in child protection services, *Child Welfare*, 85(6): 941–964.

Smyke, A. T., Zeanah, C. H., Fox, N. A., Nelson, C. A. and Guthrie, D. (2010) Placement in foster care enhances quality of attachment among young institutionalised children, *Child Development*, 81(1): 212–223.

Steele, H. (2002) State of the art: attachment, *The Psychologist*, 15(10): 618–623.

Stein, H. (2006) Maltreatment, attachment and resilience in the Orphans of Duplessis: commentary on 'Seven institutionalized children and their adaptation in late adulthood: the children of Duplessis', *Psychiatry*, 69(4): 306–313.

Stevenson, M. R. and Black, K. N. (1988) Paternal absence and sex-role development: a meta-analysis, *Child Development*, 59: 793–814.

Tasker, F. (2005) Lesbian mothers, gay fathers, and their children: a review, *Developmental and Behavioural Pediatrics*, 26(3): 224–240.

Troutman, D. R. and Fletcher, A. C. (2010) Context and companionship in children's short-term versus long-term friendships, *Journal of Social and Personal Relationships*, 27(8): 1060–1074.

Wagmiller, R. L., Gershoff, E., Veliz, P. and Clements, M. (2010) Does children's academic achievement improve when single mothers marry?, *Sociology of Emotion*, 83(3): 201–226.

Walker, J. (2008) The use of attachment theory in adoption and fostering, *Adoption and Fostering*, 32(1): 49–57.

Walker, L. J. and Hennig, K. H. (1997) Parent/child relationships in single-parent families, *Canadian Journal of Behavioural Science*, 29(1): 63–75.

Wilson, K. R. and Prior, M. R. (2010) Father involvement: the importance of paternal solo care, *Early Child Development and Care*, 180(10): 1391–1405.

12
Raising Children in Single-Parent Families[1]

JAN M. NICHOLSON, FABRIZIO D'ESPOSITO,
NINA LUCAS AND ELIZABETH M. WESTRUPP

Introduction

For many years, there has been a prevailing view that single-parent families provide less than optimal environments for raising children. This perspective is founded in evidence, consistent across many countries, that children from single-parent (typically female-headed) families fare more poorly than children living with two parents (for meta-analyses, see Amato, 2001; Amato and Keith, 1991). Most explanations for these differences assume that compromised parenting and parental mental health play a central role. However, many children in single-parent families do not have impaired outcomes (Ross *et al.*, 1998), and the factors that protect single parents in relation to parenting and mental health difficulties or place them at risk are not well understood. It also remains unclear whether these factors differ from those experienced by couple families. In this chapter we examine the contributions of a broad range of factors to the parenting and mental health of single mothers. We use three waves of longitudinal data, applying to two cohorts of Australian children aged 4–5 and 8–9 years respectively residing in single-mother families.

[1] This chapter draws on unit record data from *Growing Up in Australia: The Longitudinal Study of Australian Children*. The study is conducted in partnership between the Australian Government Department of Families, Housing, Community Services and Indigenous Affairs (FaHCSIA), the Australian Institute of Family Studies (AIFS) and the Australian Bureau of Statistics (ABS). The findings and views reported are those of the authors and should not be attributed to FaHCSIA, AIFS or the ABS. The designing of the study and the data collection were funded by FaHCSIA. The authors were supported by funding from the Victorian Government Department of Education and Early Childhood Development and the National Health & Medical Research Council (Career Development Award 390136 to Jan Nicholson).

Contemporary Issues in Family Studies: Global Perspectives on Partnerships, Parenting and Support in a Changing World, First Edition. Edited by Angela Abela and Janet Walker.
© 2014 John Wiley & Sons, Ltd. Published 2014 by John Wiley & Sons, Ltd.

Children in Single-Parent Families

Over the last 50 years, single-parent families have become increasingly common in most developed countries. This reflects a number of societal changes, most notably, greater acceptance and ease of divorce (Australian Bureau of Statistics, 2010). In Australia in 2004–6, there were 486000 single-parent families with a child under 15 years, representing 22 per cent of all families with children (Linacre, 2007). These rates are consistent with those reported for the UK (ONS, 2010), the USA (US Census Bureau, 2010), Canada (Statistics Canada, 2007) and New Zealand (Cotterell *et al.*, 2008). On the basis of these trends, a quarter of all Australian children will spend some part of their childhood years in a single-parent family following parental separation. While shared parenting arrangements are becoming more common, 87 per cent of single-parent families are female-headed (Australian Bureau of Statistics, 2010; Linacre, 2007) and the majority of care still resides with the female parent, at least for the early and middle childhood years (Cashmore *et al.*, 2010).

There is strong evidence that children in single-parent families fare more poorly across a broad range of outcome areas than children in two-parent families. In childhood this includes behavioural and emotional problems, poor school readiness, and lower literacy and academic achievement, and in adolescence and adulthood higher rates of school drop-out, health-risk behaviours, young parenthood, single parenthood and relationship instability (Amato and Sobolewski, 2001; Elliott and Richards, 1991; Rodgers *et al.*, 1997, 2011; Zill *et al.*, 1993). The consistency of these findings across countries and over time suggests there is something fundamental to single-parent families that places children at risk. As the outcomes most affected are those that are particularly vulnerable to parental influences, many causal explanations postulate a central role for parenting and parental mental health (Amato, 1993, 2005; Brody and Forehand, 1988; Deater-Deckard and Dunn, 1999).

Parenting and parental mental health as causal factors

The association between parenting and children's outcomes across the early years is well established. Existing research suggests that child outcomes are determined by a number of key parenting dimensions, including irritable, hostile parenting and a lack of parental warmth, consistency and self-efficacy (Bayer *et al.*, 2011; O'Connor, 2002; Pettit and Bates, 1989; Zubrick *et al.*, 2008). There is also emerging evidence that over-protective parenting is a risk in terms of children both internalising and externalising problems in early to middle childhood (Bayer *et al.*, 2011). Single parents have difficulties in a number of these areas. Compared with continuously married parents, they are less emotionally supportive of their children, have fewer rules, dispense harsher discipline, are more inconsistent in their discipline, provide less supervision, and engage in more conflict with their children (Amato, 2005; Lucas *et al.*, 2010).

Parent mental health problems are also consistently identified as a key determinant of poor child outcomes. Associations between maternal depression and children's socio-emotional and cognitive development are evident among both girls and boys, from infancy to adolescence (Goodman and Gotlib, 1999; Goodman *et al.*, 2011). Poor paternal mental health has also been shown to predict children's internalising and externalising of behaviour problems (Baxter and Smart, 2010; Connell and

Goodman, 2010; Kane and Garber, 2004), and cognitive development (Mensah and Kiernan, 2010). These associations are particularly relevant to single-parent families. In Australia lone mothers experience higher rates of suicidal thoughts, self-harm and depression than other women (Loxton *et al.*, 2006), and similar patterns are reported internationally (Hope *et al.*, 1999). Children in single-parent families are also at increased risk of exposure to parent mental health problems via their non-resident fathers, whose rates of psychological distress are 50–100 per cent higher than those of resident fathers (Giallo *et al.*, 2012; Huang and Warner, 2005; Jaffee *et al.*, 2001).

Children in single-parent families

Twenty-two per cent of all Australian families with at least one child under the age of 15 years are single-parent families. In 2004–2006, this equated to 486000 single-parent families. Similar rates are reported in other developed countries, and there is strong evidence that children growing up in these families fare more poorly across a broad range of outcome areas than children in two-parent families.

All children are influenced by their family environments. In particular, child outcomes are determined by a number of key parenting dimensions, as well as parent mental health. Single mothers have both greater difficulties in parenting and poorer mental health than mothers in couple relationships, which place their children's development at risk.

Determinants of parenting and parental mental health in single-parent families

There are a range of reasons why the parenting and mental health of mothers in single-parent families may be compromised. Key explanations relate to the characteristics of those who become single parents (selection effects), the disruptions associated with family transitions, and the effects of family stress and interparental conflict.

The selection effects hypothesis suggests that it is not single parenthood *per se* that places single mothers at risk of compromised parenting and mental health. Rather, single parenthood, poor parenting and mental health difficulties each arise as a result of mothers' pre-existing characteristics. These characteristics include the tendency for single mothers to be young, to have poor education, to be unemployed and to have limited financial resources (Linacre, 2007). These factors are associated both with becoming a single mother and with poor parenting and maternal mental health difficulties (Lucas *et al.*, 2010; Rubertsson *et al.*, 2005).

Modern families are dynamic in structure. Many children currently residing in single-parent families have previously lived with both parents, while some of those in couple households have experienced time in a single-parent family. The median time from parental separation to repartnering is around three years for mothers (ABS, 1994; Furstenberg, 1988; Isaacs and Leon, 1988), with nearly half of these new relationships ending within another two years (Lawton and Sanders, 1994). Each of these transitions can be considered a marker for a number of changes in intra-familial processes that extend both backwards and forwards in time (Funder, 1996; Hetherington, 1988). Changes that may start prior to a transition and endure for several years afterwards include heightened conflict between parents, disrupted parenting, reconfigured family roles and responsibilities, housing relocation and altered financial circumstances (Anderson *et al.*, 1999; Funder, 1996; Hetherington, 1987; Lawton and Sanders, 1994). However, researchers usually compare families according to their current structure, thereby overlooking the influence of prior family history. Thus, it is unclear whether the adverse effects of living in a single-parent family reflect the characteristic features associated with being a single parent, or the impact of a family transition (Brown, 2006; Cavanagh and Huston, 2006; Ruschena *et al.*, 2005).

A challenging aspect of family life for both single parents and their children concerns the burden of domestic work. In single-parent households, responsibility for domestic and child-rearing chores rests with one rather than two adults. By necessity, some things may slip. Time use studies show that when the demands on mothers' time increase, personal and self-care time is sacrificed (Bittman *et al.*, 2004)—a pattern likely to be detrimental to physical and mental health. In addition, children in single-parent families assume household chores and responsibilities for themselves and their siblings at a younger age and to a greater extent than their peers from two-parent households (Amato, 1987; Hetherington, 1987; Weiss, 1979). While such patterns may foster maturity and independence (Amato, 1987; Weiss, 1979), these increased demands provide more opportunities for parent–child conflict, potentially undermining parent–child relationships and adding to parental stress.

The majority of contemporary single-parent families are formed following separation and divorce. This period is both preceded and followed by heightened conflict between parents (Birditt *et al.*, 2010; Hetherington, 1988). Financial arrangements between parents, the sharing of parenting roles and children's contact with parents are the most common sources of ongoing conflict, issues that can be exacerbated by the repartnering of either parent (Funder, 1996; Lawton and Sanders, 1994).

In summary, single parenthood results in families being exposed to a number of adverse intra-familial conditions that place the health and wellbeing of mothers and their children at risk. However, there are also a number of adverse external circumstances that may disproportionately affect single-parent families.

Factors affecting the parenting and wellbeing of single mothers

There are many reasons why single mothers may have poorer parenting and poorer mental health than partnered mothers. It may be because of pre-existing characteristics such as low socio-economic status, or frequent changes in family structure, heavy domestic loads and high levels of family conflict.

Factors outside the family may also influence mothers' parenting and mental health. Single mothers are more likely to live in disadvantaged neighbourhoods and to have poor-quality jobs, making it difficult for them to maintain good mental health and positive parenting practices.

Extra-familial environments

Ecological models (Bronfenbrenner and Morris, 2006) highlight the fact that parenting occurs within an interrelated series of nested environments or contexts. To date, much of the research into the effects of single-parent families has focused on proximal factors—characteristics of the individual, the family or the household. Less attention has been paid to the broader extra-familial environments, which include the socio-cultural communities and neighbourhoods where families reside and the organisations and institutions with which family members interact. Financial constraints mean that single-parent families often live in poor-quality housing in disadvantaged neighbourhoods (Deater-Deckard and Dunn, 1999). These contexts shape the opportunities and pressures that families face in a number of ways. Poor infrastructure and services, lack of community support, and unsafe neighbourhoods may add to parental stress and time pressures, while restricting children's opportunities for positive development and increasing their exposure to undesirable peer models (Deater-Deckard and Dunn, 1999; Ross *et al.*, 1998).

Another contextual factor that may be important regards the effects of employment-related demands on single parents. It has long been known that employment conditions impact on employee mental health (Stansfield and Candy, 2006) and there is now evidence that non-family-friendly work conditions and poor-quality jobs adversely affect the parenting and mental health of parents of young children (Cooklin *et al.*, 2010; Strazdins *et al.*, 2007). Job conditions are not equally distributed. Those employed in the casualised workforce, women, and those in low-status employment (and hence single mothers) are likely to be over-represented in poor-quality jobs (Burgess and Strachan, 2005).

Previous comparisons of single mother and couple families show that socio-economic factors at least partly account for the increased risks of poor parenting (Chilcoat *et al.*, 1996; Knutson *et al.*, 2004) and mental health problems among single mothers (Cooper *et al.*, 2008; Hope *et al.*, 1999; Loxton *et al.*, 2006). In this chapter we extend this work to examine the additional contribution of broader contextual factors to mothers' parenting and mental health. Specifically, we compare mothers who are single parents with mothers in couple households, first when their child is aged 4–5 and then when their child is aged 8–9, to assess whether mothers in single-parent families report poorer parenting and greater psychological distress than couple mothers, and to determine the extent to which these differences are accounted for by a range of socio-demographic, family and external factors.

The Longitudinal Study of Australian Children

This chapter presents data from *Growing Up in Australia: The Longitudinal Study of Australian Children* (LSAC). The LSAC investigates the influence of family, social, economic and cultural environments on the health and wellbeing of Australian children (Sanson *et al.*, 2002). It comprises two stratified, randomly selected, nationally representative cohorts of approximately five thousand Australian children each, with data collected every two years, mainly via parent face-to-face interviews and questionnaires.

At the first wave of data collection in 2004, the Baby (B) Cohort (n=5107) was aged 0–1 years and the Kindergarten (K) Cohort (n=4983) 4–5 years. In this chapter we examine associations between the parenting and mental health of mothers at wave 3 (2008) when the children were aged 4–5 and 8–9 years (B and K cohorts respectively), taking into account a range of individual and contextual factors measured across waves 1, 2 and 3. Our principal focus is LSAC mothers (biological and adoptive) who were the sole parent of the study child at wave 3, these being compared with mothers in couple relationships at wave 3. The main outcomes investigated are maternal parenting and mental health. Sample weights and adjustment for complex sampling design were applied to all analyses.

The Longitudinal Study of Australian Children

Growing Up in Australia: The Longitudinal Study of Australian Children employs a cross-lagged cohort design. It was established by the Australian Government to provide evidence of how well Australian children are doing, and to identify the factors that influence children's developmental trajectories over the life course.

Two nationally representative cohorts of approximately 5000 infants and 5000 four-year-olds were recruited to the study in 2004, with data collection occurring every two years. Study informants include the parent who provides the primary care for the child, any other resident and non-resident parent figures, the child's childcare providers and teachers, and the child him-/herself. Direct assessments of language, cognitive ability, anthropometrics, child time-use diaries and linkage to healthcare use data are undertaken at relevant ages.

Confidentialised data are available by registration to national and international researchers. Current data releases include four waves at ages 0–1, 2–3, 4–5 and 6–7 years for the infant cohort and 4–5, 6–7, 8–9 and 10–11 years for the child cohort. Retention to wave 4 has been excellent (83% for both cohorts) although actual data available vary by data collection instrument. For more information see http://www.growingupinaustralia.gov.au/

Parenting was assessed across seven domains: maternal consistency, anger, hostility, over-protectiveness, self-efficacy, warmth and the use of inductive reasoning (Bayer *et al.*, 2009; Lucas *et al.*, 2010; Zubrick *et al.*, 2008). As these measures were generally skewed in a positive direction, total scale scores were dichotomised at the 20th percentile to create an indicator of relative poor parenting for each measure. An overall index of poor parenting was then computed as a count of the number of measures on which mothers reported poor parenting (score of 0 to 7).

Maternal mental health was measured using the Kessler-6 (K6) scale (Furukawa *et al.*, 2003). This screening tool provides a global measure of psychological distress in the previous four weeks and was dichotomised to indicate those experiencing significant symptoms of psychological distress (total score greater than 7 out of 24). A wide range of factors likely to be associated with mothers' parenting and mental health were examined. These could be classified as: child factors (age, gender, prematurity/low birth weight, sleep problems); socio-demographic factors (age, country of birth, language spoken at home, Indigenous status, education, income, poverty, financial hardship);

employment factors (employment status, work hours, job quality, occupational prestige); family factors (family stability, number of children in the house, children living elsewhere, time pressure, conflict with other parent, stressful life events); and environmental factors (housing tenure, remoteness, index of disadvantage,[2] and neighbourhood liveability, facilities and social capital). The LSAC measures are mostly standardised questions drawn from national studies such as the Australian Census or, where possible, from other Australian or international longitudinal studies (Australian Institute of Family Studies, 2007; Sanson *et al.*, 2002). In addition, three of the variables used were derived as described below.

Poverty was derived using the 2008 Australian poverty line data (Melbourne Institute of Applied Economics and Social Research, 2008). Mothers were considered to be living in poverty if they earned a wage below the published minimum income appropriate for their family structure, housing arrangements, number of children, and employment status. Job quality was measured using the Job Quality Index (JQI) developed for LSAC (Cooklin *et al.*, 2010; Strazdins *et al.*, 2007). The JQI consists of five work condition variables: family friendly leave, flexible hours, job control, job security and appropriate workload. The total JQI score is a sum of the number of conditions available to the mother, with higher scores indicating higher job quality. Family stability was determined from family structure data at each wave. Mothers were classified as being in a stable family (sole-parent or two-parent family at all three waves) or as having transitioned (at least one change of family structure by wave 3).

Characteristics of Single-Mother Families

At wave 3, when their children were aged 4–5 years (B cohort) and 8–9 years (K cohort) respectively, 10 per cent (n=449) and 13 per cent (n=545) of LSAC mothers respectively were single parents. Owing to initial non-response bias and non-random attrition over time, these proportions are 6–7 percentage points lower than expected for the Australian population of families with children of these ages (Australian Institute of Family Studies, 2009).

Table 12.1 summarises the demographic characteristics of single-mother families compared to those of couple-headed families participating in LSAC at wave 3. The study children of single mothers were no different from those of couple mothers in terms of age and gender. However, they were slightly more likely to be born prematurely (a 2–4% difference), and a much higher proportion were reported to have sleep problems (a 15–18% difference). Single mothers were younger than couple mothers by 1–2 years, were much less likely to have completed high school (47–49% as against 64–72%) and were three times more likely to be Indigenous. However, they were less likely to have been born outside Australia (a 4–5% difference) and to speak a language other than English at home (a 4–5% difference).

Differences in economic circumstances by family type were substantial. On average, the weekly household income of single mothers was one-quarter to one-third that of

---

[2]   Remoteness was classified using the Accessibility/Remoteness Index of Australia (ARIA), which is based on the minimum travelling distance required to access an urban centre containing basic services. Area-level disadvantage was measured using the Index of Relative Disadvantage from the Socio-Economic Indexes for Areas (SEIFA). Based on Census data, SEIFA ranks Australian geographical areas according to the characteristics of people, families and dwellings within that area. Relative disadvantage is associated with a low SEIFA number.

Table 12.1 Socio-demographic data for single and couple mothers

	B Cohort[a] (child aged 4–5 years)		K Cohort[b] (child aged 8–9 years)	
	single %	couple %	single %	couple %
Child factors				
Age in months[c]	57.8 (3.1)	57.6 (2.8)	105.8 (2.9)	105.5 (2.9)
Gender (male)	50.3	51.4	49.7	51.3
Premature/low birth weight	12.2	7.9	11.4	9.4
Sleeping problems	61.0	43.3	44.6	29.6
Socio-demographic factors				
Age last birthday[c]	33.8 (6.5)	35.6 (5.0)	38.2 (6.0)	39.2 (5.2)
Australian-born	87.5	82.0	83.9	78.2
Language at home not English	9.3	12.9	11.6	14.1
Aboriginal/Torres Strait Islander	6.0	1.8	5.3	1.6
Education: year 12 and above	49.9	72.4	47.1	63.6
Household income, all sources[c]	678 (397)	1985 (1344)	720 (394)	2064 (1293)
Below the poverty line	44.0	6.1	40.7	5.6
Financial hardship				
significant hardship	9.1	1.2	7.9	1.3
some hardship	32.1	14.3	32.8	12.0
Employment factors				
Not employed or in labour force	44.1	33.7	32.5	23.4
Work hours				
part-time (1–34 hours per week)	66.9	75.9	62.9	68.3
full-time (35–44 hours per week)	23.0	16.6	28.6	21.0
long full-time (45+ hours per week)	10.1	7.5	8.5	10.7
Favourable job conditions				
0–2	12.4	10.2	9.5	9.2
3	29.6	26.2	22.4	27.7
4	35.5	37.9	39.4	39.4
5	22.5	25.7	28.7	23.8
Occupational prestige				
unskilled	19.2	10.9	18.8	11.8
labour and clerical	38.8	36.5	40.8	38.5
professional skilled	42.0	52.6	40.5	49.7
Family factors				
Family transition (in last 4 years)	58.1	3.9	46.2	5.5
Number of children				
1	29.6	7.9	19.1	6.3
2	37.6	49.4	43.7	44.5
3	18.9	30.3	23.3	32.4
4+	13.8	12.4	13.9	16.8
Has a child living elsewhere	6.1	2.6	10.3	4.1
Pressed for time (always/often)	60.0	60.5	60.3	61.7
Life stresses (>1 events/last year)	69.6	55.0	73.4	51.2
Environment				
Housing tenure				
owner	22.3	77.7	39.1	81.4
renting	65.7	19.8	56.9	16.5
other arrangement	6.0	2.5	4.0	2.1

(*Continued*)

Table 12.1 (*cont'd*)

	B Cohort[a] (child aged 4–5 years)		K Cohort[b] (child aged 8–9 years)	
	single %	*couple %*	*single %*	*couple %*
Remote/very remote	4.0	3.5	3.2	3.9
Index of area disadvantage				
most disadvantaged	23.6	15.5	21.7	15.7
2nd quintile	28.7	22.1	26.6	22.0
3rd quintile	12.7	13.7	16.2	14.0
4th quintile	24.9	26.9	23.2	26.6
least disadvantaged	10.0	21.8	12.5	21.7
Satisfied with neighbourhood				
liveability	64.1	69.9	63.6	69.0
facilities	75.7	69.4	67.8	68.0
social capital	48.2	60.8	64.0	68.0

[a] B cohort: single mothers n=449; couple mothers n=3874. [b] K cohort: single mothers n=545; couple mothers n=3688.
[c] Mean (SD).

couple mothers, and rates of poverty exceeded 40 per cent for single mothers as against just 6 per cent for couple mothers. Not surprisingly, single mothers were 6–7 times more likely than couple mothers to report severe financial hardship. Couple mothers were more likely than single mothers to be in paid employment (67–77% as against 56–66%). Those who were working were more likely to work full-time hours (a 6–8% difference), and to be employed in unskilled jobs (a 7–8% difference), but were no more likely than couple mothers to experience poor-quality job conditions, and no more likely to report being pressed for time. Single mothers were 2–3 times more likely to be living in rented accommodation. Half these women lived in neighbourhoods classified as being in the lowest two quintiles (as against one-third of couple mothers) and only 10–13 per cent lived in the most advantaged neighbourhoods (as against 22% of couple mothers).

The Parenting and Mental Health of Single Mothers

Table 12.2 summarises the parenting and mental health of single and couple mothers participating in the LSAC when their children were aged 4–5 and 8–9 years. The table shows the proportions of single and couple mothers reporting poor parenting on each measure, the proportions reporting psychological distress, and the mean scores on the overall parenting problems index and on the psychological distress (K6) scale. The table also shows the odds ratios (OR) corresponding to each pair of proportions. An odds ratio of one implies that the examined outcome is equally likely in both groups. An odds ratio of greater than one indicates an increased likelihood of the outcome (e.g. OR=1.25 indicates 25% increased odds) in single mothers relative to couple mothers, while an odds ratio of less than one indicates a decreased likelihood.

Family type was strongly related to mothers' parenting and mental health. Compared with couple mothers of the 4- to 5-year-olds, single mothers had increased odds of

Table 12.2 Parenting and mental health difficulties in mothers at wave 3 of data collection

| | B Cohort[a] (child aged 4–5 years) | | | | K Cohort[b] (child aged 8–9 years) | | | |
| | single | couple | odds ratios[c] | | single | couple | odds ratios[c] | |
	%	%	(95% CI)	p	%	%	(95% CI)	p
Parenting								
Low consistency	30.8	20.0	1.92 (1.46–2.51)	<0.001	29.9	18.5	1.88 (1.50–2.37)	<0.001
Angry parenting	32.3	24.8	1.54 (1.19–1.99)	0.001	29.0	26.1	1.20 (0.96–1.52)	0.112
Hostile parenting	28.0	23.8	1.29 (1.00–1.67)	0.052	24.8	20.8	1.27 (1.00–1.61)	0.048
Over-protective parenting	29.0	20.2	1.52 (1.15–2.03)	0.004	39.9	32.6	1.29 (1.02–1.64)	0.031
Low parenting self-efficacy	26.1	18.04	1.30 (1.03–1.62)	0.025	20.1	21.3	1.05 (0.81–1.36)	0.707
Low parental warmth	21.4	23.9	0.78 (0.60–1.03)	0.083	12.6	13.7	0.92 (0.67–1.26)	0.603
Low inductive reasoning	23.6	23.9	0.90 (0.69–1.19)	0.459	23.8	21.8	1.20 (0.93–1.55)	0.168
Overall parenting index score	2.2 (1.5)	1.8 (1.4)	n/a		1.8 (1.4)	1.5 (1.3)	n/a	
Overall parenting difficulties	37.9	28.8	1.63 (1.24–2.13)	0.001	27.9	21.5	1.50 (1.19–1.88)	<0.001
Mental health								
K6 scored	4.8 (4.5)	3.0 (3.1)	n/a	<0.001	5.1 (4.4)	3.2 (3.4)	n/a	<0.001
Psychological distress	22.6	8.6	3.0 (2.2–4.0)	<0.001	25.9	11.0	2.7 (2.1–3.5)	<0.001

Note. Mothers with poor parenting outcomes are those in the least optimal 20% for their child's age group and cohort for each measure. Data collected in 2008.
[a] B cohort: single mothers n = 449; couple mothers n= 3874. [b] K cohort: single mothers n = 545; couple mothers n = 3688. CI = confidence interval. [c] Single compared with couple mothers. [d] Mean (SD).

poor parenting on five of the seven measures. Specifically, they had 30 per cent increased odds of reporting low self-efficacy and hostile parenting, 50 per cent increased odds of reporting angry parenting and over-protectiveness, and 90 per cent increased odds of reporting low consistency. Single mothers with children aged 8–9 years had significantly poorer parenting than couple mothers on three of the seven measures. They had 30 per cent increased odds of hostile parenting and over-protectiveness and 90 per cent increased odds of low consistency. There were no differences between single and couple mothers in terms of parenting warmth or the use of inductive reasoning in either cohort. When the parenting measures were combined into the overall index of poor parenting, across both cohorts, single mothers had 50–60 per cent increased odds of parenting difficulties relative to couple mothers.

Single mothers reported considerably greater psychological distress than couple mothers; 26 per cent and 23 per cent were in the symptomatic range for the older and younger cohorts respectively, as against 11 per cent and 9 per cent for couple mothers. These differences equated to a threefold increase in the odds of their experiencing symptomatic levels of psychological distress.

Maternal Exposure to Parenting and Mental Health Risk Factors

As a first step in examining whether the parenting and mental health differences between single and couple mothers were due to differences in the family and broader environmental circumstances, we conducted two multivariable regression models for each cohort. The goal was to identify a pool of factors that were associated with mothers' poor parenting and/or psychological distress. The following variables were identified as being significantly associated at a bivariate level with these outcomes: seven socio-demographic variables (younger age, non-Australian-born, speaking a language other than English, lower education, lower household income, living below the poverty line, experiencing financial hardship); four employment variables (unemployment, full-time employment, poor job quality, low occupational prestige); one child variable (child sleep problems); six family variables (family instability, larger family size, having children living elsewhere, being pressed for time, conflict with the child's other parent, highly stressful life events); and five neighbourhood variables (rented accommodation, relative disadvantage, poor liveability, poor facilities, low social capital).

To examine the extent to which mothers' parenting and mental health differed once background and contextual differences were taken into account, we then combined these variables into an overall measure of exposure to adversity (a simple count of exposure to variables predictive of poor parenting or psychological distress) which was categorised according to distribution across the whole cohort: low adversity (25th percentile and below), medium adversity (26th–74th percentile) and high adversity (75th percentile and above). The distributions of single and couple mothers across these three adversity groups for mothers of 4- to 5-year-olds and 8- to 9-year-olds are shown in Figures 12.1 and 12.2 respectively. As can be seen, exposure to adverse risk factors for parenting and mental health was very different for single and couple mothers. Single mothers were three times more likely to be in the high adversity group than couple mothers (4–5 years: 62.2% as against 21.6%; 8–9 years: 51.1% as against 22.2%)

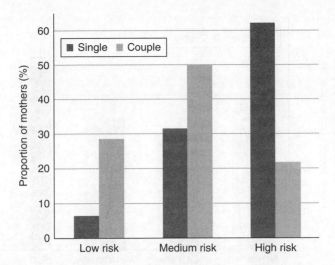

Figure 12.1 Distribution across adversity groups of mothers with children aged 4–5 years

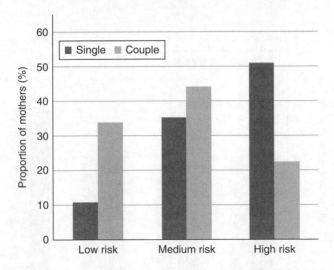

Figure 12.2 Distribution across adversity groups of mothers with children aged 8–9 years

and two to four times less likely to be in the low adversity group than couple mothers (4–5 years: 6.3% as against 28.4%; 8–9 years: 10.8% as against 33.7%).

Parenting and Mental Health of Single and Couple Mothers

Average parenting index scores by adversity status for single and couple mothers of children aged 4–5 years and 8–9 years are shown in Figures 12.3 and 12.4. Overall, single mothers of children in both age ranges reported significantly greater parenting difficulties than couple mothers ($p < 0.001$ both cohorts). There was also a clear gradient

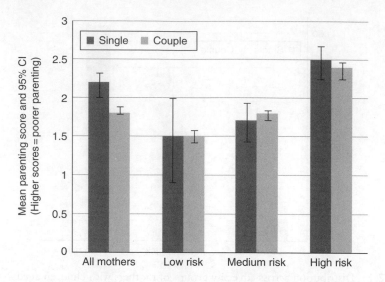

Figure 12.3   Parenting by adversity status of mothers with children aged 4–5 years

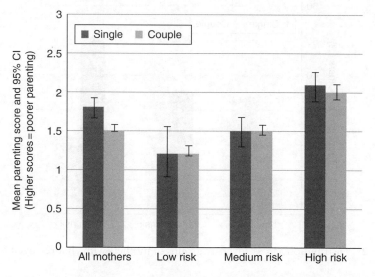

Figure 12.4   Parenting by adversity status of mothers with children aged 8–9 years

by adversity for both single and couple mothers in both cohorts, with parenting difficulties significantly higher for those in higher adversity groups ($p < 0.001$ both cohorts). The independent contributions of family type and adversity to parenting index scores were explored further using regression analyses. When considered separately, family type and adversity group both predicted parenting difficulties. When both were entered together in the regression models, adversity remained a strong predictor of parenting difficulties (4–5 years: regression coefficient 0.46 (0.04), $p < 0.001$; 8–9 years: regression coefficient 0.40 (0.03), $p < 0.001$), but being a single mother no longer predicted parenting difficulties (4–5 years: 0.06 (0.10), $p = 0.59$; 8–9 years: 0.06 (0.07), $p = 0.44$).

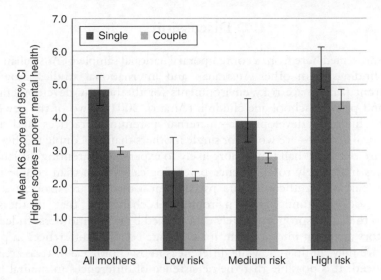

Figure 12.5 Mental health by adversity status of mothers with children aged 4–5 years

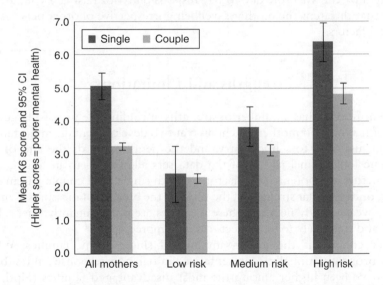

Figure 12.6 Mental health by adversity status of mothers with children aged 8–9 years

Average psychological distress scores by adversity for single and couple mothers of children aged 4–5 years and 8–9 years are shown in Figures 12.5 and 12.6. Patterns were similar to those seen for the parenting index: psychological distress symptoms were higher for single than for couple mothers (both cohorts $p < 0.001$), and there were gradient effects showing higher symptoms with increasing adversity (both cohorts $p < 0.001$). However, in the combined regression models, after adjustment for exposure to adversity (4–5 years: regression coefficient 1.22 (0.09), $p < 0.001$; 8–9 years: regression coefficient 1.38 (0.09), $p < 0.001$) single parenthood remained a significant predictor of psychological distress (4–5 years: regression coefficient 1.13 (0.30), $p < 0.001$; 8–9 years: regression coefficient 1.18 (0.23), $p < 0.001$).

Discussion

The data presented here from a contemporary national sample of Australian children confirm findings from other Australian and international studies showing that single-parent families are risky environments for the healthy development of pre-school- and primary-school-age children (Amato, 2001). Two of the key determinants of children's development—maternal parenting practices and maternal psychological distress—are worse for single mothers than for couple mothers. Single mothers are one and a half times more likely to experience parenting difficulties and three times more likely to experience psychological distress than couple mothers. However, parenting difficulties and psychological distress are strongly associated with the socio-economic and environmental challenges that mothers face—challenges that are disproportionately experienced by single mothers. Indeed, when these factors are taken into account, for both age cohorts, differences in parenting practices are fully eliminated, while differences in psychological distress are substantially reduced. It is possible that the persistence of differences in mental health in our adjusted models reflects factors not measured here. However, it is also likely that being a parent with sole day-to-day responsibility for raising a young child is a situation that threatens the mother's wellbeing irrespective of other personal, family or external factors.

Strengths and Limitations

The current research has a number of strengths, including the use of a large national sample, with a focus on mothers of children at two developmentally important ages—the period just prior to school entry, and the period towards the end of primary school. The longitudinal nature of the data sets allowed us to include changes in family structure as a potential risk factor for both single- and couple-parent families. However, one particular strength of the LSAC—the breadth of measures it employs—was also a weakness. By necessity these measures are predominantly brief self-report measures and thus likely to be subject to some imprecision.

Another concern is the under-sampling of single-parent families. While the LSAC is broadly nationally representative, initial non-response and subsequent attrition have been higher among the most disadvantaged families (Sipthorp and Misson, 2009; Soloff et al., 2006). By wave 3 when our outcomes were assessed, the proportions of single-parent families (10% and 13% for the cohorts aged 4–5 and 8–9 years respectively) were 6–7 per cent lower than expected for the Australian population (Sipthorp and Misson, 2009). As a result our data may underestimate the true extent of socio-economic and other differences between single and couple families.

While the proportion of single-parent families in Australia is similar to those in other Western countries, the experiences of single parents will vary according to both cultural norms regarding single-parent families and the availability of national welfare and other policies that may mitigate or heighten the adversities experienced. Such factors may not only change the amount of adversity experienced by single mothers, but in the case of cultural norms they may interact to exacerbate or ameliorate the effects of adversity on mothers' mental health and parenting.

Policy Implications

Poverty in Australia

Evidence that the parenting and mental health difficulties of single mothers are elevated as a result both of the risk factors for sole parenthood and of the deprivation that accompanies sole parenthood is not new. Other studies from the UK, the USA, Canada and New Zealand have similarly reported that these factors account for some or all of the differences between single and couple families (Chilcoat *et al.*, 1996; Cooper *et al.*, 2008; Hope *et al.*, 1999; Knutson *et al.*, 2004; Loxton *et al.*, 2006). What this study highlights is how stark the differences between family types can be in a contemporary Western society. At the bivariate level, this is most notable in terms of measures of socio-economic disadvantage, and particularly levels of poverty. Over 40 per cent of single-mother families in this study lived below the poverty line, as against just 6 per cent of couple families. This result challenges the prevailing Australian belief that poverty is 'something that happens in other countries' (Peel, 2003) and illustrates the failure of social policies of successive governments to meet the 1987 election commitment of former Prime Minister Bob Hawke that 'by 1990, no Australian child will live in poverty'.[3] As is shown here, for many young children being raised in a single-parent family equates to being raised in an impoverished family. What is also clear is the extent to which a wide range of adversities cluster within single-parent families. In this sample, single mothers were three times more likely than couple mothers to be classified as experiencing high levels of adversity, and conversely were two to four times less likely to experience low adversity.

Workforce participation

The LSAC study allowed us to consider a wide range of factors as possible determinants of mothers' parenting and mental health. In particular, in the case of employed mothers we were able to examine the quality and occupational prestige of their jobs, and we also modelled the effects of the family's broader social and physical environments. Maternal work and neighbourhood characteristics were both significant predictors of parenting and mental health difficulties. These findings suggest some possible avenues for improving the circumstances of single mother families via social and economic policy.

First, while maternal unemployment predicted poor parenting and psychological distress, so too did full-time employment, employment in low-prestige and poor-quality jobs, and being pressed for time. As is shown here and elsewhere, employment in low-prestige, poor-quality jobs is bad for one's mental health and undermines effective parenting (Cooklin *et al.*, 2010; Stansfield and Candy, 2006; Strazdins *et al.*, 2007). In recent decades, a number of social and economic policies have sought to

---

[3] Twenty years on, Bob Hawke noted considerable regret about having expressed this commitment: see http://www.theage.com.au/news/National/Hawke-regrets-child-poverty-comment/2007/06/16/1181414583336.html [Accessed 27.9.2011.]

increase the participation rates of single mothers in paid employment (Blank, 2002; Meyer and Rosenbaum, 2000). Such endeavours have been based on: assumptions that single mothers and their children will benefit from the economic and other gains provided by moving from welfare to work; the potential for breaking intergenerational cycles of welfare dependency; and promotion of mutual responsibility (that all citizens should contribute to society to the extent that their circumstances allow).

However, the job opportunities available to single mothers of pre-school- and primary-school-age children may not be conducive to healthy family functioning. Single mothers are younger and less well-educated than couple mothers, and therefore more likely to be employed in low-prestige occupations. Single mothers in our sample were also more likely than couple mothers to be employed in full-time jobs, despite the challenges this may entail for childcare in the absence of a second resident parent. Surprisingly, single mothers in this study were no more likely than couple mothers to be employed in poor-quality jobs or to report being pressed for time. However, both factors made an independent contribution to differences in parenting and mental health, suggesting that the effects of poor-quality jobs and time pressures may be greater for single than for couple mothers.

Studies of single mothers' experiences under welfare-to-work schemes in the USA have highlighted the challenges these women face (Dunifon *et al.*, 2005; Menaghan and Parcel, 1995). These include: employment in jobs that lack security, benefits and regular hours; the pressures associated with lengthy commute times, which mean that women are not fully financially compensated for their time away from home; and the demands placed on the children to assume increased family caring and household responsibilities. Our data suggest that a more nuanced policy approach may be required. The workforce participation of single mothers may have detrimental effects if work choices are limited to jobs that add to the pressures on them and their children. Greater investment in programmes that extend the job options available to mothers (e.g. educational and jobs skills programmes) may have more beneficial long-term effects.

Community supports

The second extra-familial set of factors that accounted for differences in the parenting and mental health of mothers in this study concerned families' social and physical environments. Living in rented accommodation and neighbourhoods characterised by socio-economic disadvantage, low liveability, poor resources and low social capital predicted poorer parenting and mental health. From intervention or policy perspectives, a range of diverse activities would seem warranted, including, for example, accommodation support, investment in neighbourhood infrastructure and services, and efforts that seek to build connections within communities.

One promising Australian approach to building the social capital and service connections of vulnerable families from early in parenthood involves play-based parent–child programmes. Traditionally, 'playgroup' programmes have been parent-run weekly groups where mothers and their infant/toddler children participate in activities designed to promote children's development through play (Dadich and Spooner, 2008). More recently, Australian state and federal governments have provided funding for facilitator-led playgroups to engage marginalised and disadvantaged families, including single mother families (Department of Families, Housing, Community

Key findings and policy and intervention implications

- The socio-economic and environmental circumstances of single and couple mother families are very different. Single mother families face heightened adversity regarding a number of aspects of their home and extra-familial environments, and are less likely to have the pre-existing personal capabilities that would aid them in dealing with such adversity.
- This study highlights the failure of successive Australian governments to substantially reduce the proportion of single-parent families experiencing poverty. Considerable numbers of single mothers and their children are living below the poverty line.
- Irrespective of family structure, the quality of parents' jobs matters. Policies aiming to increase workforce participation need to consider the increased family and household responsibilities of single mothers. Compelling women into jobs that are poorly paid and lack the flexibility to respond to children's needs may worsen the health and wellbeing of these women and their children.
- The social and physical environments to which single mothers are commonly exposed can exacerbate the difficulties they experience. These may be addressed in a variety of ways: accommodation support, investment in neighbourhood infrastructure and services, and mother–child programmes that seek to build connections between families within communities.
- Exposure to conflict not only impacts directly on children, but also affects mothers' wellbeing and parenting skills. Efforts to support all families in the resolution of conflict, and services focusing on separation and the negotiation of amicable parenting arrangements, remain a priority.

Services and Indigenous Affairs, 2010). While evaluation data remain scarce, there is some evidence that playgroup attendance is associated with improvements in mothers' non-familial social support around parenting (Hancock *et al.*, 2012). A specialised variation involving a music-based approach (Abad and Williams, 2007) has shown marked improvements in mothers' connections with other parents and use of community services (Abad, 2002; Nicholson *et al.*, 2008).

Family conflict

The findings from our current study also provide further evidence of the negative effects of conflict between parents for mothers' parenting and mental health. This builds on previous research showing that exposure to high levels of parental conflict has negative and long-lasting effects on child development (Amato, 1993; Hetherington *et al.*, 1998; Lansford, 2009). Thus, parental conflict appears to harm children both directly, through exposure, and indirectly, via mother's parenting and mental health. These findings suggest that, rather than discouraging parents from separating, policy efforts should focus on reducing the conflict associated with separation.

Some government attempts to reduce conflict between separating parents have already been made, particularly within Australian family law. In the Family Law Reform Act 1995, the terms 'custody' and 'access' were replaced with 'residence' and 'contact' (as they had been in England after implementation of the 1989 Children Act) in an attempt to move away from the impression that one parent had 'won' and the other had 'lost'. This was softened again in the 2006 amendment by its referring to who the child 'lives' or 'spends time' with (Ruddock, 2005). These changes have attempted to spark a cultural shift towards less adversarial parenting disputes and more cooperative shared parental responsibility (Family Relationships Service, 2010). In addition to these changes, enactment of the Family Law Amendment (Shared Parental Responsibility) Act 2006 involved the establishment of Family Relationship Centres nationwide (Kaspiew *et al.*, 2009). These centres offer assistance to couples at all stages of their relationship, and aim to strengthen family relationships and resolve difficulties. They also offer dispute resolution to help separating families develop mutually agreeable shared parenting arrangements (Kaspiew *et al.*, 2009). The results from the current study suggest the importance of such services for supporting the wellbeing of parents and children during parental separation.

Concluding Comments

The findings from this research provide some timely insights into the challenges faced by single mothers in contemporary Western societies. It is clear that mothers who are raising their children on their own are considerably more disadvantaged than part-nered mothers, both in terms of their pre-existing skills and capacities and the adversities they face within and outside the family. A recently released report from the Australian Christian lobby has gained widespread media attention in Australia on account of its claims of overwhelming evidence that children do best in families with two married parents. It states:

> If there is one major demographic change in Western societies that can be linked to a large range of adverse consequences for many children and young people, it is the growth in the numbers of children who experience life in a family other than living with their two biological parents. (Parkinson, 2011, p. 8)

At a simplistic level, there is some truth in such claims, with our data confirming that single mothers are more likely than couple mothers to experience parenting and mental health difficulties. However, our data also show that single mothers are not worse parents than similar couple mothers. Our comparisons of mothers facing similar levels of adversity show no differences in poor parenting practices, although single mothers remain more vulnerable to psychological distress than similar couple mothers.

Rather than stigmatising single parents, we should be seeking ways to reduce the levels of modifiable adversities they face. For all families, irrespective of structure, we should be focusing our efforts on finding the most effective means for supporting those who are most vulnerable.

References

Abad, V. (2002) Sing and grow: helping young children and their families grow together through music therapy early intervention programs in community settings, *Annals of the New Zealand Society for Music Therapy*, 36–50.

Abad, V. and Williams, K. (2007) Early intervention music therapy: reporting on a 3-year project to address needs with at-risk families, *Music Therapy Perspectives*, 25: 52–58.

Amato, P. R. (1993) Children's adjustment to divorce: theories, hypotheses, and empirical support, *Journal of Marriage and Family*, 55: 23–38.

Amato, P. R. (2001) Children of divorce in the 1990s: an update of the Amato and Keith (1991) meta analysis, *Journal of Family Psychology*, 15: 355–370.

Amato, P. R. (2005) The impact of family formation change on the cognitive, social, and emotional well-being of the next generation, *Future of Children*, 15: 75–96.

Amato, P. R. and Keith, B. (1991) Parental divorce and the well-being of children: a meta-analysis, *Psychological Bulletin*, 110: 26–46.

Amato, P. R. and Sobolewski, J. (2001) The effects of divorce and marital discord on adult children's psychosocial well-being, *American Sociological Review*, 66: 99–921.

Anderson, E. R., Greene, S. M., Hetherington, E. M. and Clingempeel, W. G. (1999) The dynamics of parental remarriage: adolescent, parent, and sibling influences, in E. M. Hetherington (ed.), *Coping with Divorce, Single Parenting, and Remarriage: A risk and resiliency perspective* (Mahwah, NJ: Lawrence Erlbaum), 295–319.

Australian Bureau of Statistics (1994) *Focus on Families: Demographics and family formation* (Canberra: Australian Bureau of Statistics).

Australian Bureau of Statistics (2010) *Australian Social Trends September 2010* (Canberra: Australian Bureau of Statistics).

Australian Institute of Family Studies (2007) *LSAC Data User Guide (Version 3.0)* (Melbourne: AIFS).

Australian Institute of Family Studies (2009) *The Longitudinal Study of Australian Children 2008–09, Annual Report* (Canberra: Department of Families, Housing, Community Services and Indigenous Affairs, Commonwealth of Australia).

Baxter, J. and Smart, D (2010) *Fathering in Australia among Couple Families with Young Children, Occasional Paper No. 37* (Canberra: Department of Families, Housing, Community Services and Indigenous Affairs, Commonwealth of Australia).

Bayer, J., Sanson, A. and Hemphill, S. (2009) Early aetiology of internalising difficulties: a longitudinal community study, *International Journal of Mental Health Promotion*, 11: 22–32.

Bayer, J. K., Ukoumunne, O. C., Lucas, N., Wake, M., Scalzo, K. and Nicholson, J. M. (2011) Aetiology of mental health problems in childhood: a national longitudinal study, *Pediatrics*, 128(4): e865–e879.

Birditt, K. S., Brown, E., Orbuch, T. L. and McIlvane, J. M. (2010) Marital conflict behaviours and implications for divorce over 16 years, *Journal of Marriage and Family*, 72: 1188–1204.

Bittman, M., Craig, L. and Folbre, N. (2004) Packaging care: what happens when children receive nonparental care?, in N. Folbre and M. Bittman (eds), *Family Time: The social organisation of care* (New York: Routledge), 133–151.

Blank, R. (2002) Evaluating welfare reform in the United States, *Journal of Economic Literature*, 15: 1105–1166.

Brody, G. H. and Forehand, R. (1988) Multiple determinants of parenting: research findings and implications for the divorce process, in E. M. Hetherington and J. D. Arasteh (eds), *Impact of divorce, single parenting, and stepparenting on children* (Hillsdale, NJ: Lawrence Erlbaum), 117–131.

Bronfenbrenner, U. and Morris, P. A. (2006) The bioecological model of human development, in W. Damon and R. M. Lerner (eds), *Handbook of Child Psychology* (New York: Wiley), 6th edn, 793–828.

Brown, S. L. (2006) Family structure transitions and adolescent well-being, *Demography*, 43: 447–461.

Burgess, J. and Strachan, G. (2005) Integrating work and family responsibilities. Policies for lifting women's labour activity rates, *Just Policy*, 35: 5–12.

Cashmore, J., Parkinson, P., Weston, R., Patulny, R., Redmond, G., Qu, L., Baxter, J., Rajkovic, M., Sitek, T. and Katz, I. (2010) *Shared Care Parenting Arrangements since the 2006 Family Law Reforms: Report to the Australian Government Attorney-General's Department* (Sydney: Social Policy Research Centre, University of New South Wales).

Cavanagh, S. E. and Huston, A. C. (2006) Family instability and children's early problem behaviour, *Social Forces*, 85: 551–581.

Chilcoat, H. D., Breslau, N. and Anthony, J. C. (1996) Potential barriers to parent monitoring: social disadvantage, marital status, and maternal psychiatric disorder, *Journal of the American Academy of Child and Adolescent Psychiatry*, 35: 1673–1682.

Connell, A. M. and Goodman, S. H. (2002) The association between psychopathology in fathers versus mothers and children's internalising and externalising behaviour problems. A meta-analysis, *Psychological Bulletin*, 128: 746–773.

Cooklin, A. R., Canterford, L., Strazdins, L. and Nicholson, J. M. (2010) Employment conditions and maternal postpartum mental health: results from the longitudinal study of Australian children, *Archives of Women's Mental Health*, 14: 217–225.

Cooper, C., Bebbington, P. E., Meltzer, H., Bhugra, D., Brugha, T., Jenkins, R., Farrell, M. and King, M. (2008) Depression and common mental disorders in lone parents: results of the 2000 National Psychiatric Morbidity Survey, *Psychological Medicine*, 38: 335–342.

Cotterell, G., von Randow, M. V. and Wheldon, M. (2008) *Measuring Changes in Family and Whānau Wellbeing Using Census Data, 1981–2006: A descriptive analysis* (Wellington: Statistics New Zealand).

Dadich, A. and Spooner, C. (2008) Evaluating playgroups: an examination of issues and options, *The Australian Community Psychologist*, 20: 95–103.

Deater-Deckard, K. and Dunn, J. (1999) Multiple risks and adjustment in young children growing up in different family settings: a British community study of stepparent single mother, and non-divorced families, in E. M. Hetherington (ed.), *Coping with Divorce, Single Parenting, and Remarriage: A risk and resiliency perspective* (Mahwah, NJ: Lawrence Erlbaum), 47–64.

Department of Families, Housing, Community Services and Indigenous Affairs (2010) *Playgroups*, http://www.fahcsia.gov.au/sa/families/progserv/Pages/parenting-playgroups.aspx [Accessed 1.12.2010.]

Dunifon, R., Kalil, A. and Bajracharya, A. (2005) Maternal working conditions and child well-being in welfare-leaving families, *Developmental Psychology*, 41: 851–859.

Elliott, B. J. and Richards, M. P. M. (1991) Children and divorce: educational performance and behaviour before and after parental separation, *International Journal of Law and the Family*, 5: 258–276.

Family Relationships Service (2010) *Response to the Victorian Law Reform Commission's Information Paper 'Review of Victoria's Child Protection Legislative Arrangements' Specifically on the Use of Alternative Dispute Resolution Processes to Assist in Child Protection Matters*. http://www.lawreform.vic.gov.au [Accessed 8.10.2010.]

Funder, K. (1996) *Remaking Families: Adaptation of parents and children to divorce* (Melbourne: Australian Institute of Family Studies).

Furstenberg, F. F. (1988) Child care after divorce and remarriage, in E. M. Hetherington and J. D. Arasteh (eds), *Impact of Divorce, Single Parenting and Stepparenting on Children* (Hillsdale, NJ: Lawrence Erlbaum), 245–261.

Furukawa, T., Kessler, R. C., Slade, T. and Andrews, G. (2003) The performance of the K6 and K10 screening scales for psychological distress in the Australian National Survey of Mental Health and Well-Being, *Psychological Medicine*, 33: 357–362.

Giallo, R., D'Esposito, F., Christensen, D., Mensah, F. K., Cooklin, A., Wade, C., Lucas, N., Canterford, L. and Nicholson, J. M. (2012) Father mental health during the early parenting period: results of an Australian population based longitudinal study, *Social Psychiatry and Psychiatric Epidemiology*, pub. online 10 Apr., doi: 10.1007/s00127-012-0510-0. http://www.springer.com/medicine/psychiatry/journal/127 [Accessed 3.7.2012.]

Goodman, S. H. and Gotlib, I. H. (1999) Risk for psychopathology in the children of depressed mothers: a developmental model for understanding mechanisms of transmission, *American Psychological Association*, 106: 458–490.

Goodman, S. H., Rouse, M. H. and Connell, A. M. (2011) Maternal depression and child psychopathology: a meta-analytic review, *Clinical Child and Family Psychology Review*, 14: 1–27.

Hancock, K. J., Lawrence, D., Mitrou, F., Zarb, D., Berthelsen, D., Nicholson, J. M. and Zubrick, S. R. (2012) The association between playgroup participation, learning competency and social-emotional well-being for children aged 4–5 years in Australia, *Australian Journal of Early Childhood*, 37: 72–81.

Hetherington, E. M. (1987) Family relations six years after divorce, in K. Pasely and M. Ihinger-Tallman (eds), *Remarriage and Stepparenting: current research and theory* (New York: Guilford Press), 185–205.

Hetherington, E. M. (1988) Parents, children and siblings: six years after divorce, in R. A. Hinde and J. Stevenson-Hinde (eds), *Relationships Within Families: Mutual influences* (Oxford: Clarendon Press), 311–331.

Hetherington, E. M., Bridges, M. and Insabella, G. (1998) What matters? What does not?: five perspectives on the association between marital transitions and children's adjustment, *American Psychologist*, 53: 167–184.

Hope, S., Power, C. and Rodgers, B. (1999) Does financial hardship account for elevated psychological distress in lone mothers?, *Social Science and Medicine*, 49: 1637–1649.

Huang, C. C. and Warner, L. A. (2005) Relationship characteristics and depression among fathers with newborns, *Social Service Review*, 79: 95–118.

Isaacs, M. B. and Leon, G. H. (1988) Remarriage and its alternatives following divorce: mother and child adjustment, *Journal of Marital and Family Therapy*, 14: 163–173.

Jaffee, S. R., Caspi, A., Moffitt, T. E., Taylor, A. and Dickson, N. (2001) Predicting early fatherhood and whether young fathers live with their children: prospective findings and policy reconsiderations, *Journal of Child Psychology and Psychiatry*, 42: 803–815.

Kane, P. and Garber, J. (2004) The relations among depression in fathers, children's psychopathology, and father–child conflict: a meta-analysis, *Clinical Psychology Review*, 24: 339–360.

Kaspiew, R., Gray, M., Weston, R., Moloney, L., Hand, K. and Qu, L. (2009) *Evaluation of the 2006 Family Law Reforms* (Melbourne: Australian Institute of Family Studies).

Knutson, J. F., Degarmo, D. W. and Reid, J. B. (2004) Social disadvantage and neglectful parenting as precursors to the development of antisocial and aggressive child behaviour: testing a theoretical model, *Aggressive Behaviour*, 30: 187–205.

Lansford, J. E. (2009) Parental divorce and children's adjustment, *Perspectives on Psychological Science*, 4: 140–152.

Lawton, J. M. and Sanders, M. R. (1994) Designing effective behavioural family interventions for stepfamilies, *Clinical Psychology Review*, 14: 463–496.

Linacre, S. (2007) One parent families, *Australian Social Trends 2007* (Canberra: Australian Bureau of Statistics).

Loxton, D., Mooney, R. and Young, A. F. (2006) The psychological health of sole mothers in Australia, *Medical Journal of Australia*, 184: 265–268.

Lucas, N., Maguire, B. and Nicholson, J. M. (2010) *Parenting practices and behaviours, Longitudinal Study of Australian Children Statistical Report 2010* (Melbourne: Australian Institute of Family Studies).

Melbourne Institute of Applied Economic and Social Research (2008) *Poverty Lines: Australia ISSN 1448-0530 March Quarter 2008* (Melbourne: MIAESR http://www.melbourneinstitute.com//downloads/publications/Poverty%20Lines/poverty-lines-australia-march-2008.pdf [Accessed 15.7.2011.]

Menaghan, E. and Parcel, T. (1995) Social sources of change in children's home environments: the effects of parental occupational experiences and family conditions, *Journal of Marriage and Family*, 57: 69–84.

Mensah, F. K. and Kiernan, K. E. (2010) Parents' mental health and children's cognitive and social development: families in England in the Millennium Cohort Study, *Social Psychiatry and Psychiatric Epidemiology*, 45: 1023–1035.

Meyer, B. D. and Rosenbaum, D. T. (2000) Making single mothers work: recent tax and welfare policy and its effects, *National Tax Journal*, 53: 1027–1062.

Nicholson, J. M., Berthelsen, D., Abad, V., Williams, K. and Bradley, J. (2008) Impact of music therapy to promote positive parenting and child development, *Journal of Health Psychology*, 13: 226–238.

O'Connor, T. G. (2002) The 'effects' of parenting reconsidered: findings, challenges, and applications, *Journal of Child Psychology and Psychiatry*, 43: 555–572.

Office for National Statistics (2010) Chapter 2: Households and families, in M. Hughes (ed.), *Social Trends*, 40: 13–26 (Basingstoke: Palgrave Macmillan). www.statistics.gov.uk/socialtrends

Parkinson, P. (2011) *For Kids' Sake: Repairing the social environment for Australian children and young people* (Vos Foundation). http://australianchristianlobby.org.au-wp-content-uploads-FKS-ResearchReport1.pdf) [Accessed 3.10.2011.]

Peel, M. (2003) *The Lowest Rung: Voices of Australian poverty* (Cambridge: Cambridge University Press).

Pettit, G. S. and Bates, J. E. (1989) Family interaction patterns and children's behaviour problems from infancy to 4 years, *Developmental Psychology*, 25: 413–420.

Rodgers, B., Grey, P., Davidson, T. and Butterworth, P. (2011) *Parental Divorce and Adult Family, Social and Psychological Outcomes: The contribution of childhood family adversity* (Social Policy Research Paper No. 42) (Canberra: Department of Families, Housing, Community Services and Indigenous Affairs, Commonwealth of Australia).

Rodgers, B., Power, C. and Hope, S. (1997) Parental divorce and adult psychological distress: evidence from a national birth cohort, *Journal of Child Psychology and Psychiatry and Allied Disciplines*, 38: 867–872.

Ross, D. P., Roberts, P. A. and Scott, K. (1998) *Mediating Factors in Child Development Outcomes: Children in lone-parent families (W-98-8E)* (Quebec: Human Resources Development Canada).

Rubertsson, C., Wickberg, B., Gustavsson, P. and Radestad, I. (2005) Depressive symptoms in early pregnancy, two months and one year postpartum—prevalence and psychosocial risk factors in a national Swedish sample, *Archives of Women's Mental Health*, 8: 97–104.

Ruddock, P. (2005) *Family Law Amendment (Shared Parental Responsibility) Bill 2005: Explanatory statement.* http://www.ag.gov.au) [Accessed 8.10.2010.]

Ruschena, E., Sanson, A. and Smart, D. (2005) A longitudinal study of adolescent adjustment following family transitions, *Journal of Child Psychology and Psychiatry*, 46: 353–363.

Sanson, A., Nicholson, J., Ungerer, J., Zubrick, S., Wilson, K., Ainley, J., Bertehlsen, D., Bittman, M., Broom, D., Harrison, L., Rodgers, B., Sawyer, M., Silburn, S., Strazdins, L., Vimpani, G. and Wake, M. (2002) *Introducing the Longitudinal Study of Australian Children (LSAC Discussion Paper No. 1)* (Melbourne: Australian Institute of Family Studies).

Sipthorp, M. and Misson, S. (2009) *Wave 3 Weighting and Non-response (LSAC Technical Paper No. 6)* (Melbourne: Australian Institute for Family Studies).

Soloff, C., Lawrence, D., Misson, S. and Johnstone, R. (2006) *Wave 1 Weighting and Non-response (LSAC Technical Paper No. 3)* (Melbourne: Australian Institute for Family Studies).

Stansfield, S. and Candy, B. (2006) Psychosocial work environment and mental health—a meta-analytic review, *Journal of Work and Environmental Health*, 32: 443–462.

Statistics Canada (2007) *2006 Census (Cat. No 97-554-XCB2006007)* (Ottawa: Statistics Canada).

Strazdins, L., Shipley, M. and Broom, D. (2007) What does family-friendly really mean? Well-being, time and the quality of parents' jobs, *Australian Bulletin of Labour*, 33: 202–225.

US Census Bureau (2010) *Current Population Survey, Annual Social and Economic Supplements* (Washington, DC: US Census Bureau).

Weiss, R. S. (1979) Growing up a little faster: the experience of growing up in a single-parent household, *Journal of Social Issues*, 35: 97–111.

Zill, N., Morrison, D. R. and Coiro, M. J. (1993) Long-term effects of parental divorce on parent–child relationships, adjustment, and achievement in young adulthood, *Journal of Family Psychology*, 7: 91–103.

Zubrick, S. R., Smith, G. J., Nicholson, J. M., Sanson, A., Jackiewicz, T. and the LSAC Research Consortium (2008) *Parenting and Families in Australia (Social Policy Research Paper No. 34)* (Canberra: Department of Families, Community Services and Indigenous Affairs, Commonwealth of Australia).

13

Sexual Orientation, Marriage and Parenthood
A Global Perspective

CHARLOTTE J. PATTERSON, RACHEL G. RISKIND
AND SAMANTHA L. TORNELLO

Introduction

Few, if any, of the transformations in family lives that are taking place around the world are as rapid or profound as those involving sexual orientation, marriage and parenthood. Whereas heterosexual marriage and parenting were once inextricably linked for the vast majority of people in the world, a number of alternative definitions and practices have recently emerged among non-heterosexual people. To identify as lesbian or gay might historically have meant forgoing marriage and parenting to make a life outside recognised family structures, but, in at least some parts of the world, lesbian and gay people now enjoy more options. There are communities in which lesbian women bear children they have conceived via donor insemination, where lesbian and gay individuals and same-sex couples adopt infants and children, and where gay men father children who were conceived and born via surrogacy. Law and practice in some countries recognise the marriages of same-sex couples, as well as the relationships between non-heterosexual parents and their children. Around the world, social and legal definitions of families are undergoing dramatic change.

Considered in a historical perspective, the pace of change in family lives among non-heterosexual people, while certainly not uniform, is essentially unprecedented (Simon and Brooks, 2009). The resulting family configurations and legal innovations are altering fundamental notions about families. In Canada, same-sex couples have been able to enter into federally recognised marriages since 2005, and their children have been assured that the government also recognises legal links between children and both same-sex parents (Simon and Brooks, 2009). While families

Contemporary Issues in Family Studies: Global Perspectives on Partnerships, Parenting and Support in a Changing World, First Edition. Edited by Angela Abela and Janet Walker.
© 2014 John Wiley & Sons, Ltd. Published 2014 by John Wiley & Sons, Ltd.

headed by same-sex couples in Canada today thus enjoy full citizenship and protection under the law, families in other parts of the world live in different circumstances. In some jurisdictions, same-sex couples may undertake legally recognised marriages but cannot adopt children; in other parts of the world, they may adopt but not marry. In still other nations, same-sex sexual behaviour is forbidden by law. In both Iran and Saudi Arabia, for example, it is punishable by death (Simon and Brooks, 2009). Overall, there is today a changing global patchwork of rights, practices and laws that includes stunning breakthroughs as well as areas of firmly entrenched anti-gay legal and social tradition.

In this chapter, we provide a brief overview of this sizeable terrain. We begin with a summary of legal environments for same-sex couples, lesbian and gay parents, and their children around the world. We then review research on lesbian and gay parents and their children, with special attention to recent work conducted outside the USA and the UK. Finally, we offer conclusions and suggestions for further research.

In the contemporary world, there are many ways to adopt non-heterosexual identities. While the majority of people who identify as non-heterosexual seem to apply the terms 'gay', 'lesbian' or 'bisexual' to themselves (Herek *et al.*, 2010), many other labels are also in use. Some identify themselves as queer, others think of themselves as transgender or transsexual, and others identify as something else altogether. Unfortunately, however, bisexual, transgender and other identities have rarely been studied or identified in the literature that we review in this chapter. Research has focused mainly on people who identify as lesbian or gay. Thus, our discussion focuses on lesbian and gay individuals, and same-sex couples, and on their offspring.

In our rapidly globalising world, definitions of sexual orientation and terminology used to describe sexual orientation can be controversial. It is not our intention to attempt to resolve any such controversies here; rather, we describe law and research findings from quantitative social science in terms that are used in these literatures. It should also be recognised that many of the topics discussed in this chapter are in near-constant flux. Thus, what was true as of mid-2012 may no longer be accurate by 2013, much less in subsequent years. It is likely that further changes will emerge over time.

What is sexual orientation?

1. Sexual orientation is a term that refers to enduring patterns of emotional, romantic and/or sexual attractions to men, women, or both sexes. Sexual orientation can also refer to a person's sense of identity based on those attractions, on behaviours related to them, and on membership in communities of others who share those attractions.
2. Research suggests that sexual orientation ranges across a continuum, but it is often discussed in terms of the categories 'heterosexual', 'bisexual' and 'gay/ lesbian'. Some people may, however, use different labels or none at all.
3. Research has examined possible genetic, hormonal, developmental, social, and cultural influences on sexual orientation, but there is no consensus among experts as to why there are variations among people in terms of sexual orientation.

In this chapter, we address three main questions. First, what are the known variations in law and policy relevant to lesbian and gay parents and their offspring around the world? Second, given their social and legal environments, how are families headed by same-sex couples and non-heterosexual individuals faring, especially in areas outside the USA? Finally, what conclusions can be drawn from the available evidence, and what are the most promising directions for future research?

Law and Policy in Global Perspective

In 2011, the Human Rights Council of the United Nations passed a resolution focusing on human rights violations based on sexual orientation and gender identity (Daugherty, 2011). Sponsored by South Africa and Brazil, this first-ever resolution affirmed the universality of human rights, expressed concern about violence and human rights violations relevant to sexual orientation, and called for further dialogue. The resolution passed on a split vote, with several African and Middle Eastern nations voting against it, and other nations abstaining. This was nevertheless a historic step towards integration of these issues into the work of the United Nations.

Just twenty years earlier, the notion that any UN body could address issues related to sexual orientation would have been difficult to imagine. In 1990, no country in the world offered legal recognition for the relationships of same-sex couples, few offered legal recognition of parent–child relationships in families headed by same-sex couples, and many outlawed same-sex sexual behaviour altogether. Public opinion, however, shifted rapidly. By 2007, a group of legal scholars had published the Yogyakarta Principles, which were an application of international human rights law to issues surrounding sexual orientation and gender identity (O'Flaherty and Fisher, 2008). One of the principles stated that 'everyone has a right to found a family, regardless of sexual orientation or gender identity'. The articulation and publication of the Yogyakarta Principles represented an important step, but they did not carry the force of law in any of the nations of the world.

Sexual behaviour with same-sex partners is still illegal in some countries, but tremendous change in recognition of family relationships has taken place in just two decades (Simon and Brooks, 2009). Law and policy regarding same-sex couples and lesbian- and gay-parent families varies substantially around the world (Simon and Brooks, 2009). Same-sex sexuality remains illegal in some countries, but in others, same-sex couples and lesbian- and gay-parent families enjoy the same rights as do their heterosexual peers. The law in other jurisdictions falls somewhere between these two extremes. In the following section we describe the international legal landscape with regard to recognition of same-sex relationships, the regulation of assisted reproductive technology, and recognition of parenthood for lesbian and gay individuals and couples.

Legal recognition of the relationships of same-sex couples

While still uncommon, legal recognition of same-sex couple relationships takes a variety of forms around the world. Full recognition of the marriages of same-sex couples is available in some jurisdictions. In other jurisdictions, same-sex couples are offered legal recognition through civil unions or domestic partnerships. In some jurisdictions, same-sex relationships are legally recognised only when the partners have entered into a legally recognised status (such as marriage or civil union) elsewhere. Below, we consider three broad categories of legal environments for same-sex couples—marriage, other forms of relationship recognition (e.g. civil unions, domestic partnerships) and complete lack of legal recognition—and describe global variation with respect to these categories.

Legal recognition of same-sex marriage

In 2001, the Netherlands became the first country in the world to provide legal recognition for same-sex marriages. Other nations soon followed suit. These nations, with the dates on which their recognition of same-sex marriages became effective, include:

- Belgium (2003)
- Spain (2005)
- Canada (2005)
- South Africa (2006)
- Norway (2009)
- Sweden (2009)
- Portugal (2010)
- Iceland (2010)
- Argentina (2010)

In all these countries, same-sex couples are permitted to marry and their marriages are legally recognised throughout the country (GayLawNet, n.d.; ILGA, n.d.).

In addition, Mexico, Brazil and Israel provide nationwide recognition of same-sex marriages. In Mexico, legal same-sex marriages can, however, be undertaken only in Mexico City (also known as the Federal District) (Agren, 2010), and in Brazil they can be undertaken only when a judge agrees to convert a civil union into a marriage, as has taken place in the state of Alagoas (Barbassa, 2011). In Israel, same-sex marriages must be undertaken in another country that allows this in order to be recognised within Israeli borders (Associated Press, 2006).

Only one country, the USA, refuses legal recognition to same-sex marriages at the federal level while providing state-level legal recognition in some jurisdictions. Within the USA, the 1996 Defense of Marriage Act forbids federal recognition of same-sex marriages and holds that no state can be required to recognise marriages of same-sex couples from other states. Thus, same-sex couples who have married in Massachusetts or New York (i.e. states in which the marriages of same-sex couples are legally recognised) would no longer be recognised as married under the law if they moved to Mississippi or New Mexico (i.e. states in which marriages of same-sex couples have no legal standing). Marriages of same-sex couples are currently recognised in Connecticut, Iowa, Massachusetts, New Hampshire, New York and Vermont, as well as in the District of Columbia and in some tribal jurisdictions. Maryland and Washington have passed laws designed to recognise these marriages, but the laws in both states were subject to voter referendum in November 2012 as to whether they would go into effect. California granted marriage licences to same-sex couples from 16 June 2008 to 5 November 2008; owing to the passage of Proposition 8, in November 2008, California no longer recognises the marriages of same-sex couples (Schwartz, 2009). California's Proposition 8 has been declared unconstitutional by a federal court, and the matter is on appeal at the US Supreme Court.

Although tremendous change has occurred in recent years, most countries still do not offer legal recognition of the relationships of same-sex couples. Israel and South Africa are the only Asian or African countries where same-sex relationships are

Other forms of recognition for same-sex relationships

More than 20 countries offer some type of legal recognition (other than marriage) of same-sex relationships. The extent of this recognition varies, as does the terminology used.

- In the UK civil partnerships carry most of the rights and responsibilities of marriage.
- In Switzerland same-sex partnerships do not carry the full rights or responsibilities of marriage.
- Austria, Denmark, Hungary, Ireland and Lichtenstein offer a form of legal recognition that carries all or almost all the rights and responsibilities of marriage.

The terms used to describe these unions include: 'civil union', 'lifetime partnership' and 'registered partnership'.

- In the USA, same-sex couples in 12 states can enter into non-marital forms of state-recognised partnerships (civil unions, domestic partnerships, more limited partnerships) (NGLTF, 2011). None of these partnerships includes rights or responsibilities at the federal level.
- Andorra, Colombia, the Czech Republic, Ecuador, Finland, France, Germany, Ireland, Israel, Luxembourg, New Zealand, Slovenia, Switzerland and Uruguay grant same-sex couples some of the benefits of marriage (GayLawNet, n.d.).

Many variations exist:

- Israeli same-sex couples who have undertaken marriages abroad, in jurisdictions that recognise them, enjoy some but not all the rights of their married peers when they return home to Israel (Amihoud Borochov Tel Aviv Law Office, 2011).
- Unlike opposite-sex couples, who are permitted to marry at any time, same-sex couples in Uruguay are not eligible for legal recognition until they have cohabited for at least five years (BBC News, 2007).
- Same-sex couples who have legally entered into what is termed a 'stable union' in Andorra must wait six months to receive benefits and are never eligible to adopt children (ILGA, n.d.).

legally recognised in any way (ILGA, n.d.). While same-sex relationships are legally recognised in many jurisdictions within Europe, North America and South America, they are not recognised in most Central American countries. Thus, considerable change has taken place, but many nations still do not provide legal recognition for these relationships.

Legal regulation of assisted reproductive technology

Even in wealthy nations, the use of assisted reproductive technology (ART) has been a recent development (Crockin and Jones, 2010). The first live human birth resulting from in vitro fertilisation (IVF) occurred in the United Kingdom in 1978. Success rates for IVF increased throughout the 1990s and its use has grown steadily, thus creating new pathways to parenthood for many people, including lesbian women and gay men.

For non-heterosexual individuals and same-sex couples who wish to become parents, various forms of ART can play a critical role. Some non-heterosexual women and men conceive children through heterosexual intercourse, but for many, this is not a preferred route to parenthood. In many cases, lesbian women may wish to conceive via donor insemination. Gay men may wish to father children through surrogacy. Gay men and lesbian women seeking to become parents may wish to employ IVF and/or additional forms of ART. Legal regulation of ART may thus have a major impact on the efforts of lesbian and gay people to become parents.

Access to ART services is regulated by law in some but not other nations. In the USA, use of ART services is not regulated by law, but in Taiwan and at least ten other nations, single women and those in same-sex relationships are forbidden to use ART services such as donor insemination (GayLawNet, n.d.; ILGA, n.d.). In contrast, 14 countries explicitly permit access to ART by law, regardless of sexual orientation: Argentina, Australia, Belgium, Denmark, El Salvador, Finland, Iceland, the Netherlands, Norway, Russia, Spain, South Africa, Sweden, and the UK. In Denmark, hospital-based donor insemination is available to lesbian women without charge, and in New Zealand, a state-funded fertility clinic supports the efforts of lesbian and gay adults who wish to become parents. In many jurisdictions, however, the law is unclear or silent; in these cases, medical professionals may act as informal gatekeepers for reproductive health services (Gurmankin *et al.*, 2005).

The legal status of surrogacy also varies considerably around the world. The practice of surrogacy involves a woman initiating and carrying a pregnancy to term with the intention that another parent or parents will rear the baby. It can be pursued as an altruistic act, in which case no money changes hands, or as a commercial proposition, in which case the surrogate is paid. The law permits altruistic but not commercial surrogacy for all individuals and couples, regardless of sexual orientation, in countries such as Australia, Canada and the Netherlands (Gentleman, 2008). In other countries, such as France, Germany and Sweden, both forms of surrogacy are forbidden for all individuals and couples. In the UK, same-sex couples can become legal parents of children conceived via surrogacy, but single individuals cannot (GayLawNet, n.d.). In India, the law bans same-sex couples from becoming parents via surrogacy, but allows individuals to do so, regardless of sexual orientation (GayLawNet, n.d.). Barriers to pursuing parenthood via ART thus exist in some but not in all nations of the world.

Adoption laws and sexual orientation

Adoption is another route to parenthood for non-heterosexual individuals and same-sex couples (Brodzinsky *et al.*, 2011; Farr and Patterson, in press). In a traditional adoption, one or two adults become the legal parents of a minor who was not previously their biological or adoptive child. In this instance, the child's birth parents give up their legal ties to the child. In a second-parent adoption, an adult becomes a legal parent of his or her partner's biological or adoptive child. In traditional adoptions, the law breaks the existing parent–child ties and establishes new ones where none had existed before, so as to provide a permanent home for a child. In second-parent adoptions, the child gains a second parent without severing ties to the first parent. Laws governing both types of adoption vary widely around the world.

Traditional adoption

National laws explicitly allow same-sex couples to complete joint adoptions of the traditional type in 15 countries: Andorra, Argentina, Belgium, Brazil, Denmark, England, Iceland, Israel, the Netherlands, Norway, Scotland, Spain, South Africa, Sweden and Uruguay (ILGA, n.d.). In joint adoptions, both members of a couple become a child's legal parents.

There are also several countries where non-heterosexual *individuals* are explicitly permitted by law to complete traditional adoptions nationwide, including Colombia, Costa Rica, Estonia, Finland, France, French Guiana, Germany, Latvia, New Zealand, Poland, Portugal and Slovenia. However, in Canada, Mexico and the USA, laws regarding adoption and sexual orientation vary by state, territory or province.

In Australia, national law does not address adoption rights, but the law in some states allows foster care by lesbian and gay adults.

Several countries, including Greece, Japan and Switzerland, explicitly ban same-sex couples from adopting children, and others, including Chile, Cuba, Ecuador, El Salvador, Guatemala, Italy, Ireland, Lithuania and Peru, explicitly ban non-heterosexual individuals from adopting children.

In many nations, however, the law on these issues is unclear.

Without severing established parent–child ties, an individual in a same-sex relationship may petition to complete a second-parent adoption of a partner's biological or adoptive child anywhere within 14 countries: Argentina, Belgium, Brazil, Denmark, Finland, French Guiana, Germany, Iceland, the Netherlands, Norway, Spain, Sweden, the UK and Uruguay. In Australia, Canada, Mexico and the USA, second-parent adoption laws vary by state, territory or province. In most jurisdictions around the world, the law is silent on this issue and the legal situation remains unclear. The extent of legal recognition of adoption for non-heterosexual adults thus varies considerably around the world today.

Conclusions on law and policy in global perspective

Law and policy relevant to non-heterosexual people and their families has undergone considerable change over a relatively short period of time. Twenty years ago, no legal system in the world recognised the relationships of same-sex couples, access to ART among non-heterosexual individuals and same-sex couples was rare, and adoptions were not readily available to most openly non-heterosexual adults. The last two decades have seen dramatic changes in these areas. Even so, the majority of non-heterosexual individuals and same-sex couples around the world today do not live in jurisdictions that offer legal recognition for their couple or family relationships. Further, most lack access to adoption or to ART services. Of the more than 190 nations of the world, only a handful offer any legal recognition for the family relationships of lesbian and gay people.

Research on Lesbian and Gay Parents and Their Children

In view of the varied legal climates in which non-heterosexual parents and their children live, their apparent resilience is remarkable. Quantitative social science research with these families began in the USA and the UK more than 30 years ago, and has produced a picture of favourable mental health and adjustment among non-heterosexual parents and their children. Below, we present an overview of the results of early research from the USA and the UK, and follow this with an account of contemporary research conducted in the Americas, Europe, Africa and Australia. We conclude with a brief commentary on the research to date.

Early research on lesbian and gay parents and their children

Research on non-heterosexual parents and their children began in the USA and the UK in the 1980s and 1990s in the context of studying families affected by divorce (Patterson, 2006). A number of studies examined adjustment among mothers who had given birth in the context of heterosexual marriages that were dissolved when the mothers came out as lesbian, and among their children. In the light of legal battles over child custody, researchers were particularly interested in learning whether non-heterosexual parental sexual orientation affected child development. Accordingly, these studies compared child and parent outcomes among divorced lesbian mothers, divorced heterosexual mothers, and their children (Patterson, 2009).

In one example of this early research, Golombok *et al.* (1983) studied a sample of 5- to 17-year-old children of divorced lesbian mothers in the UK, comparing them to same-aged children of divorced heterosexual mothers. All the children were living with their mothers. Using standardised instruments and reports from each child's parents and teachers, Golombok and her colleagues studied the sample children's gender development, behaviour problems (e.g. hyperactivity, conduct problems, emotional difficulties) and social development. Their analyses revealed no significant differences in child outcomes as a function of parental sexual orientation.

Overall, one of the most important results of these early studies, which was replicated many times, was that parental mental health was not associated with parental sexual orientation (Patterson, 1992). Lesbian mothers seemed just as well-adjusted, overall, as were heterosexual mothers. On average, reports of self-esteem, psychiatric symptoms, and preferred parenting strategies were all unrelated to parental sexual orientation. Like heterosexual mothers, lesbian mothers seemed to enjoy reasonably good mental health overall and to provide relatively healthy home environments for their children.

Furthermore, parental sexual orientation was not associated with child adjustment (Patterson, 2009; Stacey and Biblarz, 2001). On average, behaviour problems, competencies, gender development and self-esteem were all unrelated to parental sexual orientation. Children of lesbian mothers were as likely as children of heterosexual mothers to be healthy and well-adjusted. These findings were widely reported and were influential in many ways, informing many legal and policy debates (Patterson, 2009). They also set the stage for new research questions.

Contemporary research on lesbian and gay parents and their children

Almost all recent research has originated from areas of the world (the USA, Canada and the UK) where legal recognition of same-sex couples and other family relationships is most prevalent. Research produced elsewhere has often originated in nations with relatively positive social and legal climates for sexual minorities (e.g. in Belgium, the Netherlands and Australia). More recently, research has also emerged from Israel and South Africa. Notably, however, little or no research in this area has been conducted in other African, or Asian, nations, the Middle East, Central America or South America. The geographic limitations of this literature, as well as the common focus on participants of moderate or high socioeconomic status, shape current thinking about parenting by non-heterosexual individuals.

Whereas early research focused on families in which children had been born in the context of a heterosexual marriage, recent work has also addressed outcomes in families formed in the context of parents' non-heterosexual identities (Telingator and Patterson, 2008). A number of studies have examined adjustment among lesbian mothers and among children they conceived via donor insemination or other forms of ART (e.g. Chan et al., 1998; Gartrell et al., 1999, 2000, 2005). Research has also begun to include non-heterosexual adoptive parents and their children, whom the parents adopted after establishing non-heterosexual identities (Farr et al., 2010; Farr and Patterson, in press).

Chan et al. (1998) studied families who had conceived children (average age 7 years at the time of the research) via donor insemination, all assisted by a single sperm bank. These families were headed either by lesbian mothers or by heterosexual parents. Using standardised instruments and reports from both parents and teachers, the researchers reported no differences in family functioning and adjustment among parents or children as a function of parental sexual orientation. Indices of family functioning (such as interparental conflict) were more strongly associated with child adjustment than was parental sexual orientation. As in earlier research, these authors found that mental health and adjustment of children and parents were not linked with parental sexual orientation (Patterson, 2006). On average, parental sexual orientation was unrelated to child self-esteem, wellbeing, or psychiatric symptoms. Children born to or adopted by lesbian or gay parents were as likely as other children to thrive (Stacey and Biblarz, 2001; Tasker and Patterson, 2007).

In the wake of these findings, many reviewers have suggested that future research should focus also on exploring individual differences within non-heterosexual parenting communities (e.g. Goldberg, 2010; Patterson, 1992, 2009; Stacey and Biblarz, 2001). In other words, while many studies have addressed similarities and differences between children of lesbian mothers and children of heterosexual parents, several reviewers have called for studies of the conditions under which children of non-heterosexual parents suffer or thrive. In recent years, this goal has increasingly characterised the research.

Studies on variability within non-heterosexual parenting communities have emerged mainly in the USA (e.g. Goldberg and Smith, 2008; Goldberg *et al.*, 2010; Tornello *et al.*, 2011), but some efforts have also involved European and other researchers (e.g. Bos and Gartrell, 2011; Vanfraussen *et al.*, 2003). This work is beginning to identify factors relevant to the wellbeing of non-heterosexual parents and their children. For example, Tornello and colleagues (2011) examined correlates of parenting stress in a large sample of gay adoptive fathers who were geographically dispersed across the USA. The authors identified some predictors of parenting stress that would be relevant for any adoptive parent, such as the child's age at time of adoption and the extent of fathers' social support. In addition to these, however, men who reported less positive gay identities also reported greater parenting stress. Thus, research focusing on individual differences within non-heterosexual parenting communities is beginning to identify some issues that may be specific to these groups.

Researchers have also been more likely in recent years to examine contextual factors. For instance, Goldberg and Smith (2011) studied lesbian and gay couples who were becoming adoptive parents, and found that participants' perceptions of their social environments were associated with their adjustment to new parenthood. Those who reported greater social support and harmonious couple relationships reported the fewest symptoms of anxiety or depression during the transition to parenthood. Those who reported living in 'gay-friendly' neighbourhoods also reported fewer depressive symptoms during the early months of parenthood.

Other researchers have begun to study ways in which laws and policies may affect the mental health and experiences of lesbian and gay parents and their children. Some of these studies have revealed similarities in experience despite national differences. For example, in an Internet-based study, Tornello and Patterson (2012) reported that age was an important correlate of men's choices among pathways to parenthood. In this sample, gay fathers over 50 years of age most often reported that they became parents in the context of heterosexual marriages, whereas gay fathers under 50 were more likely to report that they had become fathers in other ways, such as via adoption or surrogacy. This was true for residents of Canada, the UK and Australia, as well as of the USA (Patterson and Tornello, 2010).

Researchers have also identified differences in the experiences of children with same-sex parents across national boundaries. For instance, Bos *et al.* (2008) studied the experiences of 10- to 11-year-old children with lesbian mothers in the USA and the Netherlands, comparing subsamples defined by country. Inasmuch as the Netherlands is known for its liberal laws and tolerant attitudes, the authors expected that Dutch children would be more likely to report telling their peers about maternal sexual identities and less likely to report encounters with homophobia than would American children. Results were consistent with these expectations (Bos *et al.*, 2008). Thus, the social climate for children of lesbian mothers may be more favourable in the Netherlands than in the USA, and this difference may influence children's experiences.

Another recent study examined differences in social environments across national boundaries and explored some implications of such differences (Shapiro *et al.*, 2009). The authors studied aspects of mental health among lesbian and heterosexual mothers in the USA and Canada. Despite similarities between the two countries, Canada provides a more supportive legal climate for non-heterosexual parents and their children. Consistent with expectations based on these legal differences, Shapiro and her colleagues found that lesbian mothers in the USA reported greater concern about legal problems and discrimination based on sexual orientation, but no greater concern about general family issues, than did lesbian mothers in Canada. Among heterosexual mothers, whose family relationships enjoyed legal protection in both countries, there were no such differences as a function of where they lived. These findings begin to suggest the benefits of supportive legal contexts for families headed by non-heterosexual parents.

Increasingly, scholars from around the world are documenting changes with regard to same-sex marriage and non-heterosexual parenting, and are exploring the influence of social contexts on the lives of children with non-heterosexual parents. In Australia, work by Perlesz *et al.* (2006), Riggs (2007), van Reyk (2004) and Violi (2004) has addressed aspects of non-heterosexual parenting experiences. In France (Gross, 2003, 2007, 2009), Germany (Hermann-Green and Gehring, 2007), Israel (Ben-Ari and Livni, 2006), New Zealand (Surtees, 2011), Poland (Majka-Rostek, 2011) and South Africa (Lubbe, 2008), other scholars have begun to explore dimensions of the experiences of non-heterosexual parents and their children. Research on sexual orientation, marriage and parenthood is thus becoming increasingly international in scope.

Conclusions and Policy Implications

Dramatic changes in social climates relevant to sexual orientation, marriage and parenthood are under way around the world. Twenty years ago, no nation on earth recognised the marriages of same-sex couples; today, some countries offer nationwide recognition, and a number of others offer partial recognition of such relationships. Changes in parenting laws have likewise been substantial. At the same time, however, same-sex sexual behaviour is still illegal in many jurisdictions. The world today is thus a shifting patchwork of diverse environments for non-heterosexual parents and their children.

An examination of social and legal climates for families headed by non-heterosexual parents in different nations reveals intriguing inconsistencies, even within single countries. One might expect law and social attitudes to be two sides of the same coin, such that tolerant attitudes and gay-friendly laws would go hand in hand. In some countries (e.g. Canada) this may be the case, but in others the situation may be quite different. In South Africa, for example, the law recognises same-sex marriages and family relationships, but attitudes towards homosexuality remain relatively negative (Lubbe, 2008). In Austria and Germany, same-sex couples are allowed to form a civil union or registered partnership but are not permitted to adopt children (GayLawNet, n.d.), while in Finland, same-sex couples can adopt children but cannot marry. In times of rapid social change, such inconsistencies are likely to be common.

Excluded from family life for many years, non-heterosexual individuals and same-sex couples have begun, in some parts of the world, to claim their rights to marry and rear children. In so doing, they are creating families that diverge in significant ways from heteronormative models. The families of non-heterosexual people challenge accepted definitions of parenthood, unsettle conventional views about family relationships, and question deeply held beliefs about the importance of biological linkages in family lives. The law is changing in some jurisdictions to accommodate changing ways of life, and observers from across the political spectrum agree that these challenges are profound.

Our recommendations for policy changes centre on measures that would provide recognition and support for the family relationships of non-heterosexual individuals around the world. We recommend legal recognition for the marriages of same-sex couples, and we recommend prohibitions on discrimination in matters of child custody, adoption, and access to reproductive technology. Such legal changes would help to establish and protect the rights of non-heterosexual people and their children.

Research in this area is becoming both more important and increasingly global. Studies are needed to document changes as they occur and to examine family functioning in new forms of families with non-heterosexual parents. In this effort, it will be critical to address how social and legal contexts shape and are shaped by individual and family experiences. As these fundamental shifts in family lives continue to take place around the world, a key role for social scientists is to track their impact on parents, children and communities.

References

Agren, D. (2010) Mexican states—ordered to honor gay marriages, *New York Times*, 10 Aug. http://www.nytimes.com [Accessed 15.7.2011.]

Amihoud Borochov Tel Aviv Law Office (n.d.) *Family law in Israel.* http://www.family-laws.co.il/ [Accessed 15.7.2011.]

Associated Press (2006) Israeli high court orders gay marriage recognition, *USA Today*, 21 Nov. http://www.usatoday.com [Accessed 15.7. 2011.]

Barbassa, J. (2011) Brazilian judge gives couple approval for what court says is country's first gay marriage, *Washington Post.* www.washingtonpost.com [Accessed 15.7.2011.]

BBC News (2007) Uruguay approves gay civil unions, Dec. http://news.bbc.co.uk/2/hi/americas/7151669.stm [Accessed 15.7.2011.]

Ben-Ari, A., and Livni, T. (2006) Motherhood is not a given thing: experiences and constructed meanings of biological and nonbiological lesbian mothers, *Sex Roles*, 54: 521–531.

Bos, H. M. W., and Gartrell, N. K. (2011) Adolescents of the US National Longitudinal Lesbian Family Study: the impact of having a known or an unknown donor on the stability of psychological adjustment, *Human Reproduction*, 26: 630–637.

Bos, H. M. W., Gartrell, N. K., van Balen, F., Peyser, H. and Sandfort, T. (2008) Children in planned lesbian families: a cross-cultural comparison between the United States and the Netherlands, *American Journal of Orthopsychiatry*, 78: 211–219.

Brodzinsky, D., Pertman, A., and Kunz, D. (eds) (2011) *Lesbian and Gay Adoption: A new American reality* (New York: Oxford University Press).

Chan, R. W., Raboy, B. and Patterson, C. J. (1998) Psychosocial adjustment among children conceived via donor insemination by lesbian and heterosexual mothers, *Child Development*, 69: 443–457.

Crockin, S. L. and Jones, H. W. (2010) *Legal Conceptions: The evolving law and policy of assisted reproductive technologies* (Baltimore, MD: Johns Hopkins Press).

Daugherty, J. (2011) UN council passes gay rights resolution, *CNN World*, 17 June. www.cnn.com. [Accessed 15.7.2011.]

Farr, R. H., Forssell, S. L. and Patterson, C. J. (2010) Parenting and child development in adoptive families: does parental sexual orientation matter?, *Applied Developmental Science*, 14: 164–178.

Farr, R. H. and Patterson, C. J. (in press) Lesbian and gay adoptive parents and their children, in A. E. Goldberg and K. R. Allen (eds), *LGBT-Parent Families: Possibilities for new research and implications for practice* (New York: Springer).

Gartrell, N., Banks, A., Hamilton, J., Reed, N., Bishop, H. and Rodas, C. (1999) The national lesbian family study: interviews with mothers of toddlers, *American Journal of Orthopsychiatry*, 69: 362–369.

Gartrell, N., Banks, A., Reed, N., Hamilton, J., Rodas, C. and Deck, A. (2000) The national lesbian family study: 3. Interviews with mothers of five-year-olds, *American Journal of Orthopsychiatry*, 70: 542–548.

Gartrell, N., Deck, A., Rodas, C., Peyser, H. and Banks, A. (2005) The national lesbian family study: 4. Interviews with 10-year-old children, *American Journal of Orthopsychiatry*, 70: 518–524.

GayLawNet (n.d.) http://gaylawnet.com/ [Accessed 15.7.2011.]

Gentleman, A. (2008) Foreign couples turn to India for surrogate mothers, *New York Times*, 4 March. http://www.nytimes.com. [Accessed 15.7.2011.]

Goldberg, A. E. (2010) *Lesbian and Gay Parents and Their Children: Research on the family life cycle* (Washington, DC: American Psychological Association).

Goldberg, A. E. and Smith, J. Z. (2008) Social support and psychological well-being in lesbian and heterosexual preadoptive couples, *Family Relations*, 57: 281–294.

Goldberg, A. E. and Smith, J. Z. (2011) Stigma, social context, and mental health: lesbian and gay couples across the transition to adoptive parenthood, *Journal of Counseling Psychology*, 58: 139–150.

Goldberg, A. E., Smith, J. Z. and Kashy, D. A. (2010) Pre-adoptive factors predicting lesbian, gay, and heterosexual couples' relationships quality across the transition to adoptive parenthood, *Journal of Family Psychology*, 24: 221–232.

Golombok, S., Spencer, A. and Rutter, M. (1983) Children in lesbian and single-parent households: psychosexual and psychiatric appraisal, *Journal of Child Psychology and Psychiatry*, 24: 551–572.

Gross, M. (2003) *L'Homoparentalité* (Paris: Presses Universitaires de France).

Gross, M. (2007) *Fonder une famille homoparentale* (Paris: J'ai Lu Editions).

Gross, M. (2009) The desire for parenthood among lesbians and gay men, in D. Marre and L. Briggs (eds), *International adoption: Global inequities and the circulation of children* (New York: New York University Press).

Gurmankin, A. D., Caplan, A. L. and Braverman, A. M. (2005) Screening practices and beliefs of assisted reproductive technology programs, *Fertility and Sterility*, 83: 61–67.

Herek, G. M., Norton, A. T., Allen, T. J. and Sims, C. L. (2010) Demographic, psychological, and social characteristics of self-identified lesbian, gay, and bisexual adults in a US probability sample, *Sexuality Research and Social Policy*, 7: 176–200.

Hermann-Green, L. K. and Gehring, T. M. (2007) The German Lesbian Family Study: planning for parenthood via donor insemination, *Journal of GLBT Family Studies*, 3: 351–396.

ILGA (n.d.) http://ilga.org/ [Accessed 15.7.2011.]

Lubbe, C. (2008) The experiences of children growing up in lesbian-headed families in South Africa, *Journal of GLBT Family Studies*, 4: 325–359.

Majka-Rostek, D (2011) Same-sex couples in Poland: challenges of family life, *Journal of GLBT Family Studies*, 7: 285–296.

NGLTF (2011) Relationship recognition for same-sex couples in the U.S. http://www.thetaskforce.org/downloads/reports/issue_maps/rel_recog_6_28_11.pdf [Accessed 15.7.2011.]

O'Flaherty, M. and Fisher, J. (2008) Sexual orientation, gender identity and international human rights law: contextualizing the Yogyakarta Principles, *Human Rights Law Review*, 8: 207–248.

Patterson, C. J. (2006) Children of lesbian and gay parents, *Current Directions in Psychological Science*, 15: 241–244.

Patterson, C. J. (2009) Children of lesbian and gay parents: psychology, law, and policy, *American Psychologist*, 64: 727–736.

Patterson, C. J. and Tornello, S. L. (2010) Gay fathers' pathways to parenthood: international perspectives, *Zeitschrift fur Familienforschung* [*Journal of Family Psychology*], Sonderheft, S.103–116.

Perlesz, A., Brown, R., McNair, R., Lindsay, J., Pitts, M. and de Vaus, D. (2006) Lesbian family disclosure: authenticity and safety within private and public domains, *Lesbian and Gay Psychology Review*, 7: 53–64.

Riggs, D. W. (2007) *Becoming Parent: Lesbians, gay men, and family* (Teneriffe, QLD: Post Pressed).

Schwartz, J. (2009) California high court upholds gay marriage ban. *New York Times*. http://www.nytimes.com [Accessed 15.7.2011.]

Shapiro, D. N., Peterson, C. and Stewart, A. J. (2009) Legal and social contexts and mental health among lesbian and heterosexual mothers, *Journal of Family Psychology*, 23: 255–262.

Simon, R. J. and Brooks, A. (2009) *Gay and Lesbian Communities the World Over* (New York: Rowman & Littlefield).

Stacey, J. and Biblarz, T. J. (2001) (How) does sexual orientation of parents matter?, *American Sociological Review*, 65: 159–183.

Surtees, N. (2011) Family law in New Zealand: the benefits and costs for gay men, lesbians, and their children, *Journal of GLBT Family Studies*, 7: 245–263.

Tasker, F. L. and Patterson, C. J. (2007) Research on gay and lesbian parenting: retrospect and prospect, *Journal of GLBT Family Studies*, 3: 9–34.

Telingator, C. and Patterson, C. J. (2008) Children and adolescents of lesbian and gay parents, *Journal of the American Academy of Child and Adolescent Psychiatry*, 47: 1364–1368.

Tornello, S. L., Farr, R. H. and Patterson, C. J. (2011) Predictors of parenting stress among gay adoptive fathers in the United States, *Journal of Family Psychology*, 25: 591–600.

Tornello, S. L. and Patterson, C. J. (2012) Age, life pathways, and experiences of gay fathers: life course perspective. Unpublished manuscript, Department of Psychology, University of Virginia.

Vanfraussen, K., Ponjaert-Kristoffersen, I. and Brewaeys, A. (2003) Family functioning in lesbian families created by donor insemination, *American Journal of Orthopsychiatry*, 73: 78–90.

van Reyk, P. (2004) Baby love: gay donor father narratives of intimacy, in D. W. Riggs and G. A. Walker (eds), *Out in the Antipodes: Australian and New Zealand perspectives on gay and lesbian issues in psychology* (Perth: Brightfire Press), 146–166.

Violi, D. (2004) Moving on out: the issues and experiences of nonresident gay fathers, in D. W. Riggs and G. A. Walker (eds), *Out in the Antipodes: Australian and New Zealand perspectives on gay and lesbian issues in psychology* (Perth: Brightfire Press), 167–188.

14

Parenting Teenagers

John Coleman

Introduction

In the field of family studies the parenting of teenagers is arguably one of the most
sensitive and controversial topics. There is far less research in this area than there is in
respect of the parenting of infants and toddlers, which has led to there being significant gaps in the knowledge base for families with teenagers living at home. Even
where there is good evidence, there is much debate about how best to disseminate
this among parents of adolescents, who are less likely to read books or attend to the
media to get help than are parents of younger children. The role of the school is also
different, and by and large parents of teenagers do not have the same links with the
school as do parents of elementary school children.

Perhaps most important, parents themselves often find the teenage years problematic,
even where the young person is coping well and behaving in much the same way as any
other 'normal' teenager. This is partly because of poor levels of understanding of what to
expect, and ignorance of what constitutes normal adolescent development. Parental confidence takes a significant dip at this time, influenced as much by expectations and by
what other parents report as by the actual behaviour of the young person. When things
appear to be going wrong parents often feel shame and guilt, preferring to keep family
issues to themselves rather than to share these with others. One of the most common
experiences of parents who attend a parenting group is the discovery that their teenager
is no worse than, and possibly is considerably better than, teenagers in other families.

It is important to recognise that adolescence brings with it a major change in the way
parents and young people interact with each other. Such change is gradual and, contrary to popular belief, does not bring with it a complete breakdown of relationships.

*Contemporary Issues in Family Studies: Global Perspectives on Partnerships, Parenting and
Support in a Changing World*, First Edition. Edited by Angela Abela and Janet Walker.
© 2014 John Wiley & Sons, Ltd. Published 2014 by John Wiley & Sons, Ltd.

It's very difficult to learn to be a parent of a teenager. It's the most under-rated job in the world. It's easier to be a brain surgeon than to be a really good parent. (mother of two daughters)

As we shall see, research on these matters has emphasised continuity as much as change, and there has been a greater emphasis recently on the positive role that parents can play during this stage of child development. Since the 1960s research on family relationships across the Western world has indicated that conflict is a less dominant theme than was once assumed. Many adolescents get on reasonably well with their parents most of the time, and look to them for guidance and support. Where there is conflict it tends to be over everyday things like untidy bedrooms, homework, and staying out late, rather than over major issues such as politics or basic values.

I think parents are something you can come back to and rely on, because we are supposed to be out there learning about life, but you need something to fall back on if it all goes wrong. I know that me and my Mum scream like we're going to kill each other, but she's always there. I know she's never going to abandon me if I'm in trouble and stuff. (15-year-old girl)

In setting the scene for a consideration of adolescents and the family there are some essential points to be made. A first issue to be addressed is that the very definition of family is undergoing radical change. In terms of family arrangements it is important to note the substantial increase that has occurred in Western countries in the numbers of families headed by a lone parent. As the authors in Part I of this book have demonstrated, families have changed considerably. For some couples, marriage is being postponed, or is not taking place at all. Marriage and childbearing are also occurring at a later age, and there are smaller families than in previous generations as a result of the availability of contraception. There are more family types that have to be recognised, so that we can no longer think only of the nuclear family and the single-parent family, but we have to include stepfamilies, as well as what are known as blended families where children from two different couples live together in a new arrangement. There are, in addition, more mothers now going to work. In a recent review by the Nuffield Foundation (2009) it was estimated that in the UK, of mothers with children over the age of 11 around 80 per cent are now in the labour market, at least on a part-time basis. Similar statistics apply to most European countries. This change has major implications for childcare and for the way families with teenagers function on a day-to-day basis.

Another facet of the changing family is that young people remain in the parental home for much longer today than was the case in earlier generations. This is true across Europe, as well as in North America. A review of changing patterns of leaving home can be found in Mulder (2009). The fact that the ability to set up home independently is being postponed in Western societies is related to the phenomenon of 'emerging adulthood' (Arnett, 2004). This stage is described as one of delayed independence, where adulthood is put on hold and some patterns of behaviour that are typical of adolescence continue for longer than might be expected. This has implications for the achievement of autonomy, as well as for various aspects of family life. Among other things, parents are likely to remain financially responsible for older adolescents for longer, space in the home for the young adult is needed for longer, and parents stay involved in the lives of their sons and daughters for a longer period than was the case in previous generations.

While the great majority of academic research on adolescence and family functioning stems from Europe and North America, it is essential to retain an international perspective, and to recognise that there are enormous differences across the world in the way young people relate to their families. A common distinction is that between the developed and the developing world, with continents such as Africa, Asia and South America being classed as part of the developing world. Although this distinction can be helpful, it is also the case that a distinction between rural and urban settings may be more relevant where adolescence is concerned. In many countries, those growing up in urban settings have greater access to education, and are more likely to be exposed to Western influences through the media and digital technologies. Those growing up in rural settings, however, are more likely to experience poverty, and to be regarded as needing to contribute to the economic survival of the family unit. Religion too plays a major part in influencing the way in which families treat their adolescent children, with Islam and some of the Eastern religions having quite different notions about adolescence from those to which we are accustomed in the West. This chapter considers: the development of autonomy in adolescence; conflict and the generation gap; parenting styles and adolescent development; culture and ethnicity; divorce and changing families; and the implications for policy and practice regarding parenting teenagers in the twenty-first century.

The Development of Autonomy in Adolescence

It can be argued that the development of independence, or autonomy, is one of the key tasks of the adolescent. To be free from parental restraint and to achieve control over one's life is the goal of every young person. Yet it is precisely the striving for autonomy that brings the relationship between parent and young person so sharply into focus. It is in this realm that the two generations are most likely to have different views, and the adolescent's progress towards autonomy is never straightforward. To some extent, the way independence is achieved will depend on the circumstances of the family, on ethnic background, and on the cultural, social and economic opportunities available in the environment. Gender, too, will play a part, since independence for women is understood differently from independence for men, although of course this varies from culture to culture. The development of autonomy will also depend on the relationship between parent and young person, and on the way change is negotiated in the family.

In terms of our understanding of this feature of family functioning, there have been some significant shifts over the past decades. In early writings about adolescent autonomy it was assumed that emotional disengagement from parents was a fundamental element of the move towards independence, and that unless separation and detachment occurred it was not possible to become a mature adult. This view was much influenced by psychoanalytic theory. More recently, however, empirical research has cast a different light on the matter. In the first place, from the 1960s onwards, investigators have been reporting more positive relationships between parents and teenagers than had been expected. Some of these studies are summarised in Coleman (2011).

One interesting approach to this topic is that represented by Smetana (2010), who developed what has come to be known as the social domain theory of parental authority. This theory states that parents and adolescents will hold different opinions as to who has the final say regarding different aspects of family life. For example, an adolescent might believe that she has the final say about which friends she chooses, or whether her bedroom remains tidy or not. However, she might agree that her parents should have a say when it comes to school work or decisions about career choices. Parents may take a different view, arguing that they should have a say about the state of the young person's bedroom, since it is their house. Other commentators have used this perspective to look at what are known as 'violations' of parental and teenage expectations. For example, if the parents believe they should have a say in the state of the young person's bedroom, they are violating her expectations of autonomy, leading inevitably to conflict.

These ideas can also be set in the context of broader notions of how parents and young people perceive this stage of development. Thus the adolescent may understand that with increasing age will come greater freedom and less parental direction. However, parents may take the view that it is precisely during adolescence that they need to exercise greater control, to protect teenagers from the risks and dangers in society. This debate is very current in today's social climate. The way these potential differences are resolved will be highly significant for the healthy or unhealthy functioning of the family.

Conflict and the Generation Gap

> If they [parents] say something like 'You can't do that', then I argue back and say 'Yes, I can'. And they'd say 'That's wrong'. And I'd be like 'It's right' and stuff like that. Arguing and arguing. I think that's just growing up. Quite a few people, I think, do that as well. (16-year-old girl)

Conflict and the generation gap has been the subject of more research than almost any other where parents and teenagers are concerned. What makes this of particular interest is that there appears to be a clear divergence here between the conclusions of researchers and the opinions of the general public. It is commonly believed by parents and other adults that the adolescent years bring with them conflict and disagreement in the home, as well as widely divergent views on topics such as sex, drugs and morality. Researchers, on the other hand, report that for the majority of parents and teenagers relationships are broadly positive, with little evidence of a generation gap in attitudes to careers, education, values and morality.

How can both these positions be valid? Or, to put it another way, if parents and young people are relatively close in their values and opinions, what is it that they disagree about? Disagreements occur in relation to subjects such as styles of dress, choice of music and TV programmes, the uses of phones and the Internet, and patterns of leisure activity. These choices are most likely to be influenced by friends and the immediate social environment, rather than to result from values absorbed from an early age from the wider family and the community. Studies such as those by Montemayor (1983) show that issues such as these have been the focus of family conflict for as long as the topic has been investigated, with time of coming home at night, choice of clothing and tidy bedrooms being some of the most common flashpoints. Findings also indicate that these issues are of international relevance, as shown in studies of teenagers in Hong Kong and China. The results of these studies demonstrate that exactly the same topics are relevant in these countries as in Europe and North America.

It is important to note that disagreements such as these can occur between parents and young people without relationships completely breaking down. Smetana (2010) argues that one reason for disagreements is that the generations define the problem differently. Thus, parents are more likely to believe that behaviour is a matter of convention: that is, the choice of clothing should be dictated by what would be expected by others, or by what is 'normal' in these circumstances. Young people, on the other hand, see matters like choice of clothes as a matter of personal freedom. If they can choose what they want with no reference to convention, that is a reflection of their autonomy and maturity.

Smetana and others believe that parents and teenagers are more likely to clash over the definition of an issue than over the specific details. In other words, it is more a matter of who has the authority than who is right. If young people and their parents define daily issues differently, it may be that the resolution of conflicts will prove difficult. It is at this point that communication between the generations becomes critical. In a number of studies it has been shown that the better the communication between parents and teenagers, the more likely it is that conflicts will be resolved. Thus we can conclude that there is little evidence to support a generation gap over the major issues relating to morality or fundamental beliefs. There is, however, clear support for the idea that during adolescence there will be a series of areas relating to personal choice where parents and young people will disagree. The degree of conflict in the family resulting from these disagreements will depend on a variety of factors, some of which are examined in more detail in the following sections.

Parenting Styles and Adolescent Development

One of the variables which has the greatest effect on the way parents and adolescents relate to each other is family environment. While there are many aspects of family environment which could be discussed here, one of the central topics is that of parenting styles. Stemming from early work by Diana Baumrind and Eleanor Maccoby, the notion of different parenting styles has become central to any concept of family environment. According to Maccoby and Martin (1983) four parenting styles can be distinguished. While these styles are relevant to all ages of children, they have a particular relevance to adolescence, as the following discussion makes clear.

There has been a wealth of research on parenting styles and, broadly speaking, the results are consistent. They show that, in almost all cases, children and young people brought up in families where parents use an authoritative parenting style do better on a range of outcome measures. These include having higher self-esteem, being

Parenting styles (Maccoby and Martin, 1983)

Authoritarian—parents place a high value on obedience and conformity:

- they are more likely to punish for misbehaviour and not to encourage autonomy

Authoritative—parents are warm but firm:

- they set standards and hold to boundaries
- they are more likely to give explanations and reason with the young person than be punitive

Indulgent/permissive—parents are benign, accepting and essentially passive:

- they are unlikely to set standards or have high expectations for their children
- they do not see punishment as important

Independent/neglectful—parents take little interest in their children's lives:

- they are likely to spend the minimum time on childcare activities

more advanced on such skills as perspective-taking, and having a greater likelihood of avoiding problem behaviours such as drug taking, early sexual activity, and antisocial behaviour (Lila *et al.*, 2006; Steinberg, 2008). Young people who are brought up by indulgent parents are often less mature, more irresponsible, and more likely to conform to peer group pressure. Those who grow up with neglectful parents are those most at risk, as might be expected. They are more likely to be impulsive and to get involved in high-risk behaviours.

> I have a friend whose mum is, like, really cool. Like she lets her smoke weed (cannabis) in the house, and she's really nice, and you can talk to her, but I wouldn't want her as a mum. Because it's all a bit random, like she's too much of a mate, and there's no security, rules and stuff. And I think my friend feels like that too sometimes. (15-year-old girl)

The finding that authoritative parenting leads to such positive outcomes has, not surprisingly, led many to question what it is about this style that makes such a difference. Steinberg (2008) has put forward the most convincing explanation of these results, and he makes a particular point of locating his views in the context of what we know of adolescent development. He notes that there are three key components of authoritative parenting. The first is warmth, which young people will find expressed in nurturance, support, and engagement with their lives. The second is structure, an especially important aspect of parenting teenagers. This means that young people have clear boundaries, an understanding of the rules, and an understanding of what is expected of them by their parents. Lastly, authoritative parents give autonomy support, in that they accept and encourage the young person's individuality, and their gradual moves towards taking greater control over their lives. All these components are critical in providing a family environment in which independence is facilitated while parents also set limits, provide acceptance and endorse achievement.

It may be thought that this description of parenting is too good to be true. Studies have shown that, while this may be the ideal, few parents manage to achieve this style of parenting all the time. Indeed, some studies have shown that parenting style may vary depending on the circumstances, and indeed on the behaviour, of the young person. It is all very well to imagine a benign style of parenting with a happy, responsive and well-balanced child or teenager. When faced with stress, tension and constant arguments even the most effective parents could be forgiven for slipping into an authoritarian or even an indifferent parenting mode. A further important element here is that of culture and ethnicity, and studies have shown that, as might be expected, there are important differences in parenting styles across cultures.

Culture and Ethnicity

Different cultures have different concepts of family life, and such variability is manifested in the parenting of adolescents just as much as in other areas of family functioning. Cross-cultural comparisons, however, are relatively few and far between and, as with most research endeavours, the largest body of evidence stems from the USA. In this section some of the best studies are reviewed to consider how culture and ethnicity affect the ways in which the parenting of teenagers occurs in different settings.

One topic that has received attention in the literature has to do with differences in time spent in the family environment, and variations in the emotional closeness of parents and adolescents in different cultures. Thus Cooper (1994) found greater expectations of family closeness in Chinese, Mexican and Vietnamese families in the USA than in White American families. In another study (Coleman, 2011) a comparison was drawn between the family relationships in a Scottish sample and those found in a small city in Argentina. In Argentina nearly 80 per cent of young people in the 15–16 year age range reported having meals with their parents, while only 35 per cent of the Scottish sample did so. A general picture emerges of warm and positive relationships with both parents in Argentina, similar to that found in studies of family life in countries such as Spain and Italy, where parents are close, and where young adults remain in the family home well into their twenties, or even into their thirties.

Japanese culture provides an important comparison, since, as a number of writers have pointed out, the role of the father differs significantly from that in the West. In Japan the mother is the central parental figure, with the father being 'absent' for most of the time. In addition, any open expression of discord in the family is discouraged, so that conflict is difficult to manage. Relatively little thought has yet been given to the ways in which Japanese cultural values impact on adolescent development. However, in a study by Gjerde and Shimizu (1995), the authors were able to show something of the complexity of family relationships. They examined parental agreement or disagreement regarding how the adolescent should be socialised, and linked this to mother–teenager cohesion and the adjustment of the young person. In brief, results showed that close relationships between teenager and mother (high cohesion) were adaptive so long as the parents were in agreement on matters connected with adolescent socialisation. When mother and father disagreed, however, mother–teenager cohesion was related to poor adjustment. As the authors note, these results illustrate the fact that the father's role is highly significant, even if he is away from home and participates relatively rarely in family life.

Because of the multi-ethnic nature of US society, there have been a range of studies on parenting practices. A major focus has been on the variation in parenting styles across ethnic groups. One key finding is that there is less evidence of authoritative parenting in African-American, Asian-American and Hispanic-American families than there is in White American families. This finding no doubt reflects differences in values and beliefs across different cultures. Nevertheless, young people in minority ethnic families whose parents use this style of parenting appear to benefit as much as those in European cultures.

Two further findings are of importance here. First, authoritarian parenting (where there is a greater emphasis on control and punishment) is more common in minority ethnic communities. Second, young people from white backgrounds are more adversely affected by authoritarian parenting than are minority ethnic young people. One possible explanation for this finding may be that higher levels of parental control are more appropriate to young people in communities where violence and risk are prevalent. On the other hand, it may be that these dimensions of parenting style have less meaning in non-European cultures.

Divorce and Changing Families

It was noted at the beginning of this chapter that the very notion of family has undergone substantial alteration in recent decades. In most commentary today writers distinguish between four family types—couple families, single-parent families, stepfamilies and blended families. While it was the case that for a long time research tended to focus on divorce as the topic for investigation, it is now recognised that there are many other factors to take into account. Indeed some single-parent families exist, not as a result of divorce, but as a result of parental choice. It is also recognised that the process of divorce, including the family circumstances both before and after divorce, may be more important as determinants of the child or young person's adjustment than the divorce itself.

Other factors too play their part, such as the role of the wider family, the impact of economic hardship which may occur as a result of relationship breakdown, and the differences between ethnic groups in their response to family change. Arguably one of the most significant shifts has been the emergence of parenting roles being carried out by non-biological partners, and the necessity to understand how these changes impact on family life. In past decades there was concern over the role of the non-resident father. Today, however, it is as much the place of step-parents, step-grandparents and even non-married partners that offer challenges both to biological parents and to children and young people.

A primary consideration in this context relates to a comparison of the advantages and disadvantages for adolescents growing up in intact married couple families and those growing up in other family types. Many governments struggle with the policy issues relating to divorce, and concern is expressed across the political spectrum over both the social and the economic costs of family breakdown. Much is made in cross-country comparisons and in political debate about the importance of marriage for children's wellbeing (Layard and Dunn, 2008). In Britain in 2009, 23 per cent of families with dependent children up to the age of 16 were headed by a lone parent (Coleman *et al.*, 2011). This has profound social implications, not all of which are necessarily apparent today. There are undoubtedly disadvantages for those living in reconstituted families, but these disadvantages are as much about economic hardship as they are about stress in relationships. The evidence is clear that parents who bring up children on their own are significantly more likely to be living in poverty, and this in turn has an impact on a wide variety of aspects of family life including housing, health, opportunities for further education and the transition to adulthood. (See Chs 4 and 16, this volume.)

In order to understand the impact of family change and reorganisation it is essential to recognise that events taking place before the breakdown, as well as what happens subsequently, play a larger role than the divorce itself. Reports indicate that a high level of family conflict prior to breakdown is a significant factor in determining the adjustment of young people post-divorce. Collishaw *et al.* (2004) also showed that chronic parental conflict was related to disorder among adolescents in subsequent years. Equally significant are the findings of Jenkins *et al.* (2005), who compared intact families and stepfamilies with children between the ages of 4 and 17. They showed that marital conflict which concerned children increased children's problem behaviour, but that the latter also predicted marital conflict, especially in stepfamilies. Thus problem behaviour has a two-way, or bi-directional effect. It is also important to add that siblings differed in their exposure to conflict, and thus the long-term impact is not the same for all children and young people. Variation in impact is greater in stepfamilies than it is in intact families.

Research also shows that what happens after family breakdown is closely related to young people's adjustment to divorce. The phrase 'caught in the middle' was first used in the 1980s in the USA. Following research carried out in California, writers identified the damaging effect on young people of continuing conflict between parents over contact and other arrangements. More recent research into family conflicts reflects the complexity of family relationships today. This research recognises that conflict can occur between different members of reconstituted families, including, for example, mother and former partner, mother and stepfather, and father and new partner.

> It's very stressful because I feel like piggy in the middle. It's like I'm having to be on one side and then on the other all the time, and it's quite upsetting because I … agree with my son, but on the other hand … obviously I agree with my husband too. It's so difficult, and I'm in the middle. (divorced mother, talking about her son and his stepfather)

Such complexity makes research extremely difficult, of course, but Dunn *et al.* (2005) were able to show that some types of conflict—that between mother and non-residential father, for example—were more likely to lead to poor adjustment than others. This research also led the authors to conclude that, as others have found, it was the young person's involvement in their parents' conflict that was significant rather than the frequency of such conflict. Dunn *et al.* (2005) make the point that where young people experience conflict in more than one family environment, for example at home and in a stepfamily, the impact is likely to be particularly detrimental in terms of mental health problems.

Looking at the other side of the coin, we can observe some evidence that parental divorce and family reorganisation can be a protective factor against further psychological harm. It may be that, following a change in family circumstances, young people no longer witness chronic conflict or even domestic violence. Another potentially positive experience is the opportunity to take on new roles within the family. For some young people, growing up in a single-parent family or in a reconstituted family may allow more rapid movement towards the assumption of maturity and adult roles. Adolescents may be given the chance to take on more responsibility and to play a greater role in the decision-making within the family in a way that is not possible when both parents are living together. In addition, the possibility for adolescents of making new relationships with different adults should not be ignored. As one parent finds a new partner this brings with it an opportunity for a young person to form a different relationship with someone who comes from outside the family. So much discussion and research focuses on the negative aspects of the introduction of a step-parent into a family, but there are undoubtedly many examples of positive and supportive relationships which can develop between young people and previously unknown adults.

One final protective factor has to do with the role of friends. In studies that look at the role of confidants in times of difficulty, the findings are clear. Friends play a key role, and for those who lose friends because of moving home or changing school things are more difficult than they are for those who remain in the same environment. Thus it can be concluded that it is not the family breakdown itself that is the damaging factor, but rather the circumstances that surround such an event. Serious conflict between parents both before and after separation is one of the key risk variables determining the outcome for young people, while being removed from violence or hatred between parents, and being able to keep the same group of friends, can help to mitigate some of the most damaging effects of family breakdown.

Parenting Teenagers: Implications for Policy and Practice

The topic of parenting teenagers has received greatly increased attention over the last decade or so. Books and journals dedicated to parenting have appeared in many countries, and there has been an upsurge in the number of parenting programmes available for parents of teenagers. In Britain much of this has been driven by the Government's concern over antisocial behaviour, and an associated attempt to provide greater support to parents whose sons and daughters might be getting into trouble. Quite apart from this, however, there has for a number of years been a growing focus on this topic, with researchers questioning how best to translate their findings into practical advice for parents (Kerr *et al.*, 2008; Roker and Coleman, 2007).

One important difference between parents of teenagers and parents of younger children relates to uncertainty about the parenting role. Parents of young children have relatively little difficulty in defining roles and responsibilities. Yet this is not the case with parents of adolescents, particularly in the context of changing families and the arrival of step-parents, non-residential parents, and other carers. This is connected in part with the changing nature of power and authority in the family. Today, parents of teenagers are not clear about what is expected of them in relation to monitoring and supervision, in setting boundaries and limits, regulating homework, managing the use of phones and the Internet, and so on. In addition there are issues such as confidentiality in relation to medical treatment, and the appropriate age for a young person to have sex. Many parents feel at a loss over such matters, a situation which leads to lowered self-confidence, heightened anxiety, and less effective parenting.

> It's frustrating, because you want to advise them [teenagers] but they don't really want to know, and I suppose it's that learning that in some ways they've got to just learn by their mistakes, but you don't really want them to make mistakes so you try to protect them from that but at the same time you've got to let them get on with it. (father of three teenagers)

In fact, there is much in the literature that can be used to guide and assist parents of teenagers. Questions relating to parenting style have already been mentioned, as has the management of conflict and disagreement. To take one example of a review of research findings, Kerr *et al.* (2008) highlight the importance of reciprocity in parent–adolescent relationships, arguing that for parents understanding the two-way nature of relationships offers a key to better parenting. They also identify three areas that need attention:

- the type of control used by parents
- the importance of involvement
- the provision of structure

So far as control is concerned, they draw a distinction between behavioural and psychological control, and go on to argue that both these types of control can be positive or negative depending on other factors. Control can be helpful if it aims to create rules that are perceived as reasonable and fair, and if it does not involve too much intrusion into the life of the adolescent. Control is also very much age-dependent, so that what might be appropriate for a 13-year-old will not be of any use for a 16-year-old. Parental involvement also has a part to play. This is a concept that refers to the extent that parents are interested in, knowledgeable about, and actively engaged in various elements of their teenagers' lives. The opposite side of the coin is over-involvement, or intrusiveness, which can be counter-productive and lead to tension between parent and young person.

The question of structure is an important one for any parent, and in Kerr *et al.* (2008) there is a helpful classification of six dimensions of structure that may underlie effective parenting for this age group.

Dimensions of structure that underlie effective parenting of adolescents

1. Clear and consistent communication of expectations.
2. Provision of opportunities to young people so they can meet or exceed expectations.
3. Predictability in parental behaviour.
4. Feedback of information to young people.
5. The provision of explanations and rationales for any rules or expectations.
6. Parental authority coupled with the taking of leadership roles in the home.

It is these ideas that underpin many of the parenting programmes that have been developed over the last decade or so. Roker and Coleman (2007) provide a useful review of some of the most widely used programmes. Significant dimensions to bear in mind are such things as the length of the programme, whether it is a general parenting programme or designed for problematic behaviour, whether it has been properly evaluated for outcomes, and whether there is an adequate training programme for practitioners to use before offering it to parents. While there was considerable support for making these programmes widely available in the UK during the period of office of the last Labour government (1997–2010), funding for such initiatives has now become much more scarce. However, much has been learnt over the recent past about the challenges and difficulties of running parenting programmes for parents of teenagers and, hopefully, the learning will not be lost in the coming years.

References

Arnett, G. (2004) *Emerging Adulthood: The winding road from the late teens to the twenties* (Oxford: Oxford University Press).

Coleman, J. (2011) *The Nature of Adolescence* (London: Routledge), 4th edn.

Coleman, J., Brooks, F. and Treadgold, P. (2011) *Key Data on Adolescence: 8th edition* (Association for Young People's Health). http://www.youngpeopleshealth.org.uk. [Accessed 12.9.2011.]

Collishaw, S., Maughan, B., Goodman, R. and Pickles, A. (2004) Time trends in adolescent mental health, *Journal of Child Psychology and Psychiatry*, 45: 1350–1362.

Cooper, C. (1994) Cultural perspectives on continuity and change in adolescent relationships, in R. Montemayor, G. Adams and T. Gullotta (eds), *Personal Relationships During Adolescence* (New York: Sage).

Dunn, J., O'Connor, T. and Cheng, H. (2005) Children's responses to conflict between their different parents, *Journal of Clinical Child and Adolescent Psychology*, 34: 223–234.

Gjerde, P. and Shimizu, H. (1995) Family relationships and adolescent development in Japan, *Journal of Research on Adolescence*, 218–228.

Jenkins, J., Simpson, A. *et al.* (2005) Mutual influence of marital conflict and children's behaviour problems: shared and non-shared family risks, *Child Development*, 76: 24–39.

Kerr, M., Stattin, H. and Engels, R. (2008) *What Can Parents Do? New insights into the role of parents in adolescent problem behaviour* (Chichester: Wiley).

Layard, R. and Dunn, J. (2008) *A Good Childhood* (Harmondsworth: Penguin).

Lila, M., van Aken, M., Musitu, G. and Buelga, S. (2006) Families and adolescents, in S. Jackson and L. Goossens (eds), *Handbook of Adolescent Development* (Hove: Psychology Press).

Maccoby, E. and Martin, J. (1983) Socialisation in the context of the family: parent–child interaction, in E. Hetherington (ed.), *Handbook of Child Psychology* (New York: Wiley).

Montemayor, R. (1983) Parents and adolescents in conflict, *Journal of Early Adolescence*, 3: 83–103.

Mulder, C. (2009) Leaving the parental home in young adulthood, in A. Furlong (ed.), *Handbook of Youth and Young Adulthood* (London: Routledge).

Nuffield Foundation (2009) *Time Trends in Parenting and Outcomes for Young People* (London: Nuffield Foundation).

Roker, D. and Coleman, J. (2007) *Working with Parents of Young People: Research, policy and practice* (London: Jessica Kingsley).

Smetana, J. (2010) *Adolescents, Families and Social Development* (Oxford: Wiley-Blackwell).

Steinberg, L. (2008) *Adolescence* (New York: McGraw Hill), 8th edn.

15

Working Families
Who Cares?

Simon B. Burnett, Jonathan Swan
and Cary Cooper

Introduction

For both men and women 'having it all' can be a tough balancing act. The way that many mothers and fathers manage the demands of work and home is phenomenally impressive. (Clegg, 2009, p. 12)

Prosperous as they are, the very acme of an adaptable, mutually supportive couple, both husband and wife often fear they are on the edge of losing control over their lives. This fear is built into their work histories. (Sennett, 1998, p. 19)

This chapter discusses the effects of combining work and domestic commitments in contemporary two-parent families in Britain, contributing to a politically and culturally relevant body of research and policy. It is fully acknowledged that there are other worthy familial demographics deserving of study, including those explored in Smart and Neale's publications on parenting, divorce and work (1999), and in research on the effects of single parenthood and employment (Joshi *et al.*, 1999). However, the focus here is upon parents in relationships attempting to facilitate a joint, functional work–family balance. This is for two reasons. First, it is in response to the current British Coalition Government's rhetoric about couples staying together and the proposed tax incentive for them to do so. Secondly, it stems from a desire to assess the impacts that combining employment and family in modern life yields upon working families.

The chapter begins by contextualising the extant pressures of long-hours work cultures and 'presenteeism' presently borne upon British workers in the capitalist

Contemporary Issues in Family Studies: Global Perspectives on Partnerships, Parenting and Support in a Changing World, First Edition. Edited by Angela Abela and Janet Walker.
© 2014 John Wiley & Sons, Ltd. Published 2014 by John Wiley & Sons, Ltd.

economy, as compared to pre-industrial modes of social organisation. It then discusses the history, nature and utilisation of flexible working practices, currently heralded as a measure by which to enable those who are employed to be dedicated both to their jobs and their families, thereby benefiting organisations and society at large. This leads to a discussion of the extant political and organisational efforts to understand and facilitate employees' familial needs. Finally, the chapter examines how the work and domestic care duties necessary to maintaining modern (flexible) families are typically allocated or shared in both dual- and sole-earner families. This ultimately enables us to make a logically reasoned and well-evidenced judgement about the underlying question: who cares about modern working families?

Tomorrow's World

> Do we really believe that a long hours culture, in a society where most families are working families, and the competitive pressures of the modern workplace are penal, is healthier for the family, the individual or the company? (Cooper, 2009, p. 13)

For nearly forty years, the British Broadcasting Corporation (BBC) broadcast the television programme *Tomorrow's World* (1965–2004), which regularly espoused a near future that would be disencumbered and emancipated from the mundanities of domestic and professional labour. Its catalogue of predictions included, quite accurately, mobile telephones, the Channel Tunnel and 'robot television cameras' (CCTV); and, with slightly less exactness, the ensuing ubiquity of floating bikes, paper pants and robotic housemaids (Jones, 2009). A highly popular programme, it 'captured all the promise of the future', prophesying for British employees and families fewer hours spent at work and a greater ability to be engaged in leisure owing to technological advancements.

However, a critical mass of analyses of contemporary working patterns eschews the idea of this underlying temper of modern life having become increasingly and axiomatically freer from work. Since the 1960s, congruous with the inception of the BBC's divining flagship, there has been a strong consensus among the disciplines of sociology, history and anthropology that exponential leaps in technological, industrial and political innovation have, counter-intuitively, increased the average number of hours spent performing requisite labour (Farb, 1968).

Medieval Labour

In accordance with the underlying narrative of *Tomorrow's World*, there is a general, prevailing belief that the widely available technology of the modern age has resulted in a reduction in the number of hours worked, especially when our age is compared with previous historical epochs. In 1971, *Time* magazine declared that 'it has seemed almost heretical to consider that both output and leisure could be increased together … that is the promise of [current] trend[s]' (*Time*, 1971). However, despite such common assumptions and expectations, working hours can be shown to have increased. By way of reference, in pre-industrial European societies of the Middle Ages, workers actually toiled for far fewer hours and enjoyed significantly more leisure time than their modern counterparts, with the equivalent average working day requiring less than five hours to secure the resources necessary to survive (Voth, 2000). The life of the servile labourer was not then, as popularly deemed, an exclusively drudging struggle under feudal bondage, consuming every waking hour. Rather, serfs' working hours typically lasted half of the day, and 'if they worked an entire day, this was counted as two "days-works"' (Bennett, 1960, pp. 104–106).

Comparing the holiday allowances of modern and pre-industrial societies only acts to affirm such contentions. In medieval England, the calendar was suffused with officially sanctioned recesses, including those for pious churchgoing but also for much merrymaking and resting:

> In addition to official celebrations, there were often weeks' worth of ales—to mark important life events (bride ales or wake ales) as well as less momentous occasions (scot ale, lamb ale, and hock ale). (Rodgers, 1940, p. 11)

Altogether, the time able to be spent in the pursuit of leisure equated to approximately one-third of each year. Farb (1968) thus suggests:

> Most people assume that the members of [democratically and technologically inferior societies] worked ceaselessly in an unremitting search for sustenance ... [but] a high culture emerges only when the people have the leisure to build pyramids or to create art. (p. 28)

A curious quirk of subsequent modes of modern industrial capitalism, then, is that they have greatly increased human toil, in terms of hours spent at least, while spreading the myth that they have engineered its reduction (Schor, 1993). Yet, as demonstrated above, the majority of people in medieval, pre-industrially orchestrated societies worked a far smaller proportion of each day across the year. Comparable reports indicate that an average fourteenth-century casual labourer (in what is now modern Britain) would work approximately 1440 hours per annum (Ritchie, 1962), whereas an average worker in the USA at the end of the 1980s worked 1949 hours each year (Schor, 1993). While contemporary society certainly tends to offer innumerable comparative benefits—increased accountability and enfranchisement, higher incomes, life expectancy and social mobility, and more widespread access to modern luxuries—it has also, necessarily, made the vast majority of its workers *cash-rich, time-poor* in exchange.

Modern Serfdom

Since the early 1980s, a number of advanced economies, such as Britain and the USA, have undergone pronounced transformative political, organisational and personal change, engineering 'managerialist' (Furusten, 1999, p. 1; Parker, 2002) approaches to political economy. The two contemporaneous premiers, Margaret Thatcher and Ronald Reagan, 'aggressively rejected the previously dominant hegemony of interventionist Keynesian economic theory and the notion of the welfare state' (Burnett *et al.*, 2010b, p. 538), alternatively favouring globalisation, deregulation and privatisation. In response, many employers have drastically altered their work patterns, implementing project work, teams, flattened hierarchies and knowledge workers (Burnett, 2012), with the capacity to 'change' and to demonstrate 'hair trigger responsiveness' becoming increasingly synonymous with corporate survival (Thrift, 2005, p. 130).

While this new business ecology appears fine on the surface, there are certain pressures levied upon individuals as a consequence. Consonant with what has been argued above, academic research and news reports regularly announce, for example, that British employees in particular frequently work more hours, with shorter lunch breaks and holidays, than employees in other European countries do (International Labour Organisation, 2007; Trade Union Congress, 2007). As testimony to this, a quarter of the UK's workforce regularly exceeds the Working Time Regulation limit of 48 hours per week, with 9 per cent working over 60 hours each week (Giga *et al.*, 2008). Furthermore, two-thirds of those who breached the 48-hour threshold had 'deliberately "opted out" of the directive's protection', and, 'more ominously, one in four indicated they had been given little to no choice to do so' (Burnett *et al.*, 2010a, p. 165).

The modern capitalist age is thus arguably suffused with long-hours work cultures and the demands of high 'presenteeism', even when compared to the now archaic system of medieval serfdom. Looking across the entire spectrum of employment in Britain, we see that it is professional fathers in relationships with infant children that work the longest hours of all (Burnett *et al.*, 2010a,b; Gatrell and Cooper, 2008). Such conditions have understandably led to negative repercussions being borne upon the social fabric of families (Burnett *et al.*, 2010b; Davidson and Cooper, 1992; Fielden and Cooper, 2002). Since the 1990s, research on health and employment has demonstrated clear causal links between such poor work–life balance and stress (Cartwright and Cooper, 1997), stress-related illness and stress-induced behaviours (Worrall and Cooper, 1999); and work intensification for working parents has been shown to have a negative causal impact upon relationships with partners and children (Burnett *et al.*, 2010a). Likewise, the Confederation of British Industry estimates that 'stress from work' costs employers £3.7 billion and 13 million lost work days every year (Dewe and Kompier, 2008). As Burnett *et al.* (2010b, p. 539) report, such findings led the Equal Opportunities Commission in 2007 to declare:

> The way we work no longer fits the changing world we live in. As we look to the future it looks increasingly unsustainable.

The Winds of Change

In response to these seemingly ever-heightening demands of work upon employees' time, and the associated impacts upon their health and family lives, modern British governments, trade unions and organisations have recently come to understand the wellbeing of employees as being significantly 'influenced by the landscape of work' (Haworth and Roberts, 2008, p. 2). There have hence been marked efforts to repair the 'equity between individuals' work and non-work lives', in both organisational and political policy (Burnett *et al.*, 2010b, p. 539). In order to reduce the causes and impacts of work-induced stress, evidently so harmful to individuals, and to find better ways to combine work and family life, a number of deliberately flexible initiatives have been implemented. These have grown in popularity, reportedly being desired by up to half of the British workforce (Dewe and Kompier, 2008). Their purpose is to allow employees to remain fully functional at work whilst avoiding deleteriously long hours, and thereby able to participate more fully in family affairs. The key effect of flexible working practices is to 'reconfigure temporal and spatial arrangements' of work organisation (Burnett *et al.*, 2010b, p. 539). As a consequence, their uptake has increased dramatically since the early 1990s, with part-time work, flexible hours, job sharing and working from home being the most popular options across the British workforce.

This move towards flexible working has occurred in conjunction with shifting social attitudes. Among dual-earner couples, fathers are increasingly less likely to expect their partners to mediate the child–parent relationship on their behalf, actively taking larger and more engaged roles (Gatrell, 2005, 2007). This is significant, and necessary, as in the current economic climate of recession and austerity more women than ever before with preschool-age children are remaining in the workforce (Burnett *et al.*, 2010b; Cabrera *et al.*, 2000). There is a potent need to address in detail how the British Government and organisations are presently catering for families, and how they are able to combine their work and domestic needs. For, as the current Deputy Prime Minister Nick Clegg has declared, 'having it all' is a tough balancing act for contemporary families (2009, p. 12). Many feel as though they are on the 'edge of losing control' (Sennett, 1998, p. 19). Nicola Brewer has commented:

> The truth is that the economic situation makes these issues all the more pressing. In order to recover from recession and position ourselves for the recovery we need to find a way of encouraging new people into the workforce and make better use of the skills that are available. (Equality and Human Rights Commission, 2009)

Who Cares About Working Families?

Both the British Government and employers have approached the facilitation of work and family life integration from separate and overlapping rationales for intervention and policy development. The changing nature of work and work-intensification, driven by a number of factors including, but not limited to, globalisation, the advances of technology (particularly communications technology) and job insecurity, has, in a globalised business context, meant that workers have found that work has 'crept' into areas of their lives that previously were untouched. Concurrently, the increasing participation of women in the labour market, facilitated to some extent by legislative development, has meant that traditional family arrangements typified by a working father and a mother who stays at home to provide childcare are becoming less common (ONS, 2008). Thus, organisations have found themselves having to offer and adapt (cautiously fostered by governmental support) employment policies to satisfy the needs of employees who wish to combine employment with childcare responsibilities.

Since the 1970s and the introduction in the UK of paid maternity leave, incremental increases have taken place in legislative provision which have allowed women to combine paid employment and childcare. These rights have accrued partly in connection with gender equality issues. This has been accompanied, however, by a persistent pay and job-position gap, whereby women who have sought to combine work and family care receive significantly reduced remuneration and often have to take a lower-level position than their experience or qualifications might enable them to command if they were able to work full-time (EOC, 2005). In addition, the increase in rights to work–life balance available to women via maternity pay and leave policies, and the legislation supporting these rights (in particular that relating to indirect sex discrimination), have not been matched by a corresponding accumulation of rights for fathers. The pattern of (predominantly female) reduced-hours working has become an accepted paradigm, based upon traditionally gendered roles of caring adapted to accommodate the financial needs and career aspirations of couples. As a result, many women have had to take on lower-level work roles than those which their skills and experience warrant in order to achieve the flexibility they require. This clustering of part-time, lower-level work has had the effect of reinforcing gender roles within organisations. Such organisational culture can also act as a deterrent to fathers, who in working more flexibly would contravene the often idealised always-available full-time employee model many organisations understand. Those diverging from this model may be seen as having reduced commitment to and engagement with the organisation.

Lewis and Rapoport (2009) have observed:

> Most workplaces are still structured around a cultural picture of the ideal worker who has no family or personal obligations beyond work. Hence unrealistic expectations about how people can work go unchallenged. This can lead to overvaluing and rewarding inefficient and time wasting ways of working and obscures the effectiveness of alternative working practices. It undermines not only gender equity but also workplace effectiveness. (p. 25)

Some elements of British organisations and government, however, have fully embraced the challenge of remodelling the organisation of work, and of developing policy responses to satisfy the desires of their employees to integrate work and family life more effectively. Others have not, preferring instead to adhere to atavistic workplace arrangements and making only those concessions to work–life balance that are demanded by statutory regulation (Working Families, 2011). Indeed, this latter group of employers has recently been seen to be actively pushing back against work–life balance measures, vociferously objecting to what it characterises as government-imposed 'red tape' which stifles business growth. For these employers, flexible working, if it is to be palatable at all, should operate in terms of a flexible labour force with businesses able to 'hire and fire' free from the perceived encumbrances of employment protection legislation.

Current political developments at a European level have seen the British Government being called upon to withdraw from some of the employment protection legislation provisions by business lobbies who claim that a robust economy cannot afford to have a labour force which they perceive to be 'over-protected'. Examples include the call for abolition, or suspension, of maternity leave and pay (*Financial Times*, 27 July 2011). Employed parents, and those with other caring responsibilities, thus find themselves in a British labour market where access to flexible working is variable from employer to employer, and from sector to sector.

This difference between employer practice and attitude is not just a question of some employees being concerned with improving the working arrangements of their employees and others not. Social policy, gender equality, economic participation, changing social norms, legislative pressures (such as EU regulations and directives) and the general trend of a mature capitalist economy towards enhanced working conditions are all important elements. Above all, the business case, sometimes coupled with a desire to promote gender equality, is of key importance. Employers will not enact work–life balance measures which benefit employees purely for altruistic reasons; they require a bottom-line benefit. Public-sector adoption of work–life balance measures reflects a more socially oriented approach (particularly in the context of female employment) than in the private sector, where in terms of the development of work–life policies and practices the 'business' case has always been paramount.

Work–life policy and practice—the business case

The successive incarnations of the business case:

1. Mother-supportive—mothers returning to work after pregnancy.
2. Family-friendly practices—allowing working parents (primarily women) to remain in work while raising children.
3. Flexibility—widening definition of flexible worker to include more groups of employees with caring responsibilities.
4. Wellbeing—employers recognising that work–life balance measures facilitate healthier employees (in terms of reduced stress) and better performance.

As the rationale for and framework of work–life integration policies have changed within organisations, this has influenced to some degree the way in which couples arrange work and care within their own households. However, domestic changes have not moved as far as organisational policies have, a phenomenon that can be attributed to the gap between organisational policy and practice as modified by organisational culture.

Who Cares in Working Families?

Caring patterns in families have changed considerably:

> With the growth of the industrial market economy during the past 300 years, a trend began which segmented activities associated with generating income and caring for family members. (Campbell-Clark, 2000, p. 748)

Today, the most common working pattern for couples in the UK with children is that of the father working full-time and the mother working part-time. The next most popular is the father working full-time and the mother not being in paid employment, followed by both the father and the mother working full-time. How this influences the division of caring responsibilities for children, and other responsibilities, is complex and, despite the trend towards increasing fathers' participation in childcare, the division of labour is not equal (O'Brien, 2004).

Working mothers in heterosexual couples, whether employed part- or full-time, still undertake on average substantially more domestic chores than their partners (Delphy and Leonard, 1992; Dryden, 1999; Gatrell, 2005). Men often prefer to focus on issues that involve direct contact with children, such as teaching, disciplining and rewarding, rather than on what Burnett *et al.* term 'ancillary' tasks, which are still vital but rather more indirect, such as cooking, ironing and cleaning (2010b, p. 536).

This arrangement of caring time has many shaping factors, of which workplace policy arrangements are only one. Childcare is often still perceived by couples as being primarily the woman's role (Gatrell, 2007) despite the previously noted increase in fathers' participation. Gender roles and social attitudes are entrenched by a social dialogue and stereotyped role modelling which emphasises the woman's role as the primary carer. Economic factors also prevail in households where decisions about caring are made. The persistent pay gap in the UK (Women and Work Commission, 2007) means that it is often economically imperative that the larger (male) wage is preserved when new children come in the family. If the woman subsequently reduces her working hours to fulfil domestic caring responsibilities, the pay gap is likely to increase further (EHRC, 2010), effectively trapping each partner within their role. Furthermore, housing costs in the UK have meant that, in many families, both parents need to earn an income in order to meet these costs; in real terms a sole income is no longer sufficient to support a traditional domestic arrangement. It is worth noting that reforms to the British system of state benefits for working families expected to be implemented in 2013 suggest that it may be uneconomic for women to maintain paid employment if they have an employed partner, with a possible consequence of an increase in the number of women forced to withdraw from the labour market to care for their children full-time (Working Families, 2011).

The increasing willingness of men to move away from traditional gender roles and take on more of a caring role is well-documented (Blades and Fondas, 2010). However, this is not necessarily met by an equal appetite on the part of women to relinquish caring responsibilities and increase the time they spend in paid work. Where fathers are able to rearrange their work to allow a division of caring within the household, the level to which they can realise their aspirations therefore depends upon a complex blend of the opportunities which are permitted by their employer, the framework of legislation governing flexible working, and the attitudes held within the family home.

Concluding Comments

The question of who cares *about* working families, and who cares *in* them, is, in Britain, a complex one, further complicated by the ongoing economic turmoil which is adapting the working patterns of employees at a rapid rate as employers seek to be agile in their response to fluctuating demand and an uncertain future. While there have been a number of initiatives to embrace flexible working by organisations which have deployed it as a tool to help navigate the uncertain waters of the economic recession, such as the adoption of wide-scale reduced-hours working, we have also seen counter-movements whereby working from home has stalled as employees try to display their value and commitment by working within sight of colleagues and managers at the workplace (ONS, 2011). In addition, proposed changes to the UK social support system of benefits and tax credits mean that, in dual-earner households, it may no longer be economic for the second earner in some families to continue in employment, which in turn will change how these families are able to divide and share caring responsibilities. Although social and demographic pressures in the UK may press towards a more equal sharing of the 'tough balancing act' between mothers and fathers, it is by no means certain that further progress will be made while the prevailing political and economic winds are against it.

Implications for Policy and Practice

Differing economies and employment markets across the globe make it difficult to identify a universally applicable set of implications. When different social attitudes are also factored in, the picture becomes even more complex. However, broad predictions might be made if similar (although not identical) regions are considered together. Further granularity and country-specific implications may be discussed only with a detailed understanding of a particular country's legislative framework, workforce demographics and social attitudes.

If Europe and North America are considered *en bloc*, it is possible to ascertain some mutual policy and practice implications. Among these countries the disruptive effect of the economic downturn should not be underestimated; employment has become less secure and employee behaviour has changed in so far as work–life balance policies, which allowed time for the integration of work and family life, have been subordinated to business need. Employees who feel that working flexibly for family reasons makes them more vulnerable than other non-flexible colleagues have come to adopt a defensive position of 'work comes first' at the expense of non-work life. In economies where long-hours cultures prevail, these effects are most visible. It will take some years for the disruption of the economic downturn to subside, and until this happens it is probable that quality-of-life issues will come second to business stability and growth. Whether this has the effect of re-entrenching traditional gender roles in relation to work and caring remains to be seen, but it is a very real risk.

Broadly considering the trends towards greater female participation in work, men's increasing interest in caring for their offspring, and the recent phenomenon, in heterosexual couple relationships, of females earning more than males, alongside employer interest in wellbeing and performance at work, we see that it is likely that slow systemic change will take place which allows more equitable sharing of work and caring between parents. This may be supported by legislative change, and it is here that a difference between European countries (both EU and non-EU) will occur, depending on governmental enthusiasm for enacting new laws and rights. It is difficult to foresee the UK adopting the same approach to state-subsidised childcare as Sweden, for example, and subsequently experiencing the attendant caring arrangements that families are able to make. The difference between the UK and the USA is more profound: although European and North American social structures and economies could be said to be broadly similar, the USA has scant legislation around maternity, paternity and childcare.

An interesting policy development, which illuminates the challenges to and responses of policymakers, is one that has taken place in Australia, which in 2009 announced its intention to provide paid parental leave to 'provide greater financial support to families, increase workforce participation and promote early childhood development' (Australian Government, 2009). This policy aims to prioritise the needs of children whilst at the same time improving opportunities for caring through work–life balance measures without imposing a heavy fiscal or administrative burden on employers. Additionally, initiatives like *Dad and Partner Pay* will create a dedicated payment for fathers and other partners under the Australian Government's national Paid Parental Leave scheme. Subject to the passage of legislation, the payment will be available to eligible fathers and other partners sharing the care of a child born to them or adopted, beginning on 1 January 2013. Taken as a whole, these policy frameworks seek to recognise that the parental care of children is a high priority for working families, and that providing this care is not the preserve of either sex.

A number of policy recommendations flow from the discussion in this chapter, all of which require action to promote a balance between work and caring responsibilities. These are shown in the box below.

Policy recommendations

- Increase paternal rights to time off work for caring, including childcare and eldercare, to 'level up' the gap between paternal and maternal rights that currently exists.
- Encourage, through taxation mechanisms and subsidy, the provision of good-quality, affordable childcare.
- Work with organisations to ensure that conscious and unconscious barriers to women's progression in the labour market are removed, to allow women to work to their full potential.
- Employ active measures (such as pay audits) to eliminate the gender pay gap where it exists.
- Encourage organisations to look increasingly to agile and flexible ways of working so as to remain employers of choice, and provide realistic opportunities for their employees to balance work and caring responsibilities.
- Take into account demographic and new social and economic realities. For example, in the UK retirement ages are being pushed back, eating into the availability of grandparents to take on some of the childcaring role, raising the question of how this 'care gap' will be filled and by whom.

References

Australian Government (2009) Australia's Paid Parental Leave Scheme, Commonwealth copyright (Canberra: Commonwealth of Australia, Attorney General's Department).

Bennett, H. S. (1960) *Life on the English Manor* (Cambridge: Cambridge University Press).

Blades, J. and Fondas, N. (2010) *The Custom-fit Workplace: Choose when, where, and how to work and*

boost your bottom line (San Francisco, CA: Jossey-Bass).

Burnett, S. B. (2012) *The Happiness Agenda: A modern obsession* (London: Palgrave Macmillan).

Burnett, S. B., Gatrell, C. J., Cooper, C. L. and Sparrow, P. R. (2010a) Fatherhood and flexible working: a contradiction in terms?, in S. Kaiser, M. J. Ringlstetter, M. Pina e Cunha and D. R. Eikhof (eds), *Creating*

Balance?: International perspectives on the work–life integration of professionals (Berlin/Heidelberg: Springer), 157–171.

Burnett, S. B., Gatrell, C. J., Cooper, C. L. and Sparrow, P. R. (2010b) Well balanced families? A gendered analysis of work–life balance policies and work family practices, *International Journal of Gender in Management*, 25(7) (25th anniversary edn): 534–549.

Cabrera, N. J., Tamis-LeMonda, C. S., Bradley, R. H., Hofferth, S. and Lamb, M. E. (2000) Fatherhood in the twenty-first century, *Child Development*, 71(1): 127–136.

Campbell Clark, S. (2000) Work/family border theory: a new theory of work/family balance, *Human Relations*, 53(6): 747–770.

Cartwright, S. and Cooper, C. (1997) *Managing Workplace Stress* (Thousand Oaks, CA: Sage).

Clegg, N. (2009) Modern times, flexible families, in J. Swan (ed.), *Tomorrow's World: Perspectives on work and family in the future* (London: Working Families), 12–13.

Cooper, C. (2009) Work–life balance: today's dilemma, in *Tomorrow's World: Perspectives on work and family in the future* (London: Working Families), 13–14.

Davidson, M. J. and Cooper, C. L. (1992) *Shattering the Glass Ceiling: The woman manager* (London: Chapman).

Delphy, C. and Leonard, D. (1992) *Familiar Exploitation: A new analysis of marriage in contemporary Western societies* (Oxford: Polity Press).

Dewe, P. and Kompier, M. (2008) Foresight Mental Capital and Wellbeing Project, *Wellbeing at Work: Future challenges* (London: Government Office for Science).

Dryden, C. (1999) *Being Married, Doing Gender: A critical analysis of gender relationships in marriage* (London: Routledge).

Equal Opportunities Commission [EOC] (2005) *Part-time Is No Crime* (Manchester: EOC).

Equality and Human Rights Commission [EHRC] (2009) *Working Better: Meeting the changing needs of families, workers and employers in the 21st century* (London: EHRC).

Equality and Human Rights Commission [EHRC] (2010) *How Fair Is Britain?* (London: EHRC).

Farb, P. (1968) *Man's Rise to Civilization As Shown by the Indians of North America from Primeval Times to the Coming of the Industrial State* (New York: Dutton).

Fielden, S. and Cooper, C. L. (2002) Managerial stress: are women more at risk?, in D. L. Nelson and R. J. Burke (eds), *Gender, Work Stress and Health* (Washington DC: American Psychological Association), 19–34.

Financial Times (2011) Hilton wants to abolish maternity leave, 27 July.

Furusten, S. (1999) *Popular Management Books: How they are made and what they mean for organizations* (London and New York: Routledge).

Gatrell, C. (2005) *Hard Labour: The sociology of parenthood* (Maidenhead: Open University Press).

Gatrell, C. (2007) Whose child is it anyway? The negotiation of paternal entitlements within marriage, *The Sociological Review*, 55(2): 353–373.

Gatrell, C. and Cooper, C. L. (2008) Work–life balance: working for whom?, *European Journal of International Management*, 2(1): 71–86.

Giga, S. I., Jain, A. K. and Cooper, C. L. (2008) *State-of-science Review: SR-C7—working longer: hours of work and health* (London: Government Office for Science). http://www.foresight.gov.uk/Mental%20Capital/SR-C7_MCW.pdf. [Accessed 27.3.2012.]

Haworth, J. and Roberts, K. (2008) Leisure: the next 25 years—summary, *Mental Capital and Wellbeing: Making the most of ourselves in the 21st century*, The Foresight Mental Capital and Wellbeing Project (London: Government Office for Science). www.foresight.gov.uk/Mental%20Capital/SR-C8_MCW_v2.pdf. [Accessed 27.3.2012.]

International Labour Organization (2007) *Press Release: Working time around the world*, 7 June. http://www.ilo.org/global/About_the_ILO/Media_and_publicinformation/Press_releases/lang–en/WCMS_082827. [Accessed 27.3.2012.]

Jones, B. (2009) Floating bikes, paper pants … Why *Tomorrow's World* was way ahead of its time, *Daily Mail* online, 1 Aug. http://www.dailymail.co.uk/debate/article-1202612/Floating-bikes-paper-pants-Tomorrows-World-way-ahead-time.html. [Accessed 28.3.2012.]

Joshi, H., Paci, P. and Waldfogel, J. (1999) The wages of motherhood: better or worse?, *Cambridge Journal of Economics*, 23(5): 534–564.

Lewis, S. and Rapoport, R. (2009) Modern times, flexible families, in *Tomorrow's World: Perspectives on work and family in the future* (London: Working Families), 24–26.

O'Brien, M. (2004) *Shared Caring: Bringing fathers into the frame*. Working Paper Series No. 18 (London: Equal Opportunities Commission).

Office for National Statistics (2008) *Labour Force Survey, Q2* (London: ONS).

Office for National Statistics (2011) *Labour Force Survey (Autumn quarters—all in employment)* (London: ONS).

Parker, M. (2002) *Against Management: Organization in the age of managerialism* (Cambridge: Polity Press).

Ritchie, N. (1962) Labour conditions in Essex in the reign of Richard II, in E. M. Carus-Wilson (ed.), *Essays in Economic History, Vol. II* (London: Edward Arnold), 91–107.

Rodgers, E. (1940) *Discussion of Holidays in the Later Middle Ages* (New York: Columbia University Press).

Schor, J. B. (1993) *The Overworked American: The unexpected decline of leisure* (New York: Basic Books).

Sennett, R. (1998) *The Corrosion of Character: The personal consequences of work in the new capitalism* (New York: Norton).

Smart, C. and Neale, B. (1999) *Family Fragments?* (Cambridge: Polity Press).

Thrift, N. (2005) Performing cultures in the new economy, in M. Featherstone (ed.), *Knowing Capitalism* (London: Sage), 130–152.

Time (1971) On the way to a four-day week, 1 March. http://www.time.com/time/magazine/article/0,9171,878936-1,00.html. [Accessed 27.3.2012.]

Trade Union Congress (2007) *Press Release: Real, but oh so slow, progress on long hours in London*, 20 Feb. http://www.tuc.org.uk/work_life/tuc-12966-f0.cfm. [Accessed 27.3.2012.]

Voth, H-J. (2000) *Time and Work in England 1750–1830* (Oxford: Oxford University Press).

Women and Work Commission (2007) *Towards a Fairer Future: Implementing the Women and Work Commission* (London: Department of Communities and Local Government).

Working Families (2011) *Top Employers for Working Families Benchmark* (London: Working Families).

Worrall, L. and Cooper, C. L. (1999) Working patterns and working hours: their impact on UK managers, *Leadership & Organization Development Journal*, 20(1): 6–10.

16
Children and Divorce in World Perspective

PAUL R. AMATO AND LISA M. BOYD

Introduction

During the last few decades, divorce rates have increased in many parts of the world. The rise in divorce has created concerns among researchers, policymakers and members of the public about the consequences of changes in family structure for children's wellbeing. In this chapter, we review studies of parental divorce and child wellbeing. Previous reviews of this literature have described research conducted in predominantly English-speaking countries. In contrast, we extend the discussion by using meta-analytic methods to summarise studies conducted in countries in which English is not the dominant language.

The Worldwide Increase in Divorce

Divorce rates

The crude divorce rate (CDR) is a commonly used method of understanding changes in marital instability over time. This rate is calculated by dividing the number of divorces in a given year by the total population and multiplying by 1000. Consequently, the CDR can be interpreted as the number of divorces per 1000 people in the population. The refined divorce rate (RDR), which is the number of divorces per 1000 married couples, is a more sensitive measure of divorce trends. This statistic is preferable because the denominator includes only those individuals (married partners) at risk of divorce. The CDR, in contrast, is affected not only by changes in the frequency of divorce, but

Contemporary Issues in Family Studies: Global Perspectives on Partnerships, Parenting and Support in a Changing World, First Edition. Edited by Angela Abela and Janet Walker.
© 2014 John Wiley & Sons, Ltd. Published 2014 by John Wiley & Sons, Ltd.

also by changes in the age structure of the population. Nevertheless, the CDR and the RDR are highly correlated. In the USA, for example, the correlation between the CDR and the RDR between 1960 and 2005 is 0.96 (authors' calculations). Moreover, refined divorce rates are not available for many countries. For this reason we rely on the CDR to make comparisons within and across countries over time.

Figure 16.1 displays the CDR at five-year intervals for five predominantly English-speaking countries: Australia, Canada, New Zealand, the UK, and the USA. A preliminary glance at the figure reveals that the USA has an unusually high rate of divorce. Indeed, even in the nineteenth century (when data on divorce were first available) the USA had a higher divorce rate than any country in Europe (Amato and Irving, 2005). The figure shows that the divorce rate in the USA increased dramatically during the late 1960s and 1970s and reached a high point in the early 1980s, after which it declined gradually. Despite this decline, the divorce rate remained substantially higher in 2005 than it had been in 1960. Although the other four countries in Figure 16.1 have lower divorce rates than the USA, they show similar trends over time: all of the rates increased during the 1970s, plateaued in the 1980s or 1990s, and then declined modestly. Across these four countries, divorce rates were four to five times higher in 2005 than they had been in 1960.

Figure 16.2 shows crude divorce rates for six representative European countries, three with traditionally low divorce rates (Greece, Italy and Portugal) and three with traditionally high divorce rates (Austria, France and Norway). In each country, the divorce rate increased markedly between 1960 and 2005. Portugal is an especially interesting case, with a divorce rate that increased from 0.2 in 1975 to 2.2 in 2005. In contrast to the predominantly English-speaking countries shown in Figure 16.1, the European countries in Figure 16.2 do not appear to have reached a plateau, which suggests that their rates of divorce may continue to rise in the near future.

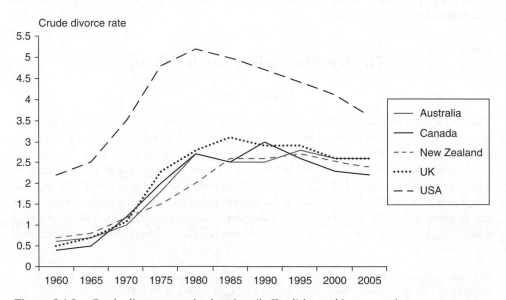

Figure 16.1   Crude divorce rates in six primarily English-speaking countries

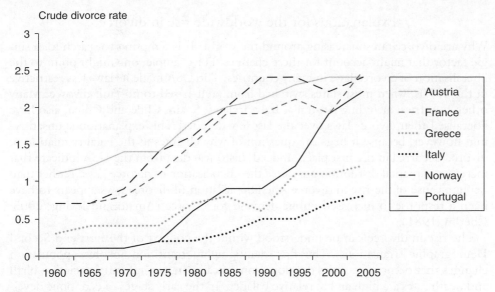

Crude divorce rate

Figure 16.2 Crude divorce rates in six European countries

Table 16.1 Changes in divorce rates (CDR) in non-Western and developing countries

Country	CDR mid-to-late 1970s	CDR mid-to-late 2000s
Japan	1.3	2.1
South Korea	0.4	2.6
China	0.4	1.4
Jordan	1.0	2.0
Kuwait	1.3	2.0
Lebanon	0.6	1.4
Turkey	0.4	1.4
Costa Rica	0.9	2.3
Panama	0.5	0.9
Jamaica	0.4	0.6
Bahamas	0.4	1.1
Mexico	0.3	0.7

Data on divorce from other societies around the world is comparatively sparse. We used available data from annual volumes of the *Demographic Yearbook*, published by the UN (United Nations Statistics Division, 2010), to assess changes in divorce rates in non-Western and developing countries (Table 16.1). Reaching a general conclusion about these trends is not straightforward, in part because not all countries have seen an increase in divorce during the last few decades. For example, the CDR in Guatemala did not change at all between the mid-to-late 1970s and the mid-to-late 2000s (it was 0.2 in both periods), and a few societies had had relatively high rates of divorce in the past that declined with industrialisation during the twentieth century (Goode, 1993). In addition, data on divorce are largely unavailable for some parts of the world, such as Africa. Nevertheless, an increase in divorce during the last few decades is the typical pattern in countries for which data are available.

Explanations for the worldwide rise in divorce

Why are divorce rates increasing around the world? It is tempting to search for a single factor that might account for these changes. For example, one might point to the liberalisation of divorce laws in many countries. The USA made its laws less restrictive in the 1970s, when most states switched from fault-based to no-fault divorce. Many other countries, including Australia, Italy, Ireland, Spain, Chile and China, also have liberalised their divorce laws over the last few decades. This explanation is unsatisfying, however, because it begs the question of why changes in the legal regulation of divorce occurred in the first place. Indeed, historical data from the USA indicate that increases in marital disruption *pre-dated* the liberalisation of divorce laws. Rather than being a cause of the rise in divorce, the liberalisation of divorce laws appears to have been a response to increased public demand for divorce (Amato and Irving, 2005; Cherlin, 1981).

The rise in divorce can be understood within the context of the First and Second Demographic Transitions. The first demographic transition involves population changes that occur as societies develop economically. In pre-industrial societies, birth and death rates are high and in relative balance. In the early stages of economic development, death rates decline owing to improvements in sanitation, nutrition, health care and education. With further development, birth rates also decline owing to the availability of contraception, a decrease in the value of children's labour in an urban economy, and increases in the amount of time and money parents invest in children. Although this model may not be universally applicable, it describes population trends in many parts of the world reasonably well.

Lesthaeghe (1983) was one of the first to describe the Second Demographic Transition (SDT). He argued that the various family changes observed in the West during the last century were not independent of one another. Instead, they were manifestations of a long-term shift in the ideas and values predominant in Western culture. The major theme underlying this shift was an increase in individualism, or the freedom to seek happiness and self-fulfilment outside traditional norms and social arrangements. Economic development led to a higher standard of living, which increased people's aspirations for the good life and enabled them to be more self-reliant. Correspondingly, the influence of extended kin networks, social norms and religion waned. As women's participation in the paid labour force increased, egalitarian views about gender came to the fore. The growth of individualism, secularisation and egalitarianism led to a variety of family-related changes, including below-replacement fertility, a rise in the age at marriage, and increases in non-marital cohabitation, non-marital births and divorce. These changes are collectively recognised as the definitive markers of the SDT.

The notion of a Second Demographic Transition is related to Maslow's (1954) hierarchy of needs. Maslow believed that economic development results in a shift from a focus on meeting material needs (food, shelter and safety) to a focus on meeting higher-order, non-material needs (such as self-esteem and self-actualisation). With such a change in the prioritisation of need fulfilment comes a corresponding shift in social values. In societies where most people's physical needs are met, people come to value individual choice and self-expression more than allegiance to tradition and social institutions. One reflection of this change involves parental socialisation of children. In the past, most parents in Western societies emphasised the values of conformity, obedience, neatness, thriftiness, traditional gender roles and religious faith. In recent decades, however, these values have been replaced by an emphasis on independence, autonomy, self-direction, inquisitiveness and creativity (Alwin, 1989). Increasingly, parents are inculcating in their children the values that underlie the SDT.

Until the end of the 1980s, features of the SDT were most noticeable in Northern Europe, the USA, Canada, Australia and New Zealand (Lesthaege and Neidert, 2006). Since then, however, family behaviours characteristic of the SDT—such as cohabitation, divorce and decreased fertility—have become common in Central, Southern and Eastern Europe. Lesthaeghe (2010) argued that evidence of the SDT is beginning to appear in some Asian countries as well. For example, Japan, Hong Kong, South Korea and Taiwan have all experienced shifts to low-replacement fertility. These same countries, along with Thailand, Singapore, Malaysia, Burma, Indonesia and the Philippines, have shown increases in age at first marriage. Although rarely studied, non-marital cohabitation has also increased significantly in Japan and Taiwan. And, as was noted earlier, divorce rates are rising in China, Japan and South Korea.

These data suggest that the SDT is occurring in many parts of the world. Of course, even if this assumption is correct, each country will make the transition in its own way, depending on historical and social circumstances. We would not expect every aspect of the SDT to unfold with clock-like precision in every country. Nevertheless, this perspective leads to the hypothesis that as societies develop economically, traditional family forms become weaker, and alternatives to traditional family forms become plentiful—especially if most people embrace a secularised culture of individualism, freedom, egalitarianism and democracy. These trends are likely to be reinforced by the mass media, which quickly spreads ideas from developed to developing regions of the globe. In summary, rising rates of divorce cannot be understood apart from other historical changes in family life, and these changes, in turn, are bound up with broad shifts in economic development and culture that are happening around the world.

Studies of Divorce and Children's Wellbeing

In the late 1960s and early 1970s, researchers in the USA began to study children from divorced families. Since then, hundreds (perhaps thousands) of studies on this topic have been published. Reviews of this research literature are available in Amato and Keith (1991), Amato (2001) and Kelly (2000). In addition, Rodgers and Pryor (1998) reviewed studies on this topic conducted in England, Canada, Australia and New Zealand. These studies typically show that children with divorced parents score lower (on average) on measures of academic achievement, conduct, psychological adjustment, self-esteem and social relationships than children with two continuously married parents. Outside English-speaking countries, however, the number of available studies is comparatively small. Because these studies have never been compiled and aggregated, it is not clear whether the gap in wellbeing between children with divorced and continuously married parents (repeatedly observed in English-speaking countries) exists in other parts of the world.

To address this gap, we located as many published studies as possible that used samples of children from countries other than the USA, Canada, England, Australia and New Zealand.[1] We imposed several constraints on the studies included in our analysis. First, because our focus was on children, we omitted studies of adults who grew up with divorced parents (e.g. studies of the intergenerational transmission of divorce). Second, we excluded studies of children living with single parents for reasons other than separation or divorce. Third, we omitted studies that did not include enough information to calculate an effect size (as described below). Finally, it was not practical to include studies published in languages other than English.

Many of the studies we included suffered from various shortcomings. For example, the number of children with divorced parents tended to be small, especially in comparison with the number of children from two-parent families. And although some studies used randomly selected, representative samples, others used convenience samples. Another complicating factor involves the manner in which parents' marital status was measured. Some studies used a dichotomous variable (divorced versus not divorced), while others divided families into multiple categories based on the number of parents or parent figures in the household, the presence of step-parents, or the level of conflict in the home. For these and other reasons, our findings must be interpreted with caution.

Overall, we located 27 published studies that met our criteria. The largest number of studies came from European nations, with the second-largest number collected from Asia. Table 16.2 summarises key information about the studies.

Meta-analytic results

To reach general conclusions about this research literature, we calculated effect sizes for each dependent variable in each study. The effect size is defined as $(M_{divorced} - M_{two-parent})/S$, or the difference in means (M) between children with divorced and continuously married parents on a measure of wellbeing divided by the standard deviation (S) of the measure. In other words, the effect size is the difference between the two groups of children in standard deviation units. Framing study results in terms of effect size is useful because this makes it possible to combine and compare outcomes with different metrics and, hence, different standard deviations. Not all studies reported means and standard deviations. Some reported percentage differences, unstandardised (or standardised) b coefficients, or odds ratios, depending on the outcome. We used established methods for turning these reported values into effect sizes, following procedures described in Rosenthal (1994). We calculated effect sizes so that a negative value indicated that children with divorced parents exhibited a mean level of wellbeing lower than that of children with continuously married parents.

Taken together, the 27 studies produced 68 effect sizes. Across all types of outcomes, the mean effect size was –0.34 ($p < .001$). This indicates that the average study

---

[1]   Many of the studies that are included in the literature review for this chapter were located via the Web of Science database, accessed through the Penn State University Libraries website. Search terms included the phrases 'children of divorce', 'children broken home(s)', 'children marital conflict', 'parental divorce', and 'child wellbeing divorce', along with a country or region name (e.g. 'children divorce Bulgaria'). These searches were repeated with 'adolescent' substituted for 'child(ren)'. Additional articles were located using the same search terms in Google Scholar. Lastly, the authors browsed the archives of several journals, including the *Journal of Comparative Family Studies* and *Journal of Marriage and Family*, to locate articles not turned up by the initial database and Web searches.

Table 16.2 Overview of studies of children and divorce

Author(s)/year	Country	Sample sizes[1]		Outcomes
Alam *et al.* (2001)	Bangladesh	329 (divorce)	2364 (no divorce)	Neonatal and post-neonatal death rates
Albertini and Dronkers (2009)	Italy	723 (divorce)	18233 (no divorce)	Educational attainment
Bockelbrink *et al.* (2006)	Germany	65 (divorce)	1844 (no divorce)	Prevalence and incidence of atopic eczema
Challier *et al.* (2000)	France	764 (divorce)	1632 (no divorce)	Tobacco use (smoking)
Cherian (1989)	South Africa	242 (divorce)	713 (no divorce)	Academic achievement
Christopoulos (2001)	Bulgaria	50 (divorce)	50 (no divorce)	Psychological problems
Chung and Emery (2010)	South Korea	198 (divorce)	256 (no divorce)	Internalising and externalising problems, self-esteem
Creighton *et al.* (2009)	Mexico	69 (divorce)	943 (no divorce)	School continuation
Dong *et al.* (2002)	China	174 (divorce)	174 (no divorce)	Depression, anxiety, behaviour problems
Dronkers (1999)	The Netherlands	681 (divorce)	9135 (no divorce)	Wellbeing (drug use, crime, school problems, depression, suicidal thoughts)
Gloger-Tippelt and König (2007)	Germany	60 (divorce)	51 (no divorce)	Parent–child attachment style
Hatzichristou (1993)	Greece	26 (divorce)	381 (no divorce)	Behaviour problems, depression, school performance
Jonsson and Gähler (1997)	Sweden	22393 (divorce)	96718 (no divorce)	School continuation
Khayyer and Alborzi (2002)	Iran	20 (divorce)	676 (no divorce)	Locus of control
Kim *et al.* (2009)	South Korea	24 (divorce)	258 (no divorce)	Full syndrome and sub-threshold ADHD
Ledoux *et al.* (2002)	France	249 (divorce)	1660 (no divorce)	Tobacco, marijuana or illicit drug use
Liu *et al.* (1999)	China	40 (divorce)	2224 (no divorce)	Behaviour problems (CBCL)
Liu *et al.* (2000)	China	58 (divorce)	116 (no divorce)	Behaviour problems (CBCL, TRF)
Mednick *et al.* (1990)	Denmark	116 (divorce)	292 (no divorce)	Recorded criminal charges
Mednick *et al.* (1987)	Denmark	102 (divorce)	241 (no divorce)	Juvenile arrests
Park (2008)	South Korea	455 (divorce)	4926 (no divorce)	Educational aspiration, school disengagement
Spruijt and Duindam (2010)	The Netherlands	148 (divorce)	1089 (no divorce)	Risky habits, number of sex partners
Steinhausen *et al.* (1987)	Germany	121 (divorce)	252 (no divorce)	Conduct disorder, neurosis

(Continued)

Table 16.2   (*cont'd*)

Author(s)/year	Country	Sample sizes[1]		Outcomes
Størksen *et al.* (2005)	Norway	413 (divorce)	1758 (no divorce)	Anxiety/depression, subjective wellbeing, self-esteem, school problems
Størksen *et al.* (2006)	Norway	1810 (divorce)	6784 (no divorce)	Anxiety/depression, subjective wellbeing, school problems
Tomcikova *et al.* (2009)	Slovakia	723 (divorce)	2815 (no divorce)	Recent drunkenness
Yannakoulia *et al.* (2008)	Greece	96 (divorce)	1002 (no divorce)	Eating style

[1] Most studies count marital separations as divorces.

found a wellbeing gap between children with divorced and continuously married parents of little more than one-third of a standard deviation. We also weighted the effect sizes to take into account the size of the samples on which they were based (Shadish and Haddock, 1994). In general, effect sizes based on larger samples should produce more accurate estimates of mean differences in the population. The mean weighted effect size was –0.24 ($p < .001$). This result indicates that when studies with larger samples were given more weight, the mean effect size declined in magnitude. Most researchers would consider an effect size equivalent to one-fourth of a standard deviation to be non-trivial but moderate (rather than strong) in magnitude.

Table 16.3 shows the mean effect sizes across outcome categories for the 27 studies included in this review. The unweighted mean effect sizes ranged from –0.26 (physical health) to –0.52 (social wellbeing), and the corresponding weighted effect sizes ranged from –0.20 (academic achievement) to –0.51 (social wellbeing). Although the weighted effect sizes tended to be lower than the unweighted effect sizes, the means all fell in a range that can be viewed as moderate in magnitude.

To provide a comparison, the table also shows comparable effect sizes from the Amato (2001) meta-analysis, which was based mainly on studies conducted in the USA. The unweighted mean effect sizes from the Amato (2001) meta-analysis ranged from –0.24 (self-esteem) to –0.33 (conduct). Correspondingly, the mean weighted effect sizes ranged from –0.15 (social wellbeing) to –0.33 (behaviour).[2] In general, the effect sizes from Amato (2001) tended to be somewhat lower than the effect sizes presented here. The remarkable finding, however, is that the results of the two sets of studies were so similar. That is, effect sizes were in the same range of magnitude in other parts of the world as they were in the USA. We return to this point in the discussion below.

Because the number of studies was small, we were limited in our ability to make comparisons across regions. Nevertheless, the mean overall effect sizes (weighted) were –0.23 for Europe and –0.31 for Asia. When restricted to studies of conduct, the mean (weighted) effect sizes for Europe and Asia were –0.21 and –0.35, respectively.

[2] Physical health outcomes were not included in the Amato (2001) meta-analysis.

Table 16.3   Mean effect sizes (ES) from studies of children and divorce

Outcome	Non-English-speaking countries			USA		
	ES unweighted	ES weighted	N	ES unweighted	ES weighted	N
Academic	−0.28	−0.20	14	−0.26	−0.16	39
Behaviour	−0.32	−0.23	27	−0.33	−0.22	40
Emotional	−0.38	−0.33	15	−0.31	−0.21	41
Self-esteem	−0.44	−0.28	4	−0.24	−0.12	28
Social	−0.52	−0.51	3	−0.28	−0.15	29
Physical health	−0.26	−0.28	5	—	—	—

Note. 'N' refers to the number of effect sizes on which each mean is based. Effect sizes from the USA are from Amato (2001). All mean effect sizes are significant at $p < 0.01$.

When restricted to studies of emotional wellbeing, the effect sizes were −0.33 and −0.29 respectively. Because of the small number of estimates, we must be cautious in interpreting these findings. Nevertheless, the pattern of results suggests that the estimated effects of divorce on children are roughly similar in Europe and Asia.

Examples of studies

We provide three geographically diverse examples of studies included in the meta-analysis. These are shown in the boxes below.

A study from Mexico (Creighton *et al.*, 2009)

The study examined the effects of divorce and paternal migration on adolescents' risk of dropping out of upper secondary school. It used two waves of the Mexican Family Life Survey, a nationally and regionally representative longitudinal data set collected in 2002 and 2005. The data set included 8440 households from 150 communities in Mexico, and the sample comprised children in these households who attended any upper secondary school between waves 1 and 2. Ninety-four per cent of wave 1 participants were re-interviewed in 2005.

As the authors noted, research from the USA and Europe has consistently shown that children living with single mothers have worse educational outcomes than children living with married parents. This is especially true in cases of parental divorce. Although research conducted elsewhere in the world has estimated the effects on children of various causes of single motherhood, Mexico is unique in that single motherhood there often results from paternal migration. For this reason, the authors distinguished between divorce and migration as determinants of single motherhood in their analysis of adolescents' school continuation.

The authors hypothesised that children living in single-mother households as a result of international migration or divorce are more likely to drop out of school than their peers whose fathers live in the household or move within their own country. The authors also hypothesised that household economic conditions partially explain the risk of dropping out for children whose parents are divorced, but not for those whose fathers are absent owing to international migration. The family structure variable was categorised as follows: two-parent family, single-mother family owing to divorce or separation, single-mother family owing to domestic migration, or single-mother family owing to international migration.

Descriptive statistics indicated that the drop-out rate for adolescents with divorced or separated parents (17%) was almost double that for adolescents from two-parent households (9%). The multivariate analysis included the following control variables: presence of a grandparent in the home, number of co-resident siblings, household socioeconomic status, urban/rural setting, and respondent sex, ethnicity and grade. This analysis showed that adolescents with divorced parents were more likely to drop out than those with married parents, although statistical significance declined with the inclusion of control variables ($p < 0.1$ as against $p < 0.05$). In addition, the hypothesis that economic differences help to explain the risk of dropping out was supported for children with divorced parents but not for children whose fathers were international migrants.

A study from China (Dong *et al.*, 2002)

This study investigated several dimensions of children's post-divorce adjustment in a Chinese sample. China's comparatively low divorce rate means that less attention has been paid to the possible ramifications of divorce there than in the USA and Europe. The sample was drawn from a larger sample of 1294 children and their parents recruited from eight elementary and middle schools in Beijing and Tianjin, both large urban centres. The sample contained 174 children with divorced parents, matched with children from two-parent families on sex, grade, school and city location. In all 174 cases, children from divorced families resided with their mother, grandparents, or both at the time of data collection. Mothers' education level was significantly higher and family income was significantly lower in the divorced group than in the two-parent family group. In other respects the two groups did not differ.

The authors' hypotheses were: (1) more behavioural problems would be observed in children from divorced families than in children from two-parent families; and (2) children's adjustment to divorce would vary with sex, years since the divorce, family income, mother's depression, and parenting style. Information on outcomes was collected by way of respondent self-reports, mothers' reports and teachers' reports. Self-report measures included the Children's Depression Inventory (CDI) and the Revised Children's Manifest Anxiety Scale (RCMAS). Parents completed the Beck Depression Inventory (BDI), the Children's Behavior Checklist (CBCL), and a parent questionnaire that included questions about family demographics and parenting style. Teachers completed the Teacher's Report Form (TRF), which is similar in content to the CBCL.

Children from divorced families reported significantly higher levels of anxiety and depression than children from two-parent families. The mean depression score for children of divorced parents was 12.26, while the mean score for children from intact families was 9.99 (a difference of about one-third of a standard deviation). In addition, both mothers' and teachers' reports showed differences in reported behaviour problems between children from divorced and two-parent families. Stepwise multiple regression analyses identified divorce status as a statistically significant predictor of total CDI score and internalising, externalising and total scores on the CBCL and TRF. The authors concluded that, of the indicators examined in the analysis, divorce status is one of the most robust predictors of depression, anxiety and behaviour problems among Chinese adolescents—a finding consistent with the idea that the negative impact of divorce is not unique to a particular culture or region of the globe.

A study from Norway (Størksen *et al.*, 2006)

This study investigated the effects of divorce and parents' psychological distress on adolescent wellbeing. As the authors noted, although Norway's divorce rate rivals that of the USA, Scandinavian countries have particularly generous social welfare systems and hold especially liberal family values. For these reasons, divorce may have fewer negative consequences for children in Scandinavia than for children in other Western countries.

Data for the study came from the Nord-Trøndelag Health Study (HUNT) and Young-HUNT, which comprise fairly nationally representative data from Nord-Trøndelag county in central Norway. Young-HUNT included adolescents between the ages of 13 and 19 recruited through the local school system. The study's aims were to: (1) estimate the effects of parental divorce or separation on adolescent adjustment and wellbeing; (2) determine whether the effects of divorce on wellbeing differ for males and females; (3) examine the role of time since separation in understanding the impact of parental divorce; and (4) investigate whether parents' psychological distress mediates the relationship between divorce and anxiety and depression in adolescents.

The authors used a five-item symptom checklist to measure adolescent anxiety and depression, a three-item subjective wellbeing scale, and a 14-item school functioning questionnaire. Control variables included family socioeconomic status. Statistically significant mean differences were observed between the divorce and no-divorce groups on five variables: depression/anxiety, subjective wellbeing, academic problems, school conduct and school dissatisfaction. Adolescents with divorced parents had means of 1.56 on the anxiety-depression scale and 5.07 on the subjective wellbeing scale, while their counterparts from two-parent families had means of 1.43 and 5.34 respectively. (These group means differ by between one-quarter and one-third of a standard deviation.) Parents' psychological distress and divorce appeared to have approximately equal effects on adolescent symptoms of anxiety and depression, with the two effects being essentially independent of one another. The findings also indicated that the gap between adolescents with divorced and non-divorced parents did not diminish with the passage of time since separation.

Additional studies

Some publications did not meet our criteria for inclusion in the meta-analysis but provided information relevant to our topic. For example, several studies examined children in single-parent households, irrespective of the cause of single parenthood. In one study, Pong *et al.* (2003) analysed the gap in mathematics and science achievement between children (3rd- and 4th-graders) from single- and two-parent families in 11 industrialised nations. With the exception of two countries (Austria and Iceland), all countries revealed a significant achievement gap between children from the two family types. The largest gaps were observed in the USA and New Zealand.

In another study, Hampden-Thompson and Pong (2005) examined academic achievement in children living with single and married parents in 14 countries. The authors also investigated whether the country's family policy environment moderated the association between family type and academic achievement. They found that the achievement gap between children in the two family types was smaller in countries with more supportive family and welfare policies, with the largest gaps existing in Great Britain, Ireland and Scotland.

Park (2007) examined the gap in reading performance between adolescents from single and two-parent families in five Asian countries—South Korea, Hong Kong, Indonesia, Thailand and Japan. He found no difference between the two groups in Korea and Hong Kong, a slight positive effect of single parenthood in Indonesia and Thailand, and a negative effect of single parenthood in Japan. He suggested that the relatively high incidence of widowhood in Asian countries may explain some portion of these contradictory findings.

Overall, the results of these studies are consistent with our meta-analysis and suggest that living with a single parent rather than two continuously married parents increases the risk of various problems for children and adolescents. These studies also suggest, however, that the association between family structure and child wellbeing depends on a wide variety of contextual factors. Additional research is needed to determine more precisely the social, cultural and economic conditions that moderate the effects of family structure on children.

Finally, not all studies have found significant associations between parental divorce or living with a single parent and child outcomes. For example, in a German longitudinal study, Walper and Beckh (2006) did not find that children in stable single-mother or stable stepfather families were worse off than children in stable nuclear families. However, children who experienced changes in family composition over time (mainly the addition of a stepfather or the separation of a stepfather and mother) reported low levels of self-esteem and high levels of depression. This study suggests that parents' marital status is less important for children's wellbeing than are *transitions* in parents' marital status.

Theoretical Issues

Why might parental divorce increase children's risk of developing academic, emotional and behavioural problems? Most reviewers of this research literature (e.g. Amato, 2005; Kelly, 2000; Kelly and Emery, 2003) have assumed that divorce is a stressful experience for the majority of children. Divorce-related stressors take a variety of forms.

For example, divorce typically results in a decline in children's standard of living owing to the loss of economies of scale associated with dividing one household into two. Similarly, marital disruption is often preceded and followed by a high level of conflict between parents. Some unfortunate children are caught in the middle between warring parents, with each parent trying to recruit the child as an ally against the other. Moreover, the turmoil of ending a marriage often depletes parents' emotional resources and interferes with the quality of care they are able to give. In the aftermath of divorce, some single parents become less responsive to their children's needs, monitor their children less effectively, and dispense harsher discipline. Correspondingly, many non-resident parents (generally fathers) become less involved in their children's lives. This is particularly true if the parent has taken on the responsibility of a new family. Many young adults report that losing contact with their fathers was the most distressing aspect of their parents' divorce. As a general rule, the more sources of stress a divorce generates, the greater the risk that children will develop problems.

Studies in this literature are correlational rather than experimental, so we cannot prove that divorce causes some children to develop problems. An alternative explanation refers to selection factors. Parents may possess certain characteristics (e.g. personality traits such as neuroticism, poor relationship skills, or an avoidant attachment style) that increase both the risk of divorce *and* the risk that their children will develop problems. If this is the case, then the association between divorce and children's problems is spurious. Although it is difficult to distinguish methodologically between the two explanations, some studies suggest that selection factors account for part—but not all—of the association between divorce and children's problems. A reasonable conclusion, therefore, is that divorce has a causal effect on children, but that effect sizes from many studies may exaggerate the degree of risk (Amato, 2010).

Given that divorce can generate a variety of stressful circumstances, one might ask why the estimated effects of divorce on children are modest rather than substantial. The risk and resilience perspective is useful for thinking about this question. This perspective indicates that the association between stressful life events and developmental outcomes is not direct or simple. Although exposure to a stressor increases the likelihood of negative outcomes, many factors can intervene in this process, resulting in a considerable degree of diversity in children's reactions.[3]

Children's reactions to stress depend on the resources at their disposal. Resources can reside in the individual child (intelligence, problem-solving skills, self-efficacy), the child's interpersonal relationships (social support from relatives, peers and teachers), and the child's physical and social environment (school quality, supporting government services). The quantity and quality of resources in children's lives not only improves their wellbeing directly, but also helps them to cope with everyday strains and major life stressors. Children from divorced families are exposed to more stressors, on average, than are children with continuously married parents. Depending on their access to resources, some children are more vulnerable than others to the ill effects of divorce. When parents manage to maintain cooperative relationships following divorce, for example, and when they stay focused on their children's wellbeing, children may be buffered from many of the strains associated with changes in family structure.

---

[3] For discussions of the risk and resilience perspective, see Cowan *et al.*, 1996; Hetherington, 1999; Kelly and Emery, 2003; Rutter, 1987.

The risk and resilience perspective suggests that social, cultural, economic and policy differences between countries might act to either exacerbate or lessen the effects of divorce on children. Although this is an intriguing hypothesis, few studies have addressed it directly. As noted earlier, Hampden-Thompson and Pong (2005) found that the gap in academic achievement between children living with single parents and married parents tended to be smaller in countries with more generous family and welfare policies. Another study, by Gohm *et al.* (1998), examined the subjective wellbeing of university students from 39 different countries. It found that students with divorced parents reported lower levels of happiness than did students with continuously married parents. The gap in wellbeing, however, was lower in 'collectivist' nations than in 'individualist' nations: individualist cultures encourage personal independence and value autonomy, whereas collectivist cultures encourage interdependence and stress the importance of obligations to others. The authors suggested that the social support available in collectivist nations helps to buffer youth against the potentially negative effects of divorce. Because the Gohm *et al.* (1998) study was based on university students, replications using representative samples are necessary before drawing conclusions. Nevertheless, the idea that large-scale social factors can moderate the effects of family disruption is a theoretically important one and should be pursued by other researchers working from a cross-national perspective.

Conclusion

Our review of recent trends leads to two conclusions. First, divorce rates are currently increasing in many parts of the world. Second, in countries for which relevant data are available, children with divorced parents have lower levels of wellbeing than do children with continuously married parents. A key question is why divorce appears to compromise children's wellbeing in so many diverse societies.

It is noteworthy that the family takes a similar form—the nuclear family—in most of the countries discussed in this chapter. Although not a universal rule, economic development and urbanisation tend to separate children from the dense network of kin and neighbours that characterise small-scale societies. Children become attached to adults who provide consistent, high-quality care. Yet, in many developed nations, the circle of people who care for children is seriously restricted. As a result, a great deal of responsibility for children's welfare is placed on the two biological (or adoptive) parents. When the small group of people essential to the child's upbringing is disrupted owing to divorce, the consequences for the child are potentially troubling.

In small-scale traditional societies, marital dissolution may be less problematic for children. In many hunter-gatherer societies, for example, divorce is common, and it is perfectly acceptable to move on to a new mate when one tires of the old one. Like many other aspects of life, parenting is flexible and transferable, resulting in a large number of people who share in the care and upbringing of any given child. This wide circle of caring and responsible adults likely safeguards children from the negative effects of losing a parent for any reason.

These considerations lead to an interesting—and troubling—conclusion. Economic development and cultural aspects of the Second Demographic Transition are raising divorce rates at the same time that they are increasing children's dependence on the nuclear two-parent family, although more research that adopts a cross-national, global perspective is clearly needed to understand these intersecting phenomena. This conclusion, albeit tentative, suggests that developed (and developing) countries need to introduce policies that protect children from the potentially harmful consequences of high levels of family disruption.

References

Alam, N., Saha, S. K., Razzaque, A., and van Ginneken, J. K. (2001) The effect of divorce on infant mortality in a remote area of Bangladesh, *Journal of Biosocial Science*, 33: 271–278.

Albertini, M. and Dronkers, J. (2009) Effects of divorce on children's educational attainment in a Mediterranean and Catholic society, *European Societies*, 11(1): 137–159.

Alwin, D. (1989) Changes in qualities valued in children, 1964–1984, *Social Science Research*, 44(2): 1–42.

Amato, P. R. (2001) Children of divorce in the 1990s: an update of the Amato and Keith (1991) meta-analysis, *Journal of Family Psychology*, 15: 355–370.

Amato, P. R. (2005) The impact of family formation change on the cognitive, social, and emotional well-being of the next generation, *Future of Children*, 15: 75–96.

Amato, P. R. (2010) Research on divorce: continuing trends and new developments, *Journal of Marriage and Family*, 72 (June): 650–666.

Amato, P. R. and Irving, S. (2005) A historical perspective on divorce in the United States, in M. Fine and J. Harvey (eds), *Handbook of Divorce and Relationship Dissolution* (Hillsdale, NJ: Lawrence Erlbaum), 41–58.

Amato, P. R. and Keith, B, (1991) Consequences of parental divorce for children's wellbeing: a meta-analysis, *Psychological Bulletin*, 110: 26–46.

Bockelbrink, A., Heinrich, J., Schäfer, I. *et al.* (2006) Atopic eczema in children: another harmful sequel of divorce, *Allergy*, 61: 1397–1402.

Challier, B., Chau, N., Prédine, R., Choquet, M. and Legras, B. (2000) Associations of family environment and individual factors with tobacco, alcohol, and illicit drug use in adolescents, *European Journal of Epidemiology*, 16(1): 33–42.

Cherian, V. I. (1989) Academic achievement of children of divorced parents, *Psychological Reports*, 64: 355–358.

Cherlin, A. (1981) *Marriage, Divorce, Remarriage* (Cambridge, MA: Harvard University Press).

Christopoulos, A. (2001) Relationships between parent's marital status and university students' mental health, views of mothers and view of fathers: a study in Bulgaria, *Journal of Divorce and Remarriage*, 34(3): 179–190.

Chung, Y. and Emery, R. (2010) Early adolescents and divorce in South Korea: risk, resilience, and pain, *Journal of Comparative Family Studies*, 41(5): 855–872.

Cowan, P. A., Cowan, C. P. and Schulz, M. S. (1996) Thinking about risk and resilience in families, in E. M. Hetherington and E. A. Blechman (eds), *Stress, Coping, and Resiliency in Children and Families* (Mahwah, NJ: Lawrence Erlbaum), 1–38.

Creighton, M., Park, H. and Teruel, G. (2009) The role of migration and single motherhood in upper secondary education in Mexico, *Journal of Marriage and Family*, 71: 1325–1339.

Dong, Q., Wang, Y. and Ollendick, T. (2002) Consequences of divorce on the adjustment of children in China, *Journal of Clinical Child and Adolescent Psychology*, 31(1): 101–110.

Dronkers, J. (1999) The effects of parental conflicts and divorce on the wellbeing of pupils in Dutch secondary education, *European Sociological Review*, 15(2): 195–212.

Gloger-Tippelt, G. and König, L. (2007) Attachment representations in 6-year-old children from one and two parent families in Germany, *School Psychology International*, 28: 313–330.

Gohm, C. L, Oishi, S., Darlington, J. and Diener, E. (1998) Culture, parental conflict, parental marital status, and the subjective wellbeing of young adults, *Journal of Marriage and Family*, 60: 319–334.

Goode, W. J. (1993) *World Changes in Divorce Patterns* (New Haven, CT: Yale University Press).

Hampden-Thompson, G. and Pong, S-L. (2005) Does family policy environment moderate the effect of single-parenthood on children's academic achievement? A study of 14 European countries, *Journal of Comparative Family Studies*, 36(2): 227–248.

Hatzichristou, C. (1993) Children's adjustment after parental separation: teacher, peer, and self-report in a

Greek sample: a research note, *Journal of Child Psychology and Psychiatry*, 34(8): 1469–1478.

Hetherington, E. M. (1999) Should we stay together for the sake of the children?, in E. M. Hetherington (ed.), *Coping with Divorce, Single Parenting, and Remarriage: A risk and resiliency perspective* (Mahwah, NJ: Lawrence Erlbaum), 93–116.

Jonsson, J. O. and Gähler, M. (1997) Family dissolution, family reconstitution, and children's educational careers: recent evidence for Sweden, *Demography*, 34(2): 277–293.

Kelly, J. B. (2000) Children's adjustment in conflicted marriage and divorce: a decade review of research, *Journal of the American Academy of Child & Adolescent Psychiatry*, 39: 963–973.

Kelly, J. B. and Emery, R. E. (2003) Children's adjustment following divorce: risk and resilience perspectives, *Family Relations*, 52: 352–362.

Khayyer, M. and Alborzi, S. (2002) Locus of control of children experiencing separation and divorce in their families in Iran, *Psychological Reports*, 90: 239–242.

Kim, H-W., Cho, S-C., Kim, B-N., Kim, J-W., Shin, M-S. and Kim, Y. (2009) Perinatal and familial risk factors are associated with full syndrome and subthreshold attention-deficit hyperactivity disorder in a Korean community sample, *Psychiatry Investigation*, 6(4): 278–285.

Ledoux, S., Miller, P., Choquet, M. and Plant, M. (2002) Family structure, parent–child relationships, and alcohol and other drug use among teenagers in France and the United Kingdom, *Alcohol and Alcoholism*, 37(1): 52–60.

Lesthaeghe, R. (1983) A century of demographic and cultural change in Western Europe: an exploration of underlying dimensions, *Population and Development Review*, 9(3): 411–435.

Lesthaeghe, R. (2010) The unfolding story of the Second Demographic Transition, *Population and Development Review*, 36(2): 211–251.

Lesthaeghe, R. and Neidert, L. (2006) The second demographic transition in the United States: exception or textbook example?, *Population and Development Review*, 32(4): 669–698.

Liu, X., Guo, C., Okawa, M. *et al.* (2000) Behavioral and emotional problems in Chinese children of divorced parents, *Journal of the American Academy of Child and Adolescent Psychiatry*, 39(7): 896–903.

Liu, X., Kurita, H., Guo, C., Miyake, Y., Ze, J. and Cao, H. (1999) Prevalence and risk factors of behavioral and emotional problems among Chinese children aged 6 through 11 years, *Journal of the American Academy of Child and Adolescent Psychiatry*, 38(6): 708–715.

Maslow, A. (1954) *Motivation and Personality* (New York: Harper & Row).

Mednick, B., Baker, R. and Carothers, L. (1990) Patterns of family instability and crime: the association of timing of the family's disruption with subsequent adolescent and young adult criminality, *Journal of Youth and Adolescence*, 19(3): 201–219.

Mednick, B., Reznick, C., Hocevar, D. and Baker, R. (1987) Long-term effects of parental divorce on young adult male crime, *Journal of Youth and Adolescence*, 16(1): 31–45.

Park, H. (2007) Single parenthood and children's reading performance in Asia, *Journal of Marriage and Family*, 69: 863–877.

Park, H. (2008) Effects of single parenthood on educational aspiration and student disengagement in Korea, *Demographic Research*, 18(13): 377–408.

Pong, S-L., Dronkers, J. and Hampden-Thompson, G. (2003) Family policies and children's school achievement in single- versus two-parent families, *Journal of Marriage and Family*, 65: 681–699.

Rodgers, B. and Pryor, J. (1998) *Divorce and Separation: The outcomes for children* (London: Joseph Rowntree Foundation).

Rosenthal, R. (1994) Parametric measures of effect size, in H. Cooper and L. V. Hedges (eds), *The Handbook of Research Synthesis* (New York: Russell Sage), 231–244.

Rutter, M. (1987) Psychosocial resilience and protective mechanisms, *American Journal of Orthopsychiatry*, 57: 316–331.

Shadish, W. R. and Haddock, C. K. (1994) Combining estimates of effect size, in H. Cooper and L. V. Hedges (eds), *The Handbook of Research Synthesis* (New York: Russell Sage), 261–284.

Spruijt, E. and Duindam, V. (2010) Problem behavior of boys and young men after parental divorce in the Netherlands, *Journal of Divorce and Remarriage*, 43(3): 141–155.

Steinhausen, H-C., Von Aster, S. and Göbel, D. (1987) Family composition and child psychiatric disorders, *Journal of the American Academy of Child and Adolescent Psychiatry*, 26(2): 242–247.

Størksen, I., Røysamb, E., Holmen, T. L. and Tambs, K. (2006) Adolescent adjustment and wellbeing: effects of parental divorce and distress, *Scandinavian Journal of Psychology*, 47: 75–84.

Størksen, I., Røysamb, E., Moum, T. and Tambs, K. (2005) Adolescents with a childhood experience of divorce: a longitudinal study of mental health and adjustment, *Journal of Adolescence*, 28: 725–739.

Tomcikova, Z., Geckova, A., Orosova, O., Van Dijk, J. P. and Reijneveld, S. A. (2009) Parental divorce and adolescent drunkenness: role of socioeconomic position, psychological wellbeing and social support, *European Addiction Research*, 15: 202–208.

United Nations Statistics Division (2010) Demographic Yearbook. http://unstats.un.org/unsd/demographic/products/dyb/dyb2009-2010.htm [Accessed 14.8.2012.]

Walper, S. and Beckh, K. (2006) Adolescents' development in high-conflict and separated families: evidence from a German longitudinal study, in A. Clarke-Stewart and J. Dunn (eds), *Families Count: Effects on child and adolescent development* (New York: Cambridge University Press), 238–272.

Yannakoulia, M., Papanikolaou, K., Hatzopoulou, I., Efstathiou, E., Papoutsakis, C. and Dedoussis, G. V. (2008) Association between family divorce and children's BMI and meal patterns: the GENDAI study, *Obesity*, 16: 1382–1387.

Part III

Global Impacts on Family Life

In the third part of the book, our attention shifts to the impacts of globalisation on partnerships and parenting. To set the scene, Melinda Mills (Chapter 17) describes four interrelated structural shifts which are linked with welfare systems, employment, training and transnational production systems, all of which impact on family life. She discusses the dismantling of national borders, rising interconnectedness through communication technology, tax competition between countries, and the world market, which is increasingly volatile. These structural shifts have generated uncertainty in modern life which influences decisions about partnership formation and parenthood. Mills looks at the opportunities afforded by digital technology and virtual communication, geographical mobility, and increased acceptance of a range of family forms. She illustrates how globalisation has fundamentally changed the ways in which families live their lives.

The impact of communication technology is developed further in Chapter 18. Monica Whitty discusses the implications of the growing dominance of the Internet in the lives of children and parents and its impact on family relationships. She draws attention to the many advantages Internet access affords, but also to the risks represented by cyber-bullying, paedophilia, sexting, fraud and crime. Whitty examines children's and adolescents' Internet use and highlights the current and sometimes heated debates about the extent to which their usage should be monitored and policed. She argues that a better understanding of the risks is essential in order to develop protective measures which do not limit young people's opportunities to benefit from an increasingly digital world.

In Chapter 19, Ubaldo Martínez Veiga explores in greater detail the impact of migration on family life referred to in Chapter 17 by Melinda Mills. Martínez Veiga

Contemporary Issues in Family Studies: Global Perspectives on Partnerships, Parenting and Support in a Changing World, First Edition. Edited by Angela Abela and Janet Walker.
© 2014 John Wiley & Sons, Ltd. Published 2014 by John Wiley & Sons, Ltd.

takes Spain as a case study in order to illustrate different kinds of migration and their impact on family life. By examining migration patterns from the Caribbean, South America, Morocco and sub-Saharan Africa we can observe the ways in which families have been split up as a result of one or other parent moving abroad to find work. Furthermore, the current economic recession has led some countries to review their immigration policies and their attitudes towards family reunification.

This is a highly sensitive and complex issue which results in deep political divisions as regards the status that should be afforded to immigrants and how to limit what some countries regard as illegal immigration. Martínez Veiga warns that unless governments cooperate in finding more constructive ways of managing migration flows, attempts at social integration will be damaged and migrants will increasingly cling to their own culture rather than adapt to the cultural norms of their host country. There is a real danger that migrants will be marginalised in their host countries, face negative social and racist attitudes, find themselves in low-paid jobs with little economic security, and experience separation from their families.

A different form of migration is explored in Chapter 20, in which Gabriela Misca examines the evidence about international adoption. In recent decades, large numbers of babies and children have been adopted in the wealthier countries of the West from poorer countries such as Romania, China and Africa. Passionate debates about the efficacy of removing children from their country of origin have resulted in several studies of outcomes relating to these children. Misca focuses on studies of Romanian children and provides critical insights into the pre-disposing factors which impact on outcomes: children who had spent less time in a variety of living conditions in Romania prior to adoption had fewer physical, medical and cognitive problems than the children who had lived there for several months or years before adoption. Although ethnic and cultural identity issues are less salient than some commentators have indicated, there is much to learn from the research about the (adverse) experiences children have had before being adopted internationally that can impact on their longer-term outcomes. Although international adoptions are usually successful for adoptees and the children concerned, this is often due to the high level of commitment and the dedication of adoptive parents. Parenting in these circumstances is both challenging and demanding. The lessons learnt from these studies have considerable significance for child adoption more generally.

Poverty also makes parenting extremely difficult, and Chapter 21 considers the struggles facing parents who are living on the margin. Angela Abela and Marie-Cécile Renoux examine the plight of families in Europe who are living in poverty. Some of the countries in Eastern Europe exhibit the highest poverty rates when assessed on deprivation indicators. The authors focus their attention, however, on the impacts of poverty on families living in more affluent European countries. They highlight the contextual risk factors which exacerbate disadvantage, including living in a poor neighbourhood, unemployment, large families, ill health, and being a single parent. Deprivation can seriously compromise parenting ability, but seeking help can be a two-edged sword since it may increase the risk that children will be taken into care and the family split up. The authors highlight the detrimental consequences of multiple deprivations and the need for more supportive early interventions and policies that address existing income inequalities. Many countries have pledged to eradicate child poverty, but this is far from easy and is likely to take a very long time. Until child poverty is a thing of the past, however, intergenerational cycles of poverty are set to continue.

In Chapter 22, Sabah Ayachi draws on her own research to explore the changing patterns of mate selection and marital stability in an area of North Africa which has experienced rapid changes in all spheres of life as well as periods of civil unrest. While customs, traditions and religious beliefs are extremely important, recent changes have promoted a greater degree of personal choice in mate selection. Ayachi uses a number of case studies to demonstrate variations in family stability and acknowledges that while governments are making efforts to tackle unemployment and to reduce drug addiction and violence against women, families are facing major challenges in maintaining stability. She illustrates the complexities which arise when global changes confront traditional values and established norms in couple relationships and family life.

East Asian countries are also experiencing extensive reshaping of family relationships and obligations across the life course. In Chapter 23, Jim Raymo considers the impacts of rapid demographic changes in Japan, Korea and Taiwan. Trends in marriage, fertility and divorce are similar to those in most Western European countries, but there is a stronger focus on educational success, the desire to produce high-quality children, 'intensive mothering', and intergenerational support. Expectations on eldest sons to care for extended family have limited their marriage prospects in recent years and have contributed to the increase in international marriages. This is likely to impact on the ability of adult children to care for older generations in the years to come. Raymo describes how globalisation has promoted policies in Japan to boost fertility, encourage marriage and facilitate a better balance between child rearing and paid work. Japan provides an important example of how a country characterised by familistic social organisation is responding to the implications of rapid demographic change.

In the final chapter (24) in Part III, we turn our attention to the way in which religious faith might provide support for couples dealing with challenges in their marriage. The practice of prayer is central to most religions, but very little is known about how prayer may be relevant to couple relationships. Frank Fincham describes a number of research studies in the USA in which one partner uses prayer to reinforce forgiveness in the couple relationship, especially after the discovery of infidelity. Since affairs are a leading cause of divorce across a wide variety of cultures, promoting forgiveness may offer a positive intervention which reduces the extent of marital breakdown. Fincham reports on an innovative randomised control trial involving African-American couples and suggests that prayer can be used in couple counselling and couple therapy to increase their efficacy. This approach is not without its critics, however, and it presents conceptual challenges for therapists. Nevertheless, it draws our attention to the significance of religious beliefs in many cultures and the potential power of prayer for strengthening relationships.

A recurring theme throughout Part III of the book is the way in which families and societies are attempting to adapt cultural norms to the challenges of globalisation. Despite cultural diversity within and between countries, these chapters illustrate the similarity of the issues and concerns relating to changes in marriage, partnerships and parenting in the twenty-first century.

17

Globalisation and Family Life

Melinda Mills

Introduction

Since the 1980s, a series of broad global transformations have emerged, representing a set of economic, political and cultural processes heralding globalisation. Research has mainly focused on the impact of globalisation on the convergence of economic, welfare and political systems (see e.g. Alderson and Nielsen, 2002), and less empirical attention has been given to the impact of globalisation on everyday life and, in particular, family life. This chapter reviews the existing literature and examines how the larger-scale transformations brought about by globalisation are impacting on family life. Following brief definitions of globalisation and family life, the chapter turns to a discussion of the central engines of globalisation, linking these to potential impacts on family life. The chapter concludes with policy implications and suggestions for future research.

Globalisation and Family Life

Before proceeding to an evaluation of the link between globalisation and family life, it is essential to clarify how the terms are being used in this chapter. Family and kinship systems organise individuals into groups and serve as an important safety net and source of distribution of resources. The family system maintains its equilibrium owing to the fact that each member fulfils a particular role, determined by institutional and cultural constraints (e.g. gender roles), negotiation within the family (e.g. division of

Contemporary Issues in Family Studies: Global Perspectives on Partnerships, Parenting and Support in a Changing World, First Edition. Edited by Angela Abela and Janet Walker.
© 2014 John Wiley & Sons, Ltd. Published 2014 by John Wiley & Sons, Ltd.

paid and unpaid work) and economic and biological constraints. When the term 'family' is used in this chapter, it refers to a system of interrelated individuals, most often biologically related. The family includes not only the immediate nuclear family, such as couples and their children, but also the broader social network of extended kin. For the purposes of this chapter, however, the focus will generally be on smaller family units and aspects related to partnership formation (dating, cohabitation, marriage, remaining single), partnership dissolution (including divorce, and widowhood), repartnering, fertility and parenting (i.e. entry into parenthood and having additional children) (see also Trask, 2010).

The term 'globalisation' refers to an inherently complex framework that represents a set of economic, political and cultural processes that change and operate simultaneously (Guillén, 2001; Held *et al.*, 1999; Raab *et al.*, 2008). Globalisation is often viewed as the intensification of worldwide social relations, where the local meets the global (Jameson and Miyoshi, 1998). The definition of globalisation used here is the one adopted by Mills and Blossfeld (2005) and takes into account four interrelated structural shifts, which are linked with domestic institutions (welfare regimes, employment, training and transnational production systems) and in turn impact on the individual life course and family life. This definition stems from the globalisation literature and captures the contemporary period of globalisation that has occurred since the late 1980s.

Four central changes fall under the heuristic of globalisation. These are listed in the box below.

Changes resulting from globalisation

1. Declining importance of national borders for all kinds of economic transactions.
2. Rising worldwide interconnectedness through the information and communication technology revolution.
3. Tougher tax competition between countries, accompanied by the deregulation, privatisation and liberalisation of domestic industries and markets.
4. Rising importance of and exposure to a world market that is increasingly volatile and prone to unpredictable disruptions.

A first key feature of globalisation is the internationalisation of markets and subsequent decline of national borders. This refers to a spate of recent changes in laws, institutions or practices that make various transactions in terms of commodities, labour, services and capital or movements such as migration easier or less expensive across national borders. Political agreements increasingly facilitate capital flows and liberalise financial markets (Fligstein, 1998), and also enable increased transnational migration across borders (Levitt and Jaworsky, 2007; Massey *et al.*, 1998; Sklair, 2001).

Globalisation can also be characterised by the intensification of competition, or the notion that capital and labour are increasingly mobile. The internationalisation and interconnectedness of financial and goods and service markets translate into increased exposure to international competition for national firms and economies. To enhance competitiveness, governments may enact what they envisage as successful liberal models and policy measures to remove or relax regulation of economic activities (deregulation), shift towards reliance on the price mechanism to coordinate economic activities (liberalisation), and transfer private ownership and control of assets or enterprises that were previously under public ownership (privatisation). Tax cuts, measures to keep inflation in check, even at the risk of increasing unemployment, strict control on organised labour, reduction of public expenditures and downsizing of government are all part of these neoliberal measures. These transformations copy the notions of efficiency, productivity and profitability, and often mean a push to adjust prices, products, technologies and human resources more rapidly and extensively (Montanari, 2001).

A third feature of globalisation is the diffusion and impact of information communication technologies (ICTs), which have evolved from microcomputers to the Internet, new satellite systems, fibre-optic cables and wireless systems (Castells, 2001). These changes have fundamentally impacted on the global networks of people, firms and financial markets. These new technologies not only accelerate the liberalisation of financial transactions, but also create the opportunity for the adoption and convergence of certain life-course behaviours by generating an instant common worldwide standard of comparison. Information communication technologies have fundamentally altered the scope, intensity, velocity and impact (Held *et al.*, 1999) of these transformations by, respectively, widening the reach of networks of social activity and power; enabling regularised connections; speeding up interactions and processes; and creating local contexts that impact upon the global context.

New technologies have also strengthened the economic interdependencies between markets and market participants and, as a result, a disturbance in one market segment or one country is likely to be transmitted more rapidly throughout the world economy than was evident in previous eras. This was readily apparent in the recent global financial crisis, which rapidly spread across many countries. Finally, the rise of global communication, and exchanges conducted via international discussion groups, Facebook, Internet matchmaking and other related technologies, mean that people are more easily able to see how others across the world shape their life course and family life.

A final aspect of globalisation is that the rapid changes within financial markets are becoming more dynamic and less predictable, which in turn heightens the level of uncertainty for individuals and families. First, the globalisation of markets endogenously intensifies competition between firms, forcing them to be innovative, to use new technological developments or to invent new products. This in turn increases the instability of markets (Streeck, 1987), a phenomenon which has become increasingly apparent in recent years. Second, modern information communication technologies and deregulation and liberalisation measures allow individuals, firms and governments to react faster to observed market changes and simultaneously accelerate market transactions (Castells, 1996). This makes long-term developments of globalising markets inherently harder to predict. Third, global prices in all kinds of markets tend to become more liable to fluctuations because worldwide supply, demand or both are becoming increasingly susceptible to random disruptions caused somewhere on the globe:

examples include the sub-prime mortgage crisis, problems in the financial sector which spread to other industries, major scientific discoveries, technical inventions, new consumer fashions, major political upsets such as wars and revolutions, and economic upsets. In other words, the increasing speed, dynamics and volatility of outcomes of globalising markets make it more difficult for individuals, firms and governments to predict the future and to make choices between different alternatives and strategies. This generates an environment of uncertainty in several places simultaneously.

The Impact of Globalisation on Family Life

Although there are undoubtedly more processes that could link globalisation and family life, the focus of this chapter is on four central aspects: first, family life and decision-making about the family in the era of uncertainty; second, the impact of new technologies, and especially ICTs, on family life; third, the impact of the fall of national borders and the growth of transnational families; and fourth, the impact on family life of changes in norms and values brought about by globalisation.

Family life in an era of uncertainty

The mechanisms underlying globalisation have generated an unprecedented level of structural uncertainty in modern societies and in family life. The promises inherent in globalisation, such as more competitive prices, more choice, greater freedom, higher living standards and increased prosperity (Edwards, 1998), are often accompanied by painful adjustments, especially in industrial societies. Salary cuts, lost jobs, redundancies, bankruptcies, severe economic crises and recessions have resulted in the perception that globalisation signals a volatile world full of uncertainty for individuals and their families. The volatile markets and deep economic recessions that began in 2007 re-emphasised the view that the neoliberal globalisation forces were unpredictable and out of control. This uncertainty in turn impacted on individuals and their families.

To understand how the large macro process of globalisation can influence individual family life, it is important to outline the potential mechanisms. The internationalisation of trade and liberalisation of financial transactions resulted in the recognition in most countries that economic openness is good for productivity growth (Edwards, 1998), and that the erection of barriers to prevent the spread of new knowledge and advanced technology would have highly adverse consequences. Not being a global player in the globalisation process was seen as severely limiting economic growth (Raab *et al.*, 2008). With the growth of supranational institutions such as the IMF and the EU, countries often felt coerced to move to lower labour market standards to become competitive, with the result that in low-income countries employees enjoy less protection, and have lower pay and poorer working conditions. This leads to increased labour market and economic uncertainty for families. This also means that the inequality between groups of workers often persists, owing to the widening gap between the wages of higher- and lower-educated workers in the industries that are more exposed to trade and international competition (Mills *et al.*, 2008).

The intensification of competition also had direct consequences for everyday life by impacting on individuals' employment careers and, therefore, family life. The major consequences are shown in the box below.

Key consequences for family life of the intensification of competition

1. Emulating neoliberal tactics often means deregulation of employment protection legislation. Less employment protection means fewer constraints against downsizing and lay-offs, and greater facility in introducing further labour market flexibility measures (Auer and Cazes, 2000).
2. Privatisation often results in changes from more to less protected public-sector jobs, given that the latter are further removed from the productivity and profitability of global competition (Standing, 1997). The result is that labour market 'outsiders' such as young people and new migrants, and also women, are increasingly vulnerable to labour market uncertainty. Recent riots across Europe attest to this growth in discontent, often related to labour market and economic uncertainty. The result is that these workers are concentrated in more precarious and lower-quality employment such as fixed-term contracts, part-time work and lower-status occupations; they are what can be termed the 'losers of globalisation' (Mills *et al.*, 2005).

When making vital life-course decisions that impact on family life, individuals face growing uncertainty, which particularly impacts on young adults, especially regarding their employment. This in turn affects the timing of partnership formation and entry into parenthood (Mills and Blossfeld, 2005). Globalisation has also had an impact on welfare regimes. The privatisation of companies has triggered the breakdown of labour unions or wage-setting agreements and other protective features that may previously have shielded employees and breadwinners within families. The current conditions of global economic uncertainty bring individual consequences such as unemployment, mortgage defaults, or the growth of temporary or fixed-term contracts.

It is also important to understand how uncertainty impacts on decision-making in family life. Owing to the process of globalisation, and the deluge of information, individuals now face three major areas of uncertainty when making decisions about family life (Mills and Blossfeld, 2005). First, there is rising uncertainty about the behavioural alternatives to family life. This becomes more important when individuals have to make choices among life-course and family life options that are already becoming progressively more blurred. For instance, owing to increased uncertainty at the national and global level it becomes more difficult for individuals to compare and rank the various options for educational, professional, family or partnership choices, simply because they know less and less about the options. The problem here is not only which option to choose but, increasingly, when to choose it.

Second, there is growing uncertainty about the probability of behavioural outcomes. This is especially acute when individuals are less and less able to reliably assign subjective probabilities to the various outcomes of their future courses of action. In the process of globalisation this uncertainty becomes particularly severe when a decision requires beliefs about choices to be made by other people (e.g. partner, employer) in the future. Third, there is increasing uncertainty about the amount of information that needs to be collected in order to make a particular decision. Collecting information is important, but also costly and time-consuming. With the accelerated spread of global networks and knowledge, the question of how much information someone should optimally collect before they are ready to form an opinion becomes more serious because the marginal costs and benefits of further information searches are increasingly unclear. One has therefore to assume that individuals—whether consciously or not—will set certain threshold limits, which, once satisfied, end the search for additional information.

A growing body of research has demonstrated that individuals postpone entry into long-term partnerships such as marriage and parenthood when they are in a more uncertain economic position or feel unable to make a long-term binding commitment (see e.g. Adserà, 2004; Kreyenfeld, 2010; Mills *et al.*, 2005). Research has highlighted two main consequences of such uncertainty, shown in the box below.

The consequences for family life in an era of uncertainty

1.   High unemployment and unstable contracts influence the timing of women having children and their opportunities for doing so. Adserà (2004), in an examination of 23 OECD countries, demonstrated how high unemployment and unstable contracts depressed fertility. This was particularly the case for young women in southern European countries such as Spain and Italy. In these countries, early skills acquisition was essential for becoming established in the labour market, resulting in many young women either postponing or abandoning childbearing.
2.   Uncertain labour market positions result in postponements in entering into partnerships and having children, with individuals sheltered in certain countries by a strong safety net. Mills *et al.* (2005), in a 14-country comparison, concluded that when young people were in an uncertain labour market position, such as having a temporary work contract, or were experiencing job instability or unemployment, they were significantly more likely to postpone starting a family. The impact of economic uncertainty on postponement was also influenced by whether there was a strong social safety net to cushion individuals from economic uncertainty. In countries with a strong safety net, such as Sweden and Norway, the effects of economic uncertainty on first birth postponement were considerably weaker.

It may be that, particularly for women, starting a family represents a strategy to reduce uncertainty. Individuals in precarious situations or lower-quality jobs may have few prospects for career advancement. They therefore opt to become parents not only to reduce insecurity, but also as a way of giving meaning and structure to their lives. Uncertainty reduction theory (Friedman *et al.*, 1994) suggests that being married and having children can serve as a strategy to reduce uncertainty, particularly among those who have limited ways of reducing uncertainty. According to this theory, while a stable and successful career is an important source of certainty for some and lowers their likelihood of forming a family, those with marginal career prospects opt for certainty by having children, a strategy that may be particularly relevant for women whose partners are considered to be the primary breadwinners.

Family life and new technology

A second impact of globalisation on family life is related to the growth of new technologies such as ICTs. This topic is considered in more depth in Chapter 18.

New technologies, and specifically ICTs, the Internet and mobile and social networking possibilities, have transformed communication in family life. Developments such as Skype, Facebook, MySpace, YouTube and related sites have broadened the scope, intensity and speed of communication between individuals and family members (Lange, 2007). Recent research has demonstrated that many users are active on social networking sites and that this type of communication is integrated into their daily lives, often through specific routines and rituals (Debatin *et al.*, 2009). Furthermore, most users upload large amounts of detailed personal information that can aid them in keeping in contact with other family members.

Johnson *et al.* (2008) found that email was an effective means of maintaining strong interpersonal relationships with family members and romantic partners across large geographic distances. In a study of the email exchanges of college students, they found that students often disclosed personal information and discussed their own social networks in order to remain close to friends and family members. In communications with romantic partners, the content of communication was not related to updating information, but rather to giving assurances about the relationship and engaging in open and positive communication. Low-cost communication options such as Skype and Facebook and similar social networking sites probably have similar characteristics.

Advances in technology mean that individuals cannot only extend their personal networks and maintain contact with geographically distant family members or romantic partners (Mahler, 2001; Parreñas, 2005; Smith, 2011), but also easily observe the family patterns of others and engage in broader social comparison beyond their own geographical context. They are able to monitor and become exposed to alternative family behaviours and systems in other global social settings, including non-marital cohabitation, gay and lesbian relationships and/or marriage, distance parenting, or living apart together (LAT) relationships, that may be less common in their own cultural or social setting. Furthermore, they are able to maintain highly personal and intense relationships with other family members at different locations in the world. The ability to communicate in an easy and affordable manner may also be related to the emergence of LAT relationships, where individuals are in a romantic relationship but do not live in the same city (Levin, 2004). This new kind of relationship is explored in Chapter 3.

People who find a partner via an online dating site are selective in the sense that they have high levels of computer literacy (Sautter *et al.*, 2010). This vehicle for partnership matching has grown in the last decade to the extent that online dating has become a widely accepted and highly utilised channel for finding a partner (Fiore *et al.*, 2010; Hitsch *et al.*, 2010; Skopek *et al.*, 2011). In a recent study of couples who formed a relationship in the USA in 2009, the Internet was the third most common way to meet a partner (Rosenfeld and Thomas, 2010). The growth in Internet dating is not only related to new technologies, but also to other transformations brought about by globalisation in the area of work and family life and the way people interrelate in developed Western societies (Barraket and Henry-Waring, 2008). Individuals not only devote more time to their professional lives, but also migrate more often for their work, leaving the traditional matchmakers of family and friends behind. As a consequence, people increasingly have to resort to other, more time-efficient means to find a partner. Online dating websites present such an alternative, offering highly systemised interfaces for browsing and getting in contact with prospective partners.

Family life, geographical mobility and transnational migration

A third key consequence of globalisation for family life is the weakening of constraints related to geographical mobility and migration. One outcome of internationalisation and the decline of national borders is the increase in transnational migration. Even though the political and cultural salience of nation-state boundaries remains relevant, family and social life increasingly takes place across borders (Levitt and Jaworsky, 2007).

Globalisation and the opening of borders (such as within the EU) facilitates not only a more rapid movement and migration of individuals, but also the direction of migration flows. Transnational mobility also has consequences for culturally based kinship systems, which diffuse and evolve when members migrate (Smith, 2011). Aspects of migration are examined in more depth in Chapter 19 (this volume).

Migration patterns related to larger-scale processes such as globalisation have occurred in several stages (Recchi and Nebe, 2003). Although they vary widely by nation or region, early migration patterns mainly involved single (male) workers who migrated to take a job. This included, for example, the unskilled 'guest workers', largely from the Mediterranean countries in Europe, who migrated to more wealthy northern European countries between 1950 and 1970. A second phase can be referred to as the 'family migration' period, where workers in a particular country often took their family with them. Since the 1980s, more mixed migration patterns have emerged, involving a heterogeneous group of individuals who migrate for multiple reasons (Recchi and Nebe, 2003; Vandenbrande *et al.*, 2006) as well as a surge in female migrants (Donato *et al.*, 2006). The nature of transnational migration varies by region and country. Vandenbrande *et al.* (2006), for example, engaged in a descriptive empirical study of geographic and labour market mobility in Europe. They concluded that Europeans are 'stayers' who do not often move across large geographic distances. In fact, only 18 per cent of Europeans had ever left their own region (within their home country) and only 7 per cent had ever moved to another country (Vandenbrande *et al.*, 2006, p. 14).

Another body of research has examined the intergenerational transmission of transnational families (Levitt and Waters, 2002; Smith, 2003). In some of these families, living in different countries across several generations has become the norm. Pries (2004) found that the need to connect with transnational family members was highly dependent on the life-course stage of individuals. Those who considered marriage, or having a baby, reconnected with people in their homeland, either in search of a partner or to reinforce cultural values and norms that they could pass on to their children.

Research has also shed light on the lives of transnational mothers and the problems that this migration may bring for both parents and children (Hondagneu-Sotelo and Avila, 1997). This relates to the more recent surge in the number of female migrants, or what has been termed the 'feminisation of migration' (Donato *et al.*, 2006). Changes in affordable and advanced Internet communication allow transnational parents to work abroad while still remaining actively involved in their children's daily lives (Mahler 2001; Parreñas 2005).

Family life and the change in values

The changes brought about by globalisation have also impacted on values and norms related to family life. Since the late 1960s, particularly in Western societies, there has been a weakening of the traditional forms of the family as an institution. Instead, as we have seen earlier in this volume (Chapters 2, 4, 9, 10), there have been increases in rates of non-marital cohabitation and divorce and a decrease in rates of fertility, increased acceptance of children born outside marriage, and a growing acceptance of and desire for voluntary childlessness. These changes link with broader cultural changes, such as the rise of individualisation, secularisation and the growth of the welfare state, and technological changes including modern contraception and assisted reproductive techniques.

In the literature, two approaches are often used to understand the changes in family life. The first is the Second Demographic Transition (SDT) framework, introduced in the mid-1980s (Lesthaeghe and van de Kaa, 1986; van de Kaa, 1987), and the second is the globalisation approach, introduced a decade later (for a review, see Guillén, 2001). Both of these can be considered as large-scale heuristic frameworks or narratives to define large ideational, cultural and economic changes in many Western societies. They are often used in parallel, or as separate or different ways of describing change in family life. However, the driving forces defined previously in relation to globalisation present many similarities with the concept of the SDT introduced by Lesthaeghe and van de Kaa (1986) and further developed by van de Kaa (1987) and Lesthaeghe (1995). The concept of the SDT was developed in order to describe changes in partnership behaviour, fertility and family formation taking place since the late 1960s in northern and Western Europe. The SDT framework has a strong focus on ideological and value changes in relation to family changes, whereas the globalisation literature has primarily focused more on institutional changes in welfare regimes, education, employment, family and gender systems. The SDT framework is characterised by a number of core features, described in the box below.

Core features of the Second Demographic Transition

1. A focus on ideational and cultural change, where family decisions are conditioned not only by economic factors, but also by the emergence of self-fulfilment, choice, personal development and emancipation in making these choices. These include factors such as personal development, but also having children as an expression and extension of one's self.
2. The contraceptive revolution.
3. The changing role and position of children.
4. Changes in living arrangements and partnership formation.

Although the globalisation literature touches upon value changes and family life, the discussion has generally centred more on broader institutional changes and the increased uncertainty and instability that these bring. In this sense, the globalisation literature offers an alternative mechanism or explanation beyond the broader value changes in relation to family life described by the SDT. Changes in values are obviously related to changes in institutional policies and regulations, but the arguments between the SDT and globalisation remain quite distinct in this respect. Mills and Blossfeld (2005) outline the theoretical relationship between the growth of uncertainty in relation to employment and temporal uncertainty with respect to family life, arguing that increased uncertainty reduces the ability of individuals to enter into long-term binding commitments such as partnerships and parenthood. This is related to the rising uncertainties described earlier in this chapter.

The emergence of new technologies, particularly the contraceptive revolution, effectively severed the link between sexuality and procreation. The contraceptive revolution is a central pillar of the SDT explanation, but was later also taken up in the globalisation literature under the auspices of 'new technologies'. The use of effective contraception in many industrialised societies has become so standard that many individuals today would find it hard to imagine being unable to engage in virtually perfect contraception and control of parenthood. Contraception not only affords more power to couples and, particularly, women, but allows postponement of parenthood. This postponement, however, has resulted in a rise in the number of older parents, the rise of involuntary childlessness, and a rise in the use of new reproductive technologies and assisted reproduction (Mills et al., 2011).

The changing role and position of children in influencing changing patterns in family formation is a third key feature of the SDT, which has received considerably less attention within the globalisation literature. In contrast to parents' need for their children to provide them with economic support and labour, the subsequent decline in the birth rate in the late eighteenth century was related to the child becoming a locus of emotional and financial investment—the 'child-king'. This refers to the situation in which parents have lower fertility in order to focus on a more limited number of children, so as to provide them with more attention and resources (Ariès, 1980). Increasingly, since the early mid-1900s in many Western societies, the child has occupied a less central place in couples' lives. Children emerged as an addition which had to be carefully planned and which might influence the partnership, lifestyle and economic wellbeing of parents. Consequently, the transition to parenthood increasingly emerged as an extended expression of individualism and self-expression. Although discussed less frequently in the globalisation literature, within the era of globalisation the role of children has also evolved in several ways.

Changes in communications and technology allow individuals to compare lifestyles and see alternative life courses with or without children. Globalisation also means that regulations have the potential to become more standardised, including stricter international regulations regarding child labour and transnational adoption.

Finally, changes in living arrangements and partnership formation are another important element that has transformed family life, particularly the rise of cohabitation. While attitudes in many Western countries towards unmarried cohabitation are often favourable, in other Western countries actual levels of cohabitation remain low, with cohabitation still often viewed as a 'trial marriage' (Heuveline and Timberlake, 2004). More tolerant attitudes to extramarital childbearing have also meant that pathways to adulthood and family systems have increasingly changed. In this sense, although the nuclear family system (two parents with children) remains a central model in most countries, the forms families take are increasingly diffuse.

Future Research and Policy Directives

This review of the impact of globalisation on family life raises several key issues and points to directions for both future research and policy initiatives. First, it remains difficult to study empirically the impact of the large-scale macro-level processes of globalisation on family life. Other factors beyond globalisation are also driving changes in family life, yet globalisation remains a useful heuristic to capture many of these changes.

Second, the growth of ICTs and the resultant possibilities for families to live and communicate in a transnational manner beyond the household is a reality that both policymakers and researchers need to consider. Family policies, tax regulations and other relevant institutional rules and regulations often implicitly assume that nuclear family members live together in one household or country. The fall of national borders and growth in the numbers of labour migrants and in varieties of family forms challenge some of these basic premises.

There is a need to focus on the impact of virtual communication on family life. Family members increasingly communicate via electronic means. How has the growth of virtual communication and detailed sharing of personal information among family members online altered family relations? It may be that, owing to increased mobility, these types of online platforms will offer a new way of building cohesion between family members that might otherwise have waned. Alternatively, virtual communication may increasingly replace physical meetings and represents a fundamentally different type of interaction. It is unclear how this impacts on family life, and thus, future policy directives and research in this area would be welcome.

Family life and decisions surrounding the life course have been fundamentally altered by globalisation, since decision-making increasingly occurs under highly uncertain conditions. The (often neoliberal) measures brought about by globalisation pressures in many industrialised countries have resulted in the rise of precarious employment, which seeps into the everyday family lives of individuals. The result may be postponement of family-related decisions owing to uncertainty, avoidance of long-term committed relationships, or the adoption of a safe or traditional family role as a means of reducing uncertainty. Globalisation has brought about a fundamental shift in the way families live their lives.

References

Adserà, A. (2004) Changing fertility rates in developed countries. The impact of labor market institutions, *Journal of Population Economics*, 17: 17–43.

Alderson, A. S. and Nielsen, F. (2002) Globalisation and the great u-turn: income inequality trends in 16 OECD countries, *American Journal of Sociology*, 107: 1244–1299.

Ariès, P. (1980) Two successive motivations for the declining birth rate in the West, *Population and Development Review*, 6: 645–650.

Auer, P. and Cazes, S. (2000) The resilience of the long-term employment relationship: evidence from the industrialised countries, *International Labour Review*, 139(4): 379–408.

Barraket, J. and Henry-Waring, M. S. (2008) Getting it [on]line: sociological implications of e-dating, *Journal of Sociology*, 44(2): 149–165.

Castells, M. (1996) *The Rise of the Network Society: The information age: economy, society and culture*, Vol. 1 (Oxford: Blackwell).

Castells, M. (2001) *The Internet Galaxy* (Oxford: Oxford University Press).

Debatin, B., Lovejoy, J. P. Horn, A.-K. and Hughes, B. N. (2009) Facebook and online privacy: attitudes, behaviors, and unintended consequences, *Journal of Computer-Mediated Communication*, 15(1): 83–108.

Donato, K. M., Gabaccia, D., Holdaway, J., Manalansan, M. and Pessar, P. R. (2006) A glass half full? Gender in migration studies, *International Migration Review*, 40: 3–26.

Edwards, S. (1998) Openness, productivity and growth: what do we really know?, *Economic Journal*, 108: 383–398.

Fiore, A. T., Taylor, L. S., Zhong, X., Mendelsohn, G. A. and Cheshire, C. (2010) Who's right and who writes: people, profiles, contacts, and replies in online dating, in *Proceedings of Hawaii International Conference on System Sciences*, 43: 1–10.

Fligstein, N. (1998) Is globalisation the cause of the crises of welfare states?, European University Institute Working Paper SPS No. 98/5, San Domenico, Italy.

Friedman, D., Hechter, M. and Kanazawa, S. (1994) A theory of the value of children, *Demography*, 31(3): 375–401.

Guillén, M. (2001) Is globalisation civilising, destructive or feeble? A critique of five key debates in the social science literature, *Annual Review of Sociology*, 27: 235–260.

Held, D., McGrew, A., Goldblatt, D. and Perraton, J. (eds) (1999) *Global Transformations* (Stanford, CA: Stanford University Press).

Heuveline, P. and Timberlake, J. M. (2004) The role of cohabitation in family formation: the United States in comparative perspective, *Journal of Marriage and Family*, 66: 1214–1230.

Hitsch, G. J., Hortaçsu, A. and Ariely, D. (2010) Matching and sorting in online dating, *American Economic Review*, 100(1): 130–163.

Hondagneu-Sotelo, P. and Avila, E. (1997) 'I'm here but I'm there': the meanings of Latina transnational motherhood, *Gender and Society*, 11: 548.

Jameson, F. and Miyoshi, M. (eds) (1998) *The Cultures of Globalisation* (Durham, NC: Duke University Press).

Johnson, A. J., Haigh, M. M., Becker, J. A. H., Craig, E. A. and Wigley, S. (2008) College students' use of relational management strategies in email in long-distance and geographically close relationships, *Journal of Computer-Mediated Communication*, 13(2): 381–404.

Kreyenfeld, M. (2010) Uncertainties in female employment careers and the postponement of parenthood in Germany, *European Sociological Review*, 26: 51–366.

Lange, P. (2007) Publicly private and privately public: social networking on YouTube, *Journal of Computer-Mediated Communication*, 13(1): 361–380.

Lesthaeghe, R. (1995) The second demographic transition in Western countries: an interpretation, in K. O. Mason and A.-M. Jensen (eds), *Gender and Family Change in Industrialised Countries* (Oxford: The Clarendon Press), 17–62.

Lesthaeghe, R. and van de Kaa, D. J. (1986) Twee demografische transities?, in D. J. van de Kaa and R. Lesthaeghe (eds), *Bevolking: groei en krimp* (Deventer: Van Loghum Slaterus), 9–24.

Levin, I. (2004) Living apart together: a new family form, *Current Sociology*, 52(2): 223–240.

Levitt, P. and Jaworsky, B. N. (2007) Transnational migration studies: past developments and future trends, *Annual Review of Sociology*, 33: 129–156.

Levitt, P. and Waters, M. C. (eds) (2002) *The Changing Face of Home: The transnational lives of the second generation* (New York: Russell Sage Foundation).

Mahler, S. J. (2001) Transnational relationships: the struggle to communicate across borders, *Identities*, 7: 583–619.

Massey, D. S., Arango, J., Hugo, G., Kouaouci, A., Pellegrino, A. and Taylor, J. E. (1998) *Worlds in Motion: Understanding international migration at the end of the millennium* (Oxford: The Clarendon Press).

Mills, M. and Blossfeld, H.-P. (2005) Globalisation, uncertainty and the early life course: a theoretical framework, in H.-P. Blossfeld, E. Klijzing, M. Mills and K. Kurz (eds), *Globalisation, Uncertainty and Youth in Society* (London: Routledge), 1–24.

Mills, M., Blossfeld, H.-P., Buchholz, S., Hofäcker, D., Bernardi, F. and Hofmeister, H. (2008) Converging divergences? An international comparison of the impact of globalisation on industrial relations and employment careers, *International Sociology*, 23(4): 561–595.

Mills, M., Blossfeld, H.-P. and Klijzing, E. (2005) Becoming an adult in uncertain times: a 14-country comparison of the losers of globalisation, in H.-P. Blossfeld, E. Klijzing, M. Mills and K. Kurz (eds), *Globalisation, Uncertainty and Youth in Society* (London: Routledge), 393–411.

Mills, M., Rindfuss, R. R., McDonald, P. and te Velde, E. (2011) Why do people postpone parenthood?

Reasons and social policy incentives, *Human Reproduction Update*. DOI: 10.1093/humupd/dmr026

Montanari, I. (2001) Modernisation, globalisation and the welfare state: a comparative analysis of old and new convergence of social insurance since 1930, *British Journal of Sociology*, 52(3): 469–494.

Parreñas, R. S. (2005) Long distance intimacy: class, gender and intergenerational relations between mothers and children in Filipino transnational families, *Global Networks*, 5: 317–336.

Pries, L. (2004) Determining the causes and durability of transnational labour migration between Mexico and the United States: some empirical findings, *International Migration*, 42: 3–39.

Raab, M. et al. (2008) GlobalIndex—a sociological approach to globalization measurement, *International Sociology*, 24(4): 596–631.

Recchi, E. and Nebe, T. M. (2003) Intra-EU migration: a socio-demographic overview. State-of-the-art report. PIONEUR working paper no. 3.

Rosenfeld, M. and Thomas, R. J. (2010) Meeting online: the rise of the Internet as a social intermediary, paper presented at the Population Association of America conference, Dallas, TX. http://www.iga.ucdavis.edu/Research/EJS/Rosenfeld%20paper.pdf [Accessed 13.7.2012.]

Sautter, J. M., Tippett, R. M. and Philip Morgan, S. (2010) The social demography of internet dating in the United States, *Social Science Quarterly*, 91(2): 554–575.

Sklair, L. (2001) *The Transnational Capitalist Class* (Oxford: Blackwell).

Skopek, J., Schulz, F. and Blossfeld, H.-P. (2011) Who contacts whom? Educational homophily in online mate selection, *European Sociological Review*, 27(2): 180–195. DOI: 10.1093/esr/jcp068.

Smith, M. P. (2003) Transnationalism, the state, and the extraterritorial citizen, *Politics and Society*, 31: 467–502.

Smith, D. P. (2011) Geographies of long-distance family migration, *Progress in Human Geography*, 35(5): 652–668.

Standing, G. (1997) Globalisation, labor flexibility and insecurity: the era of market regulation, *European Journal of Industrial Relations*, 1: 7–37.

Streeck, A. (1987) The uncertainties of management in the management of uncertainties: employees, labor relations and industrial adjustment in the 1980s, *Work, Employment and Society*, 1: 281–308.

Trask, B. (2010) *Globalisation and Families* (London: Springer).

Van de Kaa, D. J. (1987) Europe's second demographic transition, *Population Bulletin*, 42: 3–24.

Vandenbrande, T. et al. (2006) *Mobility in Europe: Analysis of the 2005 Eurobarometer survey on geographic and labour market mobility* (Luxembourg: European Foundation for the Improvement of Living and Working Conditions).

18

The Internet and Its Implications for Children, Parents and Family Relationships[1]

Monica T. Whitty

Introduction

The Internet has been around for over forty years. It has taken some time, however, to move into the homes of the majority of people in the Western world and be appropriated for social purposes. Now that it is a normal part of many people's everyday lives we need to consider the advantages and problems it brings. This chapter focuses on the implications the Internet has for children, parents and family relationships. It does so by first considering the history of the Internet and providing a brief summary of some of the existing online spaces. The argument made here is that the Internet can be both liberating and debilitating. Nevertheless, given the many advantages it affords we cannot simply block it from our own and our children's lives. The dark side of the Internet needs to be acknowledged in order for us to deal with it. This chapter considers some of the dark aspects of the Internet, including its use for crime and its potential addictive qualities. It also challenges the misconception that the Internet is a more deceptive space than any other—in fact, research indicates that more spontaneous lies are told over the telephone.

In Western countries, most children and teenagers have access to the Internet, and preventing this access could have serious educational drawbacks. Children need to be encouraged to use the Internet for informational and educational purposes. The risks that children and teenagers face online, for example, cyber-bullying, paedophilia, sexting and fraud, are also highlighted in this chapter. Finally, protective factors are considered. The ideal way to protect is to monitor, and the problems of doing so are also highlighted.

[1]   The research undertaken by the author discussed in this chapter was funded by two ESRC grants.

Contemporary Issues in Family Studies: Global Perspectives on Partnerships, Parenting and Support in a Changing World, First Edition. Edited by Angela Abela and Janet Walker.
© 2014 John Wiley & Sons, Ltd. Published 2014 by John Wiley & Sons, Ltd.

A Brief History of the Internet

The Internet has become an important vehicle for communication across the globe since the late twentieth century. Internet usage worldwide continues to grow: recently, it has been reported that 11 per cent of Africans, 24 per cent of Asians, 58 per cent of Europeans, 78 per cent of North Americans and 60 per cent of Australians have access to the Internet (Internet World Stats, 2011). In its original form, the Internet looked very different from how it looks today. Rather than being a space where people could engage in social networking, date, or surf the Web, it was intended to be a tool via which data could be moved around more easily.

The US Defense Department was responsible for the birth of the Internet (Whitty and Carr, 2006). In the 1960s, it built a system where its workers could share data. It called this system the Arpanet. Ironically, the intention was to link computers rather than people. The individuals using the system quickly reshaped it to meet their personal needs. The first Arpanet email was sent in 1971 and by the late 1970s email had become a standardised working system. The original Arpanet was gradually transformed into what we know as the Internet. By about 1985, the Internet was well established as a technology that supported a broad community, including those involved in research and development. Electronic mails (though not in the form we know them today) were being used to send messages across several communities, often with different systems. The World Wide Web was developed in the early 1990s and the commercial release of web browsers started in 1993.

Tim Berners-Lee, a graduate of Queen's College, Oxford University, is credited with the development of the very first web browser in 1990. Most people would also credit him with having helped the Web to grow. He was successful in persuading the large research organisation he was working for (CERN) to provide, on 30 April 1993, a certification that stated that web technology and programme codes were in the public domain. This allowed anyone to use and improve them. Since then, people have improved on the technology, and they continue to do so. The first of the public web browsers, MOSAIC, was released in 1993, the first version of Netscape was released in 1994, and the first version of Internet Explorer was released in 1995.

Although the Internet was not originally developed with the intention of linking people, people began to embrace the technology as a means of communication, as well as a means of initiating and developing relationships. The Internet, however, should not be understood as one generic space: it is a number of different spaces, which have continued to develop and evolve. Examples of early and contemporary Internet spaces are given in the boxes below.

Examples of early Internet spaces

1. *Bulletin board systems.* Bulletin board systems (BBs) were an especially popular space in the early days of the Internet and many of them were quite sexual in nature. They were a precursor to the World Wide Web but they looked very different from spaces currently available on the Internet. BBs

were typically single-line systems, which meant that only one user could be online at a time. Individuals could only communicate using text. Even in the early days, BBs were social spaces where people met, had discussions, published articles, downloaded software, and even managed to play games. A system's operator would sometimes censor the messages on these sites, but in the main they were fairly liberal.

2. *MUDs/MOOs.* MUDs (Multiple-user dungeons, more commonly understood these days to mean multi-user dimensions or domains) and MOOs (MUDs, object-oriented) were text-based online virtual systems in which multiple users were connected at one time. These were spaces where interactive role-playing games could be played, very similar to Dungeons and Dragons. MUDs and MOOs represented a form of synchronous communication. Participants took on a chosen character and communicated with other characters online.

3. *Chat rooms.* Chat rooms involve synchronous or 'near synchronous' communication (Whitty *et al.*, 2012). Most chat rooms have a particular theme, although this is not necessary. When a user enters a chat room he or she can type a message that will be visible to all other individuals. Hundreds of people can be in the same virtual room at the same time, typing messages to the group. Chat rooms are similar to Instant Messenger except that they can involve more than two people. Sometimes these rooms are moderated. Chat rooms were very popular in the early days of the Internet and were limited to text only. More recently, individuals have often represented themselves with an avatar. Moreover, individuals file-share photographs and videos and use webcams.

4. *Discussion boards/Usenet newsgroups.* A discussion group or Usenet newsgroup is a continuous public discussion about a particular topic. This is a form of asynchronous communication. Sometimes these groups are moderated. These groups were very popular in the early days of the Internet. They still exist today and the discussion is often in text-based form only, although pictures and video can also be posted on the sites.

Contemporary online spaces

1. *Instant Messenger.* This is a 'near synchronous' communication between two or more users over communication networks (Whitty *et al.*, 2012). Individuals can have private conversations or group discussions. The instant messaging system usually alerts users when someone on their private list is online.

2. *MMORPGs.* MMORPGs (massively multiplayer online role playing games) have now taken over from MUDs and MOOs (see previous box). In MMORPGs, players take on the role of a fictional character, typically in a fantasy world, and have agency over many of their characters' actions. MMORPGs differ from MUDS and MOOS in that they are not text-based only, but instead have sophisticated graphics. In addition to playing the game, individuals can still write text to one another and be social in these spaces. The worlds created in these games continue to evolve even when the player is

absent from the game—examples include EverQuest, World of Warcraft, Final Fantasy XI and Warhammer. The popularity of these games continues to grow. More recently, with some MMORPGs the nature of the interaction has become more 'adult'-oriented. Age of Conan, Warhammer, 2 Moons, and Requiem: Bloodymare, for example, provide increased opportunities for extreme violence and more graphic depictions of violent outcomes.

A popular MMORPG developed for children aged 6–14 is called Club Penguin, where players use cartoon penguin avatars. This space has been set up with the intention of keeping children safe, encouraging parents to be involved.

3. *Social networking sites.* Boyd and Ellison (2007) define social networking sites as 'web-based services that allow individuals to (1) construct a public or semi-public profile within a bounded system, (2) articulate a list of other users with whom they share a connection, and (3) view and traverse their list of connections and those made by others within the system. The nature and nomenclature of these connections may vary from site to site.' Friendster, which emerged in 2002, was one of the first mainstream social networking sites. This was followed by MySpace and LinkedIn. Facebook was launched in 2004 and is currently the largest social networking site in the world.

A more recent popular social networking site is Twitter. Twitter is a micro-blogging service in that it limits posts to 140 characters, known as tweets.

4. *Weblog/blog.* A blog is essentially a personal journal or diary that is placed online. Individuals regularly update their blogs. Individuals who keep a blog are known as bloggers, and they are motivated to keep their journals for a number of reasons: sometimes to gain notoriety, sometimes for personal reasons (e.g. to keep friends up to date), and sometimes for professional reasons (e.g. journalistic purposes).

5. *Online dating sites.* Online dating sites, in a fairly primitive form relative to how we know them today, started appearing in the 1980s. In the early days, online dating was stigmatised and researchers found that shyer people were gravitating towards these sites to find a mate (Scharlott and Christ, 1995). In the 1980s these sites were largely text-based, with limited space for individuals to create a dating profile and make it attractive. Currently, many online dating sites attempt to match users effectively. These sites are con-tinuing to work on refining tools to match the most suitable people together. Online daters are often expected to complete personality tests, as well as surveys about their interests and what they are looking for in a partner. From these, matches are made and often given compatibility ratings. Other sites allow clients to find their own matches, working through a sea of profiles to make their choices. In addition to the generic online dating sites that exist, such as e-Harmony, True.com and Match.com, there are also more specialised online dating sites, which gather like-minded individuals together. For example, there are sites designed specifically for Christians, Jews, vegans, Goths, or people describing themselves as 'spiritual'. Sites like these are similar to social groups one might join in the hope of finding another person who shares the same values or interests (Whitty, 2008a). Moreover, they potentially cut out some of the work involved in the search for the perfect other (Whitty, 2007a).

Is the Internet Liberating or Debilitating?

Ever since the Internet began, researchers have questioned its utility in developing and maintaining psychologically healthy (romantic) relationships. As has previously been argued:

> When we consider how beneficial it is to form relationships online we also need to consider individuals' characteristics (e.g. personality characteristics and physical attractiveness), the amount of time people spend online, the duration of online relationships, and how these relationships affect individuals' offline activities and relationships. (Whitty, 2008b, p. 1837)

Online relationships can be empowering for many people. That is, cyberspace provides a unique and potentially safe environment in which people can experience and learn about identity, relationships and sexuality. There are, however, concerns of which adults and children need to be aware.

Concerns about Internet usage

Before considering children's use of the Internet, this chapter considers some of the overall concerns about individuals' Internet usage. These concerns include excessive use, crime, and deception.

Excessive use

Excessive use of the Internet is arguably unhealthy (Cooper *et al.*, 2000; Daneback *et al.*, 2006; Griffiths, 1999, 2000; Young, 1998, 1999). Griffiths (1999, 2000) and Young (1998, 1999) have written extensively on the topic of Internet addiction, claiming that some people can be addicted to many activities online, including gambling, playing games, online sex and forming relationships on the Net. Other researchers have found support for their claims. In a revealing study, Schneider (2000) found that cybersex addiction was a major contributing factor to separation and divorce. Moreover, this study found that around half the practitioners of cybersex (52%) had lost interest in relational sex. Importantly, however, Griffiths has pointed out that many excessive Internet users are not necessarily Internet addicts. In many instances, gambling addicts, sex addicts, etc. are simply using the Internet as a place in which to engage in their addictive behaviours. Hence, we cannot blame all these people's addictions on the Internet.

Crime

The Internet can be used for a multitude of crimes, including cyber-stalking, fraud, identity theft, cyber-terrorism, drug trafficking and so forth. An in-depth discussion of these crimes is beyond the scope of this chapter, but two examples are given below.

There are numerous recorded cases that describe how individuals have used the Internet to stalk others and organisations. Perpetrators of online harassment and stalking include strangers, people who are or were close to one another, and work colleagues. Whitty (2007b) has argued that the online environment could produce a greater number of stalkers and harassers than exist offline. One of the reasons for this is that, given the absence of social cues on the Internet, people are given less feedback as to whether their behaviours are deemed appropriate or not, and so people act out certain behaviours more than in an offline setting where they witness immediate feedback. Moreover, people can often be located more easily online.

In 2011, the UK National Fraud Authority estimated that the costs of fraud in the UK exceed £38 billion a year. In 2006, the UK Office of Fair Trading predicted that UK consumers lose approximately £3.5 billion to scams each year, the average amount lost per scam being £850. The same report found that 48 per cent of the UK adult population (23.5 million people) had been targeted by a scammer and that 8 per cent admitted to having been a victim of a scam. On the basis of their findings, the authors estimated that 6.5 per cent of the UK adult population will fall victim to scams every year. Fraud not only has devastating financial costs, but can also have severe psychological effects, such as causing shame and depression (Whitty and Buchanan, 2012).

Deception

There has been much uncertainty about the Internet being a trustworthy space (Whitty and Joinson, 2009). Given this uncertainty, researchers have been interested in whether individuals lie more on the Internet than in more traditional settings. In contrast to what many theorists believed, Hancock *et al.* (2004), employing a diary study, found that the incidences of deceitful communications is greatest in synchronous, non-recorded media (e.g. the telephone), and least prevalent in recorded, asynchronous media (e.g. email). This suggests, first, that the majority of lies tend to occur in an unplanned, spontaneous manner and, second, that when engaged in deceitful communication people pay as much attention to the likelihood of a record being kept as to the absence of visual or verbal cues. Whitty *et al.* (2012) have found similar results, having added more modes of communication and having considered both planned and spontaneous lies. In cases where the lie was spontaneous similar findings were obtained. However, planned lies were more likely to be told via SMS. These studies go some way to debunking the myth that the Internet is a deceitful, untrustworthy space.

Children's and Adolescents' Internet Usage

Internet use can, of course, be highly beneficial, especially when it comes to educating young people. A key focus of this chapter is children's and adolescents' use of the Internet and the types of concerns parents might have regarding their children. In order to comprehend the concerns parents should have fully, it is important first to map out the terrain of young people's Internet usage. In 2011, the Oxford Internet Survey reported that in that year, as in previous years, young people used the Internet more than older people (Dutton and Blank, 2011). It found that almost all 14- to 17-year-olds used the Internet.

Young people's use of the Internet in the UK

Livingstone (2006) found that:

- 98% of children and young people had used the Internet
- 75% of 9- to 19-year-olds had accessed the Internet from a computer at home
- 92% of 9- to 19-year-olds had accessed the Internet from a computer at school
- 36% of children and young people lived in homes with more than one computer
- 24% of children and young people lived in a house with broadband access
- 19% of children and young people had Internet access in their bedroom

Childwise (2010) reports that 90 per cent of UK children use the Internet, the average child doing so more than five times a week and spending two hours a day on the Internet.

Young people's use of the Internet in the USA

The Pew Internet trend data (2009) showed that:

- 88% of 12- to 13-year-olds used the Internet
- 95% of 14- to 17-year-olds accessed the Internet
- 73% of teen Internet users used a social networking site
- 52% of young people used the Internet to get views or information
- 48% of young people used the Internet to shop
- 38% of young people used the Internet to share stories, photos or videos
- 31% of young people looked for health information online and 17% used the Internet to access information about health issues such as drug use and sexual health
- 14% of young people had created a blog

The Digital Divide

Researchers have suggested that, despite the rapid take-up of the Internet by young people, there are inequalities in children and young people's access to the Internet. Livingstone and Helsper (2007) found that boys, older children and middle-class children all benefit from more frequent and better-quality Internet usage than that enjoyed by girls, younger children and working-class children. Similarly, researchers found that, in an American sample, African-American children from lower-income households and children whose parents had a high-school diploma or less were less likely to use a computer at home than white children and children from higher-income families (Brodie *et al.*, 2000). Wei and Hindman (2011) point out that the concern about the digital divide ought now not to be about access or the amount of time individuals use the Internet, but rather about how they use it. They found that children from higher socio-economic groups are more likely to use the Internet for informational purposes than those from lower socio-economic groups.

There are mixed opinions as to whether children ought to be online, and parents are often concerned about what their children are doing. This is partly to do with the divide between parents' and children's knowledges of the Internet and partly to do with perceptions about young people's behaviour online. Livingstone (2009) argues that there is a polarised view about children online. She states:

> Children are seen as vulnerable, undergoing a crucial but fragile process of cognitive and social development to which the Internet tends to pose a risk by introducing potential harms into the social conditions for development, justifying in turn a protectionist regulatory environment. (Livingstone, 2009, p. 16)

The contrasting view is that children are seen as

> competent and creative agents in their own right whose media savvy skills tend to be underestimated by the adults around them, the consequence being that society may fail to provide a sufficiently rich environment for them. (Livingstone, 2009, p. 16)

The reality is that the Internet provides great opportunities for young people, but equally presents many risks.

Opportunities and risks for young people using the Internet (Livingstone, 2009)

Potential opportunities

- access to global information
- educational resources
- social networking among friends
- entertainment, games and fun
- user-generated content creation
- civic or political participation
- privacy for identity expression
- community involvement/activism
- technological expertise and literacy
- career advancement/employment
- personal/health/sexual advice
- specialist groups/fan forums
- shared experience with distant others

Potential risks

- illegal content
- paedophiles grooming strangers
- extreme or sexual violence
- other harmful offensive content
- racist/hate material and activities
- advertising and stealth marketing
- biased information or misinformation
- abuse of personal information
- cyber-bullying/harassment
- gambling, phishing, financial scams
- self-harm
- invasions/abuse of privacy
- illegal activities

If young people are not granted access to the Internet they will not be able to reap the benefits it affords, so the solution is not to ban young people from accessing the Internet. Instead, parents need to be aware of the risks and of the kinds of support they need to be offering children. This chapter now turns to consider in more detail the kinds of risks young people might be facing.

Potential Risks to Young People

Cyber-bullying/cyber-harassment

Cyber-bullying is becoming an increasing concern. Cyber-bullying is defined as intended and repeated harm caused by communication via the use of computers, mobile phones and other electronic devices. It may involve the expression of malicious or cruel sentiments to another person, and/or the posting of humiliating or embarrassing information about someone in a public online space. Children and adolescents are being bullied online, especially in social networking sites, and have then to deal with the aftermath in the playground. Wang *et al.* (2009) found that boys were more likely to be the cyber bullies and girls more likely to be the victims. Raskauskas and Stoltz (2007) found that being a victim of bullying on the Internet or via text messages was related to being a bully at school. Williams and Guerra (2007) found that Internet bullying peaks in middle school and declines in high school.

The psychological harm caused by cyber-bullying can be quite severe. Young people feel frustrated, angry, and sad. Bullied children have been known to refuse to go to school, to have become chronically ill, to have run away, or even to have attempted suicide (Hinduja and Patchin, 2007).

Paedophilia

Before the dangers of online paedophilia are discussed, the following real-life example, concerning a 13-year-old girl called Katie, might serve to shed some light on the problem. Katie was a victim of online paedophilia (Tarbox, 2000). Initially, she embraced the online attention she received from a much older man. Later, this became for her a source of fear and regret. According to Katie, a lack of understanding on the part of people around her motivated her to go online to seek like-minded people. Although she was concerned by the motivations of many of the men she encountered, she persisted in believing that she would find someone with whom she could connect:

> And they all want to know what you look like, especially your body. You can be sure that every time you go on-line someone is going to ask you your breast size. I don't really see why anyone bothers to ask. Everyone lies when they answer.
>
> It didn't take me long to figure out that a lot of the guys in the teen chat rooms were not normal guys. They were animals that wanted to be excited by someone they thought looked like Cindy Crawford with a breast size of 36F.
>
> Despite all of this—despite all of the weirdos and the creepy feeling of being detached from reality—a small part of me believed that there was someone out there on the Web like me. (Tarbox, 2000, pp. 25–26)

Eventually, Katie did meet someone whom she felt accorded with her sense of self. He claimed to be a 23-year-old called Mark, and the two discussed in detail favourite fashions. What Katie did not know was that he was older than 23, his name was not Mark, and he was a paedophile. 'Mark' remained an online friend, and Katie intimated that she and he had become so close that he had eventually displaced her best girl-friend as her closest confidant. About a year after they had first met online, Katie acceded to Mark's constant requests to meet her (she had been careful not to give out her address or surname). She organised a meeting with him while she was away in another city with her swimming team. They met in the hotel where she was staying, and Mark managed to persuade Katie to go back to his hotel room, where he attempted to assault her. Fortunately for Katie, one of her friends had followed her (without her knowing) and called her mother for assistance. While Katie avoided being assaulted, the ramifications of this event were psychologically damaging.

While paedophilia is not a new crime, with the advent of the Internet there are now new ways in which paedophiles can access children. The Pew Internet and Life Project study found that 60 per cent of the 12- to 17-year-olds it surveyed had received an instant message and/or an email from strangers (Lenhart *et al.*, 2001). Livingstone (2001) offers a descriptive summary of research on the safety of children. In one survey Livingstone instances, one in five American youths aged 10–17 reported receiving some kind of sexual solicitation in a chat room. Livingstone (2001) believes that while information is available to parents that can help them protect their children when online, many parents do not know where to find it. She also argues that 'of the various safety strategies proposed, most are more appropriate for younger children rather than for teenagers'. Needless to say, much more work is needed to understand how paedophiles conduct their activities online, how children are communicating and developing relationships online, and how best to protect children from paedophiles.

Teenagers and sexting

In recent years a new behaviour, known as sexting, has caused a multitude of problems for teenagers. Sexting is the use of a mobile phone or similar electronic device to distribute sexually explicit images. Teenagers might send images of themselves to a friend or boyfriend only to learn that the image has subsequently been distributed to his or her social network. Moreover, the images could potentially be sent to a paedophile.

Lenhart (2009) found that in the USA, of mobile-phone-owning teenagers aged 12–17, 4 per cent have sent sexually suggestive naked or nearly naked images of themselves to someone via text messaging, and 15 per cent have received such images of someone they know. Older teens were, she found, much more likely to send and receive these images: 8 per cent of 17-year-olds with mobile phones had sent a sexually provocative image by text and 30 per cent had received a naked or nearly naked image of someone on their phone.

Lenhart also found that the teenagers in her study who paid their own phone bills were more likely to send sexts: 17 per cent who paid all the costs associated with their cell phones sent sexually suggestive images via text, while just 3 per cent of those who did not pay, or only paid a portion of, the costs sent these images. Moreover, focus groups with young people revealed that there are three main scenarios for sexting: (1) exchange of images solely between two romantic partners; (2) exchanges between partners of images that are shared with others outside the relationship; and (3) exchanges between people who are not in a relationship, at least one of whom hopes to be.

Scams and children

Adults are not the only victims of fraud. Fraudsters are also targeting teenagers. Fraudsters lure young people onto websites promising them free goods, including video-game systems, iPods and so forth. The information the teenagers give out, such as email addresses and personal information, can then be sold to marketers and potentially be used for identity theft.

Teenagers are also having their ID stolen so that their grandparents can be defrauded. In a fairly recent fraud, teenagers' IDs were being stolen from spaces such as social networking sites. Their grandparents were then contacted by the fraudster pretending to be the teenager in a distressful emergency situation where they needed cash. The false narrative might be about the teenager having had their wallet stolen or even needing bail to get out of jail. In each situation the fraudster posing as the teenager asks that the grandparent should act quickly and not tell the parents.

Protective Factors and Policy Implications

Given all these online risks, what should parents do? One popular solution that has been suggested is monitoring. For example, with regard to cyber-bullying Pujazon-Zazik and Park (2010) state:

> Given that parental supervision is a key protective factor against adolescent risk-taking behavior, it is reasonable to hypothesize that unmonitored Internet use may place adolescents at significant risk, such as [of] cyberbullying, unwanted exposure to pornography, and potentially revealing personal information to sexual predators. (p. 417)

Monitoring can take the form of parents physically viewing the content that their children or teenagers are viewing, or alternatively computer software monitoring can be used. An alarm button on Facebook for teenagers to click if they believe that they have been in contact with a predator has recently been developed by the Child Exploitation and Online Protection Centre.

Parental monitoring of children and teenagers, however, is not necessarily the best solution. As Livingstone (2009) points out, parents prefer to trust their children rather than check up on them. Moreover, an important developmental step for young teenagers is to move away from being dependent on their parents, to using their peers instead. This makes parental monitoring of teenagers' online activities highly problematic. Livingstone suggests that parents become 'active co-users'. That is, parents and children go online together and talk about their experiences.

Other protective measures suggested by Livingstone include legislation, education and raising awareness, and safety by design. It takes a long time to put legislation in place, and so this is recommended as a longer-term strategy. Education about Internet risks is now being carried out in schools, but parents, arguably, need to be involved in this. Internet designers are not greatly interested in safety by design, so that in the long term society might make stronger demands on designers that they consider safety issues seriously.

The Internet is a part of everyone's lives, and increasingly so. The solution for dealing with its dark aspects is not to switch it off. Turning off the Internet in our lives, especially in children's lives, has many serious drawbacks. Instead, a much better understanding is needed of the problems that can be encountered. Parental monitoring of children's and teenagers' activities is only part of the solution. Other protective factors need to be considered, such as open dialogue between parents and their children, education, legislation, and more protective design aspects.

References

Boyd, D. M. and Ellison, N. B. (2007) Social network sites: definition, history, and scholarship, *Journal of Computer-Mediated Communication*, 13(1), article 11. http://jcmc.indiana.edu/vol13/issue1/boyd.ellison.html [Accessed 8.8.2011.]

Brodie, M., Flournoy, R. E., Altman, D. E., Blendon, R. J. M., Benson, J. M. and Rosenbaum, M. D. (2000) Health information, the Internet, and the digital divide, *Health Affairs*, 19(6): 255–265.

Childwise (2010) *Digital Lives 2010*. http://www.childwise.co.uk/childwise-published-research-detail.asp?PUBLISH=64 [Accessed 8.8.2011.]

Cooper, A., Delmonico, D. L. and Burg, R. (2000) Cybersex users, abusers, and compulsives: new findings and implications, *Sexual Addiction and Compulsivity*, 7: 5–29.

Daneback, K., Ross, M. K. and Månsson, S-A. (2006) Characteristics and behaviors of sexual compulsives who use the Internet for sexual purposes, *Sexual Addiction & Compulsivity: The Journal of Treatment and Prevention*, 13(1): 53–67.

Dutton, W. H. and Blank, G. (2011) *Next Generation Users: The Internet in Britain*. Oxford Internet Surveys. http://microsites.oii.ox.ac.uk/oxis/ [Accessed 18.11.2011.]

Griffiths, M. (1999) Internet addiction: fact or fiction, *Psychologist*, 12: 246–250.

Griffiths, M. (2000) Internet addiction—time to be taken seriously?, *Addiction Research*, 8: 413–418.

Hancock, J., J., Thom-Santelli, J. and Ritchie, T. (2004) Deception and design: the impact of communication technologies on lying behavior, *Proceedings, Conference on Computer Human Interaction, New York*, 6(1): 130–136.

Hinduja, S., and Patchin, J. W. (2007) Offline consequences of online victimization: school violence and delinquency, *Journal of School Violence*, 6(3): 89–112.

Internet World Stats (2011) *Internet Usage Statistics: The Internet big picture*. http://www.Internetworldstats.com/stats.htm [Accessed 18.11.2011.]

Lenhart, A. (2009) *Teens and Sexting*. http://www.pewInternet.org/Reports/2009/Teens-and-Sexting.aspx [Accessed 8.8.2011.]

Lenhart, A., Rainie, L. and Lewis, O. (2001) *Teenage Life Online: The rise of the instant message generating and the Internet's impact on friendships and family relationships*. http://www.pewInternet.org/pdfs/PIP_Teens_Report.pdf [Accessed 3.3.2005.]

Livingstone. S. (2001) *Online Freedom: Safety for children*. http://www.lse.ac.uk/collections/ media@lse/pdf/free_safety_children1.pdf [Accessed 2.3.2005.]

Livingstone, S. (2006) *UK Children Go Online: End of award report*. http://www.lse.ac.uk/collections/children-go-online/ [Accessed 14.5.2008.]

Livingstone, S. (2009) *Children and the Internet: Great expectations, challenging realities* (Cambridge: Polity Press).

Livingstone, S. and Helsper, E. (2007) Gradations in digital inclusion: children, young people and the digital divide, *New Media & Society*, 9(4): 671–696.

National Fraud Authority (2011) *Annual Fraud Indicator* (2011) http://www.attorneygeneral.gov.uk/nfa/WhatAreWeSaying/Documents/AFI 2011.pdf [Accessed 6.6.2011.]

Office of Fair Trading (2006) *Research on Impact of Mass Marketed Scams: A summary of research into the impact of scams on UK consumers*. http://www.oft.gov.uk/shared_oft/reports/consumer_protection/oft883.pdf [Accessed 15.8. 2006.]

Pew Internet (2009) *Demographics of Teen Internet Users*. http://pewInternet.org/Static-Pages/Trend-Data-for-Teens/Whos-Online.aspx [Accessed 15.11.2010.]

Pujazon-Zazik, M. and Park, J. (2010) To tweet, or not to tweet: gender differences and potential positive and negative health outcomes of adolescents' social Internet use, *American Journal of Men's Health*, 5: 413–420.

Raskauskas, J. and Stoltz, A. (2007) Involvement in traditional and electronic bullying among adolescents, *Developmental Psychology*, 43(3): 564–575.

Scharlott, B. W. and Christ, W. G. (1995) Overcoming relationship-initiation barriers: the impact of a computer-dating system on sex role, shyness, and appearance inhibitions, *Computers in Human Behavior*, 11(2): 191–204.

Schneider, J. P. (2000) Effects of cybersex addiction on the family: results of a survey, *Sexual Addiction and Compulsivity*, 7: 31–58.

Tarbox, K. (2000) *Katie.com.* (Sydney: Hodder).

Wang, J., Iannotti, R. J. and Nansel, T. R. (2009) School bullying among US adolescents: physical, verbal, relational and cyber, *Journal of Adolescent Health*, 45(4): 368–375.

Wei, L. and Hindman, D. B. (2011) Does the digital divide matter more? Comparing the effects of new media and old media use on the education-based knowledge gap, *Mass Communication and Society*, 14(2): 216–235.

Whitty, M. T. (2007a) The art of selling one's self on an online dating site: the BAR approach, in M. T. Whitty, A. J. Baker and J. A. Inman (eds), *Online Matchmaking* (Basingstoke: Palgrave Macmillan), 57–69.

Whitty, M. T. (2007b) Manipulation of self in cyberspace, in B. H. Spitzberg and W. R. Cupach (eds), *The Dark Side of Interpersonal Communication* (Mahwah, NJ: Lawrence Erlbaum), 2nd edn, 93–118.

Whitty, M. T. (2008a) The joys of online dating, in E. Konjin, T. Martin, S. Utz and A. Linden (eds), *Mediated Interpersonal Communication: How technology affects human interaction* (New York: Taylor & Francis/Routledge), 234–251.

Whitty, M. T. (2008b) Liberating or debilitating? An examination of romantic relationships, sexual relationships and friendships on the Net, *Computers in Human Behavior*, 24: 1837–1850.

Whitty, M. T. and Buchanan, T. (2012) The Online dating romance scam: a serious crime, *Cyberpsychology, Behavior, and Social Networking*, 15(3): 181–183.

Whitty, M. T., Buchanan, T., Joinson, A. N. and Meredith, A. (2012) Not all lies are spontaneous: an examination of deception across different modes of communication, *Journal of the American Society for Information Science and Technology*, 63(1): 208–216.

Whitty, M. T. and Carr, A. N. (2006) *Cyberspace Romance: The psychology of online relationships* (Basingstoke: Palgrave Macmillan).

Whitty, M. T. and Joinson, A. N. (2009) *Truth, Lies, and Trust on the Internet* (London: Routledge, Psychology Press).

Williams, K. R. and Guerra, N. G. (2007) Prevalence and predictors of Internet bullying, *Journal of Adolescent Health*, 41(6): S14–S21.

Young, K. S. (1998) *Caught in the Net: How to recognise the signs of Internet addiction and a winning strategy for recovery* (New York: Wiley).

Young, K. S. (1999) Internet addiction: evaluation and treatment, *Student British Medical Journal*, 7: 351–352.

19
Immigrant Families Coming to the West

Ubaldo Martínez Veiga

Introduction

Half a century ago, the anthropologist Clyde Mitchell suggested that all migratory processes involve two different or opposing forces, one centrifugal and the other centripetal (Mitchell, 1959). The centrifugal force, which drives people to leave their home and emigrate, is determined by the possibility of people improving their economic situation and finding work, or simply by the quest for survival. This force is opposed by a centripetal one which keeps people in their place of origin or, if they are forced to leave, drives them to return. While Mitchell saw these centrifugal and centripetal tendencies as elements present in all families, others, such as Löfgren (1984), constructed a typology that established a dichotomy between families or domestic units. Löfgren defined a centrifugal family as one in which the division of labour among the members is very flexible, to the extent that members can change jobs and may not always reside with other family members. By contrast, the centripetal family is characterised by a division of labour that is much less flexible and by all the members living together. While this typology should not be seen as a dichotomy which unequivocally represents all kinds of families, it nevertheless provides a starting point for studying immigration in Europe.

As borders between countries have been opened up and the European Union has expanded, it has become increasingly common for individuals and families to move to another country. At various times in the last 60 years, some governments have encouraged immigrant labour: for example, West Indian migrants were welcomed to Britain in the 1950s to work in certain occupations such as public transport, and migrant

Contemporary Issues in Family Studies: Global Perspectives on Partnerships, Parenting and Support in a Changing World, First Edition. Edited by Angela Abela and Janet Walker.
© 2014 John Wiley & Sons, Ltd. Published 2014 by John Wiley & Sons, Ltd.

labour has commonly been employed at harvest time in many European countries. However, increasing global migration has resulted in periodic concerns in host/receiving countries about the impact on employment and on social and health services, and it remains a politically sensitive area of public policy. It is important, therefore, to consider migration and its impact on family life and to understand patterns of migration. This chapter focuses specifically on immigration to Spain, using that country as a case study to illustrate different kinds of migration and the impact on family life. In an attempt to construct a model that is applicable to other European situations, the chapter considers four different immigrant groups: from the Caribbean, South America, Morocco and sub-Saharan Africa. Each of these groups illustrates a specific pattern of migration, as shown in the box below.

> ## Immigrants into Spain
>
> 1. *Migrants from the Caribbean (Dominican Republic)*. Migration has given rise to households headed by a grandmother in the Dominican Republic while the mother migrates to Europe on her own. These transnational families maintain continuous contact with each other via letter, telephone, sending money home, and reunions.
> 2. *Migrants from South America (Ecuador)*. Migration of centripetal nuclear families.
> 3. *Migrants from Morocco*. The family migrates in stages: initially the husband emigrates, followed by his wife and children.
> 4. *Migrants from sub-Saharan Africa*. Migration of individuals, with the consequence that family ties are often broken.

There are some apparent similarities between the first and fourth groups, since in both these cases men and women emigrate without their families to a new destination. An important difference exists, however, in the relationship they have with their family members. In the Dominican Republic relationships between the migrant mothers and their relatives at home are actively maintained, while in sub-Saharan Africa, possibly owing to poverty, the ties between those who emigrate and their family members at home are rather weak and often broken. In stark contrast to both these groups, emigration from Ecuador is of fully constituted nuclear families.

This chapter provides a comparative analysis of these four groups in order to develop a typology with which to understand patterns of migration to Europe more generally. An attempt is made to examine the impact of migration on families, and to determine the relationship between migration and family morphology. In the second part of the chapter, the politics of family reunification in Europe are discussed, with the aim of discerning common ideological threads. We begin, however, by examining three aspects of the migration of families to Western Europe with a primary focus on the situation in Spain: the structural changes associated with the migratory process; the impact of regulations imposed by the receptor states on the structure of migrant families; and the ideological underpinnings of regulations on migrant families.

The Structure of Immigrant Families

The structure of immigrant families is examined primarily using data from Spain. An initial in-depth study of the social integration of foreign migrants in Spain was carried out in 1992, when foreign immigration was starting to increase significantly (Martínez Veiga, 1997). The research focused on two particularly interesting immigrant groups, Dominican women and Moroccan men, but also studied the migration of Ecuadorean and sub-Saharan African families.

Migration from the Dominican Republic

Dominican women began to migrate to Spain in 1985. They originated from one part of the Dominican Republic, the north-west, and were concentrated in the Madrid region (Comunidad de Madrid) of Spain. This type of migration pattern differs from the more traditional migratory patterns, which involve men migrating first, then subsequently helping the women in the family to migrate. From a research perspective, the traditional pattern constitutes the most common migratory process for study and has been evident, for example, in the USA. Castles and Miller (1993) described the feminisation of international migration as one of the major tendencies of the 1970s and 1980s, but they devoted little attention to this phenomenon and adopted a traditional model to describe the different stages of migration—starting with the migration of men, and followed by family reunion and, eventually, permanent settlement in the new country. Cohen (1995) commented on the lack of research on female migratory patterns:

> The issue of independent women's migration remains curiously under-researched, despite the long reach of feminist-inspired studies in so many other areas of social life … One reason why independent women have remained hidden from migration history is that entry policies often insisted on family migration. (p. 4)

While the independent migration of women has certainly not been analysed in much detail, Cohen's observation is problematic, because it suggests that men always initiate family migration and women follow them as dependants. Data from our studies indicate that women are not relegated to a passive role. The ideological bias regarding the role of women in migration is present not only in the interpretations of researchers, but also in certain aspects of migratory policies, which will be discussed later in the chapter.

Dominican women who emigrated to Spain in order to work as domestics played an active role in the migratory process. Eighty per cent of Dominican immigration to Spain was initially female. Of these women, 61 per cent were married and had left their children behind, almost always with their mothers or sometimes with a sister. Throughout this entire process the husband, who did not emigrate with his wife, played no relevant role. It is important to emphasise that it was the grandmother who received the remittances sent home by these women to support their children: 49.1 per cent sent money to their mothers and only 13.2 per cent to their husbands (Martínez Veiga, 1997).

Married Dominican women who migrated to Spain were members of domestic units which were characterised by the spatial distribution of their family members in two different countries: families that can be designated multi-nuclear or bi-nuclear. The nucleus in Spain consisted of the mother who was performing domestic work, whereas in the Dominican Republic the nucleus comprised the stable family members—the children and their grandmother. The Dominican women have sent money to their country of origin particularly frequently. This and other studies have given rise to what is referred to as the grandmother's family, since the grandmother is the stable parental figure for her grandchildren, because their mother is working abroad and their father is usually absent. The Dominicans describe this situation in terms of a 'chain' which unites the migrating mother with her children and their grandmother, who remain in the Dominican Republic. Tellingly, the grandmother is described as the anchor to which the migratory chain is fastened.

In a survey conducted in the 1990s (Martínez Veiga, 1997), the Dominican immigrants were asked about the family members they wished to help to come to Spain. Forty-one per cent of them said that they would like to bring their daughters to join them because they were poor and could not leave their daughters any inheritance other than the possibility of emigrating and finding work themselves in Spain. This suggested a rich and interesting situation from the viewpoint of family organisation. In the context of family organisation, the term '*matrifocal*' was first used to describe Caribbean families in the 1950s and 1960s. It applied to families in which the women maintained the domestic unit and played a dominant role, both psychologically and economically. This role is evident even when the men live with their families (Smith, 1956; Solien de González, 1965). In the Dominican case, the mothers' desire to bring their daughters to join them also indicated a *matrilineal* form of family development. At the present time this pattern persists, as evidenced by a larger female than male immigrant population in Spain. In fact, there are more women than men in the 15- to 19-year-old age groups. This seems to indicate that mothers continue to bring their daughters to Spain. It should be emphasised that this family organisation is strictly transnational in character and represents a new migration phenomenon of long duration.

Migration from Ecuador

The second group studied consisted of Ecuadoreans. The migration pattern differed from that of the Dominican families. At the beginning of their immigration to Spain in the 1990s, couples emigrated together because this made the migration process easier, and Ecuadoreans were able to stay in Spain for up to three months without obtaining a tourist visa. Data held at the Consulate in Madrid indicate that a significant number of women were pregnant when they arrived in Spain. If the baby was subsequently born in Spain there were many administrative advantages for the couple since the child was registered as a Spanish citizen. The parents were then exempt from visa requirements because they were the parents of a dependent Spanish minor and could join the labour force under the same conditions as Spanish citizens, without needing to depend, as did other foreigners, on the national employment situation. The parents of these children also enjoyed guarantees that they would not be expelled from the country. The children provided protection for their parents in Spain, and the term 'anchor-children' is often used to describe them (Gómez Ciriano, 2004) because they bring the possibility of permanent settlement and reunification of any parents who may have migrated separately to Spain. Despite these many advantages, however, it was not unusual for the grandmother to come over from Ecuador a few months later to take the baby back home, because the parents faced many difficulties in respect of managing both their working and their family life.

The arrival in Spain of numerous Ecuadoreans has also revealed other interesting characteristics. In cases where whole families were not able to migrate, the first to arrive were frequently the women, who came to work in domestic service and who became the sponsors for bringing their husbands over. Up until 2001, this initial migration of women followed by that of their husbands was a relatively easy process, but after 2001 the administrative advantages with regard to their migration to Spain disappeared. In 2003 the visa exemption was removed and since then there has been an exponential increase in the number of applications for family reunification. Previously, family reunification had occurred de facto and had been regularised a posteriori. In the new situation, the family members who have requested reunification have been the women, if they were the first to arrive, simply because the only work they have been able to find has been in domestic service.

Various authors (Castles and Miller, 1993; Castles *et al.*, 1984; Conlinson, 1993; Hollifield, 1992) have described this phenomenon of family reunification. It has been a universal phenomenon in Europe as governments have reduced migratory flows into their countries in respect of labour migration, so that the migration that becomes of fundamental importance (personal, social and political) is that based on migrants seeking family reunion.

Migration from Morocco

Initially, migration from Morocco to Spain involved Moroccan men. The group surveyed were mostly aged 25–35, and a large proportion (80%) were bachelors. Closer analysis of the data revealed that many more married men than married women formed the workers' group, indicating that many wives remained in Morocco. Further analysis indicated that family regrouping occurred infrequently and that the families were, in many cases, based on two nuclei. When the nuclei were brought together, the second group of family members to arrive in Spain usually consisted of wives and children. An old Spanish law, based on a patriarchal family model, allowed wives who joined their husbands to obtain a residence permit but not a work permit, so they had to remain as housewives. The law interpreted female migration as a passive phenomenon and established a parallel between the patriarchal Moroccan family and the immigrant families established in Spain.

In contrast to the female immigrants from the Dominican Republic, who sent money home to their mothers, Moroccan men sent money to their own parents and consequently perpetuated the patriarchal character of Moroccan families. There was also an important difference between the Moroccan men and the Dominican women in respect of who they preferred to bring to Spain: only 12 per cent of the Moroccans wanted to bring someone to join them, the rest preferring not to bring anyone at all. The most common response from this 12 per cent was that they would like to bring a friend, and an even smaller group wanted to bring one of their children.

Migration from sub-Saharan Africa

The fourth group studied comprised immigrant men from sub-Saharan Africa, and the study included 80 interviews with male immigrants conducted in 2008. These men had arrived in Spain four or five years previously, and their journey to Spain had lasted on average three to four years, sometimes taking more than ten years (Martínez Veiga, 2011). The long journey and the conditions of detention or isolation imposed by the states through which these immigrants had travelled had greatly weakened their relationships with family members left behind, to the extent that these ties usually disappeared altogether. In spite of this, whenever possible the men still tried to send money home, all of them insisting that this represented the last link with their families. When they were interviewed in 2008, however, the majority were unemployed, with no money to send home, making it impossible for them to maintain links with family members in sub-Saharan Africa. Some of them described themselves as being completely alone.

Discussion

Patterns of migration and their impact on the family lives of those leaving their country of origin will vary according to when people migrate and the socio-economic and political factors prevalent in the host societies. It is important, therefore, to bear in mind the historical period during which these four groups of immigrants arrived in Spain. The first of the Moroccans and Dominicans arrived in 1985, when legislation regarding immigration was still somewhat undeveloped. In fact, these groups obtained legal status without difficulty. The Ecuadoreans arrived in the early 1990s, when regularisation was more difficult and the requirement that immigrants have legal status more strongly enforced. There were even proposals to repatriate them in order for them to request their work permits from Ecuador, but this was not economically viable and, in the end, they too attained legal status. The sub-Saharan Africans arrived in Spain between 2005 and 2010. For them, attaining legal status is virtually impossible. Many have been deported and those remaining in Spain have disguised their country of origin because of police persecution. After living three years in Spain they are able to regularise their status, but there are additional difficulties. In order to obtain legal status they need a work contract. This has been particularly complicated since 2008, owing to the economic crisis and increasing unemployment.

In the last decade, Western Europe has opened its doors to immigrants from the former Eastern European countries, notably Poland, Romania and the Balkan states. It has been usual for one partner to arrive first to obtain work, sending money home until it is possible for other family members to join them. Although many people migrated to the bordering countries of Germany, Austria and Italy, increasing numbers have ventured further afield, with the UK, for example, seeing the influx of many immigrants looking for work. Migration to Portugal has been particularly well-documented (Baganha, 2007): in only one year (2000–1) the number of immigrants residing in Portugal rose from 208198 to 350503—a 68 per cent increase in the immigrant population. The main group has come from Ukraine. Portugal, along with other European countries, has found itself facing considerable pressure on its resources, particularly medical care and jobs. Increasingly, receptor states have had to consider whether/how to regulate these migration flows, and the extent to which entire families should be permitted to receive social security benefits and medical care. In a global recession, free movement becomes a sensitive political issue as well as a personal family matter.

Following the economic crisis that has extended across Europe since 2008, there have been a series of transformations regarding the arrival of immigrants. First, member states have made it more and more difficult for people to enter their countries. In addition, the labour market, which has always been the fundamental determinant of migration, has deteriorated so much that, little by little, work opportunities for immigrants have decreased and one of the key drivers of migration has thereby been weakened. In Spain, for example, since 2010 migration entry numbers have fallen to become less than exit numbers: indeed, we have begun to see an increase in the numbers of migrants exiting the country, but not all of them return to their country of origin. Instead, a number of Latin American immigrants of Spanish nationality have moved to other European countries where the labour market is seemingly less severely impacted by recession (Boletín Digital de la Fundación Primero de Mayo, 2011).

Traditionally, it has been argued that poor people are less likely to emigrate. Nevertheless, migration of people from sub-Saharan Africa—the poorest migrants— has continued unabated and has remained stable despite the global recession. Another particularly poor group, Romanian Gypsies, have migrated to Western European countries, including Spain. Indeed, the numbers migrating have increased significantly, causing concern in a number of countries. These immigrants are among the poorest in their country of origin, such that even an economic recession in the rest of Europe does not deter them from moving, usually as a family group. When they arrive in a new country they are very poor and look to the host country to provide them with support.

A further problem, which was not new but which became more serious during the earlier 2000s, relates to the irregular nature of many migratory processes. There is, however, some evidence that the number of illegal immigrants into Europe has decreased in recent years (Düvell and Vollmer, 2011; Vogel, 2009). Overall, the number being arrested has reduced, largely as a result of better border controls and improved processes for obtaining visas. Moreover, immigration for reasons of work has become more restricted in the EU, and also in other countries such as the USA. The only way open for some migrants is to move as a family (Hanson, 2007; Kraler and Kofman, 2009), with considerable implications for family organisation; specifically, there have been a growing number of marriages of convenience in host countries (Boswell and Straubhaar, 2003; Düvell, 2011). In the UK, for example, there have been a number of scandals in which priests have taken money to arrange a marriage between an illegal immigrant and a British national. This kind of marriage is highly questionable and unlikely to provide a stable foundation for family life.

From Labour Migration to Family Reunification

According to some scholars (González-Ferrer, 2006), once the recruitment of foreign workers from abroad ended, the EU states which had received large numbers of immigrants were compelled by international law to admit new foreign entries owing to the right to family reunification. This shift may naively be thought to correspond to what Aristide Zolberg has described so well (Zolberg, 2006) in respect of the USA, where often, when one door to the admission of immigrants closes another (back) door opens. In Europe, the back door currently corresponds to family reunification.

The immigration associated with family reunification was thought to be of very short duration, with a slow decrease that would eventually cause it to end. As González-Ferrer (2006) has pointed out, this type of migration was expected to end quickly, since recruited workers who decided to stay at their destination brought their relatives to join them fairly soon. This consideration no doubt influenced the first adaptation on the part of the European states regarding family reunification. However, this expectation was not met, primarily because the children of immigrants often brought their marriage partners to Europe from their places of origin, thus extending the numbers arriving.

Family reunification of long duration has resulted in it being possible to distinguish at least four types of family migration (Kofman, 2004). These are shown in the box below.

Four types of family migration

1. Immigrants bringing family members (children, spouses, parents and other relatives) to the country of reception.
2. The children of immigrants bringing their spouses to the receptor country.
3. Immigrants bringing a partner they have met while being abroad.
4. The entire family migrating together.

Family reunification in Spain

For the purposes of discussing these common threads, Spain provides a useful case study. Regulations regarding family reunification were published in Spain in the *National Gazette* (Boletín Oficial del Estado, 2011), and are probably the most recent of comparable European laws. These regulations, called 'Reglamento de la Ley Organica 4/2000', were followed by a reform giving rise to what is known as the Organic Law 2/2009, described in the box below.

The Organic Law 2/2009 in Spain

This law explains which family members can be reunited.

The spouse is the most obvious candidate provided that the partners are separated neither de jure nor de facto. Since a marriage is understood as being a union in law between two adults, the reunification of polygynic families is prohibited. The law attempts to define the individuals who may be considered spouses ('*conyuge*') or as forming a 'conjugal couple'. The spouse is a person who has a relationship of affection with the sponsor similar to the conjugal one. It is clear that this text essentially refers to what is normally considered love. This affectivity must be certified by public registry and must have existed prior to the sponsor's arrival in Spain.

In a seminar (Boletín Digital de la Fundación Primero de Mayo, 2011) conducted in 2011, organised by the trade union foundation Comisiones Obreras, the Advisor to the Subsecretary for Migration and Immigration in Spain summarised the intention behind the law as being to reinforce the legal character of family reunification as a basic right. This law could be considered an essential mechanism for integration. It includes novel ideas: it allows the reunification of de facto couples and limits the reuniting of parents, only allowing this in the case of those aged over 65, and limiting the reuniting of children to those under 18. The law requires that the family has the economic means to support itself, and a stable income. If some of the requirements for the renewal of the residence permit are not met, a certificate of 'effort made towards integration' may nevertheless fulfil some of them. This is an unusual feature of the law, which states that the sponsor's effort to be integrated in Spanish society is valued even if some of the requirements for renewal cannot be demonstrated.

Many of these elements are present in the requirements for family reunification operated by most European states. Polygamous family reunification has been banned in all states, since it is viewed as contrary to Occidental values and the rights of women. Reunification of these families was permitted in France from 1980 until 1993, since this was recognised as forming part of international private law (Rude-Antoine, 1997). Polygamy is viewed negatively, along with other family structures such as female-headed households, which are considered to lead to crime, disorder and low school attendance on the part of the children, owing to a lack of male authority (Kofman, 1999). Some other customs, such as the arranged marriages of Asian women in Britain, have also been presented as arguments against family reunification. An analysis of all these factors suggests that the requirements for family reunification are largely based on ethnocentrism, when not guided by pure prejudice. The requirements for family reunification are indeed so numerous and exclude so many forms of family organisation that it is reasonable to wonder whether the family is really considered a means for achieving immigrant integration. In addition, all European legislation includes a rejection of so-called marriages of convenience. In the case of Spanish law, for example, the beginning of Article 53 states:

> The reunification could take place with the spouse if there is no *de jure* or *de facto* separation between them and when the marriage has not been accomplished fraudulently.

Betty de Hart (2006) provided a clear analysis of how this is understood at the European level. The Resolution of 1997, in Article 1, defines a marriage of convenience as:

> A marriage concluded between a national of a member state and a third country national, with the sole aim of circumventing the rules of entry and residence of third country nationals and obtaining for the third country national a residence permit and authority to reside in a member state.

De Hart (2006) commented as follows:

> The idea of a marriage of convenience not only affects the couple involved but also the general family reunification policy and genuine marriages. (p. 261)

The EU Directive on the Right of Family Reunification was proposed in 2003. Article 16, section 2b says that member states have

> the right to not accept admission or refuse the prolongation of a residence permit in case it has been established that a marriage, relationship or adoption was concluded with the sole aim of acquiring admission or residence in the Member State.

In the negotiations concerning this proposal, Belgium suggested that the Directive did not clearly refer to the case of entry into the country for the purpose of marriage. Germany and Austria agreed that the family unit was based on the fact that spouses should aim to establish a matrimonial unit. The Belgian, Italian, Luxembourg, Austrian and Spanish representatives were of the view that member states should be authorised to carry out systematic checks, even when there are no grounds for suspicion. Reunification directives limit the discretion of member states, since they require grounds for suspicion. Systematic checks are not permitted and not all marriages involving a foreigner should be subject to them. These checks are considered to be violations of the privacy of family life.

Views about migrants' marital status, as well as an insistence on identifying sham or bogus marriages undertaken for migration purposes, have had clear impacts on family reunification: in the Tampere declaration of 1999, for instance, family reunification was considered to be something that facilitated social cohesion and integration. Four years later, however, in 2003, when the EU Directive on the Right of Family Reunification was proposed, immigrant families began to be regarded as false families, and this impeded integration since these families were thought to be the result of unwelcome traditions, including arranged marriages and families headed by women.

The idea of family reunification, as a means of establishing a certain control over the migratory process (since such families appeared to be easier to manage), has been prevalent since the mid-1930s. This idea disappeared when, in 2003, Nicholas Sarkozy, the French Minister of the Interior at the time, characterised the problem of illegal immigration as that of migrating family members and asylum seekers, and complained that France had no say in who was entering the country. This phenomenon has given rise to terms that have acquired high prominence, a distinction having been made between 'immigration subie' and 'immigration choisie', or forced and chosen immigration. The second type of immigration is generally regarded as preferable to the first (Kofman *et al.*, 2010).

In parallel with this conceptual change in how family migration is viewed, there has been a change in respect of the complex issue of integration:

> … 'integration' is increasingly used as a principle of selection and understood in terms of certain characteristics of immigrants … rather than in terms of integration being a goal and a desirable outcome of the settlement process. (Kraler, 2010, p. 43)

This phenomenon is clear in the Spanish law described previously. Article 61, which addresses the renewal of the residence permit associated with family regrouping, states:

> The effort to integrate the foreigner will be evaluated … this effort could be alleged by the accredited foreigner as additional information to be considered when some of the requirements are not fulfilled.

Integration is not presented as a consequence of family reunification, but rather as an individual effort that is rewarded by the renewal of the residence permit and hence by family reunification.

Even though, in the 1970s, family reunification was considered an important means of achieving integration, in Europe this idea has always been controversial. France was the first country to promote family reunification following World War II. Across Europe, however, conditions for family reunification have become progressively more difficult. The clearest case of this is that of the Netherlands (Bonjour, 2008), where, owing to the *Gastarbeiter* ideology, it was thought that migrants' presence in the country was always temporary and hence should be controlled. In addition, owing to a scarcity of suitable housing, an immigrant worker often could not bring his wife and children to join him. Other requirements included one or two years of residence before the rest of the family could be brought in, depending on whether the immigrant was from the EU or not. Other countries gradually accepted these restrictions, and their expansion within the EU is a subject worthy of further study.

In the 1990s, the then Dutch Prime Minister, Ruud Lubers, stated that he was 'losing his patience' with immigrant problems (Scholten, 2007). He claimed that there was a need to change the direction of migration policies, away from those emphasising immigrant rights, dating from the 1980s, to ones that would insist on immigrant obligations. Lubers viewed the state as increasingly concerned with all aspects of people's lives, and as attempting to convert its members into passive and dependent subjects. He therefore argued that policies should be changed to emphasise the responsibility, activity and autonomy of citizens.

As a result of all the ideological shifts that have taken place since 1993 the conditions for family reunification have become tougher. Following the Integration Act of 1998, immigrants to Spain have been required to attend courses on integration. These courses were later introduced in Austria, Denmark, France, Germany and the UK. In France, immigrants are required to sign a 'contrat d'accueil et d'integration' or 'integration contract', and this policy has been supported in Spain by the Partido Popular.

Policy Implications

In an era when globalisation is an important phenomenon and cross-cultural interpersonal relationships are increasingly common, issues relating to human migration and discussions about regulation are both sensitive and complex. There appears to be a popular misconception about the integration of immigrant families in the EU. There has been a de facto change in the understanding of immigrant families: family reunification is no longer considered a means of promoting integration, but rather is considered an obstacle to it. This has important consequences for the attitudes of host countries towards immigrants and policies regarding immigration.

A shadow of suspicion has been cast with respect to immigrants' family organisation, as a result of which immigration is being reinterpreted as an individual behaviour. This misconception denies the educational, economic and mutual support roles that are played by the family. These changing attitudes have impacted not only via the creation of impediments to family reunification, but also via an attempt to externalise or put beyond the reach of the family all help with, and subsidies for, education and the economic subsistence of the family members themselves. All of these factors have enormous negative effects on the lives of immigrant populations, thus increasing the tendency towards negative social attitudes and social exclusion. Changes in government policies are crucial in this regard, and some key proposals are presented in the box below.

Proposals for changes in public policy

1. Pathways to citizenship should never be construed as a means of placing certain people in precarious or inferior situations. This often occurs with women.
2. The resources necessary for acquiring citizenship and family reunification have a clear gender-biased component, which often means that women have fewer economic resources. This should be remedied.
3. Sufficient flexibility is needed to prevent family members from having to renew their residence permits, and to ensure that they do not become irregular migrants.
4. The public policy element currently of most interest is the fight to prevent certain population groups (sub-Saharans in Spain and others in other European countries) from being converted into irregular migrants or perpetual 'illegals'. According the latter status to these population groups would certainly be the best way of constructing an underclass in European countries that would be unmanageable and have serious personal, social and economic consequences.

Concluding Comment

Attempting to analyse and dismantle criticism of family migration should be a fundamental task of the social sciences. To a great extent, this could serve to combat racism, both implicit and explicit. It is especially worrying that a number of policies in European states have encouraged widespread suspicion of immigrant families. Instead of these families being treated in the same way as other families are treated, they are seen as symptomatic of a rising crisis in foreign immigration. This undermines attempts at better integration. As a consequence, immigrants cling on to their own culture, traditions and ways of life rather than adopting the cultural norms of their host country. This separation between local culture and immigrant culture serves to increase prejudice and social exclusion, thus perpetrating tensions which can escalate racial discrimination.

References

Baganha, M. (2007) The migration industry: a case study, in E. Berggren, B. Likić-Brborić, G. Toksöz and N. Trimikliniotis (eds), *Irregular Migration, Informal Labour and Community: A challenge for Europe* (Maastricht: Shaker), 95–103.

Boletín Digital de la Fundación Primero de Mayo (2011) Edition of 19 May, www.1mayo.org [Accessed 4.10.2011.]

Boletín Oficial del Estado (2011) Edition of 30 April, http://www.boe.es/ [Accessed 4.10.2011.]

Bonjour, S. (2008) *Family Migration Policies in The Netherlands*, NODE Policy Report (Vienna: BMWF/ICMPD).

Boswell, C. and Straubhaar, T. (2003) *The Back Door: Temporary migration and illegal employment of workers* (Geneva: ILO).

Castles, S., Booth, H. and Wallace, T. (1984) *Here for Good: Western Europe new ethnic communities* (London: Pluto).

Castles, S. and Miller, M. (1993) *The Age of Migration* (London: Macmillan).

Cohen, R. (1995) *The Cambridge Survey of World Migration* (Cambridge: Cambridge University Press).

Conlinson, S. (1993) *Europe and International Migration* (London: Pinter).

De Hart, B. (2006) Introduction: the marriage of convenience in European immigration law, *European Journal of Migration and Law*, 8(3): 251–262.

Düvell, F. (2011) *Irregular Immigration, Economics and Politics*, CESifo DICE Report 3 (Munich: Ifo Institute for Economic Research at the University of Munich). http://www.compas.ox.ac.uk/fileadmin/files/People/staff_publications/Duvell/1210202.pdf [Accessed 5.10.2011.]

Düvell, F. and Vollmer, B. (2011) *Improving US and EU Immigration Systems: European security challenges* (San Domenico di Fiesole: Robert Schuman Centre for Advanced Studies, European University Institute). http://www.eui.eu/Projects/TransatlanticProject/Documents/BackgroundPapers/EU-USImmigrationSystems-Security-bp.pdf [Accessed 8.10.2012.]

Gómez Ciriano, E. (2004) La Inmigración Ecuatoriana en La Ciudad de Madrid en el Contexto de la Inmigración a España, PhD thesis, Dept of Social Anthropology, Universidad Autónoma de Madrid.

González-Ferrer, A. (2006) Who do immigrants marry? Partner choice among single immigrants in Germany, *European Sociological Review*, 22(2): 171–185.

Hanson, G. H. (2007) *The Economic Logic of Illegal Immigration*, Council Special Report 26 (New York: Council of Foreign Relations).

Hollifield, J. (1992) *Immigrants, Markets and States* (Cambridge, MA: Harvard University Press).

Kofman, E. (1999) Birds of passage a decade later: gender and immigration in the European Union, *International Immigration Review*, 33(2): 269–299.

Kofman, E. (2004) Family related migration: a critical review of European studies, *Journal of Ethnic and Migration Studies*, 30(2): 243–262.

Kofman, E., Rogoz, M. and Levy, F. (2010) *Family Migration Policies in France*, NODE Policy Report (Vienna: BMWF/ICMPD).

Kraler, A. (2010) *Civic Stratification, Gender and Family Migration Policies in Europe*, NODE Final Report (Vienna: BMWF/ICMPD). http://www.emnbelgium.be/sites/default/files/publications/icmpd_report_family_migration_policies.pdf [Accessed 8.10.2012.]

Kraler, A. and Kofman, E. (2009) *Family Migration in Europe Policies Versus Reality*, IMISCOE Policy Brief 16 (Amsterdam: IMISCOE, University of Amsterdam).

Löfgren, O. (1984) Family and household: images and realities: cultural change in Swedish society, in R. McC. Netting, R. R. Wilk and E. J. Arnould (eds), *Household: Comparative and historical studies of the domestic group* (Berkeley, CA: University of California Press), 446–469.

Martínez Veiga, U. (1997) *La Integración Social de los Inmigrantes Extranjeros en España* (Madrid: Trotta).

Martínez Veiga, U. (2011) *Inmigrantes Africanos, Racismo, Desempleo y Pobreza* (Barcelona: Icaria).

Mitchell, C. (1959) Labor migration in Africa south of the Sahara. The causes of labor migration, *Bulletin of the Inter-African Labor Institute*, 6(1): 12–46.

Rude-Antoine, E. (1997) *Des vies et des familles. Les immigrés, la Loi et la Coutume* (Paris: Odile Jacob).

Scholten, P. (2007) *Constructing Immigrant Policies: Research—policy relations and immigrant integration in the Netherlands (1970 2004)* (Enschede: Print Partners Epskamp).

Smith, R. (1956) *The Negro Family in British Guiana: Family structure and social status in the villages* (London: Routledge & Kegan Paul).

Solien de González, N. (1965) The consanguineal family and matrifocality, *American Anthropologist*, 67: 1541–1549.

Vogel, D. (2009) *Size and Development of Irregular Migration in the EU*, CLANDESTINO Research Project (Hamburg: Hamburg Institute of International Economics).

Zolberg, A. (2006) *A Nation by Design? Immigration policy in the fashioning of America* (New York: Russell Sage).

20

The 'Quiet Migration'
Challenges for Families with Children Adopted Internationally

GABRIELA MISCA

Introduction

Research, policy and practice interest in international adoption has grown considerably over the past five decades, as the prevalence of inter-country adoptions has increased globally. Although inter-country adoption (ICA) has been regarded as a phenomenon of interest predominantly to social scientists and social welfare practitioners, in 1984 Weil coined the phrase 'quiet migration' in respect of it. He argued for the consideration of this type of movement of children across borders as a 'significant' form of migration, highlighting how political and cultural factors play an important role in its manifestation (Weil, 1984). This chapter considers the impact of ICA as a global phenomenon on families who adopt children from abroad. Some of the early outcome studies of ICA are briefly reviewed, with particular focus on the findings from the research on Romanian children adopted abroad during 1990s. The messages from research on the challenges encountered by families with children adopted internationally will be critically reviewed, and their implications for policy and practice examined.

Inter-Country Adoption of Children as a Global Phenomenon

As testimony to the global nature of ICA, Selman (2009) estimated that in 2004 a total of 45000 children worldwide were involved in inter-country adoptions, representing a significant increase over the past 50 years (since the 'opening' of international adoptions from Korea in 1953). This increase also marks a shift from what initially used to be

Contemporary Issues in Family Studies: Global Perspectives on Partnerships, Parenting and Support in a Changing World, First Edition. Edited by Angela Abela and Janet Walker.
© 2014 John Wiley & Sons, Ltd. Published 2014 by John Wiley & Sons, Ltd.

considered a mainly humanitarian response to children who were abandoned owing to poverty and war, towards one which reflects increased demands from childless couples that they obtain a child. It has been argued that international adoption as such provides a service to childless couples in developed countries (Triseliotis, 2000). The 'migration' of children from poor countries to rich, developed countries can be illustrated by considering the social and political contexts of recent waves of ICA. For example, for a brief period during 1990–1991 Romania became the main provider of children for adoption world-wide (Selman, 2002), primarily owing to a media campaign following political and social changes in the Eastern European countries in the early 1990s and the fall of the communist regime, which showed the plight of 'abandoned' Romanian children living in large-scale 'orphanages'. The late 1990s saw the rise of China as the main source of children adopted internationally, owing to the high numbers of abandoned children resulting from China's one-child policy. More recently, we are witnessing the emergence of Africa as a potential and significant source of children, triggered by high-profile celebrity adoptions of 'orphans' from African countries (Selman, 2009).

The debate about ICA involves often passionate arguments on the part of those in favour and those against. These arguments encompass the ethical concerns about removing children from their home country and culture, and extreme positions referring to international adoption as 'the ultimate form of imperialism: wealthy nations exploiting impoverished and distressed nations by taking away their children' (Serbin, 1997, p. 85). Therefore, some studies (Saclier, 2000) have paid attention to the issues relating to a child's best interests and to international cooperation to ensure that there are safeguards in place (as reflected in the development of the 1993 Hague Convention on the Protection of Children and Co-operation in respect of Inter-country Adoption). Studies investigating the legal, administrative and social work processes involved in inter-country adoptions show that, because of the differences in frameworks between home and adoptive countries and the frequent lack of agreement between them, international adoption is difficult to achieve. Others have considered the demographic history of inter-country adoption (Selman, 2002, 2009).

Inter-country adoption has proven to be a highly sensitive and political issue. Recent debates arose around issues concerning the relationship between ICA and the use of institutional care in sending countries, and between ICA and the prevalence (or lack) of domestic adoptions in receiving countries (Chou and Browne, 2008; Gay y Blasco et al., 2008). Opponents of ICA have argued that the practice of it may contribute to the continuation of institutional care for children in the sending countries and the restriction of the number of domestic adoptions of 'hard to place' children in receiving countries. This kind of argument has been used in imposing a moratorium and a change of legislation in respect of ICA in Romania (in 2005), in the context of the country's application to join the European Union (Selman, 2009). However, proving that such relationships exist is a process fraught with difficulties, owing to the lack of accurate data on ICA and the complex factors involved in each country's child welfare provisions and permanency planning for looked-after children (Gay y Blasco et al., 2008).

Studies of Outcomes in ICA

Among the various aspects of ICA explored by much recent research, studies of outcomes for internationally adopted children are highly relevant for both policy and practice, for two main reasons. First, many of these children have experienced various degrees of adversity (war, severe poverty, malnutrition, institutionalisation, abuse, etc.) during the first years of their lives in their birth families and their countries, these adversities constituting the main reasons why the children are available for ICA. In this respect, following the children's progress into their adoptive homes is crucial for achieving an understanding of their development and for guiding policy and practice in respect of these children's lives and the support they need in their adoptive families. Second, the particular circumstances of these children may also shed light on the more general issue of the developmental trajectories of other 'at-risk' populations that encounter early adverse life experiences. In this context, studies of children adopted internationally contribute to the understanding of 'resilience', since many of the children demonstrate recovery following adoption despite their early adverse experiences.

Early ICA outcome studies

A substantial literature on the outcome of ICA started to emerge in the late 1980s and early 1990s as a result of various studies carried out in countries which were major recipients of internationally adopted children from the late 1970s onwards. Research evidence on outcomes of ICA has accumulated gradually in countries with a relatively long history of well-monitored and well-regulated ICA processes. Contributing to this evidence are two studies from the Netherlands—the 'Thai Study' (Hoksbergen, 1997) and the Dutch longitudinal study (Verhulst *et al.*, 1992)—and studies from Norway (Saetersdal and Dalen, 2000), and two from Sweden (Cederblad *et al.*, 1999; Irhammar and Cederblad, 2000). In an early UK review these studies were described as 'a qualitative step forward in analysing the "dark side of inter-country adoption" as well as its success' (Thoburn and Charles, 1992, p. 17). In another review, Tizard (1991) included studies carried out in North America as well and addressed, among other issues, the 'politically sensitive issue of cultural and national identity and experiences of racism' (Tizard, 1991, p. 752) in ICA.

Overall, these early studies on internationally adopted children, while highlighting areas of developmental vulnerability, sum up the experience in a mostly optimistic way. It is acknowledged that the vast majority (75–80%) of inter-country-adopted children and adolescents function well, although their educational performance is likely to be below that of other (in-country) adoptees and non-adopted children (Tizard, 1991). The rapid recovery of children in their first year of inter-country adoption is appreciated as being remarkable, rendering 'stunted growth as fully reversible' (Thoburn and Charles, 1992, p. 20).

The issue of cultural identity in inter-country adoptees has been highlighted in its relation to the increasing concerns about self-identity, which become relevant as the children enter their adolescent years (Verhulst, 2000). These studies showed that overall, inter-country adoptees regard themselves as having the same national identity as those born in the country where they live and, while many also show a strong interest in their backgrounds (Irhammar and Cederblad, 2000), some want to distance themselves from immigrants of a similar ethnic background (Saetersdal and Dalen, 2000). Also, there is evidence that the social and political contexts in which the inter-country adoptees grow up influence their identity formation. While cultural identity seems important for overall successful adjustment, this does not imply a denial of children's ethnic origins: the most successful adjustment is in children

Early studies of outcomes of ICA

Early studies were primarily optimistic about outcomes:

- 75–80% of inter-country-adopted children and adolescents function well.
- The rapid recovery of children in their first year of adoption is considered remarkable.
- Satisfaction with adoption by adoptive parents and adopted children is rated high or very high by over 80% of adoptive families.

whose parents are open about these issues. Moreover, a recent review found no difference in self-esteem between adoptees and non-adoptees across 88 studies, and this held true for international, domestic and trans-racial adoptees (Juffer and van IJzendoorn, 2007).

Satisfaction with adoption by adoptive parents and by adopted children has been rated as 'high' and 'very high' in the vast majority (over 80%) of the adoptive families in various studies (Tizard, 1991). While the majority of adoptive parents in these studies believed their relationship with their adopted child was strong and satisfactory, they also referred to some of the problems involved: on arrival, the children had to unlearn the 'survival techniques' they had used in their home environments (such as lying and stealing), and to reconsider their perceptions stemming from their past experience of adults as people who mainly obstructed and punished them.

However, the studies also highlighted that the risk factors involved in ICA outcomes are less certain: emotional and behavioural difficulties seem more likely to occur when children are adopted at a relatively late age, even though there is no evidence of an age threshold (problems are identified in children adopted in early infancy as well as in those adopted later). The research suggests that when these difficulties arise, they are the consequences of children's early experiences before adoption, since most of these children have experienced extremely adverse conditions such as poverty, malnutrition, institutionalisation, neglect and abuse.

Although some of the above factors are also relevant in respect of in-country adoptees and for child development in general, for children adopted internationally some of these factors may assume greater relevance, in combination with others. For example, even in the case of a child adopted at an early age, his or her medical and social history prior to birth may have been of such poor quality that even an early rescue through international adoption cannot fully compensate. Relevant factors here include the mother's poor nutrition, or abuse of alcohol or drug taking during pregnancy (Jacobson and Jacobson, 2001; Olson *et al.*, 2001). Moreover, uncertainty about a child's genetic background and lack of neonatal screening in some of the sending countries makes the early medical care of international adoptees difficult (Thoburn and Charles, 1992). As Palacios (2009) bluntly put it in his 'ecology of adoption' model analysis:

> Research on adoption outcomes has children's experiences prior to adoption as one of its black holes [and] this is especially true in the case of international adoptions. (p. 74)

Early Deprivation and ICA: Lessons from the Research on Romanian 'Orphans' Adopted Abroad

The fall of the Iron Curtain in 1989 led to an immense interest in children from impoverished Eastern European countries who were adopted in Western countries. Among these, Romanian children received particular attention, mainly because their situation in Romania was intensively publicised by Western media, and for a short period Romania was the largest source of children for international adoption (Selman, 2000). Some of the main studies of Romanian adoptees' outcomes are reviewed below, highlighting areas where the findings make a major contribution to our knowledge of risk and protective factors in ICA outcomes.

As is shown above, studies of internationally adopted children are not new, having been carried out in those countries which were the major recipients of such children (e.g. the USA, the Netherlands, Sweden, Norway). The originality of the later studies of Romanian children adopted abroad in the 1990s lies in the fact that references to 'Romanian orphans' seem to attract the attention of numerous segments of the international research community. There appears to be a common research population of children scattered over the Western world, whose main characteristic is that they were rescued from the 'terrible' Romanian orphanages, thus rendering them victims of 'severe global early privation' (Rutter and ERA, 1998). Two main theoretical approaches converge as being relevant to studies conducted on Romanian children adopted abroad: the impact of institutional rearing on subsequent child development, and the outcomes of international adoptions.

As early as 1992, academic reports were published about the adjustment of Romanian children adopted abroad. Perhaps not surprisingly, these first reports came from medical professionals, since they were among the first to be consulted by adoptive parents confronted with the health problems of their adopted children on arrival or soon after. In this review of some of these studies, a 'study-centred' (rather than 'type-of-outcome-centred') approach is used, because the heterogeneity in findings often reflects the different research questions, designs and methodologies adopted by particular group(s) of researchers.

Key studies of Romanian children adopted abroad

1. *International Adoption Clinic, University of Minnesota, USA* (Johnson et al., 1992)
   Examined the health of 65 Romanian children aged 6 weeks to 6 years over one year
2. *Winnipeg Children's Hospital, Canada* (Benoit et al., 1996)
   Reported the developmental, behavioural and health features of a small group of 22 Romanian children adopted by 18 Manitoba families, who were assessed in two stages between September 1990 and June 1992.
3. *Hospital for Sick Children, Toronto, Canada* (Marcovitch et al., 1995, 1997)
   Studied 130 Romanian children aged 5 days to 9 years, examining behavioural problems, intelligence and attachment.

4. *Case Western Reserve University, USA* (Groze and Ileana, 1996; Groze *et al.*, 1998)

    Gathered information about Romanian children adopted at an average age of 1.7 years (ranging from infancy to 13 years) across the USA, estimated to represent around 16 per cent of all adoptions from Romania between 1990 and 1993.

5. *Simon Fraser University, British Columbia, Canada* (Chisholm *et al.*, 1995; Chisholm, 1998; Fisher *et al.*, 1997; Morison *et al.*, 1995; Morison and Ellwood, 2000)

    Conducted a longitudinal comparative study of children adopted from Romanian orphanages and Canadian non-adopted children, examining attachment, development and indiscriminately friendly behaviour.

6. *London Institute of Psychiatry, UK* (Rutter *et al.*, 2010)

    Conducted a longitudinal study of 111 Romanian children aged under 2 at the time of adoption, examining development, physical and mental health, cognitive functioning and attachment.

The study at the International Adoption Clinic, University of Minnesota, USA

Johnson *et al.* (1992) examined the health of 65 Romanian children, ranging in age from six weeks to approximately six years, coming into the USA over a one-year period (1990–1991). All the children were assessed within three months of their arrival and about two-thirds of them had spent their entire pre-adoption lives in a Romanian institution. Only 15 per cent of the children were assessed as 'physically healthy and developmentally normal', and these children had been in an orphanage for 'a short length of time'. This study shows that many children adopted from Romania in the early 1990s had significant medical problems and delays in their development, and that children who spent more time in institutional care in Romania usually presented more problems than those who spent less. In spite of its limitations, such as the small number of Romanian adoptees included in the sample (which is unlikely to be representative) and the normative standards used (adopted Romanian children were assessed in terms of normative standards for the American infant and child population), this study is valuable as being the first reported assessment of Romanian children adopted abroad. Unfortunately, there was no follow-up of these children, so the long-term consequences of their medical problems or developmental delays are not clear.

The study at the Hospital for Sick Children, Toronto, Canada

Marcovitch and colleagues at the Hospital for Sick Children, Toronto, Canada explored the experiences of families adopting Romanian children in Ontario. An initial article (Marcovitch *et al.*, 1995) reports on a survey of 105 families who had adopted 130 Romanian children between the ages of 5 days and 9 years, 55 per cent of whom had lived primarily in an orphanage before adoption while the rest had lived with their birth parents. The average age of the children at the time of the study was three, and parents were asked to rate retrospectively their adopted child's status when they first met.

Marcovitch continued the study with a more focused analysis of a subset of 56 families from the initial sample (Marcovitch *et al.*, 1997), assessing at ages 3 to 5 children's behavioural problems, intelligence and general development, using Ainsworth's Strange Situation tool to assess mother–child attachment. The adoptee group as a whole was unusual in respect of attachment towards mothers: none had shown avoidant attachment, which is the most common form of insecure attachment in normative samples. The authors hypothesised that avoidant attachment may not have been adaptive in the environments from which the adopted children came. Also, there were no differences in attachment between early- and later-adopted children.

The study at Simon Fraser University, British Columbia, Canada

Among the first reported longitudinally designed study of Romanian children adopted abroad is the 'Romanian Adoption Project' at Simon Fraser University, Canada. Initially, Morison *et al.* (1995) and Chisholm *et al.* (1995) reported on the development, attachment security and indiscriminately friendly behaviour of children adopted from Romanian orphanages.

An accompanying article (Chisholm *et al.*, 1995) reports on the comparison in attachment security and indiscriminate friendliness between children from the samples described above and a third group of 29 Canadian-born, non-adopted children matched by age and sex to the adopted children. Romanian children who spent eight months in orphanages displayed significantly greater indiscriminate friendliness behaviour than Romanian children who were adopted before the age of 4 months (but comparisons with Canadian non-adopted children were not made); however, this finding was not associated with age at placement or length of time in the adoptive home. The authors concluded that Romanian children's experiences of extreme neglect contributed to their low attachment-security scores and that indiscriminate friendliness may be an important behaviour to consider in the study of attachment in institutionalised children, since this also raises concerns about the children's safety (but only three of the 46 parents of Romanian children mentioned this as an area of concern).

A three-year follow-up of attachment security and indiscriminate friendliness in children adopted from Romania (Chisholm, 1998) showed that although Romanian children adopted after eight months did not score differently from the other groups on attachment security measures, they did display significantly more insecure attachment patterns and more indiscriminately friendly behaviour. This study has shown that Romanian children, even those adopted from institutions after the age of 8 months, were able to form attachment relationships with their adoptive parents, although the attachment behaviours in these children were marked by high 'indiscriminate friendliness' features.

The study at the London Institute of Psychiatry, UK

The English and Romanian Adoptees (ERA) study team at the London Institute of Psychiatry (Rutter *et al.*, 2010) conducted a longitudinal study of a sample of 111 Romanian children aged under 2 at the time of their adoption into the UK. In line with the British tradition of research on 'maternal deprivation' (Bowlby, 1951; Rutter, 1972) and 'child institutionalisation' (Hodges and Tizard, 1989a,b), the ERA team shifted the focus from 'Romanian children adopted internationally' (which was predominant in the North American studies) to Romanian 'orphans', described as the 'victims of severe global early privation' (Rutter and ERA, 1998, p. 466).

Without elaborating on the concept of 'severe global early privation', the authors concluded that 'the conditions in the institutions [where the children came from] varied from poor to appalling' (Rutter and ERA, 1998, p. 467), even though the children included in the study came from at least 67 different institutions (Castle and ERA Study Team, 1999). A closer look at the pre-adoption experiences of this sample of Romanian children reveals that less than half of the children are known with certainty to have lived their entire lives in a Romanian institution (Rutter and ERA, 1998, p. 467). A comparison group of within-UK adoptees, placed before the age of 6 months, was selected to participate in the study.

The results (Rutter and ERA, 1998) show that the Romanian children were severely developmentally impaired at the time of UK entry, and many were also in a poor physical state with recurrent intestinal and respiratory infections. The catch-up in both physical growth and cognitive functioning appeared nearly complete (comparable to the UK sample) at four years for those children who had come to the UK before the age of 6 months and impressive, but not complete, in those placed after six months of age. The strongest predictor of the level of cognitive functioning at four years was the children's age at entry to the UK.

Attachment behaviours were also examined at age 4 (O'Connor and ERA Study Team, 1999) through a semi-structured interview with the adoptive parent. Results indicated that attachment disorder behaviours—'disinhibited attachment', similar to the 'indiscriminate friendliness' described by the Canadian study—were positively associated with the duration of severe deprivation, but a substantial number of Romanian children 'exposed to even prolonged severe early privation' did not exhibit these symptoms. In respect of attachment disorder behaviours at age 6 (O'Connor and ERA Study Team, 2000), analyses revealed a close association between duration of deprivation and the severity of attachment disorder behaviour, which in addition were correlated with attention and conduct problems and cognitive level.

A further report (Rutter and ERA, 1999) on assessments at ages 4 and 6 indicated that 6 per cent of Romanian children showed autistic-like patterns of behaviour and that a further 6 per cent showed milder autistic features. These features were not found in the UK sample. The children with autistic features tended to differ from the other Romanian adoptees in respect of their greater cognitive impairment and 'a longer duration of severe psychological privation'.

In an attempt to delineate the behavioural patterns that are specifically associated with institutional privation, dysfunction at age 6 was assessed for seven domains of functioning (Rutter et al., 2001). Attachment problems, inattention/overactivity, quasi-autistic features and cognitive impairment were associated with institutional privation, but emotional difficulties, poor peer relationships and conduct problems were not. Nevertheless, one-fifth of Romanian children who spent the longest time in institutions showed normal functioning (Rutter et al., 2001).

The UK study of children adopted from Romania represented, in the authors' words, 'a complex mix of spectacular success and worrying sequelae' (Rutter et al., 2000, p. 119). At the age-11 follow-up, the frequency of attachment disorders (disinhibited) was reduced (Rutter *et al.*, 2007a) and a quarter of children in the sample 'lost' their quasi-autistic features (Rutter *et al.*, 2007b). Importantly, at age 11, the researchers explored young people's views on adoption (Hawkins *et al.*, 2007) and the results show that children adopted from Romania differ from the UK adoptees only in respect of those who, being older at the age of adoption, found it more difficult to talk about adoption and felt more different from their adoptive families. An insightful report on young people's views on adoption is provided in the research on ICA in Ireland (Greene *et al.*, 2007), which comprised a significant subsample of children adopted from Romania.

The Experiences of Families Who Adopted Romanian Children

Reports about the characteristics of the adoptive parents of Romanian children were included in most of the studies reviewed above. For example, the Canadian adoptive parents were reported as being well-educated, married couples between the ages of 30 and 49 (Marcovitch *et al.*, 1995). Most of the American adoptive parents were white and highly educated and had upper-middle-class family incomes; 90 per cent of the adoptive families had a two-parent structure and 72 per cent of them had birth or other adopted children (Groze and Ileana, 1996).

The ERA study paid more in-depth attention to the outcome of the adoptions from Romania in terms of parental satisfaction (Groothues *et al.*, 1998/9, 2001), child relationship quality (Croft *et al.*, 2001) and the role of siblings (Beckett *et al.*, 1998). Because UK adoption policy at the time discouraged the simultaneous placement of unrelated children in the same family or of a child where there is already a biological child of similar age in the family, ERA (Beckett *et al.*, 1998) examined 95 families (from its previously reported sample) where the adopted Romanian child had a sibling, either adopted or a birth child of the family. The results show a very high level of satisfaction with the adoption (only two of the 165 adoptions had broken down). However, there was variation in the level of dissatisfaction expressed by parents and in the quality of sibling relationships. In this study sibling conflict was associated with the siblings' age-spacing (siblings closely spaced in age were reported to be more in conflict) and the parental ratings of the negative aspects of the adoption were related to sibling composition (when the sibling was a biological child). A further report concerning the age-4 assessment (Groothues *et al.*, 1998/9) found a high level of parental satisfaction, and a negative parental evaluation of the adoptions was influenced by the child's level of hyperactivity at the time of interview. The same level of high parental satisfaction was maintained at age 6 (Groothues *et al.*, 2001) and the main factor associated with lower levels of satisfaction is the child's behaviour problems. The assessment at age 6 (Croft *et al.*, 2001) found that adoptive parent–child relationship quality was related to the duration of deprivation and that cognitive/developmental delay mediated this association.

The overall conclusion of these studies is that there was a very high level of reported satisfaction and a remarkably low level of breakdown in this sample of Romanian children adopted into England. However, it is also acknowledged that these families needed and received significant amounts of support (Rutter *et al.*, 2009).

Limitations of the Studies of Romanian Children Adopted Abroad

Studies on Romanian children adopted into several Western countries have addressed various questions concerning the children's development following adoption and have employed different methodologies. They are consistent in several ways, and the conclusions supported to date are summed up in the box below.

Conclusions from studies of Romanian children adopted abroad

1. Many children had significant physical and medical problems, as well as developmental delays when they arrived in their adoptive foreign homes.
2. Children who had spent less time in Romania (in a variety of settings, mostly in institutional or hospital care) had fewer physical, medical and cognitive problems than children who had spent several months or years in Romania.
3. The physical and cognitive development of many Romanian adoptees showed impressive catch-up after their adoption, resulting in functioning that was in the average ranges within a few years of their adoption.
4. The attachment patterns of the children show features of 'indiscriminate friendliness', and a small proportion of children also show 'autistic-like' features.
5. Overall, 'duration of exposure to severe global early privation' was the most powerful predictor of individual differences in developmental outcomes.

However, before these conclusions can be accepted with confidence, certain limitations of these studies have to be considered carefully. Research on international adoption usually involves the design known as 'natural experiment' (Serbin, 1997), allowing researchers to examine the effect of interventions which cannot be carried out ethically using true experimental designs. However, the studies on Romanian children mentioned above addressed different questions relating to the development of Romanian children adopted internationally after 1990. For example, there is a marked distinction between the North American studies on Romanian children, which focused mainly on the outcome of international adoption, and the UK study, which placed a great emphasis on the previous experiences of the Romanian children, this study being more about the development of children following 'profound deprivation' in early life.

These different questions should be addressed by careful selection of certain groups. The fact that most of the research on Romanian children adopted abroad was triggered by initial reports about their poor development also raises questions about their representativeness. There is a lack of clarity in the reports regarding how the groups of Romanian children were assessed in terms of their pre-adoption experiences (institutional as against family rearing). Some studies acknowledge that a significant proportion of children from Romania were taken from their birth families rather than from institutions. However, in the presentation of findings these two groups of children were often pooled together, with the 'justification' that even children taken from families experienced 'severe early privation' (Rutter and ERA, 1998). Moreover, the emphasis is placed on the age of the child at the time of adoption (i.e. before or after 4, 6 or 8 months respectively) rather than on the type of care the child received prior to adoption.

What the studies on Romanian children adopted abroad seem easily to overlook is the fact that the influences, particularly negative influences, on these children's lives were exerted before they entered institutional care, whether this happened sooner or later after their birth. The study by the Children's Health Care Collaborative Group (Stephenson *et al.*, 1994) on a national representative sample of young children living in institutions in Romania in 1991 showed that most of the children had medical and associated developmental problems *at the time of admission* into institutional care, and in most cases these problems were the reasons why these children were referred to care. The circumstances of these children even before they entered care in Romania have to be taken into account when assessing the individual differences in outcomes and when exploring the developmental predictors.

Interpreting the findings of studies of Romanian children adopted abroad

The research studies have a number of limitations:

- There is a lack of clarity about the differences between children adopted from institutions and those adopted from birth families.
- Negative influences on children's lives were exerted before they entered institutional care.
- Most children living in institutions in Romania had medical and associated developmental problems at the time of admission into institutional care, and those factors were not taken into account.

Implications for Policy and Practice

This chapter has reviewed inter-country adoption, taking Romania as a case study, in the context of the challenges that it potentially poses to adoptive families, challenges which are mainly posed by the developmental outcomes of internationally adopted children. Undoubtedly, over half a century, ICA has become a global phenomenon, involving the migration of children from poor to developed countries, in conjunction with major social and political changes in the sending countries and attitude changes towards ICA in receiving countries.

But what is the future of ICA from a globalisation perspective, with the declining importance of national borders? Perhaps what was seen originally as a 'special' phenomenon of child migration is losing some of its stigmatising connotations as the international adoptees are brought up in increasingly ethnically and culturally diverse societies and families. Although outcome studies have shown that ethnic and cultural identity issues are not as salient as first thought for these young people's adjustment, nevertheless there is much to learn from their experiences as they reach adulthood. It seems germane that in the UK the primacy of ethnic matching in domestic adoptions has been removed, thus allowing primary importance now to be given to finding a placement that will meet the child's needs and will not delay the possibility of adoption (Department of Education, 2011, pp. 1–2).

In the context of the global information and communication technology revolution, the use of Internet advertising by ICA agencies has been criticised for potentially breaching the UNCRC and the Hague Convention (Chou *et al.*, 2007). Perhaps such disputes detract from the heart of the matter—how children's rights can best be served in a global society.

At the core of the review of early and recent outcome studies in ICA is the message that international adoptions overall are successful, with very low breakdown rates. However, such success is guaranteed by the high commitment of adoptive parents. As highlighted throughout the outcome studies, international adoptees are a high-risk group of children who need high levels of support, and such support is expensive. Therefore, service implications in terms of health, mental health and educational supports need to be considered in relation to inter-country adoptees. The assessment of children prior to international adoption, albeit desirable, in the majority of cases has been very limited or simply absent, making it difficult (if not impossible) to plan for necessary supports. However, the growing body of research offers some direction about the areas that are likely to be affected. Notwithstanding this, there remains a distinct lack of knowledge and evidence-based practice on what interventions are best suited to the needs of these children. This is an area where valuable lessons need to be learnt and applied to domestic as well as international adoption, particularly since family structures change and children and young people increasingly experience a variety of environments with a range of adult carers during their childhood.

References

Beckett, C., Groothues, C. and O'Connor, T. (1998) Adopting from Romania: the role of siblings in adjustment, *Adoption & Fostering*, 22(2): 25–34.

Benoit, T. C., Jocelyn, L. J., Moddemann, D. M. and Embree, J. E. (1996) Romanian adoption: the Manitoba experience, *Archives of Pediatrics and Adolescent Medicine*, 150(12): 1278–1282.

Bowlby, J. (1951) *Maternal Care and Mental Health* (Geneva: World Health Organisation).

Castle, J. and ERA Study Team (1999) Effects of qualities of early institutional care on cognitive attainment, *American Journal of Orthopsychiatry*, 69 (4): 424–437.

Cederblad, M., Hook, B., Irhammar, M. and Mercke, A. (1999) Mental health in international adoptees as teenagers and young adults: an epidemiological study, *Journal of Child Psychology and Psychiatry and Allied Disciplines*, 40(8): 1239–1248.

Chisholm, K. (1998) A three year follow-up of attachment and indiscriminate friendliness in children adopted from Romanian orphanages, *Child Development*, 69(4): 1092–1106.

Chisholm, K., Carter, M., Ames, E. W. and Morison, S. (1995) Attachment security and indiscriminately friendly behavior in children adopted from Romanian orphanages, *Development and Psychopathology*, 7(2): 283–294.

Chou, S. and Browne, K. (2008) The relationship between institutional care and the international adoption of children in Europe, *Adoption & Fostering*, 31(1): 40–48.

Chou, S., Browne, K. and Kirkaldy, M. (2007) Intercountry adoption on the internet, *Adoption & Fostering*, 31(2): 22–31.

Croft, C., O'Connor, T., Keaveney, L., Groothues, C. and Rutter, M. (2001) Longitudinal change in parenting associated with developmental delay and catch-up, *Journal of Child Psychology and Psychiatry and Allied Disciplines*, 42(5): 649–659.

Department of Education (2011) *Adoption Statutory Guidance—The Adoption and Children Act 2002* (as rev. Feb. 2011). http://www.education.gov.uk/ b005808/intercountry-adoption-uk-legislation-and-guidance/2005-statutory-adoption-guidance-adoption-and-children-act-2002 [Accessed 30.7.2012.]

Fisher, L., Ames, E. W., Chisholm, K. and Savoie, L. (1997) Problems reported by parents of Romanian orphans adopted to British Columbia, *International Journal of Behavioral Development*, 20(1): 67–82.

Guy y Blasco, P., Macrea, S. and Selman, P. (2008) The relationship between institutional care and the international adoption of children in Europe: a rejoinder to Chou and Browne (2008), *Adoption & Fostering*, 32(2): 63–67.

Greene, S., Kelly, R., Nixon, E., Kelly, G., Borska, Z., Murphy, S., Daly, A., Whyte, J. and Murphy, C. (2007) *A Study of Intercountry Adoption Outcomes in Ireland* (Dublin: Trinity College Dublin).

Groothues, C., Beckett, C. and O'Connor, T. (1998/9) The outcomes of adoptions from Romania: predictors of parental satisfaction, *Adoption & Fostering*, 22(4): 30–40.

Groothues, C., Beckett, C. and O'Connor, T. (2001) Successful outcomes: a follow-up study of children adopted from Romania into the UK, *Adoption Quarterly*, 5(1): 5–22.

Groze, V. and Ileana, D. (1996) A follow-up study of adopted children from Romania, *Child and Adolescent Social Work Journal*, 13(6): 541–565.

Groze, V., Proctor, C. and Guo, S. (1998) The relationship of institutionalisation to the development of Romanian children adopted internationally, *International Journal of Child and Family Welfare*, 98(3): 198–217.

Hawkins, A., Beckett, C., Castle, J., Groothues, C., Sonuga-Barke, E., Colvert, E., Kreppner, J., Stevens, J. and Rutter, J. (2007) The experience of adoption: a study of intercountry and domestic adoption from the child's point of view, *Adoption & Fostering*, 31(4): 5–16.

Hodges, J. and Tizard, B. (1989a) IQ and behavioral-adjustment of ex-institutional adolescents, *Journal of Child Psychology and Psychiatry and Allied Disciplines*, 30(1): 53–75.

Hodges, J. and Tizard, B. (1989b) Social and family relationships of ex-institutional adolescents, *Journal of Child Psychology and Psychiatry and Allied Disciplines*, 30(1): 77–97.

Hoksbergen, R. (1997) Turmoil for adoptees during their adolescence?, *International Journal of Behavioral Development*, 20(1): 33–46.

Irhammar, M. and Cederblad, M. (2000) Outcome of intercountry adoption in Sweden, in P. Selman (ed.), *Intercountry Adoption: Developments, trends and perspectives* (London: BAAF), 143–163.

Jacobson, S. and Jacobson, J. (2001) Alcohol and drug-related effects on development: a new emphasis on contextual factors, *Infant Mental Health Journal*, 22(3): 416–430.

Johnson, D., Miller, L., Iverson, S., Thomas, W., Franchino, B., Dole, K., Kiernan, M., Georgieff, M. and Hostetter, M. (1992) The health of children adopted from Romania, *Journal of the American Medical Association*, 268(24): 3446–3451.

Juffer, F. and van IJzendoorn, M. (2007) Adoptees do not lack self-esteem: a meta-analysis of studies on self-esteem of transracial, international, and domestic adoptees, *Psychological Bulletin* 133(6): 1067–1083.

Marcovitch, S., Cesaroni, L., Roberts, W. and Swanson, C. (1995) Romanian adoption: parents' dreams, nightmares, and realities, *Child Welfare*, 74(5): 993–1017.

Marcovitch, S., Goldberg, S., Gold, A., Washington, J., Wasson, C., Krekewich, K. and Handley-Derry, M. (1997) Determinants of behavioural problems in Romanian children adopted in Ontario, *International Journal of Behavioral Development*, 20(1): 17–31.

Morison, S., Ames, E. and Chisholm, K. (1995) The development of children adopted from Romanian orphanages, *Merrill-Palmer Quarterly Journal of Developmental Psychology*, 41(4): 411–430.

Morison, S. J. and Ellwood, A. L. (2000) Resiliency in the aftermath of deprivation: a second look at the development of Romanian orphanage children, *Merrill-Palmer Quarterly Journal of Developmental Psychology*, 46(4): 717–737.

O'Connor, T. and ERA Study Team (1999) Attachment disturbances and disorders in children exposed to early severe deprivation, *Infant Mental Health Journal*, 20(1): 10–29.

O'Connor, T. and ERA Study Team (2000) Attachment disorder behavior following early severe deprivation: extension and longitudinal follow-up, *Journal of the American Academy of Child and Adolescent Psychiatry*, 39(6): 703–712.

Olson, H., O'Connor, M. and Fitzgerald, H. (2001) Lessons learned from study of the developmental impact of parental alcohol use, *Infant Mental Health Journal*, 22(3): 271–290.

Palacios, J. (2009) The ecology of adoption, in G. M. Wrobel and E. Neil (eds), *International Advances in Adoption Research for Practice* (Chichester: Wiley), 71–94.

Rutter, M. (1972) *Maternal Deprivation Reassessed* (Harmondsworth: Penguin).

Rutter, M., Beckett, C., Castle, J., Colvert, E., Kreppner, J., Mehta, M., Stevens, S. and Sonuga-Barke, E. (2007a) Effects of profound early institutional deprivation: an overview of findings from a UK longitudinal study of Romanian adoptees, *European Journal of Developmental Psychology*, 4(3): 332–350.

Rutter, M., Beckett, C., Castle, J., Colvert, E., Kreppner, J., Mehta, M., Stevens, S. and Sonuga-Barke, E. (2009) Effects of profound early institutional deprivation: an overview of findings from a UK longitudinal study of Romanian adoptees, in G. M. Wrobel and E. Neil (eds), *International Advances in Adoption Research for Practice* (Chichester: Wiley), 147–168.

Rutter, M., Colvert, E., Kreppner, J., Beckett, C., Castle, J. and Groothues, C. (2007b) Early adolescent outcomes for institutionally deprived and non-deprived adoptees. I. Disinhibited attachment. *Journal of Child Psychology and Psychiatry*, 48: 17–30.

Rutter, M. and ERA (1998) Developmental catch-up, and deficit, following adoption after severe global early privation, *Journal of Child Psychology and Psychiatry and Allied Disciplines*, 39(4): 465–476.

Rutter, M. and ERA (1999) Quasi-autistic patterns following severe early global privation, *Journal of Child Psychology and Psychiatry and Allied Disciplines*, 40(4): 537–549.

Rutter, M., Kreppner, J. M. and O'Connor, T. G. (2001) Specificity and heterogeneity in children's responses to profound institutional privation, *British Journal of Psychiatry*, 179: 97–103.

Rutter, M., O'Connor, T., Beckett, C., Castle, J., Croft, C. and Dunn, J. (2000) Recovery and deficit following profound early deprivation, in P. Selman (ed.), *Intercountry Adoption: Developments, trends and perspectives* (London: BAAF).

Rutter, M., Sonuga-Barke, E., Beckett, C., Castle, J., Kreppner, J., Kumsta, R., Schlotz, W., Stevens, S. E. and Bell, C. A. (2010) Deprivation-specific psychological patterns: effects of institutional deprivation, *Monographs of the Society for Research in Child Development*, 75(1): 1–252.

Saclier, C. (2000) In the best interests of the child?, in P. Selman (ed.), *Intercountry Adoption: Developments, trends and perspectives* (London: BAAF), 53–65.

Saetersdal, B. and Dalen, M. (2000) Identity formation in a homogeneous country: Norway, in P. Selman (ed.), *Intercountry Adoption: Developments, trends and perspectives* (London: BAAF), 164–179.

Selman, P. (ed.) (2000) *Intercountry Adoption: Developments, trends and perspectives* (London: BAAF).

Selman, P. (2002) Intercountry adoption in the new millennium: the 'quiet migration' revisited, *Population Research and Policy Review*, 21(3): 205–225.

Selman, P. (2009) From Bucharest to Beijing: changes in countries sending children for international adoption 1990 to 2006, in G. M. Wrobel and E. Neil (eds), *International Advances in Adoption Research for Practice* (Chichester: Wiley), 41–70.

Serbin, L. A. (1997) Research on international adoption: implications for developmental theory and social policy, *International Journal of Behavioral Development*, 20(1): 83–92.

Stephenson, P. A., Anghelescu, C. and Bobe, N. (1994) The causes of children's institutionalisation in Romania, *Child Care Health and Development*, 20(2); 77–88.

Thoburn, J. and Charles, M. (1992) *Inter-Departmental Review of Adoption Law: A review of research which is relevant to intercountry adoption*, Background Paper No. 3, Jan. (Department of Health, Welsh Office and Scottish Office).

Tizard, B. (1991) Intercountry adoption—a review of the evidence, *Journal of Child Psychology and Psychiatry and Allied Disciplines*, 32(5): 743–756.

Triseliotis, J. (2000) Intercountry adoption: global trade or global gift?, *Adoption & Fostering*, 24(2): 45–54.

Verhulst, F. C. (2000) The development of internationally adopted children, in P. Selman (ed.), *Intercountry Adoption: Developments, trends and perspectives* (London: BAAF), 126–142.

Verhulst, F. C., Althaus, M. and Versluis-den Bieman, H. J. M. (1992) Damaging backgrounds—later adjustment of international adoptees, *Journal of the American Academy of Child and Adolescent Psychiatry*, 31(3): 518–524.

Weil, R. (1984) International adoptions: the quiet migration, *International Migration Review*, 18(2): 276–290.

21

Families Living on the Margin in Affluent Societies

Angela Abela and Marie-Cécile Renoux

Introduction

The fight against poverty continues. In spite of the targets set by the Lisbon Summit in 2000 to reduce poverty in the European Union to 10 per cent by 2010, and to reduce child poverty by half (Commission of the European Communities, 2000), 16 per cent of people in the EU-27 countries[1] were considered to be living below the poverty threshold in 2010. The poverty rates for children aged up to 17 were even higher in 21 of the member states (Antuofermo and Di Meglio, 2012). The target set in the June European Council of 2010 was to lift 20 million people out of poverty, thus reducing poverty by 25 per cent by 2020. The rate of poverty is similar in the USA: with the economic crisis, this rose to 14.5 per cent in 2009. The situation was worse for children (those aged up to 18), with more than one in five children considered to be poor in 2011 (Wight *et al.*, 2011).

In the developing world, given China's economic upturn, the proportion of people living on less than US$1 a day is expected to decrease by half by 2015. Around 920 million people are still living below the poverty line, however, and one in four children is underweight (United Nations, 2010).

In this chapter, the focus is primarily on families in Europe with children who are living in poverty, but reference is made also to families in other parts of the world.

---

[1] Belgium, France, Germany, Italy, Luxembourg and the Netherlands were the first six founding countries of the European Union. Denmark, Ireland and the UK followed in 1973, and Greece in 1981. Five years later Portugal and Spain joined, and in 1995 Austria, Finland and Sweden became members and the EU-15 was formed. In 2004, Cyprus, the Czech Republic, Estonia, Hungary, Latvia, Lithuania, Malta, Poland, Slovakia and Slovenia joined. The accession of Romania and Bulgaria in 2007 brought EU membership to 27.

Contemporary Issues in Family Studies: Global Perspectives on Partnerships, Parenting and Support in a Changing World, First Edition. Edited by Angela Abela and Janet Walker.
© 2014 John Wiley & Sons, Ltd. Published 2014 by John Wiley & Sons, Ltd.

Poor families with young children tend to form a heterogeneous group (Walker and Collins, 2004), however, making it difficult to discuss in detail all of the different types of families in one chapter. Moreover, the family life of gypsies, travellers and asylum seekers in particular is under-researched (Ridge 2009) and deserves to be treated separately. Definitions of poverty are discussed and the continuum between poverty and extreme poverty taken into account. The challenges facing families with children living in poverty and, in particular, the effect on children and parents will also be highlighted. Finally, a set of policy implications will be presented.

Families with Higher Risks of Exposure to Poverty

Families living in poverty are characterised by one common and powerful factor: they have insufficient income to meet their needs. Unsurprisingly, when the median poverty rate for the 27 EU countries was 17 per cent, in 2007 (Wall *et al.*, 2010), households of the unemployed were hit the hardest, with 43 per cent of them living in poverty. Other households with higher than average risks of exposure to poverty included immigrants from outside the EU, 30–45 per cent of whom were living in poverty, and single-parent households, in which the risk of poverty for children was doubled. Other high-risk households included those with large families (with a 25% risk of poverty) and those whose members have low educational attainment (with a 23% risk of poverty). Bradshaw and Mayhew (2011) report that those living in extreme poverty were more likely to be single parents with a low level of education, bad health and low labour market participation, and/or to be living as tenants in urban areas. Frazier and Marlier (2012) also include ethnic minorities (especially Roma) and those with disabilities.

In the USA, racial and ethnic income disparities persist (Wight *et al.*, 2011). African-American children are overrepresented in the poverty statistics and account for 36 per cent of the total. Thirty-three per cent of Hispanic children live in poverty, while just 15 per cent of Asian children and 12 per cent of white children live below the poverty line. Almost half (47%) of children in single-parent families are poor in the USA, as against 12 per cent of children in two-parent families. While unemployment is a critical risk factor for poverty, many of the poor families in the USA have at least one member of the family in paid employment: they are increasingly referred to as 'the working poor' (US Census Bureau, 2011).

In the developing countries, the families most at risk of poverty are those living in slums in the cities or in rural areas, migrant families, and those affected by HIV/AIDS (United Nations, International Day of Families, 2011). One billion people currently live in slums, 90 per cent of them in the developing world. As an example:

> Even at 70, Jiyem, an Indonesian grandmother, gets up in the small hours to cook and collect firewood for her impoverished household. Her three-year-old grandson is malnourished. Nobody in her family has ever finished primary school. Her ramshackle house lacks electricity; the toilet is a hole in the ground; the family drinks dirty water. Asked about her notion of well-being by researchers from Oxford University, Jiyem said, 'I cannot picture what well-being means.' (*The Economist*, 2010)

Definitions of Poverty

The poverty line for those living in the world's poorest countries was developed in 1990 and was set at 1 dollar a day. The $1-a-day concept became the basis of the first Millennium Development Goal, which was that of abolishing $1-a-day poverty by 2015. Ravallion *et al.* (2008), who carried out the background research which established the $1-a-day poverty line, admit that it was set arbitrarily and should have been established at $1.45 a day. They point out, however, that 'the "$1-a-day" line draws the attention of the international community on the world's poorest … in a way a slightly higher line would not' (p. 3). In 2008, Ravallion *et al.*, using a new and more representative data set of national poverty lines, proposed an increase to $1.25, but this was again arbitrary (Ravallion *et al.*, 2009). This latter amount is currently endorsed by the World Bank but has been harshly criticised, not least by UNICEF (Hoelscher, 2008a), which argued that the poverty line cannot simply be established on the basis of a minimum intake of food, ignoring the necessary conditions that provide the child with the possibility of mental, spiritual, moral and social development.

The USA has an official poverty line. The threshold takes into account household size and is based on a 'thrifty food basket' multiplied by three (Orshansky, 1969). It was originally developed in the 1960s and has continued to be adjusted for price changes, but is considered outdated as it does not take account of changes in the general standard of living. It also does not gauge the different levels of poverty in which families find themselves (Barajas *et al.*, 2008).

By contrast, the poverty threshold for EU countries is relative and based on economic income. In most countries it is fixed at 60 per cent of the national median *equivalised disposable income* of households. The scale gives a weight of 1.0 to the first adult, 0.5 to any other household member aged 14 and over, and 0.3 to each child. In the EU context, the term 'relative poverty' implies a level of poverty that is relative to a particular country at a particular time: the standard of living of those at 60 per cent below the median varies from one country to another in spite of the fact that different countries adopt the same poverty threshold.

Bradshaw and Mayhew (2011) point out that the accession in 2004 of ten new member states to the European Union complicates the understanding of what it means to be relatively poor in Europe. Accession countries have a much lower median income than the other EU-15 countries. For example, converting the national currencies of Estonia and the UK into an artificial common currency that equalises purchasing power would mean that a couple with two children living on the relative poverty threshold in the UK in 2008 would have two and a half times the spending power of an Estonian family. The authors also point out that the Romanian relative poverty threshold, which is set at €1.71 per person per day, is more an extreme poverty threshold than a measure of relative poverty. This amount is also below the $4-a-day standard established by the World Bank for the transitional economies of the former Soviet Union and Eastern Europe. In the circumstances, the European Commission decided that extreme poverty is better captured by means of a set of common indicators in all countries. The EU Indicators Sub Group (ISG) adopted a list of nine indicators of deprivation, shown in the box below.

Nine indicators of deprivation

The indicators of extreme poverty are the inability to:

- afford unexpected experiences
- manage a one-week annual holiday away from home
- pay arrears (e.g. mortgage or rent arrears), utility bills or hire-purchase instalments
- provide a meal with meat, chicken or fish every second day
- keep the home adequately warm
- have a washing machine
- own a colour TV
- use a telephone
- possess a personal car

Bradshaw and Mayhew (2011) added three further indicators of deprivation: leaking roof/damp walls/floors/foundations or rot in window frames; no bath or shower; and no indoor flushing toilet for sole use of the household. They found that countries such as Poland, Lithuania, Latvia, Hungary and, especially, Bulgaria and Romania have much higher poverty rates when households are assessed on the deprivation indicators. On the other hand, in the EU-15 countries, the extreme poverty rates are lower than the threshold, which, as mentioned above, is calculated in each country as 60 per cent of median disposable income. Bradshaw and Mayhew (2011) pointed out that families living on a very low income such as those living in institutions, those who are homeless and those from minority ethnic groups (especially Roma) are not captured in the statistics deriving from these indicators, and the European Commission is in the process of researching a wider array of indicators so as to provide a more reliable measure of extreme poverty in the EU.

A Conceptual Framework for Understanding Families Living in Poverty

Throughout this chapter a rights perspective has informed the discussion. Hooper *et al.* (2007) suggest that 'poverty is a form of societal neglect' (p. 96). In this respect the Council of Europe's stance *vis-à-vis* families living in poverty is that of protecting their human rights, including the five main social rights (the rights to employment, housing, health, education and social protection) and the rights of children encapsulated by the United Nations Convention on the Rights of the Child. Article 27, in particular, stresses the child's right to grow up in their own family, in conditions adequate for ensuring their 'physical, mental, spiritual, moral and social development', and outlines the principle of providing support to parents in order to avoid poverty-induced separation. Article 8 of the European Convention on Human Rights also guarantees the right to privacy and family life and stipulates that, where a family link exists, the state must foster the conditions which will protect that link.

The Effect of Poverty on Children and Their Parents

The impacts of poverty are considered here primarily with respect to the more affluent countries in Europe and the USA. These are described in the box below. At the same time, it is important to remember that there are very poor families living in developing countries who struggle to fulfil basic needs such as eating one bowl of rice a day.

The impacts of poverty in more affluent societies

In more affluent societies, 'poverty is a highly stigmatised social position and the experience can be particularly isolating and socially damaging … It is almost always overwhelmingly negative and can have psychological, physical, relational and practical effects on people's lives' (Ridge, 2009, p. 1).

The strong relationship between economic poverty, ill health, a low level of education, limited employability and poor integration in social life explains the insidious process by which poor families are pushed away to the margin of society such that they are precluded from participating in the normal way of life (Abela and Tabone, 2008a).

In her extensive review of poverty, Tess Ridge (2009) illustrates how difficult it is for parents to move out of poverty despite their best efforts to do so. Their best hope is to find work, but because of their poor level of education those who do find work are constantly moving in and out of jobs. Mothers, especially those rearing pre-school children, complained that childcare was not affordable. The lack of family-friendly employment was also a barrier, especially for single parents who had to look after their children. Other parents complained that the salary they were offered was so low that sometimes it was no more than the benefits they received from social services and welfare, with the added disadvantage that when they became unemployed they had to wait until they could start receiving unemployment benefits again. In the USA the average salary of mothers who succeeded in finding a job following welfare reform was not enough to keep a mother and two children living above the poverty line (Besharov, 2006).

Growing up in poverty makes it much more difficult to look after oneself and maintain a sense of wellbeing (Schoon, 2006). Lack of income and poor housing are associated with increased family distress (Conger *et al.*, 2002). In a study of mothers in Malta the lack of income was described as an everyday headache which often led to quarrels in the family; marital disagreements occurred more frequently in poor households (Abela and Tabone, 2008b). One mother on the minimum wage explained how she had to stretch her salary to have enough for the very basic necessities, 'buying only what I will be cooking this week' (p. 42). Those receiving unemployment benefits could not afford to go out for a coffee now and again, let alone take a short break once a year. One mother participated in radio competitions in the hope of winning a weekend break.

In the UK (Sharma, 2007), parents admitted that special occasions such as feasts like Christmas and Eid were a nightmare for them because they were living on a shoestring budget. In studies by Rice (2006) and Harker (2006), boys recounted harrowing experiences of other children refusing to visit their cold/damp homes, thereby precluding them from building friendships with other children.

On the basis of the indicators provided in the box below, the UNICEF Innocenti Research Centre (2012) published a league table of child deprivation in 29 European countries (Figure 21.1). The data referred to children aged 1 to 16 and were based on calculations derived from the European Union Statistics on Income and Living Conditions (EU-SILC) of 2009.

Children's material deprivation: 14 child-specific indicators

Children are considered to be deprived if they do not have:

- three meals a day
- at least one meal a day with meat, chicken or fish (or a vegetarian equivalent)
- fresh fruit and vegetables every day
- books suitable for the child's age and knowledge level (not including school books)
- outdoor leisure equipment (bicycle, roller skates, etc.)
- regular leisure activities (swimming, playing an instrument, participating in youth organisations, etc.)
- indoor games (at least one per child, including educational toys, building blocks, computer games, etc.)
- money to participate in school trips and events
- a quiet place with enough room and light to do homework
- an Internet connection
- some new clothes (not all second-hand)
- two pairs of properly fitting shoes (including one pair of all-weather shoes)
- the opportunity, from time to time, to invite friends home to play and eat
- the opportunity to celebrate special occasions such as birthdays, name days, religious events, etc.

Figure 21.1 shows the percentage of children in each of the 29 countries who lacked two or more of the 14 items considered essential for children's wellbeing, but which the family could not afford. Children in Central and Eastern European countries fared the worst. Children in France and Italy also fared badly, despite living in developed economies.

Prospects for children living in poverty

Poor parents normally want their children to move out of poverty. Mothers in Malta were very aware that educational achievement would help their children do so (Abela and Tabone, 2008b). However, although parents in poor households helped their children with their homework as much as parents in non-poor households, a statistically significant number of children living in poor families had to repeat an academic year. Wertheimer (2003) also reported that children living in poverty in the USA often repeated a grade at school. One of the mothers interviewed in the Maltese study (Abela and Tabone, 2008b) found it very difficult to motivate her children to study. She commented: 'They start mentioning others and they tell you: My friends are like

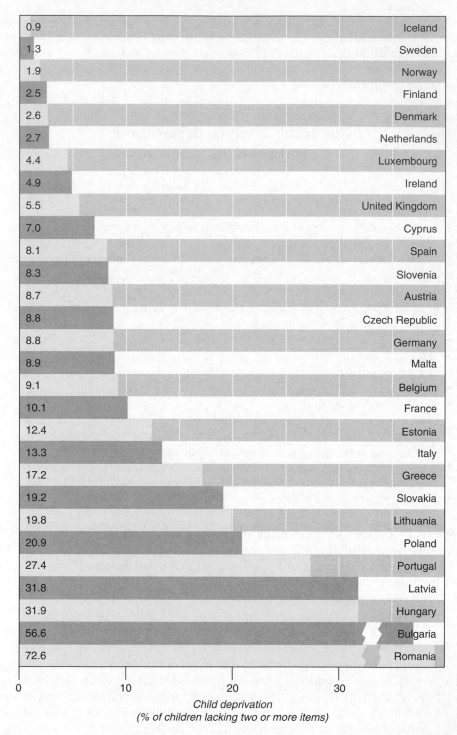

0.9	Iceland
1.3	Sweden
1.9	Norway
2.5	Finland
2.6	Denmark
2.7	Netherlands
4.4	Luxembourg
4.9	Ireland
5.5	United Kingdom
7.0	Cyprus
8.1	Spain
8.3	Slovenia
8.7	Austria
8.8	Czech Republic
8.8	Germany
8.9	Malta
9.1	Belgium
10.1	France
12.4	Estonia
13.3	Italy
17.2	Greece
19.2	Slovakia
19.8	Lithuania
20.9	Poland
27.4	Portugal
31.8	Latvia
31.9	Hungary
56.6	Bulgaria
72.6	Romania

Child deprivation
(% of children lacking two or more items)

Figure 21.1 League table of child deprivation, 29 economically advanced countries
Source. UNICEF Innocenti Research Centre (2012), *Measuring Child Poverty: New league tables of child poverty in the world's rich countries*, Innocenti Report Card 10, UNICEF Innocenti Research Centre, Florence.

that' (p. 39). Children told their parents that they study in vain, and some parents believed that their children were not good at schoolwork.

Horgan (2007) compared children living in poverty in Northern Ireland with those in better-off families in respect of their experiences of school. Children living in poverty were aware that their outcomes were not going to be as good as those of more advantaged children. Some of the boys had already started to disengage from school by the age of 9. Older children complained about being shouted at by the teachers. They did not like the compulsory nature of schooling, found the school day too long, and complained about the food in the canteen and the untidy playground.

Parents who participated in a Council of Europe project on support for parenting children at risk of social exclusion (Abela and Berlioz, 2007) were very disappointed that their children were not helped to overcome their learning difficulties. They felt that the school did not treat them as partners in the education of their children. In the Maltese study, parents and teachers blamed each other with regard to the children's performance (Abela and Tabone, 2008a). Virtuous circles of cooperation between parents and teachers can emerge when parents are interested in their children's progress and show their children that they believe in them. In turn, teachers boost the children's confidence by helping them to have high aspirations for their future (Schoon *et al.*, 2004).

Schools alone cannot respond to the challenges that poor children face. Brooks-Gunn *et al.* (1999) described five main pathways through which poverty may impact on children's wellbeing: health and nutrition, parents' mental health, parenting behaviour, the home environment and conditions in the neighbourhood. Poor children often have a low birth weight and retarded growth, which in turn impact on their cognitive development. Liu *et al.* (2004) showed that malnutrition impairs neurocognitive functioning. Barajas *et al.* (2008) cite a body of research demonstrating cognitive differences between children living in poverty and non-poor children. These disparities are already visible at age two and continue to be visible at age five or even increase. Indeed, the average cognitive scores of advantaged children are 60 per cent higher than those of disadvantaged children (Lee and Burkam, 2002).

The Need for Early Intervention

Experts in child development have focused their attention on the benefits of early education for children living in poverty (Johnson *et al.*, 2008). Poor children may suffer from a 'double disadvantage', whereby they are both 'less likely to enjoy resources in the home that promote the development of skill sets needed for school success, and less likely to benefit from resources outside the home that come from attending cognitively stimulating early care or education programmes' (Johnson *et al.*, 2008, p. 96).

Recent research has shown that high-quality pre-school education can considerably reduce the school readiness gap for disadvantaged children (Magnuson and Waldfogel, 2005). Effective childcare programmes such as 'Head Start' in the USA provide a whole array of interventions which include health services, home visits, parent education, childcare and family support. The mix of home visiting and services provided at a children's centre was found to be the most effective (Love *et al.*, 2005). Miller and Eakin (2009) also found that home-based child development intervention for pre-school children from socially disadvantaged families optimises children's developmental outcomes through education, and through training and supporting parents in their own home to provide a more nurturing environment.

The Importance of a Nurturing Family Environment for Children

Parenting plays a crucial role in child development (McLoyd *et al.*, 2006). Schoon and Bartley (2008) reported that children brought up in a stable environment by parents who showed an active interest in their children's prospect of continuing their education beyond school leaving age were doing well academically, in spite of the fact that they were living in rented and overcrowded homes with parents holding unskilled jobs. Bartley *et al.* (2007) highlighted the importance of children having a warm relationship with both parents. This was associated with a more secure attachment in adulthood, which, in turn, was associated with career advancement for those who did not have post-secondary education. Similarly, Conger and Conger (2000) reported that children were more likely to do well in school and have good relationships with other children, and were more confident and exhibited less distress, when parents were nurturing towards them. In her comprehensive study of 750 adolescents living in the Dortmund area of Germany, Hoelscher (2008b) concluded that the wellbeing of the young people depended mainly on the quality of their family life.

Nevertheless, it is very difficult for parents to contain the stress and anxiety of living in poverty in the context of what Arditti *et al.* (2010) have termed 'cumulative disadvantage'. These authors cite a host of contextual risk factors which exacerbate disadvantage, including poor neighbourhoods, parental unemployment, single-parent households with three children or more, chronic mental and physical problems, and being a member of a racially, ethnically and socio-economically disadvantaged group. Conger and Conger (2000) report that parents living in such conditions tend to become depressed and highly anxious, to the extent that parenting styles are disrupted and parent–child interactions lack the desired warmth (McLoyd, 1990). Poor parenting resulting from maternal depression can have even worse effects in terms of developmental outcomes for low-income children (Petterson and Albers, 2001; Smith *et al.*, 2001). When parents are depressed, they are less attentive and or less responsive to the needs of their children. Elder (1999) found that parental distress in situations of poverty triggered marital conflict, and that fathers were punitive towards their sons. Harsh parenting and spanking were also reported in other studies (Dodge *et al.*, 1994; Linver *et al.*, 2002).

It has been easy to point to parenting deficits when children have poor outcomes, but there is a need to be cautious when attempting to blame parents. In a study of maternal distress and parenting in low-income families in which one parent was in prison, Arditti *et al.* (2010) insisted on the importance of understanding maternal distress in context. In their examination of the links between cumulative disadvantage, maternal distress and parenting practices in poor families, they found that mothers had an intense 'desire to protect their children and to make up for past mistakes' (p. 142).

The potentially detrimental consequences for families of living in extreme poverty

Families living in extreme poverty need help and support. They are, however, unlikely to ask for the help they need, out of fear that their children might be taken into care. Renoux's (2008) description of this phenomenon is summarised in the box below.

Families with children living in extreme poverty

The majority of parents living in extreme poverty do not have the means to raise their children in such a way as to guarantee them a poverty-free future. The most revealing aspect of their lives is their fear, in particular the fear that their children will be taken away from them. This fear can result in conflict, aggression, and even subordination. Because of this fear, very poor parents will not risk asking for help or making use of services which could support them in their role as parents.

All too often, the response from social workers in many countries has been to remove a child from its family and to place the child in out-of-home care. The majority of children who are taken into care by social services are those living in vulnerable situations or chronic poverty. Very often, 'negligence' and 'educational failure' are cited in support of decisions to remove children from parental care (ATD Fourth World, 2004a,b). In these circumstances, parents living in extreme poverty are often punished for the initiatives they take to resolve matters. Arditti *et al.* (2010) report how a parent had been evicted by her housing supervisor because she had invited her sister-in-law and family to stay in her house to take care of her other children while she looked after a child who was hospitalised for three months. A mother in France who had sought help pointed out:

> We were living with two children, a one-year-old and a two-year-old, in a garage, with no water, no electricity, no toilet, nothing. So they took our children away. What we expected was a heated place to live, money for food and a job so the children could be proud of us. Instead they took our children away. (ATD Fourth World, 2004b, p. 86)

Families such as this one who are deprived economically, culturally and socially may well be split up as a result of the difficult situation in which they find themselves. Parents do not always feel empowered to challenge those in authority: they consider the 'placement' of their children to be a punishment (Renoux, 2008). There are numerous reports by children and parents which testify to the painful consequences of a decision to take children into care. This issue lies at the very heart of the lives and histories of very poor families (ATD Fourth World, 2004a). It is impossible not to recognise the link between poverty and the removal of children from their parents. Child protection and poverty go together (Hooper *et al.*, 2007). This has been documented in various European countries (ATD Fourth World, 2004b). Parents who experience vulnerability and exclusion are frequently subject to the interventions of child protection services (Arditti *et al.*, 2010). When their children are taken away from them, they feel that they have not been afforded recognition of, or support for, the efforts they have made to execute their parental responsibilities. The failure to deal with the family's problems and the rapid removal and placement elsewhere of the child merely contribute to the parents' feelings of exclusion. They are deemed incapable and considered responsible for causing the difficult family situation, a situation which they could not control and for which they needed help.

In addition to the pain these parents experience when their child is taken away from them, they are deeply wounded and bereft of social recognition: 'They told me I wasn't fit to raise my children!' (Renoux, 2008, p. 36). Research indicates that parents feel insulted, discredited, powerless and unworthy. Children suffer when others form negative opinions and critical judgements about their parents. Renoux (2008) asks how children can love a father or mother who has been discredited in this way. Moreover, separation can be hurtful and traumatic. This is exacerbated when separation is carried out hastily, more often than not generating psychological reactions which are difficult to manage. The child can develop feelings of guilt, especially in situations where they themselves might have disclosed the dysfunctional nature of their family.

Enforced separation from parents can cause a child to believe that they no longer belong in their own family. This creates deep wounds which can lead to relational and behavioural difficulties. These pose a serious hindrance to learning, social inclusion and interaction. When a family link is broken, children are affected throughout their life. The pain of separation may be further exacerbated when siblings are split up. Sometimes this is necessary, but all too often siblings are torn apart. This separation of brothers and sisters demonstrates a lack of respect for family life (Abels-Eber, 2006). If parents refuse the ruling of the authorities, they are reprimanded for not cooperating with social workers. The exclusion of parents from decisions concerning their children is not only a legal concern, but also undermines the bond that parents have with their children. This bond may be weakened further when the support necessary for planning the child's return to their family is insufficient or nonexistent. In such situations, parents find themselves alone whereas they should be benefiting from even greater support. The parent–child bond may be threatened because the time spent together is too infrequent, and meetings are too far apart, not long enough, and increasingly monitored (Renoux, 2008).

Implications for Policy

In an attempt to support families living in poverty, especially those with dependent children, a number of policy proposals should be considered. First and foremost, children and families require effective access to fundamental rights in all areas of life, including housing, health, culture, education and employment, that would allow for the promotion of the family as a whole. Helping parents to find gainful employment that gives them the possibility to move out of poverty should be a prime consideration. Single parents who live on one salary should not be left to fend for themselves when the pay cheque is insufficient to lift the family out of poverty (Besharov, 2006; Ridge, 2009). It is therefore essential to find ways of compensating for the existing income inequality relating to those at the bottom of the income distribution ladder.

Parents need to be involved in decisions about their children, particularly in respect of education and health. This approach should be adopted from pregnancy and continue after the birth of the child, allowing parents to maintain a close link with their children and develop their educational potential. When this approach is respected, children can be proud of their parents because they see them actively doing something to protect and nurture them. The United Nations Convention on the Rights of the Child makes it clear that children should have a voice in decisions which affect them.

This is being increasingly recognised in social policy and support for children living in challenging family conditions is increasing. It is now acknowledged that families living in poverty, especially families at risk of being separated, need to be actively supported. Interventions should reinforce the parents' ability to fulfil their responsibilities. Parents need to be helped to acquire the knowledge and skills to help their children develop, and they must be supported, strengthened, encouraged and monitored in the long term, especially if they have been experiencing poverty for several years.

Encouraging parents to seek help early, and removing the fear and stigma associated with doing so, are key aspects of family policy agendas. There is still a long way to go, however, to reach those who do not dare approach support services (Gregg, 2008; Renoux, 2008). Every effort must be made to develop collective and cultural activities to allow parents to form friendships through meetings with other parents. Self-help groups can help parents to overcome a sense of shame and isolation. Childcare centres and play schools are ideal venues for activities which give parents the opportunity to play a role in the development and growth of their young child. Creating the conditions for parents and children to be together, share enjoyable moments and have positive experiences helps to strengthen affectionate ties within families.

Good planning is essential. Increasingly, professionals are involving parents in the decision-making process. This builds on the strengths of the family and promotes their social networks, takes their hopes into consideration, and respects all of the people involved. In situations in which removing a child from its parents is essential, 'the aim of removal and placement must be to unite the parent and child again' (Olsson v. Sweden, no. 1, 24 March 1988, §81; Johansen v. Norway, 7 August 1996, §78; E.P. v. Italy, 16 November 1999, §64). Care plans are essential to enable families to stay in contact and create the conditions for the child to return to the family home. Encounters between parents and their children should be promoted and constructive relationships fostered.

Human rights are now enshrined in law in most countries. Respecting these is paramount; to respect the law means to respect human dignity. All families, especially the most deprived, need to be informed about their rights and how to exercise them. Examples of these rights include being able to appeal against a decision, and the right to consult the legal file at court before a hearing.

Professionals working with very poor families need support and high-quality training. Sometimes their knowledge is insufficient and there is a risk that they could form prejudiced opinions about these families. Professionals can find it useful to learn from poor people directly about their hopes, experiences and family/community relationships. Interdisciplinary training allows for an exchange of knowledge and opinions, and can increase understanding (see e.g. Fourth World University Research Group, 2007). Truly significant changes to policies for eradicating child poverty can only be carried out with the participation of very vulnerable people. This requires a commitment to build a common understanding of what it is like to live on the margin in affluent societies (Renoux, 2008).

Conclusion

Harkness (2012) has pointed out that there is 'a strong moral case for reducing childhood poverty' (p. 79). The effects on children living in poverty tend to persist into adulthood. Supporting children and their families is therefore the only effective way to break the intergenerational cycle of poverty for future generations. The current world economic recession does not augur well in this regard. The future of families with children living in poverty is bleak (Unicef Innocenti Research Centre, 2012). Globalisation will continue to widen the income gap between low- and high-skilled jobs (Harkness, 2012). The unemployed and those who are unable to work because of health problems or disability, as well as those in single-parent households, will find it increasingly difficult to move out of poverty. In this respect the statement of Paul Bouchet (in Renoux, 2008, p. 245) is highly pertinent: 'the right for each family to raise its children in dignity can only be applied if the whole of society recognises the fundamental nature of these rights and guarantees the material and moral conditions for them to be exercised.'

References

Abela, A. and Berlioz, G. (2007) Support for parenting children at risk of social exclusion, in M. Daly (ed.), *Parenting in Contemporary Europe: A positive approach* (Strasbourg: Editions du Conseil de l'Europe), 87–101.

Abela, A. and Tabone, C. (2008a) Processes of poverty and social exclusion, in D. R. Crane and T. B. Heaton (eds), *Handbook of Families and Poverty* (Thousand Oaks, CA: Sage), 144–160.

Abela, A. and Tabone, C. (2008b) *Research on the Family, No. 1: Family poverty and social exclusion with a special emphasis on children* (Malta: National Family Commission).

Abels-Eber, C. (2006) *Pourquoi on nous a séparés?* (Paris: Editions Érès).

Antuofermo, M. and Di Meglio, E. (2012) 23% of EU Citizens were at risk of poverty or social exclusion in 2010, *Statistics in Focus 9/2012* (Luxembourg: Eurostat).

Arditti, J., Burton, L. and Neeves-Bothelho, S. (2010) Maternal distress and parenting in the context of cumulative disadvantage, *Family Process*, 49(2): 142–164.

ATD Fourth World (2004a) *How Poverty Separates Parents and Children: A challenge to human rights* (Méry-sur-Oise: Fourth World).

ATD Fourth World (2004b) *Valuing Children, Valuing Parents: Focus on family in the fight against child poverty in Europe* (Méry-sur-Oise: Fourth World).

Barajas, R. G., Philipsen, N. and Brooks-Gunn, J. (2008) Cognitive and emotional outcomes for children in poverty, in D. R. Crane and T. B. Heaton (eds), *Handbook of Families and Poverty* (Thousand Oaks, CA: Sage), 311–333.

Bartley, M., Head, J. and Stansfeld, S. (2007) Is attachment style a source of resilience against health inequalities at work?, *Social Science and Medicine*, 64(4): 765–777.

Besharov, D. (2006) End welfare life as we know it, *New York Times*, 15 August. http://www.nytimes.com [Accessed 9 January 2012.]

Bouchet, P. (2008) Postface, in M. C. Renoux (ed.), *Réussir la Protection de l'Enfance avec les Familles en Précarité* (Paris: Editions de l'Atelier/Editions Quart Monde).

Bradshaw, J. and Mayhew, E. (2011) *The Measurement of Extreme Poverty in the European Union* (Brussels: Directorate General for Employment, Social Affairs and Inclusion).

Brooks-Gunn, J., Rebello Britto, P. and Brady, C. (1999) Struggling to make ends meet, in M. E. Lamb (ed.), *Parenting and Child Development in 'Nontraditional' Families* (Mahwah, NJ: Lawrence Erlbaum), 279–304.

Commission of the European Communities (2000) Contribution of the European Commission to the Special European Council in Lisbon, 23–24 March 2000 (Council Document No. 6602/00 of 1/03/2000).

Conger, R. D. and Conger, K. J. (2000) Resilience in midwestern families: selected findings from the first decade of a prospective, longitudinal study, *Journal of Marriage and Family*, 64(2): 361–373.

Conger, R. D., Wallace, L. E., Sun, Y., Simons, R. L., McLoyd, V. C. and Brody, G. (2002) Economic pressure in African American families: a replication and extension of the family stress model, *Developmental Psychology*, 38(2): 179–193.

Dodge, K. A., Pettit, G. S. and Bates, J. E. (1994) Socialization mediators of the relation between socioeconomic status and child conduct problems, *Child Development*, 65(2): 649–665.

Elder, G. H. (Jr) (1999) *Children of the Great Depression: Social change in life experience* (Boulder, CO: Westview).

Fourth World University Research Group (2007) *The Merging of Knowledge: People in poverty and academics thinking together* (Lanham, MD: University Press of America).

Frazier, H. and Marlier, E. (2012) 2011 *Assessment of Social Inclusion Policy Developments in the EU: Main findings and suggestions on the way forward*. http://www.peer-review-social-inclusion.eu [Accessed 10.10.2012.]

Gregg, P. (2008) *Realising Potential: A vision for personalised conditionality and support* (London: Department for Work and Pensions).

Harker, L. (2006) *Chance of a Lifetime: The impact of bad housing on children's lives* (London: Shelter).

Harkness, S. (2012) The future for low-income families and social cohesion, in *The Future of Families to 2030* (Paris: OECD), 57–117.

Hoelscher, P. (2008a) *The New World Bank $1.25 a Day—A Global Poverty Line for Children?* UNICEF RO CEE/CIS.

Hoelscher, P. (2008b) Children and young people's experience of poverty and social exclusion, in T. Ridge and S. Wright (eds), *Understanding Poverty, Inequality and Wealth: Policies and prospects* (Bristol: The Policy Press), 180–201.

Hooper, C. A., Gorin, S., Cabral, C. and Dyson, C. (2007) *Living with Hardship 24/7: The diverse experiences of families in poverty in England* (London: Buttle UK).

Horgan, G. (2007) *The Impact of Poverty on Young People's Experience of School* (York: Joseph Rowntree Foundation).

Johnson, A. D., Tarrant, K. and Brooks-Gunn, J. (2008) Early childhood education and care: an opportunity to enhance the lives of poor children, in D. R. Crane and T. B. Heaton (eds), *Handbook of Families and Poverty* (Thousand Oaks, CA: Sage), 82–103.

Lee, V. E. and Burkam, D. T. (2002) *Inequality at the Starting Gate: Social background differences in achievement as children begin school* (Washington, DC: Economic Policy Institute).

Linver, M. R., Brooks-Gunn, J. and Kohen, D. E. (2002) Family processes as pathways from income to young children's development, *Developmental Psychology*, 38(5): 719–734.

Liu, J., Raine, A., Venables, P. H. and Mednick, S. A. (2004) Malnutrition at age 3 years and externalizing behavior problems at ages 8, 11 and 17 years, *American Journal of Psychiatry*, 161(11): 2005–2013.

Love, J. M., Kisker, E. E., Ross, C, Raikes, H., Constantine, J., Boller, K. and Vogel, C. (2005) The effectiveness of early Head Start for 3-year-old children and their parents: lessons for policy and programs, *Developmental Psychology*, 41(6): 885–901.

McLoyd, V., Aikens, N. and Burton, L. (2006) Childhood poverty, policy, and practice, in W. Damon, R. M. Lerner, K. A. Renninger and I. E. Sigel (eds), *Handbook of Child Psychology, Vol. 4: Child psychology in practice* (Thousand Oaks, CA: Sage), 6th edn, 700–775.

McLoyd, V. C. (1990) The impact of economic hardship on black families and children: psychological distress, parenting and socio-emotional development, *Child Development*, 61(2): 311–346.

Magnuson, K. A. and Waldfogel, J. (2005) Early childhood care and education: effects on racial and ethnic gaps in school readiness, *Future of Children*, 15(1), 169–196.

Miller, S. and Eakin, A. (2009) Home based child development interventions for pre-school children from socially disadvantaged families, *Cochrane Database of Systematic Reviews 2009*, Issue 4, Art. No. CD008131, doi: 10.1002/14651858.CD008131.

Orshansky, M. (1969) How poverty is measured, *Monthly Labor Review*, 92(2), 37–41.

Petterson, S. M. and Albers, A. B. (2001) Effects of poverty and maternal depression on early child development, *Child Development*, 72(6): 1794–1813.

Ravallion, M., Chen, S. and Sangraula, P. (2008) A dollar a day revisited, research working paper No. 4620, World Bank, May.

Ravallion, M., Chen, S. and Sangruala, P. (2009) A dollar a day revisited, *World Bank Economic Review*, 23(2): 163–184.

Renoux, M.-C. (2008) *Réussir la Protection de l'Enfance avec les Familles en Précarité* (Paris: Editions de l'Atelier/Editions Quart Monde).

Rice, B. (2006) *Against the Odds: An investigation comparing the lives of children on either side of Britain's housing divide* (London: Shelter).

Ridge, T. (2009) *Living with Poverty: A review of the literature on children's and families' experiences of poverty*, Research Report No. 594 (London: Department for Work and Pensions).

Schoon, I. (2006) *Risk and Resilience: Adaptations in changing times* (Cambridge: Cambridge University Press).

Schoon, I. and Bartley, M. (2008) The role of human capability and resilience, *The Psychologist*, 21(1): 24–27.

Schoon, I., Parsons, S. and Sacker, A. (2004) Socioeconomic adversity, educational resilience, and subsequent levels of adult adaptatation, *Journal of Adolescent Research*, 19(4): 383–404.

Sharma, N. (2007) *It Doesn't Happen Here: The reality of child poverty in the UK* (London: Barnardo's).

Smith, J. R., Brooks-Gunn, J., Kohen, D. and McCarton, C. (2001) Transitions on and off AFDC: implications for parenting and children's cognitive development, *Child Development*, 72(5): 1512–1533.

The Economist (2010) The Millennium Development Goals: Global targets, local ingenuity, 23 September. http://www.economist.com/node/17090934 [Accessed 10.10.2012.]

UNICEF Innocenti Research Centre (2012) *Measuring Child Poverty: New league tables of child poverty in the world's rich countries, Innocenti Report Card 10* (Florence: UNICEF Innocenti Research Centre).

United Nations (2010) *The Millennium Development Goals Report 2010.* http://www.un.org [Accessed 15 June 2010.]

United Nations, International Day of Families (2011) Confronting family poverty and social exclusion [background note]. http://social.un.org/index/Family/InternationalObservances/

InternationalDayofFamilies/2011.aspx [Accessed 4 April 2012.]

US Census Bureau (2011) POV10: People in Families by Number of Working Family Members and Family Structure: 2010 [table]. http://www.census.gov/hhes/www/cpstables/032011/pov/new10_100_01.htm [Accessed 1 December 2011.]

Walker, R. and Collins, C. (2004) Families of the poor, in J. Scott, J. Treas and M. Richards (eds), *The Blackwell Companion to the Sociology of Families* (Oxford: Blackwell), 193–217.

Wall, K., Leitao, M. and Ramos, V. (2010) *Social Inequality and Diversity of Families.* http://www.familyplatform.eu/en/1-major-trends/reports/7-social-inequality-and-diversity-of-families [Accessed 7 October 2011.]

Wertheimer, R. (2003) Poor families in 2001: parents working less and children continue to lag behind. Brief (Publication No. 2003–10), May. http://www.childtrends.org [Accessed 30 July 2011.]

Wight, V. R., Chau, M. and Aratani, Y. (2011) Who are America's poor children?: The official story. Brief, March (New York: National Centre for Children in Poverty).

22

Mate Selection and Marriage Stability in the Maghreb

Sabah Ayachi

Introduction

This chapter examines the current criteria for mate selection operated by the younger generation in Algeria, and the lifestyle of young married couples, and marital stability, in Algeria and in the Maghreb as a whole. It draws heavily on a recent quantitative study of people in different social, educational and professional strata carried out by the author.

The Changing Social and Cultural Context in the Maghreb and Algeria

The Maghreb is the western region of North Africa. It comprises six countries, given here with their populations in 2010: Algeria (36.6 million), Morocco (32.7 million), Tunisia (11.5 million), Libya (6.5 million) and Mauritania (4 million). These countries share common values, customs and traditions. Arabic is the official language and the Tamazight (Berber) language is used in some regions in Algeria, Morocco and Libya. In addition, the French language is widely used in the administrative, economic and education sectors and in the media (except for in Libya). Muslims represent some 98 per cent of the population and the other 2 per cent comprises Christians and Jews.

The Maghreb has witnessed rapid changes in all spheres of life (mainly after independence): economic, social, cultural, political, religious, and in the media. Algeria has engaged in large development programmes based on heavy industry that have speeded

Contemporary Issues in Family Studies: Global Perspectives on Partnerships, Parenting and Support in a Changing World, First Edition. Edited by Angela Abela and Janet Walker.
© 2014 John Wiley & Sons, Ltd. Published 2014 by John Wiley & Sons, Ltd.

up the rural exodus and the expansion of cities. At its inception, this development created employment, but gradually, owing to demographic growth (young people now represent more than 75% of the population) and increasing difficulties facing heavy industry, unemployment among the young increased from mid-1980s levels, accompanied by a sharp decrease in living standards for the majority of the population. Housing shortages have exacerbated the situation. On the whole, Morocco and Tunisia have undergone fewer changes than Algeria. Their economic policies have relied on tourism, agriculture and some light industries, all of which have helped to stabilise the rural population.

In terms of social policy, Algeria has made considerable efforts since gaining its independence in 1962 to provide access to health and education for everyone. These have led to improving standards in education, particularly for women, thereby opening up access to different jobs in the public and private sectors, particularly in education, health, administration, and jobs previously reserved exclusively for men (in justice, industry, engineering, the army and the police). This shift has allowed Algeria to combine positive traditional values with modern values. Nevertheless, housing policies still fail to satisfy the demand of a growing population in the urban areas.

Culturally and in the media, Algeria displays a rich cultural diversity that combines the traditional values of the subcultures of each region with modernity: architecture, the culinary arts, fashion and marriage ceremonies are influenced by national and foreign (Western and Oriental) media, particularly TV channels, shaping young people's behaviour and conceptions of marriage and child rearing.

In family life, different policies provide for free choice in respect of marital partner, familial stability, a spouse's rights and duties, childcare and children's rights, monogamy or polygamy, divorce and inheritance. Different policies have been implemented in order to address conflicting views about family life. In Tunisia, for example, since 1956, policies have promoted equality between women and men and monogamy in marriage (*Tunisian Personal Status Code*, 1956), representing a move away from polygamy and Islamic teaching, which still allows polygamy in certain situations and under strict conditions. Algeria (*Algerian Family Code*, 2007) and Morocco (*Morocco Family Code*, 2004) have also promoted women's rights; Algeria has raised the legal age of marriage to 19, and Morocco (along with Tunisia) has raised it to 18, and both have allowed freedom of choice in respect of marital partners despite continuing to allow polygamy under certain conditions. In the Maghreb, family policy is primarily derived from Islamic legislation in order to promote stability in family life, but it has adjusted to the various changes taking place in society. As a result, some young people are choosing to cohabit or enter into a traditional customary marriage without legal bond (known as *zawage orfy*), particularly in Tunisia.

The implications for family life

All these changes in the Maghreb countries have had a profound effect on family structures, with a decline in the number of extended families and the rapid growth of families in which roles are distributed between spouses on the basis of mutual understanding rather than a hierarchical division of tasks emanating from the husband's authority over the woman's education, her access to jobs in various fields and her role as an income provider. The changes have also directly and indirectly affected the behaviour of the younger generation. Young people now tend to think differently about family life, choosing a partner, and the way in which they want to live their lives. Maghrebi women perform a variety of roles, including taking responsibility for family stability, looking after the home, bringing up the children even when they are working outside the home, and attempting to influence their husband's behaviour. Of particular importance are the changing ways of forming relationships and selecting a partner.

Radical changes affecting the mate selection process

The changes have provided:

- increased opportunities for young people to meet
- increased education levels for women
- more freedom to exercise personal choice in choosing a partner

While the process of mate selection has changed considerably, young people often make compromises to take account of their families' wishes and selection criteria in order to gain approval. Nevertheless, there appears to be a paradox: despite increased opportunities to select the 'right' partner, it can be difficult to find an appropriate mate because appearances are thought to be deceptive and expectations have become very high. Consequently, some young people fall back on more traditional methods, consulting with a range of other people before getting engaged. So while there are new and more liberating processes at work, the more traditional ways of selecting a partner have been reinterpreted, including the importance of religiosity, lineage and wealth, in order to protect family stability. Overall, however, there is much greater recognition of the need to respect the dignity and aspirations of women within marriage, to promote mutual support between spouses within the home and to encourage shared responsibility for child rearing. The more traditional religious expectations of husbands having absolute authority in the home are diminishing in favour of a more enlightened religiosity.

Theories of Mate Selection

In order to understand the research findings presented in this chapter, two theories of mate selection have been posited. The first, the theory of homogamy, postulates that 'people tend to marry those who are similar to them' (Girard, 1964, p. 27). Despite the changes from one generation to another and the growing diversity of environments and social groups, it is more likely that people marry within their own social environment than in a different one. Social homogamy (associated with location) is highly variable: it appears to be more pronounced among farmers and labourers but is much less evident among retailers, employees and middle managers. The tendency to select a partner from the same social class background has been noted in many Western industrial countries. The definition of homogamy was modified for the research reported here to take account of the criteria favoured in the Maghreb, and particularly by Algerian families, who traditionally focus on the importance of lineage, religion, morality and physical attributes.

Definition of homogamy

The theory of homogamy suggests that men and women are similar in terms of one (or more) of these specific criteria: morality, goals, educational level, physical attributes (age, height, weight), psychological or physical beauty, status, religiosity, social standing of the family, and way of life. This produces harmony between the parties.

Homogamy is a relative matter which is determined according to the values of each society; it is determined on the one hand by the maturity level of the partners and, on the other, by their parents' moral code.

The second theory is that of complementarity: Robert Francis Winch, in his socio-psychological study of mate selection in the USA (Winch, 1958), linked attraction to another person with psychological needs. There is a psychological combination which leads to attraction; each person is attracted to the other because he/she finds in him/her something that he/she does not own or did not observe in the others. Winch asserts: 'people are inclined towards those who complement their needs' (cited in Bagher, 1968, p. 17).

Definition of complementarity

Complementarity denotes the differences between partners with regard to emotion, temperament, age and biological factors which result in mutual attraction.

Social reality in the Maghreb has shown the importance of both theories and their ability to complement each other in understanding the process of mate selection and creating family stability. Young people's aspirations leading to mutual attraction between partners reflect the renewal or deepening of homogamy and complementarity.

Choice Patterns, Places of Encounter and Their Relation to Family Stability

The research reported here was the first study in the Maghreb countries and the Arab world to combine these two theories in order to examine family stability in the light of the various changes that have taken place in Algerian society. It involved a representative sample of 826 couples in 14 regions.

Choice patterns

The study attempted to assess the main changes that have affected patterns of mate selection in the Maghreb. The main factor was 'personal choice': this was favoured by couples all over Algeria, with a peak in the northern urbanised regions where nuclear families predominate over the more traditional, extended families. The majority of families regarded stability as a key factor. Family stability denotes the constancy of the relationship between members of the family, which is maintained through the fulfilment of basic material needs, homogamy and complementarity between spouses, along with the displaying of the moral qualities of tolerance and faithfulness. Stability is also determined by the complementarity between the family system and family requirements.

Personal choice in selection of a marriage partner is now more important than the choice made by families. Nevertheless, although the patterns of selection have changed radically, families still exercise some influence, particularly in the urbanised northern region of the country. Although arranged marriages are seen to secure a greater level of marital stability, mutual incompatibility and lack of complementarity in an arranged marriage can still result in marital breakdown. Some young people exercise their own personal choice but seek the assistance of their parents. They can be regarded as a transitional group who combine the wishes and desires of parents with their own personal choices. It is a compromise between the old and the new order during a time of social change. It appears to have a positive impact on family stability and offers advantages to all family members because it takes account of traditional family values as well as more modern approaches to choosing a partner. Because of these positive impacts it is emerging as a preferred approach in many regions, particularly as arranged marriages are declining year by year. A similar pattern is evident in Morocco:

> Changes have affected matrimonial structure and norms not only in Casablanca but in the whole country and we are now facing a 'composite' system sketching a new model resting upon freedom of choice where the traditional system characterised by gender segregation and the wife's obedience is still prevailing. The social status remains one of the main considerations for choice. (Aboumalek, 1994, p. 199)

Places of encounter

In the past, families encouraged endogamous marriage (the father's filiation) in order to maintain patriarchal lineage. Great changes have occurred in the twenty-first century in the ways young people meet each other. The main mode of encounter in the past was through an intermediary. In the research discussed here, 34 per cent of couples had met this way. Endogamous marriages are declining today. The intermediaries, who gained the parties' trust, might be a friend or colleague at work, a relative such as a brother, sister or uncle, or neighbours. Meeting through an intermediary does not guarantee stability, however. Ten couples in the study who met via an intermediary had experienced instability in their marriage. Some encounters had been arranged between family members: 23 per cent of the couples comprised partners who were relatives, including cousins. Commonly, marriage between cousins has been regarded as 'the privileged form of marriage that preserves descendants from the struggles that threaten family consistency' (Bonte, 1994, p. 372). Family unions have tended to lead to stability because they strengthen kinship ties and homogamy in customs, traditions and values and increase relational security.

Some 10 per cent of couples in the study had met during family visits, ceremonies and outings. Wedding ceremonies offer an important opportunity for mothers to look for partners for their children among those who appear to have the requisite qualities for homogamy. Mothers tend to seek girls for their sons who have attributes such as domestic skills, physical attractiveness and obedience. Seven per cent of the couples had met in this way. Increasingly, weddings are offering opportunities for young people to meet without their mothers' interference, however. A specific form of such encounters is still prevalent in the southern region of El Hoggar. Its population is made up of tribal groups divided into city dwellers and communities living in the Desert Mountains, especially in Harvak, and both groups are usually invited to the weddings of relatives and friends.

Encounters which happen through the workplace or in other public places reflect the changes in women's employment outside the home and changing attitudes to mate selection. Nearly 10 per cent of couples had met at work, and a further 9 per cent had met in a public place. Relationships which develop through the workplace appear to be less stable than those that evolve more traditionally.

There is considerable evidence illustrating the importance of customs and traditions. Despite the recent changes facilitating a greater degree of personal choice, Tuareg society still emphasises traditional customs. For example, during a wedding ceremony a young man from among the guests may invite a young girl onto the dance floor, and they will both engage in a traditional dance with regular symbolic movements which displays their mutual attraction. These movements are punctuated by the shouting and clapping of other women. At this point, each young person estimates the extent of their mutual harmony: if one of them (particularly the woman) stops dancing, it indicates their rejection of this partner. Often the young man's face is veiled, which shows that inner attributes have a greater importance for selection than physical attributes or material considerations.

Targui traditions differ from those in other regions because of the long duration of the 'necessary acquaintance period' between the engaged partners. During this engagement period, the couple meet in the fiancée's house. It is usual during an engagement period for the couple to meet in the girl's home. The partners are obliged to use a precise and rather restrained vocabulary, sometimes quoting poetry to assess the cleverness of each other and test each other's intellectual ability. If there is dissatisfaction on either side, the engagement is interrupted but the couple are expected to remain friends 'for God's sake'. Targui women enjoy considerable freedom and men are forbidden to exert any form of control or abuse at any time before and during marriage. The bridegroom's family usually requires the couple to live close by.

As norms change it is likely that increasing numbers of young people will meet a partner at college, in the local neighbourhood or at work. Sharing educational and other interests may contribute to the long-term stability of marriages.

Traditional Concepts of Prayer

The research looked at the resurgence of religious practices, albeit with renewed meanings. The Prophet urges Muslims to engage in supplication in prayer (known as 'Istikhara'). When embarking on a major life transition, such as marriage, Muslims should kneel down to pray and then recite a supplication (Istikhara) (El Boukhari, 2002) in order to seek God's help. Istikhara is perceived as having a number of psychological advantages during mate selection.

Istikhara's perceived psychological advantages

- It guides the future spouse to take a rational attitude, useful for morale and social behaviour in that it removes ambiguity, confusion or anxiety.
- It preserves the woman's dignity, chastity and purity and limits the scope of the relationship so as to maintain respect between the affianced parties even if the engagement is ended.
- It prevents any kind of secret engagement.
- It avoids frequent encounters that raise the level of emotional feelings or cause emotional breakdown or social crises that may result in the development of a psychological complex against the opposite sex, leading to an attempt to take revenge or a resort to suicide.

Muslims are also recommended to seek advice from others (called '*Istishara*'). Islamic law does not forbid meetings between the partners during engagement. The research showed a correlation between people with high educational achievement and the performance of rituals such as *Istikhara* before marriage, but a large percentage of research respondents expressed ignorance of *Istishara*. Those who practise *Istishara* may then go on to receive counselling.

Parental Disapproval of Partner Choice

The vast majority (92%) of couples in the study did not experience outright parental disapproval of their choice of partner. They had gained approval from the beginning of the relationship, probably because they had taken their parents' wishes into account anyway. This undoubtedly increases the chances of securing parental approval and avoids the kind of confrontation which can be very stressful for all members of the families involved. These couples also exhibited a high degree of stability in their relationship.

The couples who had experienced parental disapproval gave several reasons for why parents had disapproved of their relationship. These tend to reflect specific social values, attitudes and norms.

Reasons given for parental disapproval of choice of partner

1. The partner is a stranger in the family, tribe or region. This is a legacy of the traditional tribal social system based on endogamy.
2. There is a lack of information about the partner.
3. The partner is younger or older.
4. The partner is divorced or married already.
5. The man does not own a house.
6. The man has bad morals.

When these objectives are considered in the light of the subsequent stability of the marriage, the findings are particularly interesting. Those who married strangers, or someone who was younger or older, or someone who had been married previously, had managed to create stable marriages despite initial parental objections. By contrast, those who knew little about their partner before marriage, or married a man without his own home, or one with bad morals, had relatively unstable marriages.

When parents disapprove of the choice of partners, a negotiation process usually follows to persuade parents to change their minds. Sometimes these negotiations involve emotional blackmail, coercion and threats. Young people who are more highly educated tend to negotiate more effectively, but they may still resort to blackmail and threats (to emigrate, for example).

Protective Factors

The research looked at the protective factors of family stability. Several factors emerged as important: religiosity, fidelity, lineage, physical attributes, professional status and wealth.

Protective factors for family stability

1. *Religiosity*. Religious values emerged as the most important factor for ensuring marital harmony. Women tend to be more interested than men in their partner's religiosity (71% as against 47%). Women regard religiosity as a guarantee of good behaviour and an adequate environment for raising children. Men are more interested in their wife's abilities to run the home in line with traditional values, and their physical attributes.
2. *Fidelity*. Women and men both regarded fidelity as a critical ingredient (100% and 93% respectively). Gender differences revealed that men are more prone to infidelity and attract less stigma for this behaviour. The findings suggest that: men who lack religiosity and parental guidance tend to cheat on their wives; those who experience difficulties in their sexual relationship tend to resort to infidelity; and employment which takes the husband away from home encourages infidelity.
3. *Lineage*. Lineage is particularly important for men: being a member of a respected family and having a good upbringing promote stability.
4. *Physical attributes*. Men were more likely than women to rate their partner's physical attributes as important (31% as against 19%). Men tend to look for facial features and style while women refer to inner beauty, personality and kindness. Nevertheless, physical and personal attributes seem to play an important role in promoting marital stability.
5. *Professional status of the spouse*. This is regarded as less important.
6. *Wealth of the partner*. Algerian men consider themselves to be the provider in the household, enabling them to preserve a level of authority. The partner's wealth is therefore not a key protective factor but is considered important during difficult economic circumstances. Women tended to regard their partner's behaviour as far more important than whether they have money.

Lifestyle and Marriage Stability

The research has found that educational homogamy strengthens marital stability. Men were keen to ensure that their partner's educational level was similar to their own in order to facilitate communication and harmonise ways of thinking.

Love is also regarded as an important ingredient in Islamic Arab cultures. They have a rich history of epic love stories in literature and poetry. While being in love is not an essential criterion for getting married, its importance within marriage has been recognised by both men and women. In the study, love proved to be an essential driving force in marital dynamics and in the upbringing of children: research respondents said that love is not related only to attractiveness (beauty), but depends on tangible aspects that meet psychological, social and cultural requirements. This is likely to guarantee the psychological and social stability of family members. In addition to love, respondents valued mutual respect and understanding that extend the lifespan of the marriage by deepening mutual appreciation, enabling the couple to cope with changes and to resolve problems when they arise. Love and respect enabled couples to deal with adversity and life events, as the following comments by research respondents demonstrate:

> She was patient while I was jobless.
>
> We love each other a lot and can endure our poor living conditions.
>
> He takes care of my sick mother.
>
> I love her even more because she's the mother of my kids.
>
> He is understanding and overlooks my mistakes. He corrects me without hurting my feelings.
>
> He's compassionate and tender.

When problems arise, there is an expectation that these will be discussed between the spouses. In the past, the expectation was that women would always consult their husband about their concerns and problems. More recently, husbands are consulting their wife, behaviour that was previously forbidden because of the hegemony of the traditional patriarchal culture. This change is due in part to the decline in traditional divisions of labour in the home and, in part, to the increased family responsibilities which require continual consultation between husband and wife. Increasingly, couples are no longer sheltered by the extended family and have to manage by themselves.

Patterns of Family Stability in the Maghreb

To demonstrate the variety of family types that exist in the Maghreb, a number of case studies have been drawn from the research, described in the box below. Three illustrate stable families, one illustrates a family facing difficulties, and the final vignette illustrates an unstable family.

Case studies illustrating variations between families

1. *Latifa and Rabeh.* These young people met at college and gained their parents' approval to marry. They have four children and live a considerable distance from their parents. Latifa and Rabeh describe their marriage as stable: they combine traditional values, fulfilling Islamic duties towards each other, and display homogamy and complementarity in their relationship.

2. *Souad and Zine.* Zine was a stranger in his wife's community, but she convinced her parents that her choice of partner was appropriate by focusing on his qualities of honesty and morality. They both work outside the home and are bringing up five children, sharing childcare and domestic tasks. Their marriage remains stable.

3. *Fouzia and Hussein.* This couple met through an intermediary. They have three children and live with Hussein's parents. Fouzia stays at home and takes care of her husband's parents. Hussein's feelings deepened as a result of her care in the home but he started drinking, causing upset in the relationship. With patience and affection Fouzia managed to challenge and change her husband's drinking behaviour and their relationship has stabilised.

4. *Malika and Salim.* Salim fell in love with Malika as soon as he saw her. Since their marriage Malika has worked while also taking care of her children and the home, with help from her mother. Salim is the head of a large company and is frequently away from home. He has not contributed to family life and has been unfaithful. Malika and Salim have a high standard of living but their relationship is in difficulty. Malika has decided to do her best to save the marriage for the sake of their children and wants to avoid divorce. This entails her making many personal sacrifices.

5. *Fatima and Ali.* The marriage between Fatima and Ali was arranged by their families. She is very attractive but described as being illiterate, obstinate and stubborn. She is contemptuous of her husband, who is a teacher and heavily involved in educating their eight children. Ali is impulsive, however, and was disappointed to find that his wife shows very little emotional warmth and does little to support him. Their sexual relationship is very poor. Fatima began to turn the children against their father and family life is punctuated by disputes and abuse. This couple are on the verge of divorce.

Implications for the Future of Maghreb Families

Maghreb families are facing major challenges in maintaining their lifestyle and the stability of family members, and in succeeding in the process of educating and guiding their children, especially teenagers. This is due to the many economic, social, housing-related and other changes that have taken place in Maghrebi society in recent years.

The Maghreb countries have made considerable efforts to launch development projects and give priority to education, health, employment and housing policies.

There are disparities between the countries, however, primarily because of the varying resources available and levels of population density. Algeria has had to combat terrorism, unemployment, rising delinquency, severe economic recession and difficult living conditions. It is the most densely populated Maghrebi country and has developed a far-reaching agenda for social reform, including strategies to support families and promote stability. Efforts are being made to tackle unemployment by providing business opportunities, especially to young people (*National Action Plan for Childhood, 2008–15*), and to reduce drug addiction and violence against women (*National Strategy for Combating Violence against Women*, n.d.). In addition, positive steps are being taken to integrate women at all levels of society, increasing opportunities for their participation in public life.

The stability of family life is a key consideration for the Maghreb countries, and a number of experts and specialists are working with governments to improve the health of adults and children, support relationships and protect children. In order to fulfil the policy agenda more skilled practitioners will be needed to deliver services and support families, particularly as traditional culture is combined with modern, Western values and ambitions.

References

Aboumalek, M. (1994) *Qui épouse qui?: le mariage en milieu urbain marocain* [Who To Marry?: Marriage in urban areas of Morocco] (Casablanca: Afrique Orient).

Algerian Family Code, 2007 (Algiers: Ministry of Justice).

Bagher, S. (1968) *Le Choix du conjoint en Iran et en Occident* [Mate Selection in Iran and the West] (Paris: Librairie Générale de Droit et de Jurisprudence).

Bonte, P. (1994) *Epouser au plus proche: inceste, prohibitions et stratégies matrimoniales autour de la Méditerranée* [Marrying the Closest: Incest, prohibitions, marriage strategies around the Mediterranean] (Paris: Editions de l'Ecole des Hautes Etudes en Sciences Sociales).

El-Boukhari, S. (2002) *Summary of Sahih El-Boukhari* (Beirut: Dar El Fikr).

Girard, A. (1964) *Une Enquête psycho-sociologique sur le choix du conjoint dans la France contemporaines* [A Psycho-sociological Inquiry into Mate Selection in Contemporary France] (Paris: PUF).

Morocco Family Code (2004) http://www.pogar.org/publications/other/laws/family/morocco-familycode2004-a.pdf [Accessed 17.7.2012.]

National Action Plan for Childhood, 2008–2015 (Algiers: Ministry for the Family and Women's Issues).

National Strategy for Combating Violence against Women (n.d.) (Algiers: Ministry for the Family and Women's Issues).

Tunisian Personal Status Code (1956 [amended 2009]) http://www.e-justice.tn/fileadmin/fichiers_site_arabe/codes_juridiques/code_statut_personel_ar_01_12_2009.pdf [Accessed 17.7.2012.]

Winch, R. F. (1958) *Mate Selection: A study of complementary needs* (New York: Harper).

23

Demographic Change and Its Impact on Relationships in Japan and East Asia[1]

James M. Raymo

Introduction

As previous chapters have shown, later marriage, lower fertility and increases in numbers of divorces are reshaping family relations and obligations across the life course. These phenomena may be particularly salient in East Asian countries: Japan, Korea and Taiwan, for example, are among the lowest-fertility, latest-marriage countries in the world, and all have recently experienced rapid increases in divorce. Importantly, these countries are also distinguished by a combination of relatively low levels of public expenditures on education, welfare and family support (OECD, 2011) and a strong policy emphasis on familial provision of support for dependants. The Japanese government has promoted intrafamilial provision of support as the cornerstone of a 'Japanese-style welfare state' (Ogawa and Retherford, 1997) and others have characterised these countries as 'Confucian welfare states' (Jones, 1993). As in the 'strong-family countries' of Southern Europe (Reher, 1998), in East Asia, relatively late departure from the parental home, high rates of post-nuptial co-residence with parents (-in-law) and the high prevalence of intergenerational co-residence at older ages (Lesthaeghe and Moors, 2000; Ogawa and Retherford, 1997) facilitate the

[1] The author's research reported in this chapter was supported by the College of Letters and Science and the Graduate School of the University of Wisconsin-Madison. The research was conducted at the Center for Demography and Ecology and the Center for Demography of Health and Aging at the University of Wisconsin-Madison, which are supported by Center Grants from the National Institute of Child Health and Human Development (R24 HD047873) and the National Institute on Aging (P30 AG17266). So-jung Lim and Tiffany Yeh provided research assistance.

Contemporary Issues in Family Studies: Global Perspectives on Partnerships, Parenting and Support in a Changing World, First Edition. Edited by Angela Abela and Janet Walker.
© 2014 John Wiley & Sons, Ltd. Published 2014 by John Wiley & Sons, Ltd.

intrafamilial exchange of resources and services that in many other industrialised countries are provided by the state.

This chapter considers the implications of rapid demographic change for family relationships across the life course in Japan, Korea and Taiwan and discusses related policy responses. The chapter consists of five sections. The next section describes trends in marriage, fertility and divorce in the three countries, followed by a discussion of living arrangements and family structure at younger ages, focusing on the potential implications of lower fertility for investment in children and extended co-residence in the parental home, as well as the implications of rising divorce rates for exposure to single-parent family structure. Section three considers the potential implications of declining fertility (and associated changes in sibship structure) for marriage market dynamics and the growing prevalence of international marriages. Section four focuses on access to family care at older ages, discussing the ways in which reductions in fertility and increases in childlessness, non-marriage and divorce may limit the access that future cohorts of older men and women have to financial and instrumental support from family members. The chapter concludes with a discussion of the policy implications in response to these changes, focusing particularly on the Japanese experience.

So that it can provide a succinct overview of demographic change and its implications for family relations the chapter is limited in its focus in the following ways. First, the focus is primarily on Japan, while also discussing related trends and relevant research from Korea and Taiwan. Second, the chapter draws almost exclusively on research published in English, although there are large bodies of related research published in Japanese, Korean and Chinese. Third, the focus is limited to family change (trends in marriage, fertility and divorce), paying little attention to other important demographic changes such as declining mortality at older ages (which plays an obvious role in increasing the numbers and ages of older family members who may require care).

Demographic Change in Japan, Korea and Taiwan

Marriage trends

Figure 23.1 presents trends in mean age at first marriage since 1970 for men and women in Japan, Korea and Taiwan. Throughout this period, marriage has occurred relatively late and the mean age at marriage has increased steadily to over 30 for men and over 28 for women in all three countries. These figures are similar to those for many European countries and are substantially higher than in the English-speaking countries.

Marriage has been nearly universal in Japan, Korea and Taiwan and most young men and women indicate that they intend to marry (Kwon, 2007; National Institute for Social Security and Population Research [hereafter NIPSSR], 2007b), but delayed marriage is contributing to an increase in the proportion of people who will never marry. In Japan, for example, the percentage of women in the 1950 birth cohort who had never married (by age 50) was 5.5 per cent, but the projected figure for the 1990 birth cohort is 23.5 per cent (NIPSSR, 2007a, p. 21). Similar increases in non-marriage appear likely in Korea and Taiwan as well (Kwon, 2007). These high levels of non-marriage represent a fundamental shift in the family life course of men and women in East Asia.

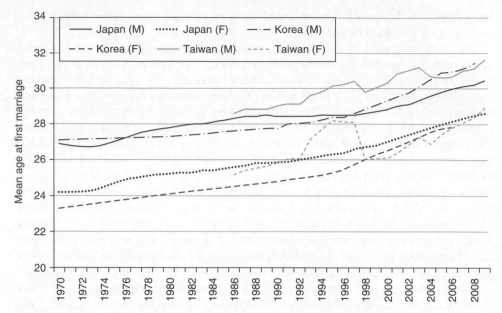

Figure 23.1 Trends in mean age at first marriage in Japan, Korea and Taiwan, by sex (1970–2009)

Note. Values for Korea are interpolated for between 1970 and 1980 and for between 1980 and 1990.

A large body of research has explored possible explanations for the increasing age at marriage and the rising proportion of those who never marry. These explanations include: increasing educational attainment and economic independence for women; changing attitudes towards marriage and family; shifting marriage market composition; and the difficulty of balancing work and family. Summaries of this literature can be found in Chen (2009), Choe (2006), Jones (2007), Raymo and Iwasawa (2008), and Retherford *et al.* (2001).

Fertility trends

Because non-marital childbearing is rare in East Asian countries, the trend towards later and less marriage has contributed to substantial reductions in fertility rates, as summarised in Figure 23.2. The Japanese total fertility rate (TFR) fell to replacement level in the 1950s, and the trend since 1970 has been steadily downward. Korea and Taiwan experienced very rapid fertility decline during the 1970s and the TFR is now well below 1.5 in all three countries. The most recent figure for Taiwan (0.90) is one of the lowest in the world. Posited explanations for fertility decline are similar to those emphasised in research on later and less marriage: increasing opportunity costs of childbearing for women, difficulties balancing work and child rearing, economic uncertainty and the high costs of raising children, and changing attitudes (Chen and Liu, 2007; Eun, 2003; Retherford and Ogawa, 2006).

The most striking feature of fertility change is the projected increase in the proportion of men and women who will remain childless. Primarily reflecting the rise in the proportion who never marry (in combination with very low levels of non-marital childbearing), 37 per cent of Japanese women in the 1990 birth cohort are projected

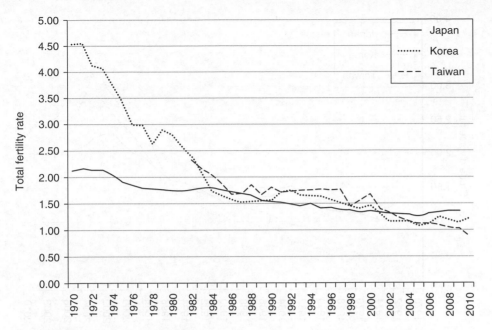

Figure 23.2   Trends in total fertility rate in Japan, Korea and Taiwan (1970–2010)

to remain childless (NIPSSR 2007a, p. 21). This represents a fundamental change in the family life course with potentially important implications for access to family support at older ages, a topic considered later in the chapter.

Divorce trends

Figure 23.3 shows a steady increase in crude divorce rates in all three countries. The current rates of 2.0–2.5 divorces per 1000 population are similar to those in most Western European countries (NIPSSR, 2011). Life table estimates of the probability that a marriage will end in divorce indicate that approximately one-third of Japanese marriages will be dissolved (Raymo *et al.*, 2004), that 22 per cent of Korean marriages will end within 13 years of marriage (Park and Raymo, 2013), and that 25 per cent of women's marriages in Taiwan will end in divorce by age 39 (Yang and Tsai, 2007).

Recent analyses of Japanese and Korean data have demonstrated that divorce is more common among those with lower levels of educational attainment (Ono, 2009; Park and Raymo, 2013), despite the very high costs of divorce for women. In Taiwan there is some support for the role of women's economic independence, with women's employment and earnings positively associated with the risk of divorce (Hsu, 1998). In Japan, over half of divorces involve children, and the fact that the mother receives sole custody of the child(ren) in most cases (NIPSSR, 2011) has resulted in rapid growth in the number of single-mother families. Paternal custody is more common in Korea and Taiwan (Ministry of the Interior, 2001). It is also clear that single mothers are particularly disadvantaged in Japan and other East Asian countries, and that a primary source of economic support for single mothers and their children is co-residence with parents.

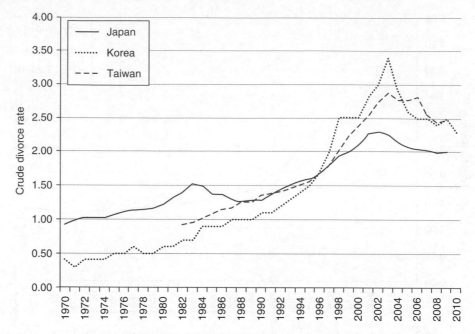

Figure 23.3   Trends in crude divorce rate in Japan, Korea and Taiwan (1970–2010)

Parent–Child Relationships

Investment in children

Theoretical linkages between smaller family size (fewer children) and increased investment in the quality of each child are well-established (Becker, 1991). A desire for
higher-quality children may contribute to reductions in fertility and lower fertility
may, in turn, contribute to increased investment of parental resources in children.
These relationships may be particularly relevant in East Asian countries where cultural
emphasis on educational success is strong (Brinton *et al.*, 1995; Tsuya and Choe,
2004) and the mother's role in fostering children's success is viewed as paramount
(Hirao, 2001, 2007). In all three countries, educational credentials play a central role
in shaping subsequent life outcomes and clear hierarchies of school quality result in
fierce competition for children to enter more prestigious schools. Public spending on
education is relatively low in all three countries (OECD, 2011) and expenditure on
private education is substantial. In Japan, for example, about 6 per cent of family
income is spent on children's education, of which around a quarter is spent on tuition
for cram schools (*juku*) or private tutors (Hirao, 2007).

Theoretical linkages between reduced family size and increased labour force participation for mothers are also well-established (Davis, 1984). In East Asian countries, however,
mothers' investment of time and energy in children's education remains substantial despite
improvements in women's own educational attainment and employment opportunities.
About two-thirds of women in Japan and Korea exit the labour force prior to the birth of
their first child, a figure that has remained unchanged since the 1980s (Lee and Hirata,

2001; Raymo and Lim, 2011).[2] Several scholars attribute this pattern to cultural ideals of 'intensive mothering' and the difficulty of balancing work and family in Japan (Nagase, 2006; Yu, 2009) and, to a lesser extent, in Korea (Lee and Hirata, 2001). The combination of reduced fertility and relatively limited change in mothers' employment suggests an increase in the time, psychological resources and financial resources that families, especially mothers, are able to invest in each child.

Extended co-residence with parents

A longstanding characteristic of Japan and Korea has been relatively late departure from the parental home (Zeng *et al.*, 1994) and extended periods of co-residence in the parental home prior to marriage have become more common in recent years (Fukuda, 2009; Raymo, 2003). The proportion of unmarried Japanese women age 20–29 living with their parents has remained stable at about 0.75 since the mid-1970s, but the overall proportion of young women co-residing with parents has risen dramatically in conjunction with the decline in marriage rates (Raymo, 2003). The proportions living with parents are even higher for young, unmarried men and women in Korea (Korean Statistical Information Service, 2012).

An inverse relationship between the number of siblings and the probability of leaving the parental home prior to marriage (Fukuda, 2009) suggests that declining fertility may also play a role in delaying the transition to independent living. Some have argued that extended co-residence with parents has emerged as an advantageous alternative to early marriage (or other independent living arrangements) as parents have become increasingly willing and able to provide their children with economic support and domestic services (Retherford *et al.*, 2001; Yamada, 1999).

Single-parent families

The number of single-parent families in Japan, the large majority of which are single-mother families, rose by 55 per cent in just ten years, increasing from 789900 in 1993 to 1225400 in 2003 (Ministry of Health, Labour and Welfare, 2005). The proportion of single-mother households among all households with children nearly doubled from 5.3 per cent in 1993 to 9.5 per cent in 2003 (Zhou, 2008). Rapid increases in divorce in Korea (Park *et al.*, 2009) and Taiwan (Jeng and McKenry, 2000) have resulted in similar increases in the prevalence of single-parent families in those countries.

Single parenthood has been linked to less favourable outcomes for children in the USA and other Western countries and there is good reason to suspect that these relationships may be particularly pronounced in Japan and other East Asian countries, where public support for single mothers is relatively limited (Ezawa and Fujiwara, 2005; Kim *et al.*, 2005). High rates of labour force participation and the stress associated with long working hours and low income may result in single mothers spending less time with their children and investing less in their development and educational success relative to their married counterparts.

---

[2]   The pattern in Taiwan is somewhat different, with a more limited labour force exit for women of prime childbearing age (Brinton, 2001).

It is possible, however, that intergenerational support may moderate relationships between single parenthood and the quantity and quality of time spent with children. Recent studies from all three countries indicate that a substantial proportion (roughly one-third) of single mothers co-reside with their parents (Hsieh and Shek, 2008; Park, 2008; Zhou, 2008). In Japan, 60 per cent of single mothers report that they have received some form of support from relatives, often via co-residence with their parents (Japan Institute of Labour, 2003). Research on the ways in which living arrangements shape the wellbeing of single parents and their children is limited, but some studies have found that co-residence with parents is positively associated with the wellbeing of both single mothers and their children (Hsieh and Shek, 2008; Raymo and Zhou, 2012).

Romantic Relationships: The Marriage Market

Sibship position and caregiving obligations

In Japan, Korea and Taiwan, expectations regarding intergenerational obligations are closely related to gender and birth order. All three societies have long histories of patrilineal family arrangements in which eldest sons carry on the family name and household or business. This system often involves co-residence with parents as part of an implicit contract in which the parental generation provides housing, childcare and promises of bequests in exchange for the promise of financial and instrumental support at older ages (Horioka *et al.*, 2000; Ogawa and Retherford, 1997). Under this arrangement, access to resources and status has historically worked to the advantage of eldest sons in the marriage market. However, shifting attitudes and increasing educational and occupational opportunities for women are thought to underlie a growing distaste for the family expectations and obligations that accompany marriage to an eldest son (Long *et al.*, 2009).

As a result of fertility decline, the marriage market is increasingly made up of eldest (only) sons and daughters with no brothers—the men and women who are most likely to expect to co-reside with and eventually care for ageing parents. In addition to the many other factors linked to later or no marriage, an increase in the difficulty of finding an attractive partner without potentially competing obligations/expectations for family care (or co-residence) may further complicate the spouse search process in these societies (Belanger *et al.*, 2010). Consistent with this scenario, Long *et al.* (2009) note that negative attitudes about marrying eldest sons have become widespread since the 1970s, and Raymo (2000) shows that eldest sons have significantly lower rates of marriage than later-born sons.

Eldest sons whose natal home is in a rural area may be particularly disadvantaged in the marriage market. Not only do they face the difficulty of finding a partner who does not have potentially competing obligations to provide care for parents, but they are also burdened with the prospect of living in regions that many women may find unappealing. All three countries are now predominantly urban, and the concentration of population, jobs and amenities in urban areas may make the prospect of marriage to eldest sons whose parents live in rural areas a particularly unattractive prospect for many young women.

International marriages

The deteriorating marriage prospects of eldest sons, as well as those of men with limited earning potential and men living in rural areas, has contributed to an increase in international marriages. Recent data indicate that the percentage of marriages involving one native-born spouse and one foreign-born spouse is 5 per cent in Japan and 13 per cent in Korea (Lee, 2008; NIPSSR, 2011). In Taiwan, the figure rose to 32 per cent in 2003 before falling to 20 per cent in 2005 (Belanger *et al.*, 2010; Jones and Shen, 2008). In all three countries, the large majority of international marriages involve a native-born groom and a foreign bride (Lee, 2008; Jones and Shen, 2008), with a significant proportion of brides coming from developing countries in Asia— especially China, Vietnam and the Philippines. The two primary pathways to international marriage are meetings between domestic men and foreign women who have come to Japan, Korea and Taiwan to work and the so-called 'mail-order' brides. The former often involves women who have come to work in the entertainment industry (e.g. bar hostesses), who more commonly marry men in urban areas, whereas the latter often involves marriage brokers or community efforts to recruit brides from abroad who typically marry men from rural areas (Liaw *et al.*, 2010).

Factors in the rise of international marriages

There are many factors underlying the rise of international marriages:

- increased labour migration
- growing gender differences in attitudes (women preferring more egalitarian relationships and men preferring more traditional relationships)
- the legacy of very high sex ratios in Korea and Taiwan (Kim, 2010)
- the difficulties faced by men (often eldest sons) in finding women who are willing to live in rural areas and co-reside with and potentially provide care for ageing parents-in-law (Jones and Shen, 2008)

The rapid rise in marriages involving native-born men of lower socioeconomic status and women from developing countries in Asia represents a fundamental reshaping of the marriage market and an increase in the diversity of these populations (Belanger *et al.*, 2010). International marriage also appears to play an important role in stemming further fertility decline (Tsay, 2004), but relatively high rates of divorce (Liaw *et al.*, 2010) suggest that many of these marriages may be strained by differences in language and customs, conflict with parents-in-law, financial worries, and other sources of marital conflict.

Elderly Parent–Adult Child Relationships

In all societies, family members play an important role in the provision of health care and financial support at older ages. The role of family is particularly important in Japan and other East Asian countries where, despite universal access to public health care, care for the frail elderly is viewed primarily as a family responsibility (Izuhara, 2002) and the main sources of such care are spouses and children(-in-law), especially wives and daughters (Long, 2008). Like health insurance, public pension coverage is universal in Japan and Korea (it is not universal in Taiwan), but relatively low benefit levels require many older people (especially the self-employed and widows) to rely on savings or the support of family members (see e.g. Lee *et al.*, 1994).

One important difference between East Asian countries and many Western countries is that the provision of care and support to older parents(-in-law) is more normatively expected and valued (Lock 1993; Yamamoto and Wallhagen, 1997), despite its well-recognised burdens. A second difference is that family provision of support is facilitated by the long tradition of intergenerational co-residence and the more recent trend toward multiple generations living separately but in close proximity (Ministry of Internal Affairs and Communications, 2006). In Japan and Korea, the proportion of elderly co-residing with children has declined over time but remains over 40 per cent (NIPSSR, 2011; Population Association of Korea, 2006). In Taiwan, the proportion is even higher (64%).

In this context, the demographic trends described above have potentially important implications for reduced access to family-provided support at older ages. Lower fertility may reduce the likelihood of support to the extent that parents with fewer children are less likely to have a child who lives nearby or does not have competing obligations to live with and care for ageing parents-in-law. The implications of the rapid projected increase in non-marriage and childlessness are even more straightforward. More elderly men and women (who are living longer, with potentially greater care needs) will not have family members (spouses and children) upon whom they can rely for support. Trends in divorce will have a similar effect—especially for men who are less likely to maintain contact with their children following separation. The separation of divorced fathers from their children is extreme in Japan, where joint custody arrangements are rare and mothers typically receive sole custody of children. For those with children, the decline in marriage and family formation in the younger generation will also reduce the likelihood of intergenerational co-residence in which daughters-in-law care for ageing parents (Takagi and Silverstein, 2006), but may increase the prevalence of care provided by co-resident unmarried sons and daughters.

The potential implications of changes in marriage, fertility and divorce can be seen by looking at projected changes in household structure. In Japan, it is clear that intergenerational co-residence—a family structure that has long facilitated the provision of care for elderly parents—is declining. Among households with a head aged 65 and over, the proportion of single-person households is projected to rise to 0.38 by 2030 (NIPSSR, 2010). The implications of demographic changes may be compounded by significant changes in attitudes as well as in the labour force participation of middle-age women. Attitudes towards old age and family provision of support for elderly parents are changing, with the proportion of older cohorts expecting to depend on their children declining and the proportion of younger cohorts believing that it is a 'good custom' or 'natural duty' for children to care for elderly parents dropping sharply (Retherford *et al.*, 1996). It is also important to recognise that families' capacity to provide care to frail elderly parents is diminished by the rising labour force participation rates of middle-aged women—the primary source of family-provided care (Ogawa and Retherford, 1997).

Policy Implications

In rapidly ageing societies like those in East Asia, slowing and reversing fertility decline and promoting labour force attachment among married women are major policy objectives. To the extent that low fertility and the exiting of women from the labour force at childbirth reflect the difficulties of balancing continued work with normatively expected mothering practices, facilitating work–family balance has become a central policy focus in Japan. Over the past several years, the government has introduced an array of measures designed to facilitate child rearing and continued work for mothers. These efforts fall under the heading of 'policies to address low-fertility' (*shōshika taisaku*) and have been introduced in a variety of policy packages including the so-called Angel Plan, New Angel Plan, and Plan to Support the Next Generation (see Retherford and Ogawa, 2006 for details). Specific changes include childcare leave, increased access to public pre-school, and increased childcare allowances (Boling, 2007), but the consensus is that these policies have had limited impact on increasing work–family balance and promoting family formation.

Recognising that the primary force behind very low fertility rates in Japan is the low rate of marriage (combined with limited levels of non-marital childbearing), the aforementioned efforts to facilitate work–family balance seek not only to promote childbearing within marriage but also to promote marriage itself. This is motivated by a belief that the perceived difficulty of work–family balance and maintaining current standards of living is a major barrier to marriage (and thus to childbearing). In addition to these efforts to promote marriage indirectly, there have been several local policy efforts to promote marriage more directly, especially in rural areas. Several depopulated areas in Japan have developed marriage promotion policies, primarily in the form of matchmaking services and cash subsidies (Kitamura and Miyazaki, 2011). In some cases, local communities have taken an even more direct approach by facilitating the recruitment of foreign brides for unmarried local men (Knight, 1995)—efforts that contrast with national policies discouraging the entry of unskilled immigrants.

Social commentators (e.g. Yamada, 1999) have made much of the problems associated with the prevalence of extended co-residence in the parental household, popularising pejorative terms such as 'parasite singles' to bring attention to the problems associated with low levels of youth independence. However, unlike many European countries, policy efforts to promote residential independence at young ages have not been implemented in Japan (or other East Asian countries). Youth unemployment has increased in recent years and policymakers presumably view access to housing and financial support from parents as a welcome resource in limiting youth poverty and the need for additional public welfare expenditure.

In response to concerns about the costs of supporting a rapidly growing elderly population at the same time that families' ability (and perhaps willingness) to support elderly parents is declining, a range of policy changes have been implemented. These include reductions in public pension benefit levels, an increase in the age of pension eligibility (Takayama, 2001), and reduced public spending on health care (Campbell and Ikegami, 2003). Two other major policy changes include the implementation of the long-term care insurance (LTCI) programme in 2000 and a law passed in 2007 that allows women who were full-time housewives to claim a proportion of their ex-husbands' pension benefits in the event of divorce (Fukuda, 2008).

Conclusion

Low fertility and population ageing pose policy challenges in all industrialised countries. This chapter has discussed several ways in which the policy challenges presented by rapid demographic change may be particularly pronounced in three East Asian societies, where public support for families is relatively limited and is supplemented by substantial intrafamilial exchange of resources and support. The Japanese policy changes discussed above represent efforts to respond to the implications of rapid demographic change in a country characterised by familistic social organisation. Subsequent efforts to compare policy responses and their effectiveness in other familistic countries in East Asia and Southern Europe would provide an important source of comparative insight into policies that are more or less effective. Such efforts may be instructive for the many developing countries in Southeast Asia and Central America that are experiencing similar patterns of demographic change.

References

Becker, G. S. (1991) *A Treatise on the Family* (Cambridge, MA: Harvard University Press).

Belanger, D., Lee, H. K. and Wang, H. Z. (2010) Ethnic diversity and statistics in East Asia: 'foreign brides', surveys in Taiwan and South Korea, *Ethnic and Racial Studies*, 33: 1108–1130.

Boling, P. (2007) Policies to support working mothers and children in Japan, in F. M. Rosenbluth (ed.), *The Political Economy of Japan's Low Fertility* (Stanford, CA: Stanford University Press), 131–154.

Brinton, M. C. (2001) Married women's labour in East Asian economies, in M. C. Brinton (ed.), *Women's Working Lives in East Asia* (Stanford, CA: Stanford University Press), 1–37.

Brinton, M. C., Lee, Y.-J. and Parish, W. L. (1995) Married women's employment in rapidly industrialising societies: examples from East Asia, *American Journal of Sociology*, 100: 1099–1130.

Campbell, J. C. and Ikegami, N. (2003) Japan's radical reform of long-term care, *Social Policy and Administration*, 37: 21–34.

Chen, C.-N. and Liu, P. K.-C. (2007) Is Taiwan's lowest-low fertility reversible via socio-economic development?, *Journal of Population Studies*, 34: 1–36.

Chen, Y.-H. (2009) A cohort analysis of the transition to first marriage among Taiwanese, *Population and Society*, 5: 25–44.

Choe, M. K. (2006) Modernisation, gender roles, and marriage behaviors in South Korea, in Y.-S. Chang and S. H. Lee (eds), *Transformation in Twentieth Century Korea* (New York: Routledge), 291–309.

Davis, K. (1984) Wives and work: the sex role revolution and its consequences, *Population and Development Review*, 10: 397–417.

Eun, K.-S. (2003) Understanding recent fertility decline in Korea, *Journal of Population and Social Security*, supplement to vol. 1: 574–595.

Ezawa, A. and Fujiwara, C. (2005) Lone mothers and welfare-to-work policies in Japan and the United States: towards an alternative perspective, *Journal of Sociology and Social Welfare*, 32: 41–63.

Fukuda, S. (2008) The system for splitting pension benefits upon divorce, *Research on Household Economics*, 80: 6–16. [In Japanese.]

Fukuda, S. (2009) Leaving the parental home in postwar Japan, *Demographic Research*, 20: 731–816.

Hirao, K. (2001) Mothers as the best teachers: Japanese motherhood and early childhood education, in M. C. Brinton (ed.), *Women's Working Lives in East Asia* (Stanford, CA: Stanford University Press), 180–203.

Hirao, K. (2007) The privatised education market and maternal employment in Japan, in F. M. Rosenbluth (ed.), *The Political Economy of Japan's Low Fertility* (Stanford, CA: Stanford University Press), 170–200.

Horioka, C. Y., Fujisaki, H., Watanabe, W. and Kouno, T. (2000) Are Americans more altruistic than the Japanese?, *International Economic Journal*, 14: 1–31.

Hsieh, M. O. and Shek, D. T. L. (2008) Personal and family correlates of resilience among adolescents living in single-parent households in Taiwan, *Journal of Divorce and Remarriage*, 49: 330–348.

Hsu, M. (1998) Determinants of the marital dissolution and female labour supply, *Journal of Population Studies*, 19: 143–160.

Izuhara, M. (2002) Care and inheritance: Japanese and English perspectives on the 'generational contract', *Ageing & Society*, 22: 61–77.

Japan Institute of Labour (2003) *Research on Employment Assistance to Single-mother Households* (Tokyo: Japan Institute of Labour). http://db.jil.go.jp/db/seika/zenbun/E2003080006_ZEN.htm. [Accessed 21.8.2012.] [In Japanese.]

Jeng, W.-S. and McKenry, P. C. (2000) A comparative study of divorce in three Chinese societies: Taiwan, Singapore, and Hong Kong, *Journal of Divorce and Remarriage*, 34: 143–161.

Jones, C. (1993) The Pacific challenge: Confucian welfare states, in C. Jones (ed.), *New Perspectives on the Welfare State in Europe* (London: Routledge), 184–203.

Jones, G. (2007) Delayed marriage and very low fertility in Pacific Asia, *Population and Development Review*, 33: 453–478.

Jones, G. and Shen, H.-H. (2008) International marriage in East and Southeast Asia: trends and research emphases, *Citizenship Studies*, 12: 9–25.

Kim, D.-S. (2010) The rise of cross-border marriages and divorce in contemporary Korea, in M. Lu and W.-S. Yang (eds), *Asian Cross-border Marriage Migration: Demographic patterns and social issues* (Amsterdam: Amsterdam University Press), 127–153.

Kim, M., Won, Y., Lee, H. and Chang, H. (2005) *Recent Divorce Trends in Korea and Policy Measures for Divorced Families*, Research Report (Seoul: Korea Institute for Health and Social Welfare). [In Korean.]

Kitamura, Y. and Miyazaki, T. (2011) Marriage promotion policies and regional differences in marriage, *Japanese Economy*, 38: 3–39.

Knight, J. (1995) Municipal matchmaking in rural Japan, *Anthropology Today*, 11: 9–17.

Korean Statistical Information Service (2012) KOSIS: Korean Statistical Information Service. http://www.kosis.kr. [Accessed 21.8.2012.]

Kwon, T.-H. (2007) Trends and implications of delayed and non-marriage in Korea, *Asian Population Studies*, 3: 223–241.

Lee, H.-K. (2008) International marriage and the state in South Korea: focusing on governmental policy, *Citizenship Studies*, 12: 107–123.

Lee, Y.-J. and Hirata, S. (2001) Women, work, and marriage in three East Asian labour markets: the cases of Taiwan, Japan, and South Korea, in M. C. Brinton (ed.), *Women's Working Lives in East Asia* (Stanford, CA: Stanford University Press), 125–150.

Lee, Y.-J., Parish, W. L. and Willis, R. J. (1994) Sons, daughters, and intergenerational support in Taiwan, *American Journal of Sociology*, 99: 1010–1041.

Lesthaeghe, R. and Moors, G. (2000) Recent trends in fertility and household formation in the industrialised world, *Review of Population and Social Policy*, 9: 121–170.

Liaw, K.-L., Ochiai, E. and Ishikawa, Y. (2010) Feminisation of immigration in Japan: marital and job opportunities, in M. Lu and W.-S. Yang (eds), *Asian Cross-border Marriage Migration: Demographic patterns and social issues* (Amsterdam: Amsterdam University Press), 49–86.

Lock, M. (1993) Ideology, female midlife, and the greying of Japan, *Journal of Japanese Studies*, 19: 43–78.

Long, S. O. (2008) Someone's old, something's new, someone's borrowed, someone's blue: tales of elder care at the turn of the 21st century, in A. Hashimoto and J. W. Traphagan (eds), *Imagined Families, Lived Families: Culture and kinship in contemporary Japan* (Albany: State University of New York Press), 137–157.

Long, S. O., Campbell, R. and Nishimura, C. (2009) Does it matter who cares? A comparison of daughters versus daughters-in-law in Japanese elder care, *Social Science Japan Journal*, 12: 1–21.

Ministry of Health, Labour, and Welfare (2005) *Report on the 2003 National Survey of Single-mother Households* (Tokyo: Ministry of Health, Labour and Welfare). http://www.mhlw.go.jp/houdou/2005/01/h0119 1.html. [Accessed 21.8.2012.] [In Japanese.]

Ministry of Internal Affairs and Communications (2006) *2003 Survey of Land and Housing* (Tokyo: Nihon Tōkei Kyōkai).

Ministry of the Interior (2001) *Survey Summary Analysis of Single Parent Family 2001.* http://www.moi.gov.tw/stat/english/survey.asp. [Accessed 21.8.2012.]

Nagase, N. 2006. Japanese youth's attitudes towards marriage and childrearing, in M. Rebick and A. Takenaka (eds), *The Changing Japanese Family* (New York: Routledge), 39–53.

National Institute of Population and Social Security Research (2007a) *Population Projections for Japan: 2006–2055* (Tokyo: National Institute of Population and Social Security Research). [In Japanese.]

National Institute of Population and Social Security Research (2007b) *Report on the 13th National Fertility Survey: Attitudes toward marriage and childbearing among singles* (Tokyo: National Institute of Population and Social Security Research). [In Japanese.]

National Institute of Population and Social Security Research (2010) *Household Projections for Japan by Prefecture: 2005–2030* (Tokyo: National Institute of Population and Social Security Research). [In Japanese.]

National Institute of Population and Social Security Research (2011) *Latest Population Statistics* (Tokyo: National Institute of Population and Social Security Research). [In Japanese.]

OECD (2011) *Doing Better for Families* (Paris: OECD). http://dx.doi.org/10.1787/9789264098732-en [Accessed 17.10.2012.]

Ogawa, N. and Retherford, R. D. (1997) Shifting costs of caring for the elderly back to families in Japan: will it work?, *Population and Development Review*, 23: 59–94.

Ono, H. (2009) Husbands' and wives' education and divorce in the United States and Japan, 1946–2000, *Journal of Family History*, 34: 292–322.

Park, H. (2008) Effects of single parenthood on educational aspiration and student disengagement in Korea, *Demographic Research*, 18(13): 377–408.

Park, H. and Raymo, J. M. (2013) Divorce in Korea: trends and educational differentials: 1991–2005, *Journal of Marriage and Family*, 75(1): 110–126.

Park, H., Raymo, J. and Creighton, M (2009) Educational differentials in the risk of divorce and their trends across marriage cohorts of Korean women, *Gender Studies and Policy Review*, 2: 6–17.

Population Association of Korea (2006) *Encyclopedia of Population* (Daejun: Statistics Korea). [In Korean.]

Raymo, J. M. (2000) Spouse selection and marriage timing in Japan. Unpublished PhD dissertation, Department of Sociology, University of Michigan.

Raymo, J. M. (2003) Premarital living arrangements and the transition to first marriage in Japan, *Journal of Marriage and Family*, 65: 302–315.

Raymo, J. M. and Iwasawa, M. (2008) Changing family life cycle and partnership transition—gender roles and marriage patterns, in German Institute for Japanese Studies (ed.), *The Demographic Challenge: A handbook about Japan* (Leiden: Brill Academic Publishers), 255–276.

Raymo, J. M., Iwasawa, M. and Bumpass, L. (2004) Marital dissolution in Japan: recent trends and patterns, *Demographic Research*, 11: 395–419.

Raymo, J. M. and Lim, S.-J. (2011) A new look at married women's labour force transitions in Japan, *Social Science Research*, 40: 460–472.

Raymo, J. M. and Zhou, Y. (2012) Co-residence with parents and the well-being of single mothers in Japan, *Population Research and Policy Review*, 31: 727–749.

Reher, D. (1998) Family ties in Western Europe: persistent contrasts, *Population and Development Review*, 24(2): 203–234.

Retherford, R. D. and N. Ogawa, N. (2006) Japan's baby bust: causes, implications, and policy responses, in D. R. Harris (ed.), *The Baby Bust: Who will do the work? Who will pay the taxes?* (Lanham, MD: Rowman & Littlefield), 5–48.

Retherford, R. D., Ogawa, N. and Matsukura, R. (2001) Late marriage and less marriage in Japan, *Population and Development Review*, 27: 65–102.

Retherford, R. D., Ogawa, N. and Sakamoto, S. (1996) Values and fertility change in Japan, *Population Studies*, 50: 5–25.

Takagi, E. and Silverstein, M. (2006) Co-residence of the Japanese elderly: are cultural norms proactive or reactive?, *Research on Aging*, 28: 473–492.

Takayama, N. (2001) Pension reform in Japan at the turn of the century, *Geneva Papers on Risk and Insurance-Issues and Practice*, 26: 565–574.

Tsay, C.-L. (2004) Marriage migration of women from China and Southeast Asia to Taiwan, in G. W. Jones and K. Ramdas (eds), *(Un)tying the Knot: Ideal and reality in Asian marriage* (Singapore: Asia Research Institute, National University of Singapore), 173–191.

Tsuya, N. O. and Choe, M. K. (2004) Investments in children's education, desired fertility, and women's employment, in N. O. Tsuya and L. L. Bumpass (eds), *Marriage, Work, and Family Life in Comparative Perspective: Japan, South Korea, and the United States* (Honolulu, HI: East–West Center), 76–94.

Yamada, M. (1999) *The Era of Parasite Singles* (Tokyo: Chikuma Shinsho). [In Japanese.]

Yamamoto, N. and Wallhagen, M. I. (1997) The continuation of family caregiving in Japan, *Journal of Health and Social Behavior*, 38: 164–176.

Yang C.-L. and Tsai, H.-J. (2007) The changes of nuptiality and fertility in Taiwan. Paper presented at the International Symposium on Social Policy in Asia organised by Public Economics Group, School of International and Public Policy and Graduate School of Economics, Hitotsubashi University, Tokyo, Feb.

Yu, W. H. (2009) *Gendered Trajectories: Women, work, and social change in Japan and Taiwan* (Stanford, CA: Stanford University Press).

Zeng, Y., Coale, A., Choe, M. K., Liang, Z. and Liu, L. (1994) Leaving the paternal home: census-based estimates for China, Japan, South Korea, United States, France, and Sweden, *Population Studies*, 48: 65–80.

Zhou, Y. (2008) Single mothers today: increasing numbers, employment rates, and income, in Japan Institute of Labour Policy and Training (ed.), *Research on Employment Support for Single Mothers*, JILPT Research Report No. 101 (Tokyo: Japan Institute of Labour Policy and Training), 26–38. [In Japanese.]

24

I Say a Little Prayer for You

Do Prayers Matter in Marriage and Family Life?

Frank D. Fincham

Introduction

Religion has influenced human behaviour throughout history, and it is estimated that somewhere between 68.08 and 88.74 per cent of the current world population (4.54–5.92 billion people) profess some religious faith (List of religious populations, 2010). The three largest religions are Christianity (33% or 2.1 billion), Islam (21% or 1.5 billion) and Hinduism (14% or 900 million).[1] Although scientists 'have generally kept their distance from religion and spirituality' (Hill and Pargament, 2003, p. 65), a small literature is emerging on religion and the family. However, most studies (79% of marital studies and 76% of parenting studies over the last decade: see Mahoney, 2010) use one or two items to measure religious variables (e.g. affiliation, attendance, self-rated importance). Although these studies generally show that religiosity is related to several positive outcomes in family relationships, they yield small effect sizes. For example, those who attend religious services frequently are less likely to divorce than non-attenders, but the average effect size is only r = 0.125 (Mahoney *et al.*, 2001). Moreover, such studies are subject to multiple interpretations. For example, they may simply reflect selection effects, the operation of third variables such as social support and so on, and provide little information about which specific, modifiable aspects of religious behaviour and spirituality are associated with positive outcomes. The need to identify specific religious behaviours that influence family outcomes is apparent.

---

[1]   If agnostics, atheists, secular humanists and people who indicate no religious preference are considered together as a group, they comprise about 16 per cent of the world's population, or around 1.1 billion people.

Contemporary Issues in Family Studies: Global Perspectives on Partnerships, Parenting and Support in a Changing World, First Edition. Edited by Angela Abela and Janet Walker.
© 2014 John Wiley & Sons, Ltd. Published 2014 by John Wiley & Sons, Ltd.

The Practice of Prayer

Central to most religions is the practice of prayer, and many individuals use prayer spontaneously to cope with their problems (McCaffrey *et al.*, 2004). But because prayer 'has been largely marginalised by social scientists who study religion' (Dein and Littlewood, 2008, p. 39), virtually nothing is known about prayer and close relationships. This chapter describes a research programme on prayer and close relationships, explores the implications of such work, and, in doing so, attempts to fill this gap.[2] First, however, it is important to briefly analyse the construct of prayer.

Prayer conceptualised

Prayer has many potential referents. William James (1902, p. 464), a founding father of modern psychology, defined prayer as 'every kind of inward communion or conversation with the power recognised as divine …'. And it has further been argued that 'if prayer is regarded as every kind of communication with the power recognised (by the pray-er) as divine, then, arguably, all individuals pray to some degree' (Breslin and Lewis, 2008, p. 10). Many types of prayer exist. For example, Poloma and Gallup's (1991) taxonomy identifies ritual prayer, petitionary prayer, colloquial prayer and meditative prayer. Given such distinctions, researchers need to be clear when describing the effects of prayer because the impact of ritual or meditative prayer could be quite different from that of petitionary or colloquial prayer.

Types of prayer

Ritual prayer.	Prayer recited through reading a text or from memory.
Petitionary prayer.	Prayer which includes requests to meet specific material or other needs.
Colloquial prayer.	Prayer which uses everyday conversational language to communicate with divine, ultimate power.
Meditative prayer.	Prayer which involves being in the presence of the divine and thinking about the divine.

In the research discussed in this chapter, the focus is on colloquial, petitionary prayer, a form of prayer that invokes the deity's help in response to specific needs, using the individual's own language rather than a set or memorised prayer. Attention is focused on this form of prayer because it may be used in response to ongoing stressors and life events, and because of its ability to serve as a point of connection with family members, but this should not be taken to imply that other forms of prayer (e.g. meditative or ritual) are a less valuable focus of future research attention or that other forms of religious and spiritual activity should be ignored.

---

[2]   The research programme on which this chapter is based was conducted in the USA by the author and a number of colleagues.

Research programme

Descriptive data show that 63 per cent of people frequently ask for help from God[3] for family difficulties (Abbott *et al.*, 1990), and that 73 per cent of spouses have prayed during marital conflict (Butler *et al.*, 2002). Finally, in qualitative research, couples report that prayer alleviated tension and facilitated open communication during conflict situations (Lambert and Dollahite, 2006).

Theoretical perspective

How might prayer influence couple conflict? Fincham and Beach (1999) offer a goal theory analysis of couple conflict in which they argue that when a conflict of interest arises the usual goal of cooperating with the partner is replaced by an emergent goal in which the task is to 'win' or, at least, not lose, setting the stage for an adversarial interaction. Building on this analysis, Beach *et al.* (2008a) argue that prayer for the partner's wellbeing (asking God to do good things for the partner, envelop the partner in God's love and so on) when utilised in this context could provide a specific mechanism that allows cooperative goals to regain their dominance, replacing revenge-oriented or competition-oriented ones. Moreover, regular (private) prayer for the partner's wellbeing, even in the absence of an active conflict, is hypothesised to prime a range of motives, setting the stage for other positive relationship outcomes. For instance, praying for God to bless, protect and guide one's partner may prime awareness of God's love for one's partner. Focusing on God's love for the partner would, in turn, be expected to facilitate the propensity to forgive and exit from negative cycles of interaction with the partner that might otherwise become self-maintaining. In addition to being self-reinforcing, such prayer is likely to be supported by the spiritual community and thereby also be maintained by natural reinforcers.

Research Design

In the absence of prior studies, this research has focused on examining the impact of prayer for a partner on the relationship. Unless otherwise stated, participants in these studies were recruited from a college population screened to identify those who prayed at least occasionally. The findings therefore pertain largely to romantic relationships in emerging adulthood and, with the exception noted below, reflect the prayer behaviour of one partner. The research began by documenting an association between prayer and relationship functioning showing that prayer predicted relationship satisfaction (both concurrently and over time) over and beyond positive and negative behaviour in the relationship, and that commitment mediated the prayer-satisfaction association (Fincham *et al.*, 2008). Although encouraging, such correlational research provides weak evidence for inferring direction of effects.

The subsequent research therefore incorporated experimental designs. Specifically, participants were randomly assigned to pray for the partner or to fulfil comparison

---

[3] Throughout the chapter, the term 'God' is used to refer generically to a range of conceptions of the deity or higher power, or transcendent aspects of life typically associated with spirituality. The usage is intended to be inclusive rather than exclusive.

conditions such as describing the partner to a parent or meditating on the partner's positive qualities. In some studies undirected prayer ('just pray as you normally would each day for the next four weeks') was even used as a comparison condition. The research has consistently shown that petitionary prayer for the partner has a greater impact on the relationship than any of the comparison conditions. The box below presents an example of the instructions used in the studies and a sample prayer.

Study instructions

Please read the example prayer below to get an idea of the type of prayer we would like you to pray on behalf of your partner:

'Dear Lord,
Thank you for all the things that are going well in my life and in my relationship. Please continue to protect and guide my partner, providing strength and direction every day. I know you are the source of all good things. Please bring those good things to my partner and make me a blessing in my partner's life. Amen.

Now, please generate your own prayer in your own words on behalf of the well-being of your romantic partner and in the space below write a short description about what you prayed for.'

The above instructions illustrate those used when participants come to the laboratory and engage in a single prayer session. Because this approach might seem somewhat artificial, the laboratory findings are always replicated using longer-term, diary studies in which participants are asked to pray each day for a month. Participants are asked to make online reports twice a week during the month in order to ensure that they are following study instructions.

Findings

Forgiveness

One set of studies provided support for the idea, articulated earlier, that prayer increases willingness to forgive a transgression by the partner (Lambert *et al.*, 2010). This is important because in relationships such as marriage each partner will certainly be hurt by the other partner and that hurt is all the more poignant as partners make themselves particularly vulnerable in close relationships. Little wonder, then, that it has been said that a happy marriage is the union of two good forgivers. In these studies it was shown that prayer led to high levels of agape or selfless love and that this love led to greater willingness to forgive.

It could be argued that such findings may simply reflect self-report biases such as socially desirable responding, but the research indicated that prayer following a partner transgression influenced actual behaviour in response to the transgression. Participants were exposed to a transgression by one of the partners in the laboratory.

Then after praying (or engaging in a control activity) participants were given the chance to cooperate with or antagonise their partner in a computer game. Those who prayed were more cooperative than control participants who, instead of praying, had been asked to think about the nature of God.

Increasing forgiveness is all very well, but what if it is not even noticed by the partner? In such circumstances it might have a limited or even a null effect on the relationship. Therefore, another study was designed to test whether partners of participants who prayed over the course of four weeks reported the participants as more forgiving. Apparently prayer had a strong enough effect on the forgiving nature of participants for them to be perceived by their partners as more forgiving at the end of the study. But the impact of prayer is not limited to forgiveness.

Sacrificing selfish interests

Successful relationships also require partners who are willing to sacrifice selfish interests for the good of the partner and the relationship. A series of studies therefore investigated the effect of prayer on satisfaction with sacrifice in a close relationship: prayer for the partner was related to satisfaction with sacrifice both concurrently and longitudinally (Lambert *et al.*, 2012b). Importantly, individuals randomly assigned to pray were more satisfied with sacrificing than those assigned to a control condition, and in a further study, experimentally manipulated prayer after a conflictual interaction increased satisfaction with sacrifice. In addition those who prayed reported fewer emergent goals and greater couple identity than control participants, and both emergent goals and couple identity mediated the relationship between prayer and sacrifice. In a final study, objective observers rated those who were randomly assigned to pray for the partner over a four-week period as being more satisfied with sacrifice than those who daily engaged in positive thoughts about their partner.

Protecting against risk factors

Clearly, prayer can facilitate positive relationship outcomes, but can it protect against risk factors for relationships? A critical risk factor for relationship dissolution is cheating or infidelity. In countries in the developed world significant numbers of spouses are unfaithful (around 2–4% each year: Allen *et al.*, 2005), with figures being even higher in some regions in the developing world (e.g. sub-Saharan Africa). Extramarital affairs are the leading cause of divorce across 160 cultures (Betzig, 1989) and among college students in committed relationships rates of cheating are even higher (up to 65%: Allen and Baucom, 2006). In a more recent set of studies it was demonstrated that, relative to those using undirected prayer and positive thought conditions, those assigned to the colloquial, petitionary prayer for the partner condition showed decreased extra-dyadic behaviour over the course of the study (Fincham *et al.*, 2010). Moreover, 'sanctification of the relationship', or the process by which secular aspects of life (in this case their relationship) become perceived as having spiritual significance and character, was shown to mediate the relationship between prayer and infidelity. Again, in one of the studies in this series, it was shown that those who were randomly assigned to pray were rated differently by trained research assistant coders, blind to study hypotheses and the condition to which the participant was assigned. Specifically, those who had prayed for their partner for four weeks were rated as more committed to the relationship, which helps explain why there was less cheating during this period even when baseline rates of cheating are taken into account.

Praying with a partner

A common saying in the Christian faith community is, 'The couple that prays together stays together.' The veracity of this statement is by no means self-evident: prayer is a motivated behaviour and wherever there are human motives, there can be good and bad ones. For example, joint prayer could be used to demean or manipulate a partner. A series of studies was therefore implemented to examine the impact of joint prayer or praying with a partner (Lambert *et al.*, 2012a). In an initial study, frequency of self-reported joint prayer predicted ratings of trust made by observers of a five-minute couple interaction. A four-week intervention study showed that those assigned to engage in joint prayer rather than a daily positive interaction condition showed increased trust of the partner by the end of the study. Two data sets were consistent with the view that an increased sense of couple unity mediated the association between prayer and trust.

The demonstration that joint prayer can increase trust in relationships does not, *ipso facto*, mean that it should invariably be used to do so. There are probably many routes to increasing trust in relationships and some may turn out to be far more powerful than joint prayer. Such considerations have implications for practice and for social policy.

Implications for Practice and Social Policy

What implications do the findings described have for practice and social policy? Each of the topics is addressed in turn below.

Practice

Although efficacious interventions have been developed for couples, a major problem in this literature concerns the maintenance of gains over time following the intervention. Because prayer comes easily to people of faith, is self-reinforcing and is reinforced by the faith community, it has the potential to address this problem. This consideration led to the development of a *primary prevention* programme, to test this hypothesis.

Primary prevention

Primary prevention refers to interventions designed to circumvent the development of relationship dysfunction. They may target the general population (universal prevention) or those at risk (selective prevention). Typically, they take the form of psycho-education where benefits outweigh the minimal costs and risks for everyone. In contrast, secondary prevention refers to interventions for those who have begun to experience a problem and attempt to halt its progress.

A randomised clinical trial was conducted to determine whether adding prayer to an established prevention programme with well-documented efficacy improved maintenance of intervention gains. A prayer-focused version (PFP) of the Prevention and Relationship Enhancement Program (PREP) was developed that included all the basic components of PREP as well as a strong focus on private, intercessory prayer for the partner. All prayers were introduced as being in keeping with the higher order goal of 'helping you to be a vehicle of God's love in your relationship'. In addition, participants were instructed not to focus on non-constructive themes, including retribution or 'praying for God to change my mate'.

The intervention was targeted at African-Americans as they are markedly more religious than the general population of the USA on a variety of measures (e.g. 76% report praying at least daily or more often; Pew Charitable Trust, 2009), leading several authors to call for greater attention to spirituality in marital enhancement programmes aimed at African-American couples (Ooms and Wilson, 2004; Wolfinger and Wilcox, 2008). Because the vast majority of African-Americans self-identify as 'Protestant' (78%; Pew Charitable Trust, 2009), prayers were used that were reflective of African-American Protestant traditions. However, the programme was offered in a non-sectarian manner and a few Muslim couples also participated. The full report can be found in Beach *et al.* (2011).

A sample of 393 African-American married couples were randomly assigned to: (a) a culturally sensitive version of PREP that included consideration of the effects of discrimination on couple relationships; (b) the same programme with an additional focus on prayer (PFP condition); or (c) an information-only control group in which couples received a self-help version of PREP. Assessments were conducted before the intervention, immediately after it was completed, and 6 months and 12 months later. There was no reliable change as a function of time in the self-help control group. Considering the two intervention groups, in the present context it suffices to note that even though wives began at similar starting points they showed differing outcome patterns over time depending on the intervention. In particular, there was significantly greater change from pre- to post-test in the PFP condition than in the traditional PREP condition, indicating a more rapid initial change process in PFP that resulted in marginally better outcomes even at 12-month follow-up. Because husbands showed equal improvement across the two intervention conditions, this study yielded only partial support for the hypothesis that prayer would improve maintenance of intervention gains over time. Nevertheless, it points to one way in which prayer might be relevant to practitioners working with couples.

The above quantitative findings do not preclude the existence of dramatic change for some participants in the PFP condition, including men. For example, one male participant reported the following:

> At the time we were in the programme, we were separated and facing divorce. Hesitantly, we started with little hope of any reconciliation. We followed through with what they asked and attended all of the sessions … I started to use the prayer cards and begin to evaluate myself and where our marriage went wrong. I can now report that we are *not* getting a divorce but we are planning to renew our vows. Prayer definitely works even if the other partner isn't praying for the marriage.

In a similar vein, a female participant stated:

> We specifically pray about matters that affect our marriage … What I find is that when I sense a disagreement brewing, I ask for guidance upfront rather than afterwards. That is the measure of my growth in using prayer in my marriage.

Couple counselling

Is there a place for prayer in counselling individual couples? A survey of marriage and family therapists showed that 72 per cent believe spirituality is relevant to clinical practice yet only 17 per cent agree that it was appropriate to pray with a client (Carlson *et al.*, 2002). Frameworks for integrating spirituality into clinical practice are rare, and hence Beach *et al.* (2008a) offered an analysis of the role prayer might play in couple therapy.

These authors argued that 'prayer-based alternatives are available that meet many of the key objectives of emotion regulation as taught in marital skill training' (Beach *et al.*, 2008a, p. 647). They went on to illustrate how colloquial prayer might even offer some advantages over therapist-directed time out from conflict or similar anger management techniques. Their arguments are summarised in Table 24.1, which shows how a prayer-based intervention achieves the same goals as some skills-based interventions. In addition, colloquial prayer provides a behaviour that partners are likely to remember to execute when experiencing strong emotions, and one that can help them return to a state of mind in which using relationship skills seems more attractive than destructive behaviour. Thus, prayer may be useful in dealing with important affective processes that skills-training methods do not always handle well. The availability of such alternative approaches to marital intervention is useful because they can provide needed flexibility in working with couples. For example, it may be useful to have an approach to couple intervention that will resonate more with those who are highly spiritual in their approach to life, as these clients prefer therapy that in some way includes their belief system and they view clinicians who integrate religion into therapy more optimistically, and as more competent than clinicians who do not (Aten and Hernández, 2004).

Beach *et al.* (2008a) also argue that prayer can be used as an addition to traditional skills-based couple interventions. This is important because couples who learn relevant

Table 24.1   Skills-based procedure and goals and corresponding prayer-based alternative

Skills-based training procedure	Prayer-based alternative
Time out	*Prayer for partner*
Regain perspective.	Focusing on divine love and its extension to partner and relationship brings new perspective.
Break negative thought cycle.	Focusing on love, compassion and understanding interrupts grievance rehearsal.
Promote relaxation.	Prayer is self-soothing and self-healing.
Social support	*Talking with God*
Engage in dialogue with supportive other.	Colloquial prayer is available 24/7 and for believers is the ultimate form of social support.

skills often do not use them when a conflict of interest arises and emergent goals dominate. These authors argue that prayer highlights the view of an important 'other' and thereby engages motivational processes that increase the ability to handle emergent goals effectively. Specifically, prayer engages 'a complex set of interrelated reparative processes by highlighting their consistency with the perceived opinion of an important other like a deity' (p. 653). Because of this, it is concluded that adding prayer to traditional interventions increases their efficacy and makes them better able to exert a lasting effect.

Finally, the Beach *et al.* (2008a) analysis notes that prayer may have transformative potential. Transformative processes have received little attention in family relationships. Fincham *et al.* (2007) therefore outlined such processes, emphasising the importance of non-linear dynamic systems for understanding relationships. It has been argued that prayer influences the fundamental components of non-linear systems (control and influence processes) and thus has the potential to bring about qualitatively different (transformative) behaviour in relationships.

Several scholars have raised important objections to the Beach *et al.* (2008a) analysis (see Marks, 2008; Sullivan and Karney, 2008, Worthington, 2008). First, objections were raised on the grounds that it will lead counsellors into the role of having to judge religious texts, which when applied to the clients' relationship may not be in their best interests.[4] It is argued that this places the therapist in an untenable dual role as both religious official and therapist. In response, Beach *et al.* (2008b) argue that the role of the therapist is not to dispute (or ignore) religious texts but to help the couple find and highlight God's love in the context of the text, remembering always that the focus is on enhancing the relationship and the wellbeing of the partners. Second, Worthington (2008) asks whether therapists can propose prayer to couples in ways that couples find acceptable. Beach *et al.* (2008b) agree that doing so requires skill and that, for example, simply doing so on the grounds of possible psychological benefits will probably backfire. A third, more telling concern, also raised by this author, is that 'prayer may not be long or strong enough to be therapeutic' (p. 688). Here Beach *et al.* (2008b) acknowledge 'that the type of prayers we recommend may not be maintained over time, and to the extent that offering prayer for the partner falters or disappears after the end of therapy, our expectation for continuing therapeutic gains could also suffer' (p. 707).

The conceptual challenges offered are not exhausted by the above examples. However, their status remains unknown since definitive tests of the hypotheses outlined by Beach *et al.* (2008a) remain to be done. Although the fate of the Beach *et al.* (2008a) analysis remains unclear, what is clear is that spirituality has been largely overlooked in couple therapy, possibly because there is some evidence that spiritual and religious diversity is not considered as important as other kinds of diversity (Schulte *et al.*, 2002). Not surprisingly, most clinical psychologists say discussion of spiritual/religious issues in psychology programmes is rare or nonexistent (Brawer *et al.*, 2002).

---

[4]   In raising this objection, Sullivan and Karney (2008) cite as examples 'If you (husbands) experience rebellion from the women, you shall first talk to them, then desert them in bed, then you may beat them' (Qu'rān 4: 34), and 'Wives, submit yourselves unto your own husbands, as unto the Lord. For the husband is the head of the wife, even as Christ is the head of the church' (Ephesians 5: 22–23).

Notwithstanding the objections noted earlier, religiously and spiritually infused interventions have important advantages. First, they may provide some advantages with regard to efficacy for some groups of people (e.g. the highly religious) or in some targeted areas (e.g. forgiveness). Second, they may facilitate maintenance of intervention gains. Third, they have the potential to enhance dissemination of effective marital enhancement and intervention. The research found that dissemination was a particularly important issue in working with African-American couples, who are often sceptical of the benefits to be derived from mental health services and therefore unlikely to seek out or advocate such services in their communities (Murry and Brody, 2004). As a result, establishing trust and making the programme culturally relevant was essential to effective programme delivery. Similar issues may be common in many groups with strong religious commitments. Such considerations may undermine any implications of this work for social policy, a topic that is now addressed.

Social policy

To the extent that the work outlined in this chapter has any implications for social policy, they concern relationship education. At its simplest, relationship education is the provision of information designed to help couples and individuals experience successful, stable romantic relationships. The goal is to impart knowledge, teach skills, and help participants develop appropriate expectations and attitudes regarding romantic relationships. The most effective interventions, arguably, focus on dynamic (relatively changeable) versus static risk and protective factors (see Ragan *et al.*, 2009). Until quite recently, most relationship education occurred in religious contexts,[5] thereby excluding those who do not profess a religious faith or who are uncomfortable is such settings.

In the USA, government policy and the emergence of a formal 'marriage movement' have led to an unprecedented emphasis on relationship education in the service of promoting healthy marriages (Amato, 2007). However, this development is not limited to the USA, since government attempts to promote couple relationship education can be found in Australia, Japan, Norway and the UK (Huang, 2005; Ooms, 2005; Thuen and Loerum, 2005; van Acker, 2003). Although these countries exhibit less rhetoric on promoting marriage *per se*, they share the same goal (to promote healthy, committed couple relationships), particularly as the strongest context for child rearing. Importantly, these policy initiatives have received funding, which has had an impact not only on their dissemination but also on marital research (see Fincham and Beach, 2010). For example, in 2005, the US government made available $150 million annually for promoting healthy marriage and fatherhood, with money funding various opportunities to develop knowledge ranging from demonstration projects to large-scale randomised trials in community settings.

As is evidenced in Chapters 4, 5 and 16 in this volume, justifying such policy initiatives offers recognition of the fact that marital problems and divorce have an adverse

---

[5] Here it has taken the form of marriage education and has been offered almost exclusively to couples. The precursor of modern programmes was Pre-Cana pre-marital counselling, now required of couples wishing to marry within the Catholic Church (Ooms, 2005).

impact not only on spouses, but also on their children (see Amato, 2010, Proulx *et al.*, 2007). Moreover, stable happy relationships are associated with a low likelihood of needing government support (Thomas and Sawhill, 2005), and persons in such relationships use health services considerably less than their distressed counterparts (resulting in about 25% lower costs; Prigerson *et al.*, 2000). As a result, strengthening marriage is viewed as an appropriate social policy goal (Amato, 2007).

But even if one accepts the last conclusion, can social policy support the use of prayer in relationship education? There is no simple answer to this question. This is because the relationship between religion and the state varies across countries. In the USA the establishment clause of the first amendment of the United States Constitution ('Congress shall make no law respecting an establishment of religion') has led to several Supreme Court cases involving prayer, the inclusion of religious symbols in public holiday displays and so on. In this context, use of prayer cannot be part of any government social policy as it is an inherently religious activity. In contrast, social policy regarding relationship education that included prayer should not be problematic, at least in theory, in a theocratic state like Iran (though cultural and political factors suggest such a policy is unlikely to emerge). Many countries lie somewhere between these two poles. For example, the French principle of *laïcité* that has ensured separation of church and state since 1905 was revisited by President Nicolas Sarkozy. His '*laïcité positive*' resulted in a new direction in the state–religion relation. In this new context, it is unclear whether relationship education that included prayer could be incorporated in social policy. In any event, whether the work described in this chapter could influence social policy is likely to vary depending on the nation involved.

Limitations and Cautions

It is important to note the limitations of the work described herein. Foremost among these is that the research described is limited to relatively small samples of people representing a single faith community (Christianity), in a specific region (the Southeast) of a single country (USA). In principle, the analysis provided is applicable to all three Abrahamic faiths (i.e. Judaism, Christianity and Islam), as well as to other religious traditions (e.g. Hinduism), even those that are less theist, or even non-theist (e.g. Buddhism, Shinto, New Age). However, such applicability needs to be demonstrated rather than merely assumed. Second, even though the results are promising, further research is needed to show that the effects documented are the result of prayer *per se* rather than a more generic other-focused activity, such as meditating on the needs of the partner.

A challenge to implementing spiritually or religiously infused relationship interventions is the need to avoid violating couples' religious self-determination and to avoid harm-doing. Not all prayer is likely to be helpful to couples in preventing future problems or responding to ongoing issues. For example, praying for the personal strength to endure the partner's transgressions is likely to be counterproductive in some circumstances and might even increase risk in contexts such as abusive relationships. Similarly, asking for divine retribution for a partner's failings could potentially focus an individual's attention on the shortcomings of the partner, supporting ruminative, blaming processes. Likewise, prayer requests that focus on changing the partner, or the way the partner behaves towards the self, have the potential to decrease the propensity towards forgiveness, again leading to less positive relationship outcomes. These concerns, at a minimum, point to the possibility of adverse effects of prayer or other religious and spiritual activities under some circumstances.

Spiritually informed prevention programmes and policies create several other potential dangers. Foremost among these are manipulation of family members by participants, and subversion of programmes by social institutions to ensure that they are consonant with institutional goals (e.g. proselytisation, secularisation). Another critical danger concerns blurring or even overstepping appropriate professional boundaries. Jacobson and Christensen (1996) captured this well in relation to couple counsellors when they stated:

> We are not secular priests, ministers, or rabbis. Unfortunately, we cannot count on our clients to recognise that. Therefore, it is our job to make sure we do not obfuscate what is already a complicated relationship by playing the role of moral arbiter. (p. 16)

Concluding Comments

A great deal of ground has been traversed in this chapter. A programme of basic research suggests that prayer may play an important role in close relationships such as marriage, especially when such prayer focuses on the wellbeing of the partner and the deity's love of him or her. Applied research on the use of prayer in a marital intervention provides evidence in support of the view that spiritually and religiously informed programmes have a potential edge because gains may be naturally reinforced by the individual's ongoing spiritual and religious commitment and by the religious community within which he or she is situated. However, there are critical judgement calls to be made when targeting spiritual and religious behaviours for intervention, and not all scientists will be comfortable with having to deal with them.

Nevertheless, our discomfort is no excuse for ignoring an important part of the lives of many couples and families. Clearly, much more work is needed if the extent to which prayer for the partner impacts on relationship outcomes is to be understood fully. In particular, the identification of the mechanisms of this impact is still preliminary. Thus far, data show that commitment, selfless concern and sanctification can mediate the effect of prayer on relationships. But other potential mediators, such as a broader time perspective, forgiveness, and activating the view of a particularly important significant other, have yet to be investigated. It is also important to identify the boundary conditions under which prayer influences relationships.

In turning to the task at hand it behoves us to be mindful of Lewin's famous observation, 'There is nothing so practical as a good theory' (Lewin, 1952, p. 169). This is particularly apposite in the present context because the ground that lies ahead is a veritable minefield. Its navigation requires a carefully delineated conceptual framework to allow a productive and ethically responsible journey. Regardless of our individual predilections regarding religion and spirituality, this is a journey that the social science community must undertake. The couples and families we serve deserve no less.

References

Abbott, D. A., Berry, M. and Meredith, W. H. (1990) Religious belief and practice: a potential asset in helping families, *Family Relations*, 39: 443–448.

Allen, E. S., Atkins, D. C., Baucom, D. H., Snyder, D. K., Gordon, K. C. and Glass, S. P. (2005) Intrapersonal, interpersonal, and contextual factors in engaging in and responding to extramarital involvement, *Clinical Psychology: Science and Practice*, 12: 101–130.

Allen, E. S. and Baucom, D. H. (2006) Dating, marital, and hypothetical extradyadic involvements: how do they compare?, *Journal of Sex Research*, 43: 307–317.

Amato, P. R. (2007) Strengthening marriage is an appropriate social policy goal, *Journal of Policy Analysis and Management*, 26: 952–956, 961–963.

Amato, P. R. (2010) Research on divorce: continuing trends and new developments, *Journal of Marriage and Family*, 72 (June): 650–666.

Aten, J. D. and Hernández, B. C. (2004) Addressing religion in clinical supervision: a model, *Psychotherapy: Theory, research, practice, training*, 41: 152–160.

Beach, S. R. H., Fincham, F. D., Hurt, T., McNair, L. M. and Stanley, S. M. (2008a) Prayer and marital intervention: a conceptual framework, *Journal of Social and Clinical Psychology*, 27: 641–669.

Beach, S. R. H., Fincham, F. D., Hurt, T., McNair, L. M. and Stanley, S. M. (2008b) Prayer and marital intervention: toward an open, empirically grounded dialogue, *Journal of Social and Clinical Psychology*, 27: 693–710.

Beach, S. R. H, Hurt, T. R., Fincham, F. D., Franklin, K. J., McNair, L. M. and Stanley, S. M. (2011) Enhancing marital enrichment through spirituality: efficacy data for prayer focused relationship enhancement, *Psychology of Religion and Spirituality*, 3: 201–216.

Betzig, L. (1989) Causes of conjugal dissolution: a cross-cultural study, *Current Anthropology*, 30: 654–676.

Brawer, P. A., Handal, P. J., Fabricatore, A. N., Roberts, R. and Wajda-Johnston, V. A. (2002) Training and education in religion/spirituality within APA-accredited clinical psychology programs, *Professional Psychology: Research and Practice*, 33: 203–206.

Breslin, M. J. and Lewis, C. A. (2008) Theoretical models of the nature of prayer and health: a review, *Mental Health, Religion and Culture*, 11: 9–21.

Butler, M. H., Stout, J. A. and Gardner, B. C. (2002) Prayer as a conflict resolution ritual: clinical implications of religious couples' report of relationship softening, healing perspective, and change responsibility, *American Journal of Family Therapy*, 30: 19–37.

Carlson, T. D., Kirkpatrick, D., Hecker, L. and Killmer, M. (2002) Religion, spirituality, and marriage and family therapy: a study of family therapists' beliefs about the appropriateness of addressing religious and spiritual issues in therapy, *The American Journal of Family Therapy*, 30: 157–171.

Dein, S. and Littlewood, R. (2008) The psychology of prayer and the development of the Prayer Experience Questionnaire, *Mental Health, Religion and Culture*, 11: 39–52.

Fincham, F. D. and Beach, S. R. H. (1999) Marital conflict: implications for working with couples, *Annual Review of Psychology*, 50: 47–77.

Fincham, F. D. and Beach, S. R. H. (2010) Marriage in the new millennium: a decade in review, *Journal of Marriage and Family*, 72: 630–649.

Fincham, F. D., Beach, S. R. H., Lambert, N. M., Stillman, T. and Braithwaite, S. R. (2008) Spiritual behaviours and relationship satisfaction: a critical analysis of the role of prayer, *Journal of Social and Clinical Psychology*, 27: 362–388.

Fincham, F. D., Lambert, N. M. and Beach, S. R. H. (2010) Faith and unfaithfulness: can praying for your partner reduce infidelity?, *Journal of Personality and Social Psychology*, 99: 649–659.

Fincham, F. D., Stanley, S. and Beach, S. R. H. (2007) Transformative processes in marriage: an analysis of emerging trends, *Journal of Marriage and Family*, 69: 275–292.

Hill, P. C. and Pargament, K. I. (2003) Advances in the conceptualisation and measurement of religion and spirituality, *American Psychologist*, 58: 64–74.

Huang, W. (2005) An Asian perspective on relationship and marriage education, *Family Process*, 44: 161–174.

Jacobson, N. S. and Christensen, A. (1996) *Integrative Couple Therapy* (New York: Norton).

James, W. (1902) *The Varieties of Religious Experience: A study in human nature*, Gifford Lectures on Natural Religion delivered at Edinburgh (London and Bombay: Longmans, Green & Co.).

Lambert, N. M. and Dollahite, D. C. (2006) How religiosity helps couples prevent, resolve, and overcome marital conflict, *Family Relations*, 55: 439–449.

Lambert, N. M., Fincham, F. D., Crow, A. and Brantly, C. (2012a) Praying together and staying together: couple prayer and trust, *Psychology of Religion and Spirituality*, 4: 1–9.

Lambert, N. M., Fincham, F. D. and Stanley, S. (2012b) Prayer and satisfaction with sacrifice in close relationships, *Journal of Social and Personal Relationships*, 29: 1058–1070.

Lambert, N. M., Fincham, F. D., Stillman, T. F., Graham, S. M. and Beach, S. R. M. (2010) Motivating change in relationships: can prayer increase forgiveness?, *Psychological Science*, 21: 126–132.

Lewin, K. (1952) *Field Theory in Social Science: Selected theoretical papers by Kurt Lewin* (London: Tavistock).

List of religious populations (2010) http://en.wikipedia.org/w/index.php?title=List_of_religious_populationsandoldid=335775267 [Accessed 4.1.2010.]

McCaffrey, A. M., Eisenberg, D. M., Legedza, A. T. R., Davis, R. B. and Phillips, R. S. (2004) Prayer for health concerns: results of a national survey on prevalence and patterns of use, *Archives of Internal Medicine*, 164: 858–862.

Mahoney, A. M. (2010) Religion in families 1999 to 2009: a relational spirituality framework, *Journal of Marriage and Family*, 72: 805–827.

Mahoney, A., Pargament, K. I., Swank, A. and Tarakeshwar, N. (2001) Religion in the home in the 1980s and 90s: a meta-analytic review and conceptual analysis of religion, marriage, and parenting, *Journal of Family Psychology*, 15: 559–596.

Marks, L. (2008) Prayer and marital intervention: asking for divine help … or professional trouble?, *Journal of Social and Clinical Psychology*, 27: 678–685.

Murry, V. M. and Brody, G. H. (2004) Partnering with community stakeholders: engaging rural African American families in basic research and the Strong African American Families preventive intervention program, *Journal of Marital and Family Therapy*, 30: 271–283.

Ooms, T. (2005) *The New Kid on the Block: What is marriage education and does it work?* Couples and Marriage Policy Brief No. 7 (Washington, DC: Center for Law and Social Policy).

Ooms, T. J. and Wilson, P. C. (2004) The challenges of offering couples and marriage education to low income couples, *Family Relations*, 53: 440–446.

Pew Charitable Trust (2009) *A Religious Portrait of African-Americans*. http://www.pewforum.org/A-Religious-Portrait-of-African-Americans.aspx [Accessed 29.6.2012.]

Poloma, M. and Gallup, G. (1991) *Varieties of Prayer: A survey report* (Philadelphia, PA: Trinity Press International).

Prigerson, H. G., Maciejewski, P. K. and Rosenheck, R. A. (2000) Preliminary explorations of the harmful interactive effects of widowhood and marital harmony on health, health service use and health care costs, *Gerontologist*, 40: 349–357.

Proulx, C. M., Helms, H. M. and Buehler, C. (2007) Marital quality and personal well-being: a meta-analysis, *Journal of Marriage and Family*, 69: 576–593.

Ragan, E. P., Einhorn, L. A., Rhoades, G. K., Markman, H. J. and Stanley, S. M. (2009) Relationship education programs: current trends and future directions, in J. H. Bray and M. Stanton (eds), *Handbook of Family Psychology* (Hoboken, NJ: Wiley-Blackwell), 450–462.

Schulte, D. L., Skinner, T. A. and Claiborn, C. D. (2002) Religious and spiritual issues in counseling psychology training, *The Counseling Psychologist*, 30: 118–134.

Sullivan, K. T. and Karney, B. J. (2008) Incorporating religious practice in marital interventions: to pray or not to pray? *Journal of Social and Clinical Psychology*, 27: 670–677.

Thomas, A. and Sawhill, I. (2005) For love or money? The impact of family structure on family income, *Marriage and Child Well Being*, 15: 57–74.

Thuen, F. and Loerum, K. T. (2005) A public/private partnership in offering relationship education to the Norwegian population, *Family Process*, 44: 175–186.

van Acker, L. (2003) Administering romance: government policies concerning pre-marriage education programs, *Australian Journal of Public Administration*, 62: 15–23.

Wolfinger, N. H. and Wilcox, W. B. (2008) Happily ever after? Religion, marital status, gender, and relationship quality in urban families, *Social Forces*, 86: 1311–1337.

Worthington, E. (2008) Can prayer be long and strong enough to matter?, *Journal of Social and Clinical Psychology*, 27: 686–692.

Part IV

Looking to the Future
The Role of States in Supporting Families

The contributors to this book have pointed to the need for social policies to support stable family relationships and protect children's best interests in a rapidly changing world. Intrusion into personal relationships and family life has often been criticised as 'nannying', however, and governments do not want to be labelled as creators of a nanny state. In this final section we consider the extent to which states should attempt to strengthen families.

Ruth Farrugia (Chapter 25) discusses the advisability of a legal definition of families and reviews interpretations of the term 'family' at the European Court of Justice and the European Court of Human Rights. She argues that the state's responsibility to its citizens is founded in its commitment to protecting human rights, which, in turn, encompasses a commitment to wellbeing. In a large number of European countries the strengthening of families has become a priority goal. Some commentators go so far as to suggest that it is a state's responsibility to provide education for marriage, relationships and family life. Attitudes vary, however, about whether all kinds of families should be supported or whether policies should reinforce marriage and more traditional family structures. As Farrugia points out, family policies are inextricably linked with political values and priorities.

Karen Bogenschneider (Chapter 26) makes a global case for family policy. She refers to a number of countries that have adopted family policy frameworks, but suggests that the reality does not always match the rhetoric. She uses the USA, Africa, Korea and Latin America as case studies. Bogenschneider takes the view that the far-reaching impacts of globalisation should ensure that family policy is at the forefront of every nation's agenda. She argues that family policies should support family

Contemporary Issues in Family Studies: Global Perspectives on Partnerships, Parenting and Support in a Changing World, First Edition. Edited by Angela Abela and Janet Walker.
© 2014 John Wiley & Sons, Ltd. Published 2014 by John Wiley & Sons, Ltd.

formation and dissolution, partner relationships, family finances, child rearing and caregiving. Furthermore, by looking at all policy through a family impact lens, we can assess and monitor the impacts on any of these family functions. Bogenschneider's rationale for ensuring that states support families is that because families make a considerable contribution to society, they are worthy of investment. Policymakers need to recognise the role families play in, for example, generating productive workers, caring for family members and promoting child and youth development. She draws attention to cost–benefit analyses which demonstrate the value of families' contributions, arguing that it would be hugely expensive to replace the functions families perform. This economic argument is increasingly evident as academics and other commentators seek to quantify the costs to society of family instability and breakdown over and above the personal costs involved.

This penultimate chapter draws together a strong and convincing message for governments about the critical importance of supporting and strengthening family life in a world that demands competence at all levels. Documenting the public benefits strong families provide to society should surely convince governments of the value of investing in supportive family policies. The author calls for the creation of a dedicated family policy champion at the heart of every government, a national infrastructure for family research, and a commitment from academics and practitioners to work in partnership with policymakers.

In the final chapter (27) of the book, we draw together the key and consistent messages from the rich and extensive knowledge accumulated in the previous chapters. Without doubt, strong, stable, supportive couple relationships, whatever form they take, strong, stable parenting, and strong, stable families are essential for global stability and for economic growth and prosperity. The growing diversity in family forms and increasing globalisation offer opportunities as well as challenges for families, communities and governments to work in synergy towards achieving these important goals.

25

Why Should States Have an Interest in Making Families Stronger?

Ruth Farrugia

Introduction

There is a difficult tension between the state supporting families and interfering in family life. This chapter asks the key question as to whether states should have an interest in making families stronger. It is divided into three parts. The first part discusses the advisability of a legal definition of families, particularly in the context of determining what renders them strong. It then reviews interpretation of the term 'family' at the European Court of Justice (ECJ) and the European Court of Human Rights (ECtHR) before examining the rights and responsibilities traditionally applicable within the family unit itself. It questions what characteristics identify strength in families and considers the element of wellbeing as a component of strength.

Part two addresses the role of the state and starts by affirming the responsibility that the state has towards the vulnerable. It develops the idea that the state has a similar responsibility towards vulnerable members of families who require support. The state therefore has an interest in promoting families to be strong so that they can take responsibility for their vulnerable members. Part two includes a comparative review of the methods currently employed by states to encourage and promote strong families, making reference to family-friendly and family-strengthening measures.

The final part deals with state intervention in those circumstances where the family is adjudged as not being strong. It discusses the impact of such action on the family as a whole and on individual members of the family, pointing out the repercussions of failure to intervene where appropriate and including a review of state liability in such circumstances. Ultimately, part three answers the question posed in the title of the

Contemporary Issues in Family Studies: Global Perspectives on Partnerships, Parenting and Support in a Changing World, First Edition. Edited by Angela Abela and Janet Walker.
© 2014 John Wiley & Sons, Ltd. Published 2014 by John Wiley & Sons, Ltd.

chapter by concluding that the state has both an altruistic and a vested interest in making families stronger. A number of policy recommendations conclude the chapter.

Definitions of Family

Defining the term 'family' is a complex issue in law, and this may reflect a particular policy determination of the state. Perhaps in this context it is advisable to look to the definition of family within the understanding of 'family law'. Family law may be described as 'the rules by which men and women establish intimate relationships that have legal consequences' (Krause, 2006). There is, however, no real consensus as to the use of the phrase itself.

Eekelaar (2001) raises the point that even if it is possible to determine precisely the criteria for identifying the members of the family (a genetic or marital basis, for instance) there would still remain the challenge of pinpointing the corresponding obligation. Bainham (2003) approaches the definition in a practical way and posits the concept of family law as being normative, so that it is expected to act both as a defender of the rights that emanate from family relationships and as promoter and enforcer of the obligations that emerge from these relationships. This continues the idea put forward by Funder and Smyth (1996), who concluded that family law is there not only to reflect perceptions and expectations of the public, but also as a means of introducing new concepts.

The state therefore has a very direct interest in determining which issues fall under the remit of family law. Where it excludes obligations or simply neglects to consider them, it is implicitly shaping a definition and agreeing to the duties that follow. Depending on its ethos, as expressed in its family policy for instance, the state may aim to widen the application of family law and definition of family as broadly as possible in order to exculpate itself from financial burdens. However, the state is not only motivated by monetary considerations: it also has other ethical, philosophical and policy deliberations to make before enacting legislation.

The EU and its court in Luxembourg have had a significant impact on notions of family and families. In deliberating issues relating to the definition of family, the ECJ was—and continues to be—asked to interpret the impact of changes in family relationships and the repercussions these have for the application of rights under EU law. Cases have addressed the rights of the spouse, of former spouses who have divorced, and of children of separated or divorced parents, as well as the features of family life impacting on sex equality, such as childcare, division of labour and work–family balance.

European courts and family life

- The European Court of Justice is asked to interpret the impact of changes in family relationships and the repercussions these have for the applications of rights under EU law.
- The European Court of Human Rights decides cases brought against state parties in relation to the right to respect for family life and the right to marry and found a family.

If the impact of the ECJ can be deemed significant in the field of families, the influence of the ECtHR can be described as momentous. On the basis of the European Convention on Human Rights, the court decides cases brought against state parties in relation to the right to respect for family life (Article 8) and the right to marry and found a family (Article 12). Although at first glance the articles may appear quite limited in scope, court judgments over the years have shown that these topics cover an extensive range of issues which impact on families and include the definition of the family itself.

For instance, the Court acknowledges de facto family ties for families living together even where there is no marriage, and may include more remote relations in the term 'private life'. Under Article 12, 'Men and women of marriageable age have the right to marry and found a family, *according to the national laws governing the exercise of this right*' (author's italics). This has been interpreted as imputing to the state an obligation to recognise this right both in principle and in practice, so that any limitation imposed must be for a legitimate purpose and must be proportionate to that aim. The Court has not sanctioned any right to divorce, although the last time it dealt with the issue was in 1986 (*Johnston and others* v. *Ireland*, Judgment 18 December 1986, Ser. A, No. 112).

In relation to children, for example, the ECtHR has decided that the family life of parents and their children is not brought to an end by the divorce or separation of the parents, so that parents and children have the right to enjoy each other's company. The Court has determined that this constitutes a fundamental element of family life. It has also decided that protection of rights clearly extends to illegitimate children, and this also within the context of succession rights (*Marckx* v. *Belgium*, Judgment of 13 June 1979, Ser. A, No. 31).

Possibly the most significant recent changes seen in the Court have been in the field of transsexuality, where the courts now provide for the recognition of a new sexual identity for legal purposes (*Cossey* v. *United Kingdom*, Judgment of 27 September 1990, Ser. A, No 184) and require states to permit transsexuals the right to marry (*Goodwin* v. *United Kingdom* (App. 28957/95), Judgment of 11 July 2002 (Para. 85) and *I.* v. *United Kingdom* (App. 25680/94), Judgment of 11 July 2002 (Para. 65)).

Courts in Council of Europe states know that any judgment they give will be subject to review by the ECtHR, should the party choose to appeal the decision by exercising the right to individual petition. This has created a situation where domestic courts may find themselves increasingly constrained to take a wider interpretation into account in the knowledge that their decision will be scrutinised and perhaps over-turned, notwithstanding the public policy issues they must take into account in the local scenario. This, in turn, has an impact on the definition of 'family'.

The term 'family' frequently has connotations of some idealised entity with stand-ardised needs and responsibilities. Legislators often make reference to 'the family' when proposing, implementing or monitoring policy even though they really mean 'families'. The difference is of fundamental importance to the individual families themselves since the needs of each family may be quite divergent from the standard-ised norm. To group all families together under the umbrella term 'the family' is to accord them little if any recognition of their specific needs, and may even result in discrimination. McGlynn (2007) expresses concern at the arbitrary definition of family within the traditional nuclear description. She claims that such an approach is discriminatory since it limits the scope of EU rights and entitlements and fails to reflect the diversity of family life. To date, states have been left relatively free to opt out of rules pertaining to different family forms and are left to use either the term 'family' or the term 'families' with little consideration of the impact this choice of terms may have.

Determining strong families

Once a family is defined as such and is therefore determined to be entitled to specific rights and benefits at law, the next stage is for the state to make a value judgement as to whether it is needful of support on the basis of its strength or otherwise. This in turn raises two issues: how should the state make such a valuation, and which criteria should it use? For the state to be in a position to strengthen families it must be clear as to who it considers to be strong, and it must be able to make such a judgment within reasonably definite criteria. As yet, there are no legal principles which may enlighten the process. It is difficult enough to reach some consensus as to who constitutes a family at law without attempting to establish a legal definition for a 'strong family'.

The relationship between family members may also have a direct impact on the considerations applied in determining the strength of a family. The state usually determines which relationships give rise to responsibilities that are actionable at law. For instance, apart from spouses and children, relatives by consanguinity have a right to maintenance if they are in need. In this way, prior to the introduction of welfare states in European countries, families were expected to support each other not just morally but also financially, and this responsibility has continued to be translated into an action available at law, particularly in civil law jurisdictions. However, where no support is forthcoming from the immediate or extended family, the onus of such provision must rest with the state. In *Cruz del Valle Bermudez* v. *Ministry of Health and Social Assistance Supreme Court of Justice*, No. 916, 15 July 1999, the Venezuelan Supreme Court held that people infected with HIV who did not have enough money to pay for the necessary drugs had a right to be provided with them. Although the state countered that it did not have sufficient funds in its budget, the Supreme Court suggested ways to raise the budget, 'but crucially left the choice of how to raise the budget to the government' (Jheelan, 2007, p. 152).

It is pertinent to ask whether searching for a definition of family or families has a wider dimension than the purely legal. The *raison d'être* of the exercise may lie in the need to identify families who are not strong so as to be able to assist and support them. Once a family has been defined as not strong or strong but in need of strengthening, those who have an interest in such strengthening would be expected to do what is necessary and invest the required resources. This means that strong families would have to fit some preconceived classification, and deviating from this would result in a variety of responses ranging from state intervention to the offer of assistance. At one extreme, for instance, this could mean that where a family does not fit the state designation 'strong', it risks having its children removed unless it does something to become strong(er). This is a controversial subject and, as Gillies (2005) points out, the state may take it upon itself to single out specific parenting practices and forward them as behaviours to be followed for the public good. In 2007 the ECtHR ruled, for example, that the taking of five children into care on the basis of the inadequate housing of the parents constituted a violation of Article 8 (*Wallova and Walla* v. *Czech Republic* (App. 23848/04), Judgment of 26 March 2007).

This could also mean that unless a family is deemed to be striving to be strong, within state criteria, it may miss out on state benefit and be denied rights accorded to families deemed to be strong or at least trying to become so. Gillies makes reference to the state's derogatory labelling of parents who decline mainstream morality defined by state policy. This is further reinforced in work on lone mothers, where Gillies, together with Edwards, found that 'what constitutes good parenting [is] ... shaped by distinct "gendered moral rationalities"' (Edwards and Gillies, 2004, p. 625).

The nature of a state's responsibility for individuals in its jurisdiction requires acknowledgement that, if individuals are to achieve the dignity fundamental to their wellbeing, which in turn leads to their strength, the state has a positive obligation to care for those who cannot care for themselves (UDHR Article 25(1)). In concrete terms this is interpreted as signifying that the state must show respect for and protection of the individual's efforts to achieve an adequate standard of living. Eide (2010) argues that states therefore have an obligation to help fulfil this right, so that they 'may have to directly provide means and resources for the satisfaction of basic needs (in the form of direct aid or social security) when no other possibility exists' (p. 236).

In the European context, while individuals who are capable of supporting themselves and their dependants are expected to do so independently, those people who are unable to care for themselves may look to the state and expect at least some assistance in order to achieve a basic minimum standard of living essential to their wellbeing. This further contributes towards the premise that the wellbeing which characterises the strong family is a state responsibility and can be founded in social and economic rights.

The Role of the State

It has been argued so far that the state's responsibility to its citizens can be founded in its commitment to human rights, and that because social and economic rights are as fundamental as civil and political ones that responsibility includes a responsibility to protect and promote the wellbeing of all its citizens. The nature or extent of that responsibility may be broader when the situation of vulnerable citizens is considered. In order to promote the rights of citizens to a position of strength through wellbeing, therefore, a state must take into account particular vulnerabilities. Ultimately all individuals (including, particularly, the vulnerable) have the right to invoke their socio-economic rights under the Universal Declaration of Human Rights (UDHR) and the European Convention on Human Rights or any one of the specific human rights conventions. The growing awareness about rights has contributed towards rendering states accountable for those obligations they have entered into.

While the relationship between a state and its citizens, in particular the state's responsibility to its citizens, is the subject of much political theory, some responsibility may be founded purely on legal, human rights grounds. The state has certain responsibilities towards persons, not least of which are those responsibilities listed under human rights law. Chinkin (2010, p. 103) states that 'sources of law provide us with the basis of legal obligation' in that they give an insight into the way older laws are repealed and new laws introduced. Although these sources may be clearly identified, different states may respond to the responsibilities set out under human rights law differently. However, it is argued that once states agree to observe binding legal instruments under international human rights law, the individual may expect a minimum standard of treatment in relation to their fundamental rights. Within the United Nations human rights canon, states are expected to respect, protect and fulfil their human rights obligations (Chinkin, 2010, citing Higgins, 2004).

In theory, at least, since all states in the world are parties to the UDHR, they have a responsibility to ensure that their citizens achieve the dignity essential to their lives as human beings. Ssenyonjo (2009) also observes that states have a responsibility to guarantee human rights, and both Covenants to the UDHR, on Civil and Political Rights and on Economic, Social and Cultural Rights, refer to the individual having human rights which may be exercised against the state in that 'the state has the primary responsibility to respect, protect and fulfil human rights' (ICCPR and ICESCR, Article 2).

Social and economic rights

Knowledge about socio-economic rights essential to wellbeing is not widely accessible, whereas most people are well aware of rights to a legal defence, a fair trial, freedom of speech and freedom to strike. Even where these civil rights are not fully respected, the average citizen knows of their existence and that appropriate remedies exist. The same cannot be said with equal confidence as regards social and economic rights. Within the context of the European Court of Human Rights in Strasbourg, the term has been accorded an even more important dimension, with a number of judgments attributing positive obligations to states, specifically in the context of Article 8. This approach has led to states being found guilty of violations in a large number of cases with a socio-economic component in respect of not providing a home which could keep a family together.

Examples of violations of Article 8

- *Wallowa and Walla* v. *The Czech Republic* (application no. 23848/04, 2006), for not providing a home which could keep a family together.
- *Hansen* v. *Turkey* (application no. 36141/97, 2004, 39 E.H.R.R. 18), for failing to enforce parental access rights to children.
- *AD and OD* v. *United Kingdom* (application no. 28680/06, 2010, ECHR 340), for placing a child in care where this was not in the child's best interests.
- *Mubilanzila Mayeka and Kaniki Mitunga* v. *Belgium* (application no. 13178/03, 2006), for failing to care for a child appropriately.

When a state decides to apportion a financial contribution from its citizens to the more vulnerable, it is obligated to make such apportionment wisely and subject to democratic scrutiny and objection (Criddle and Fox-Decent, 2008). The nature of its obligation renders the state accountable for its decisions not only to the electorate but also before a court of law. This means that care for the vulnerable using public money becomes an enforceable right. The subjection of state action (or inaction) to judicial scrutiny is in itself a measure of the development of human rights and imputes an obligation on the state to help families achieve the wellbeing that renders them 'strong'.

If socio-economic rights are to be accorded effective legal recognition, it is crucial for the judiciary also to take a stand. The courts have no hesitation in enforcing the right to free legal aid for an accused party who cannot afford a lawyer and in ensuring that the provision is made. It would be unthinkable for the state to respond that no funds are available for the lawyer, yet rights to strength and wellbeing contingent on housing, health care and education are not always treated in the same way. Strength is the result of effective access to all rights without distinction.

Cases relating to socio-economic rights

- *Airey* v. *Ireland* (ECHR decided 9 October 1979) (application 6289/73)
- *Moldovan and Others* v. *Romania* (ECHR decided 12 July 2005) (applications 41138/98 and 64320/01)

Jheelan (2007) makes the point that it may be that the state truly does not have sufficient funds to obey a court order regarding access to such rights. The question is whether that would excuse or justify non-observance. Pieterse (2004) has rightly argued that 'whether we like it or not, socio-economic rights are as justiciable as civil and political rights' (p. 204).

Assessing the strength of the family

Where a family is identified as not strong, a number of factors must be addressed. The family may not recognise that it has any issue to resolve and may be content to continue to exist within the status quo. For instance, in terms of the UN Convention on the Rights of Children (UNCRC), states have a responsibility to support parents in carrying out their responsibilities towards their children. The support may be offered directly or indirectly, and is generally part of a strategy to strengthen families. Families may, however, not perceive this assistance as being offered voluntarily (Burford and Adams, 2004). Moreover, there do not seem to be any set criteria which states apply in order to judge the strength of the family. Normally, families which are identified as not being strong are so identified because they are failing to fulfil their obligations. This reinforces the need for a definite set of criteria whereby states can gauge strength in the family rather than weaknesses. This would enable states to support families so as to help them become stronger, and to intervene where they seem to be faltering.

Once a state is convinced that the wellbeing of its citizens is a right derived from its obligations to promote and protect social and economic rights, it could be argued that it has a responsibility to take all possible steps to make this happen. Rothstein (1998, p. 215) argues:

How extensive the public commitment to the well-being of citizens should be is an altogether distinct question from whether or not the services following on this commitment should be produced by organisations which are publicly owned.

Commitment to wellbeing is a separate question from how to achieve it, so difficulties or expense in providing a response should not affect the initial commitment or constitutional or philosophical responsibility attributable to the state. The key here is that civil and political rights are as much about wellbeing as are social rights, and so at least some positive obligations rest on the state.

If the state has an interest in strengthening, and a responsibility to strengthen, families, it also has an interest in helping families to realise their potential. Ideally, each family (however described) should be able to take responsibility for itself and reach its goals unassisted. Ideally, all children should have an equal start in life which does not preclude them from progress and which ensures for them a healthy, happy and possibly prosperous future. But we do not live in an ideal world, and claims on the state to rectify imbalances of birth, upbringing, circumstance or choice are a regular occurrence. Can the state be expected to respond within its broader notion of family policy and as a result of its commitment to strengthening families?

In a large number of states across Europe, the strengthening of families has become a preoccupation common to policymakers and analysts. States also proclaim a commitment towards the happiness of their citizens. If they are convinced that such happiness is reached or bettered through strengthening families, they are aware of the significance of enabling adults to enjoy the support and comfort of family life, and of giving children every opportunity to enjoy their childhood and develop in a supporting family environment. In the final analysis, however, it is ideally the family which should take responsibility for its dependants since the state can only ever be a 'default institution, providing minimal, grudging and stigmatised assistance should families fail' (Fineman, 2004, cited in Diduck, 2008, p. 255).

State Intervention

In this context it is therefore pertinent to examine to what extent, if at all, the state can, should and does intervene in the determination of family relationships. At a theoretical level, liberal morality justifies preventive family intervention on the basis of the notion that the state should only endorse those values that enable its citizens to 'live their lives according to their own, different convictions and world views' (Snik *et al.*, 2004, p. 182). However, there are a number of issues, such as social inclusion, public morality and the environment, consideration of which cannot be based on such liberal principles alone and which may require a state to make its own independent policy. McClain (2008, p. 68), for example, holds that it is a state responsibility to play an active part in providing an education for family life, marriage and relationships, and goes so far as to contend that the state should even be directly involved in nurturing the 'preconditions for persons to form and sustain family life'.

As a matter of routine, states are reluctant to interfere in family life and are careful to show respect in terms of the European Convention on Human Rights. This is brought about by ensuring that a number of checks and balances are built into the system of law and policy whereby families are responsible for their members until such time as those members achieve independence. However, state intervention is practised reluctantly for reasons other than the purely financial. As Burford and Adams (2004) contend, people demonstrate a greater propensity to take responsibility for vulnerable members of their family when not doing so would invoke sanctions, including the removal of the right to exercise that responsibility. Gillies (2005, p. 70) proposes that states show commitment to supporting families because of 'a particular moral agenda that seeks to regulate and control the behaviour of marginalised families'.

If the state has a right to intervene when a family is not strong enough to support itself (and this includes each of its family members), it should be logical to conclude that the state also has an interest in ensuring, and an obligation to ensure, that families can support themselves. It is not obvious whether this is an automatic corollary to the promotion of strong (or stronger) families.

Before looking at the quality and/or quantum of support a state should be expected to give, it is important to identify who qualifies for it. It seems to be a given that states are ready and willing to provide financial support to parents with children with a view to assisting them in the upbringing of these children. The composition and form of the family is irrelevant, so does this mean that state support for all families undermines the more conventional family? Wikely (2007, p. 113) deduces that the welfare state tends to allocate child benefit regardless of marital status or family form: 'social security law has always treated "the family" as a protean term, depending on the respective policy goals of the benefit schemes in question.' Trends across the Western world seem to be militating against the use of public money to subsidise families who are perceived as contributing little or nothing to the state. However, one could counter that to focus on the lack of consensus in reacting to the needs of the family itself (and to those of the individuals who make up that family) is to undermine the very positive values of solidarity and social inclusion which underpin society. Nickel (2005) even proposes that individuals owe supplementary responsibility to their fellow citizens in supporting the state to provide assistance.

It remains a subject of controversy whether states that have knowledge pertaining to the strength or otherwise of families also have a responsibility to act on it. If a state knows that children brought up in strong families fare better physically, socially and academically, does it have a duty to ensure that all children are brought up in such families? One might also argue that this might render the state liable to action in child placement cases where the substitute family chosen does not turn out to be strong either. It could be argued that states that derogate from their responsibility to intervene would be just as liable as those that do and fail to deliver. Morally there may well be a difference, but the practical result is that children may be left in a family incapable of responding or unwilling to respond to their needs, with potentially disastrous effects.

Research shows that a number of measures may militate towards ensuring a strong family, although they cannot be deemed the universal panacea. Families that do not have economic worries are relieved of a substantial burden, so that employment is essential for all those who are willing and able to enter the job market. The remuneration for work should be commensurate with the standard of living identified as acceptable for strong families. If having an extra part-time job is the only way a provider can make ends meet, the opportunities for family time will obviously decrease. If low wages, high taxation and meagre job opportunities constrain both parents to work outside the home, there will clearly be additional stress involved in the care of that family.

What about those who cannot or will not work? States, particularly in the EU, have determined that women must join the labour market. When they do not work outside the home women often come under fire for failing to make any monetary contribution to the household and to society—though when they do work outside it, they are equally pilloried for not devoting themselves entirely to their children. Harris and Parisi (2005) observe that in the USA the definition of a good mother has changed from the caregiver who stays at home, particularly when the child is young, to a woman who works outside the home so that her family does not have to rely on social benefit. Mink (2001, cited in Harris and Parisi, 2005) also concludes that policy has moved drastically away from protection of women to wanting them to join the workforce and expecting them to take responsibility and work outside the home, notwithstanding the needs of their family. Where work is not an option because of ill health or unavailability of jobs, families should be able to rely on state assistance which permits them to live decently without the risk or reality of poverty.

The responsibility of states

States have a responsibility to ensure that:

- families which can support themselves do so
- families which are unable to support themselves and are in need are supported

Perhaps the solution is to respond by rewarding values of support and solidarity, so that families who stay together over a long period of time receive due recognition, provided that any incentive does not turn into a reason to keep violent families together under some financial pretext. Clearly this is an area which merits further research. Whatever the options, states that are aware of the importance of a strong family within the context of caring for children, the disabled and the elderly, as well as the wider perspective of happier adults in a happy society, really have no moral choice but to act. If a state realised that strong families give rise to happy children, happy citizens and a happy society, it would be difficult to argue that it should be able to decide not to engage in the process. Once a state acknowledged that such responsibility existed, it would arguably become legally liable to provide whatever is necessary to strengthen families.

Ferguson (2008, p. 87) comments that in Canada, the state does not actively promote marriage. If it did, it would surely warn of the risks of failure. In such circumstances

one would expect various government actions, such as government funded awareness campaigns regarding the divorce statistics and support of obligations, as well as mandatory pre-marriage counseling that included the coverage of the risks of marriage and the chances of failure.

This could apply equally in the context of strengthening families.

It is difficult to envisage circumstances where the citizen could take the state to court for failing to come up with a comprehensive family policy that encompasses strengthening families. But it is not that hard to foresee the institution of proceedings against the state for neglecting to provide due support, culminating in loss of earnings or diminished health or wellbeing. Several cases have already been successfully concluded apportioning fault and awarding damages against the state when it has ineptly intervened to care for children.

Failing to strengthen families may range from simply doing nothing to taking steps which can be shown to be seriously flawed. A decision by the state not to strengthen a particular kind of family because that family form does not fall within the purview of criteria acceptable to society would trigger an action for discrimination. So where a state decides to use punitive fiscal measures to dissuade individuals from entering into family relationships which it does not wish to encourage, would this also constitute discrimination? The decisions of the European Court of Justice and the European Court of Human Rights are crucial in swaying states on this issue.

Conclusions and Policy Recommendations

Social and economic rights which form the basis of the right to a strong family continue to be largely neglected. It is recommended that families receive information which clarifies the true range of their rights and responsibilities. The information should also make reference to the criteria applied in the assessment of the basic standard of strength which families can hope to achieve in order to support their collective and individual rights to wellbeing. The state should be expected to provide clearly defined indicators to establish criteria which provide a foundation for applications for assistance or grounds for intervention.

Accusations of state interference in the private life of the individual and criticism of state efforts to establish the ideal family model are levied against most democratic societies on a daily basis. Striking a balance is a serious challenge, which is why it is imperative for states to continue to consolidate and enhance democratic institutions which can coordinate efforts in favour of strong families. Bainham and Henricson (2005, p. 105) cite a responsibility of the state to 'invest sufficient resources in family support in order to maintain the integrity of the family unit and uphold the right to family life'.

If all states are to be deemed accountable for supporting all families to be strong, they must be made aware of this obligation in as public a manner as possible. It is recommended that civil society should, for instance through NGOs, be entrusted with promoting the desirability of strong families and with placing the onus on the state to respond accordingly.

In order for states to be held accountable, families require effective access to justice. It is recommended that each family member should be empowered to enforce the right to dignity which is evidenced in the wellbeing or strength of the family by recourse to the appropriate judicial bodies. To date, it would appear that no action has been levied against any state on these grounds under Article 8 of the European Convention on Human Rights. However, legal coercion, while potentially comforting, should be unnecessary. Instead, it is hoped that states will acknowledge their responsibilities and take up the challenge to make all families strong and strong families stronger.

References

Bainham, A. (2003) Contact as a right and obligation, in A. Bainham, B. Lindley, M. Richards and L. Trinder (eds), *Children and Their Families: Contact, rights and welfare* (Oxford: Hart), 61–88.

Bainham, A. and Henricson, C. (2005) *The Child and Family Policy Divide: Tensions, convergence and rights* (York: Joseph Rowntree Foundation), May.

Burford, G. and Adams, P. (2004) Restorative justice, responsible regulation and social work, *Journal of Sociology and Social Welfare*, 31(1), March: 7–26.

Chinkin, C. (2010) Sources, in D. Moeckli, S. Shah and S. Sivukumaran (eds), *International Human Rights Law* (Oxford: Oxford University Press), 103–123.

Criddle, E. J. and Fox-Decent, E. (2008) A fiduciary theory of Jus Cogens, *Yale Journal Of International Law*, 34: 331.

Diduck A. (2008) Family law and family responsibility, in J. Bridgeman, H. Keating and C. Lind (eds), *Responsibility, Law and the Family* (Aldershot: Ashgate), 251–268.

Edwards, R. and Gillies, V. (2004) Support in parenting: values and consensus concerning who to turn to, *Journal of Social Policy*, 33(4): 623–643.

Eekelaar, J. (2001) Family law: the communitarian message, *Oxford Journal of Legal Studies*, 21(1): 181–192.

Eide, A. (2010) Adequate standard of living, in D. Moeckli, S. Shah and S. Sivakuman (eds), *International Human Rights Law* (Oxford: Oxford University Press), 233–256.

Ferguson, L. (2008) Family, social inequalities, and the persuasive force of interpersonal obligation, *International Journal of Law, Policy and the Family*, 22: 61–90.

Fineman, M. (2004) *The Autonomy Myth: A theory of dependency* (New York: The New Press).

Funder, K. and Smyth, B. (1996) Family law reforms and attitudes to parental responsibility, *Family Matters*, 45: 10–15.

Gillies, V. (2005) Meeting parents' needs? Discourses of 'support' and 'inclusion' in family poverty, *Critical Social Policy*, 25(1): 70–90.

Harris, D. and Parisi, D. (2005) Gender role ideologies and marriage promotion: state policy choices and suggestions for improvement, *Review of Policy Research*, 22(6): 841–858.

Higgins, R. (1994) *Problems and Process: International law and how we use it* (Oxford: Oxford University Press).

Jheelan, N. (2007) The enforceability of socio-economic rights, *European Human Rights Law Review*, Issue 2: 147.

Krause, H. (2006) Comparative family law, in M. Reimann and R. Zimmermann (eds), *The Oxford Handbook of Comparative Law* (Oxford: Oxford University Press), 1111.

McClain, L. (2008) Family life, the politics of the family, and social transformation, *The Good Society*, 17(1): 68–73.

McGlynn, C. (2007) Families and European Union law, in R. Probert (ed.), *Family Life and the Law* (Aldershot: Ashgate), 247–258.

Mink, G. (2001) Violating women: rights abuses in the welfare police state, *The American Academy of Political and Social Science*, 577: 79–93.

Nickel, J. (2005) Poverty and rights, *Philosophical Quarterly*, 55: 285–402.

Pieterse, M. (2004) Coming to terms with judicial enforcement of socio-economic rights, *South African Journal on Human Rights*, 20: 383.

Rothstein, B. (1998) *Just Institutions Matter: The moral and political logic of the universal welfare state* (New York: Cambridge University Press), 215.

Snik, G., De Jong J. and Van Haafte, W. (2004) Preventive intervention in families at risk: the limits of liberalism, *Journal of the Philosophy of Education*, 38(2): 181–193.

Ssenyonjo, M. (2009) *Economic, Social and Cultural Rights in International Law* (Oxford: Hart), 17.

Wikely, N. (2007) Family law and social security, in R. Probert (ed.), *Family Life and the Law* (Aldershot: Ashgate), 113.

26

Making a Global Case for Family Policy

How Families Support Society and How Policies Support Families

Karen Bogenschneider

Introduction

Family rhetoric is politically popular. Yet in many countries around the world, a gap exists between family rhetoric and reality. The rhetoric often voiced by policymakers is that families are a basic building block of society that should be relied upon, nurtured and protected. However, reality often reverts to the usual default of viewing policy through a singular individual lens with little acknowledgement of the families to which most individuals belong. Given the pervasiveness of this individualistic perspective and the highly abstract nature of the concept of family policy, the substantive result is predictable: policy decisions are seldom examined through the lens of family impacts and, consequently, family considerations are seldom incorporated fully into the normal course of policymaking (Bogenschneider *et al.*, 2012). Four international examples (from the USA, Africa, Korea and Latin America) illustrate the mismatch between family rhetoric and reality in terms of whether a family policy exists, how it is designed and implemented, and/or whom it targets.

In the USA, political leaders across the ideological spectrum use their endorsement of families as a sure-fire, vote-winning strategy (State Legislative Leaders Foundation, 1995). In a study of the US Congressional Record over a ten-year period, family-related words and images were invoked 218 times in an average week, making their way into one-third of all speeches, statements and tributes. Across a decade, with only two exceptions, family-oriented words appeared every single week Congress was in session, leading Strach (2007, p. 25) to conclude: 'The business of Congress is conducted in the language of family.' Despite this rhetoric, a recent analysis of 173 countries revealed that only the USA and three other countries do not offer paid

Contemporary Issues in Family Studies: Global Perspectives on Partnerships, Parenting and Support in a Changing World, First Edition. Edited by Angela Abela and Janet Walker.
© 2014 John Wiley & Sons, Ltd. Published 2014 by John Wiley & Sons, Ltd.

maternity leave (O'Brien, 2011). This void in family policy makes the family rhetoric seem like empty words.

In Africa, 39 heads of state adopted a social policy framework in 2009 that named 'family' as one of 15 key themes. All these signatory countries provide some benefits for disability, maternity, old age, sickness and work injury financed by payroll contributions paid by the worker, employer and/or government. Yet these policies are available only to waged workers in the formal sector, excluding workers in the informal sector, who account for 72 per cent of non-agricultural workers (Mokomane, 2011).

Korean society is based on Confucian principles of family solidarity that subjugate individual interests to group harmony. Upon the birth of a child, South Korea offers childcare leave to employed parents, with wage replacement set at 40 per cent of their monthly salary. In lieu of leave, parents may request reduced work hours to provide family care. Yet these benefits are rarely used, serving as no more than window dressing in a workplace culture that values long working hours, a strong work ethic and uninterrupted careers. Moreover, the salary replacement for the parent who takes leave is insufficient for low-wage earners such as single parents or part-time workers (Chin *et al.*, 2012).

In Latin American culture, family remains one of the most valued social institutions, affirmed as being *very important* by over 90 per cent of citizens. One of the region's central policies for fighting extreme poverty is its cash transfer programmes. Officially, cash assistance is aimed at families, yet in practice transfers are issued in the names of women. Moreover, programme professionals tend to work more with women than with men and are criticised for not responding more specifically to children's needs (Arriagada, 2011). If policy were approached through a holistic family impact lens, it would acknowledge the important roles played by both mothers *and* fathers and bring into focus the interests of all family members, including children.

In short, we have a feast of family rhetoric but a famine of attention paid to the family concept. It remains one thing to endorse the important contributions that families make to their members and society, and quite another to systematically place families at the centre of policy design, enactment and implementation. Families may need policy support now more than ever given changing family demographics, fiscal constraints and globalisation (OECD, 2011; Robila, 2012; Trask, 2011). Taken together, these changes in families, nations and the global economy indicate that '[f]amily policy needs to be at the forefront of every nation-state's agenda' (Trask, 2011, p. 1).

Families in many parts of the world are experiencing a number of demographic shifts, including a rising age of first marriage, a lowering rate of fertility, increasing prevalence of maternal employment, and growing numbers of elderly family members (Trask, 2011). In the midst of the global economic recession, policies that support families are being systematically dismantled or substantially reduced (OECD, 2011). Globalisation has propelled the transnational movement of capital, labour and goods in ways that have devastated economic opportunities in some regions and expanded opportunities in others, prompting family members or whole family units to migrate in search of a better life. This international migration has led to a new family form, transnational families, who strive to retain roots in their own country, while putting down new roots in their host country. These families often leave behind family members needing care, young and old alike (Trask, 2011).

In this chapter the case is made that family policy and family considerations deserve to be taken seriously. First, a foundation is provided for discussing family policy by putting forward a set of key definitions. Second, on the basis of contemporary research, an evidence-based rationale is offered for what families contribute to society and how best to communicate their value to policymakers. Several examples are given of international family policies aimed at supporting these key contributions. Finally, on the basis of the author's close work with policymakers over twenty years, two approaches are introduced for bringing family impacts to their attention. The chapter concludes with next steps for moving from analysis to action.

Definitions of Family Policy and the Family Impact Lens

To be taken seriously, family policy requires a common language, its own identity, and a clear articulation of its meaning. At its root is *policy*—a plan or course of action carried out through a law, rule, code, or other mechanism in the public (e.g. government, judiciary) or private (e.g. employers, NGOs) sector. Family policy has been conceptualised so as to differentiate between explicit policies intended to achieve certain family goals and implicit policies that are not intended to affect families but have indirect consequences for them (Bogenschneider, 2006). 'Family policy' is the term used for policies with an explicit end goal of supporting the five main functions of families—family formation or dissolution, partner relationships, economic support, child rearing and caregiving (see box). Policies that fall under the family policy umbrella include adoption, childcare, divorce, family allowances, long-term care, marriage education and parental leave.

> ## Family policy explicitly supports five main family functions
>
> - family formation or dissolution—marrying and divorcing, and bearing or adopting children
> - partner relationships—providing programmes which strengthen commitment and stability
> - economic support—providing financially for members' basic needs
> - child rearing—educating, feeding and socialising children, and protecting their health and safety
> - caregiving—providing assistance for the disabled, frail, ill and elderly

The 'family impact lens' is a companion term which refers to policies that do not explicitly intend to affect family functioning but that still would benefit from an examination of their implicit effects on families (e.g. health care, housing, poverty, substance abuse and unemployment). It denotes when family is used as a criterion (a) for assessing the effects of any policy or programme on family wellbeing, and (b) for identifying situations in which families are used as a means of accomplishing other policy goals. Many policy issues are not considered family policies *per se* because they primarily target individuals rather than families, yet they would benefit from examination through the family impact lens. First, families can be used as a criterion for assessing policy and programme impacts, both advertent and inadvertent. For example, in the

USA, political discourse on prisoner re-entry policy has focused primarily on the prisoner as an individual, with little analysis of the effect of incarceration on family earnings, family relationships and parenting. Another example comes from Sierra Leone: following ten years of rebel war, discussions of reconstruction and reconciliation have largely lacked any mention of family devastation and trauma (Akinsulure-Smith and Smith, 2012). Second, the family impact lens encompasses those situations in which families are used as a means of accomplishing other policy goals such as achieving women's gender equity. Another example is when policies such as child allowances and family leave are framed as family supports, when in actuality their primary intent is to increase a nation's fertility rate.

Family policy elevates political discourse because it embodies an essential quality that is seldom advanced by special-interest groups—commitment to others even when such actions exact a personal cost. This family focus can counter individualistic, narrow or self-serving agendas forwarded by lobbyists or political action committees. Rather than concentrating on overly specific problems or solutions, a family-centred view enlarges our organising frame by moving towards a more holistic, multi-dimensional way of thinking about policy challenges. The family impact lens promotes a longitudinal lifespan perspective that considers families from the cradle to the grave and acknowledges all forms of intra-familial sharing and cooperation.

The terms 'family policy' and 'the family impact lens' move our attention beyond the individual to a relationship between two or more persons tied together by blood, legal bonds or the joint performance of family functions—a conceptual distinction that is often overlooked in policy debate. For example, children's or women's policy is often incorrectly equated with family policy even though an individual is targeted, not a family relationship or family unit. In Africa, in the event of a divorce or the death of a husband, the wife may not be entitled to unemployment or pension benefits (Mokomane, 2011). 'Family', when it is used in policy debate, is sometimes misused to represent some, but not all, relationships in families; 'family' can be used as shorthand to refer only to the relationship of the mother and child, with no mention of the father, grandparent or other partners who are intimately involved. In Turkey, for instance, childcare is widely considered a women's issue rather than a family responsibility (Çarkoğlu et al., 2012). Sometimes 'family' can be used as a code word for certain types of families, while others are undervalued or ignored. In Sweden, government subsidies cover more than 90 per cent of the cost of non-parental childcare, but no national childcare allowance exists for parents who choose to care for their children themselves (Himmelstrand, 2011).

What Contributions Do Families Make to Society?

If family policy is to secure a place on the agenda of nation states, the nature of discourse must shift to prioritising families as worthy of study, investment, partnership and political action. Most arguments encouraging public investments in family policy revolve around the functions families perform for their members (e.g. family formation, partner relationships, economic support, child rearing and caregiving). Focusing on how policies support these family functions may be less relevant to policy decisions than focusing on how family functions support society. When communicating with policymakers, it may be more effective to focus less on the private benefits of families to their members and more on the public benefits of families to society. Policymakers are more interested in the public contributions families make to the economic and social goals of society, how effectively and efficiently they do so, and the cost if they fail.

In a recent family policy decade review, Bogenschneider and Corbett (2010b) propose four societal contributions that can be used as a rationale for promoting families as a fundamental focus of policymaking: first, generating productive workers; second, rearing caring and committed citizens; third, making efficient investments to reach societal goals; and fourth, providing an effective means of promoting positive child and youth development. Each of these key contributions is discussed in turn, and illustrated with examples of international family policies.

This section begins with a caveat. The research on which this argument is based is both broad and narrow. It is broad in the sense that it is grounded in a literature review that spans a number of diverse disciplines including child and adolescent development, communitarianism, family law, family science, psychology and sociology, and draws on a number of policy reports from evaluation firms, foundations, government agencies, public interest groups and think tanks. It is narrow in the sense that it emanates primarily from research studies published in academic and government outlets, mostly in the first decade of the twenty-first century. Recently, similar arguments have been made by scholars in Asian societies (Caparas, 2011), by an international association of family enrichment programmes (International Federation for Family Development, 2011), and by parents themselves. In an online survey of European parents, 9000 messages were submitted, of which almost half (48%) called for the state and society to recognise the role and investment made by parents (Stevens, 2011).

Families as a foundation for generating productive workers

If policymakers better appreciated families as a powerful and unique engine of a dynamic economy, they would be more receptive to public policies rewarding families for their private contribution towards the public good of generating productive workers. Family policy could help policymakers perceive families, not as mere units of consumption, but rather as the contributors most responsible for the development of human capital (Longman, 2004). In the midst of a global economic transformation, every nation's competitiveness will depend more than ever on its human capital, specifically the education and social skills of its labour force (Reynolds and Temple, 2005). Human capital in these new knowledge-based economies requires cognitive and non-cognitive skills that are shaped, to a large extent, by socialisation that occurs early in family life and in pre-school programmes (Heckman, 2006). For example, in a 30-year longitudinal study in the USA, Sroufe and colleagues were able to predict which pre-school children would drop out of school 11–14 years later with 77 per cent accuracy using only one variable—quality of care up to age 42 months (Sroufe et al., 2005). Children's early experiences proved to be powerful predictors of later development, especially when considered in combination with later care, peer relationships and the immediate environment (OECD, 2011; Sroufe et al., 2005).

The political value of emphasising the role that families play in generating productive workers was documented in a study of the European Union (EU)'s adoption of the 1992 Recommendation on Childcare (Bleijenbergh et al., 2006). This was the first time that childcare policy became a topic of concern and a societal responsibility in the EU and its member nations. Beginning in the 1980s when the European debate surrounding childcare began, the authors examined the political factors that resulted in a shift in childcare policy a decade later. Over time, arguments that childcare was necessary to promote children's wellbeing became less important, and arguments that it was a contributor to economic efficiency became more important. The authors concluded that the main justification for European involvement in childcare appeared to be economic—the need for women's labour force participation to serve the larger fiscal goal of keeping the welfare state affordable in the context of an ageing population. Under this economic umbrella, the specific forces for change varied in different countries. In the Netherlands, for example, politicians defended the labour force participation of women, arguing that childcare was an efficient way to increase national competitiveness. In the UK, where participation in formal public childcare grew from 2 per cent in 1989 to 34 per cent in 2000, the debate over childcare was linked to labour market policy.

Many countries are increasing their investment in the early childhood years. A recent analysis of the expenditures of 32 countries on education, family benefits and active labour market policies for people under 27 (OECD, 2011) found that about half of these countries had increased their relative share of spending on early childhood between 2003 and 2007; most countries, however, still spend more on older children, primarily through universal compulsory education. More than other OECD countries, the Czech Republic, Hungary, and Iceland front-load their spending in the early years (OECD, 2011).

Families as contributors to the rearing of caring, committed citizens

Longitudinal studies suggest that a focus on families and the policies that support them may help a society develop a caring, committed citizenry. Secure attachment relationships (i.e. the bonds that develop when caregiving is sensitively responsive and reliably available) predict many qualities that societies value in their members. For example, in longitudinal studies in the USA, children who were securely attached to their mothers were more empathetic, more self-reliant, and less hostile to their peers (Sroufe, 1988). The attachment relationship between a mother and infant was significantly related to a number of characteristics of good citizenship at ages 15 and 16—involvement, leadership, self-confidence, and social competence in problem-solving situations (Englund et al., 2000). Moreover, the quality of caregiving at age 3½ predicted the quality of romantic relationships over two decades later at ages 23 and 26.

Countries across the world including the UK have enacted a number of policies to strengthen parenting and couple relationships, including providing substantial funding. The UK recently devoted £10 million per year to promote effective parenting. The USA allocated $150 million per year over five years to encourage marriage, strengthen couple relationships, and promote father involvement. Cowan and Cowan (2008) conducted three experimental-design studies to compare the potential effects on child wellbeing of the UK's parent-focused approach and the USA's couple-focused approach.

In one of these studies, parents and children were assessed when the children entered school, at kindergarten, and in the first, fourth and ninth grades. This was a randomised trial in which parents and children were allocated to one of three groups. The control group received a brief consultation. The treatment groups consisted of 16-week couple groups led by trained professionals: one group focused more on parent–child issues and the other focused more on couple issues. Compared to the control group, couples in the parent–child-focused group were more effective in their interactions with their children one year later; however, no changes were observed in the quality of the couple relationship. Notably, for the parents in the couple-focused group, both the parent–child and the couple relationship improved. Their children showed higher academic achievement and lower aggression in first grade and, remarkably, continued to show better school performance and fewer problem behaviours ten years later. Parents in the couple-focused group experienced a decline in depression, marital conflict and parenting stress. Focusing on the whole family system proved to be more effective for enhancing children's (and parent's) development than focusing only on the parent–child subsystem.

Family policies and programmes as an efficient investment of public resources

Families carry out a variety of functions that are critically important to society, such as child rearing and caregiving for the elderly. Economists have used different approaches to estimate the value of family functions—when fragmented families do not provide them, and when stable families do. Scafidi (2008) used data from the USA to estimate the societal costs of family fragmentation, specifically divorce and unmarried childbearing. Children growing up in fragmented families have a greater risk of poverty, juvenile delinquency, adult criminality and dropping out of school. To estimate local, state and national costs, Scafidi calculated taxpayer expenditures for programmes that address poverty, criminal justice and education along with forgone tax revenues from individuals who earn less because they grew up in poverty. His estimates included a range of cash assistance, child welfare programmes, energy assistance, children's health care, food stamps, housing and so forth. Using conservative assumptions, he estimated the annual costs of family fragmentation to be $112 billion per year or $1 trillion per decade (US currency). Given such substantial costs, even family strengthening policies with modest success rates would be cost-effective. For example, Texas recently invested $15 million over two years in programmes such as marriage education. If these efforts increased marriage stability by just three-tenths of 1 per cent, they would save $9 million per year.

Folbre (2008) also estimated the value of cash subsidies for child rearing provided by the US government: government cash subsidies represent a small portion of child-rearing costs, from 10–25 per cent of a middle-class parent's annual cash expenditures on a child under 18, to only 4–10 per cent when the estimates include the parent's time and cash expenditures. Another way to gauge the value of these parental investments in child rearing is to compute the return on investment. For every public dollar allocated to a child in a middle-class family with two parents, taxpayers receive a return of $10.50 to $25 in parent contributions.

Long-term care has been called the sleeping giant of family policy, given the extent of informal care provided by family members. In the USA, for example, the vast majority (78%) of long-term care for the elderly and disabled is provided by informal caregivers, primarily family members. The economic value of this caregiving, which does not show up in state or federal budget ledgers, was estimated to be $256 billion in 2002, or three times the $82 billion the government spent through the Medicaid programme (Normandin and Bogenschneider, 2006). In a similar analysis conducted in Canada, family caregivers were projected to save the health system $5 billion (Canadian currency) in 2002 and provide services equivalent to 276000 full-time employees (Harvey and Yoshino, 2006).

These cost–benefit analyses suggest that government cannot afford to fully replace the functions families perform for the benefit of their members and the good of society. Families do better in a supportive environment in which, for example, they have access to basic necessities such as food, water and shelter (Caparas, 2011); schools actively seek parental engagement; employers recognise that workers are also family members; agencies and organisations are family-centred in their culture, philosophy and operation; and laws support family members' roles as caregivers, parents, partners and workers. There remains a role for government to supplement and complement private investments in families in a world that is rapidly changing and becoming ever more demanding of a competent citizenry.

Family policies and programmes as an effective means of promoting positive child and youth development

Considerable progress has been made in our understanding of family contributions to the rearing of the next generation (Amato, 2005), and the efficacy of family-centred prevention programming (Spoth *et al.*, 2002). One way to estimate the value of families to the development of their offspring is to compare how youth behaviours are affected by stable versus unstable families. Amato projected that, if as many 12- to 18-year-olds were living with their biological parents in 2002 as in 1980, nearly half a million fewer US children would be suspended from school, 200000 fewer would commit violent or delinquent acts, and 28000 fewer would attempt suicide. For children who were raised by two happily married biological parents, the effects were even larger. Growing up in stable, two-parent families creates the conditions for positive cognitive, emotional and social development in childhood that extends to adulthood as well.

Turning to prevention programmes, we find that those which focus only on young people have smaller effects (Kumpfer *et al.*, 2003) than those which change family dynamics. The average effect size for universal, youth-only approaches such as life-skills or social training was +0.10, whereas the average effect size for family-focused interventions such as parenting-skills training and in-home support was +0.96. Thus, approaches that change family dynamics are nine times more effective than those that focus only on individual young people.

Many countries have introduced innovative programmes to tackle a serious deterrent to children's optimal development—growing up in poverty. One approach, known as 'Make Work Pay', was evaluated in several large-scale, well-designed and well-implemented experiments involving 12000 children in two locations in the USA and two provinces in Canada (Berlin, 2007). The results were consistent: investments in the employment of parents, particularly among fragile families (i.e. unmarried parents and their children), improved their children's school performance and, sometimes, their social development as well.

In sum, family policy can create the conditions for families to effectively and efficiently carry out the many functions they perform for their members and for society in rearing the next generation, in economically supporting their members, and in caring for those who cannot always care for themselves. Yet families can be damaged by stressful conditions such as the inability to earn a living, or afford health insurance, or find quality childcare, or send their children to good schools. Policies that support families are politically popular and typically are much more effective than policies aimed only at individuals: When the family foundation is strong today, children are more likely to develop the solid foundation they need for tomorrow to become competent workers in a sound economy and caring, committed citizens in a strong society.

Applying the Family Impact Lens to Policymaking

There is no simple, direct connection between research and policy (Bogenschneider and Corbett, 2010a). In fact, this relation may be even less linear for family policies because they touch on core and often conflicting values regarding equality, personal responsibility, sex, etc. Sometimes evidence about families is used, sometimes not; sometimes it is used correctly, other times it is misused and misconstrued for political purposes. To advance the family impact lens, both top-down and bottom-up approaches may be needed. Two such models that have proven to be successful in the USA and Belgium respectively are described in the boxes below. In the USA, the Family Impact Seminars represent a top-down approach for connecting research and policy by providing high-quality, objective research to state policymakers on timely topics; this Seminar model is operating in 21 states and the District of Columbia (Bogenschneider, 2006; Bogenschneider *et al.*, 2010). Policymakers report that Seminar information is useful in shaping policy decisions. For example, following Family Impact Seminars, a refundable childcare tax credit was adopted in Oregon, and a State Children's Health Insurance Program (SCHIP) was passed in Nebraska.

The other model is a long-standing bottom-up approach in Belgium, that organises families of all sizes, of any structure, and at every stage of the family life cycle to advocate on their own behalf and for all families (De Smet, 2011). Belgium's League of Families, known as the BOND, is an NGO that organises families in five provinces, 33 regions, and 993 local branches with support from 180 paid staff and 13000 volunteers.

Top-down approach

Family Impact Seminars in the USA provide evidence-based, family-focused information to policymakers through presentations, discussions and briefing reports.

Aims:

- to increase respect for and use of research evidence in policy decisions
- to encourage policymakers to examine issues through the family impact lens
- to provide an opportunity for policymakers to develop relationships across party lines that can overcome polarisation and build common ground

Impacts on policymakers identified in phone interviews with 15 legislators (88% response rate):

- 73% were 'quite a bit more likely' to consider how pending legislation might affect families
- 73% were 'quite a bit more likely' to see the practical value of research
- 60% were 'quite a bit more likely' to consider how legislation being developed might affect families

Bottom-up approach

The League of Families (known as the BOND) in Belgium defends the interests of families.

Aims:

- to organise political action on behalf of all families
- to promote social life at the local level
- to provide direct services to families

Impacts:

- Political: preservation of child allowances, tax reforms and work–life balance, and the introduction of family modulation (adjusting direct government support for families according to the number of dependants)
- Social: provision of education and sports programmes, parent education, and safe online environments for children
- Services: provision of consumer advice, socio-legal services, babysitting/granny-sitting, etc.

Policy Implications: Looking Ahead

This chapter aims to encourage ongoing dialogue and deliberation about how to make a global case for family policy. This evidence-based rationale for how families support strong societies and how policies support strong families may resonate with policymakers. To convince policymakers of the need for and the value of family policy, professionals may need to focus less on discussing the private benefits families provide to their members and more on documenting the public benefits they provide to society as an effective and efficient means of generating productive workers and raising caring, committed citizens.

This rationale should not be embraced without acknowledging appropriate cautions. Both the rationale and the research that supports it need careful scrutiny with an eye to their international validity in developed and developing countries. Moreover, professionals need to be aware of the potential shortcomings of family policy. First, family policy can be myopic if it fails to keep pace with contemporary families and how they are affected by a nation's changing cultural, economic and social conditions. Second, families are only one part of a vast, multi-faceted, multi-influenced political landscape, so it would be short-sighted to assert that family factors affect every issue or that family approaches are always the most effective. Third, recognising the value of family policy is a necessary first step, but it is not sufficient. Three strategies follow for placing family policy on a nation state's political agenda: the creation of a family ministry or dedicated entity located at the centre of the nation's power grid; capacity-building in the form of a national infrastructure for family research and outreach; and commitment to working with policymakers to build family-focused, evidence-informed policy decisions.

First, in many countries, formal entities exist that routinely examine the economic or environmental impact of policies and programmes. Yet few formal entities, little leadership and meagre resources are dedicated to examining the family impacts of policies and programmes (Bogenschneider *et al.*, 2012). To place families firmly on the policy agenda, nations need a family ministry or dedicated entity with sufficient organisational, fiscal and human resources to serve as a locus for forming partnerships of family stakeholders across all sectors (e.g. the academy, civil society, and governmental or nongovernmental organisations). A family ministry can also promote families as a priority for study, investment, partnership and political action. It can take the lead in analysing how families affect and are affected by policies, and in evaluating family policies and programmes (Akinsulure-Smith and Smith, 2012; Chin *et al.*, 2012; International Federation for Family Development, 2011; Robila, 2012). A family ministry can bring together multidisciplinary, cross-agency partnerships to formulate a unified voice for all families including minority, marginalised or disadvantaged families. Moreover, it can foster collaboration rather than competition and serve as a cogent force for accomplishing common aims such as incorporating families into the agenda of international organisations (e.g. the United Nations, the World Bank), and securing stable funding for family policy. For example, Italy, Sweden and some Eastern European countries have institutionalised national funding by designating a certain percentage of GDP for family and/or social expenditures (Robila, 2012).

Second, nations also need an infrastructure for building capacity for family research and outreach. Family policy is often built on demographic data on a nation's families in all their diversity. Data can sometimes be a powerful motivator for change. For example, in 2005, the South Korean government was alarmed by three demographic trends—the lowest total fertility rate in the world, a decline in marriage rates, and an increasingly large number of transnational marriages. This data was responsible, in part, for the enactment of several family policies and the establishment of the first government department exclusively in charge of family policy (Chin *et al.*, 2012). Nations also need culturally relevant family services that are available and accessible, and a cadre of family professionals trained to study, teach about and deliver family-centred services. In Eastern Europe, family life education programmes and services are limited (Robila, 2012) and, even in countries where they do exist such as South Korea, the demand for services often exceeds the supply (Chin *et al.*, 2012). Supply is limited, in part because of a critical shortage of trained family professionals and the lack of a family training component in the career preparation of other professionals (e.g. clinicians, teachers, medical staff, mental health professionals; Akinsulure-Smith and Smith, 2012). The provision of training is hampered by the absence of family life classes in secondary education and the lack of family-oriented programmes in higher education (Robila, 2012).

One of the major reasons for the success of developing family policy in South Korea is the wide consensus surrounding the need for strong family policy (Chin *et al.*, 2012). Given the extent of family rhetoric, political consensus already exists in many countries around the world, but policymakers do not necessarily have the information they need to act. Family professionals need to recognise that communicating with policymakers is as central to building strong families as their other endeavours are (Bogenschneider and Corbett, 2010a). Professionals need to invest an ongoing commitment of time and resources in top-down approaches such as building relationships with and communicating research evidence to policymakers, and in bottom-up approaches that enable families to become politically active and personally responsible for advocating for the wellbeing of all families.

Providing family-focused, evidence-based information to policymakers has the potential to generate interest in, and the momentum for, developing policies and programmes that can strengthen and support families in all their diversity across the lifespan. Communicating the value of families to policymakers can sound deceptively simple, but in reality can be quite complex and demanding. This, however, does not mean that it is not worth doing. Doing family policy can help turn family rhetoric into reality.

References

Akinsulure-Smith, A. M. and Smith, H. E. (2012) Evolution of family policies in post-conflict Sierra Leone, *Journal of Child and Family Studies*. 21, 4–13. doi:10.1007/s10826-011-9495-7.

Amato, P. R. (2005) The impact of family formation change on the cognitive, social, and emotional well-being of the next generation, *The Future of Children*, 15(2): 75–96.

Arriagada, I. (2011) Family and cash transfer programs in Latin America, paper presented at the Expert Group Meeting on Assessing Family Policies, United Nations, New York, June. http://social.un.org/index/LinkClick.aspx?fileticket=Ij_kNiT25GY%3d&tabid=1555Is [Accessed 17.10.2012.]

Berlin, G. L. (2007) Investing in parents to invest in children, presented at the National Summit on America's Children, Washington, DC, 22 May. http://www.mdrc.org/publications/456/presentation.html [Accessed 17.10.2012.]

Bleijenbergh, I., Bussemaker, J. and de Bruijn, J. (2006) Trading wellbeing for economic efficiency: the 1990 shift in EU childcare policies, in L. Hass and S. K. Wisensale (eds), *Families and Social Policy: National and international perspectives* (Binghamton, NY: The Haworth Press), 315–338.

Bogenschneider, K. (2006) *Family Policy Matters: How policymaking affects families and what professionals can do* (New York: Routledge), 2nd edn.

Bogenschneider, K. and Corbett, T. J. (2010a) *Evidence-based Policymaking: Insights from policy-minded researchers and research-minded policymakers* (New York: Taylor & Francis).

Bogenschneider, K. and Corbett, T. J. (2010b) Family policy: becoming a field of inquiry and subfield of social policy, *Journal of Marriage and Family*, 72: 783–803.

Bogenschneider, K., Little, O., Ooms, T., Benning, S., Cadigan, K. and Corbett, T. (2012) The family impact lens: an evidence-informed, family-focused approach to policy and practice, *Family Relations*, 61: 514–531.

Bogenschneider, K., Normandin, H., Onaga, E., Bowman, S. and MacDermid, S. M. (2010) Generating evidence on disseminating evidence to policymakers, in K. Bogenschneider and T. Corbett, *Evidence-based Policymaking: Insights from policy-minded researchers and research-minded policymakers* (New York: Taylor & Francis), 253–290.

Caparas, V. Q. (2011) Work–family balance and family poverty in Asia: an overview of policy contexts, consequences, and challenges, paper presented at the Expert Group Meeting on Assessing Family Policies, United Nations, New York, June. http://social.un.org/index/LinkClick.aspx?fileticket=YKoZ3tQHcQ%3d&tabid=1555 [Accessed 17.10.2012.]

Çarkoğlu, A., Kafescioğlu, N. and Mitrani, A. A. (2012) Review of explicit family policies in Turkey from a systemic perspective, *Journal of Child and Family Studies*. 21, 42–52. doi: 10.1007/s10826-011-9482-z.

Chin, M., Lee, J., Lee, S., Son, S. and Sung, M. (2012) Family policy in South Korea: development, current status, and challenges, *Journal of Child and Family Studies*. 21, 53–64. doi: 10.1007/s10826-011-9480-1.

Cowan, P. and Cowan, C. P. (2008) Diverging family policies to promote children's wellbeing in the UK and US: some relevant data from family research and intervention studies, *Journal of Children's Services*, 3(4): 4–16.

Englund, M. M., Levy, A. K., Hyson, D. M. and Sroufe, L. A. (2000) Adolescent social competence: effectiveness in a group setting, *Child Development*, 71: 1049–1060.

Folbre, N. (2008) *Valuing Children: Rethinking the economics of the family* (Boston, MA: Harvard University Press).

Harvey, C. D. H. and Yoshino, S. (2006) Social policy for family caregivers of elderly: a Canadian, Japanese, and Australian comparison, in L. Hass and S. K. Wisensale (eds), *Families and Social Policy: National and international perspectives* (Binghamton, NY: The Haworth Press), 143–158.

Heckman, J. J. (2006) Skill formation and the economics of investing in disadvantaged children, *Science*, 312 (5782): 1900–1902.

Himmelstrand, J. (2011) The concept of work–family balance seen from a Swedish perspective, paper presented at the Expert Group Meeting on Assessing Family Policies, United Nations, New York, June. http://social.un.org/index/LinkClick.aspx?fileticket=stga2FRt3Ko%3d&tabid=1555 [Accessed 17.10.2012.]

International Federation for Family Development (2011) *International Federation for Family Development Newsletter*, June.

Kumpfer, K. L., Alvarado, R. and Whiteside, H. O. (2003) Family-based interventions for substance abuse prevention, *Substance Use and Misuse*, 38: 1759–1789.

Longman, P. (2004) *The Empty Cradle: How falling birthrates threaten world prosperity and what to do about it* (New York: Basic Books).

Mokomane, Z. (2011) Session VII: Anti-poverty policies focusing on families: regional overview: Africa—introductory remarks, paper presented at the Expert Group Meeting on Assessing Family Policies, United Nations, New York, June. http://social.un.org/index/LinkClick.aspx?fileticket=2O8xXSeSFEQ%3d&tabid=1555 [Accessed 17.10.2012.]

Normandin, H. and Bogenschneider, K. (eds) (2006) *Long-term Care Reform: Wisconsin's experience compared to other states* (Wisconsin Family Impact Seminar Briefing Report No. 23, Feb.). http://www.familyimpactseminars.org/doc.asp?d=s_wifis23report.pdf [Accessed 26.3.2008.]

O'Brien, M. (2011) Father-inclusive family policies: challenges and recommendations, paper presented at the Expert Group Meeting on Assessing Family Policies, United Nations, New York, NY, June. http://social.un.org/index/LinkClick.aspx?fileticket=W14n7hnscL8%3d&tabid=1555 [Accessed 17.10.2012.]

OECD (2011) *Doing Better for Families* (Paris: OECD). http://dx.doi.org/10.1787/9789264098732-en [Accessed 17.10.2012.]

Reynolds, A. J. and Temple, J. A. (2005) Priorities for a new century of early childhood programs, *Infants and Young Children*, 18: 104–118.

Robila, M. (2012) Family policies in Eastern Europe: a focus on parental leave, *Journal of Child and Family Studies*. 21, 32–41. doi: 10.1007/s10826-010-9421-4.

Scafidi, B. (2008) *The Taxpayer Costs of Divorce and Unwed Childbearing: First-ever estimates for the nation and all fifty states* (New York: Institute for American Values).

Spoth, R. L., Kavanagh, K. A. and Dishion, T. (2002) Family-centered preventive intervention science: toward benefits to larger populations of children, youth, and families, *Prevention Science*, 3(3): 145–152.

Sroufe, L. A. (1988) The role of infant–caregiver attachment in development, in J. Belsky and T. Nezworski (eds), *Clinical Implications of Attachment* (Hillsdale, NJ: Lawrence Erlbaum), 18–38.

Sroufe, L. A., Egeland, B., Carlson, E. A. and Collins, W. A. (2005) *The Development of the Person: The Minnesota study of risk and adaptation from birth to adulthood* (New York: Guilford Press).

State Legislative Leaders Foundation (1995) *State Legislative Leaders: Keys to effective legislation for children and families* (Centerville, MA: SLLF).

Stevens, J. T. (2011) Ensuring work–family balance: The importance of family-focused solutions—the perspective of mothers in Europe, paper presented at the Expert Group Meeting on Assessing Family Policies, United Nations, New York, June. http://social.un.org/index/LinkClick.aspx?fileticket=gyhL5RWe6J0%3d&tabid=1555 [Accessed 17.10.2012.]

Strach, P. (2007) *All in the Family: The private roots of American public policy* (Stanford, CA: Stanford University Press).

Trask, B. S. (2011) Globalization and families: meeting the family policy challenge, paper presented at the Expert Group Meeting on Assessing Family Policies, United Nations, New York, June. http://social.un.org/index/LinkClick.aspx?fileticket=w3Kx6ktVVd4%3d&tabid=1555 [Accessed 17.10.2012.]

Waldfogel, J. (2010) *Tackling Child Poverty and Improving Child Wellbeing: Lessons from Britain.* http://www.firstfocus.net/sites/default/files/TacklingPoverty.pdf [Accessed 15.06.2011.]

Partnership, Parenting and Protecting Children's Best Interests
Implications for Policy and Practice

Janet Walker and Angela Abela

Introduction

The impetus for the book developed from shared beliefs that family life is central to the psychological, emotional, social and economic wellbeing of adults and children living in all types of society and in all corners of the globe, that families can provide protection and stability for their members, and that strong, stable families form the bedrock for strong, stable societies. Family structures have always evolved and changed, but immense technological advances, greater gender equality and increased globalisation have prompted widespread shifts in patterns of family formation, living arrangements, parenting practices, social attitudes and public policies. In many countries, life expectancy is higher than ever before, birth rates are lower and, increasingly, more people live in non-traditional family structures. In Western countries in particular there is more cohabitation; marriages end in divorce more often and remarriages are increasing; greater numbers of children are born outside wedlock; and parenthood is no longer the preserve of married couples. Indeed, children may spend much of their young lives in a variety of family forms and be looked after by a range of 'parental' figures. In other parts of the globe, traditional structures and institutions and gendered approaches to partnership and parenting are being challenged on a daily basis.

These shifts have been accompanied by a range of complex challenges for individuals, families and societies, and have served to draw attention to the need for sensitive, supportive family policies that protect vulnerable families and enhance child outcomes, particularly during a period of sustained global recession and widespread fiscal

Contemporary Issues in Family Studies: Global Perspectives on Partnerships, Parenting and Support in a Changing World, First Edition. Edited by Angela Abela and Janet Walker.
© 2014 John Wiley & Sons, Ltd. Published 2014 by John Wiley & Sons, Ltd.

constraints. Different countries have developed different priorities and policies and there is much to be gained from a better global understanding of the strategies that work in different cultural contexts. The contributors to this book have examined the changes and challenges, drawing on research from around the world in order to consider the implications for policy and practice in the future. In this final chapter we reflect on the key themes and summarise the learning within each of the four parts of the book, which we believe has global relevance in our fast-changing world.

Changing Couple and Family Relationships

A number of key themes have emerged throughout the preceding chapters. These are summarised in the box below.

> ### Changing couple and family relationships: key themes
>
> 1. The growing diversity in family forms is likely to continue.
> 2. Family forms and daily living experiences within families are influenced by a range of local, national and global factors.
> 3. Strong, stable relationships are central to individual wellbeing, and people value family connectedness and commitment.
> 4. Family violence and family breakdown have far-reaching impacts on adults and children and understanding these is critical to the development of supportive family environments.
> 5. Diversity in family structures offers opportunities and challenges for family life, child rearing and social support as people grow older.

At the beginning of the twenty-first century, more and more people were spending longer periods of their lives outside the conventional family unit of two married parents and their biological children (Roseneil, 2005). The emphasis in this book has been on increasing our understanding of the diversity of family forms and on how family membership changes over time. Families continue to perform a variety of functions and are expected to provide care and support for increasingly long periods as many children stay in education and live at home until they are well into adulthood and grandparent generations live longer and become increasingly dependent. Because modern families come in all shapes and sizes these tasks can be extremely demanding, and they have to be balanced with other obligations.

The way families are formed and the processes that occur within the family unit vary considerably between societies, influenced by the wider social contexts of work, education, and health and welfare services, as well as by religious affiliations and public attitudes and expectations (McKie and Callan, 2012). Natural disasters, such as droughts, tsunamis, wars and conflicts, also influence the ways in which family relationships are formed and re-formed, highlighting the complexity of factors that shape partnerships and parenting. The increased acceptance of divorce, remarriage, cohabitation and civil partnerships requires us to rethink how we define and support families. Relationship formation patterns, including 'living apart together' (LAT) and 'alone together' marriages, and same-sex partnerships, challenge traditional notions of partnership and traditional beliefs about how intimate couple relationships should be forged and maintained. Nevertheless, marriage remains the dominant type of relationship in the majority of societies, and most young people tend to regard a marital relationship as something to which they aspire. Most people value family connectedness and commitment, expect their couple relationship to last for life, and, in times of crisis, turn to their family for practical, emotional and economic support (Smart, 2007).

Drawing on data about family trends and relationships across the world in the years between 1900 and 2000, Therborn (2004, p. 314) argued that even within diverse living arrangements there is an abiding 'longing for deep, lasting and exclusive emotional bonding'. The way people talk about their families and the meanings associated with members of the kinship network indicate great diversity while still revealing shared priorities (McKie and Callan, 2012). Relationships are central to individual wellbeing, but they evolve and change at varying speeds and in different ways, requiring adaptation at all levels.

Policy and practice implications

Forming a co-residential, intimate couple relationship is one of the most important life-course transitions people make. Although family life and intimate relationships are essentially private matters, the rapid pace of change in family structures has led to ever-increasing attention from governments anxious about the consequences of more liberal attitudes towards marriage and divorce. Because families are so central to wellbeing and to the societies in which they live, they have served as a key target for public policy as more traditional concepts of family life have shifted and new structures have emerged. McKie and Callan (2012) note:

> The challenge facing all governments, at the most general level, is how to enable the development and maintenance of conditions which will protect and enhance life-enriching family relationships, notwithstanding the potential disruption that can be caused by economic recession, mobility and migration, epidemics of disease and climate change. This presents political as well as policy challenges. (p. 206)

The authors point out that, traditionally, the wealthier a country is, the more social programmes the government provides to support families, while poorer countries have had to rely on families themselves to assist their members. Looking to the future, a more comprehensive and integrated approach to policies which impact on family relationships and family life will be needed, along with more joined-up services and interventions which can strengthen families. In this context, Qatar, for example, one of the world's richest nations, has called for strong, cohesive families and effective social protection and public institutions that will support a strong society (General Secretariat for Development Planning, 2010). An increasing emphasis on strengthening adult couple relationships is evident in many European countries, the USA, Australia and India.

The Second Demographic Transition, referred to by many contributors to this book, denotes attitudinal and cultural changes and an acceptance of new family formation processes and structures which will need to be carefully considered as family policies are developed. Support services will need to take account of and be ready to respond to a range of family types and different kinds of family relationships. The challenge for policymakers and practitioners is to understand change and promote wellbeing in all kinds of partnerships. Civil unions and gay marriages will undoubtedly increase as same-sex couple relationships are recognised, freedom of choice in respect of an intimate partner is embraced across the globe, and ancestral traditions regulating marriage and family life are exposed to new norms and values. It is important that individuals are protected in their quest for intimacy and that threats to family stability such as family violence are not tolerated. Couple relationship education and therapeutic interventions will need to transcend cultural boundaries and assist families and communities to accommodate diversity. Shedding preconceptions about normative family structures must be an essential first step in developing appropriate policies and support services.

Parenthood, Parenting and Family Life

Diversity in family forms and processes is reflected in changing approaches to parenthood and parenting. These are summarised in the box below.

Changing patterns of parenthood and parenting

1. Birth rates are falling in many countries while older generations are living longer.
2. Increasing numbers of women are able to choose whether and when to have children, and many delay childbirth.
3. The transition to parenthood can be stressful and can destabilise couple relationships.
4. Families are under increasing pressure to be economically self-sufficient, resulting in the need for parents to balance home and work commitments.
5. Children may experience a variety of family types during childhood, and protecting their best interests and promoting positive child development is a major priority.

There has been a long downward trend in birth rates in many countries and, while couples are increasingly able to choose when to make the transition to parenthood and how many children to have, there is evidence that many people still have fewer children than they would like, especially in southern and central European countries and Asian OECD countries (OECD, 2011). A variety of social attitudes and public policies designed to render families economically self-sufficient have put pressure on families to balance work and child-rearing activities. As people have delayed marriage and the forming of committed relationships, so parenthood has been postponed in many societies, and there are fewer large families and higher levels of childlessness. High housing and education costs in countries such as Korea and Japan have placed further constraints on parental options.

As birth rates are declining, so life expectancy is increasing, dramatically shifting demographic profiles across the world. Population ageing is undoubtedly a key challenge for governments in the twenty-first century. Family practices and intergenerational relations are strongly influenced by societal structures and cultural and religious values, and providing care and support for the elderly will be an important consideration for all governments in the years to come. One element in ensuring future economic prosperity is the mobilisation of working-age labour market supply, which in turn means promoting female employment. The pressure on women to enter the workforce has influenced the choices they make about whether and when to make the transition to parenthood. There are clear tensions between employment, career development and childbearing, with strong evidence supporting the link between childlessness and the education level of women. Women who have received tertiary education are more likely to defer parenthood or remain childless.

Although increasing numbers of women are in paid employment outside the home and there is increasing gender equality across the Western world, enabling women to enter professions which have traditionally been dominated by men and to make lifestyle choices, gender gaps in paid and unpaid work are substantial. The wage gap has lessened over time, but the differential is still significant across the OECD countries. There is a clear link between this gap and the period of family formation, which inevitably means that women have to withdraw from the labour market, at least for a while. Moreover, the transition to parenthood tends to undermine gender equality in couple relationships as more traditional gender roles within the family are reinforced. Fathers tend to regard their primary parental role as being to provide financially for the family rather than to provide childcare and undertake domestic responsibilities. In OECD countries, even when women are in paid employment they do more unpaid work at home than men, and non-working fathers devote less time to caring than their working partners (OECD, 2011). Redressing the gender balance between earning and caring has been difficult, and even family-friendly policies such as generous parental leave, as for example exists in Nordic countries, have not necessarily resulted in fathers spending more time on childcare activities. In general, women spend twice as much time on caring tasks as a primary activity than men, and in some countries, such as Japan and Turkey, women spend between four and six times more time on care work (OECD, 2010).

The transition to parenthood marks a critical change in the life course and can impose stresses on couple relationships, which, if not addressed, can fester and ultimately result in family breakdown, separation and divorce. Awareness and understanding of the pressures on parents is relatively recent: the transition to parenthood can be fraught with tension and misunderstanding between partners, challenging the stability of family relationships. On average, some 60 per cent of mothers with dependent children go back to work, although there are significant cross-national variations. The highest rates of maternal employment are in the Nordic countries, Canada, the USA, the Netherlands and Switzerland (OECD, 2011). Decisions about returning to work can often be the trigger for further disputes between partners as expectations about roles collide and highlight the tensions between traditional gender roles and societal expectations about balancing work and home commitments.

The increase in family breakdown has fuelled concerns that parental divorce and living in a single-parent household enhance the risk factors for poor outcomes for children and young people. There is abundant research evidence documenting the potentially detrimental impacts of family breakdown on children and their parents, and indicating that children in single-parent families fare more poorly across a broad range of outcome areas than children in two-parent families. This is a complex area, and disentangling the impacts of parental conflict, the multiple disruptions which can follow parental separation, and the impact of psychological, emotional and economic pressures is far from straightforward. The parenting and mental health difficulties faced by single mothers are increased by economic hardship, deprivation and poverty. Single-parent households face the highest poverty risk, because of the constraints on earnings potential. Worries about money can then increase the risk of ill health and the inability to parent effectively, thus creating a cycle of disadvantage. Mothers who raise their children on their own are considerably more disadvantaged than mothers living with a partner.

As parenting trajectories have become increasingly diverse, it has been essential to understand the factors that promote positive child development and the ways in which children's best interests are met. Misca and Smith (Chapter 11, this volume) have shown how an ecological model of child development enables a more sophisticated understanding of the multitude of factors influencing child development, challenging some of the more negative stereotypes about lone parenting and same-gender parent-hood. It is becoming increasingly clear that the quality of the child's home and family environment, and of the relationship between the child and its caregiver(s), are more important in facilitating positive child development than the type of family structure in which children live. Studies of children raised in same-gender families have found no significant differences in child outcomes as a function of parental sexual orientation (Patterson *et al.*, Chapter 13, this volume). Importantly, lesbian and gay couples who report greater social support and harmonious couple relationships report fewer stressors associated with the transition to parenthood, re-emphasising the critical importance of the quality of parents' own couple relationships in their ability to manage this life transition well.

Policy and practice implications

Debates and concerns about the widespread changes in family structures are probably at their most heated with respect to parenting practices. Protecting children's best interests and wellbeing has become a legitimate and important aspect of family policies in many countries. The presumption that marriage necessarily provides the ideal environment in which to raise children has been challenged by recent research which has sought to understand the factors that foster good parenting and positive child outcomes. The overriding conclusion that children thrive best when they are brought up in families characterised by predictable and consistent care, and that such care is associated with stable and harmonious relationships between the parents (Coleman and Glenn, 2009), has implications for policy and practice in relation to parenting and family life.

Research indicates the importance of supporting individuals and couples during the transition to parenthood, irrespective of the kind of family structure they have chosen. Recognising the strains and tensions facing new parents and ensuring that essential support services are available requires multi-agency working and integrated services. Rather than stigmatising parenting arrangements that do not conform to traditional norms, the emphasis in policy and practice must be on seeking ways to reduce disadvantage and adversity, support the task of parenting, which is challenging for many families, and strengthen attachment opportunities between parents and their children.

Reducing barriers to parental employment while bolstering family-friendly employment practices presents many challenges for the future as more and more parents strive to balance caring responsibilities with their responsibilities to provide economic security for their children. As McKie and Callan (2012, p. 171) have pointed out, in all lifestyle choices and partnership ties, 'the acquisition and maintenance of resources, in particular, money, is imperative'. Being out of work results in a lack of resources and a lack of choice about priorities and attainable goals. Being in work can create conflicts and tensions between working and caring for children and older generations, and governments will need to recognise that the provision of adequate caring options is a high priority for working parents.

Childcare constraints play an important role in parents' decisions about work options, and childcare policies influence the ways in which mothers in particular engage with the world of work. Flexible workplace practices, parental leave arrangements and childcare provision are likely to be key considerations as economies around the world seek to climb out of recession and build stable and flourishing economic structures which enhance social and economic capital for the decades ahead. Dependence on family members to provide childcare support will be less reliable in the future as retirement ages rise and families become even more mobile. Employers have an important role to play in supporting parents and meeting children's needs for stability. With more and more young mothers in paid work, the potential trade-off between maternal employment and child development is increasingly in evidence (OECD, 2011).

Global Impacts on Family Life

Partnerships and parenting patterns play out in different ways in different cultures, but the changes that have been taking place in recent decades are slowly but surely having an impact across the globe. In addition, broad global transformations, listed in the box below, are impacting on everyday life.

Global changes impacting on family life

1. Changing communication technologies, particularly the Internet.
2. Migration of people from rural to urban areas and from country to country.
3. Demographic changes.
4. Poverty.
5. Increasing gender equality.

Changing communication technologies have opened up the world of work as access to email, telephones and social media has become readily available. Moreover, economic development facilitates the movement of people from rural to urban areas and from country to country. Looking to the future, Edgell (2006) considered that the push–pull felt by some people living in more traditional societies between obligations towards wider kinship groups and obligations towards immediate family will become increasingly more complex with the dominant prioritisation of work and the growth of urban living in global capitalist economies. The world's urban population is expected to grow by nearly 2 per cent a year until 2030 (Rosenberg and Bloom, 2004). The creation of job opportunities in the developing world is imperative if poverty is to be tackled and social unrest avoided. Greater gender equality in education and in society in general is a central aspect of economic growth. The events in Pakistan and India at the end of 2012, in which a young girl was shot because of her outspoken lobbying for education for girls, and a young woman was repeatedly raped and then killed, drew worldwide attention to and condemnation of regimes which treat women with contempt.

Ending poverty and hunger is one of the eight UN Millennium Development Goals. There is a strong relationship between economic poverty, ill health, low levels of education, limited employability, poor social integration and the marginalisation of poor families. The life prospects for children growing up in poverty are poor. Moreover, poorer, less equal societies have higher child mortality rates. There is evidence, also, that low income is significantly correlated with child abuse and neglect (Stith *et al.*, 2009). The protection of children from abuse and neglect and the eradication of child poverty are also priority policy goals in OECD countries, where more than 10 per cent of children live in poverty (OECD, 2011).

As borders between countries have been opened up, increasing numbers of individuals and families have moved to another country to find work and improve their standard of living. As the global recession bites, however, immigration has become a particularly sensitive issue for countries that have previously welcomed migrant labourers and their families. A number of ideological shifts in recent years have had a considerable impact on the ability of migrants to bring their families to a new country, and changing attitudes have had negative effects on the lives of immigrant populations, increasing their marginalisation and social exclusion.

Inter-country adoption has also become a global phenomenon that is causing concern. Wealthier nations have been accused of exploiting impoverished nations by taking their children for adoption under the guise of humanitarianism. Nevertheless, a careful review of the research evidence shows that, on the whole, international adoptions are successful, with low breakdown rates. Looking to the future, however, more longitudinal research is essential to understand the needs of children adopted internationally and the kinds of support adoptive families need to ensure positive outcomes.

Demographic changes and globalisation have had important impacts on family life which are unlikely to be reversed. Families in many countries are facing major challenges in maintaining their traditional lifestyle and family stability against a backdrop of enormous social and economic change. In the Maghreb region of North Africa, for example, on the one hand efforts are being made to give priority to reducing unemployment and drug addiction and to integrate women at all levels in society, while on the other hand, families face painful adjustments, particularly in the wake of terrorism and lawlessness. The role of families in such areas is particularly important in respect of providing care and support for older generations. In East Asian societies, the demographic changes are having significant impacts on the provision of care for the elderly.

Perhaps the most significant contributor to globalisation is the extraordinary growth in electronic communications. The Internet is rapidly becoming a normal part of everyday life: it enables instant communication across the globe and presents huge opportunities for the growth of international markets and employment. There are concerns, however, about the risks for people who are vulnerable, particularly for children and young people in respect of cyber-bullying, paedophilia and fraudulent scams. Ensuring that the Internet provides positive opportunities in all aspects of people's lives and that negative behaviours are properly monitored and eliminated are critical challenges for Internet providers and governments alike.

Policy and practice implications

Globalisation will have far-reaching impacts on partnership, parenting and family life in the years to come. Benefiting from the opportunities it presents, while at the same time reducing the negative consequences of the challenges to stability, is of the utmost importance. Global cooperation will be essential. Of course, global influences on everyday life are not new, but the movement of global capital from one country to another has affected whole societies (McKie and Callan, 2012). Changes in partnership and parenting are impacting on work patterns, particularly for women, and these in turn are influencing caring roles and responsibilities in relation to children and an ageing population. Traditional practices are evolving, blending the old with the new, promoting a mix of continuity and change in patterns of partnership and parenting.

The contributors to this volume have emphasised the importance of fully understanding this blending of tradition and innovation, recognising those who are most likely to be at risk as family stabilities are threatened, and putting in place support mechanisms which protect families and eliminate exploitation and disintegration. Finding ways to enhance integration within and across cultures and societies is a significant challenge, particularly since eliminating poverty, not least in the face of natural disasters, appears to be an almost impossible task.

Parenting programmes are increasingly popular as a means of enhancing parenting skills and creating a nurturing family environment, but the stresses and strains in family life also need to be addressed. War, civil unrest, poverty, national disasters and lack of resources all render parents vulnerable to cumulative disadvantage. Early intervention and more skilled practitioners are needed to improve the health and life chances of adults and children, and support fragile parental relationships.

It is easy to overlook the extent to which families are influenced by religious beliefs and mores. Many of the changes in family life conflict with long-held beliefs, and there are clear tensions between freedom of choice and pressures to maintain the status quo. Religion has influenced human behaviour throughout history and will continue to do so. The practice of prayer is central to most religions and innovative research in the USA has begun to explore ways in which religious belief and prayer can be used to support couples, facilitate positive relationship outcomes and encourage forgiveness between partners. Ignoring the influence of world religions is not an option in a world where many conflicts are fuelled by religious differences.

The Role of States in Supporting Families

Many of the recommendations made by contributors to this volume place the onus on governments to implement policies that address the issues and concerns relating to global changes in family life. There is a difficult tension between states supporting families and being accused of interfering in family life. The state's responsibility to its citizens is founded in a commitment to upholding human rights and to supporting parents in carrying out their responsibilities towards their children. Across Europe, strengthening families has become a central commitment of successive governments, and there is considerable agreement that governments have a responsibility to ensure that families are given the help they need.

Being in paid employment tends to be the key factor in family survival in the twenty-first century, and economic and welfare policies are moving away from a male breadwinner model of family responsibilities towards an adult worker model. For this to be effective in increasing the wellbeing of all family members there needs to be a careful rebalancing of work and care within households and societies. Given changing demographics across the world this rebalancing is a matter for urgent consideration by governments. Fiona Williams has argued for a political ethic of care which supports parents, invests in children, promotes equality and protects diversity (Williams, 2004). Worklessness and poverty are problems that cannot be addressed without state intervention. Such intervention needs to be well-informed by evidence as to what works to reduce levels of poverty and support people into work, and robust enough to avoid the stigmatisation of families living on the margin or in non-traditional family structures.

Bogenschneider (Chapter 26, this volume) makes the case for family policies to be developed across the globe with the explicit goal of supporting family formation, couple relationships, child rearing, and caregiving for the disabled, frail, ill and elderly. Family-focused policies can create the conditions in which families of all shapes and sizes can more effectively execute the many important functions families perform for their members and for society.

Looking to the Future

This book draws attention to the continuities and changes which are impacting on partnership and parenting practices around the world. People struggle to balance traditional expectations and new opportunities as they adapt to the global transformations which influence all our lives. The OECD (2011) has predicted that the number of families without children will increase in the years to 2030 and that the number of single-parent families will increase. Lone-parent families face the highest poverty risk, and poverty in childhood can have a lasting negative effect on children's development and wellbeing. Improving the living conditions of parents and supporting families at high risk of poor outcomes have to be important goals of social policies in the years to come. If governments continue to work together to address the economic, social and environmental challenges of rapid social change and globalisation, the wellbeing of families can be protected and enhanced.

References

Coleman, J. and Glenn, F. (2009) *When Couples Part: Understanding the consequences for adults and children* (London: OnePlusOne).

Edgell, S. (2006) *The Sociology of Work: Continuity and change in paid and unpaid work* (London: Sage).

General Secretariat for Development Planning (2010) *Qatar National Vision 2030* (Qatar: Doha Institute for Family Studies and Development).

McKie, L. and Callan, S. (2012) *Understanding Families: A global introduction* (London: Sage).

OECD (2010) *OECD Family Database* (Paris: OECD). http://www.oecd.org/els/social/family/database [Accessed 17.10.2012.]

OECD (2011) *Doing Better for Families* (Paris: OECD). http//dx.doi.org/ 10.1787/9789264098732-en [Accessed 17.10.2012.]

Rosenberg, L. and Bloom, D. (2004) *World Population Prospects* (New York: United Nations).

Roseneil, S. (2005) Living and loving beyond the boundaries of the heteronorm: personal relationships in the 21st century, in L. McKie and S. Cunningham-Burley (eds), *Families in Society: Boundaries and relationships* (Bristol: The Policy Press).

Smart C. (2007) *Personal Life: New directions in sociological thinking* (Cambridge: Polity Press).

Stith, S. M., Liu, T., Davies, L. C., Boykin, E. L., Alder, M. C., Harris, J. M., Som, A., McPherson, M. and Dees, J. E. (2009) Risk factors in child maltreatment: a meta analytic review of the literature, *Aggression and Violent Behaviour*, 4: 13–29.

Therborn G. (2004) *Between Sex and Power: Family in the world, 1900–2000* (London: Routledge).

Williams, F. (2004) *Rethinking Families* (London: Calouste Gulbenkian Foundation).

Index

Contemporary Issues in Family Studies: Global Perspectives on Partnerships, Parenting and Support in a Changing World, First Edition. Edited by Angela Abela and Janet Walker.
© 2014 John Wiley & Sons, Ltd. Published 2014 by John Wiley & Sons, Ltd.